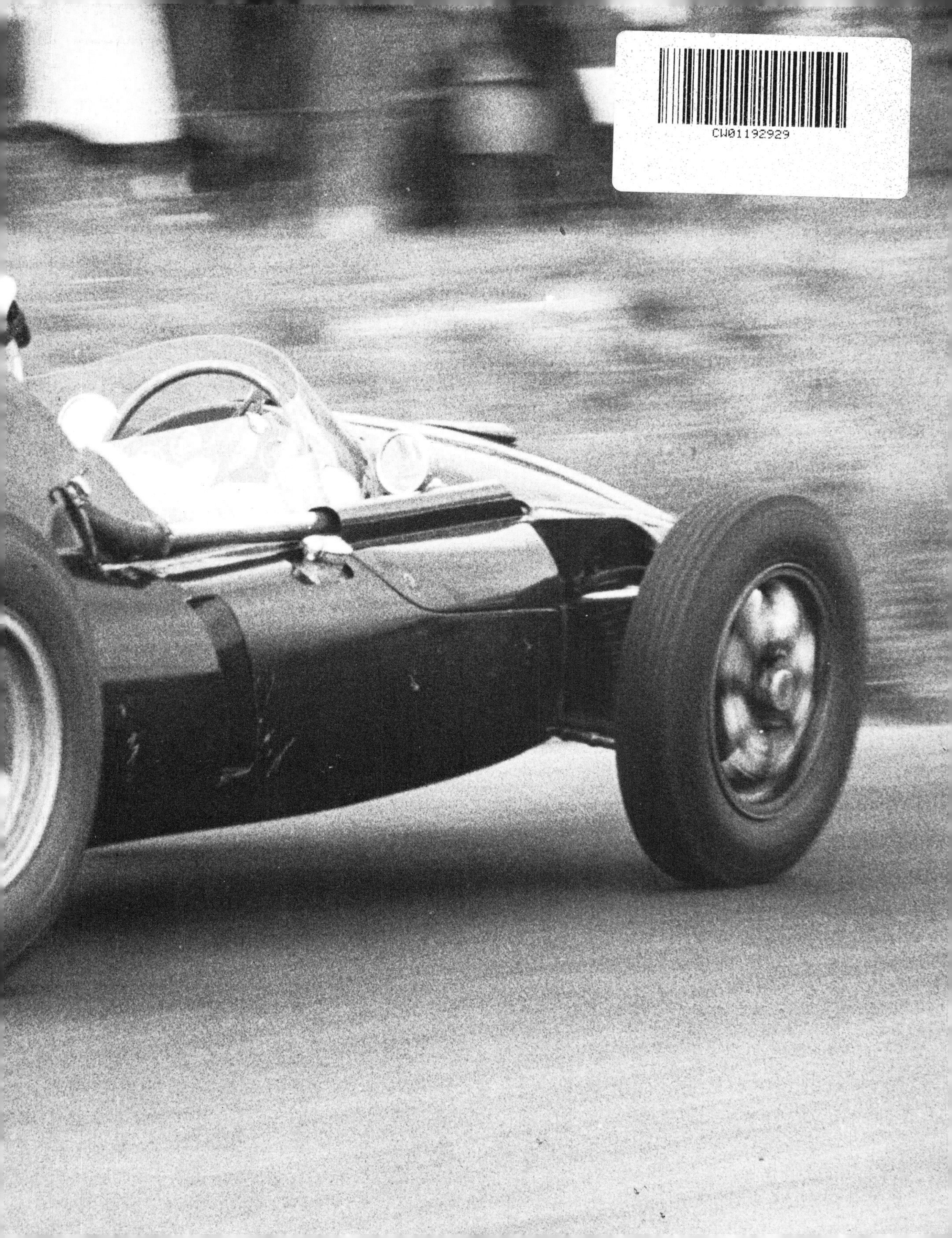

Abe #2552
2nd.
1987
£80 3/06.

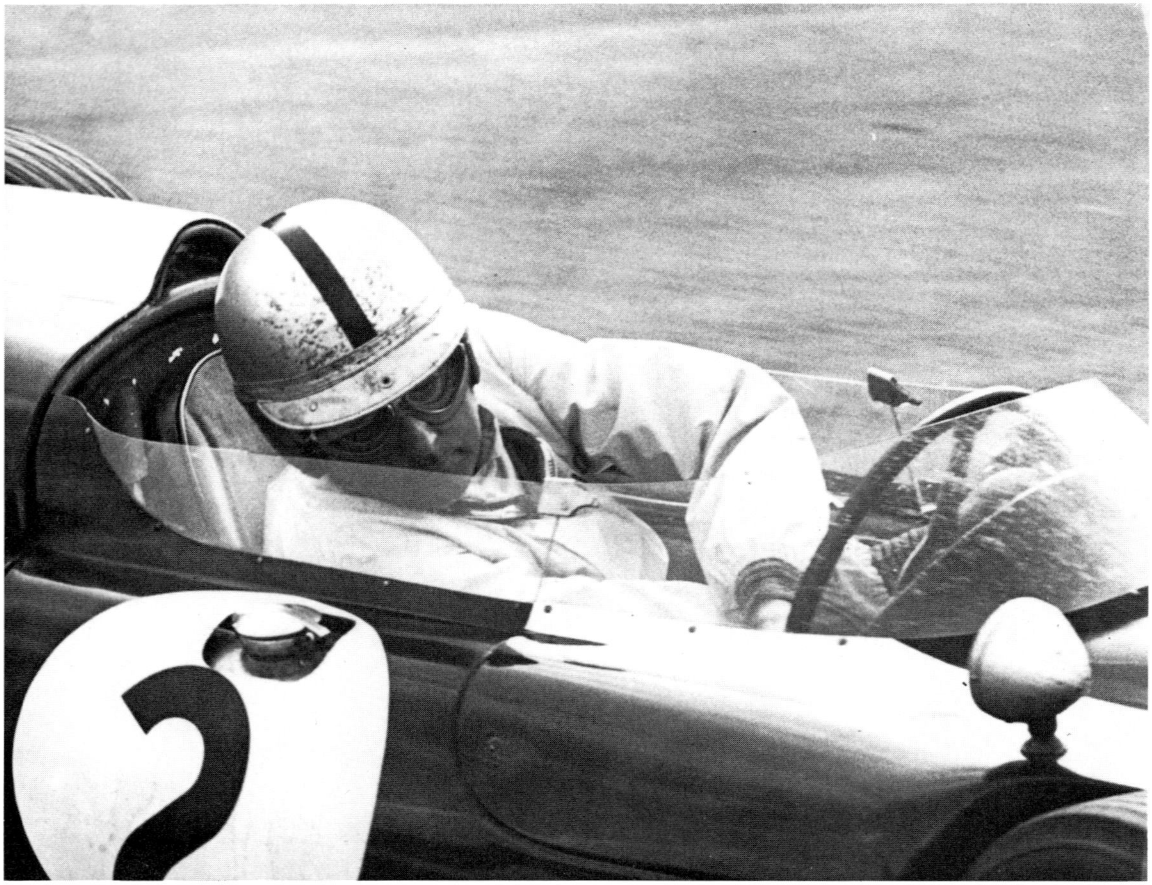

COOPER CARS

Doug Nye

OSPREY

First published in 1983 by Osprey Publishing Limited
27A Floral Street, London WC2E 9DP
Member company of the George Philip Group
Second edition 1987

Sole distributors for the USA

Motorbooks International
Publishers & Wholesalers Inc
Osceola, Wisconsin 54020, USA

© Copyright Doug Nye 1983, 1987

This book is copyrighted under the Berne Convention. All rights reserved. Apart from any fair dealing for the purpose of private study, research, criticism or review, as permitted under the Copyright Act, 1956, no part of this publication may be reproduced, stored in a retrieval system, or transmitted in any form or by any means, electronic, electrical, chemical, mechanical, optical, photocopying, recording, or otherwise, without prior written permission. All enquiries should be addressed to the publisher.

British Library Cataloguing in Publication Data

Nye, Doug
   Cooper cars.—2nd ed.
   1. Automobile racing—History 2. Cooper automobiles—History
   I. Title
   796.7'2   GV1029.15
ISBN 0-85045-828-5

Filmset and printed in England by
BAS Printers Limited, Over Wallop, Hampshire

Front end-paper *Going for it – Stirling Moss in his wire-rear-wheeled knock-off hub Walker Cooper-Climax Mark III hurtling towards victory in the 1959 Oulton Park Gold Cup. Tail-squatting, brief snatch of opposite lock, inside front wheel clearly airborne – typical '59 World Champion Cooper qualities . . .*

Half title *'Come on boy, don't lark about'. Charles Cooper doing his best to look like Tony Vandervell with Panama hat and lightweight jacket enjoys his son John's victory roll on the pit apron at Monza; Italian GP, 13 September, 1959. Stirling Moss has just won in Rob Walker's Cooper-Climax, Phil Hill's Ferrari is just crossing the line second and Jack Brabham's works Cooper-Climax will be third. The Cooper Car Company has just won the Formula 1 Manufacturers' World Championship*

Opposite title page *Jack Brabham – motive force behind such a great part of Cooper's success – on his winning way in the 'Lowline' T53 works car at La Source Hairpin, Spa-Francorchamps, during the Belgian GP, 19 June, 1960. It was the second successive GP win in his string of five that season*

Back end-paper *Geoff Goddard's classic shot of Jack Brabham, 'the nut-brown Australian', crouched in the cockpit, hurling his works Cooper through Madgwick Corner at Goodwood in the September 1957 Goodwood F2 10-lapper. He finished second to team-mate Salvadori, but set fastest lap, a new record at 96 mph. Team colours were dark BRG with red nose-band. Here the inside front wheel is just clear of the road surface and the outside rear wheel is taking a caning . . . . See the hay in the nose?*

Contents

	Acknowledgements	6
	Introduction	7
1	Beginnings . . . the family . . .	9
2	The first 500s – 1946–47	14
3	Into production	23
4	A sports car, and a designer . . .	31
5	Taking root – the season of '49	35
6	Into the Fifties . . .	41
7	The 500 line – 1951–53	50
8	Cooper-Bristols and Grands Prix	58
9	*Part 1* Mark IIs, Bristols and Altas . . .	68
	Part 2 Nine sports cars, 1953–54	92
10	Formula 3 – the later years	105
11	Changing times . . .	113
12	New beginning – Coventry Climax . . .	118
13	More Bob-tails – and beyond	126
14	First in Formula 2	132
15	Into Formula 1 . . .	138
16	1958 – The winning begins . . .	150
17	1959 – World Champions	165
18	1960 – The greatest triumph	186
19	Interlude for Two – 1958–1960	209
20	Monaco – mighty sports car	215
21	1961 – The Indy project	230
22	The Junior Coopers	236
23	The 1½-litre years – 1961–65	245
24	The minor formulae – 1964–69	277
25	The Maserati project – 1966–67	286
26	Those final years . . .	299
Appendix 1	The Mini-Coopers	307
Appendix 2	The minor leagues . . .	311
Appendix 3	The record cars	321
Appendix 4	Cooper type numbers	328
Appendix 5	Cooper chassis records	330
Appendix 6	Racing records	340
Appendix 7	Mini-Cooper serial number coding	371
	Index	372

Acknowledgements

In a work of this size where can I start? I can only list names here, which in so many cases is entirely inadequate return for their enthusiastic and unstinting help. Thanks a million to:

John Cooper; Owen Maddock; Mike Barney; Eddie Stait; Andrew Ferguson; Roy Golding; Pete Bedding; Douggie Johnson; Terry Kitson; Mike King; Sir Jack Brabham; the late Eric Brandon and his widow Sheila; Alan Brown; Roy Salvadori; Tony Crook; George Saunders; John Coombs Ken Tyrell; John Chisman; Mike Roach; Rob Walker; Brit Pearce; Ken Gregory; Mike Cooper (John's son); Archie Bryde; Phil Hill; Roger Penske; Dan C. Luginbuhl of Penske Racing; Jack Martin of the Indianapolis Speedway Museum; Georges Maitre; Antoine Prunet; Jabby Crombac; Bill Clark for enormous help from New Zealand; Tim Walton; Roddy Macpherson; John B. Blanden; John Patey; Allen Brown; John Harper; Eoin Young; *Ing.* Giulio Alfieri; Mario Tozzi-Condivi; Denis Jenkinson; Graham Gauld; Geoff Goddard; Cyril Posthumus; Dev Dvoretsky; Brian Naylor; George Pitt; Ray Fielding; Jock Watson; Jim Diggory; Jimmy Blumer; Stan Sproat; Jimmy Somervail; Arthur Birks; David Yorke; Denise Cole; Dick Gibson; Derrick Edwards; Peter Hull; Alan Stait; Peter Brockes of the National Motor Museum Library; Andrew Whyte; Mrs Laura White; Alec Rainbow; Fred Faulkner; Wakefield's of Byfleet; Mo Gomm; Tony Marsh; Michael Christie; Bill Blyth; Eric Perrin; Duncan Rabagliati; Dr K. Paul Sheldon and Mrs Betty Sheldon; Jack Knight; James A. Allington; Sid Hoole; Michael Taylor; Cliff Davis; Harold Massey of Performance Cars Ltd; Jim Russell; John Bolster; Stirling Moss; David Grohmann; John Surtees; Mike Qvale; Mike Knight; Bill Knight; Steve Sanville; Harry Mundy and Walter Hassan of Coventry Climax; Tony Mantle of Climax Engine Services; Anatoly Arutunoff; Bob Gerard; Roy Winkelmann; Alan Rees; Tom Kyffin; Jake Halligan; Bruce Halford; Bernie Ecclestone; Alan Fraser; Brian Pritchard-Lovell; Keith Hall; Peter Greenslade; Ross McKay; Don Balmer; David Vine; Hugh Clifford; Stephen Curtis; Rodney Tolhurst; Alex McMillan; Dennis Wolstenholme; Peter Scott-Russell; Bill Wilks; John Riseley-Prichard; John Bateson; Tony Mitchell; Quentin Spurring and Mark Hughes of *Autosport*; Kathy Agar and John Dunbar of LAT Photographic, which is the *Motor Sport* and *Motoring News* magazine photo archive; the late Tony Hogg and John Lamm of *Road & Track*; Michael Bowler of Pace Petroleum.

In addition for this new, revised and amended edition I want to thank so many people who have bemoaned the first edition passing out of print so quickly. Their persistence triggered this reprint. For the new colour section, photographers Geoff Goddard, T. C. 'Tom' March, Guy Griffiths and Edward Eves went to the trouble of unearthing and supplying a wide selection of superb and rare material which caused me untold frustration and agony as I had to narrow the number down to just 16. You should see what had to be left out!

Australian writer/photographer Harold 'Dev' Dvoretsky kindly provided his evocative colour shot of the team the morning after their 1959 Monaco win, and Phillip Scott of the National Motor Museum library at Beaulieu unearthed some excellent material covering that race. Thanks again to London Art tech for assistance where colour of the 1966 Mexican GP was concerned. To any whose name has been omitted I apologize sincerely, and hope the story in these pages proves worthwhile tribute.

I have also drawn heavily upon personal interviews and written material from the late Bruce McLaren, Jochen Rindt and Alf Francis, plus some extracts from the published memoirs of Sir Jack Brabham and Mike Hawthorn with permission from their publishers. Mention should also be made of Arthur Owen's source work *The Racing Coopers*, and John Bentley's *The Grand Prix Carpetbaggers*.

Reference has also been made to Cooper Car Company publications, most notably *The Golden Years* published in conjunction with Esso after that memorable 1960 season to commemorate their back-to-back double-World Championship triumph matching only Ferrari and Alfa Romeo before them. How the humble had grown.

To quote John Cooper, 1983: 'Reading about it all now, and thinking back on the way it all developed, it just seems like a fairytale, doesn't it?'

Maybe, but to the best of my ability, and barring accidents what follows is all true. I hope it does the Cooper Car Company justice.

Doug Nye, July 1987

Introduction

In the early Twenties, the small Surrey town of Surbiton was a fashionable Thames-side resort rapidly being absorbed by London's spread. It lay only 12 miles south-west of the capital's Waterloo Station, on the Southern Region Railway's direct line to Portsmouth and the sea. A few miles beyond the town, that same line flanked the vast concrete bowl of Brooklands Motor Course.

There, in 1928, a businessman–driver named Kaye Don set the first over-130 mph lap of the banked Outer Circuit, driving a V12 Sunbeam. The car was maintained for him by a burly, bespectacled mechanic named Charles Newton Cooper. He worked for Don for many years, while running his own small garage business in Surbiton.

Postwar, Charles Cooper and his son John would found The Cooper Car Company Ltd to build a long and fast-developing series of racing and sports cars. The new concern grew very rapidly, and by modern standards it was incredibly efficient. Even during its most prolific years of worldwide sales and race success its staff seldom exceeded 35, and was generally fewer than 30. Cooper cars were exported to all parts of the world. They were used by all but one of that great Fifties crop of front-line British racing drivers in their formative years. Cooper Cars became the world's largest manufacturer of pure-bred racing cars, and in 1959–60 they achieved ultimate success in twice becoming Formula 1 Champions of the World. . . .

During that period, the Cooper Car Company Ltd pioneered quantity production of proper racing cars. From 1946 to the end of manufacture in 1969, perhaps as many as 1500 racing Coopers had been built.

But not all of them by any means were completed in the Cooper factories, for UK purchase tax made cars in kit form most attractive and many Coopers were sold in this tax-free form and were completed by their purchaser and his mechanics. Therefore, what sketchy chassis production records have survived can tell only part of a very complex and obscure story.

Yet supplying so many cars in kit form enabled the company to thrive with its always compact and often over-worked staff. It minimized capital investment and overhead costs in a way close to tough, economy-minded Charles Cooper's heart.

Heart of the matter – Cooper 500s fill the grid at Snetterton, 1957. From domination in this category came two Formula 1 World titles, the Mini-Cooper saloon car line and more . . .

For much of the company's career, Cooper cars were phenomenally successful. They were only overtaken in the early Sixties by perhaps more sophisticated outfits which had themselves been founded to follow where Cooper Cars led. It was these concerns, like Lotus and Lola, which took over from Cooper to ram home the British domination of top-class single-seat motor racing which Cooper had established so sensationally.

What follows is as complete a story of Cooper's rise and fall as I have been able to compile within a viable package such as this. It is so essentially an English story that American readers in particular might find some quoted expressions tricky to understand. I can only say work on it, we suffer this way from so many TV films, and the language of their time is so quintessentially Cooper it would be wrong to alter any of it.

These pages have been a joy to research and compile, and the deep-rooted affection which so many Cooper Cars people still feel for their old company, especially in its heyday at Surbiton, has proved infectious.

This is by no means to claim that Cooper's works was a haven of peace and unity, with a jolly band of friends there, singing while they worked. Far from it, Cooper's could sizzle with discontent and friction, the atmosphere tense and combative, and nearly always because 'The Old Man' would spend no money. His men were poorly paid. They worked all hours. The works was dark, dingy, freezing cold in winter. He didn't like his lads to burn his electricity, and had a telephone-bill phobia. One time finding son John on the 'phone he listened suspiciously, with rising alarm.

''Oo y'talkin' to, boy?'

'Sssh, quiet dad, it's a very important customer in America...'

Trans-Atlantic conversation continued, Charles shifting from foot to foot, expression blackening.

''Oo's payin' for this call?'

'Sssh dad. We are – very important customer...'

BANG! The Old Man ripped the 'phone wires from the wall socket, grabbed the handset, wound the cable round it and tossed the lot out of the office window.

'I don't pay for no calls to America!'

That was quite typical, yet equally typical would be 'Mr Cooper' or 'Charles' as he was always known to his face – 'Charlie Cooper' or 'The Old Man' in his absence – pressing a £5 note into his grand-children's hands and whispering 'Go and get yourselves somethin' nice. Don't tell your dad now...' and never expecting change....

In the early days there was a shattering crunch from the workshop as somebody's attention had been distracted while raising a van on a lift, and the van's roof was caved-in against a ceiling girder. Charlie creased-up with laughter when he saw it, shattered glass still tinkling to the floor.

'Goor, you've made a mess o'that', he cried, ''Oo's is it'.

'Your's' came the answer...

Another stupendous explosion from the Old Man.

Many more Cooper stories are retold here. The Formula 1 team mechanics in California 1960 when, due to local prices, their normal £2 per day food allowance arrangement, which was quite adequate in Europe, had been altered so that the company picked-up whatever bills they incurred, and the Old Man complaining bitterly 'You're eatin' too much. Steak and ice-cream for breakfast, dinner and tea!'

The works Mini Cooper racing saloon being run-up on the roller brake when the rollers seized and the car took off, carrying its petrified garage-boy 'driver' clean through the workshop doors...

Cooper might have had its ups and downs, but life there was never, ever, dull. The company dabbled in non-racing projects. They toyed with a three-wheeler economy car around the time of the Suez Crisis, developed a lightweight scooter, the original prototype Jeenay child's safety seat, a Coventry-Climax-powered Renault Dauphine road car to project their rear-engined performance car image ... and more.

Here it has not been possible to detail Mini-Cooper saloon history without compromising racing car coverage. Since the Minis' story has been told at length so many times, here I have concentrated very much upon true Coopers, the racing cars, and the people who conceived, designed, built, maintained and raced them.

Modern enthusiasts tend to expect chassis number identification of historic racing cars. This is always a dodgy business as real life and theory generally differ. It was often expedient to transfer one given number from car to car to avoid paperwork delays at frontiers, and even more often a given identity would be passed-on despite four changes of chassis and ten changes of body panelling in a season. So what constitutes 'a car'? Here I have quoted known surviving serials, or those suggested by the few surviving contemporary records, while often referring to historic 'entities' – *i.e.* a vehicle with continuously traceable history – rather than 'historic cars'.

To complete this scene-setting introduction I quote my friend Cyril Posthumus, who knew Cooper's engaging and very popular works manager of the 'fifties, Ron Searles, very well: 'Ron would often complain about how there was no money in working for Cooper's and the Old Man's meanness in so many things, but then he'd say; "You know, I really *love* working there. I do, I love it.

'They pay bugger-all, but you'd never have as much fun anywhere else. Nobody has as good a time as us chaps at Cooper's..."'

That was the key. What follows is the story of a good time, good cars, and great days.

CHAPTER ONE

Beginnings...the family...

Charles Newton Cooper was born in Paris, France, on 14 October, 1893. He had a twin sister, Judy, and an elder sister, Lottie. They had an English father and Franco-Spanish mother, from the Pyrenees. Their's was a theatrical family with traditions dating back to Drury Lane in the 18th century. Their father, Charles Renard Cooper, ran the Swiss Express Company of touring players and performed under the stage name 'Charles Renard'. His son, Charles Newton, was not stage-struck. Far from it, he was much more interested in things mechanical.

With the children still quite small, 'Charles Renard' took his stage company touring in England and Mme Cooper moved the family temporarily to her mother's farm in the Pyrenees. Sadly she was to die quite young, while her husband moved the family again – this time to England. They took a house in Malden, neighbouring Surbiton, where Fred Emney – soon famous as a stage fat-man comedian – lived next door.

Charles the son rode a motorcycle as soon as he could hold a licence, and at 15 won an apprenticeship with Napier's of Acton. He went into their repair shop and would recall working on S. F. Edge's later record cars.

In 1914 the Great War erupted. On 28 August Charles volunteered for the Royal Army Service Corps – RASC; 'Run Away Someone's Coming!' – and was drafted into the 3rd Motor Transport Mechanical Cavalry Division. He saw considerable active service, but survived unscathed until 1918, when he was gassed at Valencienne. He was invalided home

By 1934 Charles Cooper had gone into partnership with Brooklands driver 'Ginger' Hamilton. Here in Hollyfield Road with 'the Fishponds' beyond, Charles poses in the beautifully-crafted Francis-Barnett engined special which he built for his son John. Alongside him is 'Ginger's' Alfa Romeo Monza with the owner at the wheel. Guess who won...

9

Small service – John inspecting his Cooper Spl's internals in the old front workshop at the Hollyfield Road garage. In the background is father's Rover saloon, on the right their already ancient Drummond lathe. The Spl's wheels were of the size fitted under the front carrying rack on delivery boys' bikes of the period. This old front workshop was demolished in the factory rebuild 20 years later

Opposite *Charles Cooper, having fallen victim to 'Pou Fever' showing off his Flying Flea outside the lock-ups at his Hollyfield Road Garage in the early-1930s. His home-built G-AEEI's tuned Austin 7 engine's radiator is just visible beneath the centre wing brace here. The Flea did not begin to perform until an air-cooled Henderson engine had been substituted*

and was in hospital when the Armistice was signed. After several months he'd 'had enough of them quacks' and discharged himself.

He was quite a rough diamond. He'd seen much of life and death in his 25 years. He was an experienced and capable mechanic and now he wanted to turn his training into profit.

His sister Lottie was engaged to a Mr Darby, who ran a one-man business in nearby Kingston called Darby Motors. He bought war-surplus motorcycles which he reconditioned and sold. Charles joined him briefly but soon decided to go it alone and managed to raise enough money to take the lease on a derelict builder's yard in Ewell Road, Surbiton – next to the Waggon & Horses pub – where he developed a small garage business.

Meanwhile, through riding motorcycles in competitive trials he got to know Kaye Don, who was a representative for the Avon Tyre Company. In 1921 Don began racing an ex-Harry Hawker AC at 'The Track' – Brooklands – and in 1922 bought the Wolseley *Viper* track car and asked Charles to maintain and prepare it for him.

As the years rolled by Charles Cooper became rather more than 'just a mechanic' to Kaye Don, although the assertion that he became Don's 'racing manager' seems to overstate the case. In 1922, Charles married Elsie Paul, and they took a house in Fassett Road, Kingston, where their son John Newton Cooper was born on 17 July, 1923. He was to grow up in the tiny garage business, surrounded by both the most humble road cars and some of the country's most exotic and exciting racing machinery.

In 1930 Kaye Don attacked the World Land Speed Record with the Sunbeam *Silver Bullet*, which Louis Coatalen built for him around two monstrous 24-litre V12 aero engines. Charles accompanied the team to Florida's Daytona Beach, but the car was hopelessly unreliable and fully 45 mph below Segrave's 231 mph record.

It was sold later to Freddy Dixon and Jack Field, and Charles tended it, but it repeatedly burst into flames and was no more successful. John was present at Southport Sands one time when Field tackled the British record, and vividly recalls it brewing-up yet again.

Charles crewed occasionally in Don's MG racing team and, when the Brooklands ace turned to Bugattis, he was despatched to the Molsheim factory to build up a 4.9-litre straight-eight Type 54 for him, and to learn all about it. In later years favoured customers' mechanics would sometimes be allowed to assemble their cars in the Cooper works. . . .

Charles worked hard for his daily bread. He was a good hard-nosed businessman and made the best of what he had. He was nobody's fool, and his fuse was quite short. Despite his disinterest in the stage he could be splendidly histrionic if enraged. . . . Beneath this often irascible exterior he could also be remarkably warm. He loved children, and animals, and in his later years would dote on his grandchildren, and apparently on dogs, horses, ducks and pigs as well.

John's introduction to motoring was inevitable. Charles built him a working model car which the boy could 'drive' around the Brooklands paddock while Dad was at work. This first toy was replaced in 1931, when John was eight, by a beautifully crafted self-propelled Cooper Special. It was powered by a Francis-Barnett motorcycle engine and gearbox, chain-driven to the back axle. It had half-elliptic front springs, quarter-elliptic rears and three forward speeds. Its

BEGINNINGS... THE FAMILY...

tiny wheels were fronts taken from tradesmen's delivery cycle stock, designed to fit below a carrying rack hitched ahead of the front forks. The wheels had tiny drum brakes and the 'Fanny-B' engine was good for 9–10 hp and the car would do about 35–40 mph dependent on the gradient.

Then Charles went flying. He claimed to have been the first member of the Redhill Flying Club, and he learned to fly in under two months with 30 hours in his 'book'. Coincidentally, in France, the amateur designer Henri Mignet had just successfully built and flown his *Pou du Ciel* DIY light aeroplane. He wrote a rollicking account of his activities entitled *Le Sport de l'Air*. This was taken up by the Air League of the British Empire and translated into English as *The Flying Flea*, and the early Thirties saw 'Pou Fever' sweeping Britain as hundreds of optimistic enthusiasts bought plans and kits and set to work. One of them was Charles Cooper, and quite typically he was one of the few to complete his aeroplane; using a kit which cost around £150 and included a water-cooled Austin 7 engine. But Mignet had made a gross design error, and after several fatalities the Fleas were grounded for reconstruction.

Today, some of his friends doubt if Charles ever really left the ground in his Flea. For sure the A7 engine and its radiator were too heavy, despite Charles's determined tuning to improve power-to-weight. But he eventually replaced them with an air-cooled four-cylinder ohv Henderson power unit which was much more satisfactory, and apparently he flew happily as far as Southend and back.

By this time Cooper's Garage in Surbiton was too cramped and he was looking for alternative premises. By 1934 – when Don was imprisoned briefly for the manslaughter of his MG riding mechanic in the Isle of Man – Charles had gone into partnership with another Brooklands character; this time 'Ginger' Hamilton. He raced Alfa Romeos and would later run Fisher's Garage, opposite Connaught's at Send on the A3 near Guildford.

With Hamilton's backing, Charles took larger premises at 243 Ewell Road, Surbiton. Number 243 was actually the corner shop of a small parade fronting onto Ewell Road, with a quiet side street named Hollyfield Road running down one side. Cooper's Garage would actually reopen in a large corrugated building set behind the corner shop, with petrol pumps on a forecourt opening into Hollyfield Road. Charles and Elsie Cooper would later live in the flat over the corner shop. There was then parkland called the Fishponds across Hollyfield Road, and the Ewell Road in front climbed steeply uphill towards the centres of Surbiton and Kingston. Out the back was the Tolworth Brook, a narrow stream where Charles would keep ducks. Postwar they would often parade straight through the Garage and out in line-astern onto the main road, stopping traffic....

At this time the family was living comfortably in nearby Beresford Avenue. Young John was attending Arundel House School, where in later years a Cooper driver named Jack Brabham would send his son Geoffrey.

For John's twelfth birthday, Charles replaced the Cooper Special kiddy car with a lightweight two-seat Austin 7 special. He used the redundant highly tuned engine from the Flying Flea, complete with its high-lift camshaft, twin carburettors and special crankshaft. It was installed in a cut-down A7 frame, lowered on 15 in. diameter wheels. The car weighed less than 800 lb and was good for close on 90 mph, which was prodigiously quick for that time. John was allowed to drive it on private land, and one memorable day got most of the way round Brooklands before being nabbed: 'It really was quite something; a *very* quick little car....'

Postwar, as the Cooper Car Company entered full production, this Austin 7 special would be listed retrospectively as the 'Cooper Type 1'.

John had a friend named Eric Brandon, who lived nearby in Tolworth Rise, and he was as madly enthusiastic as John himself, who was slightly younger. One of Eric's earliest motoring memories was of a bar-steering pedal car from which he removed most of the rear body and added a pram bogey to carry passengers. Running downhill six-up he slammed-on too much lock too quickly and rolled the lot, gashing his knee deeply on the jagged edge of what bodywork remained. He carried the scar for the rest of his life.

Later, he and John formed a 'club' with some other local lads to buy and race motorcycles. They paid as much as 3s. 6d. for a Rudge and two-stroke Excelsior and did a deal with a local farmer to race them on his fields. Parents approved so long as they wheeled their bikes on the public road in between. Once they were all riding when they spotted a policeman – and he spotted them: 'Yew 'aven't bin ridin' on the public road 'ave you, lad?,' he asked John. 'Ooh no sir, not me sir.' The officer leaned on the bike's cylinder head, and burned himself....

Accounts differ. One sees John dominant when he bought a dirt-track Douglas twin with the gearbox under the seat. It cost him £4. Eric responded with a Rudge, which was superior, and then he did most of the winning. It depended which you asked. Before his premature death – from cancer in 1982 – Eric recalled how it was in those days: 'The local ambulance station was up at the top of the hill past the

Rarin' to go, Brooklands Paddock, 1936. John at the wheel of the Cooper 'T1' Spl put together by Charles (centre) using the lightweight tuned Austin 7 engine removed from the Flea. Left; Charles' friend Cecil King: right; John's school chum Jasper Marsh. Charles drove the Spl down to the track in convoy with Cecil. While the Old Man worked on Kaye Don's or other clients' cars there, John did his best to sneak a lap – but was intercepted 'and given a terrific rollicking...'

BEGINNINGS... THE FAMILY...

Garage, and the police station was across the road. When there was a crash on the Kingston Bypass, down at the other end of Ewell Road, the ambulance would come whizzing down the hill, ringing its bell as it passed the police station to call them out. So you'd see the ambulance whizz by, with the police car pulling out to follow it, and then there'd be Charlie Cooper, cranking-up his breakdown truck and rumbling off in hot pursuit to get the business. And while he was away, John and I would pinch a gallon or two from the petrol pumps for the motorcycles....'

John was a pupil at Surbiton County School while Eric was at Kingston Grammar. John left at 15 and became apprenticed as a toolmaker to Hollyfield Engineering. This was a sideline business which Charles had established at the Garage, sub-contracting work from Hawker Aircraft at Kingston. It grew rapidly, other directors became involved and it eventually moved out to larger premises in Kingston.

After a few months' wage-earning, John managed to save about £12. He sold his Douglas twin for £3 and set out, unsuccessfully, to buy either a Bentley or a Bugatti! Charles eventually came to his rescue and helped him buy a 1000 cc Morgan-JAP three-wheeler: 'You could drive a three-wheeler at 16, but I was only 15 when I got mine. It had a hand-throttle on the steering wheel and went like stink. It was my first road-registered car, and I loved it'.

After the grounding of the Flying Fleas, Charles eventually managed to sell his to a film company, and later bought a much more serious Miles Hawk monoplane with a De Havilland Gypsy Major engine. Parts of his aeroplanes hung around the Garage through the war years. Postwar the Hawk was sold to Dennis Poore.

Charles could be quite inventive. He enjoyed caravanning, but appreciated the pain of storing a caravan when it wasn't in use. So he designed a collapsible 'Packaway' caravan which was hinged and bolted together so that the roof could be lifted off, the sides and wheels removed and the whole thing then stacked away neatly against a wall. It was a four-berth design and Charles had just begun production at Hollyfield Road when war broke out. John believes 'about a dozen' were made and 'father did a very good deal with one of the Ministries to take them off our hands'. Hollyfield Road then turned to war work.

Douggie Johnson, Cooper's longest-serving employee and a man who was to assemble around 1500 racing cars in his time with them, went to work there in 1941: 'I was the laundry boy, working for a chap called Ted Middleton. Mr Charles would borrow one of his vans occasionally if he wanted to shift something around, and one day in 1941 he just said to me, "I'd like a bright boy to work for us, would you fancy a job?" I said "Yes," so it was a case of "Start on Monday". Then he had a bad accident in an Austin 7 that weekend – hit a police car he did – and when I reported on the Monday there was nobody about. For some time 'til he

Enterprise immediately pre-war in the main workshop at Hollyfield; one of Charles' prototype Packaway caravans fully erected, ready for its wheels and axle with other Packaways on the floor left and right. The roof was retained by luggage trunk over-centre clips, the upright panels by through-bolts in each corner

came out of hospital it was just John and myself, larkin' about....

'The Garage was a big asbestos-roofed shed really, in a yard with a row of lock-up buildings out the back. They knocked most of them into workshops, while the engineering firm operated in more lock-ups at the far end.

'Until 1944 when I went in the Forces there were just three of us really in the Garage; me, John at first and Syd Miles, who was brought in as foreman. He brought in a lot of work, all his drinking mates from the pub round the corner! Out in the lock-ups a company called Beatty's spent the war repairing Hurricane wings for Hawker's, and we were all kept pretty busy....'

John had gone to work as a toolmaker for an Admiralty company in Chiswick, West London, entitled 'The Improved Submerged Log Company'. 'It was a curious outfit, run by a Russian named Petroff. We did a lot of work on one- and two-man midget submarines....' He wanted to join the RAF as a pilot, but the Admiralty refused to release him until the winter of 1944–45, when 'it was all over bar the shouting' and then he was drafted into the Royal Air Force as an instrument maker.

He wasn't there long, as soon after the war ended his services were more vital to ensure the Garage's future than the country's and '... the RAF let me go'.

Cooper driver-cum-historian Arthur Owen later chose a happily accurate sentence to sum up what followed: 'The youthful enthusiasm of the son combined with the more mature judgement of the father proved an ideal partnership, and the Cooper Garage prospered accordingly....'

CHAPTER TWO

The first 500s—1946-47

Before the Second World War there were probably less than three dozen worthwhile pure-bred racing cars in the whole of Britain. Motor racing in these islands had always had the image of an upper-crust rich man's sport. The Brooklands slogan 'The Right Crowd and No Crowding' summed it up. A few did succeed in making their racing pay; from men with the right background still interested in turning a profit, like Raymond Mays – father of the ERA – to the artisan racers, like Reg Parnell. But for the common man, motor racing was almost an impossible dream.

It was different in motorcycling, where just about anybody could have a go, and would be welcome. Then in the late Forties the open friendliness of motorcyling and the four-wheeled world of motor racing coalesced in the 500 cc Formula. It was rather like introducing the innate health and hardiness of a working horse into inbred pedigree bloodstock. With the new Cooper company supplying most of the cars, British motor racing simply exploded with new-found vitality.

In 1946, the war had been over just a few months and returning servicemen were hungry for many things. Somewhere on the list lay motoring in general, and motor sport. Wartime service had introduced thousands to driving and working with motor vehicles. For the first time Britain really became widely motor-minded. Postwar, car production was slow to gain pace, and any kind of road car sold at a premium. Performance cars were like gold dust. Something like a BMW 328, which had sold brand-new in 1939 for £625, could command nearly £1000 – in large white fivers – in 1946–47. Bugattis, which had been down to little more than £200 in 1939, were up above £500. Anyone with racing ambitions had to dig deep to indulge them, or otherwise club together with like-minded enthusiasts to devise some kind of competition that he could afford.

The 500 movement filled this gap. As far back as 1936 a small group of enthusiasts in the Bristol area – several of them working for Bristol Aircraft – began to race specials, mostly based on Austin 7s and GNs, round a one-mile grass track. It was cheap, harmless fun.

During the war years the specialist press put forward various ideas for a poor-man's racing formula come peacetime. The 500 cc limit for motorcycle engines in four-wheeled special chassis made all kinds of sense. Such engines were readily available and they offered a sufficient power-to-weight ratio to make quite exciting little cars.

In December 1945 'the Bristol boys' formed the 500 Club at a meeting of their own Bristol Aeroplane Company Motor Sports Club. The first secretary was John Siddall, and the new movement fostered the idea that with some degree of skill, adequate tools and raw materials, and some common sense, you could build yourself a real-type racing car for perhaps £150, maybe less.

What Charles and John Cooper would shrewdly recognize was that for every enthusiast willing to build himself a 500 cc racing car there should be five or 10 more lacking the time, talent or inclination to do-it-yourself, but ready and willing to buy a ready-made car off the peg.

The real pioneers of postwar 500 cc racing were middle-aged Clive Lones from St Mellons, Cardiff, and prematurely balding Colin Strang from Harrow, North London. They set the pace with widely differing cars; Lones's being based on an A7 Ulster frame with a TT JAP single-cylinder engine in its nose and Strang's based on a Fiat *Topolino* frame with a transverse-leaf independent front suspension, hydraulic brakes and a Vincent-HRD engine mounted in the rear, chain-driving the back axle.

Meanwhile, early in 1946, Holly Birkett of the 750 Motor

First meeting – Prescott hillclimb, 27-28 July, 1946, with Charles and his nephew Colin Darby working on the Mark I prototype which John and Eric Brandon would drive on the hill. The car aroused terrific interest with its neat Charlie Robinson-formed aluminium bodywork and Fiat Topolino *independent front suspensions fore and aft*

Eric on the Prescott startline with Mark I after its hasty overnight engine mount repairs using a plough handle and bus track-rod, the ugly hole of the forward mount visible low down behind the cockpit. Transverse leafsprings are clearly visible as are the Topo *disc wheels and tiny brake drums. Leaning on the fence, third left, apparently unimpressed is Bob Gerard, a later Cooper convert and agent*

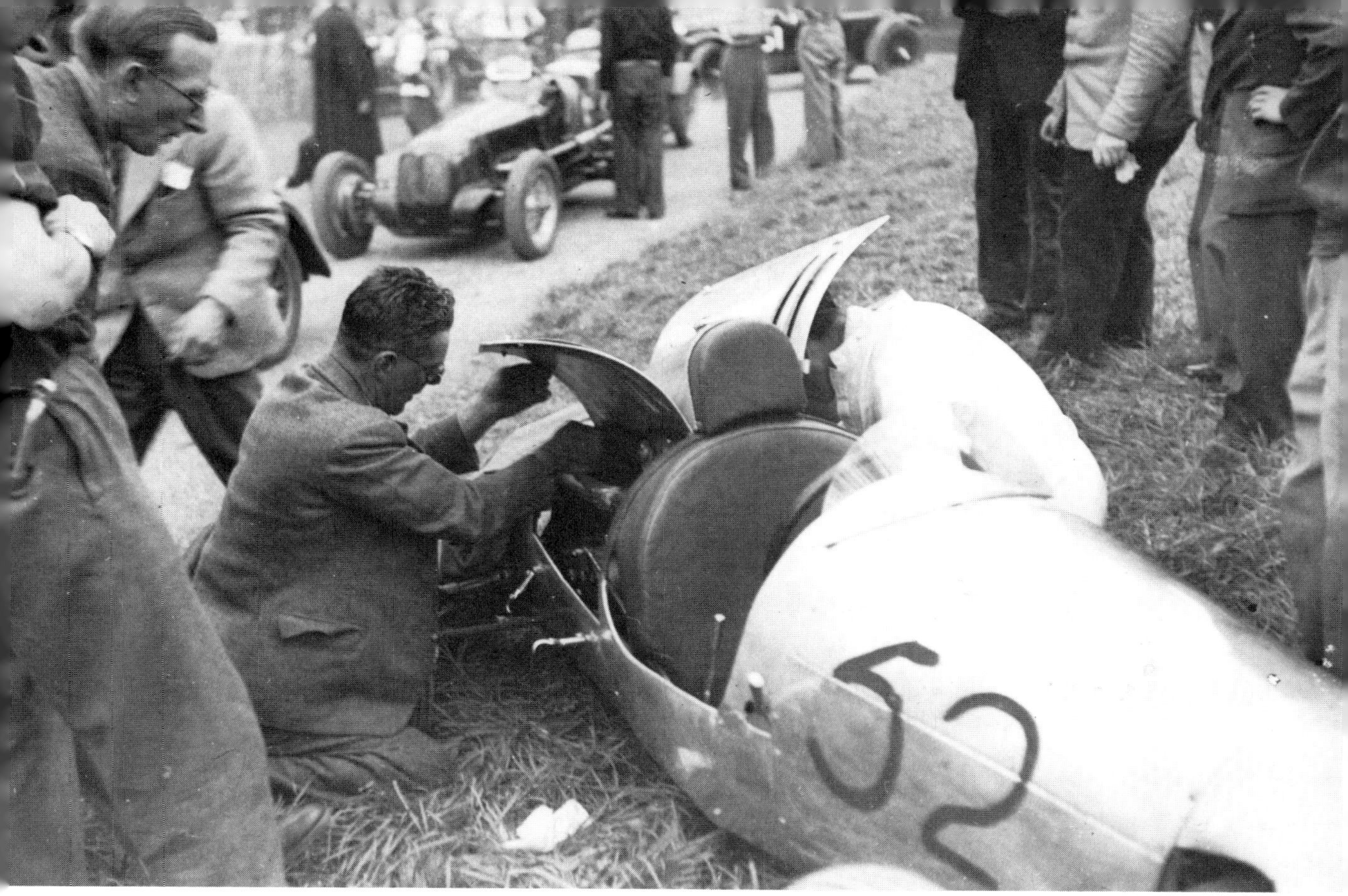
52

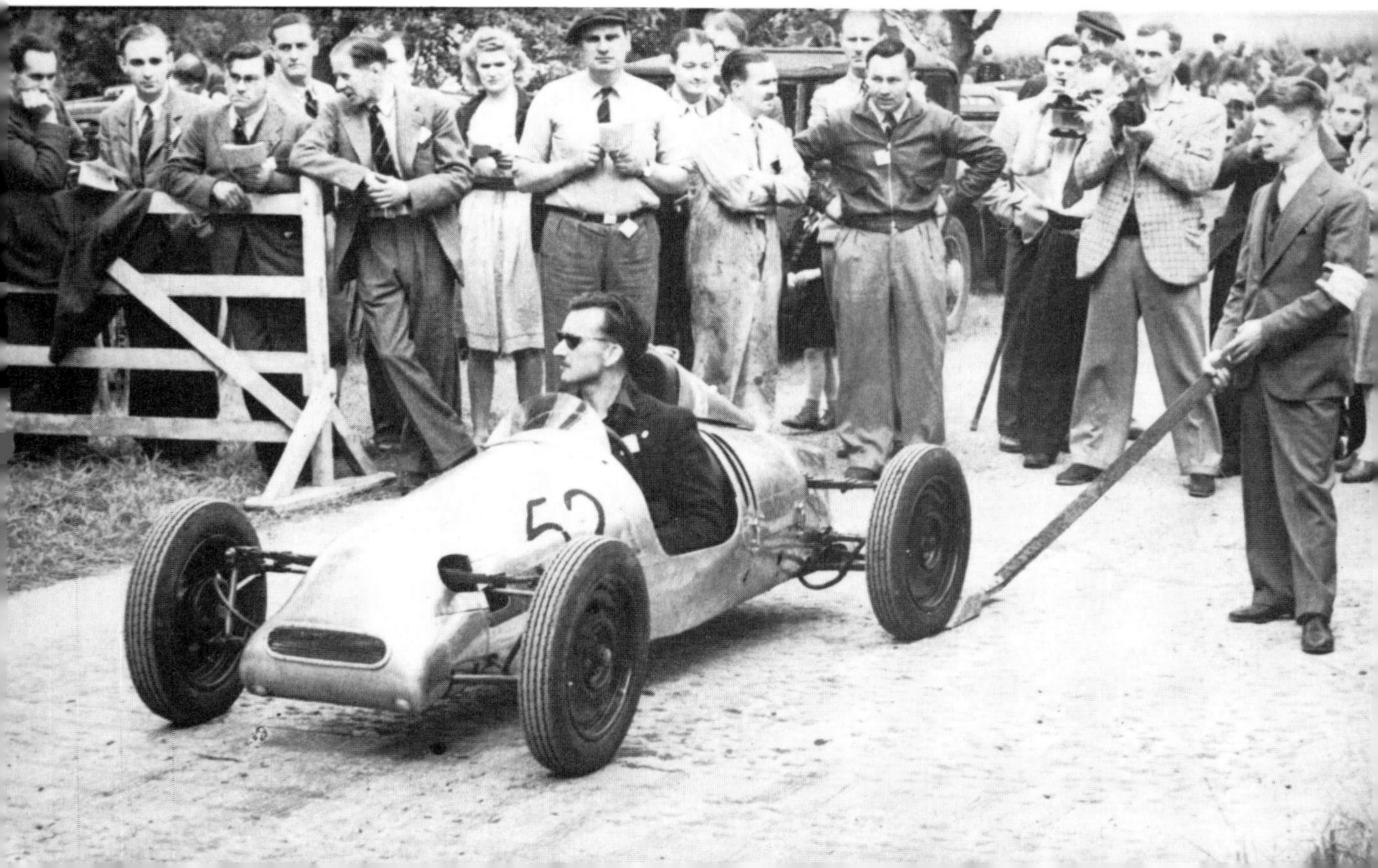
52

Club organized a mud-plugging trial at Aldershot, with a couple of speed tests added for good measure. Eric Brandon was running an MG TC at the time, registered MG 6934: 'They'd been announced the previous November and it was sold to me as only the second TC to leave Abingdon. It cost me £479 18s. and I entered it at Aldershot with John as passenger. It was hopeless! Its ground clearance was so small we got stuck and took maximum penalties on every section, but then we were quickest in both timed tests. We drove home a little wiser, talking about building ourselves a proper trials special. The Garage held a Vauxhall agency and the Vauxhall independent front end was attractive. We thought we could use that, there were plenty of scrap Vauxhalls around, we could make a nice light special, with a lot of ground clearance and take on the V8 specials. . . .

'We were still planning this car when I went off on 10 days' holiday to Babbacombe, towing a dinghy, and when I got back John had started building a competition car all right, but it was a Fiat-based 500!'

John had been down to see 'the Bristol boys', Dick Caesar and friends, who had become the power-house for 500 development, building cars along Lones and Strang Special lines. Cooper's Garage had all the facilities to build a 'proper' car. John says the catalyst was seeing an insurance write-off Fiat *Topolino* lying in the yard there. Its tail-end was badly mangled, but the front with its ifs system was intact. John torched it in half and the forepart of the frame with its precious independent suspension was laid on the garage floor as the first 'lines' of a design. Sketches and chalk marks on the floor saw the ideas flow. Parts were cleaned and shot-blasted, the steering centralized, but the problem of arranging chain-drive to a bouncing back axle remained. Then John realized that if he used another *Topolino* forepart tacked back-to-back onto the first, he'd be home and dry with an all-independently suspended racing chassis.

John Heath's Halfway Garage between Walton and Hersham dealt in Fiats. He was going into partnership with George Abecassis (they would build the HWM team of F2 cars together) and John Cooper tackled him for another tail-damaged *Topo*. He had just the thing. The deal was done and this second bent Fiat was rushed back to Hollyfield Road. Its damaged rear was amputated and both stripped chassis front halves were then butt-welded back-to-back. It was pure practicality. Cooper's never looked back . . . but right now they needed some power. . . .

John's Morgan had been JAP-engined and during his RAF service he had used a platform truck also powered by J. A. Prestwich. Now a Speedway JAP single seemed the obvious thing for the new racing car. Charles's old friendship with Kaye Don surfaced. Don knew J. A. Prestwich very well and delivery of one of his lightweight air-cooled alcohol-burning engines was arranged.

The new Cooper Mark I 500 grew rapidly.

Its simple box-section frame was almost diamond-shaped in planform with the ends squared-off by Fiat's front suspension bulkheads. These were fabricated steel hoops in effect with the transverse leaf-springs clamped over the top and the lower wishbones pivoted on axis pins within the side members. The king posts were located laterally at the top by the leaf-springs; they were standard Fiat at the front, with new welded-up Cooper uprights at the rear to accept drive-shafts.

There was just sufficient chassis width amidships for the driver's upright seat, while the side members were united by three intermediate cross-pieces plus two engine bearer tubes behind the seat. The 'five-stud' Speedway JAP engine – so-called because five studs secured its cylinder head – was bolted vertically into this frame, with drive taken by left-side chain back to a Triumph Speed Twin four-speed gearbox and clutch assembly. A secondary chain then powered a large sprocket driving the whole back axle shaft, without a differential.

The axle ran in two bearings housed in the side plates of the modified rear bulkhead, which enclosed the driven sprocket and chain. Each end of the axle shaft projected outboard of these bearings to mate with side-valve Ford Anglia universal joints driving splined half-shafts to which the standard steel-disc *Topo* wheels bolted.

Each lower wishbone axis pin carried a hydraulic piston damper on its outboard end, while the steering gear was standard Fiat mounted behind the axle, but shifted sideways to place the column on the centreline. The brakes were standard *Topo* hydraulic drums.

The JAP engine had a bore and stroke of 80 × 90 mm, displacing 498 cc. It had a compression ratio of 14:1 and on alcohol fuel gave around 38 bhp at 6300 rpm. Charles was able to improve on that. With a 14:1 compression ratio and some judicious polishing, he found a true 40 bhp-plus at around 6700 rpm, with torque to match. The use of alcohol helped cool the enclosed engine. A track-racing carburettor was used, fed by dual pipes from a two-gallon gravity-feed tank formed into the spine of the engine cowl, and doubling as a headrest fairing.

The aluminium body panels were very nicely hand-beaten by a specialist who came in to do the job. His name was Charlie Robinson. They hugged the narrow chassis lines and tallish engine as close as possible to minimize frontal area. A horizontal air intake in the thrust-forward nose fed a big-bore cooling funnel along the left side of the cockpit, blowing direct onto the cylinder barrel around its exhaust port. Slots were cut into nose and tail cowls for the transverse leaf-springs. A tall vertical slot in the extreme tail allowed exhaust gases to escape, and there was a smaller slot on the driver's right for the handbrake, which operated a simple motorcycle-type drum. Fairings bulged over the Fiat dampers on each end of the main chassis longerons. Instruments were confined to a rev-counter dead ahead of the driver, and there was a tiny Perspex screen moulding. There was a single hydraulic circuit for the brakes, while both clutch and throttle were cable operated.

The car had a wheelbase of 80 in., track $46\frac{1}{2}$ in., and it stood 35 in. high to the top of the headrest-tank. Ground clearance on those standard Fiat wheels was a huge 7 in. Weight was said to be 540 lb, which even with the JAP engine's standard 38 bhp meant a power-to-weight ratio approaching 150 bhp per unladen ton. With a startline weight around 700 lb there would still be 122 bhp per ton. Frontal area was roughly 8 sq ft, meaning 4.75 bhp per square foot, which was quite good indeed by 1946 standards.

I very much doubt if such theorizing or calculation either troubled or enthused the Coopers and Eric Brandon, as the Cooper-JAP Mark I prototype neared completion that summer. John and Charles did the bulk of the work with Eric pitching in as and when he could. He recalls the car slowly growing in one corner of the Garage, but only after hours: 'Charles Cooper would only let us work on it when the Garage was shut . . . he wouldn't let us use *his* time!'

Work had commenced in late June and in just five weeks the prototype was complete and ready for the Prescott Hill-Climb on 28 July. Its creators tested it on the Garage tradeplates — 206 PD — on a (hitherto) quiet Surbiton by-road a couple of days before the event. The gearbox mounting fractured as the clutch was banged home. Late work at the Garage put it right, and next morning the 'team' set off for Prescott with 'Mark I' lashed to one of the war-surplus Chevrolet army trucks that Cooper's had for sale at the time.

The practice day was rainy and Gregor Grant — later founder-editor of *Autosport* magazine — described what happened: 'It was fairly batting down with rain, and crowds of figures, clad mostly in WD gas capes, crowded round the interesting newcomer. After a few hefty shoves the JAP burst into life, emitting a healthy crackle. . . . John built up his revs

This way up — John gritting his teeth and hunched-up in Mark I's tiny cockpit during that first Prescott timed climb, 28 July, 1946. He had just missed his down-change into Pardon Hairpin, over-revved and bent a valve. Typically it was bashed straight over a log, refitted and the car ran again later that day. The Cooper 'team' never looked back . . .

in true Mays manner, and as the hockey stick was applied to his front wheels he banged in the clutch. The car surged forward a few inches, there was a loud clang, and then an ominous silence. Both engine bearer tubes had parted company from the frame.'

John and Eric took stock. They needed help. Eric's sister was married to a chap named Bengry, whose brother Bill – later the leading rally driver – ran an engineering and bus business at Kingsland, near Leominster. It was quite a way, but closer than Surbiton. Eric: 'We arrived at night and hunted around by candle-light because we couldn't find a torch. We were looking for something to remake the engine mounts. Obviously it was useless to merely reweld the tubes, they'd just shear again.' John eventually discovered a plough handle just the right diameter to insert into the broken tube ends, and Eric '... hacked a track-rod out of a scrap bus, cut out the section I wanted and we pinned and welded it into the other broken tube....' Gregor described the overnight repair as 'not particularly artistic'. Charles arrived at Prescott next morning with new bearers which he had made up, but they thought the Bengry yard repair would probably survive.

The rain had abated and on a dry track John attacked his practice run, only to arrive too fast at Pardon Hairpin – he hardly knew the hill at all – and miss his down-change, over-revving the JAP and bending a valve. It was roughly straightened over a log, then with the engine down on power and the car actually under-geared, John's best timed climb was an unspectacular 60.42 sec against Strang's 53.7 and Lones's 55.92. Brandon found the little car even more down on power, and was two seconds slower than John.

The Mark I was taken back to Prescott on 31 August. This time John spun on the damp Orchard Corner in practice and then snapped its new solid $1\frac{1}{8}$ in. thick bearer bars and the gearbox mounts as he took off on his timed runs.

This was serious. The JAP's take-up torque seemed too much for any uncushioned rigid mount. The solution was to adopt two transverse five-leaf springs bolted onto rubber blocks across the frame, with the engine bed-plates then bolted to brackets around the springs. This flexible mount looked promising in clandestine trials on the Kingston Bypass, and Mark I was entered again for the first postwar Brighton Speed Trials, along the sea-front Madeira Drive on Saturday, 7 September, 1946.

Opposite *500 Club at Hollyfield Road, 13 December, 1947, when their AGM was held in the Surbiton Assembly Rooms. Left to right: John Siddall, Colin Strang, S. Edwards, unknown, Stan Coldham, unknown, Eric Brandon, Bill Grose, John Cooper, unknown, Commander Christopher Yorke, C. Lang, L.B.T. Stallwood and Charles Cooper whose dealer franchises are sign-written on the workshop gable. Rear of the parade including No 243 Ewell Road looms on right*

John's Mark I pictured at the Hollyfield Road works for publicity purposes in 1947 when the rather fancy grilled engine cover was adopted on both this machine and Eric's new replica. Note the separate gravity-feed headrest tank above the cowl, short-arm driving position, Topo disc wheels and 'comprehensive instrumentation'; rev-counter only. Iota commented of the cars 'they seem rather on the short side for Motor Racing, but no doubt this is a useful asset for hill climbs...'

There was no special class for 500s, as only three such machines were actually running at the time, so the Mark I slotted into the up-to-750 cc racing car class, against prewar MGs, etc. John covered the standing-start kilometre in 35.81 sec to win handsomely, while Eric drove in the 1100 cc division and placed fourth, slower than Lones's 500, which was second.

Mark I was out again on 15 September at Westcourt, Finchampstead, in the West Hants & Dorset MC's Speed Trials. The course was a winding quarter-mile. This might sound deadly dull today, but in those spectacle-starved times with no circuits on which to race it was enough to make any enthusiast's mouth water. Mark I was the only 500 running, and Eric won with a best of 24.42 sec, which was 0.31 sec quicker than John and eighth-best of the day. None of the faster cars were under 1½ litres!

Now Mark I (with those initial engine-bearer problems solved) had proved itself a very potent and nimble machine. But there were still some other troubles... Charles – then aged 52 – had worked hard on the car with his son, but sometimes his patience wore perilously thin. John and Eric 'owned' Mark I jointly, the idea being to prove its design and then build a second car as Eric's own.

On the morning of the Westcourt Trials, Eric had arrived at the Garage early to pull out the Chevrolet truck. Charles and Elsie Cooper were by this time living in a flat above the corner shop, and as Eric quietly manoeuvred the truck across the forecourt he shattered a manhole cover with a deafening BANG!

'The Old Man came rushing out and just went purple. "That's Bloody IT!" he bawled. "That bloody car's more trouble than it's worth – I'm gunna put a sledge 'ammer through it!" I hopped out and said "All right, I'll buy out your share first." There was quite a shout-up then, but I was also running the MG at Westcourt and had to go. I got there not knowing if I'd ever see the 500 again, but then there was John driving in with the truck, grinning all over his face... the Old Man had calmed down... John could always talk him round....'

After the success there, the Mark I's creators were confident enough to set about building a sister car for Eric to drive through 1947. He had been cramped in the prototype and his own Cooper 'T3' emerged about an inch longer in wheelbase. 'The first car's Ford universal joints were designed to run in oil inside a casing. We ran them exposed, so they dried out. My new 500 used Hardy-Spicers. The chassis was again a pair of *Topolinos* back-to-back, but the webbing on the fabricated rear uprights was liberally drilled for lightness where the prototype's were plain.'

Eric's father ran an electrical wholesaling business named Halsey's Electric, and through his contacts he 'arranged' a batch of six BTH magnetos for use in the 500s – much like Charles Cooper's own friendship with Kaye Don had persuaded JAP engines out of Prestwich's. It was mutual self-help, and meanwhile Charles was already keen to turn all this activity into some kind of profit. He was keen to have a car to sell, and John's own ambitions for a production Cooper were also stirring.

At that time of continued petrol rationing, a two-seat road-going sports car based on the twin-*Topo* chassis theme with a motorcycle engine in the rear really appealed. The Garage was somehow involved in Charlie Robinson rebodying a prewar SS-Jaguar for a private owner named Paul Pycroft, who had designed florid 'aerodynamic' coachwork for it. The new sports Cooper was to carry a Robinson-beaten smaller-scale version of that bodyshell. This sports Cooper project progressed rapidly, and in April 1947 it was described by *The Motor*:

'A great deal of surprise and speculation has been occasioned of late in the Surbiton district of Surrey by the sight of a very small blue car with beautiful aerodynamic form. This turns out to be the latest version of the Cooper Special developed from the racing model which established a firm reputation at Brighton Speed Trials and other events during last year. . . .

'The new version . . . has a fully streamlined two-seater body which, by the release of one catch, can be lifted upwards from the tail to reveal the 'works', which are situated at that end. The car has a Triumph Tiger '100' motorcycle engine of 500 cc capacity, and even with the 'mock-up' engine fitted at present, speeds of between 75–80 mph are claimed to have been attained. Another Tiger engine is in course of preparation with a bronzed head, and with the use of 'dope' it is hoped that it will have an output of 38 bhp, enough to propel the car in the region of 100 mph.

'All-round independent suspension by transverse springing is incorporated, and three forward gears and reverse are provided with the change lever placed on the right-hand side of the driver. Equipment also includes Lockheed braking, together with a completely independent handbrake of the transmission type acting on the rear axle. The bonnet conceals twin head lamps, spare wheel, fuel tank and the air intake for the rear engine.

'Despite the impressive bodyshell, weight has been restricted to the minimum, total weight being 6½ cwt!

'This car is actually a prototype, and the makers, Cooper's Garage (Surbiton) Ltd., 243 Ewell Road, Tolworth, Surrey, hope, when material becomes available, to be able to go into series production.'

The Triumph engine was an overhead valve twin-cylinder. The sleek little Cooper 'T4', as LPC 500 was retrospectively listed in the company's eventual type numbering system, was to remain a one-off. Production, once it commenced, was to concentrate upon single-seaters and rather more substantial sports cars.

Nonetheless, LPC 500 gave John a great deal of fun and an entry in hillclimb and sprint sports car classes to accompany the 500s and show that these Cooper people really were capable of building something more than mere backyard special racers. Eric Brandon remembers the car well: 'I was testing it on the Kingston Bypass – I believe while John was away on his honeymoon – when the engine literally exploded and scattered pieces along the road for yards'. John had married a local girl named Pauline Brady – coincidentally born in the same road in Kingston as he himself.

The svelte little 'T4' streamliner was subsequently sold by the Garage to R. Gordon Sutherland, one of Aston Martin's many saviours, who at that time was running Abbott's of

Works team – the Cooper equipe posed against a wintry Fishponds, late-1947 with John's Mark I recognizable by its exposed gear-change pivot low on the cockpit side and flat scuttle behind the aero screen, alongside the Triumph Tiger twin 'T4' streamlined sports car and Eric's Mark I 'T3' on the far side with its fared-in gear-change pivot, integral headrest tank and (hidden in this view), upturned scuttle cowl within the aero screen

Farnham, the well-known coachbuilding company. He had a Jowett engine and gearbox installed, but the car eventually fell derelict after passing into other hands. In recent years it was advertised as 'Stirling Moss's first racing car' in *Exchange & Mart* and was discovered rotting away under a tarpaulin at the bottom of a Hampshire garden by David Baldock, a dealer from Borough Green in Kent. Into 1982 he was having the car completely restored, and by a stroke of amazing good fortune had acquired an original-type Sturmey-Archer three-speed *and reverse* motorcycle gearbox for it at a Beaulieu Autojumble. Apparently such a transmission had featured on Brough Superior sidecar combinations.

Meanwhile the 1947 season started poorly for the Cooper 500s at Prescott in May, where both John and Eric were beaten by the backyard pioneers Strang and Lones, plus 'The Wingco', Frank Aikens.

There were some rumblings about promoting 500 cc racing on Speedways, and John demonstrated his car at Eastbourne's Arlington track. 'But the idea died a natural death. . . .' There was no traction at all on the cinders.

At Shelsley Walsh in June, Strang and Aikens again beat the Cooper twins—Eric and John—3–4. There was certainly no instant domination for the Surbiton cars. . . . But now there were the first stirrings of circuit racing round airfield perimeter tracks. The Blackburn Welfare Motor Sports Club invited the 500 Club to stage a race on Blackburn Aircraft's airfield at Brough, near Hull, on 28 June, 1947. At that time there were as many as 16 500s available, but the entry dwindled rapidly to only four, each of whom hit trouble and couldn't make it. The event was cancelled.

So it fell to the Cambridge University AC and the Vintage Sports Car Club to run Britain's first postwar mainland circuit race, on Sunday, 13 July, 1942, using a 2.73-mile course at Gransden Lodge airfield, near Royston in Hertfordshire. This saw the first-ever 500-movement motor race, car running against car, rather than merely alone against the clock in timed events. Eric's highly polished aluminium 'T3' charged into the lead on the second of the four laps and won at an average of 60.21 mph. There were just three other starters – Aikens, Frank Bacon in his home-built, and Strang.

Eric was then narrowly beaten by Strang at the mid-summer Prescott 'climb, but won at Great Auclum and again at Prescott in August despite deranging his car's steering against the first-corner bank on his second run. John won the 500 class at the Brighton Speed Trials in September, covering the standing-km at 68.68 mph against his previous best of 62.48 mph. Eric's car holed its piston. John's twin-cylinder sports car was then the smallest but not quite the slowest runner in the 1300 cc sports division – but its average of 45 mph was poor.

The Cooper team then attacked the West Hants & Dorset MC's half-mile wiggly sprint at South Lytchett Manor near Poole. Eric won the class after Strang's gear selectors played up, and he and John took every class up to 1500 cc, only for near disaster on the way home. The Chevy truck ran out of fuel and while John and his cousin Colin Darby tried to prime the carburettor by pouring fuel into it the fumes ignited and John's hand and arm were quite seriously burned. Eric: 'He was in an awful mess. We ended up that night in Winchester Hospital Dental Department, which for some reason was the only place open.'

Back at Prescott for its final hillclimb of the year, Eric broke the 50 sec barrier in practice – the first time a 500 had ever climbed so fast – and in showery rain he won by over a second from Aikens, with John third.

On 20 September, the Southsea MC ran another half-mile sprint, this one on Merston airfield near Chichester. *Motor Sport* reported: 'Brandon won the 500 cc racing class with his usual masterful run in the Cooper 500, after spirited cornering, and seemed faster over the line than Cooper, who was .94 sec slower. . . .' The Cooper twins were placed 2–3 in the 850 cc class behind Ken Wharton's Austin-MG, and now several other enthusiasts were looking at the little polished-aluminium Coopers and asking if there were any plans for production?

More success the following weekend at Shelsley served to heighten such interest. Eric had the killer instinct. He wanted badly to win at everything he did, and he beat John into second place by 0.37 sec.

To round off the season the 500 Club organized a 'rally' at a remote airfield near Silverstone village, a few miles from Towcester on the Northamptonshire/Buckinghamshire border. They had permission from the landowner, but on arrival were ordered off by War Department police because they lacked the necessary Air Ministry permit. They drifted away to a pub in Towcester and there Lord Hesketh – owner of Towcester race course – invited them to run their cars on his land. Over 25 years later his son would be running a GP-winning racing team. Brandon and Cooper set fastest times on a brief uphill run at the race course, and Eric emerged as the most successful 500 driver of the year, and the Cooper-JAP was indisputably the most effective 500 cc racing car.

Same place, same day – George Saunders tries the 'T4' for size. The body was formed in one-piece hinging below the nose and lifting full-length from the extreme tail to expose the works, front and rear. LPC 500 carried 'Cooper' wheel trim centre insignia and the Robinson bodywork was beautifully finished. But the car was underpowered, unreliable and slow. It survives today

CHAPTER THREE

Into production

Into 1948 with would-be customers almost literally beating a path to Cooper's door at Hollyfield Road, Charles and John Cooper began accepting orders and deposits for production 500 cc cars.

John recalls there was a problem: 'We couldn't expect to find dozens of wrecked Fiat *Topolinos* to cannibalize. The only alternative was to sit down and design a similar type of car which we could build from the ground up in the Garage. I discussed the whole thing with my father, who was very wary of getting in too deep financially in setting up a production run. Quite apart from building the frames, could we lay our hands on enough JAP engines? They weren't cheap. Unless we could turn the money over quickly it meant tying up a lot of capital for quite some time.'

Charles cautiously went ahead, and a pilot batch of 12 new cars was planned for 1948, built it seems in two groups of six. Tooling and materials cost around £2000, and to protect Cooper's Garage from any potential claims The Cooper Car Company Ltd was incorporated on 19 December, 1947, at 243 Ewell Road. Directors were listed as C. N. Cooper, J. N. Cooper (both joint managing), P. S. Brooks, S. P. Moore and J. R. Stott, OBE. Kaye Don also assisted at the very beginning. Mr Brooks was a sleeping partner, an old friend of Charles's and a regular customer at the Garage 'who dropped a few quid in the kitty'. Mr Moore was company accountant, and Dr Stott was actually the family's doctor, an enthusiastic Bugatti OC member. He ran a Bentley and a gorgeous Type 57 Bugatti, which the Garage later sold for him '... for only £750 – ugh!'.

The new production 500 cc cars were to be known as the Cooper Mark II or 'T5' design – the beginning of the line. In general they followed the prototype form quite closely, retaining the same truncated diamond planform with box-section main chassis longerons drilled for lightness with tubular cross-members and fabricated sheet bridges at each end to support the transverse-leaf independent suspensions. A strip-steel superstructure framework was then welded onto the base frame to carry the aluminium-sheet body panels. John retained the basic Fiat suspension geometry, now using his own wishbones. The original Fiat lever-arm dampers were replaced by Newton-Bennett or Woodhead-Monroe telescopics picking up on the outboard end of the lower wishbones and reacting against abutments on the front bridge. The first two or three cars may have used Fiat steering, but Burman boxes quickly replaced the *Topo* components, centrally mounted with split track rod and a Ford production steering wheel.

The standard engine was still the 80 × 90 mm, 498 cc, Speedway JAP five-stud. The Cooper Car Co.'s prospectus for the cars listed the standard JAP output of 38 bhp at 6300 rpm, on alcohol fuel, and 14:1 cr. This represented 76 bhp per litre, making it one of the most efficient unsupercharged power units of its time, and it weighed only 78 lb complete. Lubrication was total-loss with supply from an external tank. Ignition was by BTH magneto – probably still courtesy of Eric Brandon's dad – to a single Champion LA15, Lodge BR49 or KLG689 spark plug. The carburettor was the familiar racing Amal, which was always liked because it didn't have a conventional butterfly to obstruct the airstream. When it was open, it was wide open.

A gravity-feed sprint fuel tank was still used, hung in the engine cowl spine behind the driver's head, while for longer events a further pressurized tank could be fitted under the front cowl above the driver's knees. Engine air-cooling was again provided by a nearside duct running from the nose intake alongside the driver to blow onto the exhaust port area of the head. The Burman four-speed gearbox and final-drive system was little changed from the prototype, and 8 in. Lockheed hydraulic drum brakes appeared front and rear; twin-leading shoe at the front. A simple cross-shaft carried the foot pedals, with the brake pedal operating the hydraulic master cylinder direct and Bowden cables running back for throttle and clutch. The handbrake operated a single Lockheed bisector-expander on the rear axle, again by cable. Since there was no differential there was no need to complicate matters by providing cable operation for both rear drums. The driver's seat was upholstered with Dunlopillo padding and the engine-turned dash panel simply carried a central 8000 rpm tachometer. A tiny Perspex screen gave protection.

The Press made much of Cooper's attention to minimal frontal area and good streamlining for the time, particularly since 'even the underpart of the chassis is enclosed....' Maximum speed was reckoned to be around 105 mph, with suitable gearing.

```
Telephone: ELMbridge 3346



        THE COOPER CAR CO., LTD.
             Manufacturers of the
       Cooper "500" & "1000" c.c. Racing Cars.

                                      Presented by
  243, EWELL ROAD,                    C. N. COOPER,
  SURBITON, SURREY.                   Managing Director.
```

The Old Man's business card for his new racing car production company, 1948. The reverse carried 'Cooper' capital letter script in the style soon famous, with red '500 cc' lettering interlinked, within an elliptical red rule

Production beginning in the workshop at Hollyfield Road, showing the new Cooper-fabricated basic box-section chassis with body-strips welded-on, and tranverse leafspring-supporting fabricated bridges front and rear. Centre car on the trestles has its engine cooling nose ducts installed. The Colin Darby-designed Cooper wheel castings show-off their integral brake drums with shrunk-in liners. John is working (right background) on one of the two chassis jigs visible, built from cheap wartime surplus Morrison air-raid shelter frames

Wheelbase of these production cars was 7 ft 11 in., track front and rear 3 ft 11 in. and dry weight around 520 lb. Price, open to a degree of negotiation, was just over £500, and in fact the little cars were quite remarkable for their Cooper-made content – right down to the new, and soon to become classical, design of cast aluminium road wheel, replacing the old Fiat *Topo* steel discs.

John: 'My cousin Colin Darby was a draughtsman for a firm called Celestion, who made loudspeakers in Kingston. One evening we got together and discussed supply problems with wheels. We wanted a 15 in. of our own which would be stronger and lighter than the old Fiat type which we just couldn't find any more. So with Colin we designed our own, including integral brake drums like Bugatti prewar, and patented them and had them cast in aluminium by a foundry in Croydon, I think. We then machined the castings ourselves on our old Garage lathe.'

These wheels carried 4.00-15 front and 5.00-15 rear tyres on the 1948 production cars.

Three months into 1948 Cooper held firm orders from Sir Francis Samuelson, Ronald 'Curly' Dryden, Stan Coldham, Peter Page, George Saunders, Alvin 'Spike' Rhiando and one Stirling Crauford Moss, plus the HW Motors partners George Abecassis and John Heath, while two cars were to be retained for Cooper's own use. Even Charles would drive occasionally, just to show the youngsters how. . . . The original prototype car was sold to a racing motorcyclist named Stan Goddard, while Eric retained his '47 car. Contemporary reports spoke of John having sold 'the second prototype', while Eric retained 'the original car'. Eric maintains he kept his own car throughout. Perhaps 'the second prototype' sounded more attractive when one of the cars came to be sold? Eric's mount for 1948 was updated, with the latest bullet nose cone fitted in place of the jut-chinned original fairing.

Amongst these initial original customers, George Saunders was perhaps closest to the Cooper family. He was a very successful motorcycle Speedway rider, where he'd been using and tuning JAP engines since 1934. He lived in Surbiton, where he ran the 'Atlantic Restaurant' and a small snack bar – one of the first fast-food emporia – called 'George Henry' after his Christian names. 'During the war Charles serviced a lot of fire service vehicles, and it was my job to inspect and approve them, so I knew him well . . . when they started building the cars it was a case of "Come on George you ought to have one". . . .' George eventually gave up 500 racing in 1949, but kept close contact, and in 1956 toured Europe with the works cars as 'acting unpaid honorary team manager'. After Charles's death in 1964 he bought his house on Box Hill, the Surrey beauty spot, and was still living in it – and still running Charles's last MGB – in 1982–83.

There seem to have been several seeds for the '1000' twin idea. John maintains it was all down to colourful Spike Rhiando. He was an habitually check-shirted, alleged Canadian who told journalists he had settled in England in 1933 when he barnstormed midget-car speedway racing into existence. Some of his friends maintained he'd never been closer to Canada than Greenford Speedway, but never mind, the fans loved him and his tiny, JAP vee-twin-engined Skirrow midget cars. He stored two of these machines during the war and after ordering his new 500 from Cooper he suggested it should be stretched sufficiently to accommodate one of their vee-twin engines. They weighed little more than the 500 single, and gave around 70 bhp. John realized the sprint and hillclimb potential of such a tool and did a deal with Rhiando to build the special chassis required in exchange for Spike's spare JAP twin.

Another story comes from Roy Golding, who joined the company as a fitter around this time. Motorcycle racer C. F. 'Charlie' Smith '. . . did bits for Cooper engines in his works at Clapham Junction. His foreman there was Jack Knight, who later made Cooper gearboxes. Charlie raced a JAP 1000 sidecar outfit and his passenger was a bloke called Ken Huswick, who lived near Cooper's in Alexandra Drive. He was often round the Garage looking at what was going on. He'd look at the chassis and say "Ere, John, how's about puttin' a big'un in there?"'

INTO PRODUCTION

Roy later became works manager at Hollyfield Road. He had begun work at 16 with Prince's of Kingston, crankshaft grinders. He and young Bert Prince, the owner's son, had a competition to see who could produce most in the shortest time during the war, '... working all night and most of the day. After the war I found it a bit humdrum. My pal John Hume was more into cars and motorcycles than me, and we'd often look into Cooper's Garage at the aeroplane hanging in the roof and the little racing cars. John kept saying "Why don't you get a job in there?" Charlie recognized me from Prince's – he'd been a regular customer there – and so I started, and John Hume later became John Cooper's 500 mechanic.... He always wore great big army boots. Charlie Cooper christened him "Boots" Hume, and it stuck.'

What was it like at Hollyfield Road in those formative days? 'There were just a few blokes building the cars. Jack Tolley did the welding, Fred Bedding – who'd been with Jack at Fox & Nicholl, the prewar Talbot and Lagonda racing people, doing aircraft work during the war – made the bodywork and Fred Neale, Charlie Smith and Douggie Johnson were fitters. They were all first class. Neale was a real craftsman, and Fred Bedding could do just anything with sheet metal. He could bend it, shape it, stretch it, shrink it, whatever you wanted. Later his son Pete joined to help beat panels and his other son Roy came in for a brief period as a welder.'

Roy Golding found himself running the tiny machine shop as production boomed: 'We didn't have much at all in the way of machine tools; just an Atlas lathe and bench drill, and a fly press to punch out the channel perforations for the chassis. We didn't even have a power tool to cut steel. I must have sawed-up miles of 1 in. 10-gauge steel for wishbone ends by hand, and then faced them on the lathe.... We all just did as best we could.

'Old Charlie Cooper never liked spending too much money, he wasn't a real engineer so to speak, but he was a jolly good practical mechanic and he had an eye and a feel for what was right, and what was wrong....'

In fact it was a bad time to be embarking upon racing car production at all. That winter of 1947–48 saw HM Government withdrawing the basic petrol ration. This was no problem for the alcohol-burning racing cars themselves, but how to transport them to meetings, and how would spectators get there to pay for the day's entertainment?

Still the indomitable VSCC forged ahead with an 'alcohol only' speed trial on Easter Monday 1948 at Luton Hoo Park, just north of St Albans in Bedfordshire. Six 500s were entered, including Eric's, while John Cooper shared the first production model with Sir Francis Samuelson. Eric suffered gearbox problems in practice and John beat him in the timed runs for a Cooper 1–2 overall. A huge crowd assembled despite the shortage of petrol. 'They arrived by train, coach, Green Line bus, lorry, van, private car and even on foot,' wrote 500 cc historian Austen May.

The 500 entry for the opening Prescott meeting in May included John Cooper and Eric Brandon, plus Goddard in the former 'works' car, Squadron Leader 'Curly' Dryden, AFC (who was perfectly bald) and an 18-year-old newcomer; Stirling Moss. . . .

As Stirling tells the story he had gone out for a drive one day and happened to pass down Ewell Road, where, in the corner showroom, he saw '. . . this real racing car sitting gleaming in the window. I thought it was terrific and went straight in and asked about it. After a few days I talked my father into coming out with me for a drive and we "just happened" to go past Cooper's again and "Oooh Dad, what d'you think of that?"'

John remembers this tousle-headed youngster coming in and ordering a 500 on a Friday, his irate father telephoning to cancel the order – 'He's under age!' – on the Saturday, and then both Pa Moss and Stirling arriving on the Monday to reinstate it.

Stirling had to sell his BMW 328 for £1000 to afford the Cooper plus some extra expenses, and John recalls delivering the cream-painted little car to the Moss family farm, 'The Long White Cloud', at Bray near Maidenhead. Stirling tried it on the roads of a deserted building site at nearby Cippenham. 'I was instantly impressed by the way he leaned on it from the moment he engaged the clutch. Soon the exhaust noise brought the police nosing around and we had to load up at once and do some fast talking.'

An ancient horsebox was converted to carry the Moss Cooper, towed behind either the equally aged family Rolls-Royce (father was a practising dentist) or a Jeep. A German ex-POW named Donatus Müller worked on the farm, and he volunteered to act as mechanic when young Mr Stirling went racing. . . .

At that first Prescott meeting Clive Lones beat all the Coopers, but Stirling was fourth. *Motor Sport* reported: 'Moss drove his Cooper really stirringly. . . .' It was a beginning for true greatness.

On 25 May the Manx Cup race on the Isle of Man saw Rhiando's new gold-lacquered 'Banana Split' Cooper twin make its bow with a 996 cc Fernihough-JAP engine installed. For the unusual luxury of circuit racing, car against car, it also sported rear-view mirrors clamped to each end of the front transverse leaf-spring. Early in practice the fuel tank split and then the engine seized at full throttle past the pits. Curly Dryden was also present with a 496 cc single-ohc Manx

Norton engine in his 500 in place of the standard-issue JAP, but he rolled at Cronk-ny-Mona and non-started. Rhiando repaired his twin 1000 sufficiently to collect his start money before retiring from the race. It wasn't much of a debut....

On 1 June, the Government restored a 'basic' petrol ration and the pace of the sporting calendar accelerated. The following weekend the Brighton & Hove MC ran a speed hillclimb in Stanmer Park, Brighton. Stan Coldham, a butcher, arrived with his new pale-blue production Cooper trailed behind his rebodied vintage Bentley. The Moss equipe reappeared and John Cooper arrived with his own new Cooper-JAP 1000 twin.

Alfred Moss told his son, 'Here's your chance. The others knew Prescott, here it's a new hill and you all start level....' In a dramatic battle against Brandon, Stirling's cream car won the class with a best of 58.78 against Eric's 59.20. John loosed-off his twin in the 501–1100 cc racing car class and won it easily, soaring up in 55.95 – fourth fastest of the day.

One week later Brandon won convincingly at Shelsley Walsh in his 500, while John's twin 1000 thrilled *Motor Sport*'s correspondent and broke the Shelsley unsupercharged record, '... 40.70 sec, a truly magnificent time.'

Next day at Prescott John again 'did the most prodigious things ... the car accelerating amazingly, handling superbly and being ideally suited to Prescott's difficult corners. It did in fact not only beat all the blown cars in (its) class – the real racers – but, giving away a half-litre and a blower (two blowers to be precise), broke the late A. F. P. Fane's class record with the "Shelsley" Frazer Nash by 0.66 sec.' Only Bob Gerard's blown 2-litre ERA climbed faster that day, and then by only 0.7 sec. The Cooper twin had arrived as a truly formidable hillclimb car, and it was to reign supreme in future years.

Meanwhile Britain's second postwar mainland circuit motor race was organized by the ever-optimistic Blackburn Welfare MC at Brough on 4 July. But only nine 500s appeared, one blew up in practice and another broke on the startline. Moss and Coldham in Coopers won their heats and then Stirling won the Final at 52 mph as heavy rain cut it back to just four laps. In a handicap six-lapper Stirling started from scratch and won again.

First production cars lined-up, Spring 1948 – left to right: John in the works '1000' with its ears on the engine cowl, George Saunders, Charles Cooper, Stirling Moss, Eric Brandon with his favoured beret, Stan Coldham – the racing butcher – and Moss's mechanic Don Müller in the unpainted car. Spares include fuel, fillers, wheels and tyres, tool kits, engine, gearbox, tyre inflation air bottle and pit signal board. This racing was becoming serious ...

Ecurie Moss then travelled to Jersey for the Bouley Bay hillclimb, which Stirling promptly won from Clive Lones. He won again at midsummer Prescott, where Eric Brandon in his familiar red shirt drove an ex-Harvey Noble Q-Type MG. 'It was a terrible mistake. I'd bought it in a fit of pique against Charles Cooper after one of our periodic shout-ups. It was a dreadful thing, so heavy and slow after the Cooper.' In the larger class John's unblown 1000 was beaten by Joe Fry's famous supercharged *Freikaiserwagen* special. George Saunders ran his production Cooper-JAP at this meeting . . . and it caught fire.

At Great Auclum, Stirling Moss notched his seventh win of his maiden season, beating Brandon in the Cooper, and at King's Park, Boscombe, he made it eight in a row. Then the Brighton Speed Trials saw Moss roundly beaten. *Motor Sport* sagely observed: 'The car wasn't quick enough for once, suggesting that sheer good driving may have accounted for earlier successes.' There was rather more to it than that. . . .

Peter Page made his production Cooper debut at Brighton, then back at Prescott in the wet, Brandon beat Strang and Moss, with Dryden seventh.

On Saturday, 18 September, 1948, British motor racing took a mighty leap into the future. On that day the Duke of Richmond & Gordon allowed the old Westhampnett fighter airfield on his land just north of Chichester to be inaugurated as Goodwood motor racing circuit. Short Brooklands-style races were run in a full day's programme. The first was won by Paul Pycroft's special-bodied 2.6 Jaguar – the special which had inspired the Triumph-twin sports Cooper the previous year. The three-lap 500 cc race winner was to receive a 20-guinea prize donated by *The Daily Graphic*. Page, Saunders and a 17-year-old newcomer named Peter John Collins all scratched their Cooper entries before the race, and the nine surviving starters then included Coopers for Moss, Brandon, Dryden, Samuelson and Coldham. Poor Eric stalled on the line, and it was Moss all the way to win from him and Dryden with Coldham and Samuelson 5–6. Stirling's fastest lap was timed at 73.2 mph, and in practice he had managed 77 mph. These Coopers were quick . . . and his was always very well prepared.

Pa Moss himself had raced at Brooklands and Indianapolis prewar and encouraged his son and Don Müller to tear down the JAP engine after each event, even if a whole meeting only entailed one mile's running. They carefully cleaned, polished, checked and reassembled the whole unit. Earlier in the year Stirling's first entry for Shelsley Walsh had been rejected. Now he was readily accepted, and won the class with a new hill record, after his first-run time had been bettered.

John Siddall wrote in *Iota*, the 500 Club magazine: 'I asked him [Moss] what he was going to do to get the record back – he replied that as he could not get any more poke out of the Cooper at short notice he reckoned that he would have to drive better. On the second run Moss did just that, and

Charger – Stirling Moss, still only 18, rocketed to prominence in his cream-painted production Cooper Mark II. The car was painstakingly prepared by himself and his German ex-PoW mechanic Donatus Müller with direction from Pa Moss himself. The family's equestrian interests are revealed by the horseshoe motif on the headrest fairing

the sight . . . was worth going a long way to see. Stirling arrived at the finish in 43.84 sec. A magnificent show. . . .'

More circuit racing followed, with the RAC's revived Grand Prix race run on Silverstone airfield, from which the 500 Clubmen had been evicted the previous year. The RAC organized a major 50-mile endurance race for 500s to support the main event there on 2 October. No less than 25 cars took the grid, eight of them Coopers. Rhiando, Moss, Samuelson, Coldham, Brandon, John Cooper and Saunders all used JAP engines, while Dryden ran his Norton single. He actually qualified second fastest behind Strang's special with its Vincent-HRD engine. Unfortunately the start was scrambled, as only Strang and Moss were looking when Earl Howe dropped the flag. Eric Brandon for one was actually standing beside his car when the rest set off!

Stirling led Rhiando's gold Cooper after three laps, 10 seconds clear of Dryden and Brandon, who was hammering through furiously from the back. Saunders's car broke a chain, Dryden's front engine mount parted and then Moss's leading Cooper lost drive as its engine sprocket worked loose. Spike Rhiando was able to tour home to win this first-ever serious 500 cc race at 60.68 mph from John in the pale-blue works car, then Samuelson and Brandon. Coldham was sixth and Page – whose dark green car started late after fitting a new final-drive chain – was ninth and last.

Motor Sport gave guarded approval to the RAC for running this type of race, but couldn't resist comparing its 30 per cent finishing record with the 50 per cent achieved by 1100 cc cars in the first 200-Miles race at Brooklands in 1921. John Siddall was even less delighted. He considered the Club members had blown their chance of achieving recognition as a serious racing class. The standard of driving was 'absolutely deplorable. That the road holding of the cars was not at fault was shown by the three or four who really exerted themselves, among whom Stirling Moss was almost the only one who possessed a real virtuoso technique. . . .' Some of the 'old brigade' in the RAC's corridors of power or established in the upper echelons of British motor racing didn't agree. They regarded the newcomer's scorching style with grave suspicion. It just wasn't cricket to hurl a car through corners so fast . . . even if he did look so relaxed while he did it.

One week after the Silverstone débâcle, another airfield race was run for 500s at Dunholme Lodge, near Lincoln. Dryden led Moss initially but simply couldn't hold him off before Rhiando whizzed past them both, only for his gold Cooper to seize up. Moss, Dryden, Coldham and Page notched a Cooper 1–2–3–4 finish.

There was more to racing successfully than merely buying a Cooper as-built. After the Dunholme races the Moss, John Cooper and Eric Brandon cars all came onto the second-hand market. Moss's was bought by Austen May, a prewar trials- and rally-driving contemporary of Kidderminster motor trader Pat Collins, whose young son Peter had recently taken delivery of a brand-new production Cooper, but since he was under-age he had merely learned to drive it on local airfields. May was intrigued by this little car, which persuaded him to purchase Moss's, and he later wrote this description of what he found:

'Throughout the vehicle ordinary locknuts had everywhere been replaced by the Simmonds self-locking nuts; extensive wiring and split-pinning had been resorted to, to offset that number one bogey of the single-cylinder engine, vibration: much of the chassis and body framework had been drilled for lightness; the rear shock absorbers, Newton telescopics, had been remounted [a modification since adopted by Cooper for all the cars]; the brake drums had been individually lapped-in and each road wheel had been marked so that after removal it should be fitted back only in one certain position. Small cooling ducts had been added to the front brakes.

'The Speedway model JAP engine had been converted from a five-stud to a four-stud, which simply means that only

Cooper test session on the Kingston Bypass. The circuit included a leg through suburban Surbiton on the way home to the works. Here Charles, John and the boys study progress. Local resident Alan Thomson heard the car, as so often, and grabbed his camera

The irrepressible Alvin 'Spike' Rhiando acknowledging the camera alongside his famous 'banana split' gold-lacquered Cooper twin 1000 in the Manx pits at Douglas, IoM, for the 25 May, 1948 Manx Cup. John handles the fuel at right, 'Curly' Dryden's trend-setting Mark II-Norton supports its owner-driver, left, Mrs Dryden looks on by pit wall. Note opposing angles of front and rear dampers, and rear-view mirrors demanded by real racing clipped to the front spring on Rhiando's car, on the scuttle on Dryden's. Soon after, the unfortunate Wing-Commander Dryden rolled his car and would non-start

Growing up – the Vincent-HRD 1000 twin engine for George Abecassis in a stretch chassis late-1948, hastily wheeled-out for photography here at Hollyfield Road. How hastily can be judged from the 'N/S F' – 'near-side front' – wheel mounted off-side rear with only two wheel nuts in place. The characteristic air-cooling ears of the definitive 1000 twins are visible on the open engine cowl

four cylinder head holding-down bolts were employed instead of five. The internals were polished literally to a mirror finish; there was a slightly oversize inlet valve; the piston fitted was a Specialloid type J29, with the "ears" turned off, as it had been found these tended to pick up; the plug was a Lodge type R49, which is an aircraft pattern, screened-version of the regular R49, and the fuel was methanol with a very small admixture of acetone and castor oil.

'A light sprung steering wheel padded in the centre against possible crash injury replaced the original wheel; there was a non-standard polished track-rod with special ball-joints; a mechanical petrol pump worked off a cam on the back axle to deliver fuel from the robust-looking Gallay scuttle fuel tank and the filler cap of the over-engine sprint tank had been fitted with a two-way tap. . . .'

Cooper cars had formed the backbone of 500 cc competition that season, and from 15 events started Stirling had won 11, retired once and taken a third place and two fourths. He attracted some assistance from JAP in engine parts, while Sternol gave free oil, but even after the Cooper had been sold at the end of the season as a rolling-chassis the Moss equipe still showed a small financial loss – their commitment had been so wholehearted. But the young driver attracted great publicity and it rubbed off on the car he drove.

Meanwhile John's works 1000 had proved itself undoubtedly the fastest unblown sprint car in Britain. At Brighton it covered the standing kilometre in a record 27.93 sec, again fastest unblown time of the day. The JAP twin engine used identical heads and barrels to the 498 cc singles, and was in effect two Speedway 500s mounted at an included angle of 60 degrees on a common crankcase, with one con-rod big-end forked over the other. The standard compression ratio remained 14:1 and the twin delivered 76 bhp at 6300 rpm in a car weighing only 600 lb.

Meanwhile the sister Cooper 1000 ordered by George Abecassis of HW Motors Ltd finally appeared late that year. George chose a 998 cc Vincent-HRD Rapide engine aimed more at circuit racing than sprints. It was better suited to continuous full-throttle running for this purpose. Fearless George ran the car only once, at Goodwood on 'Pool' petrol, so there was no valid comparison against the blown 1100s in the same race burning alcohol. He believed that on alcohol his engine would produce around 80 bhp since motorcycles had already raced the engine in this tune in short events at Scarborough and Eppynt. The Rapide engine had an integral gearbox so the normal Burman 'box' in the Cooper was removed to make way and the car used just a single short final-drive chain, unlike the double-drive 500 singles.

Early that winter Cooper took delivery of the latest Vincent-HRD Black Lightning twin-cylinder engine specially developed from the Rapide for racing, complete with giant carburettors and a higher compression. On its debut such an engine had taken the Belgian class motorcycle speed record to 143 mph and the American mark to 151 mph. In a Cooper chassis some real excitement was expected. . . .

Order books were full, hopes were high, and the Cooper Car Company had been well and truly launched.

CHAPTER FOUR

A sports car, and a designer...

While 500 production was getting into its stride at Hollyfield Road, John was still keen on building a sports car to use on the road. It would have to be more practical than the underpowered Triumph twin 'T4', and he appreciated that the basic box-section diamond-planform chassis could just as well accommodate an engine up front as in the back.

While the 500s were being built in one corner of the Garage, it was still operating normally for servicing and repairs. Charles Cooper was still a Vauxhall agent, and John had his eye on a four-cylinder Vauxhall Ten engine lying there in store. So the Cooper-Vauxhall sports came about, being completed during the winter of 1948–49.

The sports car chassis was identical to the 1000 cc single-seater's. As I write there's a blueprint spread beside me, dated 5 October, 1949, showing this type of frame and signed by the Cooper Car Company's new draughtsman-designer, O. R. Maddock. His name has often been misspelled, either Maddocks, or Maddox, but Owen Richard Maddock was to have immense influence upon the Cooper story.

He became an immensely popular, well-respected member of the 'family'; admired for his creativity and the artistry of his complex, fine-detailed drawings. A later assistant describes him as 'an outstanding lateral thinker'. He was quite a sensitive character. He tended to stutter. He was always on the move, and was a prodigious walker. If an argument with Charles or John upset him he would march off around Surbiton at high speed until he'd burned off his feelings. He wore a full beard, bushy and black, at a time when beards spelled either eccentricity or a maritime background, and nothing in between....

Owen was born on 24 January, 1925, son of architect R. H. Richard Maddock. Father worked mainly for Lutyens's great rival Sir Herbert Baker, who won the prize task of designing the Bank of England in the City of London. Maddock Sr spent some 16 years on site overseeing the project. The family lived in Sutton, Surrey, and Owen studied engineering at Kingston Technical College. Studies deferred his call-up for wartime military service, so he served instead in the Home Guard.

He won his AMIMechE at Kingston Tech, then spent two years in the Army 'occupying Germany' just postwar. In April 1948 he returned to the Tech on a refresher course.

Owen Maddock, Cooper's budding chief designer, on Souzaphone (left) with Beryl Bryden's Backroom Boys, alongside John Lavender (banjo), Allan Wickham (trumpet), 'Dizzie' Wood (soprano sax), Dave Stevens (piano) and Beryl herself at microphone. At one 500 Club 'do' in a plush West End hotel the regular band went home at midnight. Owen brought his own group to play into the small hours; himself on soprano sax, Pete Bedding – Cooper panel-basher – appropriately on drums and Beryl singing. The doorman turned Owen and Pete away when they arrived in the former's matt-black 1930 Riley 9 saloon with headlights on the roof – a Maddock idea to cut glare in fog. Beryl sang the double-entendre 'Race Mechanic's Blues' and cut an acetate disc of the live performance. At one point Eric Brandon cuts in on one solo instrumental to complain about '... this awful noise. Just listen!' and instantly Owen begins his saxophone solo ...

This entailed 18 months' 'workshop experience' and he looked around locally for somewhere suitable. He tried HRD, then Trojan, and eventually found Cooper, who required '... a drawer, but they didn't have enough work for someone who just wanted to draw all the time, so in September '48

I went to work there as a fitter, then storekeeper, chaser, van-driver, general dogsbody, and part-time draughtsman when they wanted something drawn. . . .

'John's cousin, Colin Darby, had drawn the first cast wheels and some other bits and pieces, but most work was done without drawings apart from a few general sketches, and some *really* technical stuff like the body sections painted on the workshop wall. When the walls were whitewashed the body sections disappeared, so they had to be drawn again! It was that kind of set-up.'

Like so many outwardly quiet people Owen was 'a raver' on the side. Most people at Cooper knew him as 'Beard', and Charles Cooper would always roar 'WHISKERS!' when he wanted him, while in his spare time Owen played jazz. . . . He played the sousaphone for 'The Mike Daniels Band', then trombone and sousaphone for the brassy, beautiful 'Beryl Bryden's Backroom Boys'. Eventually he joined 'Mick Mulligan's Magnolia Jazz Band' as sousaphone player. He could often make more money from his musical gigs than 'Charlie Cooper was paying me for the day job . . . I don't think he liked that when he found out. . . .' George Melly was vocalist for Mick Mulligan while Owen played with the band, and in his memoirs the outrageously camp Melly recalls Owen as 'a racing car designer always wearing a grease-soaked raincoat', and goes on to tell a scurrilous story about 'Beard's love of Sydney Bechet records and their effect upon his girl-friend of the time. . . . Eventually Mick Mulligan decided to go fully professional, which Owen didn't want to do, and his last public performance for the Band was actually the first jazz concert at the new Royal Festival Hall in London, in 1951. Princess Elizabeth and Prince Philip were in the audience. A year later she would be Queen.

To return to the Cooper-Vauxhall; its chassis frame was welded up from box-section main longerons in $3\frac{1}{8} \times 1\frac{5}{8}$ in. 14-gauge mild-steel channel, boxed for much of their free length with welded-on 14-gauge mild steel sheet. The suspension bridges at front and rear were fabricated from similar sheet webs, while two midship cross-members extending into body support outriggers were in $1\frac{7}{8}$ in. diameter 18-gauge mild steel tube. A third tubular cross-member fitted between the longerons, in $1\frac{1}{4}$ in. 12-gauge tube.

The longerons were spaced 20 in. apart amidships and the familiar Fiat-derived transverse-leaf suspension was mounted on the bridge pieces at front and rear, with 500-style telescopic dampers. A superstructure of something like $\frac{1}{2} \times \frac{1}{8}$ in. mild-steel strip was tacked on to this base frame to support the hand-beaten 18-gauge aluminium bodyshell formed by Fred Bedding and his son Pete, who had joined the company – 'as a short-term stop-gap' – when he came out of military service in 1948. . . . He would work for Cooper for 21 years.

Despite the shortness of the 500-derived chassis, placing the twin seats well back against the rear axle enabled the four-cylinder Vauxhall Ten engine to be mounted well back from the front axle line. The engine was installed complete with its standard three-speed and reverse gearbox and breathed through twin horizontal SU carburettors with open intakes. These were preferred to the standard single carburettor, and a smoothly branched separate exhaust manifold was another modification. Standard dimensions were 63.5 mm bore by 95 mm stroke, displacing 1203 cc, and output was around 31.5 bhp on a 6.5:1 compression. Now John believed he was seeing closer to 48 bhp.

Drive was taken from the gearbox by an open propeller shaft to a fixed diff housed within the rear bridge structure. Output shafts on either side then drove to double-UJ sliding-spline half-shafts driving the cast-alloy Cooper road wheels. By judicious bending the standard Vauxhall gear lever was brought within convenient reach of the 16 in. right-hand-drive steering wheel. The cast-alloy wheels incorporated integral drum brakes, with steel liners, which were actually sawn-off sections of Wellworthy diesel engine cylinder liners, with a retaining groove machined round them. Lockheed hydraulics were used, twin leading-shoe at the front just like the single-seaters. A 'pistol-type' handbrake cable-operated the rears.

Electrics were 6-volt by Lucas, with headlamps mounted either side of the radiator core up front behind the mesh-covered Cooper-shaped nose opening which mimicked the 500 grilles. Under new Government requirements, this mounting wasn't strictly legal.

This little prototype carried the Garage trade-plate 307 PD and was likened by *The Autocar* to the contemporary open-bodied Cisitalias and Simcas in Europe. They remarked: '. . . there may be a disposition to impute frailty to any passenger vehicle which weighs as little as 9 cwt while exerting not far short of 40 bhp [*sic*]. Such fears, however, may be discounted when it is realized that this same Cooper chassis has shown itself strong enough for the 80 bhp-plus of the big JAP racing twin, a unit which, moreover, must obviously do its work far more lumpily than a four. Furthermore, observation satisfied this journal that the new sports car, after four months of what may be called "scientific sabotage", which is the common lot of prototypes, was in no danger of "shaking itself to pieces". . . .'

John believed at that time that his little two-seater roadie was capable of 85 mph-plus with its full-width windscreen folded flat, and *The Autocar*'s man enthused about: 'First,

First front-engined postwar Cooper – the beautiful Beddings-bodied Cooper-Vauxhall prototype posed in a rain-soaked Hollyfield Road, with the old Electric Light Company buildings beyond, just along from the works. Note headlights within the mesh nose grille, well thought-out upholstery and trim, and large boot-lid in the shapely tail. 207 PD was a Cooper's Garage trade plate

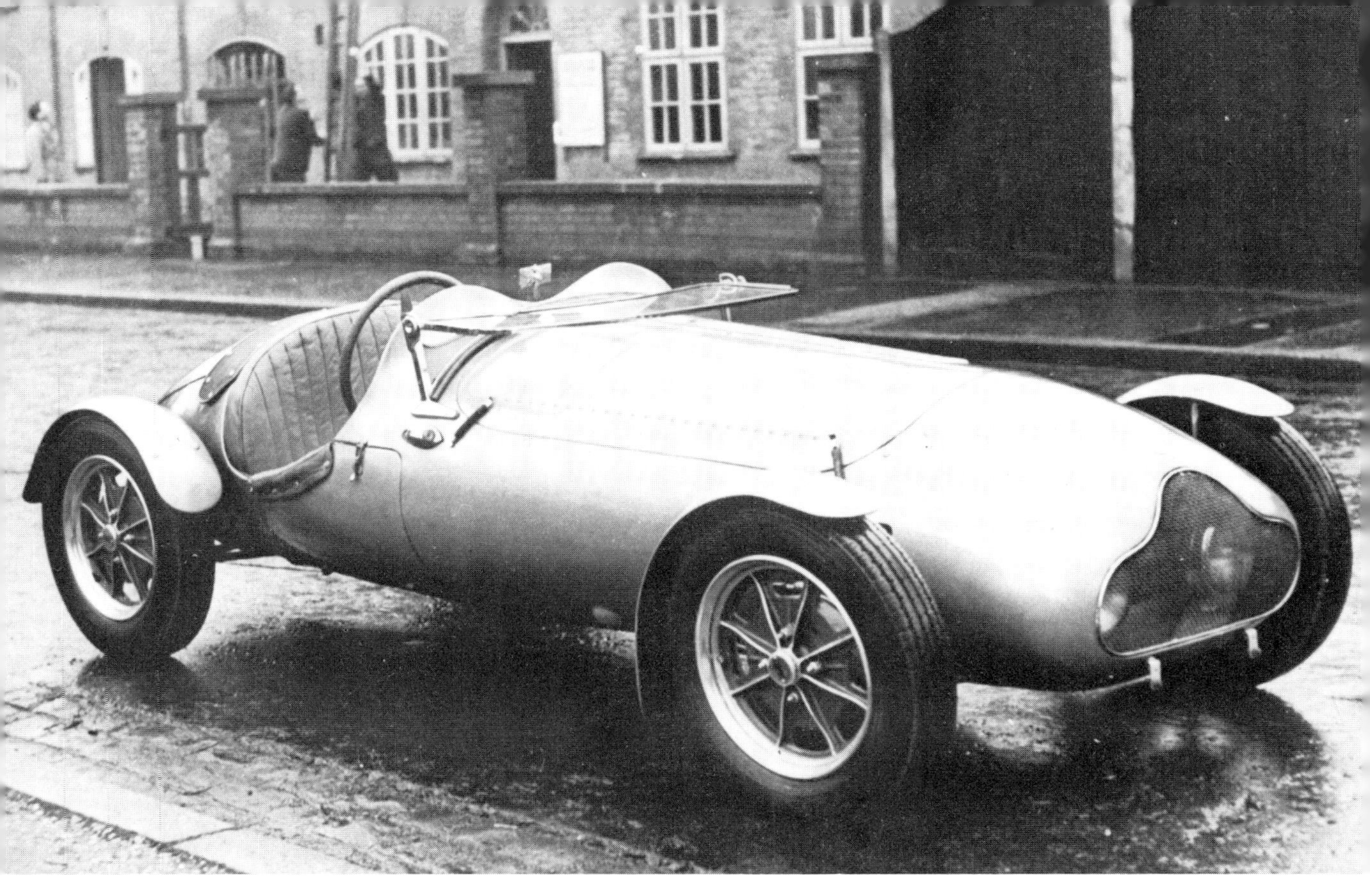

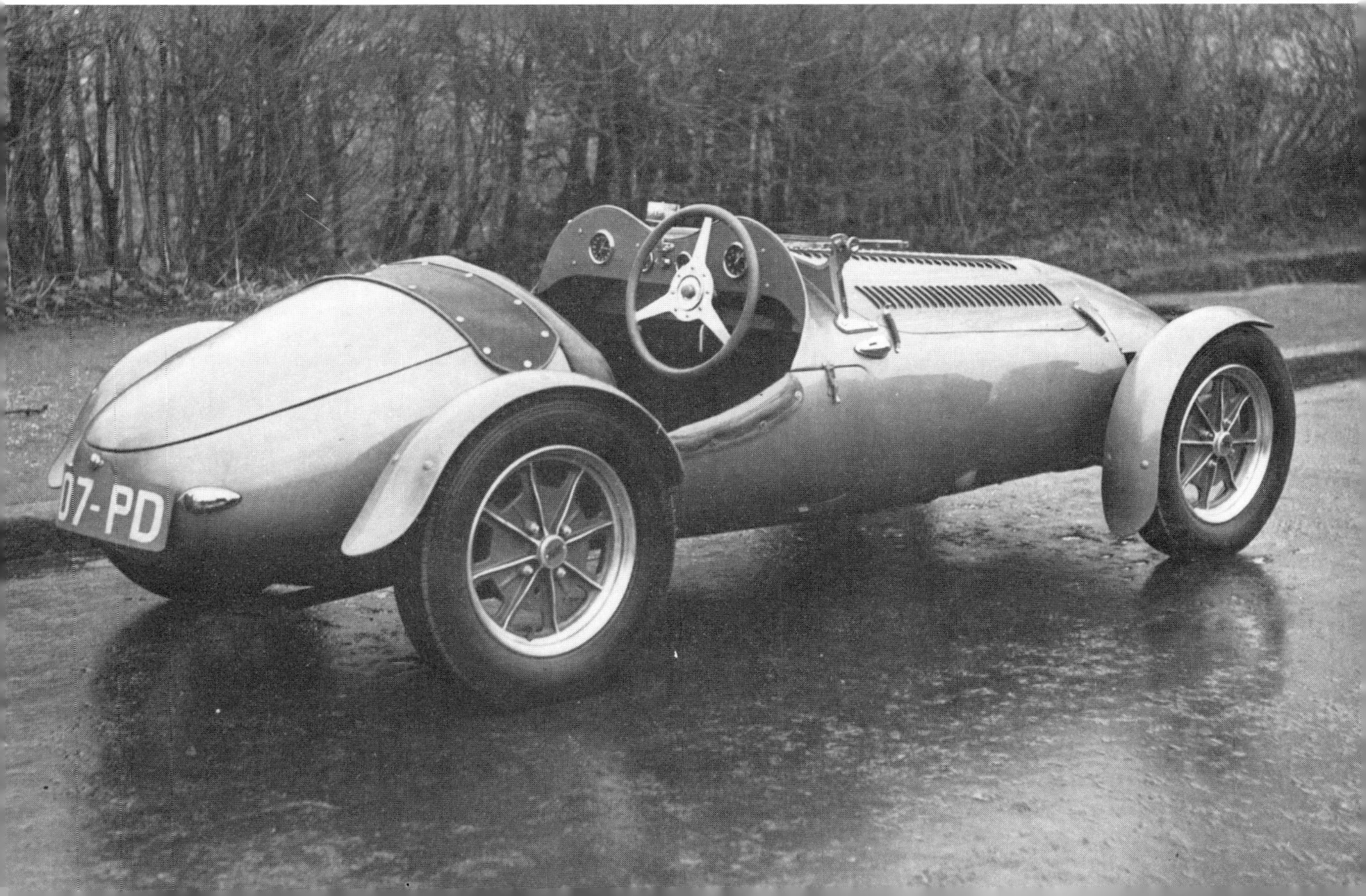
07-PD

the effortless exuberance of the acceleration; second, the hairline accuracy of the high-geared steering and fine cornering power; and third, the flatness of the ride and shock-immunity of the all-independent springing.'

Their only real criticism was that '... at present the suspension deflects excessively', predicting sacrifices in ride quality since the system obviously needed stiffening by recambering or the addition of an extra leaf in each transverse spring assembly.

The Motor also liked the little car: 'It runs true on the straightaway, and can either be steered or "thrown" round corners, according to the driver's whim, and put through open bends in a four-wheel "drift" if required. Brutal use of the tiller on sharp corners makes the tail break away in the manner made familiar by single-seat hillclimb Coopers, but the skid is always precisely under control, and the back does not "take charge".... In bodywork the little car is neat, comfortable and modern, with doors that let down, being hinged at the bottom instead of at the side. The facia is covered in red leather to match that of the elbow-pads, and the flexible light-alloy steering wheel is likewise leather-covered, giving a firm and pleasant grip.... Italian practice has inspired the lines, and the result is a car that is light, practical and aerodynamically clean....'

John raced the little car at Goodwood but realized more power was required and approached John Thornley at MG. A deal was done to provide alternative power units and as the Cooper-MG sports project evolved so the Cooper-Vauxhall lay silent at Hollyfield Road.

One day late in 1949 a Major Barker appeared, PA to the extravagant Sir Bernard Docker, chairman of Daimler, Hooper Car Bodies, BSA, etc., whose lavish-spending habits and publicity-conscious Lady wife filled the newspaper gossip columns of the time. Major Barker explained that 12-year-old Lance Docker was to have a car to drive around the family estate at Poole. Could Cooper supply?

Through the winter of 1949–50, amongst all the other production work, a special sports car was contrived for him, to use an air-cooled Sunbeam S7 vertical-twin motorcycle engine. It appears that a new frame was made for it to accept the engine plus shaft-drive to the rear wheels. John recalls: 'It vibrated so much it was completely useless, and so we never completed it. I sold him the redundant old Cooper-Vauxhall instead, and it was modified by Hooper's to carry a mock Daimler grille and flashy interior....' This was to be the most plutocratic of all Coopers. There was also a project that winter to fudge together an 1100 cc JAP engine with the gearbox integral so that it could be mounted crosswise in the frame to use shaft-drive to the rear wheels.

But the Cooper-MG approach was far more logical. It made better sense, and Charles Cooper made sure that was the path his fast-growing company would take; as and when 500 cc commitments might allow.

Uncompleted prototype – the shaft-drive JAP twin front-engined sports car photographed in a corner of the Hollyfield works by Motor Sport, *winter 1949–1950. Note 500-derived suspension layout, simple box-section welded-up chassis frame of the Cooper-Vauxhall/MG series and back-axle mounting. Leaning against the wall are two of John Hume's Cooper 'T8' trailers intended as a practical ready source of spare wheels and tyres for the 500 owner-driver. The prototype was almost certainly completed with a water-cooled in-line 4-cylinder engine of some type*

CHAPTER FIVE

Taking root–the season of '49

Motor racing mushroomed clear across Europe in 1949 and the 500 movement flourished, with Cooper chassis by far the most numerous and most successful. In many ways this caused problems. The original 'Bristol boys' like Dick Caesar had intended 500 racing to bring the sport within reach of the impecunious enthusiast. *Iota* magazine talked of cars built for £135 'of which the engine accounted for £75', while one arch corner-cutter put himself on the track for less than £40!

Now, for 1949 Cooper's new-car price was already as high as £575 and it was suggested that 500 racing should be split into quality classes, or a 'production' and 'special' division. The growing Cooper dominance was good for business at Hollyfield Road, but it did nothing for their popularity with the movement's founders. That in no way detracts from the bald fact that many drivers found their feet through buying new or second-hand Coopers when they lacked the talent or time to build specials of their own. The nimble and forgiving handling of the little Coopers provided a whole new driver training ground which traditional, still prewar-style sports and racing cars could never match.

When Bill Boddy of *Motor Sport* visited the works in February 1949 to try the Cooper-Vauxhall he wrote: 'It is not possible to be blasé on a visit to Cooper's Garage! For here British racing cars, not unjustly referred to as "miniature Auto Unions" are in brisk production.... Now the third dozen batch of Coopers is well towards completion, and they are being shipped all over the world. Last year 24 cars were produced, into three of which 1000 cc V-twin engines were installed, and this year ten owners already propose to fit such engines in their cars....'

Orders had arrived from Sweden, Denmark, Finland, Belgium and Ceylon. One car was on show in New York and used Coopers became available as their owners hammered on the door at Hollyfield Road for the latest model.

This Mark III or 'T7' 500 provided for a ZF limited-slip diff in the back axle, used new cast-magnesium wheels which were even lighter than the aluminium originals and had a new combined fuel and oil tank above the engine. An 8½- to 9-gallon long-range fuel tank could be slung under the scuttle and if necessary another could be slotted under the seat. The seat back was raked to give more cockpit space, à la Moss and his long-armed style modelled after the great Farina....

The exploits of the 1000 cc twins the previous year led to more demand from Moss, George Hartwell, Leith, Watkins, Baring, Andrews, Prosser, Patthey in Switzerland, Logan and the publicists' dream, Sylvia Bloomer. Not all of them fulfilled the rumoured orders.

Pa Moss had ordered one of the 'stretch' chassis from Cooper and his son typically threw himself into the project. The 'twins' were regarded as much more serious racing cars than the 'demented woodpecker' 500s. Potentially they could compete at international level in unblown 2-litre Formula 2.

Hollyfield Road saw regular visits from young Moss and his father, inspecting progress and suggesting mods on their new car. Rack-and-pinion steering, long-range pannier tanks and a tailor-made bucket seat for better location all appeared. This lack of lateral support for the driver showed itself in the early models as many preferred to steer one-handed while hanging on to the car's underbelly with the other! Upholstery and wheel-rim covering for Cooper was undertaken by Fulford's of Kingston.

It was clear that the Vincent-HRD Black Lightning engine was now the most potent 1000 available and Pa Moss wrote to the company to buy one. Their response was a polite brush-off, so the Moss family went to J. A. Prestwich in Tottenham, whose chief engineer, Stan Greening, agreed to supply a new 1000 twin with dry-sump lubrication, the unit worth around £200, plus spares support. Pa Moss then persuaded Mobiloil, Dunlop and Lodge to chip in with small retainers and bonuses. The old horsebox transporter was replaced by a Bedford van, blazoned with supporting companies' logos. A season was planned with the new 'two-way' Cooper Mk III running either 500 or 1000 cc engines.

This silver-green Moss Cooper lost the lead in the 500 race at Easter Monday Goodwood on the opening lap when its piston failed. Back in the paddock the 1000 twin replaced the broken 500 single and Stirling promptly beat Abecassis's Vincent-HRD Cooper to win the Second Easter Handicap at 79.76 mph. Coldham and Dryden were 1-2 for Cooper in the 500 race after Moss's departure, and that Sunday, in far-off Ceylon, a Cooper 500 scored the marque's first overseas victory, driven by a British serviceman in the St James Hill-climb over a 1000-yard tea plantation course.... Other cars began winning in Scandinavia, and the British contingent

35

prepared to go abroad as an increasing number of 500 cc internationals was mooted.

In Bois de la Cambre park in Brussels, 50-year-old fruit farmer and former motorcycle racer Bill Aston won a 500 race in his brand-new Cooper from the diminutive Don Parker's special; the Coldham and Samuelson Coopers were third and fourth. That day at Prescott Eric Brandon won his class with a record 48.40 climb.

Four Cooper 1000s tackled the Manx Cup race on the Isle of Man. They were driven by Moss, Abecassis, John Cooper and newcomer Eric Winterbottom, who was mine host of the Albert Hotel in Kingston Hill – a popular watering hole for the 500 fraternity. . . . This was serious road racing and Moss set fastest practice lap. Trying to match it, George Abecassis crashed at Governor's Bridge, wrecking his car. John's blue works machine was sick, but fifth in the race while Winterbottom's Vincent model retired. Meanwhile Moss had left the field for dead, only for his mag drive to shear with three laps to go. . . .

The British GP meeting was held early that year and another major 500 race was run as a supporting event. There were 19 Coopers in the field of 40 and Moss arrived with a 'sloper' JAP engine – just one barrel on the dry-sump twin 1000 crankcase – which caused great consternation amongst his rivals. He led throughout and won easily from Dryden's Cooper-Norton, Bill Aston's JAP and other Surbiton cars driven by names like Christie, Watkins, Reece, John himself, Pat Prosser, Samuelson and Charles Cooper – having a go 'to show the boys how it should be done.' Michael Christie's new Mark III was 'number 17, a long wheelbase model which could carry the 1000 and later 1100 twins, as well as a 500 single', as the founder of the Alexander Engineering concern at Haddenham recalled in 1983. Silverstone was his first major event with the new car and fourth place was the forerunner of great success, mainly with the twin-cylinder engines in hillclimbing.

Now Stirling Moss with his two-way Cooper was poised to wave the Cooper flag abroad. His entry for the Lago di Garda F2 race in Italy had been accepted. After setting a stunning Shelsley record of 38.57 sec in the 1000 he set off for Italy in the Bedford van, picking up a girlfriend along the way. . . . He discovered as wild and woolly a road course as only the Italians could contemplate, and found himself up against Villoresi, Tadini and Count Sterzi in V12 Ferraris. He was as fascinated by them and their cars as they were by this 19-year-old *Inglesi* and his peculiar bug-like racing car . . . which went so fast.

He qualified third behind Villoresi and Sterzi in practice

and finished third in Heat One behind Villoresi and Tadini after Sterzi had crashed – while driving over his head to hold off the Cooper-JAP!

The rest of the family had travelled down independently, and Pa Moss presided during the interval as a hole was hacked in the Cooper's undertray and its after-edge bent down to scoop in cooling air for the magnetos. In the Final, Stirling was third again behind the Ferraris, and fully four minutes clear of the next 1100 cc car. The *tifosi* gave Moss and the Cooper a terrific reception. He'd earned £200 prize money. The Cooper 1000 hadn't been able to challenge the Ferraris on even terms, but it had far outperformed everything else in the 1100 class.

On 10 July the important *Coupe des Petites Cylindrées* race was held at Reims-Gueux, accompanying the Formula 1 Marne GP. Moss ran his JAP 1000 there, alongside Abecassis with his Vincent-HRD engine fitted in a fresh chassis and Bill Aston with a 995 cc JAP twin in his car. Aston's race lasted only four troubled laps before succumbing to carburettor trouble. Abecassis's gearbox failed and Moss's chain broke on lap three. He pushed into the pits in sweltering heat, the chain was replaced and he finished eighth. On his way home he returned to Jersey's Bouley Bay hill-climb, tying for third place with Dennis Poore's big supercharged GP Alfa Romeo. He rose to third overall in the RAC Hill-Climb Championship standings, and was to finish the season there.

Back in England a new road racing circuit had been opened around Blandford Army Camp in Dorset. Both Eric Brandon and John Cooper drove twin JAPs to win heats of the Blandford Trophy. Unfortunately the Final was stopped after a multiple collision. George Hartwell and Eric Winterbottom ran their Vincent-engined 1000s, but the JAPs were better suited to the course, or perhaps Brandon and Cooper were better-matched to their cars? Certainly Eric Brandon loved his twin: 'It was the nicest Cooper I ever had, long wheelbase with a self-locker which was excellent with the twin but made the 500 worse on fast bends where there wasn't enough power to balance the car. But the 1000 was the sweetest thing I ever ran; smooth, gorgeous . . . safe and *bloody* fast!'

Cooper 500s had posted wins in Helsinki, at Skarpnack, Hedemora, Gardemoen and at Copenhagen's Kastrup airfield. Then on 30 July the biggest continental race of the season was held at Zandvoort, Holland. Moss, Dryden, Aston, Samuelson, Coldham, Brandon and 17-year-old Peter Collins, plus newcomer John Habin, ran English-based Coopers, while Dutchman Lex Beels drove his imported model. Don Parker and Charlie Smith ran their own specials.

Moss actually practised his 'two-way' car with the 1000 twin installed, hoping to persuade the organizers to give him a start in the main event Grand Prix. But they would not agree and the twin was reworked as a 500 'sloper' for the minor race.

At the start Habin's Cooper crept as its clutch dragged and his mechanic dashed on to the grid to wheel the car back to its mark. The Dutch starter dropped his flag unawares and Habin shot away, leaving the unfortunate mechanic to start back in shock – straight into Moss's path. He was bowled into the air and fell in front of Aston and Dryden, who miraculously avoided him. Stirling was sure he'd killed the man and slowed at the end of the lap, only to be waved on by reassuring officials, the mechanic was aggrieved but well enough. So he took off, stole the lead on lap three and won easily from Aston, Beels, Brandon, Dryden and Coldham. Eric recalls the organizers never did pay the promised start and prize money, and their 'free accommodation' consisted of bare beds in an army barracks. . . .

Manx Cup race, Douglas, Isle of Man, 1949: Stirling Moss's twin-cylinder stretch-chassis Mark III streaks away closely followed by Eric Winterbottom's sister 1000 which had been in trouble on the warming-up lap. Both would retire, leaving John Heath's HW-Alta (No 29 centre) to win. John Cooper's works 1000, just visible on the right of row three, finished sick, but fifth overall. Heath would build the HWM F2 team for 1950, and Moss would make his name in Europe driving those cars

Back home, Eric had won the 500 class at both Prescott and Shelsley Walsh, while young Peter Collins was slowly making his mark. He had begun racing his Mark II Cooper that season, the car painted black with red wheels and skull-and-crossbones motif on the head fairing. Now he sold it to trials and rally driver Bill Cox, and Pat Collins replaced it with a 1000 which had reputedly been built for Charles Cooper's personal use, matching Eric Brandon's with its polished alloy finish and chrome-plated suspension parts. John today doubts this story – his father just didn't think that way!

The 500 Club ran a major 44-lap 100-mile race in their Silverstone meeting on 9 July. It was the longest race yet for 500s, and the Collins family's stretch chassis had been specially prepared for it, using a postwar Manx Norton engine detuned in C. F. Smith's Clapham workshops to run petrol-benzol rather than alcohol in search of longevity.

There were 17 starters, 11 of them Coopers, and it was Peter Collins's mount which survived to win, its body smeared with oil but the detuned Norton cylinder head still cool enough to touch. 'Young Peter', wrote Austen May,

Real achievement – after learning the ropes on the British hillclimb and circuit race scene 19-year old Stirling Moss took his two-way Cooper with the twin 1000 engine to Lago di Garda, Italy for a Formula 2 confrontation with Ferrari and the strong Italian 1100 cc brigade, and utterly dominated the class. The Italian tifosi *recognized his greatness before most of his home countrymen. Here the carefully-prepared Moss Mark III shows-off its long-range pannier tank, extra seat padding, large-section rear Dunlop tyres and massive cooling intakes. The twin fillers on the headrest fairing supply additional fuel and oil tanks. On such a rough-and-ready circuit as the country roads at Garda Stirling's body-belt was an important article in the well-dressed racing driver's wardrobe. The car was anodized pale green to save the weight of paint*

'... came from comparative obscurity to the top of the class in one gigantic stride....' Coopers won every race at this meeting, save one for 'non-production' machines which fell to Jack Moor's Wasp. Brandon won one race in his Cooper-

JAP, but Curly Dryden won two with his Cooper-Norton.

At Prescott, Brandon broke his own climb record, while the new young star, Peter Collins, crashed at Orchard Corner, leaving his new car standing on its nose down the inside bank. The car ran its original JAP engine on this occasion, but generally the single-cam Manx Norton was gaining acceptance and the twin-cam or 'double-knocker' TT Norton was fast becoming a glittering attraction. There were two problems. One – the famous Bracebridge Street, Birmingham, motorcycle works showed no interest in releasing engines for car use. Two – if they did, few could afford the asking price....

At the end of August the important BRDC Silverstone meeting found Moss running his sloper engine again, but Brandon's JAP and Dryden's Norton had more power and led away. Stirling hacked past Dryden, but despite all his heroic efforts could do nothing about Eric, who hung on to win by 0.2 sec before 100,000 spellbound spectators. This was more the image of 500 racing which its instigators had planned.... It was close, hard-fought and exciting.

Dryden won at Blandford from new Cooper drivers Ken Carter – a South London estate agent – and Alan Brown, who worked for Dennis Bros of Guildford as a truck sales rep. Brown drove in immaculate pale blue helmet and overalls, which won him the nickname 'Chiron' Brown after the cultured Monégasque champion Louis Chiron.

He had served under Norman Garrad during the war. Garrad was a well-known rally driver who would run the highly successful Sunbeam-Talbot works team postwar. Working for Dennis as Midlands technical representative, Alan sold dozens of trucks through 'a bright, rough-and-ready' haulier named Bob Hamblin. He bought his first racing car through Lombard Finance, then, just before the haulage

Top of page *500 cc racing hit the big time in the British GP meeting, Silverstone, May 1949. But the start, incredibly, was so mishandled that the grid was not even properly formed at flagfall and some drivers were standing beside their cars! Here 'Curly' Dryden's Cooper-Norton leads narrowly away from Moss's two-way car with 'sloper' JAP engine and Bill Aston's standard JAP model far right*

September Prescott, 1949 – Eric Brandon doing his darndest to better Moss's twin, broadsiding his highly-polished Mark III stretch at Orchard Corner. He lost the 1100 cc racing class to Stirling by 1.05 sec. Eric disliked green, preferring his cars in polished aluminium with red upholstery, matching his habitual red shirt and helmet

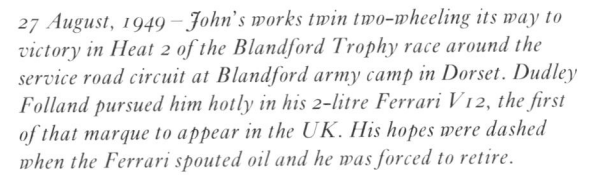

27 August, 1949 – John's works twin two-wheeling its way to victory in Heat 2 of the Blandford Trophy race around the service road circuit at Blandford army camp in Dorset. Dudley Folland pursued him hotly in his 2-litre Ferrari V12, the first of that marque to appear in the UK. His hopes were dashed when the Ferrari spouted oil and he was forced to retire.

Blandford was fast and dangerous. John's winning average speed was 80.27mph. How dangerous was shown in the accidents that day which claimed one life. Major Peter Braid was lucky to escape with bruises from his Mark III, after parking it on the guardhouse roof

business was nationalized, he and Hamblin sold huge numbers of trucks worth literally a fortune. 'Bob said, "You've done a good job for me, now what would you like?", and I said, "I'd like to go racing with a Cooper", and so he bought me the car, I bought the engines, a truck and trailer, and away we went. I started by finishing second 500 at Great Auclum, then was second to Eric Winterbottom's 1000 at Luton Hoo. At Blandford I was third in my first road race. . . . I couldn't complain!'

It was during this Blandford meeting, in the second heat, that Major Peter Braid lost his Cooper and struck the concrete base of a bus shelter which had been demolished earlier by Gordon Woods's fatal accident in a BMW 328. His little Cooper cannoned from the concrete into a tree and then bounced to rest on the guardhouse roof! Braid fell to earth bruised and shaken. Some people have no real luck. The unfortunate Major was to die in 1955 in the Barnes railway accident. . . .

At Prescott, Moss won the 1100 cc class from Brandon, and at the closing Goodwood meeting Cooper 1000s were driven by Moss, Brandon and Bill Whitehouse – another newcomer – to finish 1–2–3 in the Madgwick Cup five-lapper. John was seventh in the works car. Out again in a handicap, the Norton gearboxes in the Moss and Brandon cars succumbed to the cruel torque of their twin-cylinder engines. 'Big' race of the day – over 10 whole laps – was the *Daily Graphic* Goodwood Trophy. John Cooper lent Moss his works car for this event, but it retired after only two laps. Some of these 1000s now drew engine cooling air through an intake beneath the seat rather than through the original 'ears' on either side. Peter Collins won the 500 race using a double-knocker Norton inveigled out of Bracebridge Street by his father. Tragically Charlie Smith, who had prepared Peter's 100-mile race engine so successfully, had died in practice for the Blandford motorcycle meeting a week after the ill-fated car meeting there. Blandford would not survive long as a racing circuit.

After the Collins double-knocker Norton win at Goodwood this 79 × 100 mm 490 cc TT unit became, according to *Iota* writer Gregor Grant: '. . . Desirable Property Number One in the eyes of the majority of 500 cc drivers. Raced even as a "50/50" engine . . .' – using a mild petrol/benzol mixture – '. . . it will more than hold its own with the majority of the dope machinery. . . .'

Whatever the engine arguments; JAP 500 upright or sloper, wet-sump or dry, Manx Norton sohc or TT dohc, or Vincent-HRD, or 1000 cc twin, or 500 cc single, Cooper Cars could look back on the 1949 season and quite rightly proclaim: 'We won every important 500 cc and 1000 cc race in Great Britain and abroad. . . .' They really were going places fast.

CHAPTER SIX

Into the Fifties...

When the FIA – the international governing body – convened a meeting of its sporting commission in Paris towards the end of 1949, they decided to recognize 500 cc racing in 1950 as International Formula 3. International F3 races had to exceed 50 km, 30 miles, in length and the circuits used had to exceed 1.5 km, about 1637 yards, to the lap. Cars had to be unsupercharged, weigh not less than 200 kg, 440 lb, dry and without ballast, have a free exhaust 'not likely to interfere with other drivers' and a minimum ground clearance of 100 mm, about 4 in.

At Hollyfield Road there were some problems. Order books were now full to bursting. John's time was at a premium. He had less chance than ever to go racing, and that hadn't quite been the idea.... But clearly the existing 500 design had the legs of anything it might encounter and only minor alterations formed the new season's Mark IV or 'T11' variant, the full run of 'T'-numbers being listed here in the Appendices. In addition an inch-longer frame was developed for the 'T12' version of the Mark IV, for an all-new JAP 1100 engine which Stan Greening was developing in Tottenham for a more serious tilt at Formula 2 and hillclimbing. Design changes on the cars were of course evolutionary rather than revolutionary. They concentrated upon saving some weight, fitting 'longer' Hardy-Spicer joints and standardizing the Moss-type bucket seat. Lockheed twin leading shoe drum brakes were now standard both front and rear, and twin master cylinders were used in the split hydraulic system, with brake fluid carried in a divided Gallay reservoir above them.

J. A. Prestwich had been so impressed by Cooper's exploits with the existing 1000 twin that they specially developed the enlarged 1097 cc dry-sump twin with reshaped ports and combustion chambers, more radical camshafts and aluminium barrels in place of cast iron. Power output on alcohol was up around 95 bhp at 6000 rpm.

John's own works car was fitted with the prototype 1100 engine, driving through a Norton gearbox, while customer versions would use Burman 'boxes. These 1100s were ordered by Lionel Leonard, Bertie Bradnack, George Hartwell and the Franco-American charger Harry Schell, amongst others.

Meanwhile one stroke of Cooper practical genius had been introduced the previous season. This was the 'T8' two-wheeled trailer, which used identical wheels, tyres and brakes to the 500s and so provided a ready source of spares at a meeting. They ran on half-elliptic leaf-spring suspension and retailed for £65 each. 'Boots' Hume made them in a small shop in Browns Road, close to the Cooper works. Roy Golding respected his friend: 'John was a very knowledgeable feller – he made some good stuff....'

Another sports Cooper emerged during that winter of 1949–50, similar to the old Cooper-Vauxhall but this time carrying a 66.5 × 90 mm, 1250 cc MG TC engine. The prototype frame was a stretch single-seater 1000 twin-type fitted with twin leading shoe brakes front and rear and carrying its Bedding body on outriggers like the Vauxhall prototype. It takes the 'T7' serial in the Cooper list.

John Thornley at MG Abingdon was very enthusiastic about this idea, and Harry Weslake then assisted in tuning. This veteran airflow expert had formerly been based nearby and now that he moved his operation to Rye on the Sussex coast a former employee of his named John Lucas set up a similar tuning emporium – Barwell Engineering – in Chessington. His testbed proved invaluable for the latest optimistic tweaks from nearby Hollyfield Road. Lucas in fact developed a special Cooper-MG head with oversized valves, higher 8.6:1 compression ratio and twin $1\frac{1}{2}$ in. SU carburettor. With this head the engine gave around 75 bhp at 6200 rpm against the standard 54 bhp. Otherwise the prototype Cooper-MG was very similar to the earlier Cooper-Vauxhall, though its front cycle wings were rigidly attached to the body, whereas its predecessor's had swivelled with the front wheels.

At the time of a *Motor Sport* visit to the works in March 1950 the Docker Cooper-Sunbeam project was still under development and, coincidentally, down at Guildford in Surrey, garage owner John Coombs was completing his own variation on the Cooper sports car theme. He had bought a chassis/body unit from Surbiton and tailored a four-cylinder Rover engine down to below 1100 cc by fitting $\frac{5}{32}$ in. thick liners. The standard internals were all buffed, polished and balanced and the flywheel slimmed from $31\frac{1}{2}$ lb to only 14. Martlet pistons and a thin copper gasket raised the compression ratio to 8.5:1 and there were larger valves in the head. Uprated valve springs, electric instead of mechanical fuel pump and special RR34 bearing shells completed the conver-

COOPER CARS

Ready to run, Hollyfield Road, March 1950; five brand-new customer Mark IVs, two on 'T8' Cooper trailers, flanking (fourth right) the silent Cooper-Vauxhall prototype about to be tarted-up with a Daimler grille and Hooper body trimmings for young Lance Docker's use. Nearest camera is an older Mark III, decidedly 'used'

500 cc racing went international as Formula 3 in 1950, as here at Monaco where the most prestigious minor-Formula race of the year fell to Stirling Moss – with BRDC and 'Cooper 500 cc' badges on his overalls (and still with hair) seen with Harry Schell and his US-liveried Mark IV. In shirt and tie behind car is Harry's brother Philippe. Harry was a charmer who seldom settled his bills with Cooper but always wangled parts out of the Old Man. Eric Brandon recalled how Harry would drive off with his truck loaded to the gun'les, Charlie Cooper waving him goodbye before abruptly realizing amid all the chatter and banter no money had changed hands. ''E's dunnit again!' the Old Man would roar

42

sion, while a Ford 8 starter and enlarged ring gear replaced the bulky Rover parts to allow the engine to slip into Cooper's narrow chassis. Twin SU 1¼ in. horizontal carburettors replaced the original twin to lower the bonnet line, and a four-branch exhaust was fitted.

Hollyfield Road was fast becoming a Mecca for the special builder. A handful of Cooper-MGs were to be built, mainly by customers buying just basic parts from Cooper's and then assembling the 'kit' as they pleased. This saved purchase tax for the customer and extra workload for the hard-pressed Cooper staff. Demand for the 500s was still growing....

Pete Bedding recalls how '... we soon got so busy that my father and I just couldn't keep up with all the panel work there was to do. We had to use several outside contractors for body panels, tanks and odd bits and fittings. The Hartin brothers, Len and Roy over at Hanwell, were our main sub-contractors for bodywork, and Harold Croydon in Tolworth was another. There was also the Robert Peel Coachworks in Kingston; Freddie Faulkner and Alec Rainbow there did a lot of Cooper sheet metal parts. When production really got going there was more than enough work to keep us all hours....'

The 1950 British 500 season was again Cooper-dominated, with Norton engines to the fore. In practice for the Goodwood Easter Meeting John Cooper's latest slim-bodied lightweight works car ran a new alloy-barrel dry-sump 500 engine and set fastest practice time, but in the first corner Peter Collins's double-knocker Norton version rammed him and Curly Dryden was enabled to win in his Cooper-Norton.

Internationally, 1950 saw 16 important 500 cc F3 races, of which Cooper won 13; Alf Bottoms's self-built JBS-Norton won two and the Swede Åke Jonsson's Effyh-JAP the other. Ken Carter won at the start of his furiously busy continental career at Montlhéry when the new Formula made its French bow on 30 April.

At Silverstone's British GP meeting, Frank Aikens's 'non-production' Iota-Triumph blew off all the Coopers to win the Final after a terrific win-or-bust effort by Moss blew-up his engine. He coasted in second. Collins was third.

The first 500 races had been run round the one-mile former grass track at Brands Hatch valley in Kent. Bill Whitehouse – a tall, balding and jovial off-licence owner from South London – arrived there with a double-knocker Norton engine in his Cooper, plus motorcycle tuning wizard Steve Lancefield to care for it. 'Big Bill' was said to have paid a fortune for the engine, and it delivered the goods as he won the last race of the day. Spike Rhiando appeared in his Trimax special, a stressed-skin monocoque-fuselage car – another antecedent for the epochal Lotus 25 which would revolutionize Formula 1 come 1962, and put a nail in Cooper's coffin.... Moss's 1949 car had been sold to an enthusiast named Burgoyne, but he raced at Brands in a machine borrowed from John Cooper.

On 20 May the most charismatic 500 race of the year was run at Monaco in support of the GP. Moss had the latest JAP sloper engine flown out to him there, the single barrel sloping forward. It was disappointing, but on such a circuit Stirling's driving ability could compensate and he won his heat from Parker's Parker-JAP and Lex Beels's new home-built. Alan Brown had crashed his own blue Cooper at Silverstone and had borrowed a replacement for Monaco from Percy Bilton of Vigzol Oil. He promptly crashed it at the *Tabac* while leading Heat Two. Harry Schell won the heat from the veteran Bill Aston.

The irrepressible *'Arree* was son of Laurie and Lucy O'Reilly Schell, who had run their Ecurie Bleu Talbots in prewar GP races and at Indianapolis. He and his brother Philippe both raced, but he was the more successful and he had already won in his Cooper-JAP at Mons the previous weekend.

In the Monaco Final, Moss was unstoppable and won comfortably from Schell, Parker, Eli Bayol's French DB-Panhard and Austen May's Cooper-Norton 'double-knocker'. Schell's Cooper, fitted with an 1100 JAP twin engine, then started the GP, but went out in the famous multiple shunt at *Tabac* on the second lap. It was Cooper's first GP entry. Seven years later it would be for real.

Another alternative engine was the 500 BSA Gold Star single which Ken Wharton tried in his new Cooper, but for the Whitsun Goodwood and Blandford meetings he replaced it with a JAP. Another newcomer was Charles Headland, out in the ex-Rhiando gold car. He was to become a leading character in 500 racing; a hard, uncompromising driver who tended to crash or win, with little in between. A Maidstone dairy owner named George Wicken – 'The Maidstone Maniac' – was another new Cooper name, driving nicely prepared cars with the name *C'Est si Bon* painted on the nose.

That same Whit weekend saw a 500 race at Aix-les-Bains in support of a 2-litre unblown F2 fixture in which Stirling Moss drove for the new Heath-Abecassis HWM team from Walton-on-Thames. Their Alta-engined cars used frames welded-up in his spare time by Cooper's man, Jack Tolley.... Harry Schell won the 500 race, just as he would later that year at Grenoble. In third place at Aix was the great French champion Raymond Sommer, a superstar Grand Prix driver who loved racing for racing's sake and who had fallen for the nimble handling of the Schell team Coopers. Austen May observed: '... this was positive evidence of how amazingly the prestige of the class had increased, and what a very long way 500 racing had come in a few short seasons....'

At Zandvoort Ken Wharton won his first 500 cc race, having flown out his Cooper after running it in 1000 twin form at Shelsley the previous day. This Smethwick garage proprietor would drive anything in competition if there was money to be made. He was extraordinarily successful.

At Prescott Peter Collins, now 18, at last made ftd; in the 750 class, using a twin JAP engine put together by himself and his father. Cooper's international appeal was also emphasized by Norwegian driver Bosse Hveem winning at Andermoen outside Oslo, and now there were cars running in Malaya, Australia and penetrating the US market....

The 2 July French GP meeting at Reims saw the best-supported continental 500 race yet, but heat and pace decimated the Cooper challenge and Alf Bottoms won in his JBS-Norton. Dryden's was the best-placed Cooper, third. Moss's JAP engine briefly seized on the line in his latest lightweight Cooper and he struggled to finish sixth.

One week later, the Silverstone 100-miler fell to Ken Watkins's Cooper-JAP, while at Zandvoort on 23 July, John's own lightweight was loaned to Raymond Sommer and taken out for him specially by Charles Cooper. In practice Sommer lapped consistently 4–5 sec inside Don Parker's lap record before dropping the lot and crashing. The car's folded-back nearside front corner was repaired overnight and Sommer led the race only to miss a gear, over-rev and drop a valve. On the final lap Parker's Special broke when leading and Curly Dryden beat him to the line by 300 yards. Johnny Claes, the well-known Belgian band leader-cum-Grand Prix driver, handled a new Cooper-JAP of his own in this event. He finished fourth. These Coopers really were catching on amongst 'name' drivers.

More new names appeared in winning Coopers at Brands Hatch that month; Ian Burgess and Robin Montgomerie-Charrington. Both had some part to play in Cooper's future.

The 500 Club's own international meeting was held at Brands on August Bank Holiday Monday. The Schell brothers ran their blue-and-white US-liveried cars, Claes his yellow Belgian entry and Sommer should have appeared but was detained at home at the last moment as a huge forest fire south of Bordeaux had destroyed some of his property.

It was George Wicken's day as he won both 15- and 35-lap Finals; the first from Moss and Burgess, the second from Whitehouse and John Cooper. There were 10 races that day and Coopers won all but one; and that was the 'non-production' event from which they were of course excluded.

On 26 August it was back to the big time in the BRDC Silverstone meeting at which the legendary BRM V16 made its humiliating debut. Driven by Sommer it snapped an output-shaft on the startline. For the supporting 500 race, Moss at last deserted JAP power for Norton. Pa Moss had been trying for months to extract a double-knocker unit from Bracebridge Street, and just five days before Silverstone it had at last appeared.

There was a problem. The Cooper's engine mounts had to be remade, rapidly. John A. Cooper, sports editor of *The Autocar*, was a good friend of Stirling's. He was also a jazz fan and on a visit to The London Jazz Club he'd met a jazz critic named Max Jones. He was also a racing enthusiast and he mentioned an engineer named Ray Martin who was building an A7-based hillclimb special in his small garage near Victoria. He introduced J. A. Cooper to Martin and the technical journalist was impressed by his apparent knowledge. When 'J.A.C.' heard of Moss's engine bearer problem he recommended Martin, who made the necessary parts very quickly and completed the conversion in the small hours of practice morning. Stirling straightaway lapped at 83.86 mph, which was faster than some of the Formula 1 field! Sommer was second fastest in his borrowed works car, while the BRM Trust hierarchy plotted to persuade their superstar not to drive in the minor event – '... as it would devalue his appearance in our car'. Ken Carter equalled the Frenchman's time.

Sommer – regardless of the BRM Trustees – led the F3 race initially, but Moss beat him soundly into second place with Bottoms and Dryden 3–4. Only Sommer used a JAP engine, and he had compensated for lack of punch by sheer talent....

Eric Brandon was another man in the double-knocker queue: 'They were like hen's teeth. You just couldn't get hold of any. I even remember the numbers of mine and Stirling's when we finally got them; mine was *MN 913*, Stirling's was *MN 911*. They cost us £120 plus gearbox and as far as I know they were the only double-knocker works engines to escape direct from Bracebridge Street for use in cars. When the JAP was obviously going to be outclassed Charles and John had to start buying complete Norton bikes, then take out the engines and sell the frames bare or with JAP engines installed. It was the only way to get the engines....'

Pat Collins was better connected with Norton, and Peter's engine was reputedly works maintained. Both the Brandon

'Arree Schell gave Cooper their first start in a World Championship Grand Prix, here at Monaco, 1950 with the Mark IV twin 1100 engined. He wangled a start on the back of the grid but this happened on lap 2 at Tabac *where heavy seas had allegedly broken over the sea-wall. Farina spun his Alfa and the rest piled-in. Farina's Alfa lies bottom right, facing Rosier's fuel-gushing Talbot-Lago (16), de Graffenried's Maserati (52), Manzon's Simca-Gordini (10), the Schell Cooper and in train behind No 52 Trintignant's Simca, Harrison's ERA and Rol's Maserati. That's fuel spreading across the roadway. Schell in the white helmet, left, tells Manzon his fortune ...*

Massed start, BRDC International Trophy, Silverstone August 1950, 13 Cooper's amongst leading 17 and great French Champion Raymond Sommer showing the way in John's works Mark IV (29). Three weeks later he died in this car at Cadours, France. Here it was the only one to use JAP power against the dominant Norton engine in the other leading cars

DAILY EXPRESS TROPHY MEETING
For the Best Report and Pictures
Motor
PIRELLI TYRES
GIRLING
Autocar
LUCAS

Aix-les-Bains Formula 2, 1950 – rare shot showing how Harry Schell's Cooper-JAP 1100 twin split the Vallone and Sommer unblown 2-litre V12 Ferraris on the starting grid and headed the 4-cylinder works Simca-Gordinis. On a wet track he led until his car's clutch burned out

Left *John's handsomely sporting Cooper-MG prototype, Hollyfield Road, early 1950. Across the road a special Fiat Topolino reflects the new sports car's heritage. This one was owned by a friend of John's renowned for his swimming, known to all as 'Dipper'. The Cooper-MG has its windscreen removed for some reason, as fixing holes on scuttle show. Through 'porthole' on bonnet blister an SU dashpot is just visible. Note conventional headlight mounting compared to earlier Cooper-Vauxhall's. That's Ewell Road crossing the 'T' beyond*

Sporting trio, Goodwood paddock, 1950. Left to right; Cooper-Vauxhall prototype, John Coombs' special Cooper-Rover with its separate bucket seats, vestigial cycle-wings and tiny clear aero screen, and Cooper-MG prototype with full-width windscreen and – like its Vauxhall sister – full-width cockpit bulkhead padding. The cars in this family would be mainly kit-built with considerable variation

INTO THE FIFTIES

and Moss engines used single-float chamber dual carburettors. Brandon's had a header tank fed from the usual mechanical fuel pump which was cam-driven off the back axle. Moss's used an engine-driven pump feeding the float chamber direct. When Stirling drove out to practise at Silverstone he hadn't yet heard his new engine run. Motorcycle ace Harold Daniell's assistant, Hermann Meier, was present to tune the carburetion and check jet sizes. For Stirling all this effort paid off.

This first international F3 season ended at San Sebastian, Spain, on 3 September, where Ken Carter, Ron Frost and Stan Coldham placed 1-2-3, two Nortons leading home Coldham's JAP. Just as expected....

The following weekend – 10 September – saw the national *Trophée du Haute Garonne* race at Cadours in France. Harry Schell had suggested to Sommer at Silverstone that they should go if John Cooper would again lend his car. John agreed, offering Sommer his 1100 twin, and it was loaded on to the Schells' truck. At Cadours, Sommer was driving as exuberantly as ever when he crashed on a fast bend, and was killed....

This was the first Cooper fatality and it cast a long shadow over Hollyfield Road, particularly when the wreckage was brought home.... Eric Brandon: 'I'd tested that car at Silverstone just before it left and it caught fire. I hopped out and managed to put it out, but Jimmy Brown the track manager was dancing about calling me "A fire-raising devil" for damaging his track. After Sommer's accident I've always wished I'd let the bloody thing burn....'

By the end of that season Cooper had already produced around 100 single-seater cars and had achieved matchless dominance in 500 cc racing. But the ambitious Cooper-JAP 1100 didn't produce the expected road-race results, although it was to prove truly formidable in sprints and hillclimbing.

Both John and Eric had raced twins in the Manx Cup. Eric led his friend from the start until lap nine when John's car expired. Two laps later Eric's huge lead evaporated as the rev-counter drive between the JAP twin's two opposed magnetos worked loose and knocked one out of timing. The engine just misfired, then stopped.

Dennis Poore's big Alfa Romeo won the Hill-Climb Championship, but Ken Wharton shone with a string of successes in his 996 cc Cooper-JAP where one might have expected the new 1097 to be faster. Still, 1100 drivers like Brandon, John Cooper, Aston, Miss Betty Haig, Bradnack and Cecil Heath had their moments, and Peter Collins ran with a special JAP taken closer to 1200 cc to set a new 1500 class record at Prescott in September. Some twins were exported, and the most effective of them all was Harry Schell's in Europe.

His best performance was at Aix-les-Bains, where the tight little lakeside course was ideally suited to the Cooper's torque and good handling. When it rained '*Arree* had a double advantage, and he promptly *won* his Formula 2 heat from Raf Vallone's 2-litre unblown Ferrari! For the Final he was on the front row, flanked by the towering Vallone and Sommer Ferraris, and as the flag fell he took the lead. He was drawing comfortably away from Sommer when the little Cooper's clutch burned out and his fine drive was wasted.

Later in the year, in the F2 section of the Swiss GP at Berne, he held seventh place, dicing with Hermann Lang's Veritas, before Amal carburettor problems forced him out. Ever-ambitious, he then ran the car in the German GP at Nürburgring, but its engine broke. At the Marseilles F2 race he was sixth. Denis Jenkinson of *Motor Sport* wrote: 'It was a pity there were not more of these powerful little cars on the Continent to back up Schell's efforts....' It would come.

Meanwhile on the sports car front Lionel Leonard's

Variation taken to extremes in this Motor Sport *shot of two Cooper-MGs, British Empire Trophy race, Douglas, IoM, 14 June, 1951. Lionel Leonard is leading here in his very special* Barchetta-*bodied version, followed by Jackie Reece's more normal cycling-wing model. Reece would finish third behind Frazer Nashes of Moss and Gerard, Leonard unplaced. His enveloping-bodied* JOY 500 *later made its mark with new owner Cliff Davis*

47

They could corner too! J. H. Brooks demonstrated how well at Prescott hillclimb, 6 May, 1956 – lifting the inside wheels this high on both his runs. Note spare-wheel bracket on body side, brief grille and low headlamps etc.

Cooper-MG had made its race debut at Goodwood in May, finishing third. John was second in another race there in his works Cooper-MG and John Coombs's Rover-engined device was third in a handicap. Eric Brandon took a third in John's car in the last race of the day. One report mentioned that Coombs's car sported 'a Barnato Hassan-like air intake upon arrival, but this seemed to have fallen off before it was due to race. . . .'

In June, Moss was available to drive the works Cooper-MG at Goodwood, but it proved fractious and he was only fifth. John took over – actually wearing Stirling's helmet – in a five-lap handicap and finished second, setting fastest lap at 73.56 mph. In the final members' meeting of the year he at last achieved that elusive win, averaging 71.74 mph for the five laps and topping 100 mph along Lavant Straight. Major E. M. Mackay handled the Cooper-Rover at the Brighton Speed Trials and won the 1500 sports car class.

John Bolster of *Autosport* road-tested John's car immediately after the 12 August Goodwood victory. He explained how the transmission tunnel size had been minimized by the diff unit being fixed to the chassis frame and spring-deflection therefore not moving the prop-shaft. The engine was tuned to require benzol fuel but was '. . . smooth and flexible and starts instantly under all conditions. Power production right up the scale makes one take one's hat off to [this] engine. . . . Moving off one was immediately struck by the remarkable acceleration, and stop-watch tests proved this.'

He recorded acceleration from 0–50 mph in 7.5 sec, and to 60 mph in less than 11 sec. 'With the driver only aboard it was easy to excel [*sic*] these results, and of course some of the "one-way" performances were better still. . . . I did exceed 50 mph in second and 70 mph in third gear . . . one can cruise up quite steep main road hills at 70 mph on half throttle, and in a few seconds push the needle up to 80 with complete lack of effort. The low weight ($10\frac{3}{4}$ cwt as tested) obviously contributes to this result, but the body must be well streamlined for acceleration to be maintained at such high speeds. . . .'

John decided that the suspension was 'on the hard side' but the ride was still good on bad surfaces, there was no unpleasant kick-back in the steering, and in cornering '. . . the machine really excels'. The Cooper-MGs were to attract several customers, and appeared in club races, rallies, hill-climbs and sprints with quite considerable class success well into the mid-Fifties. Proper records of how many of these cars were produced have not survived, but several were completed with alternative engines, and it has been possible to identify at least 12 different Cooper-MG 'entities' alone.

A few more were completed in various guises, at least one with a Ford engine and of course Coombs's Cooper-Rover, which was advertised for sale in later years with a rather handsome all-enveloping streamlined body.

Peter Reece, cousin of Jackie Reece – the family involved with the very active Blakes of Liverpool sports and racing car dealership – campaigned a cycle-winged Cooper-MG registered LLV 1 in 1951–52, and sold it to East Anglian gentleman farmer Jack Sears, who was to become an excellent sports and saloon car driver. It then passed on to one Jack Hacking, who fitted an envelope body and raced it with club-level success. Jock Lawrence made his first steps towards a regular Ecurie Ecosse Jaguar drive with his car JER 547, and another Scot, Frank Dundas from Dumfries, campaigned the ex-works car registered NKC 193, largely in rallies. Paul Barwell had NRC 195, or is this a misreading of the same car's number-plate? Vic Drew of University Motors, the MG specialists, built MYH 314 and Lionel Leonard – another MG specialist – raced his cycle-fendered car extensively before selling it in late 1952 to Bristol garage proprietor Horace Gould. It was registered KOY 500 and was painted two-tone cream and maroon, Gould adding Mark I Cooper-Bristol suspension and 2ls brakes

One I. E. Davidson, in 1954, ran MOY 500 ex-Leonard successfully. Brian Lister, scion of a Cambridge light-engineering family, built himself a Cooper-MG from parts supplied, and later created those potent Lister-Jaguars. It was his JER 547 in which Jack Lawrence made his name. But undoubtedly the most famous of all these Cooper-MGs was the Lionel Leonard-assembled 1951 model JOY 500, raced subsequently, with immense success, by Goldhawk Road, Shepherd's Bush, motor trader Cliff Davis. Leonard was an MG specialist, producing bored-out 1467 cc versions of the famous 'XPAG'-series engine, and he bodied JOY 500 in 1951 with a passable imitation of the contemporary Ferrari *Barchetta* enveloping body-style. It was left in polished aluminium, and Leonard raced it in the 1951 BRDC British Empire Trophy race at Douglas, Isle of Man, but was very disappointed with it. Towards the end of that season he sold it in the Goodwood paddock to the moustachioed, check-shirted Davis, still complaining it wouldn't run reliably. Cliff promptly rebuilt the engine, and in 1952–53 he simply dominated his class with the car in British sports-racing, and added a similarly bodied 2-litre Bristol-engined Tojeiro to his stable that second season. The good looks and performance of this twin-tube chassesed car impressed the Hurlock family controlling AC Cars, and they bought rights to the Tojeiro design and the Ferrari-based, Lionel Leonard-copied body shape to produce their AC Ace – which later begat the Shelby American Cobra. . . . Cliff Davis eventually sold JOY 500 to Peter Jackson – not the Specialised Mouldings Ltd one – who continued its successful career for some time, way into the mid-Fifties.

Other Cooper-MGs to have been identified include the registrations OKB 990 and J. H. Brooks's NTO 650. Keen collector Anatoly Arutunoff in Bartlesville, Oklahoma, has what was apparently NTO 650 with wire wheels and a side-mounted spare, plus a second car carrying the Ferrari *Barchetta*-like bodywork from a Cooper-Bristol we shall meet shortly. He also owns a Cooper-MG on the company's cast-mag wheels with cycle front wings, originally registered XJH 903. Ken Flint built his own Cooper-MG on a Mark V chassis with Marshall-blown sleeved-down 1100 MG engine during 1952. Mark V was the 1981 500.

Meanwhile through the winter of 1953–54 Tasmanian-in-England Mike Cannon, noted for his trials cars, built an extraordinary little coupé on a 500 frame, using an Austin A30 engine. The car was in David Baldock's hands, still very original, in 1982. The Cooper-Rover OPC 913 was noted, together with Mrs Rosemary Seers's RKT 93 Cooper-Zephyr, GG 79 a Cooper-Riley and Johnny Goldschmidt's YM 63 Cooper-Lea-Francis: suggesting at least 17 such cars had been produced . . . and there were more powerful Cooper sports cars on the way. . . .

Rare bird – a Cooper saloon car. This is the Mike Cannon front-engined coupé special panelled by Williams & Pritchard on the ex-Peter Jopp 1949 Cooper Mark III 500 frame 'No 22-10-49' according to 1980s owner David Baldock. The car is virtually unchanged from its original Cannon appearance in the 'fifties – a fascinating little survivor. Registration was RKO 3

CHAPTER SEVEN

The 500 line – 1951-53

With 500 cc racing firmly established as International Formula 3, Cooper made several improvements to their 1951 production single-seaters; the Mark V 'T15s'. The prototype was shown to Press and public just before Christmas 1950.

While its basic chassis and suspension layout remained virtually unchanged, the body design had now been altered to improve accessibility and the body support structure had been redesigned to improve chassis rigidity. Whereas previous Coopers had had strip-steel bodyshell hoops welded permanently to the box-section base frame, the new Mark V now featured short vertical tubes welded to the base frame at around 24 in. centres, carrying at their upper ends an extra horizontal tubular longeron parallel to the main side members. This extra rail provided points from which pannier fuel tanks could be slung, which gave the basis of the new body design. The nose and tail cowls were arranged to close against these pannier sides, hingeing open fore-and-aft to expose the works.

This new layout was padded around the cockpit to give the driver much-improved lateral support, as he now sat 'in' his chassis, rather than 'on' it. There was a padded seat-back bulkhead behind his shoulders and a seat cushion braced up beneath his knees for extra comfort – upholstered by Fulford's as usual.

A simple braced-tube structure carried the dash panel and steering column, and although the body design preserved the Cooper identity from previous models – as did the dummy grille on the extreme nose – the entire flow of engine cooling air was now admitted through a belly scoop beneath the cockpit and the earlier inboard duct from the nose was gone. Incoming air was deflected up around the engine barrel – or barrels – by the oil tank, which was mounted just behind the seat-back bulkhead.

The original Cooper chassis book has survived for these Mark V cars, listing 61 orders of which two were subsequently cancelled. The chassis serials commenced at *MKV/1/51* and ran to *MKV/52/51* for the standard 500 F3s, while the 2 in. longer stretch chassis for either 500 single or 1000–1100 cc twin-cylinder engines were allotted serials *MKV/L/1/51* to *MKV/L/8/51*. One order, for car *MKV/18/51*, was altered from 500 to 1100 cc for D. Wilcocks of Butlers Motors, but nothing was recorded concerning its chassis length. This is perfectly understandable, for Cooper was never a paperwork nor bureaucracy-orientated company. What's more, since many of its cars were supplied in kit form they were exempt from purchase tax and many sales of sufficient bits and pieces to construct a complete Cooper obviously passed completely unrecorded.

Items of interest in the surviving book include Mark V chassis 4, which was built specially for permanent display at that year's Festival of Britain exhibition on the South Bank in London. It was planned originally for a white cellulose finish with red wheels and upholstery, but then changed to British racing green with green wheels and black leatherette. Cars were exported to South Africa, the USA, Spain, Italy – where they were exhibited at the Turin Show – to Harry Schell (1100 JAP twin), to Finland, to Tony Shelly in New Zealand, and seven cars – four 1100s and three 500s – are recorded bound for John Crouch, Cooper's Australian importer.

One interesting entry records: '*500 cc MK V. Norton fittings. Colour: Polychromatic blue with red wheels. Upholstery: Red. Chassis No: "MKV/26/51". Extras: Norton gearbox to be fitted. Long Range Fuel Tanks.*' The customer was '*Mr Ecclestone*' – Bernie Ecclestone, the Bexley motorcycle dealer, who was to go racing in Cooper-Norton, Cooper-Bristol and Cooper-Jaguar cars, and who in the Seventies took over the Brabham F1 team and later came to dominate the Formula One Constructors' Association.... For a time he would be the most significant force in Grand Prix racing.

Through 1951, British cars utterly dominated International Formula 3. Cyril Posthumus, reviewing the season for *Autosport*, wrote: 'Although sheer weight of numbers in respect of machines built has obviously swung the balance in favour of this country, the combination of the twin-ohc Norton engine and Cooper chassis was so powerful that the "foreign challenge" was well on the way to defeat before the start of any race. Germany is the only country which possesses 500 cc racing cars in any quantity, but it was proved beyond doubt that the horizontally opposed push-rod BMW engine, without the aid of forced induction, is a very ordinary power unit....'

But Cooper's own supremacy amongst British manufacturers was at last challenged seriously; by Alf Bottoms's JBS and by the Kieft specially designed and built, initially as a 'super-Cooper', for Stirling Moss. Tragically, Alf Bottoms was killed in May when he apparently tangled the welt of his ordinary walking shoe amongst the pedals during practice for the Luxembourg GP, and his 500 crashed into a parked car off the course. The Luxembourg GP was incidentally the only national Grand Prix race to be run solely for F3s. 'Pop' Bottoms continued the JBS business, but his youngest son then died in a motorcycle accident and the eldest boy, Charles, was injured in a 500 crash at Brands Hatch. Bottoms Sr still provided facilities for building and racing JBS cars to Alf's design, and drivers Curly Dryden, Don Parker, Frank Aikens, Peter Collins, John Habin and newcomer Les Leston kept the marque's name to the fore. However, at the last meeting of the year, at Castle Combe in Wiltshire, popular Curly Dryden AFC crashed his JBS on the opening lap, and he was killed. . . .

Still the outstanding Cooper drivers of the season were Eric Brandon and Alan Brown, driving under the Ecurie Richmond banner. Eric won the newly introduced *Autosport* £200 British 500 cc Drivers' Championship and Alan won both the Half-Litre Club's Championship and the *Light Car* Cup. He was second to Moss in the important BRDC Gold Star, while Stirling made very few F3 appearances, only fielding his new Kieft in major races, rather to the Cooper brigade's relief. . . .

While Ken Carter and Bill Whitehouse funded the works F3 team and ran their own cars alongside John's occasional entry under the Cooper Car Company banner, Ecurie Rich-

Mark V 'T15' chassis being welded-up on the Morrison air-raid shelter-based jigs, Hollyfield Road, early-1951. John Kelly is offering-up one of the new top rails to the right-hand frame which has only just been laid-down, while final welding is completed on the more advanced frame on left. In immediate postwar years various licences were required from the Ministry of Supply to acquire raw materials. The high-quality shrapnel-resistant steel corner angles and sheet panels used in wartime Morrison shelters gained a ready market, John would pay 30 bob to three pounds for them, dependent on condition. Angles formed jig bed, as here, panels were cut-up for lugs, brackets, bearers etc. Long after raw materials became easier to obtain these jig bases survived at Hollyfield. Note roll-over frame shadow thrown on far wall by welding torch flame. Cooper's works were never brightly-lit – all costs were minimized

'Boxer' at the wheel. He was a friendly mongrel living locally who simply adopted Cooper's as his own. He would arrive with the lads to start the day, patrol the works all day long, then go home when they left. Eventually he adopted panel-man Pete Bedding who took him on with the original owner's blessing. 'Boxer' loved watching the welders work, they fixed him up with a pair of goggles to protect his eyes. A photo-story on the racing team dog appeared in the London Evening News, 12 May, 1954, with 'Boxer' begoggled. He lived with Pete for many years. Here perhaps he dreams of what might have been . . . ? Note Mark V-type frame and pannier tanks

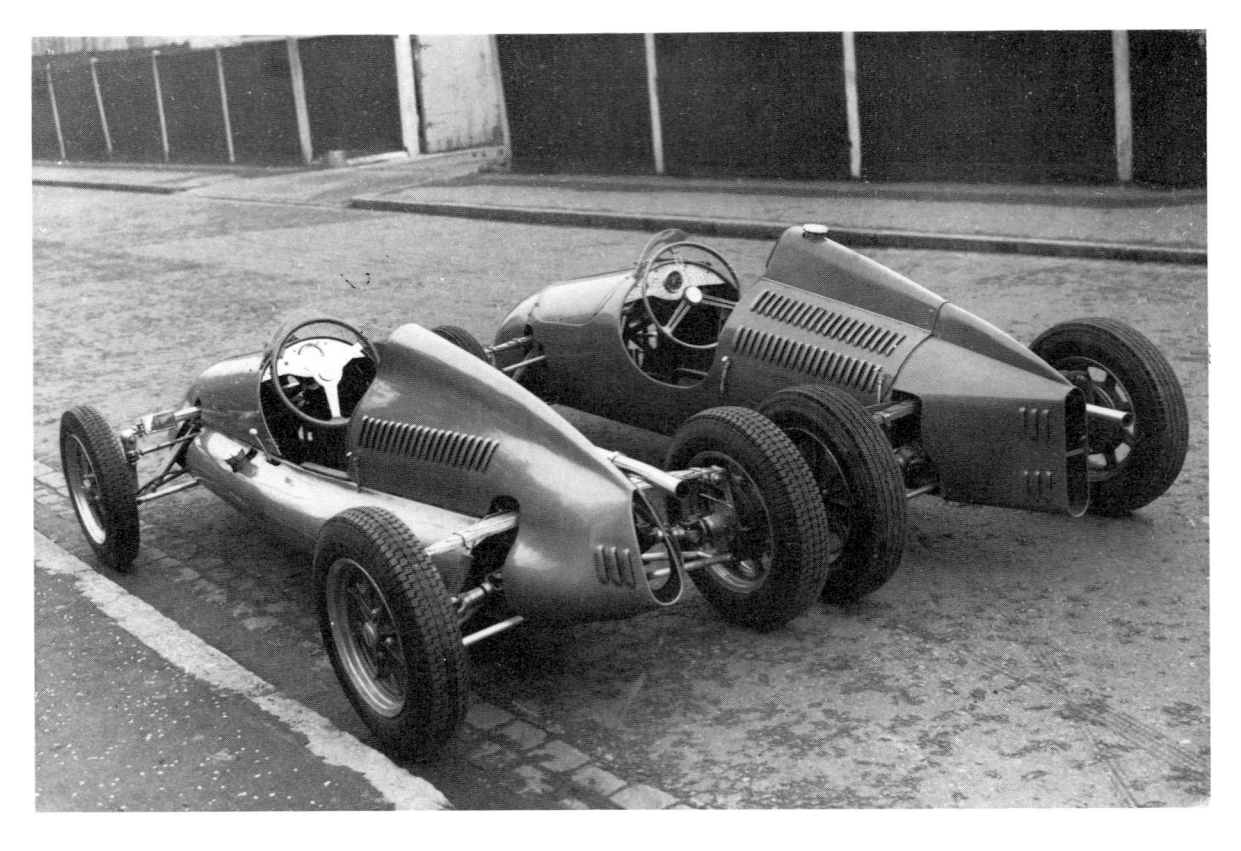

mond were more successful. Eric Brandon: 'John had asked me if I'd take his place occasionally in the works team when he couldn't get away, but it was all a bit vague. Then at the Club's annual "do" I found myself sitting next to Alan Brown. He told me he had backing from this character Jimmy Richmond, and asked if I'd like to join him and we'd go racing professionally....'

Jimmy Richmond was 27, a public works and haulage contractor from Repton, Nottinghamshire. He was keen to become involved in racing, but at 22 stones was hardly the ideal shape for Formula 3! He became friendly with Alan Brown, at 30 a coming star in Bob Hamblin's car. Eric, at 31, was building Halsey's Electric into a million-turnover wholesaling business and together they agreed to form a two-car team running Cooper cars with Norton engines and gearboxes. Jimmy Richmond provided a truck to transport the team, and bought two double-knocker Norton engines. All expenses, and any earnings from prize or start money, were to be split three ways. Steve Lancefield prepared Eric's engines and Francis Beart prepared Alan's. Both achieved great reliability; Eric's was so good he used the same engine all year – with the same big-end bearing shells – save for two German races and one at Brands Hatch.

Two full-time mechanics cared for cars and transporter; Freddie Sirkett and big 'Ginger' – Michael Devlin. The team was run from Eric's home, 4 Pebblecombe, Adelaide Road, Surbiton, and its 1951 record included 16 major victories plus 41 other heat wins and placings.

Eric: 'It was extraordinary I suppose. We became so confident we'd toss for who should win the first one, then alternate after that. We began our continental tour at Draguignan. Alan won the toss, so we passed and repassed to give 'em their money's worth. On the penultimate lap I was leading up to the line with Alan right behind when the organizers put out the flag a lap early. I promptly backed-off to let Alan go by as agreed and he had a terrific moment avoiding me!'

The whole F3 circus grew accustomed to the gypsy existence of racing across Europe, covering costs with start money, prize money and occasional travelling expenses – plus trade sponsors' bonuses if they were lucky. It wasn't too difficult to break even. For a select but talented few this was the stepping stone to stardom.... F3 was also much less expensive than attacking Formula 2, or Formula 1, or sports car racing.

Dennis Bros of Guildford, with truck sales in recession, gave Alan Brown a year's vacation without pay, but kept him on their books and paid his insurance so he could take the plunge as a professional racing driver. With 'generous sup-

THE 500 LINE – 1951–53

13 May, 1951, Monza Italy – John celebrates in company with tall, bald-headed 'Big Bill' Whitehouse after his win in the Coppa Filippini. The Cooper marque rapidly established its 500 cc F3 dominance world-wide

Left *Development by evolution, not revolution was Cooper's way. Here's a comparison between Mark V (left) with revamped chassis structure, pannier tanks and lowered lines against more upright though slender Mark IV (right). This Mark V has left-hand instead of right-hand gearchange and the rear-view mirror mounting clipped to front leafspring. It wears racing tyres in this shot while the older car has road tyres. Dependent on the owner's pocket either could be used in competition*

port' from Esso he had a superb season, its highlight being victory in the Luxembourg GP. 'I suddenly became someone, and success of course breeds success. . . .'

For John Cooper his highlight of 1951 was victory in the Corrado Filippini Cup race at Monza after team-mate Ken Carter's Cooper-Norton had won the first heat and then run into engine trouble. John's average speed for both heats combined was 81.56 mph, and he set fastest lap at 85.41. He won again later that year at Rouen.

Philippe Schell won the *Coupe des Racers* – proving *Franglais* is nothing new – at Pau in March, and at Orleans. Jacquier-Bret won at Marrakech in Morocco from other imported Cooper-JAPs driven by Limousin and Jean Lucas, while Ken Carter won at Genoa. Other international Cooper winners included Don Gray, Ian Burgess (in the formidable Eifelrennen at Nürburgring) and Bill Whitehouse.

Brandon's most satisfying moment of the year was winning the F3 race accompanying the German GP at Nürburgring, beating Brown and Whitehouse: '*What* a fabulous circuit!' he would say for the rest of his days.

Sadly the first two Cooper 500 fatalities marred this season. On 11 August in heavy rain at Boreham, Essex, David Brake crashed his immaculate black-and-white car. On 21 October at Brands Hatch in a special mechanic's race ending the day, W. H. Lowe's mechanic Harry Parker rolled their car and was killed.

In the USA the monthly magazine *Road & Track* encouraged a 500 movement. In May 1951 John Fitch's Swedish Effyh beat C. F. Wheaton's imported Cooper at Giant's Despair hillclimb. The first 500 race run at Bridgehampton, Long Island, in June and Fitch won again, beating Canadian Peter Dillnut's Cooper. Dillnut led Alexis DuPont in a Cooper 1-2 at Palm Beach that December, but only four 500s started and they were the only finishers. The 500 Club of America (30.5 cubic inch club!) was formed with Harry S. Morrow as president and L. Braxton Tabor, secretary, based in Burbank, California. One problem they faced was the 500s need to be trailed, whereas 'sporty car' owners could drive their MGs, Jaguars and Healeys on the road to their race meetings. During 1952 there were at least four Coopers in the USA, Russ Kelly's being well-known but the Effyhs were still strong. At Brynfan-Tyddyn a Kieft beat Gordon Lipe's Cooper-Triumph, 'Bud' Hoopes and R. L. Moodie in Cooper-JAPs and DuPont's Cooper-Triumph. Cliff Ricker then emerged with his Mark V-Harley-Davidson 750 on the West Coast, along with Dr Leon Becker, Bob Wittke, John Fox, Henry Manney, Richard Trimble and Bill Breeze. The movement would survive without ever really flourishing, but wider US sales would come as Cooper's sports car and single-seater range developed.

Into 1952 the attentions of the Kieft brigade led Cooper to redesign their F3 production car, to produce the Mark VI 'T18' with an all-tubular frame at last replacing the Fiat *Topolino* derived box-section base. It now employed four main tube longerons in $1\frac{1}{2}$ in.-diameter 16-gauge 45-ton steel tube, braced vertically by perforated channel pieces. The new layout was 25 lb lighter than the Mark V's.

More extensive use had been made of magnesium-elektron castings to bring total weight-saving up to more than 60 lb. Height and frontal area had been reduced and weight distribution was now more even, according to the *Iota* report 50 lb having been taken off the rear end.

An elektron casing united engine, gearbox and back axle in a single assembly with built-in magnesium engine mountings bolting to lugs on the chassis. The Burman gearbox had an elektron casting which bolted with the elektron final drive case to the spring-mounted chassis bridge. Both gearbox and engine rear mounts bolted to a frame cross-member underneath. The fuel pump was mounted on the neat final-drive housing, driven as usual by a cam on the back axle. The complete assembly was narrower than its predecessor, so allowing longer half-shafts to relieve the UJs of some of the angular loads experienced before. The final-drive sprocket itself was now in magnesium-elektron and the rear suspension uprights, brake back-plates and integral wheels and drums were all now cast in the same material. Softer leaf-springs were used to give a better ride and improve traction, while the rest of the design followed familiar practice.

One ingenious innovation was the use of the tubular top

cross-member as a reservoir for the chain-oiling system. Pannier fuel tanks were slung in the same way as on the Mark V and either JAP or Norton engines were available to choice.

Another innovation was a new cast-elektron float chamber bracket. Since a car rolls outwards in corners, in one direction fuel in the float chamber surges away from the carburettor jet. This did not affect motorcycles as they bank into corners, but the effect gave trouble in cars using motorcycle engines and carburettors. Cooper's new bracket carried two float chambers, one on either side, so whichever way the car cornered and the fuel surged, the jet was still supplied. Owen's drawing for this was dated 18-3-52.

With the exception of an unimportant Montlhéry race where there were no British entries, every F3 International of 1952 fell to a British car. Les Leston was the most successful driver in continental events with three wins to his credit, including the prestigious Luxembourg GP, while Ken Carter, John Cooper and Rodney Nuckey won two each. In the UK, Cooper's pride was dented as Parker's Kieft won the *Autosport* Championship, but apart from numerous club-level wins and a clutch of lap records he won only one International, at Brands Hatch.

Les Leston had played drums in Bert Ambrose's band at 17½. He had begun racing in a Jaguar SS100 before buying a Kieft in 1950, then the JBS in '51 and Cooper in '52.

Stirling Moss raced his Kieft with some success, some misfortune, before reappearing in a Cooper for the 2 August Boreham meeting. The *Daily Mail* International there was rated one of the most exciting 500 cc F3 races ever held. Alan Brown was in superb form in his Richmond Cooper, battling wheel-to-wheel with Moss, Parker, Brandon and George Wicken for the duration. He eventually won at 83.86 mph and set a new lap record at 90.3. Parker was second and Moss third, driving almost blind after a flying stone shattered his goggles. Stirling completed his F3 season with victories at Zandvoort, Turnberry, Goodwood and Castle Combe.

In Europe, Ken Carter won at Brussels; Brandon for Ecurie Richmond again at Nürburgring, which he loved so much, and young Stuart Lewis-Evans was a newcomer to the scene who beat John Coombs and Austen May in sister Coopers at Chimay. Stuart's father, 'Pop' Lewis-Evans, was a motor trader from Bexley, Kent, and they went racing together in a pair of dark green-and-cream Coopers.

Les Leston added wins at Orleans and Porrentruy to his Luxembourg success, while that most-travelled F3 Briton Ken Carter – who was secretary of the Half-Litre Club at this time – won for Cooper at Amiens before hurting himself in an ugly accident while on a recce of the Crystal Palace road circuit in South London, prior to its reopening. He was out for the rest of the year.

John Cooper raced purely as and when he could find the

Ecurie Richmond's famous duo of Brandon and Brown took the lion's share of Formula 3 success during their fantastic 1951 season. Here at Silverstone are (left to right) Sheila Brandon, Mrs Richmond, Jimmy Richmond, Steve Lancefield the Norton engine tuner, Freddy Sirkett (?) team mechanic, Alan Brown, Eric Brandon and Gordon Bedson who was a 500 enthusiast working full time for Vickers Aviation, Brooklands. He later designed the Mackson F3 then became chief engineer of Kieft. Ecurie Richmond Mark Vs were polished rather than painted, to save weight. Identification nose-bands were red for Brandon, blue for Brown. Note right-hand gearchanges, leafspring mirror mounts and mud-spattered screens. It had been a wet race

time, for back home the Formula 2 Cooper-Bristol front-engined cars were in production. It was a hectic time. He won at Rouen for the second year and then on 31 August at Grenzlandring near Rheydt on the Dutch-German border he fielded the envelope-bodied Cooper-Norton Mark V record car to win the first 100 mph-average F3 race. This also made him the first British driver of a British car to win a postwar race at a three-figure average speed. He covered the 12 laps, 67 miles, at 102.64 mph and set a record lap at 106.62. Brandon just edged Moss out of second place in a slipper-bodied Mark VI; Stirling was actually driving John's regular car.

George Thomas and Rod Nuckey also won F3 internationals that year for the Surbiton marque and the *Cooper Year*

The special record-breaking Mark V streamliner with horizontal steering wheel immediately after completion, Hollyfield Road 14 September, 1951, showing wheel spats, tiny cockpit opening with wrap-round screen tight against driver's face and generally fine finish. Behind are (second from left) John Kelly, flanked by John Cooper, Fred Bedding and son Pete, who built the bodywork, and John Hume in the beret. On right is fruit-farmer owner-driver Bill Aston, and beside him with cigarette, works foreman Ernie Looker. Paintwork was BRG, upholstery red

Book that season detailed 57 500 cc victories overall, including eight in British hillclimb classes. Kieft had amassed 24 wins, and other British makes only six between them. Coopers were still the cars to buy. . . .

During the winter of 1952–53, the Hollyfield Road works was heavily committed with F2 and sports cars under construction as well as the bread-and-butter F3 lines. Charles Cooper was happy that the existing Mark VI layout could handle most opposition – 'Why change it when we're winnin'?' became his theme song – and so the new 1953 Mark VII was only cosmetically updated. Francis Beart's Mark VIIA 'special' built up in his hallowed tuning establishment at Byfleet in the shadow of the old Brooklands banking was more significant.

Charles and John had backed Beart quite enthusiastically in his work and authorized a special Cooper series Mark number for the result – the Mark VIIA. The frame was the standard four-longeron layout originated in the Mark VI, now in 17-gauge wall thickness as on the Mark VII but with tubular upright linking pieces in the space between top and bottom chassis rails, instead of the perforated steel strip used by Hollyfield Road. The driver's seat was dropped 3 in. lower than standard and a 3-gallon fuel tank was sited beneath the driver's legs between the bottom chassis rails. Another 3-gallon tank was hung in the scuttle on a framework of welded triangulated tubes. The combined capacity of these tanks was judged sufficient for the type of races to be tackled and dispensing with the standard pannier tanks reduced frontal area quite considerably.

For this slimline projectile, Beart prepared a Norton engine, mounted in dural plates with gearbox as on the racing motorcycle, and the whole assembly was moved $2\frac{1}{2}$ in. further forward in the frame than standard, retained by 10 nuts and bolts of 70-ton steel. Similar fittings were used throughout, even to the wheel nuts, and those exposed to engine vibration were all split-pinned.

There had been problems with exhaust pipes vibrating themselves to destruction, and on his Mark VIIA Beart welded the pipe to the top chassis tube on two short brackets, with a section of flexible piping at the engine end, where it could be quickly loosed-off to ease engine removal.

One major innovation to experienced F3 eyes was the use of a chain guard on the upper and lower runs of the primary chain, where oiling was provided by its own light-alloy tank weighing just ounces. A split rear sprocket was fitted, allowing ratio changes without disturbing the half-shaft UJs.

Very light tubular supports were used to mount the Girling dampers and the neat cigar-shaped body panelling was by the Wakefield family business just down the road beside the canal in Byfleet. The car was finished in Beart light green enamel – by Valspar – and it was to be driven by such F3 stars as Alan Brown, Eric Brandon and Stirling Moss . . . amongst others.

By 1953 500 cc Formula 3 was very much a British-dominated class where few others were inclined to play. The Italians had sold their Volpinis to a Marseillaise team in France. The Germans, who at one stage looked like becoming serious contenders, had grown discouraged and their leading drivers like Helmut Polensky and Walter Schlüter had turned to rallying, and earned more money there. The Swedish Effyhs were over the hill, racing only at home. Coopers won 13 of the 23 major F3 races that season. Kieft won six.

The first of them, at Goodwood on Easter Monday, fell instantly to Alan Brown in the Beart Mark VIIA. He had left Ecurie Richmond in search of pastures new, teaming-up with Mike Hawthorn's former sponsor, Bob Chase of RJC Motors at Saltdean, near Brighton. Moss, despite his standing as perhaps the very best of British drivers and very much a white hope for top World Championship honours, still ran occasionally in F3, winning at the inaugural Crystal Palace meeting on 25 May and beating Brandon at the Eifelrennen. The Finn Curt Lincoln won for Cooper at Helsinki. His daughter Nina would one day marry Cooper F1 driver Jochen Rindt. Stuart Lewis-Evans won at Orleans and twice at Crystal Palace in Beart's car; Eric Brandon won at Davidstow and Agen in France; Rodney Nuckey at Skarpnack and stock car driver Johnny Brise at Amiens. His son Tony would grow into a highly promising young F1 driver before dying with Graham Hill and other team-mates on Arkley golfcourse in November, 1975, when Graham's light plane crashed in fog. . . .

But perhaps the real highlight of the 1953 F3 season was The Great Nitro-Methane Kerfuffle. In mid-season this fuel additive with its instant promise of 10 per cent extra power was being supplied by the fuel companies only to their most favoured drivers. This split race fields into two – those with nitro and those without. The effects were clear in Britain, where Moss, Parker, Les Leston in his new special and a few others would rapidly leave the rest for dead and tear away in a horsepower battle of their own.

Ken Gregory, secretary of the Half-Litre Club at this time, raced a Cooper of his own and was very close to Charles Cooper in particular, often test-driving for the company: 'I vividly recall one test-day down at Goodwood where we were experimenting with nitro fuel. What we didn't realize was that you could absorb the stuff through your skin. Dear old Charles had been handling it all morning and when we went off for a pub lunch he seemed very quiet, then suddenly sat up in the bar and said, "Where am I? Who are you? Wot's this place? I've got money in me pocket! Wot's this money? This isn't my money?" We thought he was having us on, but we soon realized it was serious; he'd absorbed some compound from the fuel and he really was away on some sort of trip. . . . I drove him home with him glaring at me and asking who I was and what was going on . . . where was I taking him? I think he was off work for a couple of days before he recovered. After that, we usually wore gloves when handling the stuff. . . .'

Rex Woodgate, long-serving Alta mechanic, remembers Cooper-Bristol driver Horace Gould being fired with enthusiasm for nitro-methane around this time: 'He'd heard about the stuff and wangled a gallon can of it out of somebody. What he didn't realize was that we'd add an eggcup to a tankful. Dear old Horace reasoned that the more you put in, the more power you would get out, so he poured the whole gallon into a quarter-full fuel tank for a sprint race at Goodwood! He was streaking down the straight with the car going like never before when there was an almighty *Bang* that you could hear in the paddock, and the whole thing blew into a million tiny pieces. . . . But even good old Horace could see the funny side. . . .'

At Avus speedbowl in Berlin, John Cooper fielded the works streamlined record car amongst a slipper-bodied field to repeat the Grenzlandring victory. But on lap one he collided with some others and had to push-start his mildly dented pancake of a car and chase after the fast receding field. He simply zoomed through them all to win at 93.85 mph. John could tiger when he wanted to. . . .

The Grenzlandring streamliner was sold the following year to John Fox Jr of California, who wanted to run it at Bonneville. It was beautifully resprayed American blue and white, with crossed Union Jack and Stars and Stripes blazoned on

Formula 3 rapidly threw up its stars in the UK and Europe and here at Crystal Palace in 1953 are three of the early-1950s' most famous; Les Leston in the hooped sports-shirt, Eric Brandon and, far side, Alan Brown in the very special slimline, lightweight Beart Cooper Mark VIIA. Eric's racing fortunes were in decline, Brown had reached his height, while Les Leston had many more years' racing in him, but would falter at Formula 1

Eric Brandon's annual pilgrimage to the Italian national 750 Formula race at Chieti always paid rich dividends. Here in 1953 the tifosi *watch him prepare for battle, running a sidecar combination Norton 600 engine in his Mark VI/VII. Note long-range pannier tanks, megaphone exhaust and the always preferred leafspring mirror mounting. 'Ginger' Devlin, Eric's long-serving mechanic, is behind the car; John Cooper 'in that shirt' on left*

the nose. The later Mark VIII(R) record-breaker was advertised for sale by Cooper's Garage in June 1954 and I believe this too went to the USA. There was quite a healthy US 500 cc movement based upon imported Coopers. Roland Keith's red Cooper-JAP was a very successful car there, facing sister cars handled by Alexis du Pont, George Perrington and others, later to include Henry N. Manney III, who would become *Road & Track* magazine's outstanding, dryly humorous editor-at-large.

Eric Brandon drove the Beart car at Silverstone, but didn't like it: 'Whenever I selected second gear it would fall right off the cam, and I'd have to grit my teeth and wait for it to get into its stride again. But it was slim, and very quick down the straights. . . .'

As 500 cc racing failed to catch on in Italy, the locals preferred a 750 class, Eric fitted a bored and stroked 600 cc sidecar Norton engine into the older Mark VI chassis that he had acquired from Vandervell Products after deciding he didn't really like the cigar-shaped Mark VII. He ran this hybrid at Chieti and won handsomely from Lewis-Evans's ordinary Cooper 500 and a flock of other F3s and converted local sports cars from Giaur and Stanguellini. 'They just couldn't live with the terrific torque of the 600, and the organizers paid out well enough to give Sheila [his wife] and I a fortnight's holiday on the Riviera. This became an annual pilgrimage. Win at Chieti, take the money, and two weeks' holiday. . . .'

Formula 3 racing had become very much 'Formula Cooper', but don't imagine they won literally everything in sight, because this simply is not true. However, their predominance forced other manufacturers out of business, and when the all-new Mark VIII or 'T31' was introduced for 1954 predominance really did become domination.

CHAPTER EIGHT

Cooper-Bristols and Grands Prix

Failure is a terrific spur to anyone competitive, especially if they have known success. While the Formula 3 Coopers had swept virtually all before them in 1951, the 1100 twins were far too unreliable for serious use in Formula 2.

At the end of 1951, established Cooper customers wanted to climb the ladder to this class, which seemed set to take over the 1952 World Championship. During the previous year most major F3 events had been curtain-raisers to F2 races – as in the *Grands Prix de France* series. So the British circus knew the organizers involved, knew how much they would pay, and how far they could be trusted. . . . With World Championship status about to be applied to Formula 2 in place of a moribund Formula 1, Grand Prix racing ambitions suddenly seemed within reach that winter. All that was needed was an economically priced, practical F2 car suitable for the private owner. . . .

There wasn't much to choose from. Geoffrey Taylor, based near Cooper in Tolworth, was offering his Alta F2s. His engines had given Moss, Collins and Lance Macklin their chance in the HWM team, but by reputation Alta cars 'were difficult'. HWM had sold their highly successful 1951 team cars, but were fully committed to building new for themselves. There was Rodney Clarke's new Connaught from Send, using Lea Francis-based engines. It looked promising, but was an unknown quantity. Real wealth could buy a Ferrari or Maserati from Italy – if you could find a place in the queue of continental and South American customers. And now there was a new Cooper. . . .

Denis Jenkinson summed up Cooper's swing towards Formula 2 like this: 'When the Cooper Car Company was first formed, to build 500 cc racing cars, one aspect that was most noticeable was the ability of John Cooper and his father to produce something in a very short space of time. Working a great deal by rule of thumb, and being very practical men, they did not have to spend unnecessary time with drawings; they were far happier to "try-it-and-see". With the rapid increase of interest in Formula 2 the Coopers soon turned their thoughts in that direction and it was not long before a 2-litre unblown Cooper was offered for sale in their catalogue. . . .'

John Cooper: 'The best available 2-litre engine was the six-cylinder Bristol, built by the Bristol Aeroplane Company car division at Filton near Bristol. It was based on the prewar BMW 328 design which we'd taken as war reparations. My father and I went down to see the Bristol people, George White was the MD, and we asked if he'd let us have an engine to try in the front of one of our chassis. He said yes, and we soon had our prototype Cooper-Bristol rolling. . . .'

This engine was a 66 × 96 mm, 1971 cc six with overhead valves actuated by cross-pushrods from a high camshaft, and three Solex carburettors. It produced around 127 bhp at 5800 rpm. This was known to be 35–40 bhp less than the contemporary Ferrari and Maseratis. It was quite a hefty and tall engine, but the Coopers were sure it would do the job. It was familiar, it was available in quantity, and parts were readily obtainable. It would also, incidentally, form a perfect 2-litre engine for a sports-racing version.

Charles reasoned that by building the lightest practical chassis and avoiding complication they could compensate for the Bristol engine's lowish power. An uncomplicated car also promised reliability.

The result was the Cooper 'T20' or Cooper-Bristol Mark I. The first prototype was shown to the Press at Hollyfield Road in January 1952. It was based on a chassis broadly similar to that of the Mark V 500, with light-gauge box-section main longerons liberally drilled for lightness, united by matching cross-members. A horizontal tube longeron ran parallel above each main box-member, linked to it by welded-on perforated strip stiffened with folded flanges. Welded between base frame and upper longerons and extending above them into body-supporting hoops were two further tubular members in the scuttle, others being welded to the suspension bridge structures front and rear.

Suspension was normal Cooper for the period, with transverse leaves offering lateral location and springing, and tubular wishbones down below. Outboard telescopic dampers were used.

The Bristol engine and its four-speed gearbox were tilted forward in the prototype car with the prop-shaft running slightly upwards towards the ENV final-drive unit, which was bolted into the front of the rear suspension bridge. John envisaged using a drop-gear final-drive arrangement in later cars, both to lower the prop-shaft and to enable speedy ratio changes. This would not happen for some time, although Bill

18 January, 1952, Hollyfield Road's first prototype Cooper-Bristol Mark I rolls out for inspection. The Mark V/VI 500-derived box-section chassis base frame can be clearly seen, with its bracing round-tube superstructure and combined tube and strip body supports, in part fitted here only to allow prototype body manufacture. Steering wheel is metal spider and rim only, as yet untrimmed, radiator has yet to be fitted, brake mechanism and piping added and half-shafts installed but Cooper's first World Championship class racing car is rolling

Aston built some specials contemporary with this 'T20' which had this feature, as we shall see. The prototype works car had a straight-cut cwp with a ratio of 3.4 : 1.

Rack-and-pinion steering was used, with the steering column stepped around the offside of the engine through two Mollart UJs. Steering ratio was 1¾ turns lock-to-lock. The central gear lever rose between the driver's shins then cranked towards his right hand. Short, splined, double-jointed half-shafts drove to the rear wheels, which were located on typical Cooper fabricated uprights.

The wheels were the familiar Cooper magnesium cast-type, with integral 10 in. diameter × 1¾ in. wide brake drums and Wellworthy centrifugally cast liners. Lockheed twin leading-shoe hydraulics were used, with separate dual circuitry.

Fuel was carried in three aluminium tanks; 14 gallons in the tail and seven either side of the cockpit to total 28. A mechanical fuel pump was driven from the camshaft. Tailor-made oil and water radiators filled the nose, beneath a neat if rather nose-heavy-looking aluminium bodyshell, with bonnet-top scoop feeding the Solex carburettors. A Ferrari-like potato chipper grille in aluminium strip followed established Cooper shape.

Body styling at Hollyfield Road was pretty much by workshop committee. Owen Maddock would have his say with a few sketches, as would John and usually Charles too. Then Fred and Peter Bedding would contribute: '. . . like, "You can't expect us to make that!"' as Pete Bedding, working for Brabham in 1982, recalled. . .

'We would outline a new shape in strip and the Old Man and John would look at it and pull it about, then we'd talk with the Beard and between us we'd sort something out which suited all requirements – and sometimes Owen would draw it to scale, we'd make jigs and if necessary put them out to our sub-contractors. . . .'

The Mark I's wheelbase was 90 in., track 50½ in, and dry weight was quoted most Imperially as '9 cwt 3 qr 12 lb'. The wheel rim sizes were 15 in., carrying Dunlop Racing 5.00–15 front and 5.50–15 rear tyres.

COOPER CARS

Details were published in mid-January. A deal for two cars, possibly a third, had already been made with Jimmy Richmond, Alan Brown and Eric Brandon. Now very significant new interest was shown.

It came from a former Naval Commander, an engineer based in Saltdean, Brighton, where his company, RJC Motors Ltd, were main dealers for GM commercial, industrial and marine diesel engines, plant and vehicles. His name was Bob Chase, and he was an old friend of a Farnham, Surrey, garage owner, whose name was Leslie Hawthorn. . . .

During 1951, Leslie and his 22-year-old son Mike had raced a pair of venerable Rileys with great success. The cars looked tatty but were mechanically superb and very fast indeed. Leslie was a most capable tuner, and his Tourist Trophy Garage business in East Street, Farnham, was well known among enthusiasts. During that winter the Hawthorns pondered on single-seater racing, in Formula 2.

Mike later wrote: 'Father had given up racing and was putting everything into pushing forward my career, which meant not only using all his skill to give me cars that were fast and reliable, but also negotiating with people who might give me a drive, while I was away continuing my engineering studies. . . .'

He test-drove a Connaught at Goodwood, but spun it when trying too hard. John Heath tested him for HWM as Moss was leaving the team, but Peter Collins was chosen instead. He had single-seater experience; Mike had not.

Now Bob Chase had been in bed, suffering from 'flu, reading the week's motoring press when he saw details of the new Cooper-Bristol. He telephoned Leslie Hawthorn and offered to buy one of the cars for Mike to drive and TT Garage to maintain. He then called John Cooper to place his order, but John hedged. 'We're only building three,' he explained, 'and they're all spoken for. . . .' Then Chase explained it wasn't for himself, but for a young fellow called Hawthorn. John had seen Mike driving his Riley at Goodwood. Chase's order was accepted, rather – one senses – to Richmond's disgust, as neither Brandon nor Brown had heard much about the newcomer.

Eric Brandon: 'The deal we finally did was for our mechanics, Ginger Devlin and Bernie Rodger, to assemble our cars plus Mike's at Cooper's, and we could have ours for £1200 apiece. Our blokes progressed our cars as quick as they could. If some shortage meant a car was going to lag behind, it was obvious which one it would be. . . .'

The Hawthorns went to Filton, Bristol, to ensure early delivery of a third racing engine, and Leslie specified a rather special unit with high-compression head, tuned to burn nitro-bearing fuel. Mike then went to Hollyfield Road with soft-spoken, gentlemanly family friend Hugh Sewell, who liked nothing better than getting his fingers greasy in a racing car's internals. They helped progress the car, which they would subsequently maintain at TT Garage alongside mechanics

Top of page *Proud father – Charles Cooper at the wheel during initial testing of the prototype Cooper-Bristol Mark I on a misty winter's day at Odiham Aerodrome, Hampshire. The car wears its original potato-chipper grille and shows off its neat, uncomplicated lines with bonnet-top intake to feed the Bristol engine's triple Solex carburettors, blister to clear distributor (on right) and neatly faired-in rearview mirrors*

Makings of an historic team. Mike Hawthorn poses proudly with the spanking new Bob Chase-owned Cooper-Bristol Mark I which will project him towards Britain's first World Drivers' Championship title. Beside him outside father Leslie's Tourist Trophy Garage showrooms in East Street, Farnham, is mechanic Brit Pearce. Leslie Hawthorn's influence on this car's development shows in its extended carburettor intake duct wrapped over the nose cowl. The engine was tuned to run nitromethane fuel and with Mike's driving the combination was very special

60

COOPER-BRISTOLS AND GRANDS PRIX

Famous photo, famous day — Easter Monday Goodwood, 1952, the four Cooper-Bristol Mark Is then extant lined-up against the paddock stalls. In foreground is Alan Brown's Ecurie Richmond car flanked by team-mate Eric Brandon in his, reigning World Champion Juan Manuel Fangio guesting in John Cooper's prototype (with mesh radiator grille replacing original potato chipper) then Hawthorn in unpainted, just completed Bob Chase machine. Behind, third from left, is Ginger Devlin, behind Fangio stand Jimmy Richmond, Charles Cooper with his twin sister Judy, then sitting on Hawthorn's rear wheel is John Cooper and behind him, in light overalls, Brit Pearce

Fangio drove the Alan Brown Richmond car into a misfiring sixth place in the Formule Libre Chichester Cup race at Easter Goodwood. Here he is wearing a borrowed helmet. Note Brown's Bluemels moulded-finger-grip standard steering wheel unlike the Cooper racing wheels on the Brandon and prototype cars — Hawthorn's was a special 4-spoke of his own preference

Briton Pearce and Joe Bickell. Joe's late brother Ben Bickell had been a very effective racing motorcyclist before crashing fatally, and Leslie himself was a motorcycle tuner of old. They had great experience with nitro-methane fuel additives – as yet little used in cars – and Brit recalls how: '. . . we got the stuff in drums and mixed it up at the Garage, and kept it quiet. I don't think even Bob Chase knew we were using it. . . .'

All three new Cooper-Bristols were ready four days before the Easter Monday Goodwood meeting. On Good Friday they tested briefly at Lasham Aerodrome, beyond Farnham, but while both Richmond cars behaved well, Chase's lost compression – its valve-seats had warped.

The Hawthorn crew worked all night at TT Garage using an old worn out cutter to remake them. Then early Saturday morning, with practice that day, they put the car into a big Austin six-cylinder transporter that Leslie had borrowed from Connaught. Brit Pearce chocked its wheels with timber but just a mile outside Farnham – within yards of me as I write – 'There was a rumble and bang and the car had run up over the timber – there'd have been hell to pay if Leslie had found out; he had a terrible temper!'

At Goodwood, Mike immediately and sensationally set second fastest practice time in his unpainted new car, behind only the $4\frac{1}{2}$-litre *ThinWall* Ferrari. The Richmond cars were painted pale metallic green, Brandon's with a red noseband, Brown's dark blue. John Cooper drove the old prototype car, now with a wire mesh intake grille like its sisters, replacing the potato chipper.

Fangio was at Goodwood and was fascinated by the new cars. Should his expected BRM fail to appear on the Monday, John offered him the prototype for one of the day's races though he also tried Brown's.

Easter Sunday saw the Hawthorn car being race-prepared by Hughie Sewell, Leslie, Brit and Joe at TT Garage. Mike told the story of that historic Monday: 'I was on the starting line when I realized that I had never practised a racing start in the car. I had no idea what revs or how much wheelspin to expect. Suddenly there flashed into my mind something I had read in *Motor Sport*. It said somebody ... at the Brighton Speed Trials took the revs up and then held them instead of blipping the throttle.... Down went my foot, the flag dropped, I let in the clutch and away I went.... When I got a chance to size up what was going on behind I simply could not believe it. I was well in the lead.'

And he won the six-lap Lavant Cup to give both himself and his new car a sensational debut. Brown and Brandon followed him home for a Cooper-Bristol 1-2-3 grand slam.

Out again in the six-lap Formule Libre Chichester Cup, Mike won again, leading all the way after another steady-rev start. Fangio's Brown car finished sixth. The day's feature race was the 12-lap Richmond Trophy, including F1 cars, and Mike actually led Gonzales' *ThinWall* before it got into its stride and thundered ahead. Mike still finished second, 26 secs behind, to complete his fantastic day. Fangio's prototype car non-started with valve trouble. According to John this was due to its high test mileage, according to Hawthorn part of a Bristol plague at that time, his own engine had needed more attention that very morning. Alan Brown then won a Handicap race in his Richmond car, and the Cooper-Bristols had most sensationally arrived.

The Hawthorn Cooper-Bristol season of 1952 is now familiar motor racing legend. He won minor races at Ibsley and Boreham, but his international exploits rocketed him to fame, and a Ferrari works drive for 1953. At the May Silverstone meeting he had a fright in practice, spinning into the straw bales on the very fast Abbey Curve. Undeterred he still won his heat and was leading the Final from Jean Behra's Gordini when 'I found my gear-lever flapping uselessly'. The stop for repairs dropped him to 18th. The Richmond boys had objected to the between-legs gearchange while building the cars, and had rigged a right-hand remote like Veritas used. Eric Brandon: 'Then Charles saw what we'd done and blew up because we were messing about with his design. He insisted we replace the original lever, so we did, on the Chase car....' It was Richmond's revenge....

The Richmond boys set off on their continental tour with the Cooper-Bristols and 500s, and on 18 May the Swiss GP saw Alan Brown finish fifth and score Cooper's first-ever World Championship points. Eric was eighth, despite leaving the road at one point: 'A gasket had gone and I was just limping round to finish. I was looking round for Farina. He was an absolute thug with back-markers, and when I looked back to see where I was going I was charging off the road along a ditch!' Alan Brown admired Eric's driving but felt he was always happier in the 500s than the larger cars. Eric didn't have much time for his Cooper-Bristol: 'It was just horrible. It wasn't competitive and I didn't enjoy driving an uncompetitive car. It would run out of brakes as soon as you stamped on them, and we couldn't afford a spare engine so we had to do the best with what we'd got and not break it. The biggest problem was changing the diff to get an axle ratio to suit different circuits. But it was strong, and surprisingly stiff. That chassis gave the impression it would break before it would flex....'

Hawthorn had his reservations too: 'The Cooper ... handled well in the wet, steered well and drifted the corners with great ease, although the wheel adhesion was not all it might have been. Perhaps the weakest point was the braking system ... the integral drum liners sometimes distorted and cracked, so that the car pulled to one side or the other when the brakes were used. Spare wheels were almost unobtainable

Morning after Hawthorn's meteoric rise to fame at Goodwood, the newshounds were beating at TT Garage's door in Farnham. Here posed rather self-consciously with the car are family friend Hughie Sewell, Leslie and Mike Hawthorn, and (right) Brit Pearce. Hawthorn already preferred four-spoke steering wheels like the thick-rimmed one seen here. This preference would persist throughout his racing career

Opposite *Mike Hawthorn doing his steady-revs start trick to make the most of his first-ever race getaway in the Chase Mark I, setting off to lead the 6-lap Lavant Cup all the way and win at 83.18 mph – Easter Monday Goodwood meeting, 1952. This was the first event of the day, for unblown 2000 cc (Formula 2) cars. Beyond Hawthorn stand Brit Pearce (second from left) beside Hughie Sewell, with Leslie Hawthorn in the dark sports jacket and tie immediately beyond his son's screen Ginger Devlin next in line. On the grid, George Abecassis' new HWM is next up, with Brandon on row two, Brown on the front row, and Bill Aston's new Aston-Butterworth just visible beyond him with its curious cast-alloy wheels*

and we had to make do with (just) two for the whole season....

'We had no spare engine and so the one engine together with the rest of the car had to be checked over in detail after every race, which meant long hours of day-and-night work by my father and the mechanics ... the engine was not extensively modified, but it was very carefully assembled ... there had been hardly time to do anything before my first Goodwood meeting except cure the valve-seat trouble. We decreased the valve-seat angles to improve the gas-flow and changed the ignition and carburettor settings.... Choice of fuel was fairly critical. The mixture recommended didn't seem to us to be ideal, so we mixed our own.... There were only two combinations of crown-wheel and pinion available and the ratios in the Frazer Nash gearbox were too wide for use on a racing single-seater. We had only two available tyre sizes, so we often had to put up with gearing which was far from ideal.... However, it was a wonderful year, and I shall always be grateful to those who made it possible....'

His first European foray had been to the Belgian GP on 22 June, and while the Chase car was being carefully prepared for it Leslie Hawthorn borrowed the prototype car from its new owner, A. H. 'Archie' Bryde, for the Ulster Trophy at Dundrod. In practice there its water pump failed. There was no spare, but Mike discovered a Major in Belfast who owned a Bristol road car. He and Jimmy Hall of Castrol talked the proud owner into 'loaning' its water pump, and Leslie and Hugh rebuilt the Bristol race engine overnight, only to find its head gasket blown next morning. They filled the system with Colman's mustard, and the leak dried-up....

Mike led early on before the road dried and Taruffi powered his *ThinWall* Ferrari ahead. After a stop for more water and oil Mike finished second: 'The Major's water pump was of no further use to him or to anyone else, but Bristol's gave him a new one....'

Leslie Hawthorn might have been a tetchy character, but he had a fine sense of humour. Now he had a 'Colman's Mustard' advertisement painted on TT's converted Bedford bus transporter.

In Belgium, in the Chase car with its characteristically large induction cowl on top, Hawthorn fought a long duel with Ken Wharton's new F2 Frazer Nash. 'Ken had more experience of this type of racing than I had ... then I got in front and I noticed he was missing.' Wharton had spun into the woods beneath a barbed-wire fence, which plucked the shirt from his back as he ducked under it! Misfiring on low fuel caused Mike to stop twice near the end to top up, and he finished fourth to score his first World Championship points on this his GP debut. The Richmond cars were sixth and ninth, Brown and Brandon. The cars were too slow to be competitive, but they were reliable and if well driven could inherit finishes in the points, and the money.

Mike drove the Bryde car at Reims, but its head lifted and the overheating engine broke. Brandon used a detuned engine to survive this long, hot race, and after Brown's sister car broke its engine he took over Eric's to finish 11th. Capable of about 130 mph flat-out, the Cooper-Bristols could match neither the Italian cars nor the French Gordinis on such a high-speed circuit.

The Bryde car was rebuilt at Cattaneo's in Paris and Mike then enjoyed himself hugely driving it on the road to the French GP meeting at Rouen, escorted by the owner's Bentley. Archie Bryde, living in Germany in 1982, remembers how they '... came up to a rather flash Packard white convertible, driven by a young man with a very pretty dolly sitting on his right. Mike first came level on the correct overtaking side, did a double take, and continued to pass. He then slowed right down, and the Packard went to pass him. Mike allowed him alongside, and, naturally, at this point the bird was next to Mike. This went on for two or three kilometres and it's the only time I have ever seen somebody trying to chat-up a bird while driving a single-seat racing car....'

The Cooper's battery was found to be flat just before the start of the GP, and it was replaced by one from a police motorcycle. Mike inherited fifth place before the header tank split, shorting out the plugs as water sprayed over them. After two stops he was out.

Meanwhile, Hollyfield Road had completed more production Mark Is; one going to the George Hartwell–Alan Fraser Syndicate for Bournemouth-domiciled Belgian charger André Loens; another to a Billingsgate fish-merchant named John Barber; and a third to David Murray's Ecurie Ecosse team from Merchiston Mews, Edinburgh.

John Barber had appeared as a young unknown armed with a Cooper 1000 cc twin at the Lydstep hillclimb early in 1951, and promptly capsized it in the deceptive top corner there. André Loens was a cheerful extrovert garage proprietor, based in Bournemouth, although Belgian-born, another 500 and big twin exponent.

The British GP was at Silverstone on 19 July and five Mark Is ran there; Chase's car with its engine rebuilt to '135 bhp' form; Reg Parnell driving Bryde's; David Murray the Ecosse car, and Brandon and Brown. Barber's entry was accepted only for the supporting Libre race. Hawthorn finished third in the GP behind the uncatchable Ferraris, Parnell seventh. Brandon was 20th and Brown 22nd after a string of mishaps. Murray retired. Barber was seventh in his race, learning the ropes.

André Loens took the new Fraser-Hartwell car to Mont Ventoux, and was second in class in the classic French mountain climb, while Boreham airfield on 2 August saw another brilliant Hawthorn drive in heavy rain.

This race was a combined F1/F2 200-miler, including Hawthorn, Brown, Brandon, Murray, Bryde, Barber and Loens in the seven Mark Is extant. In heavy rain Mike caught works Ferrari driver Luigi Villoresi for the overall lead, despite an early spin, and then pulled away 5 secs a lap. Then the rain stopped, and the circuit began to dry. His 40 sec lead evaporated with the puddles. His Bristol engine began stammering. He was down to 4700 against the normal 5800 rpm. Its flywheel was breaking adrift. Villoresi and Brazilian Ferrari driver Chico Landi both went ahead, but Hawthorn hung on for third overall, winning the F2 category by miles from Brown, with Brandon fifth, and setting F2 fastest lap near the end on the dry track. Murray was seventh and Bryde 13th while Barber and Loens retired.

Bryde retired his car at Comminges, and then on 17 August the Dutch GP at Zandvoort saw Hawthorn qualifying third fastest alongside the Ascari and Farina Ferraris. He ran second and finished fourth in the race. This was his first full(ish) season of racing and he had already driven in four World Championship GPs, finishing three times; fourth, third, fourth. *Maestro* Nello Ugolini and Aurelio Lampredi of Ferrari talked quietly with Leslie Hawthorn about Mike driving for them in '53.

Ecurie Richmond meanwhile raced at La Baule, finishing 9-10, and at Grenzlandring the cars were outgunned by the German AFM V8s, Brandon placing tenth, while Brown's water-pump drive failed.

The Italian GP at Monza saw Richmond running both cars again, alongside Hawthorn, with Wharton in the Ecosse Mark I. All qualified well though slower than Stirling Moss's Connaught. None had high-enough final-drive ratios. Eric found: 'You could go all-out for a quick lap in practice and after using those under-sized brakes to the full just once or twice they'd burned out and there was nothing left. And we were running out of revs on the long straights. It was hopeless....'

Yet from the start Hawthorn slipstreamed Taruffi mercilessly, only for his distributor drive to shear. His crew got him running again after an hour's work, but he was not classified as a finisher. Wharton drove a steady non-stop race, but the cars were far outclassed.

The Richmond boys were always staggered by the Chase car's speed compared to their own. Eric: 'On the rare occasions we saw it back at Cooper's we'd crawl all over it, open the filler cap, sniff the tank and look in the carbs, but the tanks were always cleaned-out and they'd taken the jets out of the carburettors.... It was only later we found they really had been using nitro....'

At Monza, the Ferrari management – urged on by bearing manufacturer Tony Vandervell, whose *ThinWall* had been driven by Hawthorn at Turnberry in Scotland – invited Mike and his father down to Modena to try a Ferrari for the city GP the following weekend. There was talk of a green-painted Ferrari for the Englishman, while Roy Salvadori would take over the Chase Cooper-Bristol.

Mike tried a Ferrari in practice, and Leslie then suggested he drive the Cooper for comparison. The boy promptly tried to brake at the same point as the fabulous Ferrari and those

The other Hawthorn car – Mike hustling the Archie Bryde-owned prototype Mark I around Dundrod during the Ulster Trophy meeting. He led initially until the road dried allowing Taruffi to use the 4½-litre V12 ThinWall Ferrari's power and thunder by. The Mark I's engine overheated despite Leslie Hawthorn's ministrations with Colman's mustard! Despite race failure the TT Garage Transporter was suitably adorned next day, here with Ron Flockhart sharing the joke. The transporter was an obsolete wartime coach, bought from E. J. Baker of Farnham and panelled-in with hardboard, leaving the original glass in place...

14
16

TOURIST TROPHY GARAGE
FARNHAM
ENGLAND
COOPER-BRISTOL
WE USE COLMAN'S MUSTARD
297 PO
KRF 119

Cooper's first-ever World Championship points were notched by Alan Brown's Ecurie Richmond Mark I-Bristol in the Swiss GP at Berne's daunting Bremgarten forest circuit, 18 May, 1952. Here during the race he holds off Moss, charging up the inside at Jordenrampe *in the works HWM, while 'Toulo' de Graffenried looks on in his Maserati. Note the Bristol engine's huge projecting sump and the Hawthorn-style 'schnorkel' which was becoming so popular amongst Mark I runners*

Hawthorn's Grande Epreuve *debut came at Spa-Francorchamps in the Belgian GP, 22 June, 1952. It was wet and treacherous high in the Ardennes but despite two late stops to top-up a leaking fuel tank Hawthorn finished fourth overall behind the works Ferraris of Ascari and Farina, and Robert Manzon's Gordini six. His stops lost him a lap to this trio*

treacherous integral drums locked-up. At around 75 mph the Cooper-Bristol broadsided into some straw bales and rolled, tossing Mike out and inflicting severe abrasions and a damaged lung. While recovering in hospital he still signed for Ferrari; the first British driver to join a major European works team since Dick Seaman in 1936–37.

Back home, Alan Brown took a third at Goodwood in the closing meeting of the year, while Duncan Hamilton drove the repaired Chase car, only for its unique engine to disintegrate totally along Lavant Straight. For Castle Combe, a Frazer Nash-Bristol engine was installed and Wharton drove, finishing second ahead of F3 Cooper driver Ninian Sanderson, trying his hand at F2 in the Ecosse machine. Barber and Brown collided, without injury. Wharton was third in the unlimited race; an excellent result in this outclassed car. He drove it again at Charterhall.

Meanwhile, back at Easter Monday Goodwood, Bill Aston had emerged with his Cooper-derived Aston-Butterworth F2, using a flat-four air-cooled AJB engine made by Archie Butterworth in Frimley, Surrey. The car used a Mark I-type Cooper-Bristol frame with drop-gears behind the final-drive to lower the prop-shaft, running Borrani wire wheels with separate Alfin bimetal drums. The AJB engine drove through an MG TC gearbox and Aston tried swing-axle rear suspension originally, but soon scrapped it in favour of a conventional Cooper layout. Robin Montgomerie-Charrington had heard about the project and asked Aston to build him a sister car, identical in most respects apart from expensive new six-spoke cast-alloy Dunlop wheels. Charrington's car was finished in blue and white as he held American nationality, and he put up the type's best performance at Chimay when he looked set to finish third only to run out of fuel on the last lap. He ran seventh in the Belgian GP before refuelling with the wrong mixture, which gave his engine severe indigestion and caused him to retire.

In practice at Reims the Aston-Butterworth's step-up gears stripped, but Charrington miraculously found a local gear-cutter who machined new gears for him while he waited! A

The well-used prototype Mark I-Bristol in Archie Bryde's ownership was raced widely around the UK and Europe both by its new owner and by Hawthorn. Here Mike locks over on the pavé *for Thillois Corner at Reims-Gueux during F2 GP de France qualifying round there on 29 June, 1952. He was classified seventh, though the engine broke after 66 of the 71 laps. He had his favourite steering wheel fitted to the prototype, compare with that on this car at Goodwood. Non-availability of larger-diameter bolt-on rear wheels handicapped the Mark I's overall gearing and restricted its suitability for high speed circuits like this*

Inevitably, Hawthorn again, this time in his supreme drive versus the 4½-litre V12 Ferraris at Boreham in the rain, 2 August, 1952. Relaxed, confident and amazingly quick through the corners, Hawthorn humbled Villoresi in the Formula 1 Ferrari and also Ken Wharton and Froilan Gonzales in the V16 BRMs before the Chase car's flywheel worked loose, the track dried and two F1s moved ahead leaving 'The Farnham Flyer' to finish third overall and still win the F2 category by miles. One month later he was signing for Ferrari, the first English driver to win a place in a serious Continental factory GP team since Dick Seaman had joined Daimler-Benz for 1937

half-shaft UJ then broke in the race and he was so discouraged that he abandoned his racing ambitions and returned to the USA.

The veteran Bill Aston continued to enjoy his racing as a hobby. It was such a shoe-string operation that any major breakage was devoutly to be avoided, and when 'nasty noises' intruded in the German GP at Nürburgring he stopped before something expensive broke. At Monza the car was utterly outclassed. Aston was sure restricted breathing gave no hope of higher speeds from the engine, and he failed to qualify. He started two late-season races at Goodwood, but retired from both with loose valve inserts.

So Cooper's first serious season of Formula 2 racing yielded the marque's first World Championship points, brilliant results for Mike and Leslie Hawthorn, rather less so for the other customers. But it was obvious that the Mark I recipe offered a light, good-handling platform for more powerful engines.

Peter Walker, who had raced ERAs widely, aimed at sprint and hillclimb success by buying a slightly lengthened rolling-chassis Mark I to accommodate a six-cylinder single-stage supercharged ERA engine originally built up for his friend Peter Whitehead in 1949. The new Cooper-ERA made its debut at Brighton, where Walker just missed FTD by 0.3 sec as a piston collapsed within yards of the finish. The car, with just under 200 bhp, showed blistering acceleration, and at Prescott hillclimb proved incapable of putting all that power through to the road, suffering uncontrollable wheel-spin. The engine gave trouble at Goodwood, but at Castle Combe Walker pressed Bob Gerard's normal 2-litre ERA very hard, and finished a close second. In the British season finale at Charterhall in Scotland, Walker finished fourth in a major 40-lapper. Wharton's Chase car battled with Poore's Connaught for the lead until its timing chain broke after nine laps.

There was obvious further potential for alternative power units in the basic Cooper-Bristol frame, and there were still busier times ahead for Hollyfield Road. . . .

CHAPTER NINE

Part 1 Mark IIs, Bristols and Altas . . .

While the composite box-and-tube section Cooper-Bristol Mark Is were making their name during 1952, the all-tubular Mark VI 500s had been very successful, easy to build and profitable. Clearly their simple all tubular frame was the way to go, and during the autumn Owen Maddock laid out such a chassis for the coming season's Mark II 'T23' F2 car.

The prototype Mark II was displayed at the 1952 London Motor Show in October. It was impeccably prepared, standing on a special display of Britain's new F2 cars, and was finished in bright mid-green.

Its lighter tubular frame was obviously the most important new feature. Its top rails ran alongside the engine bay at cylinder head level forming deeper trusses than ever before. The tubes themselves were 16-gauge $1\frac{1}{2}$ in. diameter steel. Maximum frame depth was at the scuttle, tapering fore and aft to the suspension pick-ups. At the front the top rails and a single main diagonal on either side converged above the transverse leaf-spring. At the rear the dipping top rail and rear bay diagonal converged beneath the spring. Lower wishbones pivoted on the bottom rails, which still retained the diamond planform.

While the earliest Mark Is had used a spiral-bevel rear axle, a hypoid type had later been adopted to lower the prop-shaft slightly, and in turn the driver's seat. This hypoid axle was retained for the Mark II, but John had persuaded his father to invest in a new magnesium final-drive casing with an ENV nose-piece. It might attract orders from other manufacturers. It was mounted with the pinion shaft inclined slightly downwards to lower the prop-shaft still further, and in turn the driver's seat.

Cooper's integral light-alloy wheels-cum-brake drums had been a major Mark I limitation. Now large 11 in. diameter separate Alfin linered light-alloy drums were fitted; two leading shoe front and rear and $2\frac{1}{4}$ and $1\frac{3}{4}$ in. wide respectively. There was a Vernier brake balance adjustment on the linkage between the two master cylinders. The new brakes were carried on lighter cast-magnesium combination back-plates and stub axle carriers, smooth-shaped to reduce aerodynamic drag. The steering rack housing was cast in magnesium-elektron to save more weight. Another new detail was the ingenious little remote gearchange linkage modelled after Veritas and Ecurie Richmond practice. The Mark II was altogether a better-engineered car than the rather cobbled-up, made from available parts, Mark I.

Up front, Owen had another brainwave. To lose the ugly bonnet-top air scoop of the Mark Is he split the radiator core and spread the two blocks thus produced apart at their feet, with a common header tank over the top and a horizontal oil cooler down below. Carburettor air was guided in through the gap, while the uncontrolled discharge of hot air into the engine bay, which made the Mark I require such heavy bonnet louvring, was slashed by the use of proper radiator ducting to guide hot air away through the suspension cut-outs either side. This permitted a neat, smooth un-louvered bodyshell carefully faired around the cockpit and including a moulded Perspex windscreen lip.

The Mark II's wheelbase was 7 ft 6 in., front track 3 ft 10 in., rear track 3 ft $10\frac{1}{4}$ in., overall length 11 ft 3 in., overall height 3 ft 3 in. and ground clearance 5 in. It weighed $9\frac{1}{4}$ cwt. It was obviously possible to fit engines other than the Bristol if so required, as Peter Walker had done in his Mark I-ERA.

Into the winter of 1952–53 the Argentine Club was offering

The prototype Cooper-Bristol Mark II or 'T23' ready for display at the London Motor Show, October 1952. It was handsomely show-prepared, with chromed damper barrels and stub exhausts. The oil cooler ahead of the splayed-leg radiator is visible inside the nose, and the remote gearchange projects in the cockpit. The ducted radiator saved the unsightly bonnet louvres of the Mark I. At right here in Hollyfield Road is works foreman Ernie Looker. Note cooler has starting handle hole, though there is none in the grille

Preparing for the 1953 Argentine GP in a Buenos Aires garage, John Barber works on the London Motor Show prototype Mark II, showing off its engine-turned firewall, now blued-chrome stub pipes and the unique Mark II radiator-cum-oil cooler layout. There is strong evidence to suggest this car was later sold to Australian customer David Chambers, in turn becoming Jack Brabham's historic RedeX Special *after Chambers' suicide. In background Bernie Rodger, Alan Brown's mechanic, tends his Mark I*

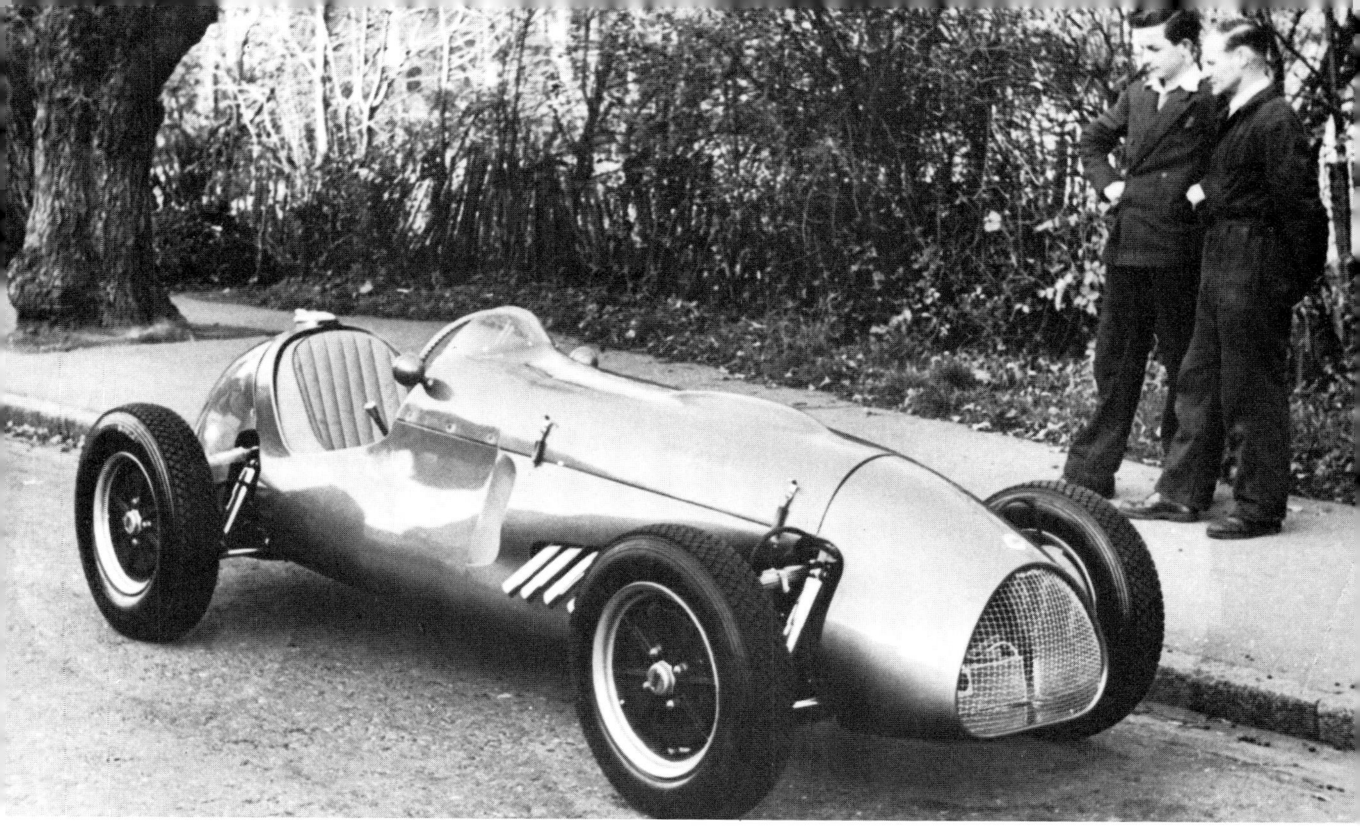

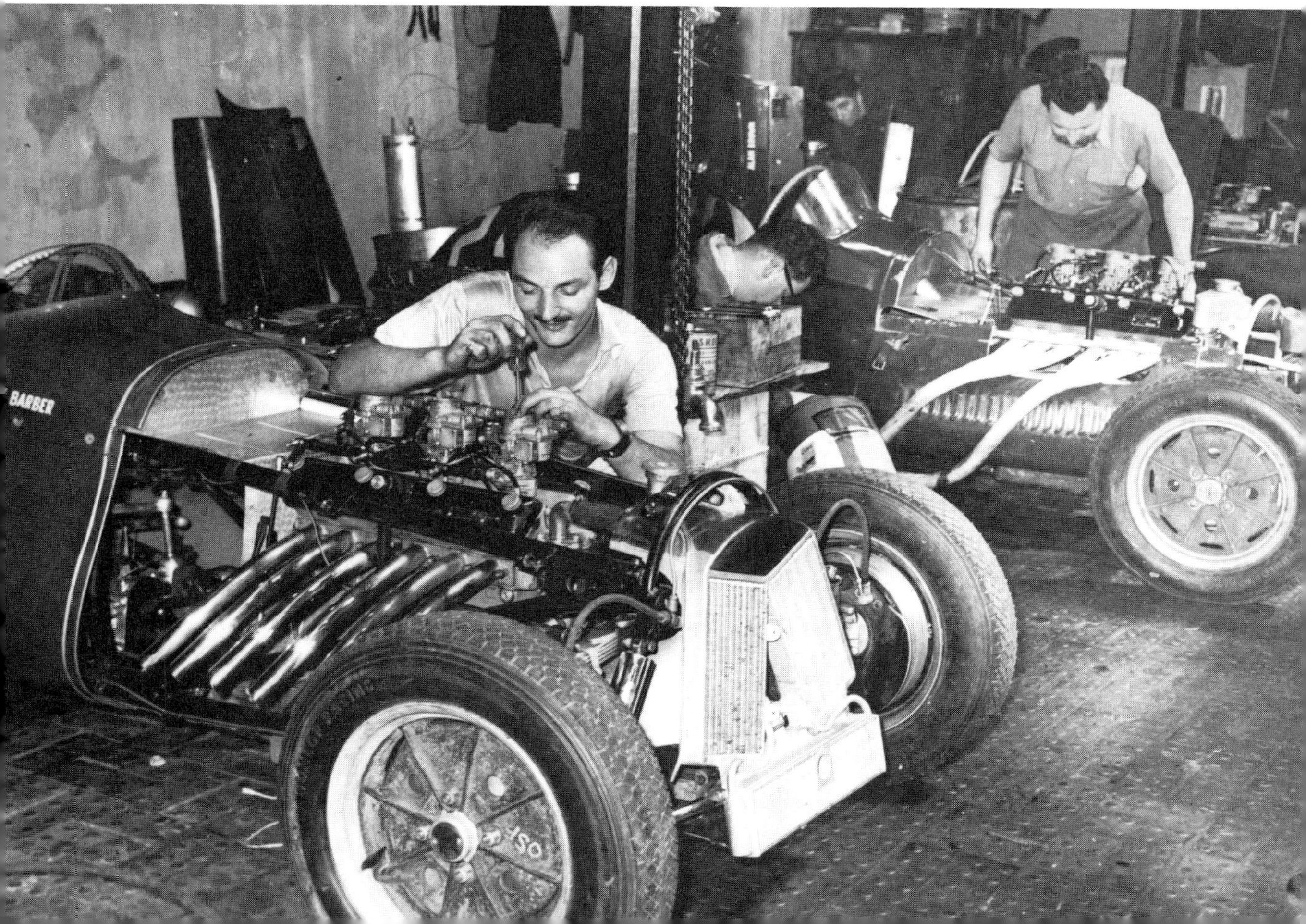
BARBER

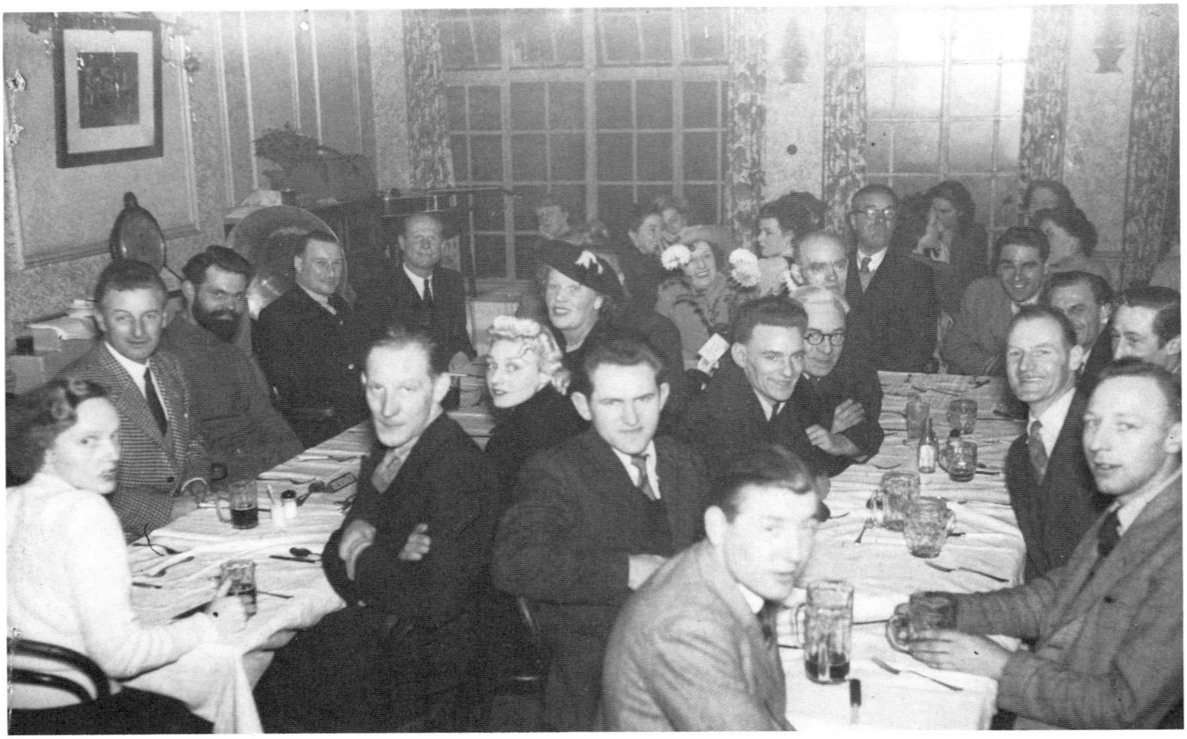

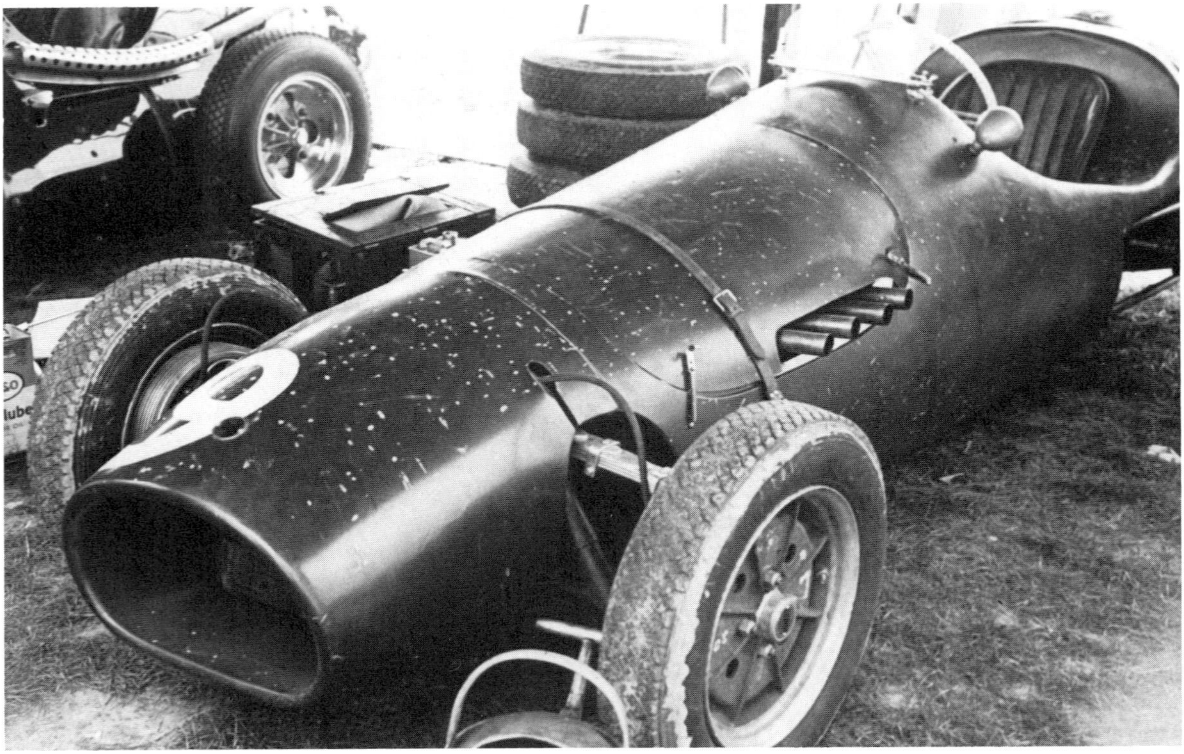

Part 1 MARK IIS, BRISTOLS AND ALTAS...

The handsome Tom Cole replacement car seen with Belgian team patron Jacques Swaters during Silverstone May meeting, 1953 when he swopped his Ecurie Francorchamps Ferrari 500 with Cole, whose first Mark II had been burned out in its debut race at Syracuse. Cole was scion of the Vidor battery family, crippled by a spinal problem in childhood. He spent years bedridden before recovery, and thereafter lived life to the full, motor racing, flying, sailing and skiing. After a terrific fourth overall in the Mille Miglia he raced his private Ferrari at Le Mans. It had a rigid metal tonneau over the passenger seat and when it ran into straw bales and overturned poor Cole could not duck, and was killed

Below *The Peter Whitehead Mark II-Alta leading his Cooper-Jaguar Mark I driven by Peter Walker in the closing Snetterton meeting, 9 October, 1954, showing mid-1950s club* Formule Libre *as it was, with Boulten's Connaught, Geoff Richardson's RRA Spl, an ex-Whitney Straight Maserati 8CM and another A-Type Connaught in pursuit*

Opposite top *Christmas 'do' in nearby Royal Oak pub for Hollyfield Road staff and friends. Seen here at left is Miss Fahy from the office, John Lucas of Barwell Engineering beside Owen Maddock, John Hume to Miss Fahy's right, beside him Miss Garnett from Cooper's Garage and beside her John's mum-in-law, and behind the flowers Mrs Elsie Cooper, John's mum. At right-hand table, foreground, is Douggie Johnson, behind him a Polish staff member who changed his name to the most English name he could think of, apparently 'De Havilland', to his left is Jack Tolley, beside Fred Neale, 'Pop' who ran the Garage petrol pumps, Charles Cooper looking merry, and John. On right from John forward are Fred Fox, Ernie Looker, Don Pearman and Bert Westwood, who managed the Garage business at the time*

Opposite *The Bernie Rodger-built* Equipe Anglaise *(Alan Brown/Bob Chase) Cooper-Alfa Romeo Mark II on its muddy debut in the paddock, Easter Monday Goodwood, 1953. It used from new this Ferrari-like bodyshell, the stub-pipe Alfa 1900 engine and de Dion rear suspension, twin radius rods for which are visible under cockpit. The cockpit side formation with the body panelling wrapped over around the seat was unusual. It survives today. That's a Connaught beyond, look at its sophistication with cast-alloy wheels still safe for historic racing into 1983 while Colin Darby's simpler, lighter 500-based castings have long since been condemned, though Minilite produce a design very similar to Cooper's later Maddock-designed eight-spoke type*

71

Cooper-Bristols in South Africa, starting the 1956 Cape Grand Prix with Jimmy de Villiers in the ex-Whitehead ex-Brabham Mark II (4) using the Bristol engine which Jack had fitted in the UK, just shaded off the line by Gordon Lindsay in the ex-Brandon ex-Somervail/Border Reivers Mark I with its distinctive slab-sided bonnet airbox. In later years what was most probably this car went to George Cannell, seen right, with a Chevrolet V8 engine installed, plus oversize disc rear wheels and tyres

good terms to attract entries for its Grand Prix in Buenos Aires, opening the 1953 World Championship series. Alan Brown had opted-out of Ecurie Richmond and Dennis Bros to join Bob Chase as 'Manager, Car Division and Motor Racing Department', and he entered his Mark I, alongside the Fraser-Hartwell Syndicate car and the works prototype Mark II to form a full 'works' team of three Cooper-Bristols. Charles Cooper made the long trip south as team manager, and John Barber went along as driver of the stub-piped Mark II. Local driver Adolfo J. Cruz Schwelm rented the F-HS Mark I with Jesus Ricardo Iglesias – who was rated higher by the Argentine press – as reserve driver.

Unfortunately Cruz Schwelm's ageing Mark I broke a stub axle and nearly lost a wheel during the race, and later Farina's works Ferrari ploughed into the uncontrolled crowds, killing many. Brown was unable to avoid a young spectator running into his path, but continued with his Mark I's nose stove in. After three stops to top up the leaking radiator he finished ninth and last. Barber survived all this carnage to place eighth.

The team also contested the Buenos Aires City *Libre* GP, in which both Cruz Schwelm and Brown retired, while Barber

drove the new Mark II quietly home 11th – according to most reports. . . . Argentine lap-scoring was chaotic. Charles was doing a deal with the ACA to import '26 500s for driver training', and one twin demonstrated at the Autodrome by Harry Schell; Fangio also tried it for size. Much publicity followed this order but I have found little evidence that it was fulfilled. . . .

Hollyfield Road was already bursting at the seams. The original Cooper's Garage business had run down almost completely. Owen Maddock recalls one nail in the coffin: 'My little drawing office out under the stores had a fanlight window above the door and in the dust there our tea-boy had written something very rude backwards; telling everyone inside to "Go away". One morning John came rushing in saying Quick! Clean that flipping window, Vauxhall's are coming! The Vauxhall people arrived and found the place full of racing cars. They didn't like it at all. In effect they said "Stop messing about with racing cars or lose your agency" . . . so Cooper's lost the agency. . . .'

Jack Tolley had long gone, to be replaced as resident welder by John Kelly. Ernie Looker became workshop foreman. Terry Kitson, who welded Cooper frames alongside Kelly in later years, remembers Ernie well, also the problems he had rewelding split fuel tanks: '. . . Ernie had several explode on him and go hurtling through the roof!' Roy Golding knew the trick: 'You just filled 'em with car exhaust fumes before you started. . . .'

Now they were beavering away helping customers' mechanics complete new Mark IIs, finishing-off production Mark VII 500s and contemplating John's plans for a new 2-litre Cooper-Bristol sports car, as described shortly.

It appears that at least 14, maybe 16, Mark II single-seater

Part 1 MARK IIs, BRISTOLS AND ALTAS . . .

'entities' were supplied in 1953–54, possibly under only 13 serial numbers; 12 with Bristol engines, two with Altas, for which a third was also intended, and one more was completed by Bernie Rodger at RJC Motors, Saltdean, using his own brand of de Dion rear suspension and an Alfa Romeo 1900 dohc four-cylinder engine. It seemed like a good idea at the time. . . . Then there was an extra Mark II delivered after its main chassis rails had been literally jacked further apart to form a '1½-seat' sports-cum-F2 hybrid car which could run in the former class with cycle wings and lights fitted, or in F2 with the road equipment stripped off. Two other Mark IIs were similarly converted.

As with the Mark Is there is no surviving works Register of chassis built and customers supplied. There is considerable interest in all the Cooper-Bristols today due to their historic racing eligibility. They are relatively as simple and inexpensive to maintain and race today as they were in their heyday. Some parts are still available off-the-shelf and just as in 1952–53 they are also still relatively easy to build. . . .

Inevitably the closely interwoven histories of the original cars have become muddied by time and the motor trade. I know nobody who can state hand-on-heart that he has their story 'stone cold'. By his own admission that includes current Mark II owner Roddy Macpherson in Scotland, who, in addition to being an utterly outstanding historics driver, has I believe a better grasp of the cars than most – myself included.

That accepted, for the sake of clarity we had better take an overview of the 1953 season before examining what can be deduced of the cars' as-new and subsequent histories. . . .

The rising star of the Mark I's first season, Mike Hawthorn, was beginning his works Ferrari contract. The new European season commenced at Syracuse on 22 March and Ecurie Richmond arrived with Brandon's Mark I accompanied by new team mate Rodney Nuckey and his brand-new Mark II. The Atlantic Stable were also there, with two new Mark IIs; the BRG Alta-powered model for Peter Whitehead, and a blue-and-white liveried Bristol for naturalized American sports-car driver Tom Cole – British-born to the Vidor battery family. The entire Ferrari team was sidelined by a bad batch of valve springs and Nuckey emerged ahead of Brandon and Whitehead for a lucrative 3-4-5 Cooper team finish. It was not Tom Cole's day. It seems a tyre burst and his new car hurtled into a wall, igniting its fuel tank. He was lucky to escape unscathed as the car was burned out. Mechanic Arthur Birks recalls: 'We just swept up what was left and put it in the transporter, then started building a new car all over again at Cooper's. . . .'

At Easter Goodwood the Bob Chase/Alan Brown Equipe Anglaise Mark II-Alfa Romeo appeared with its de Dion rear end and Ferrari-like bodywork, to be driven by Paul Emery. Neither it nor Stirling Moss's new Cooper-Alta Special – which in truth owed very little to Hollyfield Road – would perform with distinction. Jimmy Stewart's Ecurie Ecosse Mark I won a handicap race.

Ken Wharton emerged in his new quasi-works Mark II-Bristol, using an ENV pre-selector gearbox of the type fitted in the Peter Bell ERA, which he was sprinting and hillclimbing with success. Bob Gerard also unleashed his brand-new Mark II-Bristol and these two were to be the outstanding

André Loens not quite as cheerful as usual in pouring rain at Boreham, Essex, 1952 with the Fraser-Hartwell Syndicate Mark I-Bristol, CB/5/52. The car survives today, with Bill Clark in New Zealand. Note Belgian and Union flags on 'schnorkel'

Mark II drivers of the year – in the northern hemisphere....

May Silverstone saw Wharton on pole and finishing second to Hawthorn's Ferrari in Heat, then fifth in the Final after misfiring. Moss was second in Heat but retired from the Final. Gerard's day yielded eighth and 11th. Next day Rodney Nuckey won in Helsinki's Djurgards Park and three days later won again at Tampere.

A week after Silverstone, Wharton was second to Hawthorn in Heat and Final of the Ulster Trophy at Dundrod. Graham Whitehead drove the replacement Cole car there, as he would in the Coronation Trophy at Crystal Palace. The car had appeared at Silverstone, but Cole preferred to swop it with Jacques Swaters of Ecurie Francorchamps; he drove Swaters's Ferrari and the Belgian drove his Mark II-Bristol.

Cole was back in the Cooper at Albi, where Whitehead's Cooper-Alta finished fifth in the Final, second F2, but they were both outpaced on the fast circuit. Ken Wharton attacked World Championship GPs with his immaculate car, but at Zandvoort a wishbone broke. At Rouen Gerard was eighth and Moss 10th, but they were outpaced again, though 'Mr Bob' was second F2 home behind a Gordini. These two cars then went to Reims to join Wharton in the French GP. Of course the superfast course was no place for a Cooper-Bristol or Cooper-Alta to be competitive and they were utterly outclassed. Reliable, stolid Gerard finished 11th, while Wharton's pace ran a big end and Moss's clutch exploded after an awful race in the Alta Special, pieces of disintegrating bell-housing gashing his leg. He would never race the car

Jimmy Stewart's Ecurie Ecosse Mark I-Bristol skating round the straw bales at Boreham, 2 August, 1952, showing off car's Hawthorn-type 'schnorkel' and St Andrew's saltire motif on Scots-blue painted nose. This car sold to Alastair Birrell, he passed it to Border Reivers to replace their first ex-Brandon Mark I and Gordon Pick in September 1958 dis his best to demolish this perfectly good timing box with the obsolete car at Prescott hillclimb, right

again, and in 11 days a replacement Cooper-Alta Mark II was built for him at Hollyfield Road, where the works staff responded brilliantly to assist Alf Francis and Tony Robinson, the Moss mechanics.

In the British GP at Silverstone six Coopers ran and only two finished; Wharton and Whitehead 8–9, way behind the pack after numerous troubles. Alan Brown appeared in a new Mark II-Bristol. It had been ordered originally by *Belfast Telegraph* newspaper proprietor Bobby Baird for himself and Roy Salvadori. Baird already had a Ferrari and the Cooper-Bristol would seem entirely superfluous in such company. Brown had tried to race the Cooper-Alfa Romeo one last time at Crystal Palace but was stranded on the starting grid. Now for the German GP at Nürburgring the de Dion car was fitted with a Bristol engine in place of the troublesome Italian job, and sprayed silver for Porsche star Helm Glockler to drive. He rodded the new engine in practice and could not start. Brown charged hard there in his new Mark II, fought nobly

Part 1 MARK IIS, BRISTOLS AND ALTAS...

against horrific handling when a spring anchorage parted, but had his engine blow half-a-lap from the finish. Moss ran strongly with his new 11-day wonder Mark II-Alta and finished sixth, while Rodney Nuckey impressed with a drive, delayed by damper mount breakage, into 11th place.

Nuckey was a brave driver, and at Berlin's banked Avus track he led before a wishbone broke and he was forced to slow, finishing fifth. Brown crashed his car there, but had the consolation of sixth ftd at the difficult and majestic Freiburg hillclimb.

Wharton ran his Mark II alone in the Swiss GP, finishing seventh, and was sixth at Cadours. At Monza he drove bravely to compensate for his engine's lack of power, but eventually pushed the broken car across the line, exhausted, only to be too far behind to classify as a finisher. Moss's Alta engine had been tuned to run nitromethane fuel and it staggered the Italian establishment by running hot and hard, fifth with the works Maseratis and Ferraris, before numerous piffling troubles dropped him back to 13th, just behind the reliable Alan Brown.

At the end of the year Gerard and Moss both shone in minor British events, along with Tony Crook's F2 Cooper-Alta and – into 1954 – his 1½-seat Cooper-Bristol Mark II, which was to become one of the outstandingly successful British club racing cars of all time; referred to as his 'Formula XYZ' car. This machine was modelled after northern quarry-owner Jack Walton's offset single-seat car – delivered mid-1953 – which was similarly successful in sprints, hillclimbs

and circuit racing, while Bristolian garage proprietor Horace Gould – stepping up the ladder from his potent little Cooper-MG sports car – began to make his wild and woolly reputation in another new Mark II-Bristol F2.

At the end of 1953 Formula 2 died, to be replaced in 1954 by the 2½-litre Formula 1. The Cooper-Bristols, both Marks I and II, raced on, some having been converted to sports racing cars, as we shall see, while others like the Gerard and Gould cars in particular were to have a very successful time in *Libre* and occasional F1 races, Gerard's especially being continuously developed with ever-larger Bristol engines, eventually achieving 2246 cc. The cars were still very much part of the British major race-meeting scene through 1955, but into 1956 they were creaking into obsolescence and faded away. Not until the Sixties would they re-emerge as immensely practicable and inexpensive historic racing cars. Their second coming was upon them....

Before going on to examine the Mark IIs more closely, I should clear the decks of the remaining Mark Is: Chassis numbers applied to the cars are in some cases prospective, but in simple terms their careers seem to have developed like this....

The Archie Bryde prototype:

This of course was the only Cooper-Bristol other than the Bob Chase Mark I to be raced by Mike Hawthorn. As such it has special significance. Its number was supposedly *CB/1/52* and Archie continued racing it in British events into the early part of 1953. Bernie Ecclestone then appeared with a schnorkel-nosed Cooper-Bristol, as at Thruxton in midsummer, when he 'became entangled with the straw bales and then continued at a slower pace before retiring'. He was later fifth at Crystal Palace. Bernie recalls the car typically crisply as: 'Ex-Hawthorn with the gearchange between your legs. It was prepared for me by Leslie Hawthorn and Brit Pearce at TT Garage, Farnham....' Brit can't remember that, while Archie Bryde cannot recall who bought his car, but I am convinced it was Ecclestone, and it then seems highly probable that he sold it in turn – he can't remember what happened either – to West Country salvage-man Fred Tuck. He accompanied Horace Gould on a trip to the New Zealand GP at Ardmore in January 1954, running 'an old Mark I' alongside Horace's rapid Mark II, which had all kinds of good components built into it, fresh from Bristol's works, which was 'just over the wall for his lads....' Tuck clouted a marker drum early in the NZ GP and covered very few miles more before retiring. There was no Cooper-Bristol raced in New Zealand for some time thereafter, so presumably neither of these cars stayed there. Certainly Gould brought his Mark II home for the British season, before buying a Maserati 250F in 1955. Tuck sold his Mark I out there, however, and 'early in 1954' a reputedly ex-Bryde Mark I appeared in Australia, driven by its new owner, Stan Coffey. He named it the *Dowi-*

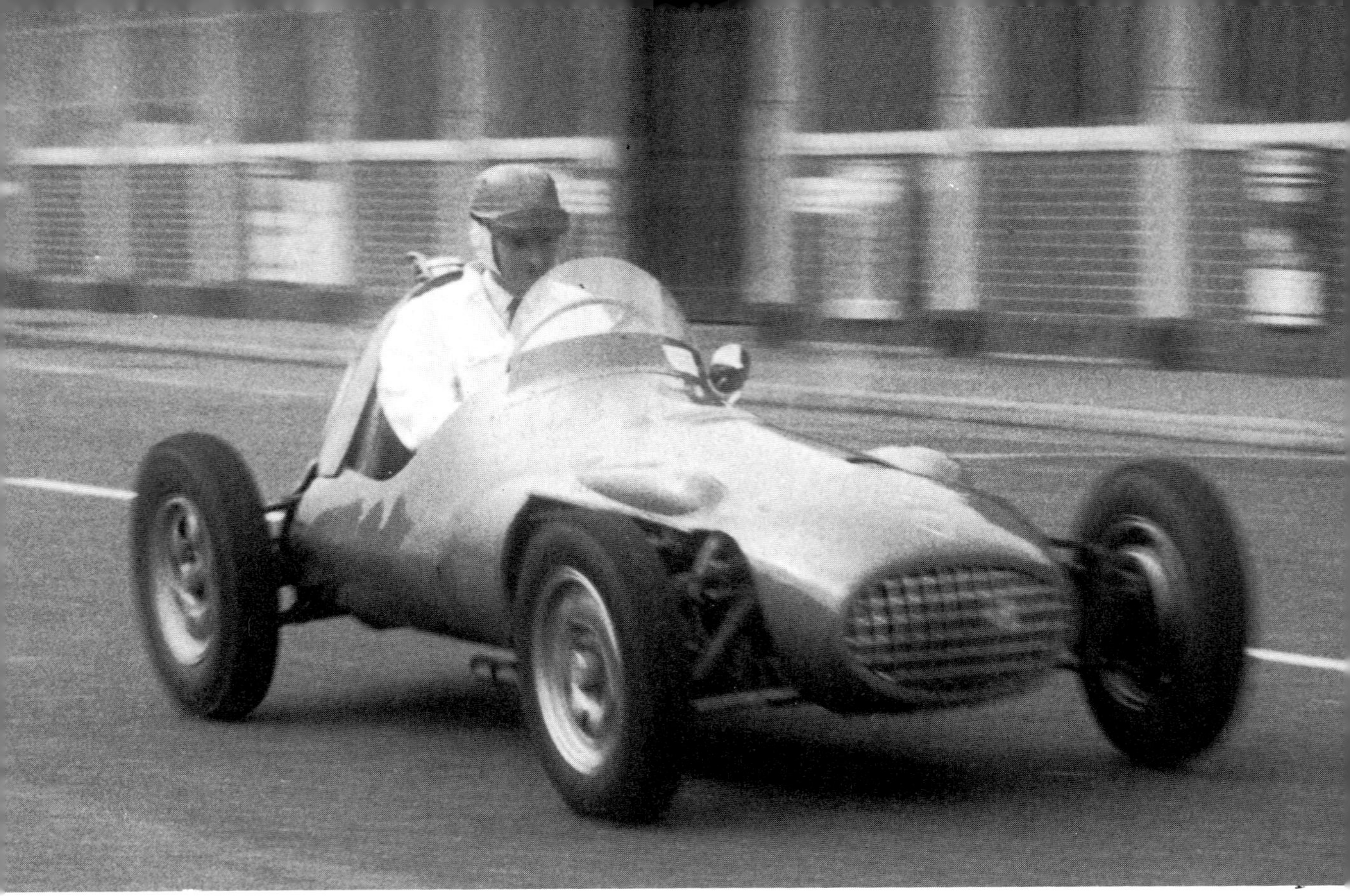

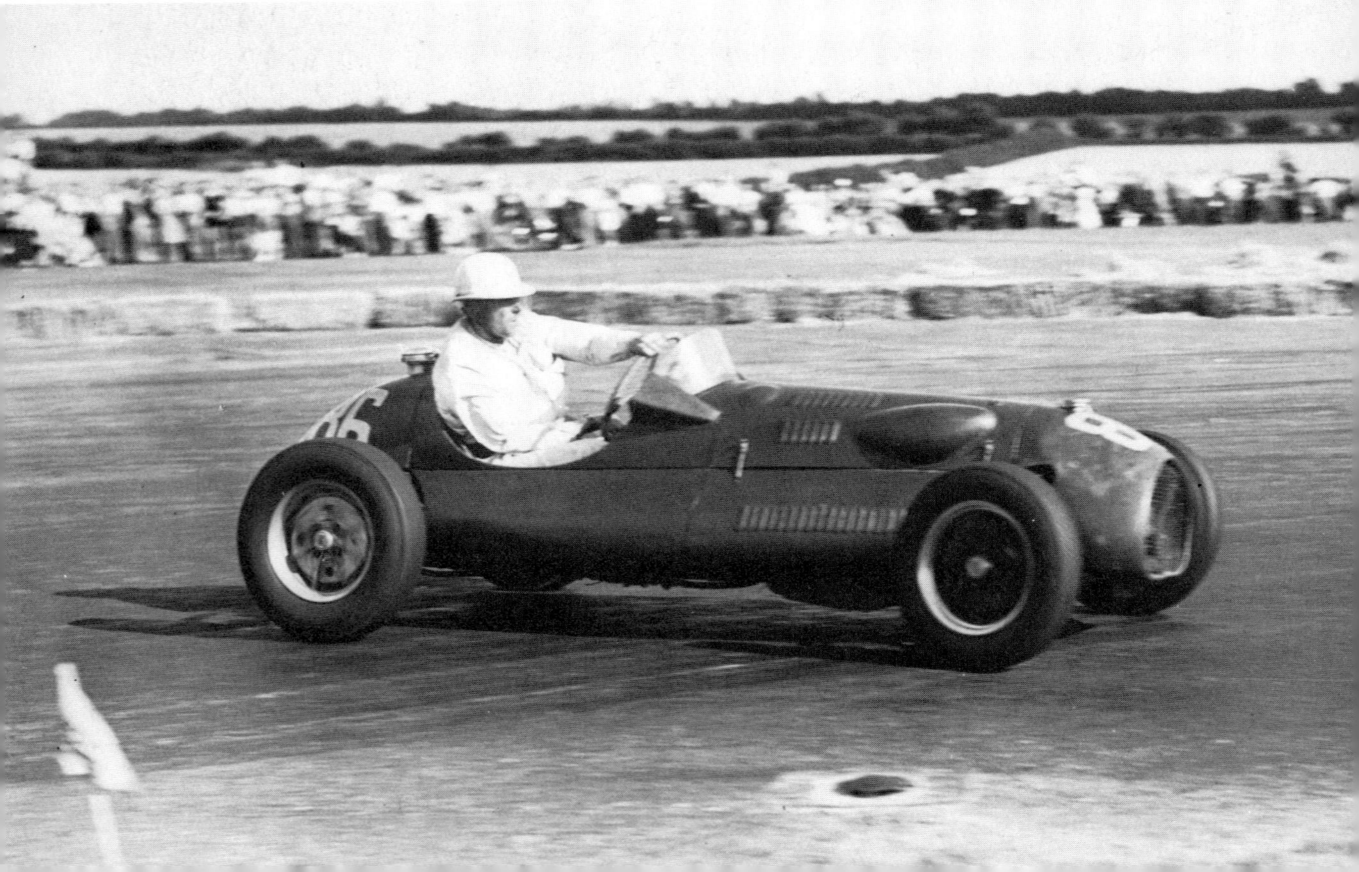

Part 1 MARK IIs, BRISTOLS AND ALTAS...

Opposite top *One of Bill Aston's two Butterworth-engined Mark I-type chassis Formula 2 specials with flat-four air-cooled AJB engine attacking the Brighton Speed Trials standing-start kilometre in 1956 driven by L. H. Pittaway. The wheels suggest this was Charrington's car. VSCC racer Bill Wilks later acquired it to complete an historic racing Mark I with best parts remaining from the Ecosse car. The Aston chassis survives today, with Nigel Woollett of F & N Garage, Aldershot.*

Opposite *Peter Walker at Thruxton with the long-wheelbase basically Mark I Cooper-ERA special in 1953. By common consent it had too much power for its own good...*

Top *'Europe, here I come' – Jack Brabham making his name down-under in the luridly sponsored Mark II-Bristol RedeX Special 1953–54. His clashes with authority over such blatant advertising on the car came close to seeing his licence withdrawn. They drove him abroad, and his role in making Cooper double World Champions should never be under-estimated. This was almost certainly the ex-Motor Show, ex-Barber Argentine prototype car, with its chromed dampers...*

Above *9 May, 1953, International Trophy, Silverstone – Ken Wharton pressing on in his quasi-works Mark II-Bristol with ENV pre-selector gearbox projecting below the undertray. He started on pole for Heat Two and was beaten only by Hawthorn's works Ferrari. A very successful season followed. This is the car raced in historic events of the 1980s by Roddy Macpherson. Note starting handle holes in both oil cooler and inset stoneguard grille, and neat airbox shape*

dat Special after one of his principal sponsors, apparently a spanner and tool company. Coffey had little success with it, raced it in the 1955 NZ GP at Ardmore, but retired. Then, at Port Wakefield for the 1955 Australian GP, he rolled it and subsequently sold the mildly damaged car to Jack Myers of Maroubra, a noted touring-car racing driver. Myers knew all about Holden engines, and the Bristol engine and gearbox were removed and sold and Myers fitted a very special dohc 2440 cc Holden-based engine built for him by Merv Waggott. According to Australian racing car historian John Blanden 'only the original Holden crankshaft and conrods were retained'. Myers's completed special appeared at Bathurst in October 1956 but retired, then set a new Australian record of 25.46 sec for the standing kilometer at Schoefields on 18 November, 1956. Stirling Moss was in Australia to race Maseratis, and he tried the car briefly at Parramatta Speedway dirt track! In December it was the first Australian car home in the GP at Melbourne's Albert Park.

At Bathurst in October 1957 Myers crashed heavily, and then to overcome the handling problems caused by too much power in the old Mark I frame he started from scratch to build a new chassis, and the old Bryde/Hawthorn frame was apparently junked. Although the Myers car survives today in Australia's Birdwood Mill Museum, *CB/1/52* really died in Jack Myers's workshops during the Australian summer of 1957–58.

The Ecurie Richmond cars:
Ostensibly chassis *CB/2/52* and *CB/3/52*. One would suspect that competitive little Eric Brandon would have taken what he considered the better of the pair, and probably preferred the later number '3'. Alan Brown was involved in a multiple collision at Castle Combe with his car right at the end of the 1952 season, when it was damaged together with John Barber's Mark I and Peter Whitehead's Alta F2. Once he joined Bob Chase's RJC Motors team for 1953 they had two Mark I F2s, his own and the ex-Mike Hawthorn classic, and the new Bernie Rodger-modified Mark II-Alfa Romeo was on the way. The Hawthorn car was judged surplus to requirements and it was converted – as will be described shortly – into a *Barchetta*-bodied sports racing car. Alan's own Mark I followed suit soon after.

Eric raced his Mark I in the early part of 1953, as at Syracuse and Silverstone, before concentrating on building up his business. He sold the car to Jock Somervail of the Scottish Border Reivers team. This was a syndicate based in the Scottish border country, a group of enthusiasts who pooled their resources. The car was raced by Somervail, Keith Hall, the Newcastle draper who had been making considerable impact in 500 cc F3, and by Jock McBain. The car was prepared in McBain's garage at Chirnside, Berwickshire, by mechanic Bobbie Hattle. Keith Hall was most successful with the car and enjoyed it: 'It was a super thing, light and easy to handle, underpowered of course but a very nice car to drive, and maintain....' One time at Crystal Palace: 'I was leading on the last lap; thought I was coming up to the chequered flag, relaxed too much and Horace Gould came up on me. I then had to go so hard I was watching my mirrors, got off line on to some marbles and slid into the bank, where the car rolled and threw me out. I broke my collar bone and banged my knee. The car wasn't too badly damaged – and it certainly taught me that no race is won until it's over....'

Jock Somervail and his brother Jimmy recall that the car was sold eventually to Gordon Lindsay, who raced it back home in southern Africa in 1956, while the ex-Ecosse/Birrell car appeared in Reivers' hands in its place. It was later sold in Rhodesia to one George Cannell, who raced it with a Chevvy V8 installed. Eric Glasby, Rhodesian owner of the ex-Whitehead Mark II and later Bob Gerard rear-engined BG-Bristol, wrote in 1977: 'The nearest information we have is that it is in some basement in South Africa....'

The Bob Chase-Hawthorn car:
Modified by Bernie Rodger for RJC Motors and Alan Brown racing as Equipe Anglaise during the winter of 1952–53, emerging as *Barchetta*-bodied sports racing car, HPN 665.

The Fraser-Hartwell Syndicate car:
Alan Fraser was a young estate manager controlling some 13,000 acres at Ibsley in the New Forest when he became very friendly with George Hartwell, the Bournemouth Rootes Group dealer and well-known competition motorist, around 1948. Hartwell and Jack Fairman talked him into driving a Sunbeam-Talbot with them on the 1952 Alpine Rally and from this experience of competition grew the F2 Syndicate and their Mark I undertaking. Fraser drove the car several times in British meetings, while André Loens handled it at international level. For 1953 another Bournemouth garagist, Jeff Sparrowe, was invited to drive after its return from Argentina. Although they remained the very best of friends, Fraser finally decided that the Syndicate seemed to be 'George's name and my money', and decided against investing any more in the project. Eventually Alan authorised Hartwell to sell the car; 'After it had lain dormant for some time.... He had built another body for it, but that didn't happen so the car was sold, I have no idea to whom....'

They transported the car in an ex-WD left-hand-drive converted Chevrolet ambulance, painted two-tone blue. It was prepared at Hartwell's dealership and engineer Brian Pritchard-Lovell, today working at Weslake's in Rye after Grand Prix service with Connaught's, instantly recalled the car when approached: 'Ah yes, old *CB/5/52*....' The car was evidently sold to New Zealand, as Bill Clark of Rokanui today owns a Mark I with that original chassis serial clear in its paperwork; although the chassis plate is now missing he discovered the serial '3/52' stamped into a lower chassis tube.

Part 1 MARK IIs, BRISTOLS AND ALTAS...

'Mr Bob' – Gerard at his immaculate best in his bright green Mark II-Bristol with its white wheels, kicking down through the gearbox into the Goodwood chicane in 1953. His car sported the neatest 'schnorkel' treatment of them all, and had a rear anti-roll bar conversion. With ever-larger engines, preparation was immaculate as Gerard's motor trade franchises included both Cooper and Bristol distributorships in Leicester

The old car was sold through Jack Brabham to George Palmer of Hamilton, now the New Zealand Porsche distributor, whose son Jim played a major role in Tasman racing through the Sixties. It looked brand new, he recalls, when he bought it, while Jack Brabham seems to have obtained it via Fred Tuck, Hartwell's having advertized it in 1955. . . . The car was handed over to Palmer at Ardmore apparently before the 1956 NZ GP '. . . but I had major engine problems, mainly loss of oil pressure when hot, and owing to parts not arriving with the car I was unable to start the race. The car won the first race at Levin later that year, but I was forced to retire it in spite of much arm-waving from Alf Francis [who helped him get the thing running properly] when leading the second race as the oil gauge showed zero. . . .'

Later in the year Palmer telephoned Horace Gould for spares and was offered 'two Cooper-Bristols. The very excellent one he had raced at Ardmore and one which had belonged to Alan Brown which Alan had raced with a four-cylinder Alta engine fitted. I agreed to buy both cars providing the Alta engine was replaced with a Bristol. This was done and they were shipped to me. . . .'

With these Mark II cars on the way George sold the ex-F-HS Mark I to Gavin Quirk from Te Awamutu. The ex-Gould Mark II arrived for George in time for the January 1957 NZ GP at Ardmore, where he finished commendably sixth overall. Quirk's Mark I broke in practice, and allowed Horace Gould's pal, W. F. Morice, into the race for which he had originally non-qualified – despite journeying half-way round the world from England – in another very mysterious Cooper-Bristol, ostensibly the second car just sold to Palmer, i.e. the ex-Brown Cooper-Alta.

However, Ken Tyrrell would still be racing this car in the UK six months later, so was Morice's mount another car masquerading as the ex-Brown car, which as we shall see was also the famous ex-Moss 11-day wonder 1953 methanol car?

However, in June 1957, while Ken Tyrrell was racing Brown's Cooper-Alta at Mallory Park, George Palmer was winning the Southport Road Race at Christchurch in his ex-Gould Mark II, while Quirk was out again in his Mark I. Then Quirk replaced the old Mark I with a Maserati 250F, the Cooper-Bristol selling to Johnny Mansell, who raced it in New Zealand in 1958. Brian Prescott of Auckland took over the car and his road registration documents for it survive today, revealing chassis number *CB 552* with Bristol engine *108*; '*Seating accommodation: 1 persons; Type of vehicle: Racing Car. . . .*'

During the Sixties he sold it to Peter Elford, who cut away the body support frame and as Bill Clark observes '. . . actually fitted a two-seater fibreglass body for a couple of years. Thank God he kept the body panels. . . .' Dave O'Connor bought the car from Elford then passed it on to Bill, in whose sympathetic hands it has been exquisitely restored to racing order today.

The Ecurie Ecosse car:
Believed fairly reliably to be *CB/6/52*, the David Murray Mark I was bought for the team by its benefactor Major Thompson, MD of the Ben Line shipping company. The

car was one of new Ecosse mechanic Stan Sproat's first responsibilities when he joined the team: 'It was very much a side-show compared to the sports racing Jaguars at that time....' Still the car with its St Andrew's cross blazoned across the radiator mesh was raced extensively by drivers like Jimmy Stewart and Jock Lawrence through 1953–54. It was sold eventually to Alastair Birrell to replace his famous ex-Mays ERA 'R1A', which went to a promising young driver named Bill Moss. Birrell does not seem to have been very impressed with the Cooper-Bristol, and when the Somervails sold their ex-Brandon Border Reivers car to Rhodesia in the winter of 1955 he would loan them the ex-Ecosse machine for various outings in 1956.

This twist in the story has confused many Cooper-Bristol researchers ever since, for the Reivers began advertizing 'their' Mark I – now the ex-Ecosse car – for sale, together with their Mark VIII 500 from mid-May 1956, and when the F2 car subsequently passed to the Chaseside Motor Company it was advertized again, quite rightly, as 'ex-Reivers' rather than 'ex-Ecosse', as its more charismatic previous ownership would have warranted. Many have since become understandably befuddled over *the* Reivers car; whereas in fact there were the two....

From Chaseside the ex-Ecosse/Reivers car went onto the hills in the hands of George Keylock and Gordon Pick, the latter creating a sensation at Prescott in September 1958 when he lost control and smashed right through the finish-line timing hut, virtually demolishing it without hurting either himself or the aggrieved occupants. Around 1960–61 he sold the old car to Bernard Worth, who confirmed its number as CB/6/52. Bernard paid £400 for it, and sold it to Bill Wilks for £330 around 1962.

Wilks was a very good practical engineer in the best Cooper tradition, and he built himself a sports car using the running gear from the old Ecosse single-seater. He added a body of his own making, and the result was registered 51 PH. It was powered by an engine from a touring Bristol. He also obtained what was apparently the ex-Bill Aston Aston-Butterworth F2 car, which used a Cooper Mark I-type chassis frame. He was actually '... an observer at a 750MC Debden meeting when it ran out of petrol at my point. I looked at it, it had a Ford engine, and I offered to buy it there and then. He finally accepted £32 10s. and it was mine.... I collected it from a flat near Walker's garage in Dorking....'

Wilks swopped most of his sports special for another Cooper-Bristol-based sports car with 'a peculiar razor-edged body rather like a DB3S', the Wilks Special going off to Dulwich. From bits of the Ecosse and Aston-Butterworth cars he then built himself an historic racing Mark I, which excelled in VSCC events in Britain. The car eventually moved on as the Ecurie Ecosse Mark I through the historic racing fraternity and survives today.

The John Barber car:
Something of a mystery. At the end of the 1952 season its body was damaged in the Castle Combe collision, and the Billingsgate fish merchant then raced the works Mark II prototype car in Argentina. There is one report that he raced his F2 car at Crystal Palace in May 1953, but, soon after, he appeared at Snetterton in an extraordinary sports Cooper-

Rodney Nuckey's smooth-bodied stub-pipe Mark II-Bristol was run under Eric Brandon's Ecurie Richmond banner, 1953. Here he is at Snetterton where at the end of the season this car would be effectively written-off in a comprehensive accident. It was subsequently completely rebuilt around new parts, the original engine and drive-train going into Bernie Rodger's Warrior-Bristol, named after the Nuckey family company

Part I MARK IIs, BRISTOLS AND ALTAS...

Bristol eccentrically styled after the Alfa Romeo *Disco Volante*, registered NXH586 and known as the Golding Cooper – presumably constructed for him under the direction of Ron Golding, John Lucas's partner in Barwell Engineering of Chessington who had much to do with Coopers at this time. The car's subsequent history as far as I know it is related shortly.

The Peter Walker Cooper-ERA:
This long wheelbase special with its 16 in. wire wheels and ERA engine raced briefly into 1953, and was then sold for 1954 to Derek Wilkinson, who was a partner in Dove's of Northampton and a greetings card company. He hillclimbed and sprinted the car together with Bentley-man Jack Williamson. The ERA engine was removed for Wilkinson's ERA chassis, and the Cooper then lay dormant for some years in Wilkinson mechanic Jim Abbott's garage at Weedon. Ken Yeates of the BARC then bought the car, to join his ex-Hawthorn Mark I/Brown sports car HPN 665. Both these cars were bought from him by John R. Brown of Burnley, who intended building up a Cooper Bristol single-seater from the pair for historic racing. The former ERA car's 16 in. wheels would over-gear the car for short-circuit racing, so Brown 'decided to use the 15 in. wheels from the two-seater as well as the engine and gearbox. Unfortunately the brake drums on the Cooper-ERA were too large for the smaller diameter wheels and when we tried to exchange these many of the suspension parts differed, so that eventually we changed over most of the front suspensions!'

Brown completed the long-wheelbase single-seater satis-factorily using those ex-Hawthorn car components, and sold it to Don Balmer, a Birmingham estate agent. He became the most daring historic driver of the mid-Sixties; to paraphrase the late John Cobb, he regularly leaned further and further out of the window, and eventually, inevitably, fell out....

Don Balmer: 'I really enjoyed driving that car, until at Silverstone a little bolt came out near the dipstick and oil dropped onto the left-hand rear wheel. I was having to hold it in gear and had spun at Becketts, then slid at Woodcote and finally went off at Copse, caught the ruts and flipped. It fell on top of me, and busted my ribs, and flattened a lung, and I was burned right round my body against the road. I lost my spleen but it could have been worse, and I was up and about two or three weeks later. The car was repaired, Rubery Owen straightened the frame and I sold it all to David Vine with bits of the ex-Jack Walton Mark II, RUM 2....' The former Cooper-ERA survived with Hugh Clifford in Lancaster; the last of the eight Cooper F2 Mark I cars built and raced during 1952.

Looking back on the 1953 season with Cooper's front-line Mark IIs, clearly the names of Wharton and Gerard stand out from a British and European viewpoint, but the benefit of hindsight shows clearly that only one Mark II was as significant as the Hawthorn/Chase Mark I of 1952. It was the Australian *RedeX Special*, campaigned in 1953–55 by John Arthur 'Jack' Brabham....

Jack Brabham and the RedeX Special
Jack was the only son of a greengrocer, born in Hurstville,

'Big Orrice' – Horace Gould, the tough Bristolian garage proprietor characteristically bulging out of his Mark II-Bristol as he muscles it round Crystal Palace in 1953. The two large fasteners retaining the scuttle panel were characteristic of all Mark IIs, but nose, carburettor air intake, exhaust, mirror and occasionally detail dash panel and tail vent treatments differed considerably between individuals. The distinctive double-cranked exhaust system survives on this car preserved today in New Zealand

COOPER CARS

Part 1   MARK IIs, BRISTOLS AND ALTAS...

Sydney, on 2 April, 1926. He was a second-generation Australian, his grandfather having emigrated from London's East End in 1885. Jack's father was a keen motorist who taught his son to drive as a boy. Jack was fascinated by mechanical vehicles and at 15 began work in Ferguson's Garage, Treacy Street, Hurstville, where his father's cars and trucks were maintained. Father bought him a 350 cc Velocette motorbike, and Jack was to cover thousands of miles on saddle or pillion in his teens. He soon started his own tiny business, buying ancient bikes to renovate and resell. He took a three-year evening course at Kogarah Technical College, but only completed two years of it before joining the RAAF, at 18. The war was raging in the Pacific and he wanted desperately to fly, but was trained as a flight mechanic.

Out of the forces in 1946 he set-up a modest engineering shop at the back of his grandfather's house. A retired engineer friend, Bill Armstrong, taught him machine skills. Then he met a midget-car driver named Johnny Schonberg. He was an American, ex-USN, married to a local Australian girl, and he introduced Jack to midget racing. They decided to build a new car for Johnny to drive, working with Bill Armstrong and another midget-car owner named Ronnie Ward. The car was completed with a JAP 1000 engine, and ran in the season of 1946–47. It gave trouble, but was improved and enlarged with help from local motorcycling personality Art Senior, who ran a nearby machine shop. The JAP twin engine was enlarged to 1100 cc, and Schonberg won twice.

Jack produced most of a special 1350 cc engine for the car and it was very successful. But Mrs Schonberg pressured her husband to retire, so Brabham took over driving the car. On his third night he scored his first win. He stole the NSW Championship at Sydney Showground in his first season. But when a thrown rod cost him the South Australian title one night in Adelaide he decided to give up this silly game and enter the trucking business instead, with his father. Only when a truck purchase deal collapsed did he have second thoughts.

A customer at his machine shop was Ron Tauranac, an engineer who was building and racing his own Ralt Special with his brother Austin. In 1951 both Ron and Jack – with the midget – ran at the Hawkesbury hillclimb and the track car won. This was anathema to the conservative organizers, who could not accept that their road racers had been bested by a 'freak' car from the dirt-tracks. They ruled it out because without front brakes it didn't qualify as 'a proper car'. This was the first of Brabham's clashes with Australian motor sporting authority. His hackles rose and with four-wheel brakes fitted he returned to win that year's Australian Hill-Climb Championship at Rob Roy, Victoria, beating Cooper importer John Crouch's brand-new Mark VI. . . .

Now Jack was keen to go road racing, but the midget was clearly unsuitable, so he bought an ancient Cooper Mark IV instead. When his first self-built BSA/JAP hybrid motor proved to him that 500 cc racing held no interest, he fitted a 1000 cc Vincent-HRD twin instead, then enlarged it until it blew-up regularly. A Mark V Cooper was then acquired, and Jack fitted it with an 1100 cc alloy JAP big twin. At this point enter the Cooper-Bristol Mark II, and the unfortunate David Chambers. . . .

He was an enthusiastic if apparently rather dilettante member of the Australian Racing Drivers' Club, and on a visit to England in 1949 he had bought – supposedly ex-Salvadori – a Maserati 4C, chassis 1521. He raced it only briefly in Australia, but then for 1953 ordered one of the first Cooper-Bristol Mark IIs. It may actually have been *the* first car, the Argentine prototype, but by the time it arrived down-under David Chambers had committed suicide. . . .

The F-HS Mark I was back from Argentina in time for the Easter Goodwood meeting, and it seems highly probable that when the works Mark II returned – if indeed it was not sold in Argentina, and there is no evidence to suggest it was – the Chambers order was waiting to be fulfilled, a cash prospect from some unknown Aussie. The car could have been cleaned-up and diverted on to an Australia-bound freighter very quickly, if indeed it was not sent direct from Buenos Aires. Irrespective, after Chambers's death the car was offered for sale by his executors. This can often be a lengthy business, but Jack Brabham and his father attracted backing from the then little known RedeX additive company, and were able to run the car in its first down-under race at Leyburn as early as 23 August that year. Jack won the Queensland Road Racing Championship with it, his class in the NSW Hill-Climb Championship at Newcastle in September and at Orange in October set fastest lap. But at Melbourne's Albert Park for the Australian GP a big-end ran in practice and he could not start the race.

He then ran into more trouble with the authorities, who simply hated advertizing on racing cars. The *RedeX Special*

Opposite top left *Tom Kyffin bought the Gould car for his Equipe Devone team in 1955, where it joined the ex-Brown Mark II-Alfa Romeo re-engined with a Bristol unit for Bruce Halford, as seen here. What is almost certainly this car is shown right in 1983, owned by Ross McKay at Washdyke, NZ*

Tony Crook's Mark II-Alta being tended before the 1953 International Trophy, Silverstone by (right) Alta manufacturer Geoffrey Taylor. Tony's own mechanics Frank Sharpe and Reg Cope maintained all his cars at his Town End, Caterham Hill establishment where into the 1980s the Caterham 7 Lotus-lookalike has been in production for many years. This Mark II-Alta was modified by Bristol as a 1½-seat F2/sports car using their engine for 1954. Note typical Mark II aerodynamically smooth combination upright-cum-brake backplate

lettering blazoned on the Mark II was considered disgraceful and Jack could not talk them round. They threatened to ban him, and he had to erase the lettering and lost his sponsorship.

In disgust he took the car to Auckland, New Zealand, for the inaugural NZ GP in January 1954, meeting other Cooper-Bristols driven by Gould and Tuck, and he placed sixth. His furious cornering to overcome his car's power deficiency against the V16 BRM and Ferrari opposition enthralled the 70,000 crowd.

He raced through 1954 in Australia, then returned to Auckland for the 1955 NZ GP, in which he placed fourth in what would be his last drive in the car. There he met two visitors from the UK, Dean Delamont of the RAC and Dick Jeffrey, newly appointed head of Dunlop Competitions. Dean had heard about the 29-year-old Aussie, and when they met was fascinated by his evident skill, knowledge, ambition and approach. Jack drove him back to his hotel after a party thrown at Reg Greason's house, one of the GP organizers. They sat in the car far into the wee small hours while Dean painted a picture of British and European racing for the dark, taciturn Australian. He returned home to Sydney, decided that he was going to Britain for the 1955 racing season, and since the *RedeX* could not possibly be competitive in such company, he sold it to Stan Jones. That was his only mistake, for he had made the decision which would have as much influence upon Cooper's future as upon his own.

Jones had destroyed his famous Maybach Special during the AGP at Southport late the previous year and he needed the *RedeX* as a stand in. He raced it at Fisherman's Bend that February, where he was third, then after a race at Albert Park in March a new Maybach was ready and he entered the Cooper-Bristol instead for Ern Seeliger. He was second in the Bathurst '100', and Jones then sold the car to Tom Hawkes of Geelong.

His diminutive engineer Murray Rainey helped Hawkes fit a Holden engine with Repco head, as Murray recalls: '... as such it was very fast. It could keep cars like Jones's 250F Maserati and Davison's 3-litre Ferrari honest indeed. In 1958 I altered the suspension to the then fashionable Lotus type ... and of course fitted coil-springs. Without even road-testing the car it went straight to Bathurst for the AGP, where it ran third, 200 yards behind Davison's Ferrari, and Ern Seeliger in the Maybach. After this race Hawkes decided that we should fit a Chev Corvette engine (against my wishes, but he had the money).... It was all supposed to be ready for a race at Albert Park late in 1958 but it didn't make it. At this meeting Moss and Brabham were driving 2.2 Cooper-Climaxes, also Teddy Gray was in the Tornado with a Chev Corvette engine. The Coopers passed the Tornado like nothing and Hawkes gave me 'very definite' instructions not to bother finishing the mods. Some years later ... around 1962, when Hawkes was in England building the Ausper FJ cars, I sold the *RedeX Special* to Earl Davey-Milne of Melbourne, he finished fitting the Chev and got it running....'

The old car, substantially altered to accept the Chevy engine and power, is still there today.... Supporting the contention that it began life as the Barber Argentine car is its chassis number, reliably reported to be *CBMk2/1/53*.

The Ken Wharton car:

Wharton bought his Mark II with money from Shell, his first retainer that year. It cost him around £1700 but he would enter it as a virtual works car, which gave him extra pull with continental race organizers. He had an ENV pre-selector gearbox fitted, like that in Peter Bell's ERA, which he hill-climbed very successfully. The Smethwick garage proprietor was at the peak of his career at that time, driving the V16 BRMs in Formula 1, and now effectively the works Cooper-Bristol in F2.

His mechanic, Bernard 'Bill' Blyth, built the car at Hollyfield Road, and remembers how 'Ken had his own special-mix dark-green paint and I had to take tins of it down with me. He also had some fiddle to get free tyres and didn't want to pay Charlie Cooper for a set, so we had to heave the car up into our truck on its rims....'

The car was finished dark green with primrose-yellow nose cowl and wheels. They used three engines, mildly tuned, although Blyth spent ages grinding valves and 'two or three days a time scraping the head and block to Grade A surface plate, because the biggest problem with the engine was the block/head joint.... We experimented running on SU carbs, but settled for the Solexes after the crank broke while warming-up on the SU rolling road dyno in Birmingham. That made a fair mess; I took the engine back to Bristol in a sack....'

They operated the car from the Wharton Garage in Hume Street, Smethwick, 'which was a modest little Ford sub-agency. We had another filling station round the corner, which did good business, and when we went off racing Ken would stop by to get some ready cash out of the till.... It was that kind of operation....'

The car was the widest-raced and most successful of its type during 1953. Wharton's race record looked like this:

6 April	Lavant Cup F2 Goodwood	Sixth
18 April	Snetterton *Formule Libre*	First
9 May	International Trophy, Silverstone	Fifth, fastest lap
16 May	Ulster Trophy, Dundrod	Second
23 May	Charterhall F2, Scotland	First
7 June	Coronation Trophy, Crystal Palace	Second
5 July	French GP, Reims	Retired, big-ends
18 July	British GP, Silverstone	Eighth
23 August	Swiss GP, Berne	Seventh
30 August	Cadours F2, France	Sixth
13 September	Italian GP, Monza	Unclassified
26 September	Goodwood, Madgwick Cup	Fourth
3 October	Castle Combe F2	Third

Part 1 MARK IIs, BRISTOLS AND ALTAS . . .

The Ray Martin/John A. Cooper Alta Spl first time out, Easter Monday Goodwood, 1953, with a worried Stirling Moss at the wheel already wondering if he has done the right thing. Note special body wrapped round special chassis, disc brakes with behind-the-axle calipers, and special coil-spring suspension with twin radius rod-located de Dion rear end. Tony Robinson, in beret, had years of Cooper racing ahead of him

'This Aussie is a real presser-onner' – Jack Brabham displaying his talents, first time out in the UK, Easter Monday Goodwood, 1955. The car is his deeply disappointing ex-Whitehead Mark II-Alta with its distinctive potato-chipper grille and large diameter wire wheels housing the biggest possible drum brakes. He soon fitted a Bristol engine, sold the Alta unit in Australia 'though it has not raced since', and sold the car to Southern Africa

Bill Blyth: 'He really took to that car. The Silverstone problem was misfiring caused by something in the pipe interconnection between the tanks. At Monza the reports say we lost the crankshaft damper and the car shook itself to bits. That's not right. We didn't lose the damper, but Ken was really ear'oling it to compensate for lack of power and the pounding and vibration shook things apart. We'd been troubled all season by the Solexes throwing out as much fuel as the engine burned, and at Monza fuel consumption really worried us. We fitted little Japanese lantern gadgets in the schnorkel, so that any fuel flung up would be caught and directed back into the carburettors. They were attached by little 6BA nuts and bolts and the general pounding and vibration made them chatter loose and they dropped straight down the carburettors and it all came to a grinding halt. Ken pushed the last half-mile or so, and was really done-in at the finish. He hadn't covered enough distance to be classified as a finisher. . . .'

At Berne, Wharton had split works Maseratis mch of the way, but he was using personal skill and courage to match their lap times; it said more about him than about his car. . . .

For 1954 the Wharton Mark II was sold to Bristol distributor Tony Crook, who had already raced an F2 Cooper-Alta Mark II and a Mark I-chassised Bristol sports car, and now had his special '1½-seat' ex-Alta Mark II-Bristol. The Wharton car arrived less engine but still with the ENV 'box, but Crook found this device far too heavy and with too much drag for his liking. The car sat little-used until, he recalls: 'I sold it to an Australian. . . .'

Roddy Macpherson's Mark II, believed to be the ex-Wharton car today, has an Australian history extending back to 1957, when it was imported by Ray Gibbs, who had reputedly discovered it in bits at Hollyfield Road – it would appear – while working there during 1956. He fitted a Holden engine and raced it until 1959, when it passed to Tony Osborne. In the mid-Sixties it went to Bob Punch, who advertised it for the first time as the ex-Wharton car. It was brought back to the UK by Stephen Curtis, who identified it as indeed the Wharton car due to its apparently unique starting handle hole in the nose and the presence of 'odd gearbox mountings on the frame, suggesting at some time it had carried something like a pre-selector'. The car's bodywork, with its undertail louvres for example was pure Wharton. Stephen fitted a Bristol engine and the car subsequently became an integral part of the British historic scene, performing most spectacularly in Roddy Macpherson's hands in recent years.

The Bob Gerard car:
Immaculately prepared, reliable and fast among British company – this was the car campaigned by Bob Gerard from his Parr's of Leicester headquarters, where facilities were available for some most advanced engineering work. He raced the car at Rouen and Reims in 1953 and it became most distinctive with the neatest ramduct treatment above the nose of any of its type. 'Mr Bob' was regarded very much as an elder statesman of British racing during the mid-Fifties – he was 40 in 1954 – when his 2-litre car won at Aintree, Oulton Park, Snetterton, Castle Combe, Charterhall, Crystal Palace and Goodwood. The engine was first stretched from 1971 cc to 1997 '. . . and later,' he recalls: 'we pulled the liners out and ran to 2170. Bristol's then produced a true 2.2 [2246 cc] for Le Mans and we tried both engines, but our own 2170 was always better. And we ran six port heads. . . .'

He ran in 2½-litre Formula 1 events as well as the national-level *Libre* races into 1955–56, and in 1957 he replaced the old but still immaculately maintained car with his rear-engined Cooper-BG-Bristol special. He sold the Mark II to veteran enthusiast Jimmy Stuart from West Hagley, Worcestershire, who had formerly bought a Gerard ERA, and he raced it quite extensively and hillclimbed at Shelsley Walsh and Prescott. At the end of the year the car was sold to Jim Berry, another experienced club competitor, who had been sprinting and hillclimbing his ERA Special with great success. This car was based on a Horace Richards HAR tube-frame ordered originally by Bertie Bradnack. Now the 2-litre supercharged ERA engine was shoe-horned into the Cooper frame and the Jim Berry 'ERA Special' in this form proved very potent. In the 1960s the old car was rebuilt as a Cooper-Bristol historic car by Dick Crosthwaite in Buxted, where he runs this country's leading restoration company, and the Mark II has been racing 'historically' every since.

The Nuckey car:
Rodney Nuckey's family ran the Warrior Tap & Die Company of South Mimms, Hertfordshire, and he ran his early-delivery Mark II-Bristol alongside Brandon's Mark I in Ecurie Richmond, 1953, the duo also campaigning a pair of F3 500s in parallel. He won with the F2 car at Helsinki and Tampere, Finland, and led at Avus until a wishbone broke, but still finished fifth. Unfortunately in the final Snetterton meeting that year he upended the car rather seriously. It was very badly mangled, and Bernie Rodger was commissioned to build the salvaged engine and gearbox into a new tubular sports racing car frame of his own design, which was christened the Warrior-Bristol. Both Nuckey and Roger Biss drove this car in 1954 sports car events, and it later appeared out in Singapore. The Nuckey Mark II-Bristol was meanwhile resurrected, presumably round a replacement chassis frame, and he raced it in 1954. Australian visitor Alec Mildren then acquired it through the Cooper factory, and it arrived in Australia that December. It was not a lucky car for him and he sold it to Syd Negus of Western Australia for 1957–58. Following engine trouble at Bathurst in 1958 it was fitted with a Holden power unit. It was used in this form for some years before Jim Harwood bought it in the mid-1960s. He rebuilt it with a Bristol engine, but was not very enthusiastic

Part 1 MARK IIs, BRISTOLS AND ALTAS...

about the result and eventually sold it via visiting Briton Cameron Millar to Cecil Bendall. It went into the historic scene, being used notably by Richard Pilkington of the Totnes Motor Museum before going to Julian Majzub in more recent times. When first retrieved from down-under it was thought to be the *RedeX Special*. Its chassis number seems to have been *CB/5/53* during its Australian period, while *CBMk2/3/53* and *8/53* have been linked with it in Britain, the earlier number possibly being most appropriate in view of the car's debut at Syracuse as early as March '53.

The Tom Cole car:

This car was completed alongside Peter Whitehead's Mark II-Alta at the Hollyfield Road works by Whitehead's mechanics Stan Ellsworth and Arthur Birks. It was totally destroyed by the Syracuse fire, the frame distorted and unusable. It was rapidly rebuilt around a fresh frame and reappeared at Silverstone driven by Jacques Swaters – while Cole handled the Belgian's Ferrari – and at Dundrod and Crystal Palace, where Peter Whitehead's half-brother Graham took over. Cole was out in it again at Albi, then lost his life at Le Mans in the 4.1 Ferrari with which he had earlier scored a magnificent fourth overall in the mighty Mille Miglia. Arthur Birks is the only surviving member of the Atlantic Stable technical crew and cannot recall the blue-and-white car's subsequent fate. Neither can former Atlantic Stable team manager David Yorke, who later became famous controlling the Vanwall Formula 1, Essex Wire GT40 and later Gulf-Ford and Gulf-Porsche endurance racing teams. The problem of what became of the Tom Cole Mark II, the most handsome of all these cars, seemed insoluble when even Boy's surviving sisters could shed no light on its fate. Then the problem emerged of what Cooper-Bristol did Barnstaple garage proprietor Dick Gibson campaign during 1954?

Dick, living today in Mesa, Arizona, USA, supplied the answer: 'I bought the Cooper-Bristol from the Bristol factory at Filton in 1954. It had belonged to the young American, Cole ... unfortunately he was killed and I bought it from his trustees. I raced this car with moderate success before buying the ex-Johnnie Claes 2-litre Connaught from Alan Brown. I sold the ex-Cole car to a man in Sydney, Australia. The car was shipped there, I would say, in about 1956....'

Where this car fits into the known histories of the Australian Cooper-Bristols is very obscure. It was unusual in having a horizontal exhaust pipe run, which with its blue-and-white colour scheme helped make it the most handsome of all these cars. One horizontal-pipe car to appear in Australia was Reg Hunt's 1955 machine known as the 'Last of the line' and reputedly brand-new when he acquired it. Dick Gibson began racing his A-Type Connaught in the UK during 1955. Hunt's car was almost certainly Gibson's ex-Cole.

The Bob Chase/Alan Brown Mark II-Alfa Romeo:

This de Dion rear-axled Ferrari-like bodied special was a disaster. Alan Brown recalls its back axle falling out when Duncan Hamilton attempted to race it at Goodwood, and at Crystal Palace Brown himself had it expire on the grid. He then acquired the 'ex-Baird' Mark II-Bristol as a replacement, having temporarily parted company with Chase. Once they were reunited the first Mark II had its Alfa engine removed and a Bristol fitted in its place. It was sprayed silver and taken to Nürburgring for local Porsche ace Helm Glockler to drive in the German GP. No doubt the start money was very attractive, but poor Glockler rodded the engine in practice and that was that.

The car was subsequently sold for 1954 to Tom Kyffin's Equipe Devone, based around his Torbay Speed Shop in Torquay. It was to be driven by Bruce Halford, and the story as they understood it was that it had been rebodied 'for some film'. It was a decidedly peculiar confection, which mechanic Jake Halligan freely admits he never could get running right .... more shortly.

The Alan Brown ex-Baird car:

Bobby Baird bought this car when he had been persuaded to retire from racing by his *Belfast Telegraph* board. Roy Salvadori was to have the choice of Baird's Ferrari or this Cooper

The catastrophic Moss Alta Spl was replaced by the 'eleven-day wonder' pre-selector gearbox Mark II-Alta seen here with Moss hurtling his nitro-fuelled way round Monza in his sensational 1953 Italian GP drive

87

but when the Ulsterman opted to continue driving he wanted the Ferrari and Salvadori opted out. The Cooper was then sold to Alan Brown. He appeared with this car in the 1953 British GP, and subsequently shunted it at Avus while setting a good sixth ftd at the major Freiburg hillclimb. In the German GP he ran well until the suspension began to fall apart. He battled on, determined to finish, only for his engine to fail half a lap from the chequered flag. He loaned the car to American driver John Fitch for Aix-les-Bains, but neither was on form. In the Italian GP at Monza Alan was outpaced, of course, but survived reliably to finish 12th. He subsequently sold the car to Alex McMillan, who had it converted into first a Crook-type '1½-seat' sports-cum-F2 car, then with a Rochdale fibreglass wheel-enveloping body to become the Bristol Barb... see page 96.

The Horace Gould car:
The rough, tough, popular Bristolian garage owner had made his name racing the ex-Lionel Leonard Cooper-MG KOY 500 when in mid-1953 he appeared with this F2 Mark II-Bristol. He gained an entry in the British GP meeting *Libre* race rather than the GP itself, and subsequently began building his wild and woolly reputation with some very fast but roughly spectacular drives. He was a great crowd-pleaser, bulging out of the Cooper's cockpit. Cyril Posthumus of *Autosport* dubbed him 'The Gonzales of the West Country, and Silverstone commentator Nevil Lloyd neatly turned this about to describe how: 'The large gentleman climbing into his red works Ferrari is familiar to us all as the Horace Gould of Argentina....'

Gould took the car to the 1954 NZ GP, and may have won. The lap scorers became confused and lost count. He claimed he had completed one more lap than Stan Jones's Maybach, which they placed first. Initially the organizers placed Gould fourth, then elevated him to second after he had protested. Who knows? He then set second ftd at Wairamarama hillclimb behind Gibbons's Cooper twin, then shipped the Mark II home for a full British season. He bought a Maserati 250F for 1955 and sold the Cooper to Tom Kyffin.

Jake Halligan: 'This was much the better of our two cars, and Tom quite enjoyed driving it, though his real love seemed to be the ex-Brown Cooper-Bristol sports car we ran at the same time....'

Kyffin's mother was one of the Wills tobacco family daughters and when he was 21 he had come into some money and took his friends motor racing: 'He was a very nice feller, but he couldn't spot a crook. He tended to do deals secretly so that we wouldn't find out and shout at him!'

Kyffin, living in Wales today, admits as much: 'Eventually an Australian bought the cars from me, took them away, and left me with only half the agreed money....'

I hesitate to speculate upon the identity of this purchaser, but doubt that he took both cars, because the ex-Gould/Kyffin Mark II was advertised for sale by Performance Cars of Brentford early in 1956. It was subsequently raced through that season by Flt/Lt W. F. Morice, who had previous experience with a Cooper-MG and who was apparently a good chum of Gould's, also living in the West Country.

He drove the Mark II very slowly in minor races at Oulton and Mallory Park and then took it to the Caen GP in Normandy, where he survived to finish sixth in a small field, though many times lapped.

The car was then sold to George Palmer in New Zealand to replace his earlier Mark I, which went, as already related, to Gavin Quirk. Confusion surrounds this period, because Morice travelled with Gould to the NZ GP in January 1957 and while Palmer finished sixth in the race with his new 'ex-Gould Cooper-Bristol Mark II' Morice also-ran another Cooper-Bristol. According to the official race history Morice had the Cooper's gear-lever snap early on and became 'the first casualty of the race'.

The question remains, what car did Morice drive at Ardmore? He was actually New Zealand-born, ex-RNZAF. A scrap dealer, he recalls the car as being ex-Kyffin.

Bill Clark writes: 'Jack Malcom bought a Mark II off George Palmer, and believes it had an Alta engine originally, and raced at Ardmore with Morice. It had a Bristol motor in it at the time of purchase....' However, George Palmer has told how Gould offered him both his own former Mark II and 'the ex-Alan Brown Cooper-Alta', which George insisted should be refitted with a Bristol unit. We know that Alan's Cooper-Alta was the ex-Chase/Brandon/Moss 11-day wonder car, which would make the Palmer/Malcom machine surviving today in New Zealand quite famous. But it doesn't fit chronologically, because while the 1957 NZ GP was being run, the Brown Cooper-Alta was still in the UK and would be raced there by Ken Tyrrell as late as June that year.... But what it could well be is the ex-Brown/Kyffin Mark II-Alfa re-engined – note Alfa not Alta.

In New Zealand, at Washdyke, Timaru, in the South Island, there is the strange Coper owned, as Brian Middlemass of the Queenstown Motor Museum describes: '... by Ross McKay. He has had it for about 15 years [writing in 1979] without an engine, and Lotus and Minilite wheels. It looks like an early Mk 2 with different tubing to [our] *CBMK2/11/53*. Odd engine mountings, doesn't look as though it ever had a Bristol engine in it. Said to have come from Australia, where it had raced with a Holden engine in it. Wonder if it started life as a Cooper-Alta as it looks so different to our one....?'

According to Bill Clark the McKay car is the Mark II sold to George Palmer as the ex-Brown Cooper-Alta: 'Jack Malcom subsequently fitted a Holden motor after breaking the crankshaft at a race in Dunedin. The car was eventually sold via a dealer to Ross McKay at Washdyke, where it still lies – no identification plate attached....

Part 1 MARK IIs, BRISTOLS AND ALTAS...

However, to revert to the ex-Gould Mark II ... the old car survives there today, after being raced by George Palmer, then Lenny Gilbert in international events. Gilbert later fitted a pontoon affair to carry a second seat, thus forming a sports car. The liners were removed to take the engine out to around 2.1-litres *à la* Gerard. The car much later went to Peter Pinckney, who was Chairman of the Queenstown Motor Museum, until his tragic death in a helicopter accident in 1982. The chassis number is reported to be *CBMk2/11/53*.

The Whitehead Cooper-Alta:
Using the dry-sump, dohc eight-plug Alta racing engine from his 1952 Geoffrey Taylor-produced F2 car, this machine was very neat, powerful (about 160 bhp) and generally reliable, and the wealthy wool-industrialist had a good 1953 season with it, mainly in the UK but with occasional forays to Syracuse, Bordeaux and Albi when sports car racing commitments – mainly with the Jaguar works team – allowed. At the end of the following year the car was offered for sale and when Jack Brabham came to England early in 1955 he bought it, but soon discovered his mistake. 'It wouldn't keep running for more than five minutes.' He fitted a Bristol engine in place of the obstreperous Alta unit, but then became involved in his rear-engined Bob-tail-Bristol F1 project, which was a far more sensible and far-sighted proposition. Jack had believed that his own old Cooper-Bristol Mark II would not have been competitive in British company. It seemed he had been wrong and buying the Cooper-Alta was a bad and expensive mistake. He soon put it right, and sold the ex-Whitehead car with the Bristol engine to Jimmy de Villiers in Rhodesia, the car arriving there in October that year, 1955. It subsequently passed to Scuderia Lupini for South African Ian Frazer-Jones and according to Eric Glasby of Glasby Motors, Bulawayo, who was 'instrumental' in de Villiers importing the car, it later passed to Tony Kotze, Guthrie, Maritz and then to Les Tempest, who replaced the damaged Bristol engine with a Mercedes 300SL unit. Glasby's son Bruce then acquired the car and restored it to Bristol 100B2 form. In 1983 it was still with Bruce Glasby in Zimbabwe, while his brother Ivan, who owns the later ex-Bob Gerard rear-engined Cooper-BG-Bristol described later, had emigrated to Australia, and was racing the car there.

The Tony Crook cars:
The Caterham Bristol enthusiast and dealer must have been the most popular man at Cooper's in the spring of 1953. He not only ordered a Mark II-Alta F2 single-seater like Whitehead's but also a Mark I-type chassis frame on which to build a Bristol sports racing car of his own.

He made his debut with the F2 Cooper-Alta at club level before attacking the British GP, where the car died on the grid. Later in the season he had it running very well until at Snetterton the clutch exploded heading along the main straight into the hairpin. 'The bell-housing disintegrated, and attached to one of the fragments which went overboard was the brake pedal. ... I went hurtling straight off between marquees and people, way into the fields, where I was knocked out by a flying cabbage. ... I didn't really have much use for the car after that and it lay around for a long time before I decided to sell the engine and have the car modified by Bristol's at Filton into an offset-seat dual purpose F2 which could carry wings and lights for sports car racing. It was powered of course, by Bristol engine. ...'.

Thereafter the 1½-seater, or Formula 'XYZ' car as it became known, went on to become perhaps the most successful individual car in British racing during the Fifties. Crook raced it in all manner of events, including the Goodwood 9-Hours of 1954, when he had decided to retire from racing, and sold it to Dick Gibson, who was his co-driver there. Gibson raced and hillclimbed the car, then Crook grew restless, bought it back and continued an enormously successful programme of club races, sprints and hillclimbs. It was the only Cooper-Bristol ever to be supercharged – at one period of its long, long, long life – and Tony retains the car to this day, utterly original and still in his maroon racing colours.

His Mark I-framed envelope-bodied sports racing car and Jack Walton's Mark II 1½-seater RUM 2 are described in the following chapter.

The Moss cars:
Into 1953 Stirling Moss desperately wanted a British-built Grand Prix car worthy of his talents. His friend John A. Cooper of *The Autocar* suggested they should build a special F2 car employing a version of the new Cooper Mark II frame, with advanced de Dion rear suspension, disc brakes and an Alta dohc dry-sump pure racing engine. There were some moves to obtain a 2-litre Jaguar dohc four-cylinder for this car, and experiments were under way but this project would not come to fruition. 'The other' John Cooper organized a small team to engineer and build the car, including Ray Martin, who had helped on Stirling's Cooper and Kieft 500s, and Polish ex-serviceman turned racing mechanic, ex-HWM, ex-Whitehead, known in England as 'Alf Francis'. Further help came notably from Londoner Tony Robinson, and Moss, Francis and Robinson would all have a greater role to play in the Cooper story.

It rapidly became apparent that it would be easier and cheaper to start building a new frame from scratch rather than modify one of Hollyfield Road's, and the eventual Moss 'Cooper-Alta Special' owed the first part of its title more to courtesy than anything else. When it proved 'an unmanageable, unreliable, thoroughly upleasant pig of a thing to drive' even the word 'courtesy' looks misplaced. Designer Ray Martin smartly left the team, while Francis and Tony Robinson tried to salvage what they could from the wreckage of his and John A. Cooper's bright ideas. ...

The car was retired, eventually being sold by Moss's business manager Ken Gregory two years later and appearing in sand races on the Channel Islands. Today it survives in fine order in the Doune Collection in Perthshire.

Its replacement was the 11-day wonder Mark II Cooper-Alta, which was rushed together at Hollyfield Road with the Alta engine driving through an ENV pre-selector gearbox to avoid use of a conventional clutch, like the one which had exploded between Stirling's shins in his swansong with the Special at Reims. Francis planned to mount the ENV 'box in unit with the final-drive behind the cockpit to alter weight distribution, but there was no way to do this on the standard frame. So John Cooper offered use of the company's jig and welder for Alf to tailor a frame to suit. Within seven days, with the whole-hearted support of Hollyfield Road's staff, the car grew. Girling instead of Lockheed (as favoured by Cooper) provided the drum brakes.

Meanwhile Francis had gone to Barwell Engineering in Chessington to extract more power from the Alta engine. By juggling the valve timing, reshaping the ports and careful assembly he found an extra 19 bhp. John Morris of SU persuaded the team to try fuel injection but it refused to run cleanly and SU carburettors were quickly refitted.

The new car emerged with a virtually standard-looking Mark II body, bolt-on wheels, etc., and was completed in only 11 days from cutting first metal. This is the true Moss Cooper-Alta and it behaved quite well at Nürburgring only to jam in second gear while warming-up before the start of the GP. But as the flag fell it miraculously cured itself and Stirling finished sixth out of 30. At Sables d'Olonne the following week he was third. Running SU injection the car retired from a minor race at Charterhall, whereupon Alf refitted carburettors for the afternoon's *Libre* event. Stirling ran well in an early dice with Rolt's Walker Connaught before the carburation – perhaps understandably – went off tune.

Back at Barwell's, Alf re-tuned the engine onto injection and with nitromethane fuel additive claims to have exceeded 200 bhp – past the magic 100 bhp-per-litre mark. On nitro, fuel consumption fell to near 4 mpg, but the car would be very fast. Next race was the Italian GP at Monza, a 'power circuit' indeed, and Moss chose the nitro option, regardless of three refuelling stops this would entail and the necessity of carrying their own fuel into Italy, where nitro was not then obtainable.

Alf Francis: 'The car went like a bomb in practice ... it fairly streaked round on that first lap. When the field came past the pits I could hardly believe my own eyes. There was a bunch of four red cars and, right on their tail, the green Cooper-Alta.... At least we were showing the massed Italian crowd that a British car and driver could keep up with the Italian aces....'

Moss's pace was too great for the standard 6.00-15 tyres, which he was forced to use by the non-availability of larger Cooper wheels. The car's pace was exceeding its road-holding capabilities, and although they had adopted a rear anti-roll bar the whole affair was very dicey through Monza's high-speed corners. By Ferrari and Maserati standards the 11-day wonder had no road-holding and no brakes and with its tiny wheels there was soon no tyre tread left either. Moss stopped first to investigate oil fumes blowing out of the crankcase breather, but this was unnecessary, merely due to insufficient oil-warming before the race began. He restarted in mid-field, still lapping as fast as the best Italian cars, but then a fuel tank sprung a welded seam and leaked. The tank was drained and sealed off, and he rejoined again. Then came a stop to change the worn-out rear tyres, a lengthy business with the bolt-on Cooper wheels, and after a succession of such delays he finished 13th while the winning Maseratis and Ferraris ran non-stop. Both Alta engine and fuel-injection equipment had run perfectly, surviving 300 miles at an extraordinary if often interrupted pace.

Back home Stirling then won both heats of the London Trophy at Crystal Palace, and next day took the F2 class and fourth ftd at Prescott hillclimb. In the closing Goodwood meeting a works Connaught saw him off into second place, and then he placed fifth in the F1 race behind the *ThinWall Special* and two V16 BRMs. The lubrication system failed in a third race that day and he retired. It was his last race with the car, for it was not ready for a planned outing at Castle Combe, and Eric Thompson took over for the last race of the season at Snetterton, only to crash mildly on the first lap.

Competitive little Eric Brandon was fascinated by all this and he bought the car for 1954, but it was further modified by Barwell and would never run so well again. He passed the car on to Bob Chase for 1955, when it was driven mainly by Mike Keen. Later the car appeared only sporadically, and early in 1957 Alan Brown advertised it for weeks on end, 'Ideal for beginner'. It did not sell and was later advertised further by Sidney Marcus Ltd of Sloane Street, London. 'Brownie' stored the car at his friend Ken Tyrrell's timber yard and during 1957 'Chopper' raced it occasionally.

There is then the strong story from George Palmer in New Zealand that he bought the car through Horace Gould, but its last-known British owners cannot recall its fate at all and Palmer is vague about the date of his Bristol-engined ex-Cooper-Alta's arrival; his inferred date clashing with Tyrrell's racing the car still in the UK. However, if the New Zealand car did not in fact appear there until late 1957/early 1958 the story would be complete, but it is indeed now certain that the NZ car is the one-time Alan Brown Cooper-Alfa and 'the wonder' sold to Stutz Plaisted in the USA, who still retained it in 1987 (see page 208).

The last of the line ... :
This heading is applied to a car known as *CBR/2/9/53* in the records of Australian authority John Blanden. It was repu-

Part I MARK IIs, BRISTOLS AND ALTAS...

tedly the last Cooper-Bristol to be built and was supplied new to the order of Reg Hunt early in 1955, for Kevin Neal to drive in Australia. It would presumably have been constructed sometime in the summer of autumn or 1954, over a year after the last of its older sisters, if it was indeed new.

It made its debut at Fisherman's Bend on 19 February, 1955, where Neal was fifth in the Victorian Trophy. In 1956 it was third in this event, and fourth in the important Australian GP. In October 1956 Len Lukey – of 'Lukey Muffler' exhaust fame – bought it. He was a most capable engineer and driver, and in his hands the car was quite successful without actually winning anything against Maserati 250F opposition through 1957–58. On 28 September, 1957, at Coonabarrabran, NSW, Lukey created a new national record in class of 147.4 mph over the flying kilometre. Early in 1959 Lukey bought a rear-engined Cooper-Climax; the car Jack Brabham had brought in to race at Orange in January that year. Lukey lent his front-engined special to visiting English driver David Piper for races at Phillip Island in 1960, and later to Frank Coad at the same venue, using the original body. In 1961 the car went to Eddie Clay, who had the old Bristol engine disintegrate expensively. In January 1963 it was racing again, with a Holden engine installed, driven by Ken Cox. It passed through various hands through the 1960s, until Peter Menere restored it to Bristol power. 'Jumbo' Goddard, English engineer-enthusiast resident in Australia, bought the car in 1974 on behalf of his friend Tom Wheatcroft, founder of the British Donington Collection of Single-Seater Racing cars, and, finished in a representation of the Wharton colours, it stands in the Collection's halls at Donington Park race circuit today, representing the whole Cooper-Bristol breed, which boosted Mike Hawthorn and Jack Brabham towards the World Championship.

None of my Cooper contacts can recall a Mark II being built new 18 months after its sisters. This was surely the ex-Gibson, ex-Tom Cole second Mark II of 1953, as sold 'to a man in Sydney'....

At Easter Goodwood, 1954, Eric Brandon emerged in this ex-Moss eleven-day wonder Mark II-Alta. Ginger Devlin on left, Bernie Rodger with moustache and cigarette, having developed the engine at Barwell Engineering. It never ran as well again according to Eric, though subsequent owners Alan Brown/Bob Chase campaigned it with some minor success, 'Brownie' and Mike Keen driving. This handsome car sold eventually to Stutz Plaisted in the USA. Note distinctive Brandon grille, and two-into-one Alta exhaust on the car from new

Part 2 Nine sports cars, 1953-54

It was Alan Brown and Bernie Rodger who set a minor trend when they schemed their *Barchetta* sports-bodied conversion on the famous Bob Chase/Mike Hawthorn Cooper-Bristol Mark I through the winter of 1952–53.

Emphasize the word minor, for not many of the F2 cars followed suit. In more recent times as historic racing cars have appreciated in value, this minor trend has often been overstated. 'Aah now, most of the F2 Cooper-Bristols were converted into sports cars you know . . .' is something I have heard many times, and as an assertion it simply is *not* true. It is a reasonable and understandable assumption, but so far as the majority are concerned it is certainly groundless. . . .

Through the years 1953–54 there seem to have been nine front-engined sports-racing Coopers put together, other than the 1954 Jaguar-engined cars. They line up as follows:

The Alan Brown ex-Hawthorn Mark I:
As described in the last chapter, this Bob Chase-owned car was surplus to requirements as an F2 once Alan Brown had joined Chase's Saltdean team with his own Mark I and Rodger was putting together his own ideas in the de Dion-axled Mark II-Alfa Romeo. Alan thought the old Mark I would make an excellent basis for a sports racing car: '. . . and Bernie was responsible for putting it all together. I told him what I wanted and he welded together a cage profile for the new bodywork which was sent to Wakefield's of Byfleet to be skinned. It copied the Lionel Leonard Cooper-MG bodies, which he had copied from the Ferrari *Barchetta*. . . .'

It was planned initially to carry a 2.6-litre Aston Martin Vantage engine, while there was talk of a similar works-built car being supplied to Ken Wharton after being ordered originally by Bertie Bradnack. This car might have had a hardtop body fitted on the *Barchetta* base, in part aimed at a Wharton Bristol-engined entry in the Mille Miglia 2-litre class, but it didn't happen. . . .

Alan Brown drove the Chase car under their Equipe Anglaise banner, commencing with the opening Goodwood meeting. It was still Bristol-engined; the Aston Martin conversion would not be made for a couple of years. Under the registration HPN 665 the Brown Cooper-Bristol became a familiar entry in British racing through 1953, and really came on song in 1954 when Alan won the important British Empire Trophy race with it at Oulton Park, and also the 2-litre race in a major sports-car meeting at Zandvoort replacing the World Championship Dutch GP.

'The sports car was exactly to F2 spec,' Alan Brown told me, 'save for Bernie lowering the compression ratio to something like 10.5:1 and running 100-octane petrol instead of a fuel mix. The Bristol engine was always problematic with fuel mixtures and ran a lot better on straight petrol. It was a very fast little car and still is, we could see off a D type round Silverstone and when I won the Dutch race for sports cars we lapped faster than all the D types in the unlimited-capacity race apart from Ninian Sanderson's. . . .'

Mike Keen also raced the car with some distinction until it was sold to Tony Everard for 1955. Now a 2.6 Aston Martin engine was fitted in place of the Bristol, and it was maintained and prepared for him by Don Christmas at Rob Walker's Pippbrook Garage, Dorking. Everard raced, sprinted and hillclimbed the car widely before selling it to veteran Midland enthusiast Austin Nurse, who raced regularly at Mallory Park and other nearby venues. The car seems subsequently to have passed through the hands of one M. Taylor and lady Frazer Nash campaigner Betty Haig. Writing in the Historic Sports Car Club newsletter for June 1974, she recalled: 'I myself owned the car for a time. It was then fitted with the ex-Archie Scott-Brown Bristol engine BS4 Mark 2, though the previous bills which came with the car contained records of the Aston Martin engine. I had the car up at the Cooper works at odd times and Charles and John Cooper confirmed that this was the ex-Hawthorn chassis. I sold it in 1959. . . .'

The car was advertised by Wayside Garage (Rusper) in 1960 and it was acquired subsequently by Ken Yeates of the BARC. He sold it around 1964–65 to John R.Brown, who ran a specialist-car garage business in Burnley, Lancashire. He explained in 1967: 'The Cooper-Bristol HPN 665 was purchased by myself from Kenneth Yeates, then of the BARC, along with the ex-Peter Whitehead [*sic.* – means Peter Walker] Cooper-ERA single-seater, which was minus engine and gearbox, with the object of making up a Cooper-Bristol single-seater for historic events.

'The Cooper-ERA had 16 in. wheels, which over-geared the car for short-circuit events, and we decided to use the 15 in. wheels from the two-seater, as well as the engine and

Part 2 NINE SPORTS CARS, 1953–54

Alan Brown's ex-Hawthorn/Bob Chase Mark I when first rebodied by Wakefields of Byfleet and converted by Bernie Rodger into the 2-litre Cooper-Bristol sports car HPN 665. This entity survives today, the closest one can get to that historic unpainted Mark I of Easter Monday Goodwood fame, 1952 .... Note distinctive side vents, number disc light for Goodwood 9-Hours here in 1953

Tom Kyffin was very happy with his ex-Alan Brown Ecurie Richmond Mark I conversion, UPF 440. This was another Bernie Rodger job, and its extensive racing career included the Bol d'Or 24-Hours at Montlhéry. The body survives on one of Anatoly Arutunoff's Cooper-MGs in Oklahoma into the 1980s, the chassis entity survives once more as an F2 single-seater

gearbox. Unfortunately it was found that the brake drums on the Cooper ERA were too large for the smaller-diameter wheels, and when we tried to exchange these many of the suspension parts differed, so that eventually we changed-over most of the front suspensions.

'When the single-seater had been finished, with the aid of a new bonnet top to suit the Bristol unit, we then set about the two-seater, and I acquired a Bristol FNS unit which had belonged to Doug Haig and had been taken out of his ex-Josh Randles Frazer Nash Le Mans, and I also obtained a gearbox from another source. The car was then sold, not completed, to Mr E. A. Dixon . . . of Ponteland, Northumberland. . . . The single-seater was sold to Donald Balmer. . . .'

In 1974 Miss Haig's newsletter story mentioned John Brown telling her that in his efforts to produce a Cooper-Bristol single-seater for historic racing the Chase/Hawthorn Mark I-cum-sports car and the ex-Walker Cooper-ERA 'have been scrambled somewhat so that I have virtually the ex-Hawthorn chassis and engine from HPN 665 with the Whitehead [sic.] single-seater body and wider rear end. This I have run in the last Snetterton historic racing events in August and September, finishing second to Bill Wilks . . .' inferring his single-seater used HPN's frame.

However, the long-wheelbase chassised single-seater

Libre *racing, Mallory Park, 16 September, 1956, with the obscure W. F. Morice charging away in his ex-Gould ex-Kyffin Mark II-Bristol flanked by (left) Niall Campbell-Blair's ex-Baird/Salvadori, ex-Brown Mark II converted by Dennis Wolstenholme into the Bristol Barb. The car is in its last few weeks of life, being destroyed in a massive shunt at Oulton Park the following month*

While Bernie Rodger's conversion work on the Hawthorn and Brown F2 Mark Is was under way at Saltdean and Byfleet, here at Hollyfield Road the works' own Bristol-engined sports car project was under way. This is the frame, without the characteristic stamped lightening holes of the single seaters', showing off its Bristol power unit and gearbox, transverse-leafspring suspensions and Mark II-type streamlined hub-carrier castings-cum-brake backplates. Pity the throttle pedal seems to be falling off. In rear is a 500 cc F3 Mark VII-Norton, showing its all-round tube and stamped strip chassis construction. The Wakefields sports body was damaged in John Coombs' Goodwood 9-Hours crash, but later rebuilt and possibly re-chassised the car went to the Hon Edward Greenall, then Roy Winkelmann. It's an 'historic' single-seater today

Part 2 NINE SPORTS CARS, 1953–54

which Brown subsequently sold to Don Balmer equates better with being the Cooper-ERA frame than the original Hawthorn chassis, so either Miss Haig's quotation of the story may be at fault, or Brown not only scrambled the cars but also his memory. Irrespective, his candour in explaining what had been done to the two cars is to be applauded.

Old HPN 665 then lay fairly quiet until 1974, when Alan Brown bought back his old car. He was running Connaught's on the A3 at the time and it was restored for him by the staff. He still owns this most famous of all Cooper-Bristols 'entities' today, in 1983, although how much of its metalwork experienced Mike Hawthorn's driving—or Alan's own pre-'55—is a moot point.

The second Alan Brown Mark I:

As the 1953 season progressed, with Alan Brown, Paul Emery and Duncan Hamilton each trying their hands with Bob Chase's latest Mark II-Bristol and the catastrophic Mark II-Alfa Romeo single-seaters, so Alan's own ex-Ecurie Richmond Mark I in turn became surplus to requirements upon its return from Argentina. The success of the ex-Hawthorn, Equipe Anglaise sports-car conversion prompted the team to convert this remaining Mark I similarly, *Barchetta* bodywork again being fitted by Wakefield's of Byfleet.

The new car was registered UPF 440 and was sold early in 1954 to West Country wheeler-dealer David Watts, who promptly set a new hillclimb record with it at Trengwainton in Devon. He passed it on almost immediately to Tom Kyffin's ambitious new private team, Equipe Devone. Kyffin raced the car widely in British club and national events, featuring strongly in 2-litre sports-car classes. He and Bruce Halford also took the car to the 1955 Bol d'Or 24-Hours at Montlhéry: '... where the spare wheel broke loose in the tail and started to demolish the bodywork. The first I knew of something being seriously wrong was when the door started flying open round the banking, because the tail section of the bodywork was moving backwards. Eventually it fell off and the wheel went hurtling off miles into the countryside....'

Old UPF was regarded as 'a good honest car' and it seems to have passed in later years to Aubrey Taylor *c*. 1959, Eric Castle *c*. 1963, Harry Pattison *c*. 1963, to Stephen Curtis before 1967. He apparently separated body and chassis in order for the original F2 single-seater to be restored for historic racing. The car was built up as a single-seater once more by John Roberts, who raced it with some success before replacing it with a more modern Lotus 16. The single-seater went to Peter Van Rossem and then to Barry Simpson and survives in good order within the historic movement today. Meanwhile old UPF's *Barchetta* body had been fitted to an, at this range anonymous, Cooper-MG chassis, and was subsequently sold to Anatoly Arutunoff of Bartlesville, Oklahoma, USA, under the original Cooper-Bristol sports-car registration. He describes it as having 'mag Cooper wheels, a door in the driver's side only and a *huge* fuel tank filling the tail...' and he cherishes it dearly, alongside two other Cooper sports cars – an MG model with wire wheels, side-mounted spare wheel and UK registration NTO 650, and a Ford 120E-powered version on mag wheels, with cycle front wings and the UK registration XJH 903.

The ex-Alan Brown Mark II Bristol Barb:
At the close of the 1954 season Alan Brown sold his 'ex-Baird' Mark II-Bristol to enthusiastic club-racer Alex McMillan from Cheshire. Alex recalls: 'At first Dennis Wolstenholme, who looked after all my cars for me in Prestbury, widened the car slightly into a 1½-seater like Tony Crook's and Jack Walton's, with cycle wings and what we chose to describe as road equipment. It made the scrutineers laugh, it had a kiddy car hooter and two very small sidelights. I remember the first time we presented it to them they said "all you need is a fairy on the top and you've got a Christmas tree..."'

Dennis Wolstenholme: 'I was always very conscious of advising Alex to buy good cars, not junk, and we only bought the Brown Cooper-Bristol after a careful test session at Silverstone. Everything was loose, Brown had two or three different cars and he obviously had different people looking after them all. But essentially it was very sound and we bought it, fitted with a BS1 engine.

'We had built-up a Cooper-MG with cycle wings for Niall Campbell-Blair – I can't recall doing the same with the Cooper-Bristol [photographic evidence shows they did in fact] before... taking a Rochdale fibreglass body and fitting that to produce a very modern-looking sports car. The chassis was all round-tube [hence a Mark II] and we kept the main lateral tubes while fitting outriggers to support the Rochdale body, and cutting and altering the top frame rails to offset the driving position....'

The finished offset-two-seat sports car with its enveloping fibreglass body was sprayed white with a black stripe, and was very attractive indeed, and McMillan road-registered it LBU 349. By September 1955, when Rochdale Motor Panels – with whom both McMillan and Wolstenholme were associated – advertised the Barb for sale, its record included 35 events, yielding no less than 20 firsts, three seconds, three fourths and three fifth places. The asking price was £1700.

Niall Campbell-Blair bought the car and he, McMillan and Johnnie Higham – another long-term Cooper adherent – raced jointly as Ecurie White Rose. Again the Barb was very successful until right at the end of the 1956 season at Oulton Park, where Campbell-Blair crashed heavily and mangled the car beyond economic repair.

Dennis Wolstenholme: 'It was smashed to pieces really, and the sweepings went to an enthusiast in Ashton-under-Lyne named Maurice Burrill. He never raced, he just loved the cars. There was no longer a chassis with the bits, it was scrap....'

In later years the Bristol Barb 'sweepings' formed the basis of a new historic racing F2 Cooper-Bristol single-seater. Unfortunately it was rebuilt as a Mark I with the box-section chassis, which wasn't very bright. It survives today as a perfectly adequate replica but the 'ex-Baird' Mark II really died that bleak autumn day at Oulton Park in 1956.

The works production 'cars':
In *The Motor* for 19 August, 1953, the new Hollyfield Road-built Cooper-Bristol sports car was described: 'Following the astonishing success of last year's Formula II Cooper-Bristol it was not surprising that the concern should turn once more to the design of a two-seater... and a small series of Bristol-engined cars is being laid down, the prototype of which it is hoped will appear in the Nine-Hour race at Goodwood on 22 August. A similar, but not identical, car has already made several appearances this year in the hands of Alan Brown....'

The new works car used a similar box-section chassis to the Mark I single-seater's with the important difference that the main members were undrilled. The 18-gauge steel upper framework bowed outwards to accept Wakefield's bodywork, following Bernie Rodger's *Barchetta*-derived original very closely, though without the distinctive side vents of the Bob Chase/Alan Brown original. Cross-members were formed by the front suspension bridge, a centre member supporting the tail of the gearbox and another bridge at the rear enclosing the diff unit. Suspension was identical with the contemporary Mark II single-seater, with the exception that its Armstrong rear dampers picked-up on the built-up cross-member instead of on the side tubes. The Mark II-type brakes were fitted; 11 in. diameter by 2¼ in. wide at the front and 1¾ in. at the rear; the lining area of 164 sq. in. was considered very large for a car weighing less than 12 cwt.

Tony Crook's basically Mark I-type chassised sports-racing Cooper-Bristol made its debut, top, Silverstone International Trophy meeting, 1953 with Cooper-type meshed radiator intake as shown. Note single-block radiator shape just visible through the mesh with separate oil cooler, but unlike Mark II's, and hefty frame cross member from which exhaust hangs. The second shot shows Tony approaching the Goodwood chicane during the 9-Hours race, 22 August, 1953, when he shared with Guy Gale to finish fifth 2-litre. By this time the whole front end had been remade with this Bristol-type grille, more curvaceous lines and improved wrap-round screen. The twin exhaust is new too. Crook's race test results fed back to Filton as part of their development programme. After Bert Rogers' tenure, TPD 1 or Mucky Pup as he called it, went to ground. These remains of the Cooper-Aston Martin in Australia have a radiator identical to the Pup's unusual one, and the frame cross-tube seen here would coincide with that supporting the sports car's exhaust .... Amputated body outriggers are also clearly visible.

Part 2 NINE SPORTS CARS, 1953–54

The Bristol engine's output was rated as 141 bhp at 5750 rpm with maximum bmep of 163 psi at 5000 rpm. the unit retained its standard dynamo and starter, but the air cleaners were removed from the three Solex carburettors and there was no fan. A bonnet-top scoop directed air into the induction system. Two three-branch exhaust pipes united in a single tail-pipe.

The remote-change Bristol gearbox had ratios of 1.0, 1.292, 1.825 and 2.92:1. A single dry-plate clutch was fitted, and a very short prop-shaft drove to the ENV final-drive unit, which offered alternative ratios of 3.27, 3.64 or 3.916:1. Alternative tyre sizes were 5.00 or 6.00-15, on the larger size, road speed per 1000 rpm in top gear being quoted as 'about 24 mph'. The car was very stark and spartan, its rather heavy lines belying its light weight, for much of the thin aluminium body panelling enclosed merely air. The cockpit was furnished with two leather-covered bucket seats, and there were alternative Perspex screens – a full-width type or a tiny semi-wrap-round for the driver, in which case the passenger seat would be covered by a metal tonneau. The body included a full-length undershield, and was sprayed British racing green with cream wheels and upholstery. Plans were announced to build 'about 25 cars at a basic price of approximately £2000', but this would not happen in practice, as the tiny factory was working flat-out on other production models and it seems most likely that the works-built Cooper-Bristol sports car of 1953 was to remain unique.

It was loaned to John Coombs for the Goodwood 9-Hours race, in which he shared it with Tommy Sopwith, facing amongst other 2-litre cars the Alan Brown/Mike Currie Bob Chase car and Tony Crook's special-bodied Cooper-Bristol box-frame TPD1. John Coombs: 'It was a brand-new car and after trouble with the brakes locking in practice we took them down and found three different brands of brake lining inside.... They were replaced but we had no chance to bed them in, so had to do that during the early stages of the race. Then Dunlop ran out of tyres, but we were quite well placed, when just before the finish, in the dark, I spun on oil at St Mary's and ran off into the plough, where the car dug in and cartwheeled three times. It took the screen off, while I'd ducked under the metal tonneau. I still have a vivid recollection of seeing the following cars' headlights flash through my field of vision on every roll.... The car went back to Cooper's rather damaged....'

It had run at Goodwood under Cooper's trade plates, but subsequently reappeared road-registered UPA 261. It passed subsequently to the Hon. Edward Greenall of the Midland brewery family. In an *Autosport* interview he described the car as having been 'ex-Ecurie Ecosse', but I have been unable to trace their racing such a car during this period, when Jaguars were their front-line armament. Ecosse mechanic Stan Sproat cannot really recall them owning such a car, but has misty memories of selling 'a car' to Greenall.

Certainly the Hon. Ted raced the Cooper-Bristol in 1955 with some good results at club level before turning to Lotus for 1956. The Cooper-Bristol sports then lay fallow until sometime later that year, when English-born American Roy Winkelmann bought it from the Chequered Flag dealership in Chiswick.

Roy had served in the Royal Navy and emigrated to the States just in time to be drafted into the US Navy to fight the Korean War! He became deeply involved in security and

Tony Crook's original F2 Mark II-Alta was modified à la Jack Walton's car to form his famous 'Formula XYZ' all-purpose 1½-seater. The conversion work was carried out by Bristol's at Filton. Tony retains the car into the mid-1980s. Colour is maroon

Part 2 NINE SPORTS CARS, 1953–54

intelligence work. Building up his own Armoured Car Company business he returned to the UK and went racing as an absorbing hobby, 'spending all my money'. The Cooper was painted white with a blue stripe in deference to his American naturalization. His brother Bob reworked the chain-driven camshaft engine and Roy raced it for two seasons, during which he recalls magazine comments like 'Winkelmann drove with more bravado than skill'. The old car threw a wheel at an Easter Goodwood international and he eventually took it back to his adopted home in Denver, Colorado, for 1959.

There he was activities chairman of the local SCCA branch, organizing and competing in meetings at airfields like Buckley (Aurora) to the north-east, La Junta to the south-east, where he took third overall and second in class, and then at Continental Divide close-by to the south-west. He was leading there when 'the brakes went, and I shot helplessly up an escape road. Unfortunately there was a guy crouching there taking photographs, with his back to me. It was a hot day, he'd stripped his shirt off, and I hit him in the back and crippled him. . . . It was a terrible thing, but when I went to see him in hospital he bought the car from me. "That bugger crippled me," he said, "I might as well keep it. . . ."'

More than a decade later, English classic-car dealer Stephen Langton was in Denver seeking CanAm cars when he was shown a rotting car lying on its side behind some lock-ups. He recognized the wheels as Cooper castings and bought the wreck on the spot for a song. The bits reputedly included a perforated Mark I F2-type chassis frame and Stephen was told the story of the car having been owned by someone who had been 'run over by it'. He was unable to contact the elusive Roy Winkelmann and subsequently sold the car, which was rebuilt by Barry Simpson Engineering as an F2 single-seater. It would appear that if UPA 261 indeed began life as the works prototype sports car it was indeed re-chassised after its debut upset in the Goodwood 9-Hours and that a (probably spare) perforated single-seat chassis frame had been pressed into service. The only possible missing Mark I to give up its chassis for such a car would be that which Bob Gerard says he owned before his Mark II, although we can find no record of his having competed in such a car before his famous Mark II came along.

Meanwhile, during the Sixties Roy Winkelmann went on to form his illustrious F2 team, whose Brabham and Lotus cars utterly dominated the class, notably in the hands of Jochen Rindt. Roy had learned a lot since those days. . . .

The Tony Crook/Bert Rogers car:
Early in 1953, when Anthony Crook had placed his order at Hollyfield Road for the F2 Cooper-Alta Mark II, he also ordered a box-section Mark I-type frame on which to build an enveloping-bodied pure sports racing car. 'I styled a body to mount on the box frame, and had it made by a sub-contractor of Bristol's who was based in the Reigate/Redhill area. . . .'

The new sports car was completed with a very distinctive bodyshell which had scalloped side panels and initially a standard Mark II-shaped radiator intake fitted with a mesh stoneguard. Tony registered the car TPD 1 and it made its debut at the major Silverstone meeting in May 1953. He raced it quite widely that season, but for 1954 preferred the replacement open-wheeled 1½-seater, which was built-up by Bristol Car Division on a Mark II tubular frame bought from the works. He sold the envelope sports car to Riley saloon-car racer A. P. O. 'Bert' Rogers. A veteran of 46, he had raced MGs at Brooklands as early as 1930, and postwar became one of the most popular figures in the British club racing scene. He was a cockney from Bow, running the SunPat peanut butter business. Silverstone commentator Peter Scott-Russell, at that time racing a Frazer Nash, became a close friend: 'Bert was a large, jolly cockney. He and his wife Bluebelle lived near Golders Green and their large house was always full of other people's maimed or deficient or somehow sub-normal kids; they loved giving such children a good time, sharing their comfortable life with them. Bert also loved racing cars and he grew very fond of "*Mucky Pup*", as he christened TPD 1. It was very fast and it made such a shattering noise that you couldn't really drive it on the road, so we trailed it everywhere. . . .'

Rogers featured in 2-litre sports-car races at Goodwood, Brands Hatch, Silverstone and Crystal Palace in the main, anywhere within easy reach of London. He also took it to the 1954 Dutch GP meeting for sports cars at which Alan Brown shone in 'HPN'. 'Bert loved his battles with *Mucky Pup*,' Scott-Russell recalls; 'I drove it occasionally, and when I told him one time how the thing had nearly killed me he roared with laughter and said "no you've just got to kick the little bugger, and it loves it!"'

Rogers continued racing the car through 1955. One time at Oulton Park, Peter Scott-Russell was driving when '. . . it developed even more of a mind of its own than usual and I could see the marshals peering at it as I went by, and then it wouldn't respond at all and we went off at Old Hall Corner and I managed to get it stopped on the grass. A marshal laid down to look under it and said "I thought so, this thing's broken in half. . . ." The frame had broken and one jagged end had punctured the fuel tank; I was very lucky it didn't catch fire.' The owner then rolled this car at Melling Crossing, Aintree, during the 1955 British GP meeting; co-drove Percy Crabbe's Tojeiro in the Goodwood 9-Hours—and rolled that too. . . .

For 1956 Bert Rogers bought himself a new Tojeiro-Bristol, which he christened the *SunPat Special*. Scott-Russell: 'It was my wedding anniversary, 2 April, Easter Monday Goodwood. Bert's new Tojeiro was a horrible thing, all over the road in practice. We warned him to take care. My Lotus-Bristol Mark X broke a drive-shaft on the way down on the road. We welded it in a garage and drove on and when we arrived at Goodwood the first race was over and old Bert was dead. On the first lap his new car had rolled and broken his neck....'

There is no further trace of *Mucky Pup*, the discarded Cooper-Bristol, and I have been unable to unearth any real clues to its fate. There is one faint possibility relating to a mysterious single-seater currently in Australia. According to John Blanden this device, which has undrilled box-section main chassis rails supporting a Mark II-type upper frame in round tube, 'came to Australia around 1957 and lay unused for quite some time. It is thought someone associated with Reg Hunt was responsible, for in *Australian Motor Sports* in 1958 an advertisement appeared. Reg Hunt Motors in Elsternwick were inviting enquiries and the price was quoted at £1400....' John's intensive researches could only conclude that the car's early history was obscure. It housed an Aston Martin engine mated to a pre-selector gearbox clothed in what the Australians considered to be an Alta bodyshell. 'Around 1955 it was sold, less engine, to a driving school who fitted the Aston Martin engine and used it for training ... it is alleged that it was involved in a fatal accident and in support of this suggestion, the left-hand chassis tubes show evidence of major repair....'

Certainly in the end-of-season national F1 meetings at Snetterton and Brands Hatch in 1956 a driver named Leslie Hunt, possibly related to Reg Hunt, the Australian-domiciled British-born motor trader-cum-racing driver, competed with a Cooper-Aston Martin. The box-section frame with its undrilled plating suggests works-type sports-car frame, and the uniquely-shaped Cooper type radiator matches uncannily that shown in photos of TPD. Could *Mucky Pup*'s shattered frame at Oulton Park have been repaired in a manner suggesting repaired crash damage? Could the old sports-car frame have been modified with superstructure rails as a single-seater? If so, why was the work done in this way—and was the sports body destroyed in the Aintree shunt?

Is there any link at all between *Mucky Pup* and the mysterious Cooper-Aston Martin.... Do you know?

The Tony Crook and Jack Walton 1½-seaters:
Both these cars were formed around Mark II single-seat chassis in which the main longerons were almost literally jacked apart to accommodate an extra seat and then united by wider-than-normal cross-tubes. Tony Crook loved his car: 'It held numerous sports-car lap records, and one day at Crystal Palace in 1954 we were first or second in four races and broke the outright sports-car lap record regardless of engine capacity. We were second to Tony Rolt's Walker Connaught in a *Libre* race that day as well as running in the sports-car events. We broke the Shelsley Walsh hillclimb record, running the engine supercharged, it was the only Bristol engine to be supercharged in fact. I did 33 events with it in 1954 and Salvadori never beat me in his 2-litre Maserati and Archie Scott-Brown never beat the car, either, in his Lister-Bristol.'

Tony decided to retire from racing and sold the car to Dick Gibson from Barnstaple for 1955. But in the 1955 Goodwood 9-Hours they shared, it, and were running well near the end when Tony unfortunately discovered fresh oil at the chicane and spun, Moss's Porsche ramming the Cooper-Bristol very hard indeed. Tony subsequently bought back this, his favourite, Cooper-Bristol from Gibson and retains it to today, in 1983.

The Jack Walton car, meanwhile, was the first 1½-seater to appear, a half-season before Crook's. It was finished metallic pale-blue and registered RUM 2. Both Walton and Peter Bolton drove the car, which appeared initially with a BMW-built version of the Bristol six-cylinder engine installed. Walton raced it widely on northern circuits and in hillclimbs and sprints from mid-1953, later ordering a Cooper-Jaguar Mark I as a replacement the following year. The cars were maintained for him by Stan Hauxwell, who later advertised RUM 2 for sale fitted with a very pretty enveloping body made for it by Williams & Pritchard in Edmonton, North London. Poor Jack Walton had fallen victim to cancer, and died in Harrogate in February 1956.

His son Tim, now an active Frazer Nash enthusiast: 'The car was raced purely in UK events, apart from one trip to the Curragh in Eire for the Wakefield Trophy. It was never damaged racing and was very reliable, and once the 1½-seat body had been removed it hung up in one of our garages for about three years....'

Old RUM 2 in W & P envelope-bodied form passed subsequently to club-racer Ben Moore of Hull, and around 1965 he sold it to John R. Brown in Burnley; who already had HPN and the ex-Walker Cooper-ERA single-seater. Included in the Brown purchase from Moore was 'a Bristol BS5 engine, which I had rebuilt by Don Moore, and this was possibly from the 2-seater. This engine was in the single-seater when sold to Don Balmer and he also purchased the 2-seater ...' ie RUM 2.

Don recalls he robbed the sports car of its running gear to graft them onto the single-seater if necessary: 'I sold the registration number to the Rum distillers for 50 quid, and sold the bare frame and body to Richard Barker in Wednesbury....' He in turn recalls the chassis/body but cannot

Jack Walton's original 1½-seat Mark II-Bristol emerged in mid-1953 with a BMW-built power unit installed. With wings and tiny lights fitted, as here, it qualified as a sports car. With them stripped away it became eligible for Formula 2 racing car classes. Here top RUM 2 bellows through the courtyard, Kinneil hillclimb, Bo'ness, Scotland, RUM 2 was subsequently rebuilt as a pure sports-racing car with this Williams & Pritchard body, Jack Walton driving in one of his last events, the 1955 British Empire Trophy, Oulton Park. Whereabouts of the ensemble are unclear as we go to press

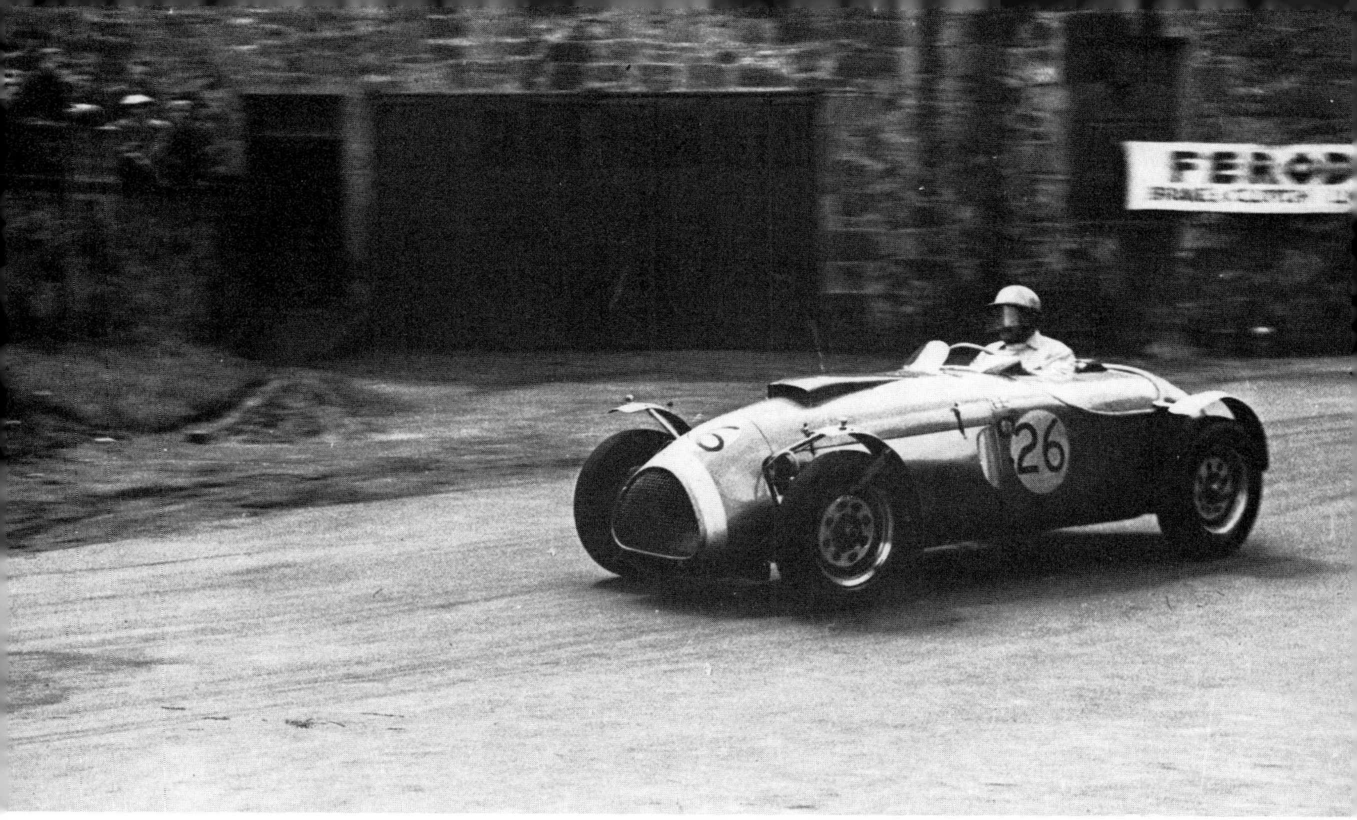
26

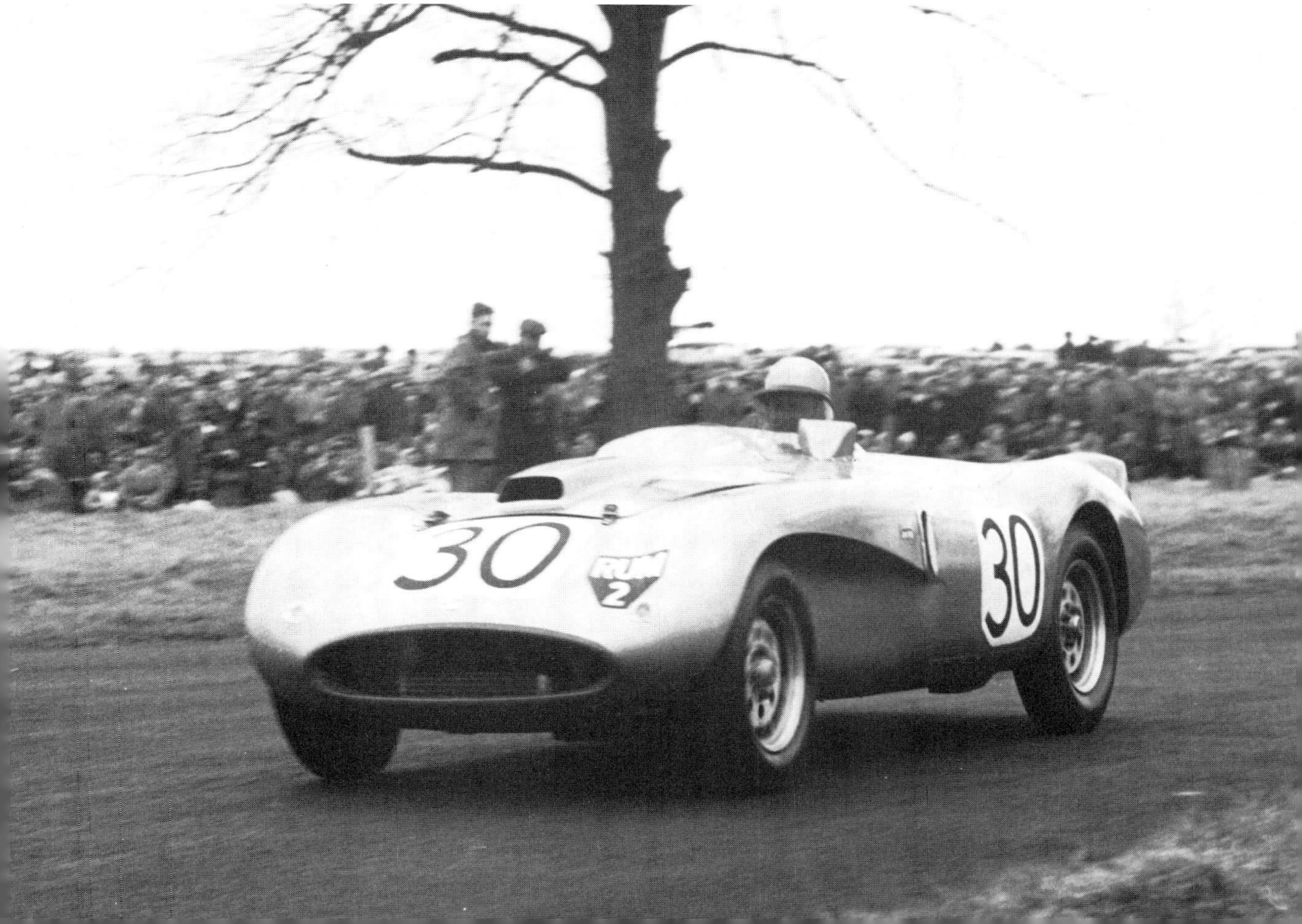
30
30

Mystery car – John Barber's Golding-Cooper has provided the author with persistently frustrating questions. Was the exaggerated Disco Volante *shape with those huge overhangs based on the Owen Maddock late-1952 sketch plan for an under-slung radiator streamliner? Was it part of the rumoured Ken Wharton Mille Miglia project? Why on earth was it left-hand drive when used on clockwise English club circuits? We could not contact those who might have the answers. But, after damage, weird body was removed and Peel's of Kingston built the razor-edged Aston Martin type in its place, seen here – with right-hand drive – in Sir Clive Edwards' hands at Prescott two years later. John Cooper bought the car from Barber and traded it on in this form . . . . Body survives into the 1980s, the frame having long since gone into an historic Mark I single-seater . . . having begun life in Barber's F2 Mark I according to Sir Clive who hugely enjoyed the car*

recall its fate, feeling he sold or swopped it with somebody 'possibly around Devon. . . .'

The trail in effect ends there.

The Golding-Cooper:

This is by some way the weirdest of all Cooper-Bristols, built apparently to the commission of Billingsgate fish merchant John Barber apparently by Ron Golding of the Golding-Lucas Barwell Engineering partnership. It may have been based on Barber's 1952 Mark I F2 car following his collision during the final Castle Combe race meeting of that season.

During the winter of 1952–53, Owen Maddock had been working on designs for a floridly aerodynamic sports-racing or Coupe car with the radiator housed in a pod slung beneath the nose section. A general-arrangement drawing of the car survives. This may have been the progenitor of the still-born Ken Wharton Mille Miglia Coupe project, which may have been under-written by Walsall industrialist Bertie Bradnack.

In any case this project came to nothing at Hollyfield Road, but within six months the Golding-Cooper emerged looking remarkably similar, with its radiator slung in a pod beneath the nose, the most wildly overhung 'flying saucer' enveloping bodywork ever seen and – staggeringly for clockwise circuit racing – a left-hand-drive cockpit. Perhaps the project was aimed at America when it began, or was this the Mille Miglia background?

The result was road registered NXH 586 and Barber drove it in its debut at Snetterton in June 1953. Soon after, he took it to Douglas, Isle of Man, for the British Empire Trophy race meeting, but while running there with this entirely unsuitable car on the Manx street circuit he was involved in a very unpleasant incident. Peter Scott-Russell, driving a Frazer Nash that day, saw it: 'James Neilson, a Scot, was driving the maroon ex-Crook Frazer Nash when the dreaded A-bracket broke and it just rushed up the wall and turned over and I saw him fall out. I was following John Barber in

Part 2 NINE SPORTS CARS, 1953–54

that weird *Disco Volante* thing and poor Neilson landed in his path. Barber didn't hit him but he was convinced he had and when Neilson died from head injuries he was beside himself.... We looked after him after the race, walking him round and talking to him. I was a witness at the BRDC inquiry which followed and testified that Barber hadn't run over his head at all, as first reports suggested and as Barber clearly believed....

'The Barber car itself was very strange, a kind of dirty green, it looked tatty and the bodywork all seemed to be loose, it was obviously very light and it all rattled and shook as he drove along....'

John Barber '...a very nice, friendly bloke', seems to have appeared with the mysterious Golding-Cooper once more, at Snetterton, before retiring from racing. Through BRDC and RAC records I traced him to his 1978 address at East Grinstead, but he had moved and the trail went cold there. I eventually found his brother, still in the fish trade, but John had retired incommunicado to the Mediterranean....

Meanwhile, trying to discover who built the body, I could only find the Robert Peel Coachworks who recalled anything at all about such a car. Partners Alec Rainbow and Fred Faulker seem to have had it brought into them, badly damaged 'with this awful old body, very thin panels on spidery tube, and we scrapped that and fitted a more conventional sports body like an Aston Martin DB3S'. John Cooper recalls buying in a Cooper-Bristol with 'a body like a DB3S' and he resold it... to Sir Clive Edwards.

Some years later, into the Sixties, Bill Wilks was about to enter historic racing with what was thought to be the ex-Ecosse single-seat Mark I. While collecting suitable spares he built himself a sports special which he called a Cooper-Bristol and registered 51 PH. This car he later swopped with a gentleman from Dulwich, South London, in exchange for an apparently genuine but 'extremely tatty Cooper-Bristol Mark I-based sports car with a "razor-edged" body'.

Up in the Manchester area John Bateson and Tony Statham were two enthusiastic motor traders who enjoyed restoring and racing Altas, HWMs and the like. John recalls: 'We'd found what was apparently a Cooper-Bristol single-seater body up here, complete with schnozzle on the bonnet and side panels but no tail. It was a dirty brown colour and was sitting on an Austin 7 special in the back of a garage. At that time Austin 7 specials just weren't wanted. I offered Bill Wilks the body, but he said "I've got a chassis" and so we eventually took his sports car which had a body very reminiscent of a DB3S, painted dark green, with Cooper magnesium wheels. It was obviously based on a Mark I – with the box-section frame – and you could clearly see the stumps where the superstructure tubes had been sawn off. It would be easy to rebuild it from the stumps....'

Other projects intruded, and the whole collection of bits was traded to Tony Mitchell in Gloucestershire, who at that time was rebuilding the Cecil Bendall believed-*RedeX Special* freshly extracted from Australia. Mitchell advertised the rebuilt Australian find and sold it promptly to Richard Pilkington of the Totnes Motor Museum. Another response to the advertisement came from Tony Bailey of Sonning, Berkshire, who – finding he had just missed the Pilkington car – purchased the ex-Dulwich/Wilks/Bateson sports-car chassis with a BS1A Mark III Bristol engine. Bailey succeeded in restoring the car to F2 form after 'a three-year conversion. I tried to copy Hawthorn's bodywork as closely as possible [and] after several seasons of racing in VSCC events I sold it to Frank Rout....' This car survives in historic circles today very probably the Barber Mark I.

A body thought to be the Williams & Pritchard shell from RUM 2 still survives hanging today in a store in Oxfordshire. Tim Walton has examined the shell and says it bears no real resemblance to the W&P body fitted to his late father's car: 'If anything,' he remarked, 'it looked like an Aston Martin DB3S with the round indentation at the front for a Cooper badge....' This is most surely the replacement body built by Peel's on what remained of the John Barber Golding-Cooper.

The John Riseley-Prichard Disco Volante:
This is really something different, not a Cooper-Bristol at all but a distantly related car raced during the 1953–54 period and often discussed in the same breath with HPN, UPF, Mucky Pup and the outlandish Golding-Cooper....

John Riseley-Prichard was a city stockbroker and member of Lloyds who became an enthusiastic and really very promising amateur racing driver. He told me in 1982: 'I became involved with commissioning a special Cooper sports car after buying the 1100 and 1500 Rileys from Leslie and Mike Hawthorn in 1952. They were very fine, fast cars but really were just too heavy in modern company. I sold one of them to Mike Hawthorn's friend Don Beauman but kept the other for quite some time.

'Then, looking for a lighter sports car to carry my spare Leslie Hawthorn-tuned Riley 1500 engine, I got a Cooper 500 chassis and had it widened – much to Leslie's horror. He lost interest after that because the 500 frame was grossly under-braked for it.... I did part of the work myself, with a couple of boffins.

'Early in 1953 I picked up a copy of *The Autocar* and there were photographs of the Alfa Romeo *Disco Volante* prototype. I thought the body was beautiful and took the magazine to Wakefield's of Byfleet – a father and three sons – and asked if they could build me a body like this, and they said "make us a model out of stiff garden wire and show us exactly what you want". They did me a superb job, beautifully finished, really far superior to the little 500 Cooper chassis hidden away underneath. They charged really a derisory sum, only about £240 I think.... It was originally red, and then dark blue

Wakefields of Byfleet showed how to produce a beautiful Cooper-chassised Disco Volante *in John Riseley-Prichard's F3-framed Cooper-Connaught seen here leading the 1955 British Empire Trophy race at Oulton Park's Lodge Corner. It had made its debut the previous year with an ex-Hawthorn Riley power unit. Here it is in Rob Walker Scots-blue livery, over-powered, and under-braked, but gorgeous even so*

'Last of the Line' – Len Lukey's immaculate horizontal exhaust pipe Mark II-Bristol tackling the Templestowe hillclimb, Victoria, 1959. None who were at Hollyfield Road at the time recall a new Mark II being produced 12-18 months after the original run had ceased, and it seems likely it was one of the earlier cars 'tarted-up' as new. But which one?.... Very probably the Tom Cole car sold to Australia by Dick Gibson ... the chronology fits ...

when I began driving for Rob Walker [in his Connaught] and the Cooper-Riley was prepared for me at Pippbrook Garage....'

He was driving this very attractive special at Thruxton in an early outing when the Riley 1500 engine abruptly threw a rod and disintegrated, red-hot fragments severing a fuel line and causing a fierce fire. Riseley-Prichard managed to bale out with only minor injuries and the car – although scorched – suffered no lasting harm.

He then invested in a 1500 Connaught engine, which cost something like £1 per cc – a huge sum in those days – and the revamped Cooper-Connaught *Disco Volante* really began to perform. He qualified on pole for the 1500 Heat of the 1954 British Empire Trophy at Oulton Park and led from Moss for 16 of the 20 laps until a half-shaft broke. 'That kind of performance brought me to notice and I went on to drive Rob Walker's Connaught and graduated to Aston Martin, so then I didn't really need a sports car of my own....'

There was no chance to sell this delightful and sophisticated little special: 'One day it was taken out on test on the Dorking–Leatherhead Bypass by one of the Walker mechanics, and he got over-exuberant I think and had an almighty accident at well over 100 mph and was thrown out. He survived but the car was a write-off. I know I had a problem with the insurance because at that time the Connaught engine alone cost more than a new Jaguar XK120, complete....'

Presumably the wrecked Cooper-Connaught joined Walker's other racing-department detritus, bulldozed deep into the Dorking tip.

CHAPTER TEN

Formula 3 – the later years

As Formula 2 World Championship racing died at the close of the 1953 season, Cooper tightened its grip on Formula 3. In October the first new Mark VIII 500 was unveiled. The prototype was actually a streamliner broadly similar to the earlier record-breaker, as described in the Appendix. The slipper-bodied road-racing Mark VIII was then acclaimed as the sleekest Cooper yet. Evolution had taken Charles and John Cooper and Owen Maddock a stage further in tubular frame design, introducing the now famous Cooper 'curved-tube' concept, or aberration as some engineers would describe it. . . . A true spaceframe will use only straight tubes, each one in compression or tension to perform its proper stress function. It is 'bad engineering practice' to use curved structural members, and to join one tube to another in the middle of a long unsupported run. Cooper defied both precepts; here Owen explains why:

'John was away somewhere. I'd been told to lay out an improved frame for the 500. I did various schemes which I showed to Charlie Cooper and he kept saying, "Nah, Whiskers, that's not it, try again, try something else boy." I'd tried all sorts of straight-tube designs and always the same response. Finally I got so fed up with it that I sketched a frame in which every tube was bent. It was meant just as a joke. I showed it to Charles and to my astonishment he grabbed it and said, "That's it. . . ."

'He was a good intuitive engineer. I think most of our blokes just looked upon him as a bit of an old garage mechanic; a blacksmith. But he certainly had a good feel for what "would do", whatever else might have been "theoretically correct". In the early days I'd seen a road crash come in apparently written-off and Charles said, "I'll straighten that", and with a blow torch and a hammer he worked away just by eye, and when they measured it up it was absolutely true.

'When John returned we discussed the curved tube idea, and it did make all kinds of sense. Curving the top frame rails down to meet the bottom ones reduced wracking through the frame. You could run curved tubes where they wouldn't interfere with fuel tanks and suchlike. One of our very good welders always told me he preferred simple joints, with just one tube jointed into another, to multiple joints with three or four tubes involved. We didn't like weld overlapping weld and so tried to arrange things to avoid that. With curved tubes we could follow the body lines more closely, so we didn't need the old strip-steel frame to support the body panels. What had started as a joke began to look quite logical, and very practical. . . .'

This framework for the Mark VIII was welded-up from $1\frac{1}{2}$ in. diameter 18-gauge mild-steel tube. The body was in three; tail-cum-engine cowl, nose, and undershield. Nose and tail were arranged to open clamshell style on rubber-mounted hinge bolts and were secured by spring clips. The undershield was fixed by Dzus fasteners. It took only two minutes to remove the body panelling completely. Fulford's comfy seat was slung low in the undershield to lower the driver. Both gear and brake levers were within the scuttle.

A welded light-aluminium 8-gallon fuel tank was fitted above the driver's legs, bungee-corded to the top rails. The earlier panniers were junked in a move to increase the car's polar moment of inertia. In effect this meant the Mark VIII's designers were seeking to separate the major masses to either end of the car to increase its so-called 'dumb-bell effect'; the machine's inherent resistance to changing direction rapidly. With major masses like engine, driver and fuel load gathered around the centre of the wheelbase, the 'dumb-bell's weights can be visualized as being slid together around the centre of the bar. If one spun the dumb-bell it would require little effort to stop it spinning and reverse its direction. Slide those major masses out towards either end of the bar and it would require greater effort to start it spinning, and to stop it, and to reverse its direction. The dumb-bell with the weights amidships on the bar has a 'low polar moment of inertia'; with them spread apart it has a 'high polar moment of inertia'. Experience with the earlier 500s had shown them too prone to swop ends. Now Cooper wanted extra stability at higher speeds in faster curves. For this same reason the Mark VIII's oil tank was overhung in the extreme tail.

Rigid engine mounts had proved best, replacing the one-time leaf-spring palliative. Now the engines – usually Norton – were supported in chassis-mounted plates, plus a stay to the gearbox and another from frame to cylinder head.

A magnesium bearing housing supported the final-drive sprocket and fuel pump as on the Marks VI and VII, and a gear-type differential could now be fitted to reduce solid-axle drag.

The so-called Mark VIII(R) streamlined record-breaker commissioned largely by Eric Brandon to emulate the Montlhéry feats of the Bill Aston Mark V model. The company projected it as the prototype of slipper-bodied 500 cc F3 production for 1954 but it used the earlier straight-tube Mark VII-type frame, like that behind John Cooper in this Hollyfield workshop shot. Pictured outside, 16 October, 1953, it shows off its bare aluminium enveloping shell — it was run at Montlhéry like this, unpainted — the multi-curvature wrap-round screen and angled steering wheel, unlike the flat wheel of the 1951 record car. The blanking plates on the nose top are interesting. They cover openings through which a nose steering fin and its steering arm projected, above the conventional gear inside. The fin stood some 18-inches high and was neutral airfoil in section. Owen Maddock recalls it testing briefly 'possibly at Goodwood' but nobody was keen to bite the bullet and try it at really high speed to see if it would kill understeer which original car suffered. It was deleted. At Montlhéry the little car's best lap with 500 cc Norton power averaged 116.33 mph

The familiar transverse leaf and wishbone all-independent suspension was retained, but it had matured at last. During 1953 a fashion had flared and died for zero rear roll-stiffness. Some drivers preferred free movement of the leaf-spring instead of clamping it firmly on the centreline. Now the Mark VIII's rear leaf-spring was firmly bolted down against the top frame members, but at the front Owen came up with an ingenious idea, using the classical anti-roll effect of the transverse leaf-spring.

He had been working on Cooper's sub-contract design of the first Vanwall Special F1/F2 car, and Vandervell's *Thin-Wall Special* Ferrari had been in the Hollyfield Road works for study. 'I got the idea for wide-spaced control of the transverse leaf-spring from that,' Owen explains. 'My invention was the "curly leaf", which was another spring sitting above the main one and clamped to it amidships. The curly leaf's outboard ends then wrapped round through-bolts in brackets above the top chassis rails. This meant the curly leaf located the main spring laterally on the chassis but allowed some measure of free movement vertically. The outboard ends of the leaf-spring passed over rollers bearing against its underside on each side of the chassis frame. As one end of the leaf-spring was deflected over a bump so the centre could drop slightly. You could space the rollers wide for greater roll-resistance, while the suspension remained soft in the vertical plane. By moving the top rollers further outboard you gave shorter wishbone effect and reduced the tendency for the spring itself to flex and twist. It was better all round, and gave the new car extra stability by introducing some understeer....'

The Mark VIII's wheelbase was 7 ft 3 in., front track 3 ft 10 in. and rear track 3 ft $7\frac{1}{2}$ in. The familiar cast-magnesium wheels were 15 in. diameter with integral drums.

This curve-tube chassis 500 heralded the generation of Cooper cars which was to see the company reach its peak, and in turn convince many observers who should have known better that Owen Maddock never had a straight-edge in his draughting kit, only some French curves. In fact, Owen explains, 'I never had a set of French curves at all – all my non-circular curves were drawn freehand and, if full-size transferred to production templates by carbon paper. Fred Bedding would stand there and cut out the templates as I drew them.'

During 1954 the Mark VIIIs were very successful, and Les Leston won the major F3 Championship in his car. There were over 50 F3 internationals, the majority in the UK, but others in France, Germany, Switzerland, Finland and Sweden. Cooper still didn't have it all their own way as little Don Parker flew the Kieft flag high, and lost the major championship by only half a point to Leston. Reg Bicknell's Revis cars from Southampton also did some Cooper-baiting. But generally rival constructors had abandoned F3 to Cooper, and now their former customers joined the queue at Surbiton's door. Of 48 principal F3 races that year Cooper won no less than 37, with Leston victorious at Goodwood, Snetterton, Ibsley, Oulton Park, Brands Hatch and Charterhall.

Stirling Moss – campaigning his private Maserati in Grand Prix events – still appeared in F3 in the special Beart-Cooper and he took the cream of 500 cc races at the May and British GP Silverstone meetings, the Aintree inaugural and the second event there in October, plus the Oulton Park Gold Cup and the Eifelrennen at Nürburgring.

Frail and skinny Stuart Lewis-Evans was to develop alongside Moss and Peter Collins through Cooper 500 experience to win a Formula 1 works drive with Vanwall. He was Cooper's works driver alongside Les Leston for 1954 F3, and his Mark VIII won at Brough, twice at Brands and at Orléans in France. He also won a 750 cc race with his 500 at Senigallia in August. Rodney Nuckey and Eric Brandon were still running as Ecurie Richmond – 1–2 in alternate order at both Bressuire and Montauban. It was like the old days of Brandon and Brown. Nuckey also won at Falkenburg in the team's annual Scandinavian tour, during which Eric took the F3 events at Hedemora and in Helsinki's Djurgards Park, before winning from Nuckey versus the 750s at Chieti. Bellocchio, Italian Cooper owner, featured there.

Sponsorship of racing teams is nothing new. Eric: 'We were nearly all signed up with somebody. In the latter days I'd get a thousand pound signing-on fee for the year from Shell, plus bonuses for good placings, maybe up to £100 for a win, dependent on the meeting's status. We'd get similar deals from Dunlop, Ferodo, Lodge ... and dear old Jack Newton's "Notwen Oil" in the early days – and from Mobiloil in 1951. Whether the fee was £50 for the year and 10 or 15 quid for a win you could still pay your way, even outside the top bracket. But what I always found difficult was running my electrical business while spending so much time away racing. At one time I was away six weeks in a row and got home to find my business had almost folded....'

Other Cooper winners in the 1954 season included the German Adolf Lang, who toured with his team mate Kurt Kuhnke. He won three major races in France; at Porrentruy, Montlhéry and Agen. And for Cooper there were two major discoveries that year; both British garage proprietors racing their own private cars. One was dark, rugged-looking 34-year-old Jim Russell from Downham Market, Norfolk. The other was rotund, comic 31-year-old Ivor Bueb, from Cheltenham, Gloucestershire.

Russell just erupted onto the scene with wins at Brands Hatch (two in a day), Snetterton and Silverstone, where he won the second 100-miler and the Commander Yorke Trophy – one of the Half-Litre Club's most prized awards. In September 1954, incidentally, the Half-Litre Club became the British Racing & Sports Car Club or BRSCC. Bueb came good towards the end of the year with wins at Skarpnack in Sweden, then Crystal Palace, Brands Hatch, Cadwell Park and the inaugural Boxing Day Brands Hatch.

Jim Russell, in 1983 running his highly successful international racing drivers' schools: 'I'd bought my first 500 from Cooper's in 1952. It had a JAP engine. I only did the latter part of the season with it and realized that the Norton double-knocker was the thing to have, so for 1953 I got one which was tuned for me by Steve Lancefield, and began to win a bit. Then along came the slim Mark VIII; I put the Lancefield engine in it and we began winning everywhere. I beat Moss in the *Daily Telegraph* meeting at Brands' – a rare defeat for the Beart-Cooper – 'which was the blue riband of 500 racing at the time....'

His car was prepared at his garage by mechanic Johnny Giles, while Bueb's was run from his establishment, Turks Motors, North Place, Cheltenham, by his mechanic Pip Preece.

'Ivor the Driver' had grown up in Dulwich within earshot of the Crystal Palace circuit prewar. He never missed a meeting there. After wartime service in the RAF he began trading in ex-WD vehicles in Newport, Monmouthshire. He then sold out and went into partnership with Geoffrey Turk in the Cheltenham garage business. He joined the Cheltenham MC and met a fellow enthusiast named Jack Welton. In 1952, when Welton bought a Mark IV Cooper-JAP, Ivor helped tune it, and drove occasionally. His own first Cooper followed, an early model 'much-pranged'. It proved a mistake, and he replaced it with Fred Tuck's Iota, and began winning. For 1953 he bought an Arnott, which he, his mechanic Pip Preece and helper John Denley modified extensively, lengthened 8 in. and christened the Bueb-Arnott. He won at Crystal Palace, was handicapped by not running nitromethane and was refused an entry for the big Silverstone 100-miler. 'Pop' Lewis-Evans came to the rescue, loaned him his Cooper together with its reserved entry and Ivor finished third. 'After

Advent of the curved-tube Cooper chassis frame – the definitive 1954 500 cc Formula 3 Mark VIII pictured on the Hollyfield forecourt, 25 December 1953. The scuttle fuel tank, lowest possible seat mounting and double-knocker Norton engine with megaphone exhaust can be clearly seen, also the different section front and rear Dunlop Racing tyres. But for improved lines, lighter weight and disc brake developments the Cooper 500 had reached its development peak. The 1955 Mark IX and subsequent models up to Mark XIII were virtually annual serial changes only

King of Formula 3 – Jim Russell, the Downham Market garage man who later founded his world-famous racing drivers' school, winning the Snetterton F3 International, 14 August, 1954, in his Mark VIII, soon after beating Moss at Brands Hatch. From 1955 he would dominate the class

that I was convinced that I should drive a Cooper,' he wrote later. 'When the Motor Show came round I went to John Cooper and ordered a new Mark VIII. I had it without rev-counter, engine, tyres, gearbox or paint, but I took away a handful of parts for around £2 10s. I remember Charlie Cooper saying at the time that it cost him nearly as much as I had paid to make the thing....'

The new car arrived in February 1954 and Ivor and Pip stripped it '... and as I was really rather heavy for 500s I got down to drilling and sawing where I could, and so lightened the car by 20 lb.'

Jim Russell and Ivor became good friends, and John Cooper signed them both as his works F3 drivers for 1955. 'Ivor was a lovely character,' Jim recalls, '... always thinking of his tummy. We'd often be in the middle of a race meeting, having lunch, and all he could talk about was what he was going to have for dinner!'

For 1955 the production F3 Mark IX retained the curved-tube layout of the Mark VIII, but Owen resited the transverse front leaf-spring rollers 15½ in. apart and the rears 12 in. to give increased front-end roll-resistance, retaining the ingenious 'curly leaf' lateral location. Magnesium castings appeared as rear uprights and the new cars left Hollyfield Road set up with one degree positive camber front/one-degree negative rear.

Armstrong telescopic dampers were fitted, more nearly vertical than hitherto for a better operating angle, matching Beart practice. The double-knocker Norton engine was vital if you wanted to win, but supplies were still restricted and so the only Mark IXs to be delivered complete with engine retained the old-faithful JAP.

The Norton engine mounting in the Mark IX raked the unit backwards 15 degrees from vertical, reducing head height. The mounting plates were slotted to facilitate primary chain adjustment. The Norton gearbox was to be carried between thick dural plates extending rearwards to a cast magnesium-alloy final-drive casing. The gearbox could be pivoted around its bottom fixing bolt to adjust secondary chain tension. The final-drive casing itself carried a cross-shaft in two ball races, with the final-drive sprocket mounted on the left and a splined flange on the right. This was designed to carry the major Mark IX innovation, which was a single disc brake acting on the diff-less back axle. The caliper was anchored to a plate welded onto the top rear chassis cross-member, and the disc itself was liberally drilled to save weight. It was free to float slightly on the splined flange; the prototype car's was made from mild steel, but Meehanite cast-iron discs were to be used in production. HRG Engineering made them, just down the road in Tolworth.

The rear hubs revolved on wider-spaced bearings than hitherto and of course the rear wheels no longer carried integral brake drums. At the front they were now less readily detachable, the old separate hubs having been discarded.

They were completely machined, and lighter than ever. Front brakes were 8 in. diameter × 1¾ in. wide Lockheed drums with two leading shoes.

A 7-gallon light-alloy fuel tank resided above the driver's legs, strapped down onto rubber pads by bungee cords. The 18-gauge aluminium clamshell body featured spring-clipped opening front and rear sections, while the undertray was retained by Dzus fasteners. The designers had discussed using fibreglass mouldings, then in their infancy in Britain, and Fred and Pete Bedding made some aluminium masters on which an outside contractor laid-up panels. Pete Bedding: 'When the first fibreglass panel came in it was a horrible thing. It was floppy and willowy and not man enough for the job at all. . . .' Subsequent mouldings were used, however, and a great fuss was made about so-and-so's Cooper 'with special fibreglass body. . . .' It was 'the material of the future', but traditional aluminium still had more to recommend it. Owen recalls one rejected GRP panel which lay for months in the back of the works with '*Ron Mooper Special*' scrawled across it, disparagingly. It must have been one of John's ideas.

Overall the new Mark IX F3 car was slimmer, lower and lighter than its immediate predecessors. Its wheelbase was 7 ft 3 in., front track 3 ft 9 in., rear track 3 ft 7 in. and overall length 10 ft 8 in. Maximum height (top of screen) was only 2 ft 7 in. and maximum body width a mere 1 ft 11½ in. Dry weight with the Norton engine/gearbox was 530 lb – somebody had forgotten earlier claims of 520 lb for the prototype cars. . . . Price ex-works less engine was £620, with JAP installed £718. The single rear disc brake was a £20 extra. It was a far cry from 1946, and a racing car for £150.

Of course the 1955 racing season was curtailed by the Le Mans catastrophe in June, but F3 racing was more Cooper-dominated than ever. In Europe interest had grown in 750 cc cars, particularly in Italy. Still the CSI were considering extending International F3's life through 1958–59. *Autosport* commented: '. . . there are many at home and abroad who persist firmly in regarding 500 cc racing cars as "four-wheeled motorcycles", dislike their noise and monotonous similarity of design, and dismiss them as "circus stuff". In defence it can be pointed out that Formula 3 (a) provides a technical exercise (in proving rear-engined cars); (b) it constitutes an admirable training ground for racing drivers . . . and (c) it undeniably produces extremely close and exciting racing, not be it said, between rival marques, for it is virtually a Cooper monopoly, but between rival drivers. . . .'

Most of the rivalry that season was seen amongst Jim Russell, Ivor Bueb, Don Parker, Stuart Lewis-Evans and Colin Davis – whose father was S. C. H. 'Sammy' Davis, the pre-war Bentley boy and long-time sports editor of *The Autocar*. Jim Russell won the national championship handsomely, while newcomer Henry Taylor won the JAP and Clubman's titles, and Don Parker's Kieft actually took the *Light Car* competition from Boshier-Jones.

'Ivor the Driver' — Ivor Bueb with mechanic Pip Preece (in cap) and their painstakingly prepared quasi-works Mark IX ready for battle, closing Goodwood meeting, 28 September, 1955. Pip trimmed the car down below 500 lbs. He had to . . . look at Ivor

Henry Taylor was 22. He had built an A7-Ford special with a fellow student from agricultural college named Bob Anderson; himself destined to become a very effective racing motorcyclist and later Formula 1 privateer. Henry entered F3 at Brands Hatch in 1954 using a £100 Mark IV Cooper chassis and borrowed Vincent Comet engine. He showed promise. His father bought him a JAP engine for 1955 and Henry responded with 11 firsts, six seconds and six third places plus class wins at both Shelsley and Prescott. He too was on his way to Formula 1.

Ivor Bueb was given a drive in the works Jaguar team at Le Mans, and paired with Mike Hawthorn he actually won. Pip Preece recalls Ivor's 1955 works Mark IX like this: 'I built the engine and gearbox for that car and did all the lightening and preparation work on it. In the end we got it down under 500 lb; we had to, because Ivor went around 15 stones, while Jim Russell weighed probably 13 stones at the most. But Ivor always told me he could corner inside any other car with it. Saving weight and friction was what 500 cc racing was all about for us. For short races we'd run without any oil in the wheel bearings, just polished surfaces, and for longer races we'd wipe them over with RedeX. We had our own little racing workshop in a back lane behind the Electricity company in Cheltenham. We could stand the 500 outside on a windy day, and the wind would blow it along. . . .'

Bueb and Russell between them won 15 of the season's leading 28 F3 races; Jim nine to Ivor's six. Lewis-Evans won four major events, while previous year's star Les Leston was usually beaten in his Beart-Cooper. Other talented F3 names

FORMULA 3 — THE LATER YEARS

Nearing the end of its life, Formula 3, 1957, saw these names doing regular battle; Stuart Lewis-Evans (44) in the Beart Cooper, Jim Russell (43) taking the middle line and young Trevor Taylor (52) on the outside, in the sleekest and quickest Cooper 500s yet...

– all Cooper-mounted – that year included Dennis Taylor, Keith Hall, Cliff Allison, George Wicken, Donald Iszatt and happy-go-lucky André Loens, who won at Kristianstad and Skarpnack in Sweden and in the 750 race at Caldaie in Italy. The Welshman Boshier-Jones won the major F3 race supporting the Oulton Park Gold Cup. Hard-charging Ken Tyrrell – partner with his brother in a 'round timber' business based at Ockham, near Ripley, Surrey – had been in Formula 3 for three seasons now and he was always towards the front of the pack. He won at Karlskoga in Sweden after a much-photographed collision at Kristianstad in which the Dutch KLM pilot Henk Hutchinson's Cooper cartwheeled several times. Ken's cars carried a woodman's axe symbol painted on their flanks and he won the nickname '*Chopper*' – partly in reference to his driving.... Football had been his game in the late 1940s, fresh out of the RAF. He didn't even read about motor racing until his football club one day ran a trip to Silverstone: 'When I saw the Formula 3 race I thought, "Well, I'm sure I could do at least as well as him, and him, and it all started from there. I wanted to have a go myself."' He soon took a part-share in an F3 Cooper-Norton and drove his first race in it at Snetterton in 1952.... He later played a major part in Cooper's minor-Formula story.

During 1955 the Mark IX had acquitted itself so well that all opposition apart from Parker's pestiferous Kieft had been killed off. Charles Cooper's 'Why change it when we're winning?' catchphrase was heard again. The Mark IX's successors were therefore merely cosmetic updates of that 1955 design, renumbered as the years rolled by.

Into 1956, countries outside Britain lost virtually all interest in 500 cc F3. It became a visiting side-show class when international promoters could afford nothing better; such as a sports car race, then becoming widely popular. At home, F3 had become a battle between drivers rather than cars. Jim Russell was again works driver and British F3 Champion, winning no less than 14 of the 31 principal races. Stuart Lewis-Evans was his main opponent in the Beart-Cooper. Occasionally he could beat the man from Norfolk. On one spectacular occasion at Mallory Park they actually dead-heated – that rare result in motor racing at any level.

Ivor Bueb had left the works team to run his own cars under the name Ecurie Demi-Litre. He began the season well with a win in the important Earl of March Trophy at Goodwood's Easter meeting and later won again at Crystal Palace. George Wicken was still driving his maroon '*C'est si Bon*' cars and won twice before his home crowd at Brands Hatch. Colin Davis's Beart-tuned car, wearing one of the early fibreglass bodies, won at Aintree. Beart used Continental tyres which were 6 lb lighter per tyre than Dunlop. May Silverstone saw a typically merciless battle between the contemporary stars of F3; Russell – who won – versus Lewis-Evans, Bueb, Boshier-Jones, Cliff Allison and Davis. British bobsleigh team member Henry Taylor won twice at Silverstone meetings. Diminutive – 8-stone – Don Parker was driving as hard as ever, but now in a Cooper, and other significant winners that season included Phil Robinson, Ian Raby, Solve Andersson – at Roskilde, Denmark – and a youngster named Tom Bridger, who looked most promising.

Jim Russell won the RedeX Trophy at Brands for the third successive season, so kept it as his own, while Lewis-Evans for the fourth year in a row made the long trip to Teramo, Italy, for the 750 cc race. He won his Heat and broke the lap record, but his car failed in the Final. Taraschi's Giaur 750 won, while Kuhnke's Cooper was third.

There were some successes for non-Cooper cars. Jack Moor's latest Wasp won at Mallory in a clubbie, and in Europe Loens's *Loweno* special won at Narbonne. But Cooper's grip on the formula is typified by the British GP supporting race grid, where 14 Coopers occupied the first 14 places.

Boshier-Jones won the prestigious Commander Yorke Trophy 100-miler at Silverstone after Russell broke a driveshaft. Henry Taylor took second place on quick refuelling, only for his engine to seize as he switched-off across the finish line! He beat Ivor Bueb into third place – it was 'Ivor the Driver's' regular lot that year....

By 1957 opinions were divided in Britain. Was F3 in decline or not? Its vociferous supporters claimed not, but internationally it was virtually dead. An ember of technical interest flared in August when the Commander Yorke meeting at Silverstone included a 51-miler for F3s on pump fuel instead of the traditional alcohol brew. But this was an experiment which was not repeated for some time, until the dying formula

111

saw double-knockers confined to pump fuel, and the rest ran alcohol to attract larger fields.

Jim Russell again ran the works car 'which I actually bought and ran under their name from my garage'. It glistened in polished aluminium *á la* Brandon's cars of earlier years. He won seven principal races, against Lewis-Evans's four for Francis Beart and two each for Gordon Jones and Tom Bridger. The light Beart car actually used *heavier* 16-gauge lower frame longerons and extra bracing, saving weight elsewhere. A young Yorkshireman named Trevor Taylor began making his name with heroic drives in the black-and-yellow car immaculately prepared by his Rotherham garage-proprietor father. He won at Mallory, beating both Russell and Boshier-Jones, and was third in the Silverstone 100-miler behind Russell and Bridger.

As fields shrank, Don Parker featured regularly. August Bank Holiday Monday showed the remarkable enthusiasm of Alan Cowley, who collided with Parker at Crystal Palace, straightened his car and drove immediately to Brands Hatch to finish third in another race that day! Lewis-Evans beat an amazed Jim Russell at Brands. Young Stuart had been black-flagged to secure a flapping engine cowl and tore right through the field to catch the Downham Market man right on the line. They were keen in F3....

But it could still be a rough, tough game, and at Oulton Park at the end of the season one of the regular multiple shunts injured Phil Robinson, Boshier-Jones and Ivor Bueb, who was at first feared for.

Through 1958, F3 plunged into steep decline. Fewer fresh faces were seen. Crowds lost interest. This was no longer a starved public, hungry for spectacle. Now motor racing had blossomed. Fields were rich with modern and rapid sports and single-seater cars. Formula 2 had taken hold, *Libre* races included F1 entries and against such proper racing cars with proper water-cooled racing engines the spidery clamouring F3 'one-lungers' seemed unimpressive and crude.

As fields shrank the racing was less competitive. Still, Trev Taylor emerged as a real new talent during that season, beating the mighty Russell himself, but never at Snetterton, where Jim was king.

Don Parker and Tom Bridger both won four major races, but at Brands Hatch on Easter Monday long-simmering needle between Parker and Cowley erupted into a nudging and nerfing match which ended in a serious collision. Parker was severely reprimanded by the RAC Stewards and Cowley lost his licence. It was a sad blot on the class and upon Parker's respected career.

Meanwhile Stuart Lewis-Evans continued to support F3 despite his fully fledged Formula 1 stardom with Vanwall. On his day he could out-drive Moss and Tony Brooks in the Vanwall team; he was that good. But his frail frame lacked stamina – he had ulcers and his great friend Bernie Ecclestone remembers '... carrying buckets of milk round for him wherever we went racing'. His presence made any F3 race something special, and he won three major events – Easter Goodwood, British GP supporting race and August Brands, all in the usual Beart-prepared and entered Cooper. Right at the end of the year his Vanwall engine threw a rod and locked-up in a fast curve at Casablanca. The car speared off course into some trees, splitting its fuel tanks on a road marker along the way, and Lewis-Evans was fatally burned. It was virtually the end for Formula 3....

No longer did the class have real stars nor feature in major race programmes. It became just another club class, surviving merely because there were sufficient owner-drivers still willing to run. It spluttered on into the early-Sixties. No accurate chassis records, nor even good works of fiction, survive for total Cooper F3 production, but figures reliably quoted for their declining years tell the tale. In 1957 there were 19 Mark XI versions built of the basic 'T42' Mark X. In 1958 only six Mark XIIs left Hollyfield Road, and in 1959 just four Mark XIIIs. For 1960 the new in-line, water-cooled Formula Junior Cooper-Austin was introduced, and the taproot of all Cooper Cars had finally been grubbed-out.

The late model Cooper 500s like this Mark XI were virtually man-carrying bullets on wheels. Here rising star Henry Taylor applies all his double-knocker Norton engine's horsepower leaving a turn, Tempsford sprint, 13 May, 1957

CHAPTER ELEVEN

Changing times...

On New Year's Day, 1954, 2-litre Formula 2 had died and was replaced by a new 2½-litre unsupercharged Formula 1 for World Champion-status races. Cooper retained an interest in the Grand Prix class through Guy Anthony 'Tony' Vandervell, head of the Vandervell Products bearing company. His team had wielded the fearsome Ferrari *ThinWall Specials* with great success. He was also a director of Norton Motors, and was very proud of their long competition history. Once the new Formula 1 had been announced he involved them in development of a racing engine of his own. It was intended to appear first in 2-litre F2 form, but by the time it was ready the old Formula was no more.

Rugged old Vandervell was also well aware of Cooper's F3 exploits with Norton engines. He knew that a full works engine from Bracebridge Street would see off the production double-knockers then being taken for F3 use from complete Norton bikes. 'GAV' as he was known inside his empire, put pressure on Gilbert Smith of Norton and his notoriously conservative chief engineer Joe Craig to provide such a works engine for F3, and contacted John Cooper for a car.

In the British scheme of things at that time 'GAV' and John should never have 'clicked' the way they did. Their difference in age and status was considerable, but each found the other's enthusiasm infectious. Vandervell would phone John for a chat about racing on Sunday mornings and eventually told him of his plans for a Vandervell F2 engine. He suggested it should be carried by a Cooper-built chassis, like the Cooper-Bristol's, but reworked to incorporate *ThinWall Special* Ferrari technology. During the winter of 1952–53 he commissioned John to design and build such a car....

Meanwhile the Cooper 500 had been delivered to Vandervell Products' Acton works and Joe Craig loaned a 1952 works Norton engine for it. GAV pulled some more strings and a half-dozen Manx Norton engines were supplied direct to Cooper as 'the icing on the cake'. Alan Brown drove the Vandervell Cooper-Norton at Goodwood, but its power curve was so peaky it demanded at least a six-speed gearbox and the project flopped. During later tests a valve broke and junked the engine, and GAV's brainchild was quietly forgotten. The empty frame was sold to Eric Brandon to replace his new 'slimline' car, in which he never 'felt at home'.

At Hollyfield Road, Owen Maddock then laid out the new 'T30' Cooper frame for the Vandervell-Norton F2 engine. It was tailored to accept Ferrari suspension, steering and transmission, and the latest *ThinWall Special* stood hidden behind a curtain in the rear of the Ewell Road showroom for weeks while Owen examined and measured and pondered....

At last the Vandervell F2/F1 engine was ready – still in 2-litre form – early in 1954 and during one Sunday morning chat with John, GAV asked if he could suggest a suitable driver. 'Try Alan Brown, you know, he drove the 500....'

So the bespectacled Guildfordian tested the new *Vanwall Special* prototype at Odiham aerodrome and on 15 May, 1954, gave the machine its debut at Silverstone. It was very promising and ran third in the Final before finally retiring when an oil pipe parted. The car felt remarkably taut and well engineered compared to earlier Coopers. GAV then brought in Peter Collins to drive the car in the British and Italian GPs and the September meeting at Goodwood. Best GP placing was seventh at Monza, while Collins was second in one race at Goodwood before handing over to Mike Hawthorn, who placed fourth in another. The engine had been progressively enlarged, first to 2.3 then full 2.5 litres. The Vanwall team was on its way towards GAV's avowed intention of 'beating those bloody red cars' – whose bearings he readily supplied.

Late in October the car was taken to Barcelona for the Spanish GP, but Collins tail-ended it into a tree during practice. The wreckage was brought home, where the Pearl Assurance Company adjudged the frame a write-off and paid £1473 8s 6d for its loss. In 1955 a team of four similar cars was built at Acton, but it was not until 1956 – after Colin Chapman of Lotus had totally redesigned the Vanwall – that it would begin winning. Lotus would wrest away Cooper's mantle in years to come, but not before Hollyfield had celebrated immense success....

While the Vandervell project was nearing completion, another customer had appeared with a special commission. He was Peter Whitehead, well pleased with his Cooper-Alta and now asking Charles and John to build him 'a lighter C type Jaguar ... to make better use of the XK engine'. Cooper had never built anything around such a large and powerful unit as the 3.4-litre Le Mans-winning six-cylinder twin-cam, but John was fired-up and overcame his father's reluctance.

Owen set John's ideas down on paper and as usual honed them with his own thoughts. Between them they produced an all-new chassis frame using large-diameter steel tubes curved and looped in the Mark IX manner. The prototype Cooper-Jaguar Mark I or 'T33' emerged with its John Kelly-welded 1½-in.-diameter 14- and 16-gauge tubular frame featuring four main longerons curved into half-ellipses and forming effectively a central backbone for the car. Similar cross-tubes then curved laterally to extend either side of this backbone into lateral formers over which the bodyshape could be wrapped. The driving position was outrigged far to the car's offside with the seat-back just ahead of the right rear wheel, and the pedals were slung just behind the right front wheel. The passenger was similarly 'sidecar' seated out on the left.

Since they had moved up a league in power and torque, John and Owen knew they could no longer rely on the transverse-leaf and wishbone system, so they adopted double wishbones, which relieved the transverse leaves from lateral location duties and freed them to act purely as a springing medium, controlled in the Mark VIII manner with Owen's 'curly leaf' on the centreline and outboard rollers. Armstrong telescopic dampers were used and steering was by Cooper rack-and-pinion. Peg-drive Dunlop perforated disc 16 in. wheels were attached by three-eared knock-off hub nuts and

15 May, 1954, the wet International Trophy race at Silverstone – Alan Brown splashing round in Tony Vandervell's prototype 2-litre Vanwall Special *(or Cooper 'T30') using chassis design by Owen Maddock, and Ferrari-derived suspension thinking and components. The gilled-tube surface radiator arrangement across the nose was not a trend-setter...*

Peter Whitehead's prototype Cooper-Jaguar Mark I was the largest-engined car ever attempted by Cooper at this stage when it made its debut in the same Silverstone May meeting as the Vanwall Special. Still unpainted, it has the under-nose shark's mouth radiator air intake with draught includer, top-duct exit for hot radiator air, far-offset sideslung driving position, recessed aviation-style exhaust box, rear wheel spats and Dunlop disc-type alloy wheels enclosing that super-expensive disc brake set. Later painted BRG this car was road-registered UBH 292

carried 6.00 and 6.50 section Dunlop Racing tyres front and rear. The wet-sump engine was rated at 225 bhp and was mounted well back in the frame with a normal C type Moss gearbox. A short universally jointed prop-shaft drove to a version of the Cooper-Bristol Mark II magnesium final-drive unit. John reasoned that there could be quite a market for similarly independently suspended sports cars, in which case such a final-drive unit would be much sought-after. Bill

CHANGING TIMES...

Heynes, Jaguar's chief engineer, was always willing to listen, and at that time was toying with irs for his own cars. He showed interest in the Cooper-ENV final-drive and John recalls it was partly this interest which helped release competition XK engines from Allesley for Cooper to use. Another new departure in the big sports car was the adoption of Dunlop multi-pad disc brakes with Plessey servo assistance. At a time when the whole car cost something like £4000 this brake system alone set Whitehead in for around £750. The new car had a wheelbase of 7 ft 7 in., and its wide track was 4 ft 4 in. It was comparatively light at around 16½ cwt – while the new monocoque D type from the Jaguar works would scale just on 17 cwt.

Cooper split their 'big-banger's fuel load between a large main tank mounted behind the seats and a subsidiary tank housed beneath the passenger-seat. They then clothed the body in an aerodynamic and Porsche-like aluminium bodyshell – as usual in 18-gauge aluminium – with each panel secured by Dzus fasteners and so quickly detachable. The design featured a flat drooping snout and clean nose, with the radiator air intake slung underneath like a shark's mouth, and the radiator matrix itself laid flat and ducted out through the bonnet top within. John hoped that this feature would give another 10–15 mph top speed, but recalls '...that comical system. I tested the car extensively on the Dorking Bypass, but it kept getting hotter and hotter and each time we had to make the radiator bigger and bigger, until finally we gave up and mounted it behind a proper hole....'

Charles Cooper regarded such experimentation with grave suspicion: 'The Old Man was a good engineer, he'd built up a good business making cars we understood, and he didn't want to see me lose it all by making cars we didn't!'

Whitehead drove his new car with his usual careful aplomb. They made their debut, the car still unpainted, in the wet May Silverstone meeting which saw the *Vanwall Special* make its bow. Later the shark-mouth nose was replaced by a conventional radiator layout. The car was sprayed BRG and road-registered UBH 292. Whitehead beat two C types as planned to win a minor race at Snetterton and then began an international programme. At Oporto he was third (though lapped twice), while Duncan Hamilton and Peter Walker both drove the car later.

Two more of these rather peculiar-looking T33s were built that year, going to Bertie Bradnack of Walsall and Jack Walton of Leeds. They were eventually registered PDH 33 and UUG 3 respectively, and appeared during 1955. Poor Walton drove his only briefly before succumbing to cancer in February 1956. Meanwhile burly, jovial Bradnack shared his car with hillclimber Tony Marsh in the Goodwood 9-Hours and after a terrible time with brake servo failure they finished 17th....

Whitehead ordered a new improved Cooper-Jaguar for 1955; the Mark II 'T38'. He sold UBH to Cyril Wick, who enjoyed considerable success in it.

The new Mark II car was displayed at the Brussels Show in January with its aluminium body panels removed to show off the works. The design was a simplified and tidied Mark I, but the car was now powered by a full dry-sump XK engine rated at the normal 'customer' level of 250 bhp. The 4-gallon dry sump oil tank was mounted on the left side of the engine, which was again mounted well back in the frame and canted 8 degrees from vertical to allow a lower body profile. The virtual backbone formed by the four main chassis longerons enclosed the gearbox tightly amidships to allow the seating positions to be drawn more closely together inboard, but the far-back engine mounting had pushed the gearbox back, so that the gear-lever itself now sprouted up somewhere by the driver's left elbow; he almost had to reach back for it. Even so, the new Mark II was a handsome-looking beast bodied in more conventional style than the weird-looking prototype cars.

The Whitehead Mark II was apparently never road-registered. Two more T38s were built; one for Tommy Sopwith, son of Sir T. O. M. Sopwith of aviation and America's Cup yachting fame, and the other for Lt-Col Michael Head, completed early in 1956.

Tommy Sopwith was only 22 at the time and he was to enter his car under the name of Equipe Endeavour, honouring his father's famous racing yacht. The car was sprayed dark blue, road-registered YPK 400 and initially was planned to accept nothing so mundane as a Jaguar XK engine. Sopwith wanted to use a Turbomeca gas turbine instead....

The Turbomeca was being developed in England by Blackburn Aviation. John recalls visits to their factory to inspect the power units. But progress was slow and Sopwith eventually decided to wait no longer, and used an XK.

Many of Cooper's staff relate how prone John could be to 'going off on flights of fancy' once his enthusiasm had been fired. His father was just the opposite. He loved to see the money coming in and became very restless when John talked of spending it. Charles was particularly phobic about telephone bills and there were regular explosions when he saw John putting across more than two sentences at a time on it. Owen Maddock: 'One day the Old Man was giving us a lecture on how not to use the telephone. "You're spendin' all me profits," he was saying, when the phone beside him rang. He picked it up and said, "'Allo! *NO!*" SLAMMM – smashing it back onto its rest. "There," he said triumphantly, "that's the way to talk on the telephone...."' Perhaps the Turbomeca project is one example of John's enthusiasm being fired before realism intruded. His workforce's outlook lay somewhere midway between father and son. The mixture is what made Cooper work so well....

Peter Whitehead ran his new Mark II at Silverstone in May 1955 and then tackled Le Mans, co-driving with his half-brother Graham. They lasted three hours before the XK engine's oil pressure zeroed and the organizers black-flagged them for dropping oil on the course. Whitehead ended the season fourth at Oporto, lay third before the gearbox broke at Lisbon, fifth at Aintree and retired from the TT at Dundrod with a very rare Cooper failure – the chassis broke.

Another front-engined Cooper project during 1955 was the one-off front-engined Cooper-Maserati sports car produced for Syd Greene's Gilby Engineering concern from South Woodford, Essex. He was an enthusiastic private entrant of Maseratis driven by Roy Salvadori, and in 1954 his Formula 1 250F had been the first to reach Britain. He had also entered a 2-litre A6G sports car for Roy, registered XEV 601, which had been very successful, but the engine impressed more than the hefty chassis. For 1955 Cooper's produced a simple Mark I frame with transverse-leaf suspensions and their familiar cast wheels to carry the Italian power unit. It was certainly lighter than the A6G, but it proved dreadfully unreliable that season and Roy scored only one fairly lucky win with this 'Cooperati' special, at the Snetterton meeting, which witnessed—as we shall see—a terrific battle between Moss's F1 250F and Jack Brabham's prototype F1 Cooper.... The one-off Cooperati frame sold to New Zealand, eventually returning to UK ownership in 1987.

Syd Greene would subsequently buy a new Cooper-Climax sports car for his teenage son Keith to drive, and they aspired later to F1 with a Cooper-Maserati....

CHANGING TIMES...

Meanwhile, in the winter of 1955-56, Peter Whitehead took his Mark II Cooper-Jaguar down-under to New Zealand and sold it there to Australian garage proprietor Stan Jones – who had an enthusiastic young son named Alan. Stan Jones had considerable local success with the car. For the first time in its life it was road-registered, with the Victoria plates GLP 333. It later sold to John Aldis and in 1958 to Ron Phillips. Ern Seeliger prepared it properly for him and Phillips was second in the 1958 Australian TT. Cooper's first Le Mans car still survives today, with Dave Robinson in Australia.

Meanwhile the Michael Head Mark II was commissioned as a roadworthy sports-racer. Head was military attaché in Scandinavia and raced widely there, driving on the road from course to course, plus a club programme in the UK. His son Patrick would later design the Williams F1 cars in which Alan Jones became World Champion.... His light, low, slim Cooper-Jaguar was registered HOT 95 and John Bolster road-tested it for *Autosport*, finding a top speed of 137 mph at 6000 rpm in top gear and covering the s/s quarter-mile in 14.8 sec.

The first Whitehead car, UBH 292, was sold by Wick to Dick Steed, who with John Hall tackled the 1957 Mille Miglia in it. The Bradnack car sold to Bernie Ecclestone, who fitted a handsome new body closer to Mark II than Mark I styling,

The major Longford, Tasmania meeting, March 1960, which saw Jack Brabham's first appearance on home soil as reigning World Champion also featured this supporting sports car race in which Ron Phillips' ex-Whitehead ex-Jones Cooper-Jaguar Mark II (42) showed the way from the Finch and Matich D types, and the former Bill Paterson Bob-tail (8). Phillips' ageing ex-Le Mans front-engined Cooper finished third behind Doug Whiteford's big Maserati 300S (10) and Derek Jolly's Lotus 15

and it was driven for him by Lewis-Evans and Peter Jopp, but thereafter went to ground. David Shale and later Peter Mould raced YPK 400 successfully, and Walton's UUG 3 was Colin Murray's before apparently selling to the USA.

Old UBH seems to have been virtually destroyed in John Harper's Castle Combe crash in 1966. Its remains laid fallow for years before being rebuilt. It is now in Michel Gosset's collection in France. The ex-Walton/Murray car is apparently that raced in recent years in the UK by Ken Rogers. The other two Mark IIs are both in France in 1982; HOT 95 chassis CJ/2/55 is with Roland Urbain and YPK 400 chassis CJ/3/55 is with Dr Philippe Renault in Paris.

Smaller-engined sports cars were the next development in the Cooper saga....

CHAPTER TWELVE

New beginning – Coventry Climax...

During 1953, when the days of 2-litre Formula 2 racing were numbered and the new 2½-litre Formula 1 was fast approaching, the British specialists like HWM, Connaught, Kieft and Cooper all began the hunt for suitable engines to keep them in the Grand Prix class.

Dear old Geoffrey Taylor was building a suitable Alta engine, but something less fragile, with perhaps more industrial muscle behind it, would be preferable. It was at this time that motor racing appealed to a company manufacturing commercial engines and fork-lift trucks in Widdrington Road, Coventry. The name was Coventry Climax Ltd, run by Mr Leonard Lee.

Between the wars Climax engines had powered Morgan, Crossley, Triumph and Swift cars. In the 1930s this market shrank and Lee began building Swift-type engines for Government pump and generator contractors. Soon he tendered for manufacture of the machines complete, and won the contract. He borrowed design expertise from the Hale Fire Pump Company of America, and Coventry Climax pumps performed heroic service throughout World War Two.

In 1950, the Korean War triggered a spate of new Government contracts. The existing Swift-originated Climax firepump engine was an 800 cc cast-iron side-valve giving around 20 bhp on a good day. Now the Government specified a replacement with twice the pumping capacity for half the weight.

Walter Hassan, ex-Bentley, ERA and Jaguar, had recently been appointed chief engineer of Climax and he began work on this contract in September 1950. He worked with Harry Mundy, an old friend ex-ERA and BRM, with whom he forged a brilliant engineering relationship which would culminate in possibly the world's finest production engine – the 5.3-litre Jaguar V12.

The concern with light weight, efficiency and the best possible power-to-weight ratio in a firepump engine was much the same as that for motor racing. Both Hassan and Mundy had racing in their blood. Now Mundy laid out in just three weeks a basic scheme for a new firepump engine and Leslie Johnson's ERA concern at Dunstable then did most of the engineering drawings. The all-aluminium 1-litre four-cylinder engine emerged with a single overhead camshaft and inclined valves in wedge-shaped combustion chambers. One target was 35 bhp at 3500 rpm, and when first run in April 1951 the new Hassan-Mundy unit immediately delivered 37 bhp!

They called it the Climax FW – for 'FeatherWeight' – and won a vast Home Office order for 5000 units. It was Climax's biggest-ever order at that time and from this design would grow a long line of racing engines. Not that there was any conscious decision to enter racing with the FW....

Climax built several marine engines and took a stand in the marine section of the Earls Court Motor Show. Old motor racing friends of Hassan and Mundy saw them there, and Leonard Lee was besieged with letters from Charles Cooper, John Heath of HWM, Rodney Clarke of Connaught and Cyril Kieft asking if he would supply a 2½-litre engine for the 1954 Formula.

Lee was willing, and he was finally convinced at the Shell Oil Motor Show party in October 1952. So Hassan and Mundy produced a 2½-litre Formula 1 V8 later known as the *Godiva*. In first bench tests it delivered 246 bhp on SU fuel injection, but Lee became wary of risking Climax's reputation if there was any danger of proving uncompetitive. The press at that time was trumpeting news of prodigious power claims from Ferrari, Maserati, and Mercedes-Benz and Climax got cold feet and opted out. Only in retrospect would they realize nobody should ever believe what they read in the newspapers. Had the V8 been raced it might have proved more than adequate.

Meanwhile, the British specialists had discovered the little single-cam FW. Interest was growing in 1100 and 1500 cc sports car racing, and the Coopers joined Colin Chapman of Lotus and Cyril Kieft in pestering Climax for suitable power. Stock-block MG and Ford engines were by that time proving fragile and costly in racing, and Lee gave his engineers approval to tune the FW for automotive use – but this must not interfere with commercial work....

The standard FW displaced 1020 cc. Now the FWA – 'FeatherWeight Automotive' – emerged with the bore enlarged to 72.4 mm to displace 1098 cc with the 66.7 mm stroke. The first units were available in midsummer 1954 and the first FWA went straight into the Alan Rippon/Bill Black Kieft for the Le Mans 24-Hours. With an 8.8:1 compression

NEW BEGINNINGS — COVENTRY CLIMAX...

it delivered 72 bhp at 6100 rpm. It ran wet-sump with its oil washing around under acceleration, braking and cornering loads. Last-minute sump baffling was vital for any hopes of survival. Yet in the race the FWA ran like clockwork in the Kieft, and it was the back axle which failed after 10 hours.

Climax put the FWA into small-scale production with a 9.8:1 compression and a reliable 75 bhp at 6500 rpm. In the RAC TT at Dundrod two Kiefts and a Lotus used Climax engines, and one of the former won the class.

At that time Owen Maddock had just begun serious design of Cooper's variation on the 1100 cc sports car theme. The thinking behind what became renowned as the 'Manx' or 'Bob-Tailed' Cooper was summed-up in *The Autocar* in May 1955: 'When there is only 75 bhp available and the aim is to produce a car with a speed around 125 mph, saving of weight and frontal area are of paramount importance. In conceiving the new 1100 Cooper fitted with the Coventry Climax FWA engine, John Cooper decided that the rear engine layout offered the greatest possibilities. Furthermore he has had a lot of experience of the road-holding problems of such vehicles including those fitted with the 1096 cc V-twin JAP engine.'

In developing this design John had in fact tested the old 500 cc record car with its engine bay ballasted to FWA weight distribution, and he had liked what he found: 'It was easily tameable – no problem at all. . . .'

The new car's chassis frame mirrored Mark IX/Cooper-Jaguar practice with four main longerons in the usual 1½ in. 18-gauge stock, curved down to simple points at front and rear but with transverse bracing hoops extended right out to two-seater enveloping body width. All suspension pick-ups were provided by the familiar Cooper welded-on brackets and, taking a leaf out of Kieft's book, John chose to place his driver's seat on the centreline, with the legalizing passenger seat outrigged on the left in the space between the cross-hoops. This frame weighed only 65 lb complete with all attachment brackets. It was a good start.

Below *Amateurs at Le Mans, 1955; Edgar Wadsworth/John Brown's Bob-tail 1100 seen here finished 21st and last overall but third in class behind two Porsches, averaging over 72 mph for the 24 hours. The centre-seat position was legal that year. Note 'hick' mirror, integral spot-lights still protected on this, the Saturday afternoon with the long night ahead, and pit identification light just behind the number disc, on rear cowl*

Below left *Tale of a tail – chopped-off transom of the new 1100 cc centre-seat Cooper-Climax sports car in 1955 won it the 'Bob-tail' or 'Manx-tail' nickname, both of which have stuck ever since. Here at Dundrod, RAC Tourist Trophy, is Ivor Bueb in 750-1100 cc class-winning works car shared with his chum from Cheltenham Mike MacDowel. They finished tenth overall. Mike's budding career as a works-supported Cooper driver took a knock when he was called-up for National Service in the RAF. This shot emphasizes the Bob-tail's low built, curvaceous lines. Note rear-intake carburettor bulge on centre engine hump, hot-air exit ducts and vertical exhaust-pipe slot in tail. John Cooper had an aerodynamicist friend named Vyvyan Stanbury who assisted Sir Sydney Camm, Chief Designer of Hawker Aircraft at Kingston-upon-Thames. Stanbury helped-out with aerodynamic advice on occasion; so far as John is concerned cut-off rear end treatment should be 'Camm-tail' rather than 'Kamm-tail', as is normal, after the German physicist who described the long-tail streamlining mimic effect of air turbulence around a truncated tail way back between the wars*

Geoff was there! While hunting for Bob-tail photos the author held little hope of finding much showing the Jack Brabham Formula 1 Bristol special under construction. Hey presto, Geoff Goddard produced this superb shot, showing half-finished car in the Hollyfield works. The curve-tube frame concept is clearly visible. Note how body-side sections follow cross-hoops; cross-pushrod Bristol 2-litre 6-cylinder engine and transverse leafspring suspension, with Owen Maddock's 'curly-leaf' lateral location between frame rails on top. Tanks, gearbox, full instrumentation, steering, plumbing and wiring are yet to be fitted. Note the gear-lever, ex-Ford Zephyr saloon column change. If it was there, cheap, practical, and man enough for the job, Cooper would use it . . .

Denis Jenkinson of Motor Sport *took this happy snap,* **top***, of the Brabham rear-engined F1 Cooper-Bristol's engine installation at Aintree ready for the British GP, 16 July, 1955. It was a tall bulky power unit, and while the entry claimed dimensions of 69 × 96 mm, 2200 cc (sic) it was in fact a normal 1971 cc unit as that bore and stroke suggest. Dean Delamont of the RAC gladly gave Brabham and Cooper their first Formula 1 chance. This view emphasizes Cooper curved-tube structure. Note ducted oil cooler set into firewall, and convoluted rubber hose, typical of period.*

In the race Jack Brabham is seen cornering, heading more serious British hopes – Leslie Marr's Connaught streamliner and Harry Schell's Vanwall with its basically Cooper-designed chassis

Suspension was by transverse leaf-springs at front and rear with single tubular lower wishbones and Armstrong telescopic dampers. The method of clamping the leaf-springs between outboard rollers was retained with the curly leaf amidships, the rear spring now being 2 in. longer than the front with this extra length between the roller and the spring eye, so giving rather lower roll stiffness than the shorter-overhang spring at the front.

There, fabricated steel uprights swivelled between the top spring and lower wishbone, while at the rear the now familiar heat-treated cast-magnesium hub carriers were used. Height between hub centre and the spring eye was 2 in. greater at the rear than at the front, which was actually straight Mark IX 500. Wheel deflections from static were identical fore and aft — $3\frac{1}{2}$ in. to bump and $2\frac{1}{2}$ in. to rebound stops.

Cooper rack-and-pinion steering was used, the rack housing extending right across the forward frame with short track rods connected to behind-the-axle steering arms either side. Steering ratio was just $1\frac{3}{4}$ turns lock-to-lock. In this early form drum brakes were retained as on the Mark IX, cast integrally with the wheels, and they were tiny, only 8 in. diameter and $1\frac{1}{2}$ in. wide, which raised some eyebrows. When he unveiled the car to the press at Hollyfield Road John was already talking of using larger 10 in. drums, and possibly adopting discs if their unit cost would reduce 'to more realistic levels'. Separate hydraulic master cylinders were mounted on the front frame cross-member.

Behind the cockpit the FWA engine was mounted on the centreline with a separate header tank for the cooling system bolted to the headrest above it. The three main-bearing unit breathed through twin SU $1\frac{1}{2}$ in. downdraught carburettors and Cooper listed its power output in this form with a 9.7:1 compression ratio as 75 bhp at 6200 rpm.

The engine was mated to a $7\frac{1}{4}$ in. Borg & Beck clutch, and the problem of arranging transmission with a rear-mounted power unit had been solved, at Francis Beart's suggestion, by using a Citroën *traction avant* (front-drive) unit turned about face and enclosing special close-ratio gear clusters and shafts made by ERSA of Paris, whose four-speed conversions for the standard production three-speed transmission were very popular at that time. Beart drove a Citroën Light-15 and was a great enthusiast for the marque. The four-speed gearbox used helical-cut constant-mesh gears. Its first motion shaft, driven by the clutch, passed rearwards above the diff and past the crown-wheel to carry the free-running gears and selector dogs. The second motion shaft gears were all fixed, and the forward end of this shaft was forged to form the bevel pinion. This light-alloy cased transaxle was attached to the rear of the engine via a separate bell-housing, part of which was cut out to clear the starter pinion. All ERSA's gears were crash-type, unlike Citroën's, which had synchromesh standard on the upper pair. Standard overall ratios with a 4:1 final-drive were 4:1 for top, 5.17:1 for third, 7.56:1 for second and 10.9:1 for first. Cooper also offered a 4.5:1 final-drive and a 'Le Mans' 3.7:1.

Since this transaxle was turned about-face its shafts rotated in the opposite direction to standard, and the oil return scroll had to be replaced with a synthetic rubber oil seal to prevent the gearbox pumping its oil forward into the clutch housing. Initial testing also revealed an irritating problem with top gear jumping out of engagement, but dog modifications cured it.

Engine mounts were four Silentbloc bushes, bolted through a lateral plate on the front timing cover and at the rear through another plate sandwiched by the clutch housing attachment bolts. Two further mounts on the gearbox merely controlled sideways movement of the transaxle.

On the right side of the cockpit a light diagonal tube welded to the outer hoop bay carried the gear-lever mechanism and pivots from which a system of rods and levers push-pulled back to the gear selectors. It was as direct and rigid a system as could be devised and it worked well enough despite the distances involved. Reverse was engaged by clearing a spring-loaded lock-out button, which enabled the lever to move forward beyond first gear position.

Drive to the rear wheels was by telescopic Hardy-Spicer shafts with twin UJs, while clutch operation was hydraulic, obviating any mechanical linkage problems.

This essentially simple but so practical package was clothed in a neat, stubbily, attractive, centre-seat bodyshell. The tail section opened rearwards, the nose section, including the deck extending alongside the cockpit to the driver's right, hinged forward. There was a two-piece drop-down door on the passenger's side, the top panel of which could slide down inside the lower section if a passenger was to be carried, otherwise forming a closed tonneau. A full-length undertray was attached by Dzus fasteners. The cockpit was faired with a wrap-round windscreen and the headrest fairing extended to the cut-off tail, incorporating a left-side carburettor air-box plus an air outlet vent in the extreme tail. Similar vents were cut in the tail of each rear wheel hump and the twin exhaust pipes emerged through a neat transom slot, cut just left of centre.

Cooling was accomplished by a radiator mounted neatly in the nose section, which hinged with it as the nose was opened. Cooling air was ducted round the radiator from the nose intake, while behind the core a vee-shaped deflector despatched hot air up through a bonnet-top vent and half downwards through a vent in the undertray. The engine water pump drew cooling water through pipes strapped to the lower-left main chassis rail, similar pipes strapped to the top-right rail feeding return water from the headrest tank back to the radiator top. A spare wheel was bungee-strapped over the driver's shins in a three-piece steel cradle, and the battery was sited well forward in the radiator deflector. Overall this was a very neat little car, based on a 7 ft 5 in. wheelbase, with tracks front and rear of only 3 ft $9\frac{1}{2}$ in. and 3 ft 11 in. Overall length was 10 ft 10 in., width 4 ft 9 in. and height to headrest 2 ft 10 in. Ground clearance was listed as $4\frac{3}{4}$ in. and dry weight was only 896 lb. Fuel was carried in an 8-gallon aluminium tank strapped outboard just behind the right-front wheel, but a 14-gallon long tank could fit there if required.

With the driver and 8 gallons of fuel aboard, weight distribution front/rear was 44/56 per cent.

It was the little sports car's chopped-off Kamm tail which attracted most comment. It was Owen Maddock's idea: 'I'd been reading somewhere about this German aerodynamicist Professor Kamm and his theories about cutting off the rear of an aerofoil and making the airflow mimic its shape, so you get as low drag as with a long trailing section without the extra material and inconvenience it entailed. I don't think John ever really approved of its looks, but he told everybody we had to cut it off because it wouldn't fit in the transporter otherwise, and everybody was happy....'

At that time Eric Brandon was going his own way, Ginger Devlin building the first of his two ultra-low Halseylec sports cars which took their name from the telegraphic address of his electrical company.

Ivor Bueb drove the works' first Bob-tail in its debut race at Easter Monday Goodwood 1955. The little rear-engined 1100 finished third after an early battle with two 1500 Connaughts before they drew away. Several other 1500s were left in its wake.

A second works Bob-tail was completed for Jim Russell and the first customer car sold to Tommy Sopwith, registered NUO 400. In practice for May Silverstone 'Ivor the Driver' lapped faster than all other 1100 and 1500 cars and in the race he equalled Archie Scott-Brown's fastest 2-litre lap with the Lister-Bristol! Ivor finished ninth overall, ahead of all the 2-litre cars, and won the 1500 class from the Connaughts of Leston and McAlpine which had beaten him at Goodwood....

The Bob-tail sold for £1350 and such performances brought the orders rolling in. Leston's 1500 Connaught beat Bueb and Sopwith at Ibsley, but Ivor won at Brands Hatch, still with 1100 cc FWA power. Clearly the little Cooper's power-to-weight ratio was a match for the Connaught and at Crystal Palace Bueb slashed past Leston under braking near the finish to win the Anerley Trophy.

Lotus were still using MG power at this time, but Chapman realized that the Climax-powered Coopers had more to offer, and quickly followed their lead. Jim Russell shunted his new car at Snetterton, where Sopwith drove very well. Meanwhile Edgar Wadsworth and John Brown were having a Bob-tail prepared for Le Mans. It was trailed to the Sarthe at the last moment, with John Cooper and Harry Mundy in attendance. A new Lotus-Climax was running. It led the class, with the new Cooper third into the night. Then a water hose burst in the Bob-tail and under the regulations it had to complete another eight laps before water could be added. Somehow the little engine survived. The Lotus was disqualified for reversing against race direction after slithering into a sand-trap, and the class fell to two works Porsches with the inexperienced Cooper pair third. They were 21st and last overall, having lost some 2½ hours through the hose incident, but averaged 72.05 mph nonetheless. And Ivor Bueb shared the victorious Jaguar D type with Mike Hawthorn.

Sopwith won twice at Whitsun Goodwood, and Russell too at Snetterton. Meanwhile, Jack Brabham had arrived in Britain, encouraged to make the trip by Dean Delamont of the RAC, and he had been hurling the ex-Whitehead Cooper-Alta round in wild and woolly style. He had made his British debut at Easter Goodwood. Gregor Grant wrote then: 'This Aussie is certainly a presser-onner and possesses remarkable control over his car. More will be heard of this young gentleman....'

The lads at Hollyfield Road knew of his reputation down-under in the *RedeX Special*, and today recall the dark-tanned, taciturn young man quietly looking around, soaking up knowledge. He had driven hard for a fourth place at Ibsley in the New Forest only for the Alta engine to break before the finish; so he bought a Bristol unit to replace it. He had been keeping the car at Whitehead's racing shop in Motorwork garage at Chalfont St Peter, but now moved his worldly goods down to RJC at Saltdean. The Bristol engine was fitted there and the broken Alta returned to Geoffrey Taylor for repair. It was refitted late in the year, but Jack then took it home and sold it.

Meanwhile he joined the Cooper team more or less by osmosis. John explains: 'He didn't so much start working for us as just start working *with* us.... He just began coming in more often, and we got used to having him around. He acted as a kind of unpaid fitter-cum-welder-cum-driver – and he was bloody good at all of it....'

NEW BEGINNINGS — COVENTRY CLIMAX...

He was asked to drive the Cooper truck to Goodwood for early Bob-tail tests and was nabbed for speeding on the way. He gave Cooper's address and when the summons arrived John scrawled a note on it explaining that Mr Brabham was 'a temporary overseas visitor' and had since returned whence he came, leaving no forwarding address. Jack warmed to the friendly, pipe-smoking car builder and that spring began a major project in the Hollyfield works.

He was keen to build a Formula 1 version of the Bob-tail around a 2-litre six-cylinder Bristol engine. He persuaded John, and through him Charles, to let him use the works chassis jig. His wife Betty had arrived from Australia, and they stayed with Peter Morris, one of the RJC mechanics, for a fortnight before taking a flat in a private house on Ewell Road.

Douggie Johnson remembers him well: '... working quietly away on his own, welding-up his own chassis and building his Grand Prix car in one corner.' It was allegedly going to use a 2.2-litre Bristol engine modified like Bob Gerard's renowed *Libre* racing special. The Bob-tail frame was stretched 2 in. in wheelbase to accommodate the longer unit and the gearbox was modified by removing first gear. The car was so light that with over 140 bhp first would be unnecessary and it was in any case the weakest part of the system. Normal sports car road equipment – lights, etc. – was omitted and a virtually standard body fitted. Dean Delamont was keen to foster Brabham's career, and when the engine enlargement never happened a standard 2-litre was nodded through into the British GP, though official sources carefully quoted it as '2.2'. The F1 special was completed in a frantic rush the night

Perhaps the most significant single race in Cooper history, 25-lap RedeX Trophy, Snetterton, 13 August, 1955, saw this terrific duel between Moss's private Maserati 250F and Jack Brabham in his Cooper-Bristol Bob-tail special. While Vanwalls finished 1–2 driven by Schell and Wharton, Stirling set fastest lap and Jack – ferociously competitive for the first time at this level – was narrowly beaten by him for third. This performance determined the Australian to come back for more the following season, and dispelled any idea he might have had about going back home, and staying there ...

before the GP at Aintree. On race morning the clutch failed, so Jack had to start clutchless from the back of the grid. He boomed round unobtrusively until the engine overheated and put him out. This was a low-key debut for the rear-engined Formula 1 Cooper breed – nobody could be blamed for failing to read the writing on the wall.

Subsequently this Cooper-Bristol Bob-tail was properly sorted, and at Snetterton Jack had a wonderful battle with Moss's Maserati 250F. The Vanwalls were away first and second as they disputed third place. Jack Brabham: 'They called it "a classic contest" ... it was certainly a landmark for me. If it hadn't been for that race I might have gone back to Australia for good.... We raced in close company for about 16 laps, then the track started to dry and with about four laps to go I spun off when in front of Stirling.... I finished fourth.' He also raced the car at Brands, Charterhall and Crystal Palace before taking it down-under that autumn, on the *Himalaya*.

The pale-green car made its Australian debut at Bathurst on 1 October, but ran its bearings in practice. Two days later at Orange it led a prelim before an oil line blew and Jack coasted home second. The engine was damaged and he retired after one lap in the main event. A week later he won the Australian GP at Port Wakefield. At Auckland's Ardmore aerodrome circuit for the New Zealand GP in January 1956 Jack retired, then took second to Whitehead's Ferrari in the South Pacific Road Race Championship. After a final fling in the Victorian Trophy he sold the car to Reg Smith. The old car subsequently aroused little interest, going to Tasmania, where it was converted with lights and road equipment as a sports car. After long disuse it survives in remarkably good order with Frank Cengia of Hobart. Its chassis number is – perhaps predictably – *CB/1/55*.

Meanwhile back in Britain Bob-tail sports cars appeared with increasing success towards the end of 1955. At Crystal Palace on 30 July Colin Chapman's works Lotus-MG beat Bueb and Sopwith, who had a terrific tussle for second place in their Bob-tails. The Air Kruise Trophy at Brands on August Monday saw Chapman beat Russell in Heat One, and new Bob-tail owner Peter Gammon, a draper from Guildford, beat Bueb in Heat Two. Gammon's bare aluminium XPG 2 led Bueb and Chapman in the Final, but they forged ahead until Chapman's extra 400 cc gave him the lead. Near the end his engine ran rough and he was instantly swamped by Coopers; Bueb leading Russell home by 1.6 sec. for a works 1–2.

At Craigantlet hillclimb in Ulster, Chris Lindsay took two awards in the ex-Le Mans Bob-tail – apparently then registered SZ 4423 – and at Snetterton Roy Salvadori drove Sopwith's car in the meeting which saw the terrific Moss–Brabham duel. Roy had his doubts about handling a car 'with the engine in the wrong end', but soon found 'It was absolutely superb. I hadn't driven such a light car before. It could easily have been front-engined, it was so nicely balanced, but you could hang the tail out and it was so much better on brakes and road-holding. I was delighted with it. . . .'

He destroyed a quality field including John Coombs's powerful Lotus-Connaught, which was second. John Cooper noted Roy's prowess and talked to him about driving for the works in 1956. . . .

Down at Saltdean, Bob Chase's RJC Motors company had built a Bob-tail Bristol similar to Brabham's, but adapted for 2-litre sports car racing. Mike Keen drove it unpainted in its debut at August Brands Hatch, an outing best remembered for the car's new nose being crumpled in the paddock. Later that month Keen shared the car with Mike Anthony in the Goodwood 9-Hours. He was leading the 2-litre class when the car ran wide at high speed through Fordwater curve, cartwheeled along the verge and burned out. Mike Keen died.

The Bueb/Russell works car was second in class behind the well-driven Leston/Scott-Brown Connaught, and Watling-Greenwood/Barthel's Bob-tail was sixth. The Sopwith/Blond car failed.

Goodwood's enduro had its humorous side. Ivor Bueb had a promotional contract with Ribena, and in practice the works Bob-tail lurched and dived for the wall through the tight chicane. Ivor and Jim were discussing the problem with John in the pits when the Ribena man arrived and left some crates on the counter. The team were still deep in discussion when the BBC commentator arrived to ask what was happening. His hovering irritated John who was trying to brainstorm the problem. When he asked 'What's the trouble?' John straightened-up, gripped his pipe and explained confidentially, 'Well, it's the water pump – see that Ribena, we're putting it in the radiator because fruit juice lubricates the pump and has a higher boiling point than water. Good God man; you don't think we drink the stuff do you?'

The story went out verbatim and Beecham's, who produced Ribena, were not best pleased.

Ivor took a Bob-tail to Skarpnack, Sweden, to win a 2-litre race, while Salvadori and Russell were 1–2 at Oulton Park. The World Championship TT was held at Dundrod in September, when John entered two works cars, for Bueb with a friend of his from Cheltenham named Mike MacDowel and Russell/Dennis Taylor – and the O'Shea Racing Organisation fielded a third Bob-tail for Jim Mayers/Jack Brabham. On the third race lap, seven cars went missing, decimating the small-capacity classes. Glass manufacturer Jim Mayers had made a desperate attempt to pass a slow-driven Mercedes 300SL coupé, which had been holding back a whole queue of quick boys. He had lost control, rammed a gate-post and died as his Bob-tail disintegrated in a shower of blazing wreckage, which others ploughed into. Bill Smith died in his works Connaught and Jim Russell crashed avoiding the fires. Ivor Bueb and Mike MacDowel won their class and were fourth in the Index of Performance.

Bueb was really in tune with the Bob-tail by this time and he slaughtered the Lotus best at Castle Combe in October, but Chapman was avenged at Brands a week later. Lotus would eventually win the battle of the 1100 cc sports cars with their Mark 11, released the following year, but the Cooper-Climax Bob-tails had scooped most custom, and most success, in 1955. . . .

In addition to their original Bob-tail 1100, Sopwith's Equipe Endeavour had attacked the 1500 class with a Connaught-engined Bob-tail. This car ran at Snetterton in October 1955 driven by Reg Parnell, but he was plagued by clutch-slip and finished second behind Peter Gammon's regular 1100. Reg also drove Sopwith's Cooper-Jaguar there. At the Guild of Motoring Writers' Motor Show test day at Goodwood King Hussein of Jordan was a guest, and he drove the works Bob-tail under the respectful eye of John Cooper

NEW BEGINNINGS — COVENTRY CLIMAX...

and Ivor Bueb. A rear-engined Cooper sports car of a different hue was racing in the USA that season, Seattle VW dealer Pete Lovely having fitted a 1500 Porsche engine in the tail of his record car, known as the 'Pooper' in fact the ex-Grenzlandring-John Fox machine. At Grand Central, California, that November he actually beat two regular Porsche 550 sports racers.

Syd Greene of Gilby Engineering had ordered a Bob-tail for his 17-year-old son Keith. The car was late completing so for Keith's competition debut at Stapleford hillclimb in his home county of Essex they borrowed Bueb's works car. Keith — running the Ford C100 endurance project into 1983 — recalled: 'Alan Stacey was there with his very quick Lotus and when he saw me arrive he was thrilled to bits. "Here's my chance to beat a works Cooper," he said, but I beat him instead. We became the best of friends after that. . . .' Keith's own Bob-tail was registered 30 FVX when it arrived, using a Stage 1-tuned engine in 1956, uprating to Stage 2 for 1957. Other registration numbers identified for the cars from 1955 to 1957 include: LFR 419 W. A. Towse; 555 LRE 1956 works; TOL 444 Mr and Mrs Lionel Mayman; PHO 6 the ex-Leston 1956 car sold to Patsy Burt for 1957; J 31 Arthur Owen; XKX 1 Len and Bluebelle Gibbs; SZ 4425 — later 577 PRE — George Nixon/Alan Eccles; BSS 180 Tony Marsh; TOF 264 Tim Parnell; KNJ 800 J. F. Dougherty; RUB 406 G. H. Lambert/Chris Bristow 1957; and TMY 400 a third Sopwith car. In addition to 21 known UK registrations, including some recorded elsewhere in these pages, there were at least eight other British-based 'entities' plus those exported to the USA and down-under; total production was clearly in excess of 30 as an absolute minimum. . . . pro-

Latter-day RedeX *Special — Jack's 2-litre Bob-tail-Bristol in downunder warpaint during 1956 New Zealand GP, Auckland's Ardmore airfield circuit. He retired but had already won Australian GP with car at Port Wakefield. It still survives today*

bably nearer 50 including the 1956–57 numbers.

It had been a frantic time for everyone at Hollyfield Road. Owen Maddock: 'We worked regular 6½-day weeks doing the Cooper-Jaguars and central-seat 1100s and the 500s all at the same time, but I was pleased the way the Bob-tail worked out. I think I was one of the few people ever to ride in the passenger seat of one, with an Australian customer named Alan Mackay, up to a bed-and-breakfast near Silverstone. I drove one back from Brands too. It was the first time I'd ever driven over 100 mph. . . .'

Jim Russell enjoyed the Bob-tail too, but in later years found its successor, the Monaco, even better. He has obvious affection for his Cooper days and recalls Owen's devotion to duty: 'You'd just have set your car up nicely in a *big* slide aiming at a marker tub somewhere and suddenly you'd spot his big black beard jutting out from behind it. He was lying on his tummy watching how his cars behaved. . . .'

Another time Jim had come to Hollyfield Road with Reg Tanner of Esso to sort out a contract after declining an offer from Lotus. 'We were in Charles's office when one of the girls knocked at the door and said a young man had arrived for an interview for a job. Charles just asked "Has he got a beard?" and when she said "Yes" he said "Send 'im home, I've got enough trouble with the one I've got!". . .'

CHAPTER THIRTEEN

More Bob-tails – and beyond

The successes of the Bob-tail Cooper-Climax during 1955 made the adoption of full 1500 cc engines an obvious move for 1956. Another attraction was the knowledge that a new 1500 cc Formula 2 would begin on 1 January, 1957, and that a number of dress-rehearsal races would be run under these rules during the coming season.

Coventry Climax had impressed customers with the standard of their engines and service back-up. They had delivered seven prototype 1100 cc FWAs during 1954 and had put through a production batch of 100 in 1955, selling for £250 each. Now Climax laid down a larger number of FWAs, plus 24 enlarged 76.2 × 80 mm, 1460 cc FWBs. Head design was unchanged despite the enlarged bore and stroke. Output was 100 bhp at 6000 rpm with a little extra mid-range torque, but for Formula 2 the single-cam FWB was to be merely a stop-gap until a new twin-cam head could be developed.

At Hollyfield Road, the 1956 Mark II Bob-tails carried 10 in.-diameter brakes within new eight-spoke four-stud-fixing cast-magnesium road wheels designed by Owen Maddock and separate from either drum or disc brake options. The cockpit was enlarged slightly, the opening widened and the screen moved forward. To save weight 22-gauge Duraluminum body panels replaced the original aluminium. Heavier rear dampers were adopted to prevent wandering at high speed. Works drivers were to be Roy Salvadori and Ivor Bueb's protégé Mike MacDowel, while Jack Brabham had sold his rear-engined Cooper-Bristol to finance a return to Britain, and he arrived to buy the Owen Organisation's Maserati 250F. This very special car had been bought to give Owen's BRM team 2½-litre race experience while their own new F1 design was being completed. Its purchase – like that of the Cooper-Alta – was a terrible mistake for Jack, but again John Cooper came to his rescue.

Sports car racing up to 1500 cc that year was dominated by Cooper versus Lotus, with Porsche and OSCA playing a major part in Europe. No production records of any kind seem to have survived for the Bob-tailed Coopers, but most of those who helped build the cars seem to think perhaps as many as 40 or 50 may have been completed. Several were sold in kit form for their new owners to complete, and many were exported. American interest in Coopers was growing. A hardy few, including names like Tippy Lipe, Cliff Ricker, John Fox and Alexis du Pont, had invested in 500s and now the rear-engined sports car began to appeal to this highly sports car-orientated nation. Two Bob-tail 1100s were entered under the Cooper Car Company name in the 1956 Sebring 12-Hours, driven by Cracraft/Byron and Ed Hugus/ John Bentley. The former pair finished only 21st overall but won their class, while Hugus/Bentley went out after 117 laps with dynamo failure and a flat battery.

John entered three works Bob-tails for the Goodwood Easter meeting listed with 1460 cc FWB engines for Salvadori and Jim Russell while Mike MacDowel's ran a 1098 cc FWA. During practice, John invited Stirling Moss to sample Salvadori's car and he was impressed enough to order one for himself, rather to his mechanic Alf Francis's disgust. On the Monday, Salvadori and Russell scored a works 1–2 in the 1500 cc sports car race, with Les Leston third in the Willment Speed Shop's gaily striped new Bob-tail FWB. Reg Bicknell's works Lotus was fourth, but more Bob-tails – Bueb's Ecurie Demi-Litre entry and MacDowel's works cars – were fifth and sixth.... The works FWB drivers shared fastest lap at 1:38.8, only 3 sec slower than Moss's best in the unlimited race driving a 3-litre works Aston Martin.

Goodwood had its tragic side, for immensely popular Bert Rogers of Cooper-Bristol *Mucky Pup* fame, crashed his replacement Tojeiro-Bristol and was killed instantly. Tony Dennis also died there that day in a D type Jaguar.

At Brands Hatch, Peter Gammon's very carefully prepared lightweight Bob-tail won two races, with FWA power, and Cooper cars won every race on the programme; Hall, Bridger and Wicken victorious in 500s, and Gammon in the two sports car races. A young De Havilland aircraft engineer named Maurice Phillippe was sixth in one of these, driving his monocoque MPS-Ford special.... Ten years later he would be designing epochal Lotus Formula 1 cars for Colin Chapman.

Two weeks later the important British Empire Trophy meeting at Oulton Park saw ten Bob-tails competing, driven by Moss, Salvadori, Russell, Bueb, Dennis Taylor, Leston, Gammon, Tony Marsh, George Nixon and New Zealand Speedway star Ronnie Moore. Moss's car was MacDowel's RDG 474 re-engined with an FWB and entered by the works.

The British Empire Trophy was an important but curious race, organized in three varying capacity class Heats and a

MORE BOB-TAILS — AND BEYOND

Bob-tail Mark II under assembly at Hollyfield Road, 1956, showing its enlarged 10-in. instead of mere 8-in. diameter front brake drums, Climax FWA/FWB engine on twin SUs, banana-section cooling system headrest header tank, barrel-at-bottom damper mounting etc. Convoluted hose takes water runs low on left/high on right between engine and nose radiator which mounted within nose body section and hinged open with it

Left *Equipe Moss on parade at Hollyfield Road with van donated by Standard Motor Co Ltd of Coventry and Mark II Bob-tail freshly-completed under Alf Francis' steely eye. The car shows its slightly enlarged cockpit compared to original Mark Is, faired-in mirror mounting and top-ducted radiator layout, allowing cooling air to enter through the nose aperture, pass through radiator matrix, then exit over body's upper surface*

combined handicap Final. In the 1500 cc Heat Ivor Bueb led from the flag, but only as far as Druid's Corner, where he rolled his Bob-tail out of the race. Chapman's Lotus 11 went on to win from Salvadori, Hawthorn in Bueb's Lotus 11 and Moss. Heat Two was for 1501–2700 cc cars and Heat Three for over 2700s. In the Final the 1500s were given a 15 sec start from the 2700s and 40 sec from the unlimiteds. Moss took the lead and fought long but unsuccessfully to hold off Colin Chapman. But the Lotus constructor led only briefly before spinning, so Stirling won with Colin second. Salvadori was third, Hawthorn fourth and Leston and Russell 5–6 for Cooper-Climax. The first six cars all ran FWB engines.

Meanwhile Moss's own Bob-tail was being completed at Hollyfield Road under Alf Francis's eye. He took it to Modena and fitted Weber carburettors, rather to Climax's disgust for Walter Hassan in particular took a dim view of customers playing around with the specification of his engines, and twin SUs were the standard wear. Stirling gave the car – registered BPB 777 in deference to his sponsors and his own superstitions concerning the number '7' – its debut at the Aintree '200' meeting. Fortunately he won the main F1 race in his Maserati because the new Bob-tail was a disas-

Les Leston's multi-hued Willment Speed Shop-entered Bob-tail Mark II hustling round North Tower Crescent at London's Crystal Palace parkland circuit with Stirling Moss wrestling his ill-handling sister car behind. Charles Cooper was convinced Alf Francis' fitting Weber carburettors to the Climax FWB engine in place of its original SUs had upset handling by altering engine's response and torque curve. Jack Brabham and Alf subsequently discovered otherwise...

Engine bay of ex-Moss car still on Webers but owned late '56 by Robin Mackenzie-Low. This shot shows Mark II Bob-tail's latest-style Owen Maddock-designed eight-spoke Cooper cast-magnesium bolt-on wheels, replacing earlier Colin Darby-designed ex-500 cc type used on Mark Is. Early-type Citroën-ERSA gearbox is also visible, offering normally four forward speeds without reverse – which was quite illegal in international racing though few people really seemed to care – though reverse was later fiddled-in. Complex gearchange linkage required at this time is visible above 'curly-leaf'

ter in the 1500 cc sports car event, handling murderously badly. He was placed fifth, way behind Hawthorn's winning Ecurie Demi-Litre Lotus and Salvadori's second-place Cooper. Colin Chapman won the 1100 race in his Lotus, heading the Bob-tails of Gammon, MacDowel and hill-climber Tony Marsh.

While Francis wrestled with the problems of Moss's new Bob-tail, Stirling won the BRDC International Trophy for Vanwall, and the 1500 sports car race there saw 11 Bob-tails in a field of 21. Jim Russell was unable to take part and John gave Brabham his car instead. It became the only Cooper to retire – with gearbox failure – after Jack had been harrying Chapman's Lotus for second place, in Roy Salvadori's wake. Chapman spun again, promoting the Australian to second place, and then the gearbox bug struck. Roy won easily, setting fastest lap at 1:49.00, 96.67 mph, Leston and Taylor placed 3–4 and Gammon won the 1100 class from MacDowel and Marsh – a Cooper-Climax 1–2–3.

Today, living in Monte Carlo, Roy recalls the 1500 Bob-tail with immense pleasure: 'The extra power made all the difference and that Kamm-tail body helped enormously I am sure, the slight lip at the tail perhaps forming the original "spoiler"? The car was very small and low and very light for the time, and handled too good for words. It was also

MORE BOB-TAILS — AND BEYOND

Later years: ex-Moss ex-Mackenzie-Low, Jimmy Blumer's Bob-tail, 1957, Mallory Park, chased hard by Hon Edward Greenall's Lotus 11, the sophisticated lightweight which would topple the Bob-tails' grasp on their class. In background is David Shale in his ex-Sopwith Equipe Endeavour Cooper-Jaguar Mark II, the car originally planned to use Blackburn-Turbomeca gas-turbine power! Jimmy's Bob-tail sold subsequently to the Jim Russell Racing Drivers' School, who removed body, amputated overhanging cross-hoops and converted it into open-wheeler training car. This was fate of several Bob-tails. Few survive today despite quantity production

immensely quick, almost too quick for a 1500. There was super torque from that engine, and the body shape I am sure was great... I really loved it....'

Over Whitsun Lotus reigned supreme, with Chapman's new works Mark II winning at both Brands and Goodwood. But despite Lotus' resurgence the Bob-tails' season included three wins in a day for Leston in the Willment Speed Shop car at Oulton Park, two in the day for Gammon at Brands and Bueb victorious there on August Monday. Ivor's Ecurie Demi-Litre mechanic Pip Preece: 'He really liked that central-seater — it was a car he could do almost anything with. It was works built and we had a works mechanic looking after it while I prepared the 500s and the Lotus 11 which we ran for Mike Hawthorn. Late in the year at Oulton Park, Mike somersaulted the Lotus right over Roy Salvadori's works Bob-tail and left a scrape in Roy's crash helmet! Mike was only bruised but with good reason, Roy retired — he was pink round the gills after coming that close....' The works mechanic was Gordon Whitehead.

For Le Mans 1956 John was approached by the enthusiastic ex-Sebring American amateurs Ed Hugus and John Bentley. Revised regulations now demanded two properly accessible seats, and a Le Mans special Bob-tail was built-up for them at Hollyfield, with extra stiffening longerons passed through the cockpit centreline, leaving space either side for suitable driving and passenger seats. The little car was finished in American white and blue and they survived the 24-Hour grind to finish eighth overall, and second in class to the winning Lotus 11. They were reckoned to have covered 2102 miles and averaged 87.607 mph, finishing only nine miles behind the Hornsey car. John Bentley would meet John again in the Seventies and pen *The Grand Prix Carpet baggers* with him, which is virtually a tape transcript of John's many humorous memories of the Cooper Car Company's life.

Charles Cooper and George Saunders took the works Bob-tails to several Continental races. Roy won handsomely at Oporto in Portugal, and later he and Jack Brabham finished 5–6 at Avus in Berlin, outclassed by the Porsches and East German AWEs. Still Roy had lapped almost as fast as them in practice but '... we had overheating trouble. The Porsche people wouldn't believe we only had a 1500 and when we had to strip the engine down and renew the head seal – Jack doing the work as usual in a garage by the track – von Hanstein and Trips came in to have a look; I'm sure just to see how big the bores and pistons really were. In the race a wishbone bent, the cars couldn't stand that banking, and we had to slow down as the handling went to pot....'

In the 1500 cc sports car race supporting the German GP at Nürburgring Hans Herrmann's works Porsche was uncatchable, but Roy harried it mercilessly in his Bob-tail and held Moss's works Maserati 1500S at bay: 'My car was very much quicker on the straight but it didn't handle as well as I'd expected over the bumps. In no time at all the wishbones were bending and the dampers were fairly clapped. I was always able to pass Stirling on the straight, but towards the end the car became lethal so I had to let him go and settle for third. I think the Cooper's speed shook Stirling though.... At Oporto, on a smoother surface, the little car was in its element and won without much trouble. It was superb fun to drive, especially on a good surface....'

The new F2 single-seat Cooper, derived from the Bob-tail, made its debut at Silverstone in the mid-season British GP meeting, and later in the year Jack Brabham was fully established as team driver-cum-mechanic-cum-general dogsbody. When he asked Charles and John if there was any chance of a proper works drive for 1957 Charles's response was typical: 'Yeah – you can 'ave a works drive. You can drive the transporter down to Imola!'

A major international sports car meeting was held there on 30 September, and the Lotus and Cooper visitors gave the local OSCA and Maserati brigade a nasty fright. Cliff Allison's Lotus and Salvadori's Cooper harried Castellotti's leading OSCA until the Lotus broke a hub-shaft and the Bob-tail its distributor drive. Jack inherited second place in his Bob-tail. Denis Jenkinson reported: 'Although the British cars had stirred things up at Imola they all suffered from inexperience of the more serious type of road racing, bits falling off, shock-absorbers failing, engines proving fragile or gearboxes not being meant for racing.... Now that the works Cooper and Lotus cars are beginning to tackle the Italians on their home ground there is every opportunity of sweeping the field, but more care and attention will have to be given to the job. The British contingent at Imola did not disgrace itself by any means; in fact it created an excellent impression for a change, but preparation and know-how is far from perfect....' For the first time in years here were two British teams who were willing and able to learn.

Jack also learned at Imola 'what life might be like as a Cooper works driver'. They had taken the third Bob-tail there for the Australian tourist driver Alan Mackay and late in practice its gearbox broke, the casing split and Jack had to weld it back together and rebuild the internals: 'So I worked virtually all night and didn't get to bed at all. In the morning John came down and the car was just about complete and everyone wanted to get to the circuit. My car hadn't even been looked at. By the time we started the race I was ready for bed, and I had just begun to realize how much hard work motor racing could be....'

Meanwhile Moss had entered his Bob-tail 1500 at Crystal Palace for its first race since its hapless Aintree debut. In the meantime it had been carefully checked at Hollyfield Road but seemed perfect. At the Palace when Stirling again rubbished its handling Charles bluntly blamed the Weber carburettors; 'They've altered the engine's characteristics and up-

Great race – Roy Salvadori drove as hard as he knew how in 1500 cc sports car event supporting 1956 German GP, Nürburgring. While Hans Herrmann's works Porsche had long gone in the lead he harried Moss's factory Maserati mercilessly until the bumps wore-out his Mark II-FWB's dampers, it became unmanageable, and he had to settle for third

set the handling. . . .' Alf Francis began to feel persecuted as he refitted SUs and Stirling won, but only after driving like a demon to hold off Leston. When Alf asked him what to do with the car Stirling replied crisply 'sell it'.

A week later Alf and Jack Brabham tested the car at Brands and discovered the problem. The chassis had been misaligned in its original jig and the front spring was bottoming out against the damper brackets. Packing pieces raised the spring and Jack then claimed the car felt as good as his works machine.

A last-minute entry was made at Reims in the 1500 cc 12-Hours race supporting the French GP. Stirling was to share it with Phil Hill, and set best practice time. He led the first half-hour, at least 5 sec per lap faster than the opposition, but then the FWB engine ran rough. Phil took over, but soon retired with overheating caused by running lean in the hot high-speed conditions. The following weekend saw Peter Jopp handling the car at Rouen, but on his first race lap he rolled it spectacularly, possibly due to an unscrubbed new tyre having just been fitted. Alf Francis left Equipe Moss, and went to work for Rob Walker at Pippbrook Garage in Dorking, Surrey. Coopers were not yet out of his hair. . . .

The Moss Bob-tail was repaired and sold to Robin Mackenzie-Low, in whose ownership the original BPB 777 registration was curiously reversed to 777 BPB. At Oulton Park in August the car was one of nine Bob-tails facing Moss in the gaily striped Willment machine, its usual driver Les Leston having spiked his foot on a nail. Stirling won after the Hawthorn–Salvadori attempt at mirror aerobatics already described, beating two Lotus 11s, and Brabham fourth for the works.

Towards the end of October, after the Avus and Imola outings, George Saunders trucked the works Bob-tails way south to Rome's Castelfusano circuit, stopping off on the way at Monza, where the Jerseymen Arthur Owen and Bill Knight were attacking records in their car – see Appendix. In the combined 1100–1500 cc race at Castelfusano, Roy led until sidelined early on by electrical trouble. Les Leston took over in his Bob-tail until its water pump failed and Luigi Musso won for OSCA. Arthur Owen's heavyweight special Bob-tail was the fourth 1100 home. In the accompanying 750 cc racing car event Colin Davis's Cooper won, the sister cars driven by Vroomen and Dave Latchford 5–7.

The original ex-Equipe Moss Bob-tail was sold subsequently through Ian Raby's Car Exchange at Brighton to north-easterner Jimmy Blumer, who had been racing the ex-Peter Gammon MG TC, a Jaguar XK120 and an Austin-Healey 100S. Jimmy became an enthusiastic Cooper owner-driver, and recalls: '. . . I paid £1150 for the Moss car and drove it up from Brighton on the road. It was a fantastic fun car and gave me a lot of groundwork in race driving during 1957. Its worst feature was that dreadful ERSA gearbox – awful thing. Eventually I sold it to Jim Russell for his school and they cut the outrigger hoops off the frame and converted it to an open-wheeled single-seater, along with several similar Bob-tails – I bought a Lotus 11 in its place. . . .'

In effect this conversion from Bob-tail sports to slipper-bodied single-seater was what formed Cooper's first water-cooled rear-engined Formula 2 car in midsummer 1956. It was the move which set them on the road to the World Championship. . . .

Works Bob-tail Mark II-FWB in the Sudkehre *turn at* Avus *in* Grosser Preis von Berlin *sports car race, 16 September, 1956 – Jack Brabham tigering hard to compensate for the super-streamlined speed of the East German AWE* Rennkollektiv *entries sandwiching him, driven by Arthur Rosenhammer (11) and Egon Binner (12). Up ahead, team-mate Roy Salvadori placed fifth, Jack finally sixth. This season saw the Cooper Car Company's first serious forays abroad other than as a Formula 3 team*

CHAPTER FOURTEEN

First in Formula 2

After the CSI announced that from 1 January, 1957, a new 1500 cc unsupercharged Formula 2 class would be recognized internationally, the British Racing Drivers' Club was quick to recognize its potential and organize a race to the forthcoming regulations as part of their programme for the British GP meeting at Silverstone on 14 July, 1956.

Charles and John Cooper immediately recognized the customer potential of Formula 2. The Climax FWB single-cam engine would suit and there was a twin-cam-headed version on the way for 1957. A Cooper-Climax F2 was projected simply by amputating the body outriggers from the Bob-tail frame and fitting a single-seat slipper body and FWB engine.

Owen redrew the frame just wide enough to accommodate the driver. It looked much like the Mark X 500s, but at 40 lb bare it was around 15 lb lighter, due largely to the simpler engine mountings for a smooth-running four-cylinder water-cooled unit. Transverse-leaf suspension reappeared fore-and-aft with 'curly leaf' location. Many parts were interchangeable with the 1100–1500 Bob-tails; wheelbase and tracks were identical.

Fuel was housed ahead of the cockpit around the driver's legs; one tank in the scuttle and two more on either side. Ahead of them lay the battery for the 6-volt coil ignition and fuel pumps, and the radiator with ducting to exhaust hot air through the suspension cut-outs either side. The radiator mounted in the nose cone, and hinged with it. The FWB engine was behind the cockpit in unit with the Citroën-ERSA four-speed and reverse transaxle, with its wider third and fourth gear wheels than used in 1100 Bob-tail trim. This separation of major masses throughout the length of the frame was aimed at raising the polar moment of inertia slightly to give a more stable platform.

The gearchange linkage was complicated by the narrow frame. It was impossible to arrange a straight run like the sports car's, so reverse-motion levers were used, pivoted on the left side behind the seat and operated via a cross-shaft beneath the seat from the right-hand lever to an ingenious spring-loaded cam arrangement zeroing on neutral. This linkage then operated the main change-rods passing aft to the driver's left. The under-seat cross-shaft both rotated and slid axially to select the required ratio.

The slipper body was beaten and rolled in 18-gauge aluminium, arranged clamshell style. The upturned nose shape jarred, but Owen chose it to centre the intake's horizontal axis with that of the radiator within. The water header tank was fitted to lugs welded onto the chassis hoop, which formed roll-over protection behind the cockpit.

The latest cast-magnesium wheels were fitted, around separate finned drum brakes in the first prototype, while John announced that discs would be optional in production.

Alcohol fuels were forbidden in the new Formula, so premium grade pump fuel promised modest fuel consumption. It was hoped that the new Cooper-Climax would survive a 200-mile race on only 12 gallons. Weight distribution, with five gallons of fuel aboard plus a 170 lb driver, was said to be 43/57 front/rear. Dry weight was just 694 lb, which with the SU-carbureted FWB's 100 bhp meant 323 bhp per ton. Frontal area was a tiny $5\frac{1}{2}$ sq ft. The twin-cam Climax FPF then under development promised 425 bhp per ton and *The Autocar* rightly predicted: 'This should produce an exceptional performance ... the twin-camshaft FPF engine on many circuits will permit top speeds approximating to those achieved by the present Formula 1 cars.'

Roy Salvadori drove this first prototype Cooper-Climax F2 Mark I car at Silverstone in the dress-rehearsal race at the British GP meeting. He qualified easily on pole against a field of stripped sports cars running on pump fuel less lights, dyna-

Towards the big time – John Cooper tries first prototype 'T41' or Formula 2 Mark I for size in the Hollyfield Road shop. The frame shows family affinity with concurrent Bob-tail sports. Welded aluminium fuel tank is visible alongside John's legs. Drum brakes are retained, and gearchange still uses Ford Zephyr column lever, straight off the shelf.... The stub axles were also humble Ford saloon components but they did the job and continued to take the strain until the advent of Alford & Alder forgings as employed by Standard-Triumph

Ready to go at Silverstone – Roy Salvadori watching the rev counter as mechanic Gordon Whitehead tunes twin SU carburettors. The car had been very hastily completed and rushed to Silverstone just in time for the meeting

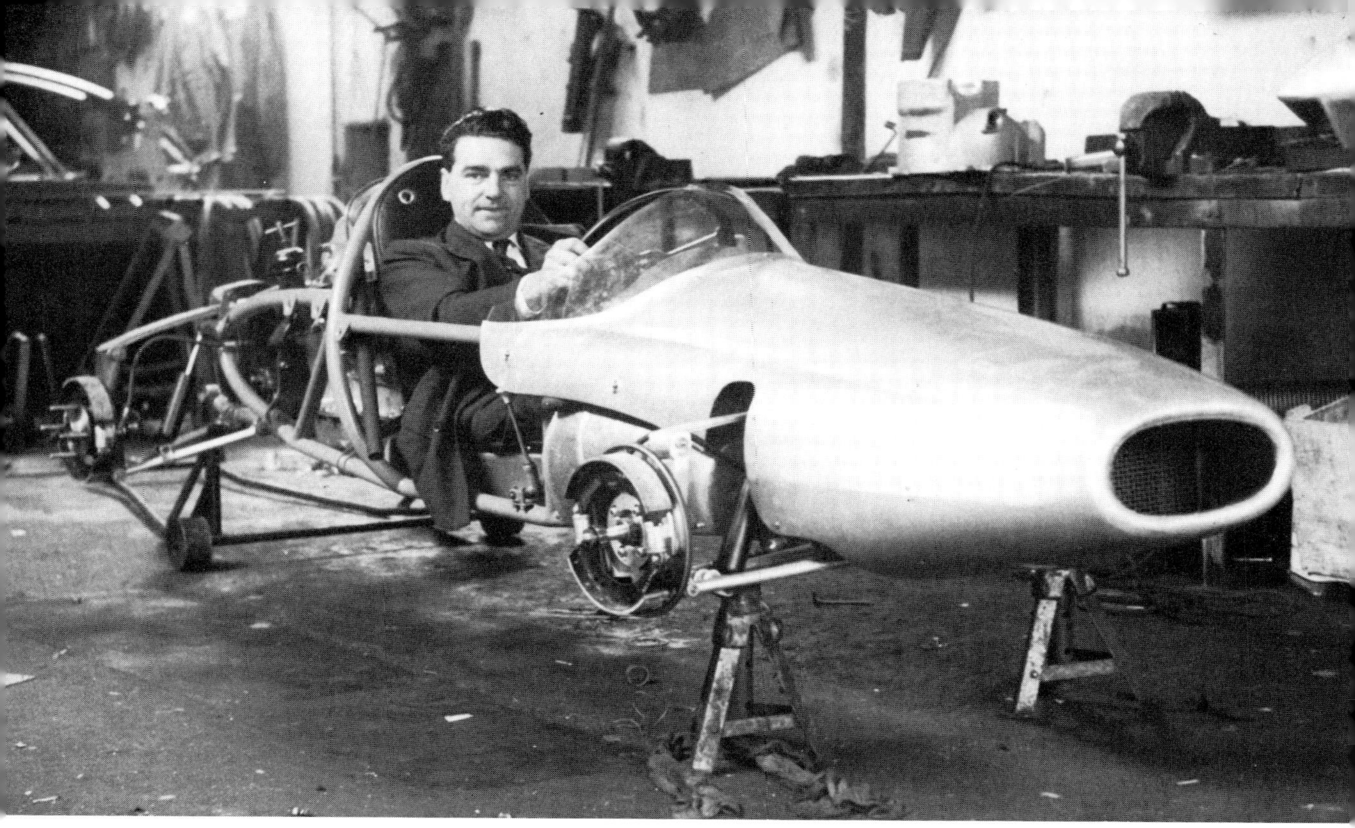

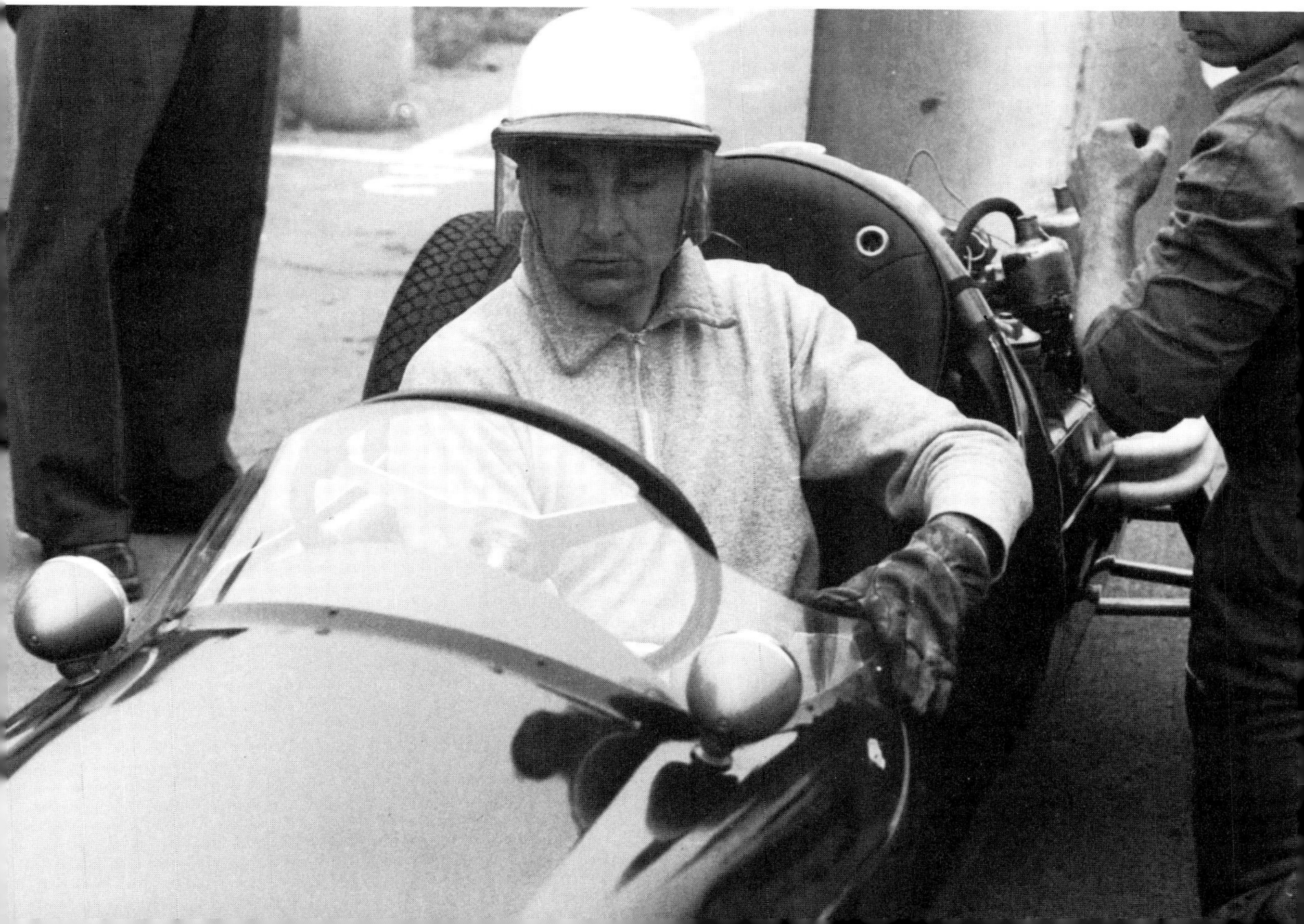

COOPER CARS

Left *Winning first time out against a field largely composed of stripped sports-racing cars the prototype Cooper-Climax Mark I F2 excelled through the corners as the Lotus 11s were much faster along the straights. Roy always went well at the airfield circuit. An air intake scoop is visible beneath the cockpit, feeding engine bay*

Right *Mark Is at Oulton: Tony Brooks hurtled round to take pole position in Rob Walker's machine during practice but could not match Salvadori's race pace in the works car. This shot spells out the extreme simplicity of the new Cooper F2. Hardly any photos of Ken Wharton's Mark I have been published. Here he is at Lodge Corner in his BRG car, built at Hollyfield by his mechanic Bill Blyth, on the way to fifth place. Owen Maddock styled the upturned nose cone to place the intake centreline level with the radiator core centre. John didn't altogether approve . . . the aerodynamic effect may be imagined, though it was evidently not as bad as one might expect*

Below *The £1000 first prize for the Oulton Park Gold Cup race in September set many eyes a'popping, but Cooper scooped the pool. Here at the start Tony Brooks lags on pole position in Rob Walker's new Mark I while a determined Salvadori, head down, takes an immediate lead. Third fastest in practice, Jack Brabham crouches even lower in his unpainted works Mark I while behind Brooks on row two Ken Wharton is just visible in his new privately-owned sister car*

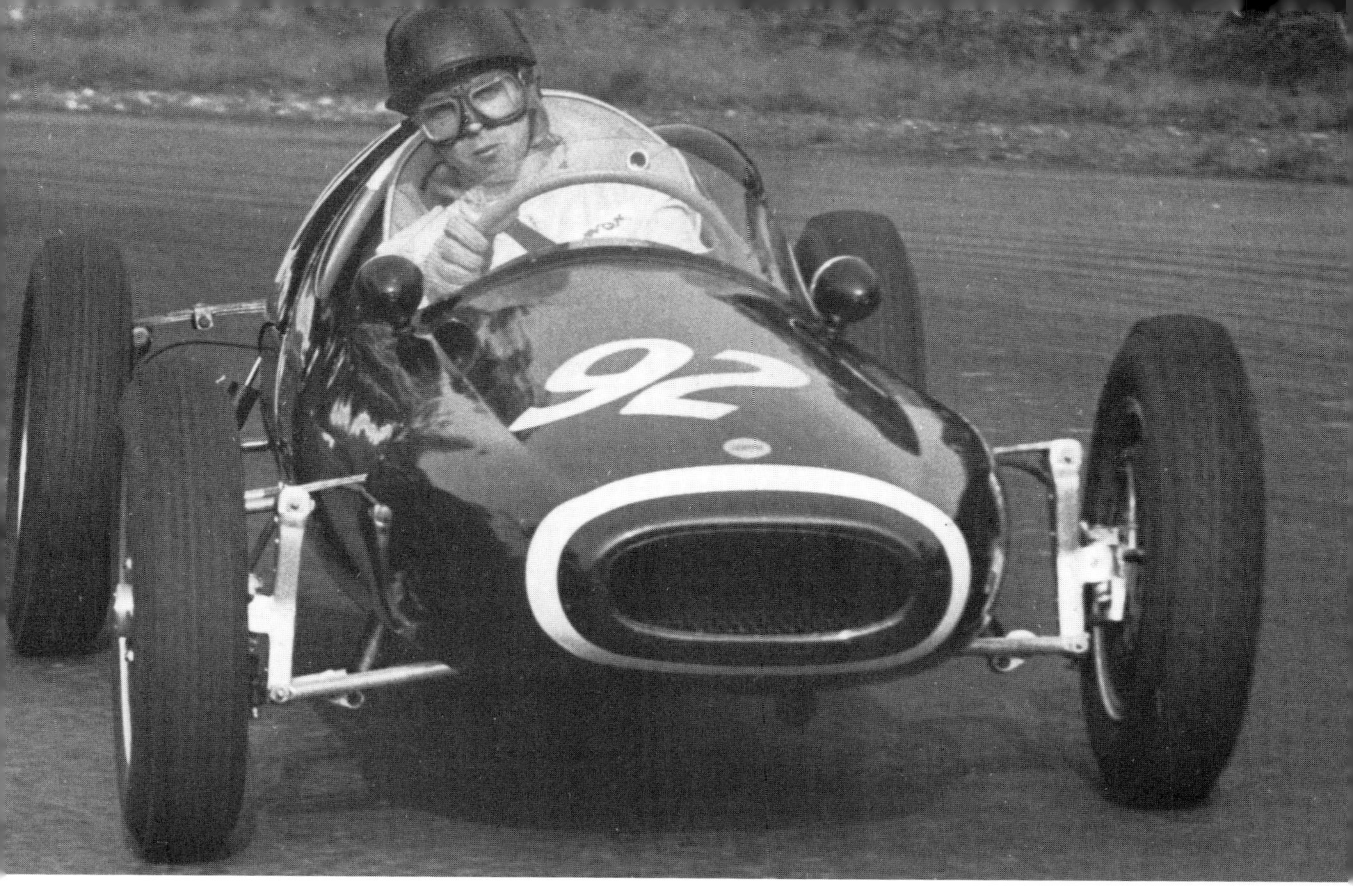

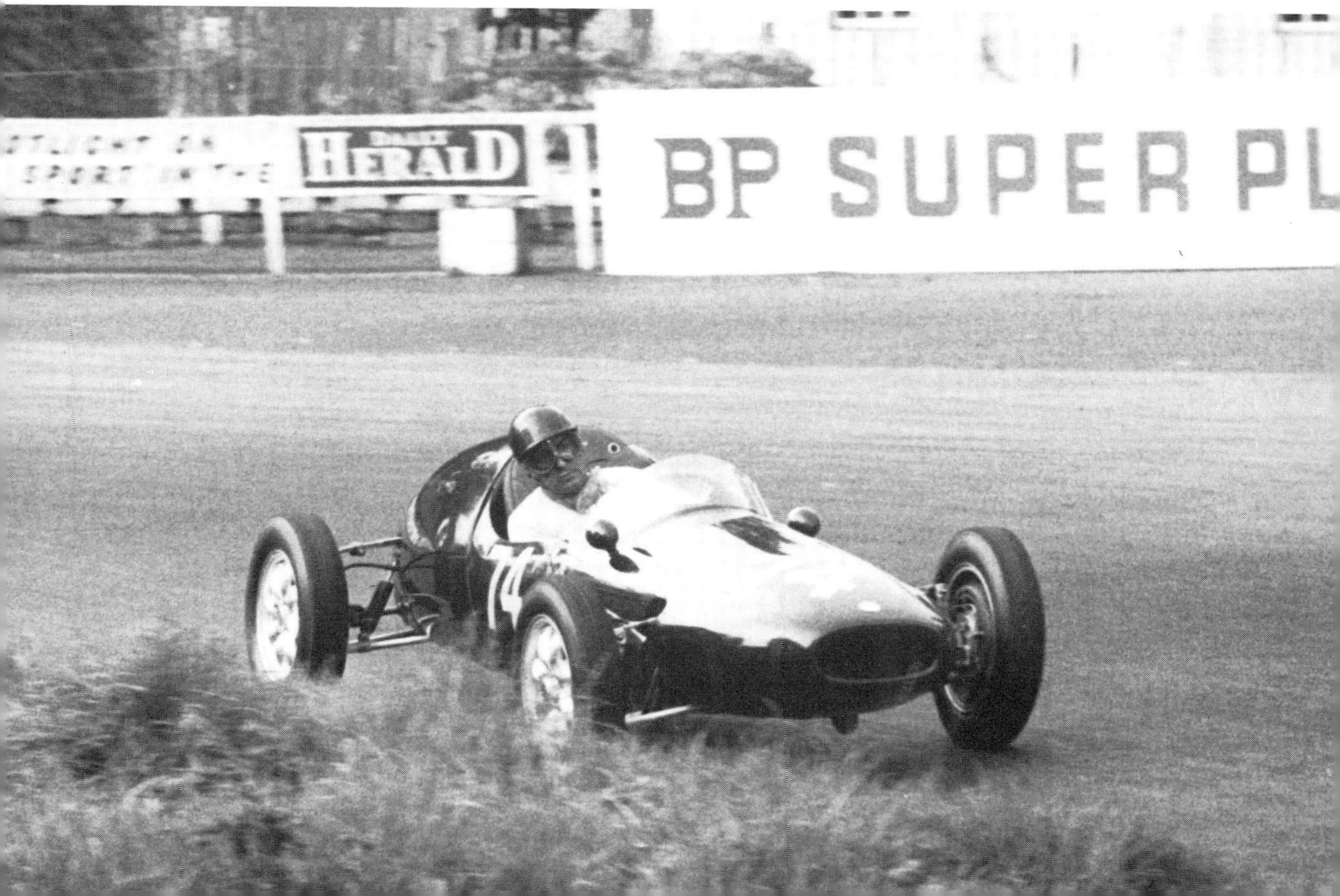
HERALD
BP SUPER PL

mos, etc. His time of 1:49.0, 95.79 mph, compared with Moss's GP pole of 1:41.0 and equalled a BRM and a Vanwall on row five of the GP grid. André Pilette's elderly Gordini was the only other open-wheeled single-seater in the race, but Roy's Cooper had suffered handling problems pre-race. Mark X 500 springs hurriedly fitted at the last moment minimized them, and the prototype car had actually been finished-off hurriedly with reference to Theo Page's part-imaginary cutaway drawing in *Autosport*!

Roy followed Chapman's Lotus 11 gently off the line, took the lead after nine of the 25 laps and won by over 30 seconds. Chapman set fastest lap and his sports-bodied Lotus was clocked at 123.71 mph down Hangar Straight, against the open-wheeled Cooper's 119.21 mph.

Three weeks later, August Brands saw the Mark I racing again, but rain swept the course, and in a preceding sports car event Roy smashed the works Bob-tail against a marshal's post. He emerged unaware that tenderness in his chest announced two broken ribs. He still won the F2 race easily in the Mark I from Bicknell's Lotus and Dennis Taylor's Bob-tail, and was third behind two 2½-litre Connaughts in a *Libre* race before being carted off to hospital as the pain became unbearable.

Jack Brabham took over the single-seater for part two of the *Libre* event and was third again, behind the Scott-Brown and Leston Connaughts. It was the nut-brown Australian's first race in a rear-engined Cooper-Climax open-wheeler.

Meanwhile the first customer order had been placed by that enthusiastic private entrant Rob Walker. He was great-great-grandson of Johnny Walker of whisky fame and after racing cars like a TT Lea-Francis, Austin Sevens, a 'flat-iron' Thomas Special and a pair of Delahayes around the war he later began entering various cars for other drivers once he had promised his new wife that he would not race himself. His Scots-blue cars with their white nosebands had been handled by Tony Rolt, Reg Parnell, Peter Walker and Peter Collins and were exquisitely prepared and maintained in his Pippbrook Garage business at Dorking. Now Rob ordered an F2 Cooper-Climax, which he invited Tony Brooks – just recovered from a crunching BRM crash at Silverstone – to drive for him.

While the car was being completed, John Cooper loaned Walker the works car for the Brighton Speed Trials. They both drove and perhaps diplomatically Rob was quicker; second in the 1500 cc racing car class behind Instone's blown Djinn Special. Incidentally one L. H. Pittaway ran an ancient Aston-Butterworth, owned by W. C. Jackson, in this meeting.

The following weekend saw the BARC September Goodwood, where Salvadori set fastest time during practice of all 68 cars at the meeting – 1:36.8 – and won both his races in the F2 prototype as he pleased: getting down to a lap of 1:35.4, 90.57 mph.

On 22 September the Oulton Park Gold Cup was run for Formula 2 with *The Daily Herald* offering £1000 first prize. Four F2 Mark Is did battle; the original prototype and an unpainted second car entered by the works, plus the glistening new blue-and-white Walker car and another private entry for Ken Wharton in opposition.

The works Lister single-seater was withdrawn, so the field was completed by 11 Lotus sports-cars, 11 Bob-tails, Ian Burgess's new Beart-Rodger *monoposto* with OSCA engine, an Elva and Horace Richards' elderly HAR special.

The works FWBs ran 11:1 high-compression heads, while Walker's was standard, but Brooks's delicate skills still gave it pole position, 0.4 faster than Roy and 0.6 ahead of Brabham in the other works car. Chapman's Lotus took fourth place on the outside of the front row, with Wharton on row two.

Alf Francis, Walker's new race mechanic, admits he ruined Brooks's chances in the race. He fitted a brand-new set of tyres and after the warm-up lap the young Dukinfield dentist was asking, 'What *have* you done?!' Its handling felt ruined,

Tiddler: Jack's Mark I sets off in 1957 Australian GP, Caversham aerodrome, Perth, flanked by Lex Davison's towering Ferrari 500/750 4-cylinder. The little F2 'bug' placed third

Opposite *Heavy metal thundering off the line to start the Lady Wigram Trophy race on the operational RNZAF aerodrome outside Christchurch, 1957, with Mark Is of Syd Jensen and Jack Brabham (3) rushing off behind. Leading here is Reg Parnell's 3-litre engined* Squalo *Ferrari (4) flanked by Ron Roycroft's 4½-litre Ferrari 375 V12 (19) with Parnell's team-mate Peter Whitehead's sister* Squalo *(5) behind and Horace Gould's Maserati 250F (2) on far side. Whitehead won from Brabham, Jensen finished fifth*

Brooks was put off his stroke, and Salvadori tore off into a start-to-finish demonstration to win the £1000. Brooks and Brabham duelled in his wake until Jack's fuel pump lead came adrift – John believes because his young son Geoffrey had been bouncing up and down in the car's seat before the race.... Roy won from Brooks with Brabham 20th to secure the team prize for Cooper – another £250. Charles was ecstatic.... Wharton finished fifth.

Another unofficial F2 race took place at Brands on 14 October, where in late-autumn sunshine a claimed 37,000 crowd saw Brooks win in the Walker car. Alf Francis ran it on part-worn tyres and fitted his favourite Italian Tipo Mona fuel pump, which 'definitely improved performance. Where previously the power had dropped off at 5800 rpm it now kept going to 6500 rpm and over....' Brabham's works car lost second place before a piston failed, but set fastest lap at 75.15 mph. Dennis Taylor's Bob-tail inherited the place, only for Ivor Bueb to snatch second by 0.4 sec on the line in the works Bob-tail.

The British season over, Jack returned to Australia with a 1500 Bob-tail, while what was presumably his Oulton Park and Brands Hatch Mark I F2 single-seater was despatched direct to New Zealand. The Olympic Games meeting in Melbourne's Albert Park saw Jack win the Argus Trophy with the Bob-tail and he followed up with two wins in a day at the inaugural Philip Island race meeting.

John had instructed him to sell the Coopers down-under. Jack had originally entered his unloved Maserati 250F for the New Zealand GP in Auckland in January 1957, but now talked the organizers into letting him race the modern Cooper F2 in its place. Jack was preparing it and the Bob-tail in RedeX New Zealand executive Geoff Wiles's back garden when two visitors arrived to have a look. One was 'Pop' McLaren, who ran a garage in the pleasant Auckland suburb of Remuera. The other was his 19-year-old son, whose name was Bruce....

Ken Wharton's F2 Mark I was shipped out to Auckland alongside the John du Puy 250F and *Monza* Ferrari sports car which he was also to drive. He rented the Mark I to local driver Alex Stringer for the NZ GP, while another Kiwi, Syd Jensen, had bought the other ex-works Mark I, presumably the Salvadori prototype car....

Sadly, Wharton crashed the *Monza* fatally in the sports car race, in which Brabham's Bob-tail finished second behind Gibbons's Jaguar D. All three F2 Coopers disappointed in the GP itself; Jensen and Stringer both retiring; Jack 10th with persistent overheating.

Interestingly George Palmer finished sixth in the old Cooper-Bristol which Horace Gould had taken out for the 1954 NZ GP, while slow west of England driver W. F. Morice made the grid as reserve but retired his Cooper-Bristol.

Jack's Mark I finished second to Whitehead's powerful *Squalo* Ferrari at Christchurch, where Jensen's was fifth and the Wharton entry was understandably scratched, his Mark I was on its way back home.... Jack also won the sports car race in his Bob-tail and both Cooper-Climax cars made an enormous impression upon the local racing fraternity. He was second again, this time to Parnell's *Squalo*, around the houses in Dunedin, and back home early in March placed the F2 car third in the Australian GP at Caversham aerodrome, near Perth and was second to Davison's Ferrari back at Albert Park.

He had left the Bob-tail in New Zealand, with Buzz Perkins, secretary of the New Zealand International Grand Prix Association (NZIGP). Perkins was a regular customer at McLaren's garage and told 'Pop' he ought to buy it. Young Bruce McLaren was enthralled and after selling their other cars the family scraped together enough to settle the deal. The ex-Brabham Bob-tail became the McLaren family's first Cooper-Climax racing car.

Now, at the start of the 1957 European racing season, Cooper cars were poised for greater things....

CHAPTER FIFTEEN

Into Formula 1 . . .

During the winter of 1956–57 the customer production Mark II or 'T43' Cooper-Climax was finalized for Formula 2. It differed from the prototype Mark I cars in its 2 in. longer wheelbase – reaching 7 ft 7 in. – its restyled bodywork and the introduction of the completely new twin-cam Climax FPF dry-sump engine.

Chassis changes accommodated the lengthened wheelbase and reshaped engine. Where the prototype Mark I frames' vertical tubes either side of the scuttle were welded into the top longerons just behind the dash cross-member, the Mark II's were welded-in ahead of it. The Mark I's tall frame hoop forming the perimeter of the seat-back bulkhead was braced by two diagonals. In the Mark II it was unbraced, but the top chassis longeron abeam the engine bay was braced against the lower longeron by a three-piece inverted 'Y'. The usual $1\frac{1}{2}$ in. diameter tubing was used.

John's aesthetic sense had persuaded Owen to redesign the nose cowls, so they now swept down quite handsomely to a low-set air intake in place of the horizontal centreline affair on the Mark Is. While the Mark I side panels had wrapped tightly around the section described by the lateral chassis hoops, the Mark II's were bulged into midship panniers to house extra long-range tanks if required. These bulged panels were held clear of the frame hoops on light-gauge outriggers. The radiator was still attached to the forward-hingeing nose cowl – opening with it – while the engine cowl raised rearwards for easy access. For races up to 200 miles a 5-gallon tank would be slung either side ahead of the dash, piped together with a $5\frac{1}{2}$-gallon standard scuttle tank which incorporated the filler neck. Long-range tanks strapped beside the driver's hips would give a total 25 gallons – sufficient for a full 500 km Grand Prix distance on pump fuel, or for 200 miles on alcohol.

The twin-cam Climax FPF engine was to become the first genuine production racing engine ever built in Britain. Its design was largely by Harry Mundy, schemed before he left Climax to become *The Autocar*'s best-ever technical editor. It used many components from the still-born $2\frac{1}{2}$-litre V8 *Godiva* project, and was developed after Mundy's departure in search of journalistic riches by Walter Hassan, Peter Windsor-Smith, Gray Ross, Ron Burr and Hugh Reddington. Harry Spears became responsible for assembly, overhaul, customer engine testing and liaison – he was to become a familiar face to all Cooper customers.

The FPF emerged as a compact in-line four-cylinder with bore and stroke of 81.2×71.1 mm, displacing 1475 cc. It had a five main-bearing crankshaft and was dry-sumped with a single pressure pump and two scavenge. It breathed through newly developed twin-choke SU DU6 carburettors with $1\frac{3}{4}$ in. bores. In effect they were individuals with a common float chamber sandwiched between. Climax claimed on the test-bed they were as efficient as Webers. . . .

In the Cooper the FPF's oil was pumped through flexible piping strapped to the chassis rails into a 3-gallon nose tank, vee-shaped in plan to deflect hot air from the radiator up front.

The F2 FPF ran a standard compression ratio of 10.0 : 1 and peak power was quoted as 141 bhp (nett) at 7000 rpm. It drove through a $7\frac{3}{4}$ in. Borg & Beck clutch to the now familiar about-faced Citroën-ERSA transaxle, now in a stiffened casing with straight-cut stub-toothed spur gears, closer ratio than hitherto. Full-length splines were introduced to locate the gear wheels better on the first motion shaft, and the engagement dogs on third and top gears were wider. The crown-wheel bearing mounts were also stiffened to accommodate the extra power and minimize wear.

The Mark II frames retained transverse-leaf/narrow-based wishbone suspension, with $10 \times 1\frac{3}{4}$ in. Lockheed drum brakes standard and Girling discs an optional extra.

The prototype car was completed around a mock-up FPF, the engine being installed at a compound angle to minimize height and to pull the carburettor bellmouths back within the 'headrest' cross-section. It tilted down 5 degrees from the half-shaft centres towards the front, then canted 18 degrees to the right, relative to the still upright transaxle. The prototype was rigged with coil-and-distributor ignition driven from the front timing gear train, but a lighter magneto would be used in racing.

Today it is tricky to decide which of the prototype Mark I cars went where. The 1956 production records, like all those relating to the Cooper-Bristols and Bob-tails, have been lost, but those from 1957–67 survive in a dog-eared 'Ideal' series No 4450/1 maroon-bound notebook. It mentions just one 1956-numbered F2 car, this being *F2/P/56* with engine

INTO FORMULA 1...

FWB/8/6624 on which £851 7s. tax was paid and reclaimed under then-current laws on 6 March, 1957. The car is listed as 'Works', with the abbreviation 'Aust.' added subsequently. Today the Mark I machine which Brabham took out to Australia during that far-off winter apparently survives with this number.

Something as evocative of 'first-off' as *F2/P/56* should logically apply to the Salvadori British GP meeting car, but simple logic in paperwork and bureaucratic terms was never Cooper's strong suit. . . . Any written records must in some ways be regarded as a work of fiction or barely calculated vaguery; that's the way it was; if a mangled chassis had to be replaced overnight they did it *now* and caught up with the paperwork later. Paperwork doesn't win races. . . . 'Twas ever thus.

No record has survived of the Walker and Wharton Mark Is, but Rob's raced in Europe into 1957 and after Wharton's fatal accident his car was sold by his estate to Bill Whitehouse back in England. Two more Mark Is were built with Owen's original upturned nosecone design and slimline bodies. They sold to the New Zealand speedway riders Ray Thackwell and Ronnie Moore, both with FWA 1100 cc single-cam engines, and were exported to them in South Africa ready for the early-1957 Springbok series of races. According to the surviving Register they were numbered *F2/1* and *F2/2/57* – see the chassis Appendix. . . . Later in the year the Kiwis took delivery of FWB-engined F2 Mark IIs numbers '*17*' and '*18/57*' for racing in the UK and Europe. The rapid Rhodesian Mike Stafford apparently bought one of their Mark Is, a compatriot named Guthrie the other. Sadly Stafford was killed in his at Bulawayo.

Other customers for Mark II's included Bill Whitehouse, Les Leston, Bob Gerard, Alan Brown, Rob Walker, Tommy Sopwith, George Wicken, Tony Marsh, George Nixon, Brian Naylor, Jack Lewis, Tommy Atkins, Joe Lubin – the Los Angeles agent in the USA – and Alec Mildren in Australia.

The first works experimental car is recorded as *F2/3/57*, earmarked for Roy, before works' *F2/8* and *F2/9/57* became available for him and Brabham. At least two further cars went

Below left *The new 1957 'T43' Formula 2 Mark II chassis frame propped against work-bench at Hollyfield Road, showing off pannier tank support frames, 'Y'-bracing in engine side bays, tall seat-back hoop providing some roll-over protection, and simple front suspension layout. On left is the special offset driving position Bob-tail being completed for use in the Driver Training Division and at Le Mans following the Hugus/Bentley performance in similar conversion at previous year's 24-hour classic*

Grand opening of the Cooper 'School' at Brands Hatch, 20 March, 1957, saw the Hon Gerald Lascelles, cousin of the Queen and a great racing enthusiast, on hand to watch the goings-on and drive the cars. Here he shakes hands with the first paid-up student, Master-Sergeant Henry Kliner of Rock Island, Illinois and the US Army, after completing some rapid laps with John Cooper in the side-by-side Bob-tail. The extra centreline chassis brace structure is visible dividing the cockpit in place of the original twin longerons passing either side of a centre seat. The little Bob-tail, with its broad-humped engine cowl and top-ducted radiator is flanked by the School's two Climax FWE-engined single-seaters. They were all painted pale blue

to US owners; for a customer named Woodward and for the Woolworth's heir, Lance Reventlow, who raced his in England.

Roy Salvadori was to have a busy year, having signed with BRM for Formula 1, Cooper for Formula 2 and Aston Martin for sports car racing. In March his new Mark II lapped Goodwood in 1:32.2, 3.2 sec within his best Mark I-FWB record set the previous September.

Meanwhile at Pippbrook Garage, Alf Francis was building up his own version of the FWB engine after testing on the Alta bed with twin Weber carburettors, the Mona pump, his own inlet manifolding and some experimental fuel mixing. With magneto ignition he claims to have seen 113 bhp. The Walker Mark I car was tested briefly at Goodwood, where both Peter Walker and Peter Whitehead tried it, and then it was whisked away to Syracuse, Sicily, for the first official F2 meeting on 7 April, 1957.

These were troubled times again for British motor racing in the wake of the Suez débâcle. Petrol rationing was to be reimposed and it looked as if motor racing would be banned. Ron Searles, storeman-cum-general manager at Hollyfield Road, suggested to John they should open a racing drivers' school to cushion the effect. Thickly bespectacled, humorous Ron had dabbled in racing 500s and 1000s. Charles and John were agreeable and they took an ad in *Autosport* announcing Climax-engined single-seater open-wheel racing cars would be available to students and that Brands Hatch was the chosen 'training centre'. Response was staggering! Around 2000 hopefuls applied, flooding Hollyfield Road's tiny offices with correspondence. John did a deal with Brands Hatch promoter John Hall, who took a fee for each pupil using the track each week in the new Cooper Training Division's regular Tuesday and Thursday sessions.

Steve Sanville had joined Cooper's as a fitter at about the time the first F2 car had been built. Perhaps he showed his better education than some, for he was suddenly presented with a cardboard box full of letters, a typewriter and a stack of CCCo orange-headed notepaper, and overnight he became 'secretary to the Driver Training Division'. Steve soon left to join Lotus, for whom he would work on gearbox and engine projects before establishing his own Norvic Racing Engines Co, still running into 1983.

The Division's courses were inaugurated on 20 March, 1957, by which time nearly 5000 applicants had been sifted to produce 1000 pupils for the first intake. Classes were arranged for up to 20 drivers at a time, using a replica of the centre-tube Le Mans 1100 Bob-tail with its side-by-side seats and a pair of new Mark II open-wheelers using 1250 cc FWA engines with single carburettors. These first two school cars are recorded as numbers *F2/4* and *F2/5/57*.

The instructor would first take his pupil for a few introductory laps in the Bob-tail. He would then despatch the novice on pain of a severe rollicking if he should bend one of the F2s. The staff would then pick those 'with aptitude' for further tutelage at the school's expense. Trainees not chosen could buy more time to prove their worth. Cooper couldn't lose... Charles was delighted....

Ron Searles was the Division's first manager and Les Leston its first – and rather unlikely – schoolmaster. Soon they had acquired an ex-Bristol Corporation bus to transport the sports car and single-seaters, which were painted uniform grey-blue. Ian Burgess and Sir Francis Samuelson's son Dickie became instructors. Ginger Devlin and a teenage recruit named Terry Kitson maintained the cars, and the Division was to run very happily, and profitably, for some years to come, without producing any star drivers....

Organizing the School could be soul-destroying and Steve Sanville soon opted out. Urbane Ian Burgess, ambitious racing driver, took his place and in answer to an ad in *Autosport*, young Andrew Ferguson became his assistant. Andrew's enthusiasm for motor racing had been fostered by Kay Petre – glamorous prewar lady racing driver turned motoring journalist. He'd worked briefly for Allard, then as a Daisy-Fresh cake salesman, then a dog-meat man before joining Cooper.... He would become responsible for their works team bookings and travel, before leaving in 1961 to manage the Camoradi F1 team, and then joining Team Lotus in 1962. He became secretary of the Formula 1 Constructors' Association in its formative years and apart from a brief spell with the American VPJ F1 team has been with Lotus ever since

A typical scene in a Cooper School day at Brands Hatch, with chief instructor Ian Burgess looking on (left) while Ginger Devlin (foreground) and Terry Kitson tend one of the single-seaters and Andrew Ferguson wonders if it will be ready in time to earn its day's keep. The converted coach School transporter was typical of its time...

Monaco – Jack Brabham scuttling out of Mirabeau Supérieur, down towards the Station Hairpin at Monte Carlo during the Monaco Grand Prix, 19 May, 1957, which demonstrated the potential of a larger-engined Cooper-Climax in Formula 1 World Championship racing. This is the F2 car brought along originally as Walker/works team spare which Jack had to take over for the race after crashing their purpose-built F1 special, only the 1960 cc engine being transferred

– still running team affairs in 1983.

Andrew is a man of wicked wit and a bottomless source of motor racing stories. He was amongst kindred spirits at Cooper's and recalls his time there with deep affection: 'I don't think there was ever a day at Cooper's when I didn't go home chuckling because something hilarious was going on. . . .'

'The day I joined, I was in my office in the front shop when the door burst open – Charlie Cooper seldom used the handle, he'd just thump a door with his shoulder or forearm and burst it open – and he brought in an upright electric fire. "'Ere Boy," he said, "take that round the pub and leave it with the landlady. . . ." I thought this was a bit strange, but I took it round and the landlady didn't seem at all surprised. "See you later dear," she said, and sure enough she did, I was in and out all day bringing round electrical appliances which Charlie kept bringing in. Finally she explained the Electricity Board inspectors were coming round and he was trying to reduce his rating! That was typical. . . .

'Another time we were in the pub and the Old Man kept nudging me and pointing at a couple of pin-striped city gents at the bar, speaking real Oxford English. "'Ark at them poofs," he kept saying. Then one of them turned to us and asked if we knew where some local address was. Charlie got up and said, "Yes cock, you want to go up 'ere . . .", jabbing his thumb at the street, and then he started to draw a map on the bar top with his finger. But it wouldn't show on the polish. He was a rugged old boy with huge hard hands and thick fingers, and now he just plonked his finger unconcerned in this chap's lager and drew a map that everyone could see. I'll *never* forget the look on that man's face. It was typical Charlie Cooper . . .'

Dickie Samuelson also worked on 'The School'; '. . . but it drove him to distraction. We ran two days a week at Brands, perhaps 20–24 pupils a time, so we'd have to type out reports on around 320 laps a week, and we had to answer all the correspondence, which was *massive*! Dickie got so uptight with some of those people. He was very British and proper, and I remember he threw away one letter just because the stamp was stuck on upside-down so someone had stood the Queen on her head. He soon left as well. . . .'

Ian Burgess was regarded as a rogue, but a likeable one. He was the only member of staff allowed to call Charles

Cooper 'Charlie', apparently because the Old Man considered he was a rogue and it didn't matter if a rogue didn't show you respect. Owen's latter-day assistant draughtsman, Eddie Stait: 'The one thing the Old Man couldn't stand was Burgess rolling in late, around ten in the morning. "Where's that bugger Burgess?" he'd grumble, and when he heard the door bang you'd hear his own office door go, then he'd stamp down to Burgess's office and you'd hear raised voices, then an amiable murmur, then Charlie again speaking normally. Eventually the door would open and the Old Man would come out saying: "That's all right, then boy, you fix up your drive for next weekend and g'luck; mind 'ow yer go, boy . . ." Old Burgess could always twist him round his little finger. . . .'

John Cooper: 'We evolved an almost foolproof method of building the school cars – after we had written-off the first batch. We built the chassis in heavy 12-gauge tube, which was almost crash-proof, whereas the suspension wishbones were made much lighter than usual. So, if a car did go out

Opposite *To Le Mans 1957 – one of the works' Ford Thames vans heaves the School Bob-tail up the ramps onto a Silver City Bristol Freighter en route to France and the 24-hour race. Shared there by Jack Brabham and Ian Raby it placed 15th overall and third in class, then back to the training routine at Brands Hatch, two days each week . . . round and round . . .*

Monaco – the long push home after the little car's fuel pump mounting had fractured, parting the pump-drive and losing a sensational third place behind Fangio's victorious Maserati and Brooks' Vanwall. Anxious to avoid outside assistance which would disqualify the car, here Jack pants towards the quayside finish line, escorted by John, Alf Francis and behind the car Colin Chapman and Charles Cooper. Colin's presence is interesting as no Lotuses ran that weekend. He took a rare holiday, anxious to see how a lightweight car could perform with an enlarged Climax engine. Original intended driver Roy Salvadori missed out. His works BRM failed to qualify

of control and leave the road, the suspension was knocked off without hurting anything else. . . . Our mechanics became so skilled in effecting repairs that if a crashed car was brought back in the morning it could be serviceable again the same day. Often to save time the work was done at the side of the track, which probably made the offender squirm a bit too, which was all to the good. . . .'

It was during this year that the old corrugated Cooper's Garage buildings were demolished and a new factory-cum-office block built for the Cooper Car Company. It had a curved frontage; 'Owen Maddock must have designed it'. Nearly right – the architect was actually Owen's father, Richard. In 1961 a penthouse drawing office would be added on the roof of the original two-storey structure. The building division of the Willment organization did the work, while the car company and works team operated from lock-ups behind the 'Royal Oak' pub, reached by a footbridge across the Tolworth Brook.

Meanwhile, down at Syracuse the planned F2 class within the F1 GP flopped, probably due to the lack of any suitable Italian entry, and only three Coopers appeared to do battle with the 2½-litre F1s. Rob Walker invited Jack Brabham to drive his Mark I; Maidstone dairyman George Wicken ran his first customer Mark II – *F2/6/57* – with FWB power, and Bill Whitehouse ran the ex-Wharton Mark I-FWB. Jack was sixth, Wicken – misfiring – seventh and last, while 'Big Bill' retired. Denis Jenkinson wrote: 'Brabham's speed in the little single-cam 1500 cc Cooper was quite remarkable and augurs well for the time when a twin-cam becomes available. . . .'

The FPF emerged soon after at Easter Goodwood, where the works Mark IIs for Roy and Jack were so equipped. But only eight of the 17 F2 entries arrived and Tony Brooks's Walker single-cam Mark I lapped 3.8 seconds faster than Salvadori in practice. When the works driver's clutch failed in the race, Brooks won by 18.2 sec from Brabham's surviving works car. The stewards later docked Brooks a token 5 sec for jumping the start. Salvadori's fastest lap was at 91.52 mph, Wicken placed fourth and Noel Cunningham-Reid drove Sopwith's latest Mark II.

Brabham then drove his F2 car in the 32-lap Formula 1 feature race that day and finished fourth behind two Connaughts and a BRM, while Roy's BRM drive fizzled with locked brakes. In the 1500 cc sports car race his FPF-engined Bob-tail ran third behind the Lotuses until a pluglead came adrift. He set fastest lap again, at 89.07 mph, but it really wasn't his day. . . .

Early in May, Michael Christie drove the Walker Mark I-FWB to second ftd behind Marsh's Cooper-JAP 1100 at Prescott hillclimb, but at Pippbrook Garage a far more exciting development was under way.

During the pre-Syracuse testing at Goodwood, Salvadori had driven both Walker's Mark I and his F1 Connaught. He found the carefully prepared little F2 car with its single-cam engine was almost as quick as his twin-cam Mark II; as Brooks later proved. John was there, and they began discussing prospects for the coming season. Roy had grasped the true potential of what Cooper-Climax could do. He floated the idea of enlarging the FPF sufficiently to tackle Grand Prix racing under Formula 1.

John believed that a long-throw crankshaft, new liners and pistons could take it close to 2 litres. Cooper couldn't afford the cost, but Rob was fascinated. . . . Alf Francis agreed that 180 bhp in an 800 lb car could match the F1s on suitable courses. Rob's vast enthusiasm was fired, and he ordered a new chassis plus 2-litre engine there and then. The target date was 19 May, the Monaco GP, on the ideal street circuit.

Walter Hassan at Climax wasn't so keen. He doubted the FPF had sufficient reserves of space and strength to permit a stretch, but was persuaded to take a gamble. Yet again the Climax people were showing almost excessive caution. Again it paid off, and there was nothing madcap about what would follow. . . .

The special 'F1' Cooper-Climax went together at Hollyfield Road with Alf Francis chewing over its design with John, Owen, Charles, John Kelly, the chassis welder, the Beddings and anyone else who could contribute. It was to carry 25 gallons of fuel in enlarged panniers; a 65/35 100-octane petrol/alcohol mix. Alf went to Weber's in Italy to see his friend Galetti, who recommended 42 mm chokes. A Tipo Mona pump was fitted half-submerged in the pick-up tank and the special crankshaft was collected and delivered to Widdrington Road by Francis, who spent the next three days there assembling the special 'Grand Prix' engine. At midnight, Friday, 10 May, 1957, it went on the test-bed. It peaked at 176 bhp at 6500 rpm, with peak bmep of 204 lb/sq. in. at 5000 rpm – a new high for an unsupercharged engine. The new bore and stroke were 86.4 × 83.8 mm, 1960 cc. Hassan was thrilled with the performance of undersized ports and high gas velocities in producing meaty mid-range torque. He became even more entrenched in his distaste for 'engineers' inclined to 'improve' his engines by opening out their ports....

Francis rushed the new engine back to Hollyfield, where the car was completed frantically by a team working through the Saturday night and Sunday. Alf wrote: 'John Cooper, in shirt sleeves and pulling away at an empty pipe, was on the job with us all the time, together with Jack Brabham, who had been signed-up to drive at Monte Carlo, as our original choice – Salvadori – was under contract to BRM.... Brabham put all his enthusiasm into the project and he "lived" the 1960 cc Cooper together with the rest of us....'

There was no time for the planned Goodwood test, so Jack merely blasted the car around sleepy Surbiton and along the Kingston Bypass before the Walker truck set off for Monaco at 4.30 pm on Monday. Jack was late arriving in Monte Carlo and Walker asked Salvadori and Peter Collins to try the little car. Eventually the apologetic Australian reported for duty and next day in the usual 6 am practice session he sped away, forgetting unadjusted brake balance. At the top of the Beau Rivage climb he tore into the Hotel de Paris left turn, only to find the brakes locking solid: 'I found myself in the road where it drops off to the right and wasn't able to make the bend. I went straight into the barrier, which was made of sandbags and telegraph posts . . . and knocked a post up and as it went up I went under it. It crashed down on the bonnet of the car right behind my head. That put the car into an irreparable state, by quite a bit....'

Luckily they had a spare. It was Jack's Goodwood Mark II in F2 trim, which Les Leston had been attempting to qualify for the GP, only for its engine to blow in the first session. Now the 1960 engine was fitted into the F2 frame in a hectic eight-hour session. Jack qualified 13th amongst the 16 starters.

Race morning – more panic. The gearbox was oozing oil. A bearing cap nut had cracked and loosened. It was replaced. The F2 car lacked the 'special's' extra tankage. Alf insisted they practice refuelling. The filler was too small to accept a 5-gallon 'chuck-in'. An exploratory push-start then revealed no fuel pressure. Alf stripped the pump. Nothing wrong. Refitted it. Still no pressure. Fit a spare gauge. Push-start, successfully, but still no pressure. The spare gauge must be faulty too, they hoped. The F2 hybrid car took the Monaco GP start with no visible fuel pressure and merely the *de facto* evidence of the engine running cleanly to calm Brabham's mind.

As the flag fell the gauge soared into life and Jack was away into Cooper-Climax's first World Championship Grand Prix. After 10 laps Moss, Collins and Hawthorn – a Vanwall and two Ferraris – were already out and Jack lay sixth in his tiny green car. He rose to fourth in a duel with Flockhart's BRM and Rob decided to call him in for refuelling at 60 laps instead of the scheduled 50 to give the BRM less chance to retake the place. Alf Francis: 'To me and to most people it was absolutely incredible that our car was still runing. Here we were holding our own with the big boys....'

Jack rushed in to refuel on lap 62, but the starter then refused to turn. Alf called for the jack to lift the rear wheels and start the engine in gear by spinning them, but Charles Cooper, quivering with tension, shouted 'Push it, push it . . .', although that should disqualify the car. The crew flung themselves at the car and pushed. It fired and Jack was away almost instantly.

On circuit it was going splendidly and Jack was really racing. He caught and passed two Maseratis. On lap 96, with nine to run, Trips's Ferrari blew up and crashed. Fangio's Maserati led from Brooks's Vanwall, and Jack was *third* for Cooper-Climax. But on lap 100 its stretch-engine died on the descent from the Casino past the railway station. Jack coasted despondently down to the sea front and rolled to a halt just short of the famous tunnel. Vibration had finally broken the fuel pump mounting, and as it fell its drive had parted.

'In those days I didn't like to be beaten, so I got out of the car and pushed. I was eager! I pushed the thing down to the chicane, up to the *Tabac* corner and along the harbour side to finish sixth – and last.... The worst thing wasn't so much the exhaustion as losing third place; and the really scary part was going through the tunnel with all these cars screaming past in the near dark...' Dropping three places so dramatically avoided any potential protests.

It was an heroic effort all round. Cooper-Climax ingenuity and Rob Walker's enthusiasm had produced what was going to become the most potent Grand Prix contender for years . . . but not, be it said, just yet....

The works team contested 14 more races that season, including the French, British, German and Pescara World Championship GPs, and the non-Championship Moroccan race at the end of the season. Their F2 programme began post-Monaco at Brands on Whit-Sunday, where Brabham and Salvadori finished 1–2 in the first race that day for the class, and Jack won from Mackay-Fraser's Lotus in the second after Roy's car shed a steering arm. There were 10 Coopers running, including Brooks in the Walker Mark I, qualified in his absence by Peter Gammon, but on lap 2 of the first race he spun off most uncharacteristically and crashed heavily at Paddock Bend reportedly due to mechanical failure.

Dennis Taylor drove Bill Whitehouse's new Mark II – *14/57*. Lance Reventlow also ran his US white-and-blue Mark II. Les Leston's twin-cam Mark II was third in the second race, followed by the Kiwi Equipe single-cam Mark II-FWBs of Moore and Thackwell. Jack set fastest lap in both F2 races, plus a new class record at 75.4 mph. But a sound Cooper defeat by the Lotus 11s in the 1100 sports car race demonstrated the Bob-tail's passing; and in the 1500 race Salvadori's works Bob-tail was also defeated by Colin Chapman.

INTO FORMULA 1...

Top *Salvadori picking up World Championship points with fifth place for the works Mark II in the British GP at Aintree, 20 July, 1957. Moss/Brooks shared the victorious Vanwall in this great day for British racing which saw the first home victory by an all-British team/driver combination, heading three Lancia-Ferraris and the 1960 cc works Cooper. Jack Brabham's similar Walker-entered Mark II retired* **left**, *but he drove hard – as usual. Note disc brakes with front-mounted calipers, opened-out radiator intake on the Alf Francis-prepared Walker car, and rear damper pick-up inboard on the bottom rear wishbones. This caused trouble over the bumps at Nürburgring . . .*

Next day at Crystal Palace, Brabham beat Salvadori again – something he rather relished – to take the F2 London Trophy two-part race on aggregate. Roy won Heat One, but gearbox trouble dropped him to third in Heat Two. He then led the 1500 sports cars in his works Bob-tail, only to be beaten by a nose on the line – again by Chapman's Lotus.

At Mallory Park that day Tony Marsh's new Mark II won two *Libre* races. The field included Jimmy Stuart in the ex-Gerard Cooper-Bristol Mark II and Ken Tyrrell in the Alan Brown/RJC Motors ex-Moss, ex-Brandon Cooper-Alta. . . .

The following weekend saw the F2 Prix de Paris at Montlhéry marking the class's true continental debut. It was an appalling introduction for would-be promoters, as only Brabham, MacDowel, Marsh and Bueb in Mark II single-seaters faced Naylor's sports Lotus-Maserati, Mercedes 300SL, GT Ferrari, Porsche and Austin-Healey makeweights, and they finished 1-2-3-4 in that order. Cooper domination had already killed F3, now it threatened to do the same to a poorly supported F2. At least Lotus were taking up the challenge with their Type 12 single-seater, but they had a long way to go to become reliably competitive.

Cooper school activities at Brands Hatch were suspended for a week while their Bob-tail side-by-side seat 1100 was raced at Le Mans by Brabham and Ian Raby, finishing 15th overall and third in class; out-paced by the Lotuses. On the following Tuesday the car was back at Brands, droning round with instructor and pupil hard at work. Charles moaned about the school's week off; 'That's cost us three 'undred pound. . . .'

Marsh continued his fine home season, winning two more races in a day at Mallory, where Jimmy Blumer also shone in his ex-Moss Bob-tail. The little transom-tailed cars were still thick on the ground. Ian Raby was racing old XPG 2 with his familiar *Puddle Jumper* title in script on its flanks, finishing second at Roskilde, for example, where other Bob-tails were driven by Arthur Owen and local man Andreas Geil. Nelleman was another Danish Bob-tail driver. Innes Ireland raced Equipe Endeavour's 1500 car and won, the Mayman husband and wife team shone at club level, as did Chris Summers and Chris Power, and Johnny Highham of Ecurie White Rose ran his ex-Wadsworth Le Mans/McMillan car as team mate to Alex McMillan and Niall Campbell-Blair. Chris Bristow's John Hume-prepared Bob-tail took three first, four seconds and five thirds to propel him towards Formula 1. George Nixon had sold his '56 car to Alan Eccles, replacing it with a new F2. Tim Parnell, son of Reg, was successful in TOF 264, and the American visitor Lupton Rainwater III won at Mallory Park, where he beat David Shale's big Cooper-Jaguar, also hillclimbing his ex-Endeavour machine. Down in New Zealand both Merv Neil and Ian

145

McKellar were local Bob-tail campaigners....

But now the latter half of 1957 saw Cooper's pace accelerating in Formula 1....

The works and Walker teams were to combine, and their three dark green Mark IIs arrived at Rouen-les-Essarts for the French GP. Jack was to drive the 1.9 special, curiously on drum brakes, until one appreciates how drivers preferred their 'feel' to discs at that time, while Mike MacDowel handled a standard F2 1500 on discs, with a sister car as spare. They proved way under-powered on the gradients, the F2 was totally outclassed and in the race Jack went out after an early incident with Gould's Maserati. MacDowel was called in and the Australian took over to finish seventh and last, nine laps behind Fangio's winning Maserati.

From Rouen the team travelled to Reims, where continental F2 at last took off in earnest. A full field of 12 Coopers and five Lotuses had real works opposition at last from Maurice Trintignant's Ferrari Dino V6, with a sports OSCA and Porsche completing the grid.

John fielded two works Mark IIs for Salvadori and Brabham, plus the 1500 Bob-tail sports in stripped F2 form as a 'streamliner'. Roy found it very fast, but disliked its wandering 'feel' in practice. He took the Mark II open-wheeler instead. Big Bill Whitehouse – so long a Cooper customer – had broken his Mark II's engine in practice and borrowed the works Bob-tail 'streamliner' to collect his start money in the race.

The works Mark IIs fought a fantastic duel with the powerful front-engined Ferrari. Denis Jenkinson described it as 'the closest-fought race seen for many a day' as the red Ferrari blared ahead on the straights only for the two green Coopers to scuttle round it in the curves or under braking. But on lap 24 Jack's engine failed and on lap 31 the Ferrari wailed up from Thillois alone and Roy's Cooper stammered by slowly, eventually parking beside Jack's just short of the finish line, from where both pushed home at the end. Trintignant won from Jean Lucas's borrowed Cooper, Marsh, Salvadori and Goethals' sports Porsche.

In the blistering heat down the long Soissons Straight ending lap two, Bill Whitehouse's borrowed Bob-tail had apparently burst a tyre under braking for Thillois corner and somersaulted along the verge and burned out, and he had been killed.

His was the first fatality to come so close to the Cooper 'family' and he would be sorely missed at Hollyfield. Douggie Johnson: 'He was a super bloke. You've got to understand that any customer was welcome to wander into the shop to see what was going on and have a chat. There was none of this business about visitors being led away to the office and kept clear of the workers. The first thing Bill Whitehouse would do when he arrived outside was to go to the sweet shop next door and buy two dozen choc ices – then he'd give 'em out round the works before doing his business with Mr Charles or John.... You missed blokes like that....'

After the finish Jack prepared to do battle with the 1.9 in the afternoon's Formula 1 race over a full 61 laps, 506 km. The usual chaotic Reims organization saw him motoring round the back of the starter towards the rear of the grid when the flag fell, and he was still bare-headed! John actually scampered alongside offering crash-hat and goggles and after taking the flag Jack stopped to don his battle-dress before rushing off after the field. He could never improve on last place with only 175 bhp against nearer 300, but survived the distance to finish 12th, again nine times lapped....

The following Sunday saw the British GP at Aintree, with two 1.9 Mark IIs running; Jack in the Walker car, Roy in the works car, both disc-braked, while a third 'Formula 1' Cooper was entered by Bob Gerard.

His Parr's of Leicester workshops had modified a new Mark II – *F2/21/57* – to accommodate the very special 2246 cc ex-works Bristol engine which he had retained after selling his BRM-baiting Cooper-Bristol Mark II the previous year. The rear-engined frame was not stretched, but the rear cockpit hoop was set more vertically to enlarge the engine bay. The Bristol unit was inserted well forward in the frame. The claimed weight difference between Climax FPF and Bristol was only 20 lb and it was hoped to maintain the standard weight distribution. 'Mr Bob' planned to drop the engine lower either by inverting the Citroën-ERSA transaxle to raise output shaft level or to produce a special 'box. Time was short and a normal Cooper 'box was retained. Some frame tubes were reshaped or deleted to house the tall engine, while the owner emphasized that its light-alloy six-port head, crankcase, magneto and alloy Solex carbs saved weight. The mag prevented the standard Cooper engine cowl closing, but with coil-ignition it fitted perfectly – if the carburettor bells were removed. The large sump projected through the undertray for cooling. This 'Cooper BG-Bristol' could be refitted with an FPF if required for F2 racing.

The Walker-works team 1.9s were by no means the slowest runners at Aintree and they overshadowed Gerard's rather ungainly 2.2 special. Salvadori was in terrific form, relieved to have escaped from his BRM contract after Monaco and fresh from a one-off Vanwall drive in France. Les Leston was in the BRM team now, and Roy and Jack Brabham in the Walker car both carved past the front-engined four-cylinder and left it for dead. They then harried Trintignant's works Ferrari V8 mercilessly and so embarrassed the Italian team management that they called in the Frenchman for a driver change....

Roy was sixth and Jack seventh until the distance and pace told. Jack's clutch failed, and with only five laps to go Roy's gearbox shattered and he pushed across the line fifth for Cooper's first World Championship points of the $2\frac{1}{2}$-litre Formula. Gerard's special was sixth, but Roy had lapped it three times before breaking.

INTO FORMULA 1...

The two interim F1 Coopers were then rushed straight to Caen in Normandy for a minor F1 race. Tony Brooks drove the Walker car, Roy the works 1.9 and Jack was left with his works 1500 F2. Brooks was second fastest in practice to Behra's BRM with Roy completing the front row in a thin 11-car grid. The Behra and Schell BRMs dominated the race, with Brooks and Salvadori leading the private F1s. Tony held third easily until the clutch broke again, as at Aintree, and Roy inherited second place when Schell's BRM dropped out. Brabham retired early with ignition trouble.

Clearly the extra grunt of the 1.9 engine was too much for the Walker car's drive-line and Alf Francis fitted a Maserati clutch to transmit it more reliably, worrying now that the gearbox would break instead.

August Brands saw a two-heat F2 race for the Rochester Trophy. Wicken, Brabham and Salvadori attacked Heat One with gusto, Jack winning from Wicken while Roy retired. In Heat Two Jack won again, as he did overall on aggregate from Wicken, Ronnie Moore and Lance Reventlow's US-liveried Mark II.

The German GP at Nürburgring incorporated an F2 class. Walker ran a new Mark II car – F2/7/57, a number which would delight the superstitious Stirling Moss. Brabham drove it in Germany, while Roy Salvadori ran the works Mark II and private cars were entered by Tony Marsh, Brian Naylor – F2/23/57 – and Dick Gibson. Paul England – an Australian tourist – ran his ex-Wharton/Whitehouse Mark I.

Against works Porsche Spyder opposition on their home ground the Coopers went incredibly well. Roy drove with immense heart and courage – just as he drove normally on the public road – and he was locked in battle with Barth's leading Porsche most of the way until a Cooper rear wishbone broke on the bumps. The tortuous circuit and rugged surface had knocked-out the car's dampers, leaving the bottom rear wishbones to take the shock as the dampers bottomed-out. Not unnaturally, they couldn't stand much of that. Marsh's car suffered similarly and he replaced the broken wishbone in the pits, using one cannibalized from the works car. Barth won the F2 class from Naylor, de Beaufort's Porsche and the dogged Marsh. Brabham's gearbox broke, along with Gibson's steering and England's distributor drive. The Coopers had been well beaten, but had again put up a terrific fight against full factory cars and had fallen honourably. Continental interest in F2 grew....

On 18 August, the Championship Pescara GP was run in Italy, where Cooper ran two 1500 F2s for Brabham and Salvadori. Roy: 'It was a bit cheeky to run under-sized cars at all in the GPs, but the starting money was attractive, they were inexpensive cars to make and race and although even the 1.9s were not that quick they certainly handled well and their brakes were superb....'

He tried too hard at Pescara and wiped-off a wheel on a

4 August, 1957, German GP, Nürburgring with Salvadori on top form in F2, here leading Edgar Barth's works Porsche in the German's own back yard. But Barth had lapped 3.8 sec quicker in practice and although Roy lowered his qualifying time by 2.2 sec to set fastest F2 race lap his Mark II's hammered suspension fell apart and put him out, leaving the East German defector to win the division, 12th overall

marker stone while Jack ground round alone. Roy showed him a pit signal announcing 'I am going swimming' – and Jack growled home seventh and last, two long, long, laps behind Moss's winning Vanwall, totally outclassed.

In early September, Walker's slender-bodied Mark I was fit again after Brooks's most uncharacteristic Brands accident and Rob himself won the 1100–1500 cc racing car class with it at the Brighton Speed Trials, beating Marsh and Wicken. Miss Griffen took the Ladies' award in Marsh's car from Patsy Burt in the Walker 1.9. Michael Christie drove the 1.9 at Prescott for second ftd behind Dick Henderson's blown 1100, after his second run saw the gearbox split ... it really was vulnerable.

The Suez Crisis had pushed the BRDC's International Trophy meeting at Silverstone back from May to 14 September, with the main F1 race in two Heats and a Final. Vanwall stayed away, so Brooks was free to drive the Walker 1.9 again, facing Brabham's works car and BRM. Private Maseratis completed the field with some F2 Coopers and Gerard's BG-Bristol.

Silverstone in the Eighties might be one of the world's fastest circuits, but in Fifties company it was merely medium-quick, with no really fast straights nor really slow turns. This made it ideal for a 2-litre lightweight with Tony Brooks aboard and he qualified on pole for Heat One, 1:43.0 equalling the Moss/Hawthorn, Maserati/BRM best of 1956. But as the flag fell for the start Tony's hopes were demolished along with the car's crown-wheel and pinion – which stripped.

Brabham stuck out his neck in Heat Two for second place behind a BRM, and in the Final he was deep in combat with two Maseratis until oil began splattering around the cockpit and he stopped. John retired the car as an expensive engine failure looked imminent. With both interim F1 cars broken, a planned trip to the following weekend's Modena GP was then cancelled.

Meanwhile a horde of F2 Coopers had started the Silverstone Final, driven by Marsh, Innes Ireland, Leston, Fairman, Wicken, Graham Hill, Cunningham-Reid, Salvadori, Burgess, Gibson, Thackwell, Jim Russell and Ronnie Moore.

George Wicken won the Martini Trophy at Brands in his Mark II after smashing his gearbox on the startline in a preliminary race. He had rushed back to his Bexleyheath garage to collect the 'box from the late Bill Whitehouse's car, then fitted it back at Brands....

The September Goodwood meeting included a 10-lap F2 race. Brooks was on pole again, but, mindful of his car's transmission, muffed the start and let Salvadori and Brabham score 1–2 for the works. Roy's average of 94.43 mph made this the fastest-ever Goodwood race at that time. Jack's new F2 lap record was 96.00 mph, just 0.4 sec outside the outright F1 mark. Cliff Allison's Lotus 12 was third. They were looking competitive at last....

The £1000 Oulton Park Gold Cup attracted a full F2 field, including Brabham, Salvadori, Burgess and Russell in works cars – Brooks in the Walker team's Mark II and Noel Cunningham-Reid in their Mark I. Brian Naylor had broken his leg at Goodwood and entrusted his Mark II to Bruce Halford.

Tony Marsh took pole in practice alongside Allison's Lotus, Brooks and Brabham. Again the Walker car's final-drive stripped at the start and Brabham was able to lead throughout to win from Allison, Marsh and Burgess. Cunningham-Reid's car broke its water pump, while poor George Wicken suffered an ugly accident, somersaulting into a brick wall on Clay Hill, breaking a leg and hurting his head and chest. More significantly for motor racing's future, Graham Hill's front-engined Lotus 12 set fastest lap, and the Lotus team of Hill, Keith Hall and Allison took the team award from the Bueb, Moore and Gibson Coopers. Surbiton was not having it all its own way in F2 – it was a positively healthy sign.

Tony Marsh won a final Oulton clubbie *Libre* race before the British season ended, but the non-Championship Moroccan GP remained at Casablanca. Rob Walker entered his 1.9 for Brabham, while Salvadori ran the works car, and Brooks returned to Vanwall. Jack outpaced Roy in practice, but the race regulations demanded electric starters. Francis and the Walker crew had to remove their special Maserati clutch to fit a standard Borg & Beck plus starter ring which the Italian clutch lacked. In the middle of practice the clutch lining tore out, leaving Jack without drive to the rear wheels.

Despite this discouraging incident Jack went well – if briefly – in the race, clinging to the tail of the works team bunch until the gearbox broke after only four laps. He retired straight to the paddock, Roy's works car soon following with a similar problem. But the field was being decimated and Equipe Walker realized that if they could resurrect their car they might inherit a good placing. They actually fitted a new gearbox and Jack rejoined '... down the back of the pits when no one was looking'. Portly Toto Roche, the Clerk of the Course imported from Reims, informed Rob Walker that his man would be black-flagged. Unfortunately, looking back up the circuit from the pits meant staring straight into the setting sun: 'Every time my car came along Rob would tap him on the shoulder and start talking to him.... This went on for two or three laps and Toto had already done his biscuit; so he swung round and waved his black flag violently at the first car that came by. It just so happened that it was Fangio the World Champion!'

He drew in to ask what was wrong, with the Maserati crew going berserk and Roche beset on all sides. The crowd began jeering him, and nearing apoplexy he threatened Rob's licence unless Brabham was pulled in. There was no point in spoiling the joke so Jack was flagged down; his mistake having been to retire to the paddock in the first place, instead of stopping in front of his pit. If the work had been done on the pit apron his return to the fray would have been legal....

Roy Salvadori has one fond memory of Casablanca: 'We went to a party on Lord Tredegar's yacht, where we were introduced to his step-daughter and her friend, both very attractive girls. Lady Tredegar asked if we'd take them along to practice and introduce them to other drivers.... John and I were very keen on the idea. They thoroughly enjoyed first practice, but ended up hot, dusty and thirsty, and we took them back to the hotel to freshen up before returning them to her Ladyship. We were all in my room and the girls decided to have a shower; one went in first and the other sat on the bed wearing my dressing gown and talking to John and myself. Just then there was knock at the door and it was Charles saying, "Roy! I want to talk to you; can I come in, the door's locked?" John immediately lost his cool and said, "My God, don't let him see me in here!" and he rushed off into the bathroom and slammed the door.

'I didn't see any alternative so I opened the door and Charles came in, looked at Bridget Russell sitting there in my dressing gown, looked at me and said "*Salvadori*! At it *again*! I've 'ad enough of this – I'm going to tell John and you'll be hearing from him!"... and he slammed the door and stamped off....

'John never did tell me what his father said, but ever since I've regretted I didn't have the neck to say, "Well, if you want John he's in the bathroom here right now with Bridget's friend...."'

The Suez Crisis had seen the BRDC International Trophy meeting at Silverstone postponed from its traditional May date to 14 September. Here Salvadori hurries his F2 works car into Maggots Curve, showing off the simplicity of its transverse leafspring suspensions. Radiator is partially blanked-off – it was a cool day despite the sun

CHAPTER SIXTEEN

1958 – The winning begins...

When the 2½-litre Grand Prix Formula began in 1954 it was planned to run for three seasons, to the end of 1957. The CSI later decided to extend it for a further three, through to the end of 1960, but with some far-reaching changes. From 1 January, 1958, the regulations would ban methanol fuels, and their replacement was 100/130 octane AvGas aviation spirit; and at the same time race distance was slashed from a minimum 500 km or three hours' duration to only 300 km, or two hours'. Racing engine consumption on AvGas was far more modest than on methanol, so fuel tankage could have been reduced even without the accompanying cut in race distance. Under the new Formula cars could be smaller, lighter, less committed to long-distance endurance... in short they could be built like Coopers, and Lotuses.

Through the winter of 1957–58 the major British teams of Vanwall and BRM slaved away to adapt their alcohol-burning engines to AvGas spirit. In Italy, wily old Ferrari had already introduced AvGas-burning Dino V6 F1 cars based on his pump fuel F2 late the preceding season. Then the Argentine club put a cat amongst the pigeons by applying at short notice for the opening race of the 1958 World Championship, to be run at Buenos Aires Autodrome on 19 January. To the horror of the British establishment the CSI accepted. The ACA invited British entries. Tony Vandervell – who in any case was incensed at the way the oil companies had foisted AvGas on Formula 1 – refused to enter on principle. His team had always been aiming at Monaco in May for the start of their AvGas-engined campaign. BRM needed more development time, also aiming at Monaco, and they declined as well.

This left the ACA with a thin all-Italian field from Ferrari and – even though the company was on its beam-ends – from Maserati for Fangio's sake on his home soil. But meanwhile Stirling Moss had agreed verbally with Rob Walker – they would never bother with a written contract – to drive his Cooper-Climax cars in F2 and in F1 races which Vanwall did not enter. GAV readily gave Stirling his blessing if Rob Walker could provide his 1.9 Cooper Mark II for the Argentine race. The eager ACA agreed attractive terms, which included expenses-paid return air travel for Stirling, his wife Katie, mechanics Alf Francis and Tim Wall, and the car.

This last-minute entry was made while the British RAC registered an official protest on behalf of Vanwall and BRM against the race's World Championship status. Typically the CSI agreed to decide on the case at Monte Carlo during the Rally.

While this controversy was growing, the traditional Boxing Day Brands Hatch meeting of 1957 saw Jack Brabham driving the Walker car to victory and a new lap record of 58.85 sec, 75.92 mph in the main *Libre* race. Some reports would later maintain this was an AvGas-fuelled shakedown for the Argentine sortie. Not so. The car ran alcohol as usual. There were no track tests with AvGas prior to Buenos Aires, which frankly worried Walker, but left Alf Francis as confident as ever. Back at Dorking he changed carburettor chokes and jets, and a dyno run on 100/130 octane AvGas showed 180 bhp against a previous alcohol best of 182. The car had also been changed pre-Brands to include top radius rod location for the rear suspension.

Meanwhile, at the F2 Prix de Paris meeting the previous October, Anglophile Swiss enthusiast 'Jabby' Crombac – later to found *Sport Auto* magazine – had won the 1100 sports car race in his Lotus. He and Jack Brabham became good friends, and that winter saw Jabby take Jack around ERSA's Parisian factory. Obviously the prospect of more F1 racing was appealing, but the Cooper cars' transmissions just had to be stronger. Jack wrote: 'I went down to the foundry and I can remember trying hard to explain to them what we needed in the way of a stronger case.... I finished up with all the patterns spread out on a bench, putting Plasticine on them and scraping out the cores and so on. We made about six gearboxes, all cast with extra strengthening ribs....'

While the Walker crew prepared their car for its Argentine trip, John Cooper rushed to ERSA by air on a day-trip to collect the first strengthened casings; one destined for the Argentine car. Back at Heathrow with three casings in his baggage he was anxious to clear customs rapidly. To the question 'Anything to declare?' he answered honestly with a long rambling list of valueless knick-knacks, burying a mumbled 'three gearbox casings' in amongst them. The customs officer seemed poised to clear John's baggage, when he suddenly did a double-take: 'What, sir? Three *gearbox* casings?' John had been rumbled, and he had to spend most of the night clearing them through the proper channels. In the wee small hours he

1958 – THE WINNING BEGINS...

rushed to meet Alf Francis and the Walker 'box was built-up just in time to catch its long flight south.

Air-freighted to BA the car was hastily prepared and Moss found it '... felt fast, although the handling was no better than fair, particularly on the slow corners ... it handled far better with a full load of fuel, of which it used $3\frac{1}{2}$ gallons on my 15 practice laps, which ended when the gearbox drain plug came out....'

This caused anxiety, for the gearbox was already the car's Achilles' heel without running it dry. Then that night Katie Moss accidentally stuck her finger in Stirling's eye, scraping the cornea. He completed practice with an eye-patch and pain-killers, but more trouble was forecast: '... we had put 4.50s on the front, which improved the handling, but we heard that our tyres should last for 30–40 laps; the race was 80.' There were no knock-off hubs on the Cooper, but four fixing studs, so a tyre-change could only be disastrously time-consuming. 'I only did three laps on the Saturday to conserve the tyres and also because my eye was still very painful and my vision blurred....'

Stirling started seventh on the 10-strong grid. The race began in the late afternoon after the blistering heat of midday had cooled slightly, and his eye was much better. He began well, fourth behind Fangio's and Behra's Maseratis and Hawthorn's V6 Ferrari, and stole third place only for drama on lap 4 centred on the gearbox clutch interlock mechanism, which had been introduced to help resist it jumping out of gear: 'The gearbox jammed in second and I did almost a complete lap like that. I tried to change gear all the time ... running up to 6000 rpm, putting out the clutch and trying to move the lever, but it was jammed solid. I was just going to pull into the pits ... when suddenly it freed. It was one of the luckiest breaks I have ever experienced....' The clutch had broken and since the change interlock device was only actuated by the clutch releasing, when the clutch broke the interlock held second gear. Now a stone had miraculously flown up, jammed beneath the mechanism and opened it for him! Stirling called it '... the most incredible stroke of luck'; he was right....

He had lost 15 seconds and Musso had gone by in his Ferrari. Now Stirling caught and passed the heavier car and chased as hard as he dare, mindful of tyre wear, creeping round the tight corners and finding optimum traction without wheelspin away from them. He closed on Hawthorn for second place, nipped him out into one of the turns and then when Fangio stopped to refuel and change tyres he inherited the lead on lap 35. At 40 laps – halfway – he was 21 sec clear of Behra, who still had to stop, and Fangio was flagging behind. Into the closing stages the Ferrari team management suddenly realized that the Cooper's 'inevitable stop' just wasn't going to happen. The Walker crew had spare wheels ready on the pit apron, but it was only to lull the opposition's fears. Moss was attempting to run race distance non-stop!

Above *Boxing Day Brands Hatch, 1957, saw Jack Brabham out again in the Alf Francis-developed Rob Walker Mark II, winning the main* Formule Libre *event and setting a new 75.92 mph lap record on the way. It was a gloomy day. Here he rounds Druid's Hairpin, showing off the Scots-blue and white car's single radius rod rear suspension location and modified nose treatment*

Top *Swiss-born 'French' journalist 'Jabby' Crombac took this shot of John triumphantly brandishing the Jack Brabham redesigned Citroën-ERSA transaxle casing which at last gave the hard-pressed mechanism some chance of surviving 2-litre Climax FPF torque and power. Jack's redesign was pragmatic in the extreme, as Jabby recalls he 'redesigned it on the spot at ERSA's using plasticine to add the reinforcing ribs'. It was on the way home to London with the first casings that John had his little spot of bother with HM Customs ...*

The first of many – Stirling Moss, waving joyfully, takes the chequered flag in the Walker Cooper to win the World Championship-qualifying Argentine GP, Buenos Aires Autodrome, 19 January, 1958. His tyres were worn through to the canvas by his non-stop run and luck was on his side against a small though more powerful field. To combat the heat various slots have been cut into the Mark II's bodywork and air deflectors fitted, like that visible under the nose to enhance radiator flow

Waking up to the fact too late Musso began a late charge to catch that disreputable little English special.

Phil Hill, reserve Ferrari driver: 'We were all sitting around content, knowing this damned little bug was going to have to change tyres and then its bolt-on wheels would kill its chances. But Stirling just went on and on, and then came the awful realization they'd been bluffing and he was going right on through. Musso ran out of laps to catch him ... we'd been sitting round waiting for the Cooper to break or blow a tyre, but it just went round like clockwork....'

Stirling: 'From about the halfway mark I had been glancing at my tyres ... at last with 14 laps to go I saw a little white spot flick past.... After that I kept looking at them – the spot became longer, became a continuous white band around the tyre and then began to broaden; an undulating band of white on both back tyres...' they were wearing through to the canvas.

Terrified of them bursting he kept to the oily sections of track, pussy-footing round as Musso bit great chunks out of that time-cushion. But lap 80 came and ended with Stirling still 2.7 sec ahead; he and the Walker Cooper-Climax had won the Argentine Grand Prix.

Phil Hill: 'After the race Amorotti, our team manager, was wandering around the paddock, with his hands palm upwards, fingers interlocked and waggling in the air – a sign like a bug on its back waggling its legs. He couldn't believe his masterpieces had been beaten by this horrible iddy-biddy thing with its engine in the wrong end....'

Stirling: 'It was quite staggering and I could hardly believe it, as the odds were all against a 1.96-litre car lasting 80 laps without a tyre change and with such little preparation. Alf Francis had done nothing but change the jets and tune it for petrol, and the car had averaged 83.57 mph....

'Above all, it was a British victory.... I was very proud....'

In Surbiton, John Cooper was having a drink at home with friendly Keith Challen, motoring correspondent of *The News of the World*. Keith called his office to ask if the agency tapes had brought in the race result yet. He beamed, and broke the news to John. He rang Salvadori and some of the other lads 'and some serious drinking began....'

Before returning home the Walker car ran in the *Formule Libre* BA City GP at the Autodrome, retuned to run alcohol. Stirling qualified second fastest to Fangio's Lightweight Maserati, but it rained on race day and the Cooper's gearbox jammed briefly in second. Still Stirling plumed third into the first turn, but as he braked he was rammed heavily from behind by Iglesias' Chevrolet Special. Neither driver was hurt, but both cars were out.... In fact it seems the Cooper was rebuilt around a brand-new chassis, the bent one being discarded, though the Walker team would know the repaired 'T43' as their 'Argentine' car, irrespective....

Now with eight World Championship points to Moss and Cooper the RAC protest to the CSI about the Argentine GP's status was quietly dropped, and Stirling led the World Drivers' Championship into 1958 courtesy of Cooper-Climax, which as a marque led the newly instituted Manufacturers' Cup competition! Rob Walker was the first true private entrant ever to win a World Championship-qualifying Grand Prix road race.

Consider now that at that time only Vanwall had previously achieved all-British success at this level, and they had won only three GPs – this maiden victory for Cooper-Climax was only the fourth of a new age of British dominance.

1958 — THE WINNING BEGINS...

Jack Brabham winning the New Zealand GP **top** *at Ardmore aerodrome in his ex-works car using a 2.2-litre engine which he confirms today he had manufactured himself. Typically he made little song and dance about it, and the '2.2' NZ entry subsequently appeared to be engine development of the race promotional variety. Alf Francis' FPF stretch to 2015 cc pre-dated Climax's own production of their first 2.2-litre engine, but Sir Jack with his own Laystall crank, and pistons and liners made for him by Repco in Australia, showed them both the way. Also in New Zealand, after finding his feet in the ex-Brabham Bob-tail sports through 1957, young Bruce McLaren was armed with this bored-out ex-works Mark II-FPF 1.7 by Brabham for the 1958 summer races there. Here he is in the Ardmore '50', heading Ron Roycroft's giant Ferrari 375 on the way to fifth place after an enforced pit stop. Jack had developed his Cooper-Bristol's suspension with advice from Australian engineer Ron Tauranac, and after moving to the UK and joining Cooper he maintained a regular technical correspondence with him. Ron's advice for Cooper mods included geometry changes, the addition of top rear wishbones and drop-gears to aid ratio-changing. He had the first drop-gear set made for Jack in Australia, though they were not fitted until his return to England*

Meanwhile, in New Zealand, Bruce McLaren had been finding his feet in the ex-Brabham Bob-tail sports car through 1957. The day after buying it he had won his class in the Horahora hillclimb: 'It was a dream to drive,' he would recall; 'I'd never experienced such responsiveness to the controls. . . .' He notched three wins in a day at Levin and the Bob-tail broke its class record at every hillclimb entered. He and a racing friend named Phil Kerr had ambitions to run the car at Sebring. Through 1957 he corresponded with Jack Brabham in England, who said he would bring out a '1.7' Cooper for Bruce in the 1958 NZ GP. In discussion with Buzz Perkins about a possible Sebring entry, the NZIGP man suggested there might be an even brighter chance ahead. The Association planned to sponsor a Kiwi driver for a year's racing in Europe. Bruce was on the short-list. He'd stand a better chance in Jack's promised single-seater, so the Australian was asked to bring the car down for the McLarens to purchase, and they sold the Bob-tail to Merv Neil to raise the cash.

Contemporary reports suggest that Jack had a '2.2' Climax FPF engine in his NZ GP car. According to Climax's history it was surely a regular 1.96 with, according to Bruce, a 1.7 in the ex-Salvadori works car – presumably *F2/8/57* – for him. Climax's own 2.2 stretch FPF would not be out for months, but today Sir Jack confirms this was indeed 2.2 which he had made-up himself and which was 'later taken up by Climax'. Mechanic Derrick Edwards also brought out Dick Gibson's latest brand-new Mark II and Bruce was all over it in eager anticipation of Brabham's arrival with his new car.

The NZ GP was run at Ardmore the day before that historic Argentine race; Jack Brabham notched victory on his fifth attempt with Gibson sixth and Ron Frost seventh in another Cooper. It wasn't Bruce's day. He was second to Jack as planned in a prelim, but while he and his friend Colin Beanland were warming-up the car for the GP itself its gearbox broke. Jack had brought out a spare for Gibson's car and 20 minutes before the start a gearbox change began. Then the organizers found mysterious oil patches on the course, sufficient to delay the GP until the final bolts were being tightened as the flag fell. Bruce joined in half a lap behind the rest and gained eighth place before misfiring began. Plugs were changed, but then the hastily fitted gearbox cover worked loose, the oil gushed out and he retired with red-hot gear clusters. At the presentation that night he won huge consolation – he was named as the NZIGP's first 'Driver to Europe'.

He won a locals-only race a week later at Levin, where Jack won the feature and Bruce was third behind Archie Scott-Brown's sports Lister. The Scot won the Lady Wigram Trophy, as both Brabham and McLaren had gearbox trouble. Merv Mayo drove Frost's Cooper home fifth after the owner had hurt his arm by tipping the car over at Levin.

Brabham sold his Mark II to Merv Neil and left for Australia, while Bruce took his to Dunedin, had two confidence-rocking shunts in practice, then finished second to Ross Jensen's Maserati in the feature, beating Scott-Brown. Dick Gibson had qualified on pole, but spun and finished fifth. Merv Neil's ex-Brabham Mark II won a prelim.

Having completed his business in Australia, Jack Brabham returned for the Teretonga Park race where he drove in ordinary shoes and caught the welt between brake and throttle pedals while striving to catch Jensen. After retrieving a lurid moment he was third; Jensen won, Bruce was second, Merv Neil fourth and Gibson seventh.

Both Bruce and Jack had sought more grip on the shingle-surfaced track by fitting Michelin X rear tyres. Dunlop's rep was philosophical: 'At least we can still say Dunlops crossed the line first if you win. . . .'

On 1 March at Ardmore the final race of the NZ season saw Jensen win to take the Gold Star award, while Bruce slowed with a plug lead adrift. He finished fifth, then prepared for Europe, with Colin Beanland and a new F2 Cooper.

The new Mark III – T45 – car for 1958 had been shown to the Press in January. The usual Cooper design committee had made a major change in adopting coil-and-wishbone front suspension in place of the original transverse leaf, although the leaf was retained at the rear, where it still doubled as top lateral location for the wheel uprights. For much of the coming year, however, the works cars would adopt double rear wishbones too. . . . In addition the winter of gearbox developments in conjunction with ERSA and Jack Knight had reached fruition with a pair of step-up spur gears introduced within the bell-housing to enable a $2\frac{1}{2}$ in. lower engine mounting and easier ratio changes for differing circuits.

On the earlier cars, engine height had been dictated by the Citroën transaxle layout in which the primary shaft from clutch to gearbox passed above the inner drive-shafts taking power to the wheels. To lower the engine's centre of gravity as much as possible in the Mark IIs it had been mounted inclined downwards towards the nose and canted to the right. Now the step-up gears enabled the rear of the engine to be dropped to a level mounting within the frame. Owen Maddock recalls it as 'Jack Brabham's idea originally . . . he was always working with the cars, looking at them, thinking about them, and I'm sure it was his suggestion that led to the step-up gears being adopted . . . now we could change overall gear ratios in a matter of minutes by removing the gearbox and swopping the step-up gear wheels'. In fact Jack had been in close touch with Australian engineer Ron Tauranac since *RedeX Spl* days, and Ron made many suggestions like the drop-gears which made the Coopers work. With John's connivance Jack got many things past Charles; 'I flew over to Germany one day to get us some ZF diffs old Charlie wouldn't pay for. John fixed the money. I get the bits. We'd never have won a race without 'em. . . .'

The gearbox now included a ZF diff as standard, and the gear-wheels were made in stronger EN39 steel, while the John-cum-Jack reinforced ERSA transaxle case was cast in

1958 – THE WINNING BEGINS...

heavier-duty aluminium alloy with more beefy mounting flange and external ribbing, and the new internal ribs. The old 'round the houses' gearchange linkage was replaced by a much more straightforward right-side single-rod system, including two UJs, and the existing Citroën gearbox lid with bolted-on fabricated bracket for the selector lever was replaced by a new casting. The heavy steel engine rear mounting plate of the Mark II was replaced by a lighter magnesium casting.

Chassis frame changes were few, being confined to lowering the whole structure about $1\frac{1}{2}$ in., while the front end was altered to provide pick-ups for upper wishbones and a coil-spring/damper unit top abutment. The inboard pivots for the lower wishbones were above the bottom frame rails instead of below them. Both top and bottom frame longerons were more widely spaced than the Mark II's, with less tube curvature.

The top wishbones were welded tubular fabrications carry-

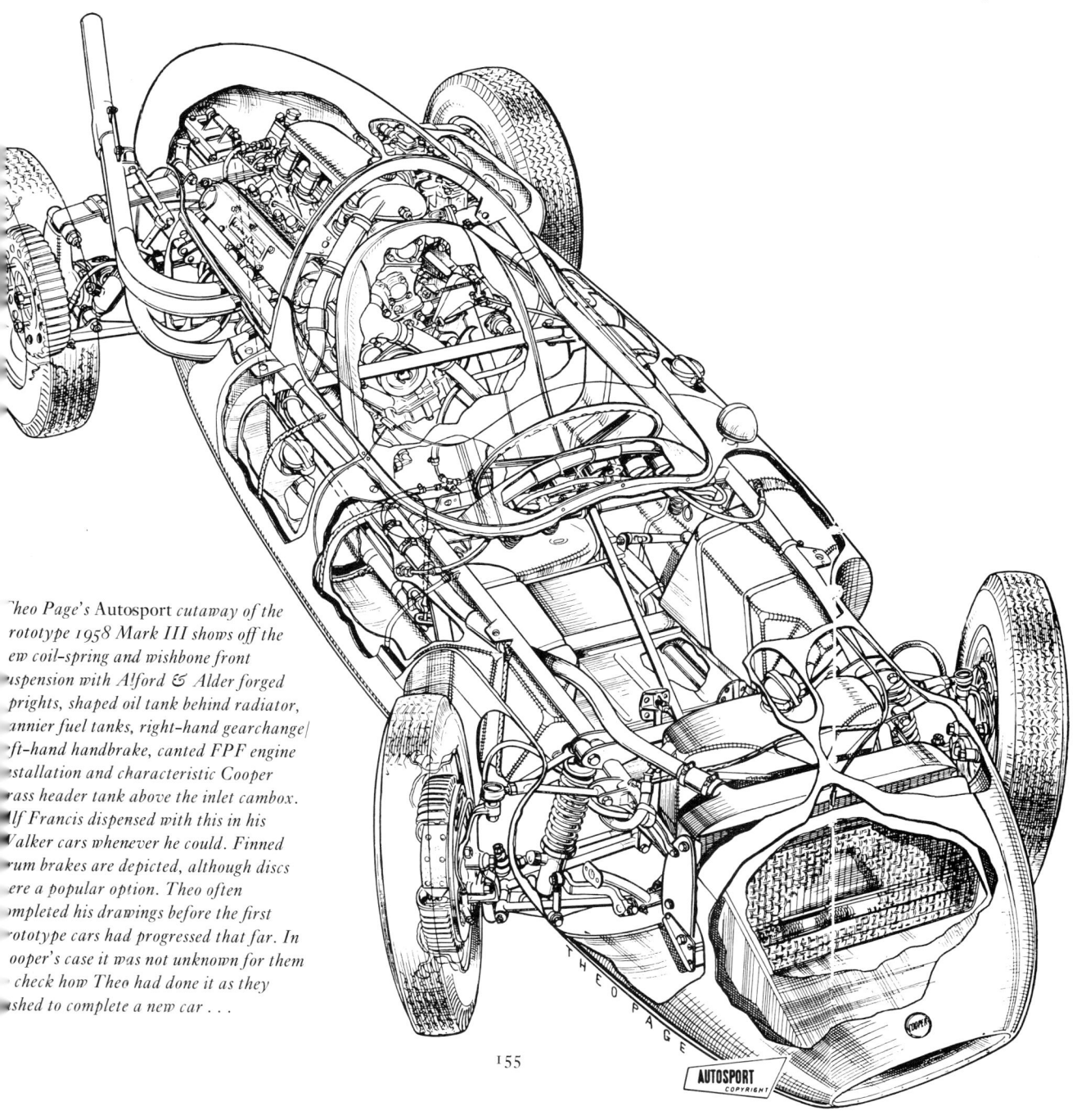

Theo Page's Autosport *cutaway of the prototype 1958 Mark III shows off the new coil-spring and wishbone front suspension with Alford & Alder forged uprights, shaped oil tank behind radiator, pannier fuel tanks, right-hand gearchange/left-hand handbrake, canted FPF engine installation and characteristic Cooper brass header tank above the inlet cambox. Alf Francis dispensed with this in his Walker cars whenever he could. Finned drum brakes are depicted, although discs were a popular option. Theo often completed his drawings before the first prototype cars had progressed that far. In Cooper's case it was not unknown for them to check how Theo had done it as they rushed to complete a new car...*

ing a threaded Chorlton ball-joint on their apex. Alford & Alder forged uprights and stub-axles were adopted, the upright being Standard 8 and the stub Triumph TR3. The lower screw-thread trunnion was retained and all external surfaces were polished and cadmium-plated. Roll-stiffness, which had previously been maintained by Owen's curly leaf, was maintained by a transverse anti-roll bar passing through the foremost bottom frame cross-member.

At the rear the widely spaced trunnion mountings for the transverse leaf-spring were retained, but the curly leaf was replaced as lateral spring location by a single short link pivoted on the left-side frame trunnion and bolted to a centre clamp around the leaf-spring. The original curly leaves had been effective, but in hard use tended to adopt a permanent set. The bottom rear wishbones were now more widely based both on the bottom frame rail and at the foot of the uprights, and the outboard mount for the telescopic damper was more rigidly sited on a cross-brace between front and rear elements of the wishbone. On the Mark II it had been clipped to the forward wishbone tube and this had broken on occasion – as at Nürburgring. Now the weakness had been seen, and corrected. It was typical Cooper design by evolution; learning lessons, and learning them well.

The Armstrong telescopic dampers fitted front and rear were adjustable by means of a knurled knob on the bottom of the unit, and had been introduced on the interim F1 cars the previous season.

Unusual not to see some smiling faces amongst the works team. Here on the grid for the Formula 1 Glover Trophy race at Goodwood, Easter Monday 1958, Roy Salvadori sorts-out his kit, Charles poses, John ponders, Jack Brabham just sits, characteristically alert but inscrutable, while chief mechanic Bill James investigates his upper set. Tom Bridger, behind in the new F2 BRP Mark III will end his race against the safety bank but emerge unhurt

Drum-type two leading-shoe brakes by Girling, 10 in. diameter × 1¾ in. wide, reappeared front and rear, operating in laterally finned and linered magnesium alloy drums, but discs were available as an attractive option. Lengthened pannier fuel tanks were used as standard without the additional scuttle tank of the Mark II, which could be fitted in the Mark III if extra range should be required. John announced initially that four Mark IIIs would be built – two each for F1 and F2 use to be driven by Jack Brabham and Roy Salvadori. Similar models would be available in customer production from Hollyfield Road. *The Autocar* explained: 'Racing cars are subject to purchase tax, recoverable from a Government research fund, so that, less PT, this Cooper can be bought for £2350 – an amazingly low figure.'

For Formula 1 a new 2.2-litre version of the Climax FPF twin-cam racing engine was on the way.

After their sometimes encouraging outings with the

1958 – THE WINNING BEGINS...

Fresh from their Argentine victory Moss and the Walker Mark II stalled at the start of the Glover Trophy. Here Alf Francis and Don Christmas desperately push him off pole while Harry Schell's BRM booms away along with Bridger and the rest. Stirling set a joint new lap record tearing back through the field until the 1960 cc engine failed. Had he finished he would have been penalized for the push-start. This car was based on a new frame carrying the Argentine engine and possibly some of the earlier body panels. The GP winner had been shunted and Rob Walker would always replace a damaged frame rather than merely repair it. Though this Mark II would retain the 'Argentine' car's identity, its frame had never been to Buenos Aires...

1960 cc FPF 'stretch' engines in 1957, both John Cooper and Colin Chapman had pleaded with Hassan and Lee at Coventry Climax to go further. Hassan didn't want to push his luck too far, but the FPF was to grow from 1500 cc to 2.7 litres.

The initial step authorized by Lee was for four-only 2.2-litre units to be shared; two to Cooper, two to Lotus for Formula 1. They were 'square' engines, both bore and stroke measuring 88.9 mm, to displace 2207 cc. The extra stroke demanded longer liners and the only way to accommodate them, since they protruded above the standard block's top deck, was to insert a packing piece, about a quarter-inch thick, between block and head. Hassan disliked such fudgery, but with regular inspection it sufficed. These 2.2s produced around 194 bhp at 6250 rpm on AvGas, with a peak bmep of 204 lb/sq. in. at 5000 rpm. The first new engine would be available in May. Meanwhile Alf Francis again led the way for Walker with an interim FPF 'stretch' of his own, to 2015 cc, using 0.9 mm oversize-bore liners and pistons. Moss was to use it in a new Walker team Mark III frame.

The surviving Cooper Register discloses orders for 25 Mark 'III' F2s, one bound for a Portuguese named Monteiro subsequently being cancelled, although he raced such a car in the UK. Two were works cars – the second *F2/23A/58* – actually being completed during the 1958–59 winter as a new works Mark IV for the following year. Plain *23/58* had already been supplied to Jack Lewis late in the '58 season. Other customers appear in the Appendices. Two significant new teams were to emerge.

Former Cooper 500 driver Ken Tyrrell had joined forces with fellow Guildfordians Alan Brown and Cecil Libowitz, who ran a local concern named Weyside Engineering. They bought two F2s – chassis *2/58* and *17/58* – for Ken himself and Keith Ballisat, amongst others, to drive. Moss's business manager Ken Gregory likewise formed the other team with Pa Moss and BP backing. It was to be called the British Racing Partnership; BRP for short. Their base was at the contemporary Moss home, 'White Cloud Farm', at Tring in Buckinghamshire. Chief mechanic was Tony Robinson, who since his earlier stint with Stirling Moss Ltd had maintained Bruce

Halford's private Maserati 250F. BRP drivers were to be Stuart Lewis-Evans, when Vanwall commitments allowed, and the promising young Tom Bridger, ex-F3.

The Autocar F2 Championship that year, open only to British licence holders, included for the first time all the major class events abroad as well as in the UK. Lewis-Evans would lead this affair into its final round – the F2 category of the Moroccan GP at Casablanca – but there Brabham and McLaren would surpass his points total as the Londoner was committed – tragically as it turned out – to Vanwall.

The season commenced on 7 April, Easter Monday Goodwood, with the 15-lap Lavant Cup contested by nine Coopers and three Lotus 12s. Brabham drove the works' new wishbone Mark III, Salvadori the new car entered by Tommy Atkins, proprietor of High Efficiency Engineering of Elmbridge, close by the Cooper works, and Lewis-Evans the pale-green BRP car. He had a radio link to the pits, but it proved inaudible at racing speeds. Roy led before crashing at Lavant. Jack fought a torrid duel with Graham Hill's progressively disintegrating Lotus and won by 0.4 sec. Allison's Lotus was third, Lewis-Evans fourth.

F1 and F2 cars combined in the main 42-lap Glover Trophy race that day and Brabham and Salvadori both drove works 1.96s, Moss his Argentine car and Ian Burgess took over Jack's still-warm F2. Hawthorn's Ferrari Dino won from Jack and Roy, while Stirling stalled at the start, but recovered to share a new lap record of 1:28.8, 97.30 mph, while Hawthorn then had his engine throw a rod, Brabham spinning in the smoke and oil. Cliff Allison won the F2 class for Lotus; Hornsey's first defeat of Surbiton. Tom Bridger mangled the new BRP car against the Madgwick bank.

That same day at Pau five Coopers contested the F2 GP, and the veteran 40-year-old French driver, Maurice Trintignant, made his debut for the Walker team. While Moss was contracted to Vanwall for the rest of the year's GPs, *Le Petoulet*, mayor of the small town of Vergeze, would handle the British privateer's Coopers. He was vastly experienced, smooth and reliable and he won on his Cooper-Climax debut at Pau, handling Walker's ex-Leston Mark II – chassis *F2/16/57*. Hernano da Silva Ramos was second in the Tyrrell-Brown Mark III, while Ken's older Mark II broke a half-shaft. The Kiwi Equipe Mark IIs for Moore and Thackwell ran twin-cam FPFs for the first time in place of single-cam FWBs and respectively finished fourth and broke a gearbox.

At Surbiton, Bruce McLaren had recently arrived, with Colin Beanland. The driver was 20, his mechanic 22. Buzz Perkins had arranged a works F2 drive for him in the Aintree '200' on 15 April. Jack Brabham met him at Heathrow and introduced him to John at Hollyfield Road. 'Pleased to meet you, boy,' said the pipe. Bruce recalled: 'All round the workshop were Coopers in various stages of assembly. I asked where my car was. "Your car, boy?" said the pipe, "In the tube rack I reckon. . . ." I couldn't see any car in the pile of chassis tubes, but it slowly dawned on me. I felt very small. . . .'

It was Cooper kidology. A fresh-painted frame was ready and Douggie Johnson took Bruce in hand to complete the car: 'On discovering I was a New Zealander he announced to the shop, "Here's another one – lock up your tools or you'll lose 'em. . . ."'

While Bruce would be settling into the Cooper 'system', the works team as always operated with minimum personnel. Ginger Devlin, Eric Brandon's former Ecurie Richmond mechanic, had dropped out with Eric when they went off to build the Halseylec sports-racing cars. Eric then took up hydroplane racing on water, and left motor sport behind him. Ginger became an integral character in the Cooper Car Company, for many years maintaining the School cars while doubling-up as required on the works team at home or in the field. He would eventually act as midwife in the birth of the Mini-Cooper saloon in 1960–61, and would run the works saloon car team for the following eight seasons.

Bald-headed veteran Bill James was the works team's chief mechanic during the late-Fifties. His habit of parking lighted cigarettes behind his ears as he became engrossed in his work mesmerized his workmates. Two stripes of nicotine run up either side of his bald head. . . .

Then there was lean, often mean Mike Grohmann, a young racing mechanic formerly with Connaught. The story was that he'd been thrown out for slinging a punch at the boss, Rodney Clarke. But he was a fantastic, utterly dedicated, totally committed racing mechanic. He struck up a close relationship with Jack Brabham – another man prepared to work all hours, and to eat, drink and sleep racing and racing cars.

Mike Grohmann's sharp features won him the nickname 'Noddy', after the Enid Blyton character. He had been trained as an engine fitter on National Service in the RAF. He later had various jobs in the motor trade before joining Connaught around 1955. His parents were in the antiques business, and he was single and lived with them in a sizeable house in Godalming, about 20 miles south from Surbiton. He was a sombre person in some ways. He'd state ideas and contentions and then openly challenge contradiction. 'If he didn't like what you said,' a friend told me, 'he'd bop you one with his fist. . . . He seemed to punch people about three or four times a year; but at the same time he was a very humorous bloke and he had the most terrific sense of outrageous fun. He got up to some incredible things; he was an absolute law unto himself. He told everybody, including old Charles, to f—— off if he felt like it and he worked all hours. . . . And he couldn't stand Bill James, and Bill James couldn't stand him. . . .'

For Aintree, Bruce McLaren was to drive Jack's Mark III prototype ex-Goodwood. But Charles didn't approve at all – who was this schoolboy anyway? John smoothed it out, provided Bruce paid £50 insurance on the car. The Aintree orga-

1958 – THE WINNING BEGINS . . .

While Moss handled his works Vanwall in the 1958 World Championship classics, Rob Walker gave Maurice Trintignant a choice of cars as here at Monaco where the veteran Frenchman chose the newer Mark III with Francis-modified nose cowling, underslung oil cooler behind a protective grille, 2015 cc engine and Francis single radius rod rear suspension. The works cars used upper wishbones to relieve the rear transverse leafspring of lateral location duties. Here at the Station Hairpin, on his reliable way to Walker's second successive Cooper-Climax GP victory

New arrival: Bruce McLaren testing his new Mark III F2 at Brands Hatch on a Cooper School day. On the left stand Ginger Devlin and Terry Kitson, Colin Beanland is behind the car in woolly hat; Ian Burgess has been offering advice and former Daisy Fresh cake salesman Andrew Ferguson ponders beneath that cap . . . . Bruce's NZ Mark II with leafspring front suspension was shipped to England but sold to Steve Ouvaroff on arrival

nizers were paying £60 start money, so Bruce was already in profit.

The race was to be another combined F1/F2 affair and Moss would be driving the latest Walker Mark III with Francis's 2015 cc interim engine. From the surviving Register one may conclude this car was chassis *F2/9/58*, but we must be careful. Cooper frames were quite easy to make and John Kelly undoubtedly welded-up more than were recorded and the Register does not include 'kits' of the kind which Walker bought whenever one of his existing cars showed too much wear and tear. Neither is there any evidence at this range of what was actually stamped on the metalwork of any of his cars. The Dorking team also fielded two F2 Coopers at Aintree; one, the Argentine Mark II re-engined with a 1500 for Tony Brooks, and the other the ex-Leston car, again for Trintignant. John ran the two works wishbone-suspended 1.96s for Brabham and Salvadori.

In the race, Moss's Mark III led from Behra's BRM until the front-engined car's brake fluid boiled and Brabham tail-wagged his way into second place. Moss's clutch then failed, but he drove on. Both Jack's and Roy's clutches began slipping, but the Australian still barged into the lead only for Moss to pull out a breath-taking manoeuvre in the last turn to win by 0.2 sec! Brooks was third in the Walker F2 to win the class and give the team a double victory. Salvadori's crippled works 1.96 limped home fourth, ahead of Lewis-Evans's F2 and Harry Schell's pale-blue F2 Cooper taking his Owen Organization BRM entry. Bruce was ninth on his British debut.

After this Cooper triumph against the hapless BRMs the Silverstone May meeting saw Ferrari re-entering the fray. Salvadori's 1.96 Mark III took pole from Brabham and Moss's Walker special, all faster than Collins's quickest Ferrari on the outside of the front row. Charles Cooper was so proud he took a colour photo of the line-up for the family album. The F2 field included a full complement of Coopers, while Bob Gerard was out again in his F1 BG-Bristol special, down the grid.

As at Goodwood, Moss stalled, Behra's BRM and Collins's Ferrari outpaced the Coopers as expected and the Italian V6 won, with Salvadori a distant second. Jack's carburetion played-up and he finished fifth. Allison's F2 Lotus placed sixth overall to beat Lewis-Evans and McLaren for the F2 class – Surbiton's second defeat by the Hornsey marque. Bruce drove his newly completed Mark III. During the hectic assembly work at Hollyfield Road, where other customers like Syd Jensen and Alan Mackay were also beavering away to finish their cars, Douggie Johnson recalls returning from lunch one day to find Bruce's frame with a 125 Villiers two-stroke sitting proudly in its engine bay. . . .

Another Cooper with something strange in its engine bay at this time was actually one of the rare Formula 1 cars to take advantage of the 750 cc supercharged section of the basic 2½ litres unsupercharged regulations. This was optimistic Bruce Gleed's special, the Formula 1 Gleed-MG, mounting a supercharged prewar 'R'-Type MG four-cylinder engine in an elderly 500 frame. It never started an F1 race, if it ever started any races at all. . . .

Bruce McLaren's car appears to have been *F2/5/58* recorded as *Works Car No 1* followed by the pencilled letter '*B*' – although this could apply equally to Brabham's Goodwood prototype. The works F1s seem to have been *F2/30/57* and *31/57* for the paperwork buffs; both Mark II serials recorded the previous December and transferred to the first Mark IIIs for '58. There are no other candidates for the McLaren car in the Register and equally there is no telling now what carnets it subsequently travelled under. . . . The Formula 1 Register have taken it as '*31/57*.

For Walker, Silverstone was a disaster: Moss's gearbox suffered from the start, Trintignant's 1.96 overheated and Brooks retired his F2 with 'power loss'.

Bruce won a five-car F2 clubbie at Silverstone a week later, despite flak about running 'works cars' at club level, then at Whitsun Brands he beat Ken Tyrrell in one Heat, then George Wicken and Ronnie Moore in another. Charles' attitude to the newcomer softened – 'that Brabham' had been right, he did show promise. Bruce had practised at Brands during a School day, and had a wild spin. Ginger Devlin remarked to Colin Beanland: 'That mate of your's will either be bloody good or he'll kill himself. . . .'

At Crystal Palace on Whit Monday, Ian Burgess won from Tom Bridger's BRP entry with Bruce third. Ivor Bueb's private Lotus 12 won heat one. Bridger and Wicken jointly set a new lap record, and the pace was so furious that the race average was actually higher than the preceding record. . . .

At Brands Hatch in June Lewis-Evans won for BRP hounded by Burgess and Dennis Taylor. New Zealand tourist Syd Jensen shared a new lap record with the Lotuseer.

The second French race of the season followed at Montlhéry where Coopers filled the first six places in the Prix de Paris, Henry Taylor notching another one for BRP from Guelfi, McLaren, Burgess, Marsh and another Kiwi visitor, Merv Neil.

Syd Jensen won at Crystal Palace on 5 July, succeeding on aggregate in face of fierce opposition from Jim Russell's Cooper and Ivor the Driver's Ecurie Demi-Litre Lotus.

Meanwhile the Cooper Car Co's Bedford transporter ground its 25 mph way south to Monaco for the GP on 18 May and unloaded three works cars; two 1.96 Mark IIIs with new fin-styling on the tail cowls, plus a sister Mark III with the latest 2.2 FPF 'stretch' engine. Equipe Walker ran the Argentine Mark II leaf-spring car, with the latest wishbone front suspension Mark III in company. Both featured the Francis radius rod rear suspension, while the works cars all used double-wishbones front and rear. The Walker Mark II's gearbox had a bracing clamp over the gearbox drawn down

1958 – THE WINNING BEGINS...

Alf Francis in one of the experimental Walker F2 streamliners tested at Reims-Gueux. The tack-on side pod fairings made the cars extremely unstable at high speed and were thankfully set aside before the race began

to the frame by tension rods to resist flexion. Both engines had the 97.3 mm bore liners and pistons, for 2015 cc.

In the works camp, Brabham and Salvadori drew lots for the larger-engined works car, while the Walker entries were handled by Trintignant and the experienced Scot, Ron Flockhart. He was handicapped in the older car by unsuitable gear ratios, because it didn't have the step-up gear facility of the Mark IIIs. Jack had drawn the works 2.2 and he and Trintignant were amongst the front-runners in practice with cars ideal for the street circuit. Jack qualified on the front row with Salvadori and Trintignant on row two, but poor Flockhart couldn't qualify.

Roy's starts were always terrific and he led into the first hairpin at breakneck speed only to slither wide. Bumping his way back into the pack his car's steering arm bolts were stretched and he stopped immediately to replace them. The leading 2½-litre cars were really racing, and Brabham and Trintignant were outpaced 5–6 until lap 22, when Jack stopped to have a loose anti-roll bar remounted. He rejoined just ahead of Salvadori, who was firmly last.

The Vanwalls retired, and Hawthorn's Ferrari was left with a half-minute lead from Trintignant's steadily driven Cooper until lap 46, when the Italian car's fuel pump mount broke and parted its drive – just like Brabham's Cooper failure the previous year. Trintignant was thus handed the lead and he drove a model race, as he had in 1955 for Ferrari, to win the Monaco GP after faster opposition had retired. Not that he drove slowly, for his race average of 67.99 mph was a new record, although we should remember that the race was five laps shorter that year. Jack finished fourth, three laps behind, while Roy's gearbox had failed after 56 of the 100 laps. The Walker crew couldn't believe it. The winning car had smoked all the way.

Denis Jenkinson mused on other aspects of the race: '... The chummy atmosphere in the little British teams is refreshing.... Brabham just will not stop working on all the Coopers. Their "science" gives one to think; John Cooper was seen using his finger as a dip-stick on one of the Coopers – at least he's not likely to mislay it....'

Incredibly, with two consecutive World Championship GP wins to its credit, the Cooper-Climax marque still led the Constructors' Cup competition, and Rob Walker became the first private entrant ever to win two races of such status in succession. But Argentina had been won by Moss and kidology against a sparse field, and Monaco was now a proven Cooper circuit, which had broken faster cars. It would be hard for the small-engined Coopers to do so well on the faster courses to come....

So it proved, beginning with the Dutch GP eight days after Monaco. Brabham and Salvadori swopped cars – 1.96 and 2.2 respectively – for this race and would take turns with the 'big gun' for the rest of the year. Trintignant was out again in the Monaco Mark III with the 'Argentine' Mark II leaf-spring car in reserve. While Vanwall monopolized the front row, Jack got onto row two, and Trintignant and Salvadori shared a time behind him. In the GP, Roy soared into fourth place and finished there, lapped once by Moss's victorious Vanwall and two BRMs. Jack was 8th and Trintignant 9th.

At Spa, of course, the Coopers were utterly outclassed, Walker stayed away and Salvadori's daring with the 1.96 works car saw him close to Jack's 2.2 and lead him in the race until clutch-slip intruded. He fell back to finish a lapped eighth while Jack retired with head-joint failure.

Reims followed; the speed weekend included the French GP and the most important F2 race of the season. Walker's two F2 Coopers appeared with bolt-on body farings to streamline their wheels on the superfast straights. Moss and Trintignant were to drive, while John fielded two works F2s for Jack and Roy. Main Cooper opposition would come from Collins's works Ferrari Dino V6 and Jean Behra's centre-seat Porsche special.

Practice soon proved to the Walker drivers that they didn't like the streamline option, while Behra took pole from Collins and Moss. As practice ended Trint's car caught fire, singeing his neck, but despite extensive damage the machine was repaired for the race. On the grid Brabham's engine threw a rod, Behra led from Moss and Collins, while Wicken's Cooper rammed Allison's recalcitrant Lotus in the tail. Roy retired, Moss stole the briefest lead, but on lap 11 was out with no oil pressure. Behra won from Collins with a delighted Wicken third ahead of Burgess, McLaren and Taylor. That a one-time Le Mans sports car could so humble the cream of F2 proved the value of proper streamlining on such a high-speed circuit.

161

Only the works Coopers started the GP, Walker again opting out at such an unsuitable venue, Jack finished a lapped sixth in the 2.2 and Roy – handicapped throughout by clutch-slip – was classified 11th, 13 laps behind Hawthorn's winning Ferrari.

Two weeks later the British GP at Silverstone – Salvadori's favourite circuit – saw John field three works Mark IIIs, all with double-wishbone rear ends and disc brakes all round; Roy in the 2.2, Brabham and Burgess with 1.96s. Trintignant had driven a BRM at Reims and now reappeared in the 'Argentine' Walker Mark II with its leaf-spring front end, the team's other two cars going to Caen that weekend....

Roy drove brilliantly in practice to qualify third-fastest alongside Moss's Vanwall and Schell's BRM, 0.4 sec quicker than Hawthorn's Ferrari Dino on the outside spot. Again all the Coopers were outpaced at the start, but Jack and Roy ganged together in a cut-throat dice for sixth place against Ferrari, Lotus and BRM opponents. Roy won and inherited third place, which he defended despite the close attentions of Lewis-Evans's Vanwall and roasting cockpit heat. Jack finished sixth and unhappy: 'My reputation was more for Formula 2 in those days.... Roy drove very well and people began to look upon him as possibly one of the few top Grand Prix drivers....' Trintignant, twice lapped, finished eighth in the old Walker car.

Overnight, drivers rushed to Caen in Normandy for a combined F1/F2 race that Sunday. Walker fielded their 2.2 Mark III for Moss and the ex-Leston Mark II for Trintignant as a 1500 cc F2. Stirling won as he pleased after a dice with Behra's BRM and Trintignant's fourth overall brought Walker the F2 class as well.

On 27 July the Louis Rosier circuit was inaugurated in the hills above Charade, Clermont-Ferrand, and there Maurice Trintignant was uncatchable in Walker's car, beating Bueb with Lewis-Evans (just) shouldered back to third.

Only eight F2s ran in the Vanwall Trophy at Snetterton, where once in front Ian Burgess proved quite uncatchable, Bruce finishing second when Henry Taylor spun George Nixon's Cooper.

On 3 August, the German GP at Nürburgring saw Peter Collins crash fatally while in hot pursuit of Brooks's leading Vanwall. This was another combined F1/F2 event, though a World Championship round, and with *Autocar* Championship points at stake and good class money John dropped Jack Brabham into the 1500 division with McLaren while entering Salvadori in the 2.2. Moss drove for Vanwall, while his Caen-winning Walker Mark III was entrusted to Trintignant and the team's F2 Mark II went to Wolfgang Seidel. Burgess drove the Atkins F2 Mark III, with Brian Naylor, Dick Gibson and Goethals other Cooper runners.

Some, Brabham included, covered less than the required six training laps in practice so were demoted to the back of the grid. This led to the quicker boys, again like Jack, rocketing through the grid at the start. His luck ran out as he rammed Bonnier's Maserati in the rump. Cliff Allison, also from the back row, actually caught and passed Roy's 2.2 on the opening lap, which made the Cooper man view the Lotus with new respect....

After Jack retired, Roy ran sixth behind Allison. As the front runners dropped out they inherited places and when the Lotus's radiator split Roy was second, and there he finished behind Brooks's Vanwall, with Trintignant third on his heels. Bruce McLaren drove brilliantly on his first visit to this daunting circuit, and won the F2 class. As Roy crossed the line John was so delighted he turned a joyful forward roll on the pit apron. Huschke von Hanstein of Porsche captured the moment on movie film. It was to become a regular ritual... a Cooper team trademark.

The major August Monday meeting at Brands Hatch next day featured a two-heat F2 race; the first falling to Jack Brabham after a duel with Lewis-Evans, with Russell third. Heat Two was a repetition of the first, though Russell retired, and the inevitable McLaren – growing in stature all the time after his German drive the previous day – was third.

At the end of August the Kentish '100' saw the circus back at Brands, where Moss won brilliantly for Walker. In the first heat both Stirling and Jack Brabham hacked into the lap record, and in the second, Moss the maestro lowered it still further.

At Oporto for the Portuguese GP, Brabham was given the precious 2.2, Salvadori the 1.96 and Walker's 'Argentine' Mark II was towed out on a trailer behind the Bedford, with a 1.96 engine for Trintignant. The Frenchman's smooth precision on this difficult road circuit out-qualified Salvadori's similar 1.96. In the race Brabham, Trintignant and Salvadori finished 7–8–9, Roy two laps down after bending his car's suspension on a kerb.

The Italian GP at Monza offered little prospect of further Cooper honours, the circuit was too fast. Still the interim cars ran; Roy in the works 2.2, Jack the 1.96 and Trintignant having a choice of Walker's 2.2 Mark III or 1.96 Mark II, understandably preferring the former. Roy's car had the top rear wishbones removed as he preferred the oversteering characteristics of the leaf-spring top location.

Brabham rammed Gendebien's slow-off-the-line Ferrari at the start, while Trintignant and Salvadori were outpaced again, running 10–11 until Roy stopped with his car's cooling system airlocked. Trintignant's car was running a special 'long' top gear made by Alf Francis and he went out when it stripped. Roy rejoined and as other cars hit trouble he inherited fifth place at the finish, for another World Championship point.

On 21 September the Avusrennen in Berlin saw Masten Gregory victorious in the streamlined Behra-Porsche, winning from Jim Russell and Jack Brabham in their Mark IIIs, but the unfortunate Ian Burgess had a huge accident and injured himself quite severely, not returning to his Training Division duties at Hollyfield Road and Brands Hatch until the turn of the year.

The unfortunate Montlhéry organizers saw another poor entry for their F2 Coupe du Salon in October, Russell winning from a field of only eight. Jack was second after being shunted on the startline when he lost bottom gear. He was just ahead of bobsleigh driver Norman Barclay's Mark III, with Keith Ballisat fourth in Dick Gibson's car.

In Formula 1, a long break had followed the Italian GP before the Moroccan race at Casablanca on 19 October. This race would decide the World titles between Moss and Hawthorn, Vanwall and Ferrari. An F2 race was being run concurrently and John again entered Brabham and McLaren in this division, while Salvadori would drive the 2.2 and Jack Fairman was enlisted to handle the 1.96 works car. Walker's Mark III was entered for Trintignant, while his ex-Leston F2 was rented to French sports car driver François Picard. Lewis-Evans was driving for Vanwall so could not defend his narrow *Autocar* F2 Championship lead in the BRP car, Tom Bridger driving instead, while André Guelfi and Robert la Caze handled private Coopers.

Jack qualified no less than 5.3 sec faster than McLaren in the F2 category, finished 11th overall and won the class and the Championship; Bruce, la Caze and Guelfi finishing 2–3–4. In 20 F2 races that year, Cooper-Climax had won 16 against two each for Lotus and Porsche.... Meanwhile Moss won the race and the Constructors' Cup for Vanwall, but Hawthorn's second place in the Ferrari was sufficient to make him Britain's first World Champion Driver. Roy was seventh in the GP and Fairman eighth, while Trintignant had retired early. Roy finished fourth in the Drivers' Championship; Jack was 18th....

Meanwhile, out at the high-speed curve down to the sea by Sidi Abderhaman Forest, Brooks's Vanwall had blown its engine and gushed oil. Gendebien, Picard and Bridger all crashed there; poor Picard being very badly hurt and the Walker F2 written-off. Its remains were bulldozed into the Dorking rubbish dump, like most Equipe Walker detritus, including chassis frames. Lewis-Evans's Vanwall also blew-up and crashed, the driver suffering fatal burns. It was a cheerless Championship for the team ... a mixed day for Britain and a sad end to a season which had seen the first British winners in both Championships, and Cooper's first major victories. But for the Cooper boys it had also been a frustrating year since Monaco, for the interim Coventry Climax engines were not competitive – there really was no substitute for cubic inches.

On 30 November, Stirling Moss and Jack Brabham appeared in Walker and works Coopers respectively in the Melbourne GP around Albert Park, in Australia. The race was run in two 25-mile Heats and a 100-mile Final. Rob Walker had taken delivery of a brand-new Mark III, evidently in the usual kit form, as it passed unrecorded in the surviving Register, and it was assembled for this Australian trip with a 2015 cc FPF installed. Jack's car was apparently a new one, probably *F2/22/58*, which he had bought as his own property, new that September. Moss won his Heat, Brabham the second at a higher average speed and so took pole for the Final.

The Heats had only lasted eight laps, but that had proved sufficient for the Walker car to lose half its water. The engine bay side panels were removed for the Final and the dark blue car survived, with Stirling leading Jack from start to finish despite having to cruise the last half-dozen laps as virtually all the coolant had gone. A huge crowd of around 70,000 flooded the track at the finish, as Moss was whisked away by helicopter. One report ended: 'The winning Cooper was wheeled away, completely dry of water, and had it been dark it would have glowed like the Coca-Cola sign in Piccadilly....'

It had been a wonderful year for Equipe Walker, and the frustrations of the works team could only be relieved by new full-size 2½-litre engines from Coventry Climax. Now they were on the way....

Salvadori shining again, British GP, Silverstone, 19 July, 1958, when he won this close-quarters battle with Stuart Lewis-Evans' powerful Vanwall and finished third overall for four more World Championship points. Here the car used the big 2.2-litre engine while it was Brabham's turn to run the team 1.96. I'd heard the bar-room tale about Roy using a two-headed coin to toss for the big engine. Sir Jack: 'No, Roy didn't have a double-headed coin. He just tossed the coin in the air and said "Heads I win, tails you lose"'. Note the top rear wishbone visible beneath the leafspring here. The nose top intake directed cooling air into the cockpit. The foot pedals, hard against the dry-sump oil tank and water radiator, always grew very hot

Measuring up...

In 1960 other Formula 1 teams had followed Cooper's lead and mounted their engines behind the driver's cockpit. The first of them had been BRM and on November 9 that year engineer Tony Rudd of BRM completed this report comparing the anatomy of a 1958 Mark III Cooper with that of his own team's latest F1 car. It makes fascinating reading, and highlights major differences between the enthusiast's built-to-a-price Cooper approach, and the Rolls-Royce style 'proper engineering' of BRM. The Mark III in question bore the plate *F2/12/58* – the number originally allocated to Bruce McLaren's 1958 F2 frame.

'*Examination of 1958, $1\frac{1}{2}$-litre Cooper No. F.21258.* The car had been rolled over, damaging most of the body, and bending both front stub axles. The gearbox differential assembly had been removed, leaving the half shafts and clutch case in place.

Throughout this report the equivalent figures of latest BRM components are given in brackets where significant; but it should be remembered that this car is two years old, and was built for sale to a private owner and lacks some of the features of the Works cars.

Weight as received, with oil & water, but less gearbox .. .. 922 lbs
Front wheel, 5.00 × 15, 4″ rim, Dunlop D.9.S, with hub races .. .. 25.4 lbs
(BRM 5″ rim, knock on hub 24.8 lbs)
Rear Wheel, 6.00 × 15, 5″ rim, Dunlop D.9.S. .. 32 lbs
$1\frac{1}{2}$-litre Climax engine with SU carburetters, magneto, etc. .. .. 290 lbs
Water Header tank, 20 SWG brass, $\frac{3}{4}$″ OD. 7″ bore inlets, $1\frac{3}{8}$, 1.25 bore outlet, no steam separator, pressure cap .. .. 3.8 lbs
Fuel tanks, 20 SWG Alum. secured by rubber strap, 2″ Monza filler each tank, $\frac{1}{4}$″ bore cross feed, two baffles. LH side, capacity 14 gallons .. 17 lbs
RH side, capacity 12 gallons .. 15 lbs
(BRM Fireproof 6 lbs, cap. 15 galls).
Body, 20 SWG Alum. no reinforcements. Dzus fastened – nose section, less windscreen .. 17 lbs
Front undertray & cockpit sides .. .. 16.5 lbs
Tail, hinged at rear, with two quick release spring fasteners .. .. 11.5 lbs
Engine underpan .. .. (56 lbs) 11.0 lbs
(Mark II BRM with fuel tank boxes 50.5)
Exhaust Pipe, 18 G. Mild Steel Alum. sprayed, slip joint in twin section, no other slip joints – 4 × $1\frac{1}{2}$, 16″ long 2″ × $1\frac{1}{2}$″, 20″ long 1″ × 2″, 18″ long .. .. 12.5 lbs
(Mark II BRM for $2\frac{1}{2}$-litre engine) .. 14 lbs
Oil Pipes, $\frac{7}{8}$″ OD. 18 G. Alum. with $\frac{7}{16}$″ bore high pressure flexibles, wet weight .. .. 5.8 lbs
(BRM $1\frac{1}{4}$″ × 1″ 18 G. Alum. $\frac{3}{4}$″ bore flexibles wet weight) .. .. 13.6 lbs
Water Pipes, $1\frac{3}{8}$″ OD. 18 G. Alum. wet weight .. 9.2 lbs
(BRM $1\frac{3}{4}$″ 18 G. Alum. wet weight) .. 20.8 lbs
Radiator-Oil Cooler assembly (Brass) .. 29 lbs
($2\frac{1}{2}$-litre BRM radiator 26, oil cooler 10).
Oil tank with $1\frac{1}{4}$ lb. filler cap, 20 SWG 3 gall. capacity, one baffle .. .. .. 9 lbs
(Mark II 18 SWG 5 gall. capacity, two baffles). 9.8 lbs
Front roll bar assembly, $\frac{9}{16}$″ dia. 24″ long, with adjustable levers, set 4″ long, .75″ wishbone ratio 6 lbs
FRAME, $1\frac{1}{2}$″ dia. 14 & 16 g. tubes, torsional stiffness 365 ft.lbs. per degree over wheelbase, with body brackets and brake pipes .. 101 lbs
(Mark II 82 lbs, stiffness 2020)
Steering Rack, with track rods, 2 turns of wheel, $4\frac{1}{2}$″ rack movement on 5″ long steering arms, Zero Ackermann (Mark II 5.75) .. 8 lbs
Caster Angle 7° 20, too damaged to measure kingpin offset or camber .. .. ..
Hardy Spicer halfshaft 11″ long, $1\frac{1}{4}$″ stroke weight 9.5 lbs with 200 ft lbs torque applied requires 180 lbs to slide, 140 to sustain sliding
(BRM 14″ long 2″ stroke, 2 to 3 lbs to slide and keeps sliding) .. .. 12 lbs
Rear Hub casting with races. .. .. 3.4 lbs
(Mark II fabricated steel $6\frac{1}{2}$ lbs)
Rear Wishbone, $\frac{7}{8}$″ dia. 16 G. tube on $\frac{3}{8}$″ pivots, in Cleevite bushes Top (Mark II 2.6 lbs) .. 2 lbs
Lower (Mark II 5.2 lbs) .. 2.8 lbs
Front wishbones, same construction, top adjustable (Mark II 2 lbs) .. .. 1.8 lbs
Lower (Mark II 4.1 lbs) .. .. 2.8 lbs
Lower wishbone stiffness .0017 per 100 lbs load. (Mark II .0011 per 100 lbs load)
Girling Brakes, discs. $9\frac{1}{2}$″ dia. $\frac{3}{8}$″ wide; weight .. 8 lbs
Calipers, part stripped, Light alloy body .. 5 lbs
Front unsprung weight with wheel .. 42.4 lbs
(Mark II 49.8)
Rear unsprung weight, less transverse leaf spring 59.2 lbs
(Mark II 66.1 lbs less spring)

From the foregoing, it will be seen that although many Cooper components are heavier than BRM equivalents, principally (with the exception of the frame) to reduce expense, the unsprung suspension parts are much lighter and nearly as strong as their BRM equivalent. Also life has been sacrificed for lightness as is indicated by the omission of grease and dust seals on the suspension. The second significant weight gain on the Cooper is on oil and water pipes, which are smaller and shorter than on the BRM.

9th November, 1960.   A. C. Rudd'

CHAPTER SEVENTEEN

1959 – World Champions

After their experience with the interim FPF engines during 1958 and those two encouraging victories in Buenos Aires and Monte Carlo it took little time for Charles and John Cooper, and Colin Chapman, to persuade Leonard Lee of Coventry Climax to sanction development of a full 2½-litre engine for 1959.

A modestly revised block was cast to accommodate bore and stroke dimensions of 94.0 × 89.9 mm, 2495 cc – dimensions dictated by available space. Peter Windsor-Smith wrestled with problems of accommodating crankshaft balance weights, and adopted an expensive GEC heavy alloy to keep them small. The existing twin-cam head was remodelled for the larger capacity, and at first was purposely under-valved to restrict power in case the new crankcase proved weak. Once this 'full-size' FPF was running it became obvious there was strength to spare, and enlarged ports were soon adopted with bigger valves. But detail design had not commenced until 1 December, 1958, and only four months would elapse before the first 'two-and-a-half' units would run their maiden race in the rear of Walker and works Coopers. . . .

At Hollyfield Road, meanwhile, the latest 'T51' or Mark IV F1/F2 Coopers entered production, little changed from the Mark III and attracting 28 recorded orders as in the Appendices. Meanwhile, a new sports car, named the 'Monaco' in honour of the 1958 GP victory there, was also beginning production – see Chapter 20.

Roy Golding was also back as works manager, having been away for some years, in part working with John Hume and Albert Zains building Azum karts in Epsom. Charles had asked him to return. 'I can't,' Roy said, 'You know you don't pay enough. . . .'

'Aah,' said the Old Man, 'That was in the old days when we was makin' pennies, Boy. Now we're makin' pounds. . . .'

Roy returned to find Formula Junior production being set up alongside the Monaco sports and customer F1/F2 cars. 'But we still had the minimum in equipment and even the new works was dark and gloomy, and freezing cold in the winter. The old man hated people using his electricity. He'd go round and switch off the lights on the welders. "Welders don't need light," he'd say. "Welders make their own light. . . ." Another time, one bitter winter, the blokes weren't doing any work because it was just too cold. The only way to get the circulation going in your fingers was to stand around the stove in the middle of the works. I went to Charlie Cooper and said, "Look, you'll have to do something about installing central heating. . . ." "Central heating?" he said. "What's the matter with you lot" – pointing at the stove – "What can be more central than that? . . ."'

The new year's racing commenced as always in Australasia, where Moss won the NZ GP in his Melbourne-winning

Lady Wigram line-up, New Zealand, 1959; Ron Flockhart's BRM P25 on pole flanked by the McLaren 1.96 and Brabham 2.2-litre Mark III Coopers. The front-engined car won from Brabham and Bruce . . .

Right *Glover Trophy, Easter Monday Goodwood, 1959; first two 2½-litre Coventry Climax FPF engines overcoming Cooper rear-wheel traction at flagfall, leaving Moss's Walker car slithering sideways and Jack Brabham matched off the line by the Maserati 250F while Schell and Behra tear away in their front-engined BRMs. Once Stirling caught and passed Schell he handled various problems to score another handsome win. Inside wheels just lifting, Stirling is seen hammering on in his slender-nose bodied Mark III (left)*

Walker car with the Francis 2015 cc engine. Brabham's works 2.2 was second and McLaren's 1.96 third. Stirling had broken a half-shaft while leading his preliminary heat from Ron Flockhart's BRM, but Jack gave him his own spare for the GP; a fine gesture. As at Albert Park the Walker car was boiling in the closing stages and oil pressure was falling below 30 psi. . . . Again it all survived just long enough.

After Ardmore, Bruce won two minor races in the day at Levin, then Flockhart beat the Coopers for the Wigram Trophy; Brabham, McLaren and Syd Jensen's F2 finishing 2–3–4, Merv Neil's 1.96 and Lenny Gilbert's venerable ex-Gould Cooper-Bristol 7–8.

On the Waimate street circuit in a freak downpour Bruce won a national race from Ross Jensen's Maserati, which spun out of the lead after Bruce's 1.96 had spun at the start.

Brabham won one prelim Heat, McLaren the other, at Teretonga, and in the 60-mile Final Bruce 'simply mowed down the opposition to come home an easy winner in record time . . .' as one report put it. His Mark III ran single rear wishbones, Jack's double wishbones, and the older system's inherently marked oversteer was better-suited to the Invercargill track. Bruce would later recall how he and Jack had raced wheel-to-wheel into the first turn and 'for the first and only time in my career he nodded me through. . . .' After Bruce's win, Jack '. . . was strangely quiet . . . and has never waved me past since when we have been in equal cars. It was the first time I had beaten him fair and square and I was pleased with myself. . . .'

Teretonga marked the end of the international tour, but Bruce then won a local race at Ohakea with his 1.96. Spectating that day was a young MG driver from Te Puke named Denis Hulme. After the race he bought Merv Neil's 1.96 Mark III, while George Lawton from Whangarei – who had been driving the ex-Brabham/McLaren/Neil 1500 Bob-tail – bought Bruce's car. Hulme and Lawton would be chosen jointly as NZIGP Drivers to Europe for 1960.

With support from Esso and promise of a works F2 drive Bruce was to return to England that year, and he suggested Jack Brabham should take on a friend of his named Phil Kerr to help in the Australian's newly opened garage, near the Cooper works in Chessington. Back in England, Bruce found a flat for himself and Phil in Lovelace Gardens, Surbiton. He bought Betty Brabham's two-door Morris Minor 1000 as road transport. Imagine his delight when he heard that with increased Esso backing John had decided to run a three-car Formula 1 team; initially with a new 2½-litre car for Jack Brabham, and 2.2s for the stocky, bass-voiced Kansan Masten Gregory and McLaren. He had been hoping for an assured F2 contract. Now he would drive in the minor class for Ken Tyrrell, and he was in Formula 1 with the works. 'Will that be all right, Boy?' asked the pipe . . . would it!

Roy Salvadori was no longer in the team. Why? It wasn't that Charles and John didn't want him; they simply could not afford both Salvadori and Brabham. Roy had driven for David Brown's Aston Martin sports car team for some years. Now Aston was entering Formula 1, but their cars probably would not be ready for the full season. David Brown wanted Roy's services in the single-seaters, and also made an attractive offer to Jack Brabham on Roy's recommendation. The Coopers found themselves faced with improving the Aston offer or losing both their established drivers. They took their problem to Esso, who responded with more backing, but not enough to match both Aston offers. In effect the problem solved itself. By the time the extra money became available, Roy considered himself too deeply committed to Aston to go back on his new agreement. Jack felt he was not so committed and opted to stay on with Cooper, as number one.

At that time Salvadori might have had the brighter reputation, but Jack's greasy-fingered technical dedication made him a kindred spirit to John; a valuable engineering asset as well as a driver of obvious potential. Just how much we would soon see.

It remains an interesting question; could Cooper have taken the World Championship in 1959 if both Salvadori and Brabham had remained in the team? John believes not; the balance of probabilities suggests that each would have robbed the other of Championship points at some stage during the year, and it was going to be the closest-run Championship thus far, with three teams and drivers still in contention right into the final round. . . .

So Salvadori went to Aston Martin, and for F1 races they could not enter he was invited to drive for Tommy Atkins's private team run from a lock-up in Chessington by his mechanic Harry Pearce. Since the new 2½-litre Climax FPF would be in short supply and deliveries to private owners could not be guaranteed, Atkins invested in a 2½-litre sports Maserati four-cylinder engine to power his new Cooper frame, the car being built-up by Pearce from parts supplied by Hollyfield Road and Modena.

The engine had been developed by *Ingegnere* Giulio Alfieri and his Maserati staff from the 1500–2000 cc sports car design used in their 150 and 200S models. Bore and stroke of 96 × 86 mm now displaced 2489 cc. Twin overhead camshafts were spur gear-driven from the crankshaft nose, and inclined valves in hemispherical combustion chambers were controlled by hairpin springs. The aluminium head carried two spark plugs per cylinder, fired from Marelli magnetos driven from the tail of each camshaft. The block was in aluminium, with cast-iron dry cylinder liners. The crankcase was split on the crankshaft axis. The engine breathed through two 45DCO3 twin-choke Weber carburettors and with a compression ratio of 9.75:1 developed 238 bhp at 7000 rpm. This was some 40 bhp more than the most reliable figure for the 2.2-litre Climax engine, which was Atkins's only sensible alternative that winter. The engine weighed around 330 lb complete with clutch, which was the reliable Maserati all-metal multiplate affair. Harry Pearce mated this unit to the standard Cooper gearbox with its step-up spur gears housed in a new purpose-built casting which bolted onto the back of the engine.

While the Climax engines were mounted inclined in the frame, the Maserati was upright and was still 1¾ in. lower at the top of the cam-covers. The crankcase was not as slim as Climax's, however, and a housing on its right side for the starter motor pinion necessitated mounting the unit offset to the left of the frame with unequal-length half-shafts driving to the wheels, and that on the left demanding greater angular movement in its UJs. Pearce had to resite some chassis tubes, notably where clearance had to be found for the carburettor bell-mouths. The roll-over hoop section of frame abaft the seat was made detachable, and the engine was mounted on a pair of front bearers low on the crankcase and on a single rear mount above the bell-housing around the clutch. This was clamped between collars to a detachable cross-member. A fourth mount, a steady for the final-drive assembly, was provided on the rearmost cross tube, picking-up on the back of the gearbox casing. The Maserati engine demanded a larger radiator and oil tank than the Climax FPF, but carried a coolant header tank like the FPF's above the cam-covers. Maserati had designed a specially shortened exhaust system for this application. The Atkins equipe had run Ian Burgess's impeccably prepared F2 Mark III the previous season, and they had a new F2 car for '59 to run alongside the F1 hybrid. It was also possible to mount either a 2½- or 1½-litre FPF in the Maserati frame with minimum further modification. There are no C. T. Atkins or High Efficiency Motors entries in the 1959 chassis Register, since these cars were built outside the Cooper Car Company's aegis, though using chassis frames from the Hollyfield Road jig.

Rob Walker now had Stirling Moss driving for him regularly as Vanwall had withdrawn from racing; he didn't want to go with Tony Brooks to Ferrari, and he still mistrusted BRM unreliability and disorganization. He also loved being cast as the underdog, and the prospect of driving for a private team against the factory battalions very much appealed, but BRM power was magnetic. . . .

The scheduled 1959 Argentine GP was cancelled, so the new Championship series would not commence until Monaco in May. Stirling discussed prospects with his business manager Ken Gregory, his father Alfred, Rob Walker and Alf Francis. The idea of combining BRM's powerful four-cylinder engine with Cooper's nimble handling was suggested, especially for Monaco. Rob was agreeable if the Owen Organization would loan his team an engine. He had a 2½-litre FPF on order and would obviously prefer not to buy both. Gregory contacted Sir Alfred Owen, who instantly agreed. A BRM P25 engine was delivered to Pippbrook Garage to be built into a special Cooper frame.

While Charles and John would happily provide frames, running gear and body panels for Walker and he could arrange his own engines, they could do nothing about suitable transmissions. Owen Maddock and Jack Knight were producing their own gearbox, but it was a long-term prospect, and clearly the standard Citroën-ERSA-based unit was not really suitable for Grand Prix racing even with 2.2-litre power, never mind 2½ litres....

But both Moss and Francis knew Maserati's former chassis and transmission designer very well. His name was Valerio Colotti and he had just left the Trident to set up his own *Studio Tecnica Meccanica* – 'TecMec' for short – in Modena. He agreed to design and produce a suitable transaxle for them.

When Bruce McLaren returned to England in March he found three cars ready to run in the works team's cramped dark and dingy 'shop at Hollyfield Road. The pilot 2½-litre FPF was ready in Jack's chassis and 2.2s for Gregory and himself. Testing at Goodwood, neither Brabham nor Salvadori in the new Atkins special were very quick. Roy put it down to the wind direction, 'It's a slow day.' Bespectacled Masten Gregory grinned slowly and drawled, 'It's a slow day all right, 'cause Moss and Brooks ain't here.' Bruce was impressed. It was a no-excuses attitude he'd never forget.

Formula 1 and Formula 2 events were closely entwined this season, but Cooper activity in both was so extensive I have split them and cover Formula 2 elsewhere.

The season was set rolling at Goodwood on 30 March, Easter Monday. After much testing, Moss ran the Melbourne and NZ GP-winning Walker car with 2½FPF to face Jack's sister works entry, Salvadori's special, the BRMs and some ageing Maseratis in the Glover Trophy. While the Walker car retained leaf-spring top location for the rear suspension with radius rod control, the works cars this season would be all double-wishbone jobs with the rear leaf-spring relieved of all lateral location duties.

Moss's steering came adrift in practice when a bracket bolt loosened and he clouted the wattle fencing at Fordwater. The race 'was tough going ... the throttle was sticking, the clutch was adrift and the gearbox packed-up on the last lap', but he won; first-time victory for the 2½-litre Cooper-Climax. Alf Francis had fitted the car experimentally with knock-off rear hub conversions to speed potential GP tyre-changes, but the adaptor-sleeves and plates were not right and by the end of the race the fixing had split and the wheels were wobbling....
The Motor observed, 'Rarely have we seen Stirling driving so hard....' Roy had qualified the Cooper-Maserati second quickest, but spun out at Lavant when he couldn't see through dirty goggles. Jack's 2½ made it a Cooper-Climax 1–2 success, while Gregory and McLaren finished 5–6.

The 1959 works chassis are recorded as *F2/23A/58* – fitted initially with 2.2 engine *FPF430/3/1082*; plus from the 1959 series *F2/4/59*, *F2/7/59* and, in October, an additional car listed as *Works Car IV*, serial *FII/27/59*. In the Register the Roman 'II' replaces the Arabic '2' from chassis 12 onward, except for Australian Alec Mildren's *F2/22/59*, which entry is written by a different hand. I am not convinced this style extended to all the chassis plates concerned for I have seen plates numbered both ways. Perhaps it shows which plates are genuine and which have been fudged ... but I cannot prove which is which.

The Aintree '200' combined F1/F2 race followed, with Ferrari and BRM facing Cooper and Equipe Walker, whose Cooper-BRM was ready to run. It was based on a standard Mark IV frame, and Walker mechanic John Chisman recalls how: 'Alf, Mike Roach and I knocked it up at Dorking, hacking it about 'til everything would fit.' The frame's rear end was cut about and many curved tubes replaced 'by nice straight ones' and the major tube junctions were boxed and gusseted, while the driving position was moved forward slightly to give room for the engine. The big but light aluminium BRM radiator was outrigged far forward with a Bourne oil tank behind it, and blisters were necessary to fit the nose-cone round the oversized rad. The twin mags on the front of the BRM engine would have sat one in each of the driver's ears in the Cooper, so they were remounted either side of the block, driven by US dragster-style internal-toothed rubber belts within casings bolted onto the original three-stud mag flanges. The special was completed with wider than

The Walker Cooper-BRM special nears completion in Modena **opposite top** *where Alf Francis, Valerio Colotti and Giorgio Neri combined to fit the rapidly designed and built Colotti Tipo 10 five-speed transaxle seen here. Note tight fit for the BRM P25 4-cylinder engine, its awkward tuned-length exhaust manifold run and straight engine-bay tubes inserted by Walker crew. Back at Walker's racing workshop in Dorking* **right** *Alf Francis and John Chisman refit the engine in the near-completed car. The blisters necessary to accommodate the large but light-weight BRM radiator within the nose are clearly visible. At Aintree* **top right** *Moss gave the ungainly-looking hybrid its only race, here leading its front-engined sister from Bourne's works team, but the experiment was an expensive failure. The car later appeared in F1/F2 Climax trim before selling to South Africa, then returning to the UK for restoration in the 1980s*

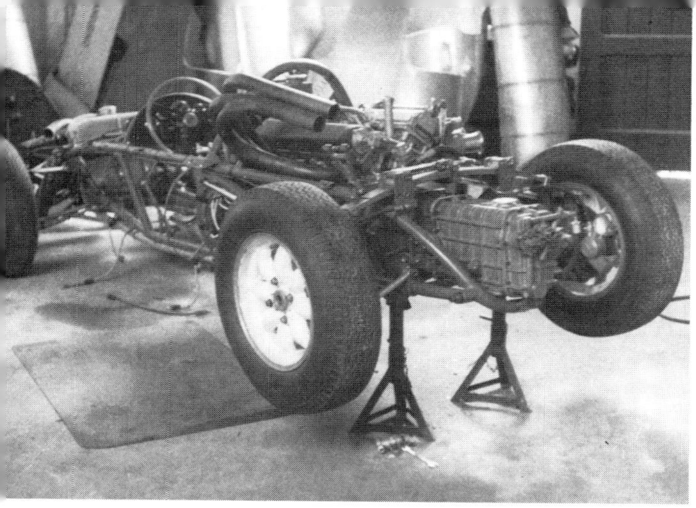
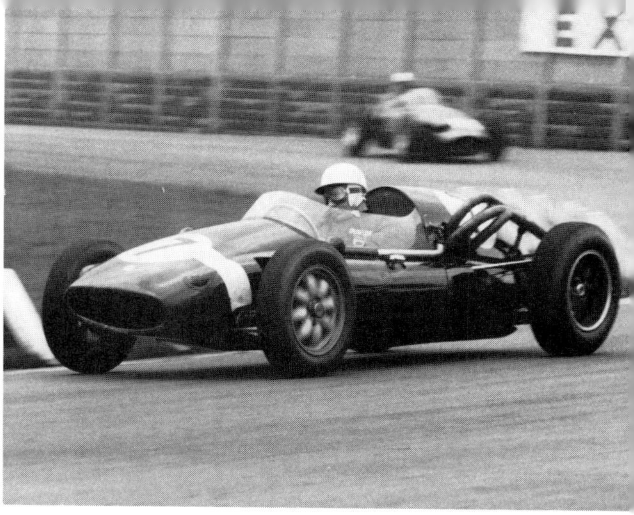
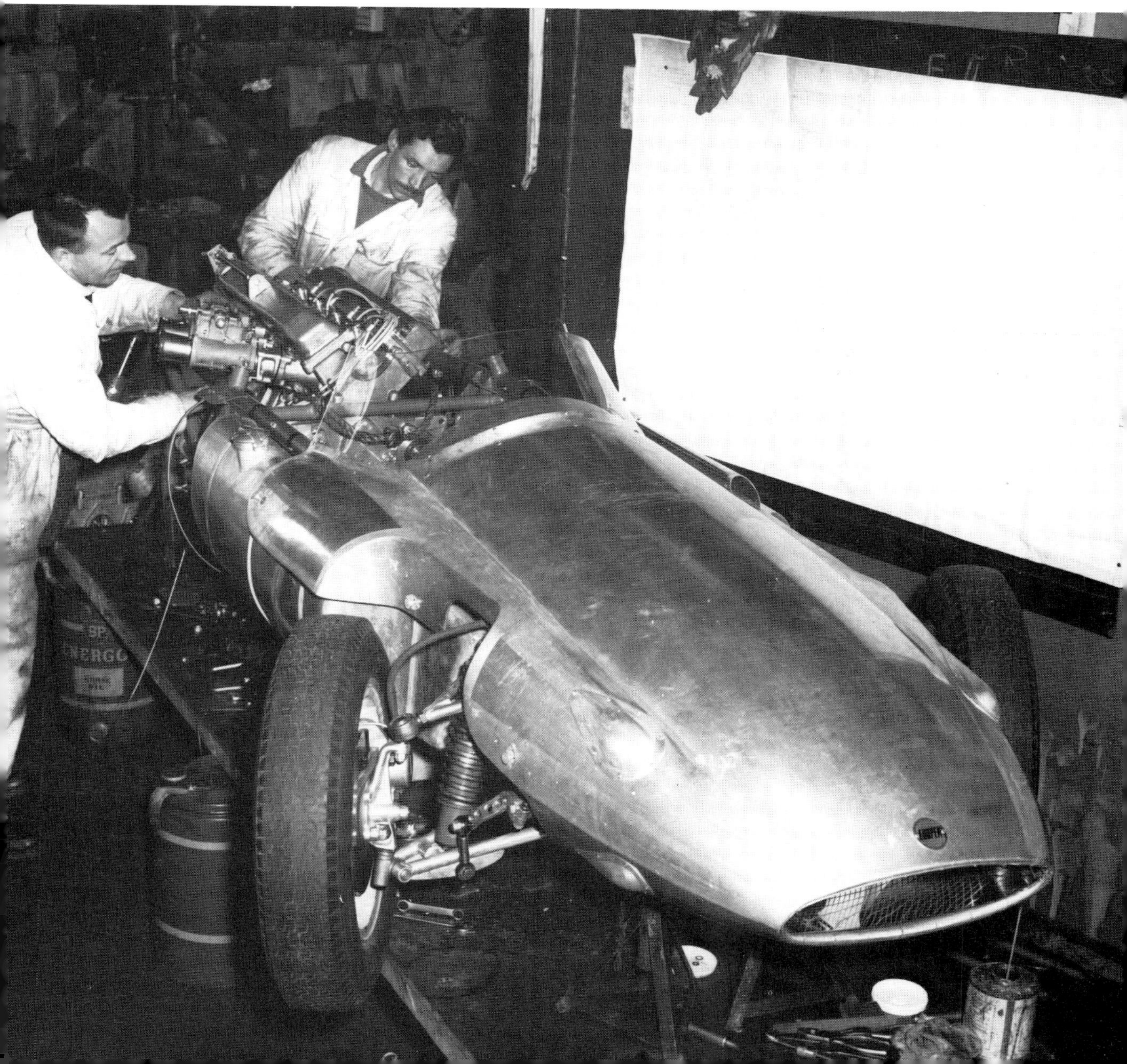

The Cooper works team's first Formula 1 victory came at Silverstone in the BRDC International Trophy race, 2 May, 1959. It was Jack's race all the way in slender-nose Mark IV, leading Salvadori's brand-new factory Aston Martin DBR4/250 which stole fastest lap. While Jack won with relative ease he drove hard all the way. Here he has his new 'T51' works car tweaked into understeer, tightly hugging one of the airfield circuit's then-characteristic breeze-block marker walls

standard front track, non-standard bodywork and Alf's single top radius rod leaf-spring top location rear suspension.

In Modena it was always possible to get castings made and gears designed and cut at blinding speed. This had always been one of Ferrari's and Maserati's great strengths. Colotti enlisted help from ex-Maserati mechanic Giorgio Neri's new workshop in assembling the new Walker gearboxes as soon as parts became available. They housed the final-drive and limited-slip diff in one casing bolted to a bell-housing to which BRM, Climax and the new F2 Borgward engine, then about to be used by both Walker and BRP, could be attached. Drive from the clutch passed through step-up gears like Cooper's, enabling easy ratio changes, then via torsion shaft past the diff into the overhung gearbox proper. On the end-plate was a starter-dog shaft and an oil pump feeding the gears and shafts under pressure, while the crownwheel picked up its own oil from a sump. This Colotti Type 10 gearbox had first been discussed around Christmas 1958. Now in April it was ready and Moss tested the Cooper-BRM at Modena and promptly bettered Ferrari times around the town's *Aerautodromo*.

John Chisman developed immense respect for Alf Francis: 'Looking back, it's obvious that Alf was very clued-up for that time. He had trained as a locksmith in Poland before the war and really was a first-class engineer. He could adapt and manufacture all kinds of things. When Alta packed up we bought all their presses and tools, and I remember there was one huge drill there, and Alf said, "With this drill we can make anything," and he showed how we could use it as a mill and all kinds of tricks. One fad of his on the Coopers was his dislike of their big copper header tank on top of the cam covers for the cooling system. He always did away with it and fitted his own system; we didn't even have a header tank on the Argentine car despite the heat. People used to look at these ideas of Alf's and laugh, until his car beat theirs. . . .' After the Goodwood incident when Moss's steering column pulled out, Walker's were always cross-drilled and pegged behind the rev-counter. Alf also denied his drivers the 'tell-tale' needle zeroing button on their Smiths rev-counters. He would put a $\frac{1}{16}$ drill through, and peg them. He also beefed-up the pedals on his cars, some being machined from the solid, and they tried pendant pedals, too.

At Surbiton, Bill James prepared Brabham's car for Aintree, Noddy Grohmann worked on Gregory's and Bruce McLaren cared for his own. Jack's was now fitted with larger 58 mm Webers, wider front wheels and tyres, special disc brakes and some new suspension thinking was built in. Its discarded F2-sized wheels and tyres, old-type brakes and 50 mm Webers were grafted onto Masten's car, which had the team's second $2\frac{1}{2}$-litre FPF installed. Bruce later wrote: 'In practice Masten was warned not to do too many laps in case something fell off before the race . . . imagine when the timekeeper announced that Masten had just broken the circuit record . . . he was flagged in. "If that car's bad," he drawled, "leave it bad. . . ."'

He took pole position, the only driver under 2 minutes. Moss's Cooper-BRM was slower than the works front-engined BRMs and he was bitterly disappointed. His new special shuddered violently at the front under braking. Masten led the race for 19 laps until his clutch broke, Moss took over from Schell's BRM and Behra's Ferrari. On lap 29 Stirling set a new lap record at 1:58.8, but next time round went out with gearbox failure. A tab washer locating a nut on one end of a gearbox shaft had broken and allowed the nut to unwind, which allowed the shaft to slide axially and pull the gearwheels out of mesh. Giorgio Neri was in the Walker pit.

He was heartbroken. Behra and Brooks placed 1–2 for Ferrari, with Bruce's works 2.2 third. Salvadori's transmission broke in the Cooper-Maserati and Brabham retired on lap 18 'with a reputed blown cylinder head gasket'.

Two weeks later at Silverstone, Moss drove a front-engined BRM loaned to BRP and qualified on pole. Salvadori's brand-new Aston Martin was sensationally third quickest behind Brooks's Ferrari, and Brabham's works 2½-litre Mark IV completed the front row. He led away before Moss stormed by, only to spin out almost immediately with brake failure. The works Cooper then roared away to win easily. Jack '...drove like one possessed, sliding the tail of the Cooper out of the corners', reported *Motor Sport*, to earn himself and the Cooper Car Company's own team its first-ever Formula 1 victory. Now Charles, John and their men looked optimistically towards Monaco.

Jack Fairman placed fifth in the Atkins Cooper-Maserati at Silverstone, while Bruce drove a Tyrrell F2, Masten Gregory non-started after baling out of his crashing Ecurie Ecosse Lister-Jaguar during sports car practice, and Ian Burgess drove the works 2.2 into a twice-lapped eighth overall.

Two days later, the teams set off for Monaco. Charles and John entered their three works cars, two 2½s and the lone 2.2 for Bruce. Masten had recovered from skidding along Silverstone's track on his backside and his 2½ engine carried 48 mm Webers as he preferred their mid-range punch to the better top-end of the 58s on Jack's power unit.

Walker arrived with three Coopers for Moss and Trintignant; Stirling to choose between the Cooper-BRM and Trint's old Mark III winner from the previous year, now with a 2½ FPF installed plus Colotti gearbox, while the Frenchman was to drive Moss's ex-Melbourne/NZ GP frame with 2½ FPF and Colotti gearbox plus k/o Rudge hubs front and rear carrying Borrani wire wheels to speed tyre changes should a stop be necessary. John Chisman: 'Alf had experimented long before with converting standard Cooper bolt-on wheels to knock-offs by inserting a steel sleeve through the centres, but the sleeve kept cracking. So we ordered these beautiful Borranis with aluminium rims and superbly machined very light hubs ... they cost a fortune....' The F1 Cooper entry was completed by the Maserati-engined Atkins special for Salvadori.

John and his team stayed at Roquebrune, some five miles round the coast from Monaco and close to Lance Macklin's mother's villa. Lady Macklin gave them free run of her garages to prepare the cars. At this range it's sobering to picture Bruce McLaren and Phil Kerr driving down from Surbiton in their second-hand ex-Betty Brabham Morris Minor and being passed on the way by Graham Hill of Lotus, flat-out in his Speedwell-tuned Austin A35 ... the days of jet-set superstardom and big-money GP racing were far ahead.

When Bruce arrived, he found all three cars stripped out and his seat already installed in Jack's winning Silverstone frame, probably *F2/4/59*. Masten would try his assigned car, find its engine really strong, and emphasized the terrific spirit within the team by instantly offering it to Jack for the race. So the Kansan's engine and brakes were fitted to Bruce's originally assigned car, probably *7/59*, for Jack to drive while Masten took over the former 2.2 frame *23A/58* fitted with Jack's discarded engine and brakes; leaving Bruce the Silverstone-winning car with his 2.2 hastily installed. Australian journalist Dev Dvoretsky was close to Jack at this time. He recalls clearly helping unrivet a chassis plate to swap cars like this without troubling the scrutineers and losing ready-worn practice times....

For the first time, F2 cars had been accepted to fight for a place on the 16-strong grid, including four Coopers, but none made the race. Among the F1s Moss was fastest on the Thursday, Brabham on Friday. The Cooper-BRM proved unstable and, on the Saturday, Stirling took pole from Behra's Ferrari and Jack's works Cooper in his Climax-engined Walker car. The Cooper-BRM proved down on power and to have a faulty gearchange in a couple of brief laps, so it was put aside.... It would eventually be sold, less engine, to South Africa and only return to England many years later, in very tatty order, but unmistakable with its gusseted part-straight-tube frame....

Jack had a brush with the straw bales in practice and found his foot pedals getting too hot for comfort. Overnight, Bill James and Noddy Grohmann fitted radiator heat deflectors to protect his feet.

Behra led from the start, but would retire with engine failure. Moss inherited the lead from Brabham and by half-distance the Walker car was 40 sec clear and Jack's gearchange was sticky; he reckoned it cost him 2 sec a lap in the hairpins. And those foot pedals had heated-up again, burning his feet. Masten's clutch and gearbox had broken as early as lap 7, while Bruce had been the meat in a BRM sandwich until Harry Schell punted him up the tail at *La Portière* and he spun and knocked a rear wheel out of line against the sea-wall. He restarted with the car understeering on left-handers, oversteering on rights. John urged him to stick with it – at Monaco merely finishing can score you points.

Brooks's Ferrari was challenging Brabham's second place when the Australian began to fight back hard. Moss seemed uncatchable out ahead until lap 81, when the Walker car suddenly zoomed into its pit. There was a vibration in the transmission. Francis checked anxiously. Nothing could be seen. Moss restarted, but before the *Gazomètre* hairpin an awful grinding noise sank all hope. The bolts holding the crown-wheel to the diff cage had been threaded right down to the bearing surface by a manufacturing oversight and, predictably, had sheared off. Now the amputated bolt heads had picked up in the gear teeth, and Moss was out.

This left Jack Brabham leading for the works. His pedals were almost too hot for him to press, but the pressure was

COOPER CARS

10 May, 1959 – Monaco GP. Jean Behra's snub-nosed Ferrari Dino 246 leads into the Station Hairpin on the opening lap, with Moss's Walker Cooper hot on his heels and Brabham close behind in the 'bitsa' works car, hastily assembled from the best available collection of parts during practice. Phil Hill's Ferrari is next out of Mirabeau Supérieur in background, chased by Bonnier's BRM, Trintignant's ex-Moss Walker Mark III, and just visible over wall Brooks' Ferrari and Flockhart's BRM. Trintignant's car – seen broadsiding round the Station Hairpin later in the race – was one of the most handsome F1 Coopers ever assembled, with its special Borrani light-alloy wire wheels and centre-lock hubs. It was the ex-Moss Melbourne GP/NZ GP winner from the preceding winter, which Stirling had also used to win at Goodwood. Superb Monaco – but where are all the people?

172

off; Brooks, overcome by heat and fumes, vomiting in his cockpit, was lolling in the Ferrari, settling for second place. Jack won for Cooper by 19.7 sec!

Trintignant's strikingly pretty wire-wheeled car finished third, twice-lapped and handicapped by a sticky throttle, while Bruce was classified fifth, four laps down. Salvadori's special had stripped its final-drive, but he pushed across the line to qualify sixth, 17 laps behind. The Cooper-Knight gearboxes finished out of oil, almost red hot: 'If you spat on them, it sizzled and flashed into steam....'

It was the works team's first *Grande Epreuve* victory and their first over their favourite customer – Rob Walker. Charles was intensely proud, quivering with glee. There was an uproarious celebration at the *Hôtel de Paris* race dinner that evening – including a strawberry fight... victory was sweet.

The season roared on. Trint's wire-wheeled Monaco car in F2 trim won at Pau for his and Walker's second consecutive victory there and then came the Dutch GP at Zandvoort. The organizers would not accept Bruce's entry, preferring their own man, Carel Godin de Beaufort, in a sports Porsche. To conserve their gearboxes, the works Coopers now had small gravity-feed oil tanks strapped above them. The drivers could top-up the oil level in mid-race by turning a tap connected to a Bowden cable and cockpit lever. A brand-new works car was available, *F2/27/59*, identical save for alternative rear wishbone pivot holes to change geometry.

In practice Masten was depressed by his slow times and Jack tried his car, diagnosing gear selection problems and adjusting its carburetion. Like Alf Francis, the Australian had developed a particularly good 'ear' for tuning Webers, working closely with the rep from Bologna. As they brought the instruments into tune so Jack lapped progressively quicker, and quicker.

Meanwhile, Walker ran the Monaco Climax cars for Moss and Trintignant; the former's now fitted with double rear wishbones *à la* works spec, at last discarding the Alf Francis top radius rods. Both cars ran 2½ FPFs with Colotti gearboxes. Bonnier's BRM took pole position, Jack later equalling this time to line up on the front row with Stirling on the outside. To combat left-front tyre wear during the race, a thick-tread Dunlop sports car tyre was fitted on Jack's car. Gregory, rather to his own surprise, was on row three, and he made an electrifying start to take an early lead! As Andrew Ferguson wrote in the Esso-sponsored booklet *The Cooper Golden Years 1959–60*: 'Until lap ten he spent his leisure moments wondering where everyone had gone, but then trouble in selecting third gear solved the mystery for him. Bonnier and Jack passed him on successive laps. followed by Stirling....'

The Brabham/Bonnier battle raged for 15 laps, but Jack lost second gear, vital for the *Hunzerug* turn behind the pits, and Moss passed them both to run away towards another apparently certain victory. But after only three laps in the lead a bell-housing ball-race supporting the clutch shaft broke and the blue car was out again. Bonnier went on to score BRM's maiden victory at this level, after 10 years of trying, with Brabham nursing his car home second and Masten third.

Owen Maddock: 'With the 2½-litre engine, the Citroën-based gearboxes were being twisted under load, despite the strengthened casings we'd adopted the previous year. Once the engagement dogs had taken on a twist, drive torque was trying to force them apart out of engagement, and it was only the selector forks then which held gears in. So they took one hell of a pounding, and after every race we'd have to replace the lot; gears, dogs, forks.... There was never sufficient oil capacity for the work the gearbox had to do, and as they got hot most of the oil would come out of the breather anyway. Obviously we had to design and make a new gearbox of our own, and I eventually designed it in six months through 1959 – with a broken back and cased in plaster....'

He had taken up gliding as a hobby.

Having completed one flight successfully he took off for another, but inadvertently left the air brakes extended. His Slingsby failed to complete the circuit, crash-landed on the opposite side of a main road to the airfield perimeter, slithered across it and smashed head-on into the high kerbstone on the airfield side.... He was lucky to escape with his life.

There was a break before the French GP at Reims on 5 July since the Belgian round had been cancelled. Rob Walker was desolated at seeing Moss robbed of two consecutive apparently certain victories by Colotti gearbox breakages and recommended Stirling to try another car while the problems were resolved. Stirling consequently turned to BRP's BRM for the French and British rounds. Meanwhile, at Hollyfield Road, John was off on one of his occasional 'flights of fancy' as his men would recall them....

The Beddings were briefed to build a special wheel-enclosing streamlined body for Jack's F1/F2 cars. The memory of the Behra Porsche and Walker's fairings there in 1958 was still fresh. Surely the works could do better? Owen made a model body from *papier maché* over a welding-wire frame. Andrew Ferguson remembers how 'Charlie discovered the model in the drawing office. "'Ere, what's this?" he demanded and when I told him he just brought his knee up and smashed the model over it. "There!", he said, "It never would've been strong enough! Bloody *aerodynamics*!..."'

At such times there would often be a furious family row for all to hear. Very occasionally it would get out of hand and one, usually Charles, would take a swing at the other. If you happened to be caught in between it was your bad luck. John normally avoided his father's wrath, and could later talk him round. When the F1 team developed its own 'shop in Langley Road, about a quarter-mile up the hill above the Hollyfield works, it became John's refuge.

Andrew again: 'You'd hear a row start, then the office door

173

On their way to the Cooper Car Company works team's first Grande Epreuve *victory, Jack Brabham and what was probably chassis 'F2/7/59' tail-wag out onto the seafront at* La Portiere *and accelerate right-handed towards the famous tunnel. The Australian suffered painful burns to his feet despite all efforts to insulate the car's foot pedals against radiator and oil tank heat. The nose-top cool air intake provided little relief, but it was sufficient to win. Note Mark IV or 'T51' car's engine bay air intake on body side, raised tail-fin spine*

would bang, pause, then you'd hear John's Zodiac rev up outside and a mighty squeal of tyres as he smoked away to Langley Road. It was always interesting just to study the road surface. You'd always know there'd been a row when you could see black tyre marks shooting out of Hollyfield Road and turning right up the hill, and often there'd be great wiggly skid marks coming down the hill where a trolley-bus had locked-up everything 'cos John had shot out in front of it....'

The aerodynamic body was tested briefly in the rain at Silverstone but conditions at Reims – 98°F in the shade, 130°-plus on the road surface and 170° in the cockpits – were immensely different, and it was much faster. With the usual F2 race supporting the GP there were Coopers everywhere. John fielded four F1s, one with the streamlined body, which was effectively a Monaco sports car nose mated to an old 1100 Bob-tail centre-section. The shell was in two parts, split horizontally at hub-height, and the works F2 car present had a second full-width under-section to accept the unique streamlined top half. A standard slipper-body panel set was available in case the streamliner didn't work out. It didn't – lifting at 180 mph on the straights and feeling decidedly 'squirrelly' in the curves. The slipper body was to be used in both F1 and F2 races. New-material gearbox bushes were tried in practice, but were prone to seizure, and all three race gearboxes had to be stripped and the original bush material refitted.

Walker ran three cars, a choice for Trintignant and the F2 Cooper-Borgward for Moss, who would drive BRP's BRM in the GP. This F2 car was apparently the Monaco and Dutch GP Mark III, since re-engined. Trintignant had tested it at Zandvoort post-race and liked its behaviour on double rear wishbones. Consequently his own wire-wheeler

Opposite top *Cooper's new works team mechanic Mike Barney was a keen photographer. He took these evocative shots in the old team shop at the Hollyfield Road production factory in summer, 1959. 'They really sum up the place for me, dark and gloomy, tools and bits all over the floor and cars low down on axle stands or wheels. We spent hours working on our knees .... It was good though'. The Mark IV chassis was simple in the extreme but was stiff enough, light enough and good enough with the 2½-litre Climax FPF engine to challenge the best F1 opposition. The four works cars (nose of fourth on right) also shown, display the cam-box mounted header tank and supplementary oil tank as they lurk there in the gloom...*

Right *Superb shot of works Mark IV preparation under way in the Hollyfield Road shop, with the chassis welder's tube store beyond. At left is 'Noddy' Grohmann, who headed the Cooper works crew. Behind the gearbox, with its supplementary oil tank, is a Dutch boy who worked for the team for some months, named Hein, while on right towers tall Mike Barney. He had worked formerly for Dee's of Croydon where a fellow race enthusiast was a young salesman named Peter Gethin. They went to see the 1958 British GP together; within a year Mike was working for Cooper's and after a long racing career Peter Gethin would win the fastest-ever Championship GP, the 1971 Italian, at 150.75 mph. See the characteristic Cooper wishbone pivot mounts on the chassis? Cooper's had struggled to cut them out of surplus sheet stock in the early days, then Bertie Bradnack bought a Cooper and offered to stamp them out* en masse, *at his Walsall Pressings company. Ever after they were known by Cooper people as 'Bradnack lugs...*

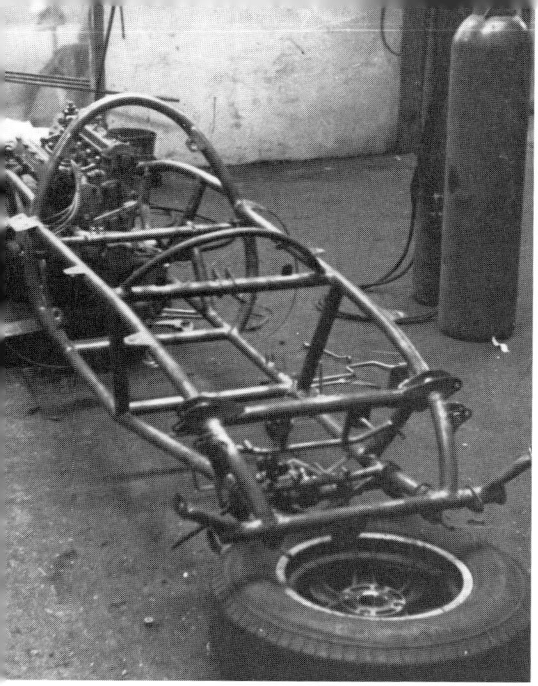

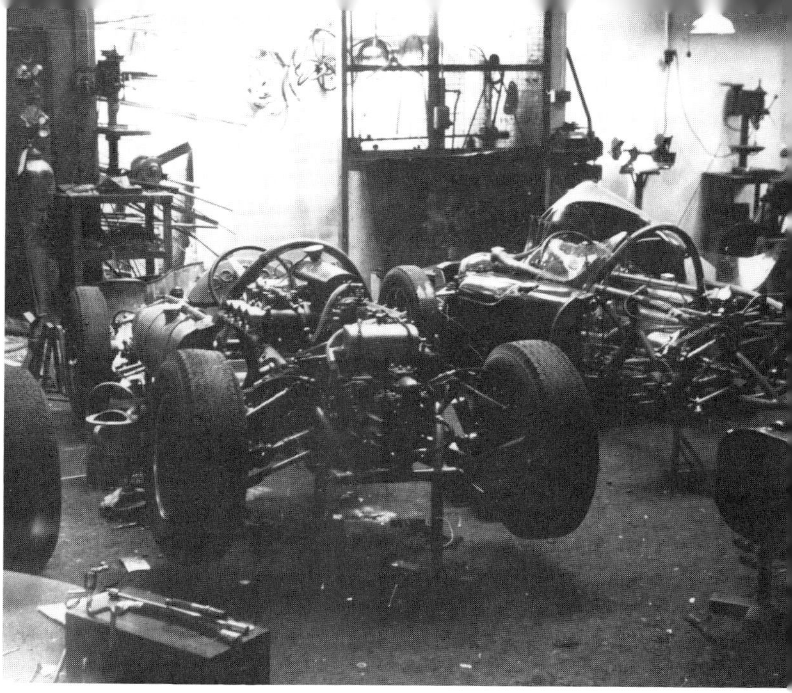

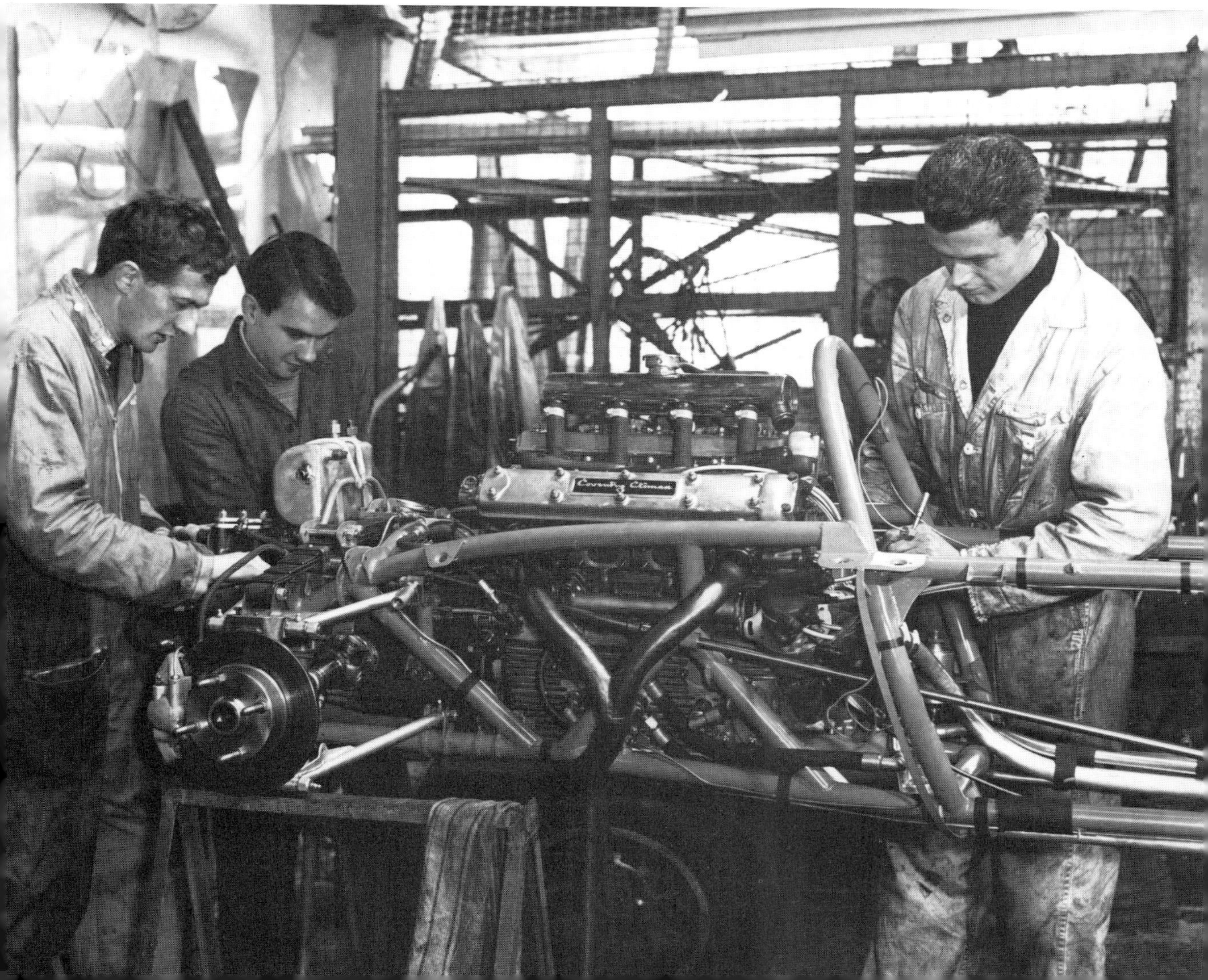
Coventry Climax

'Black Jack's flying machine – the all-enveloping streamliner body tested on Brabham's F1 car briefly in the wet at Silverstone and then more seriously in practice for the 1959 French GP at Reims is pictured here before its departure for France, on the new Hollyfield Road works' forecourt. At high speed on the superfast Reims straights the front end became airborne, the car wandered 'and the steering went rather light'. Second shot shows under-body sections attached to basic Mark IV to carry top enveloping shell

had now been modified to match for Reims. The third Walker car was the old Cooper-BRM, now fitted with a $2\frac{1}{2}$ FPF, the resited frame rails allowing it to stand upright rather than canted as in other Cooper-Climaxes. The engine mounts were re-made to give a lower tail line. It was also altered to double wishbone rear suspension, the old Francis radius-rod layout finally being scrapped at last. All three cars used Colotti gearboxes.

Newcomers were the Italian Scuderia Centro-Sud, run by 'Mimo' Dei with two Cooper-Maseratis – chassis *12* and *13/59* – similar to Atkins's and entered for Ian Burgess and Colin Davis.

All the works cars ran $2\frac{1}{2}$ FPFs, and Jack Brabham qualified between the Tony Brooks and Phil Hill Ferraris on the front row, but Brooks led throughout the race for a superb win. Out in front was the place to be, for the merciless sun had melted the road surface, which was rolled into missiles and thrown up by passing cars. On lap 7 Masten Gregory was smacked in the forehead by a glob of tar and stone after setting a new lap record. Overcome by pain and heat he pulled into the pit and could not be revived quickly enough to rejoin. Bruce's $2\frac{1}{2}$-litre car had only 35 psi oil pressure and he avoided slipstreaming as far as possible to minimize temperatures. Then he became engaged with Gendebien's Ferrari and took '... a fearful battering from flying stones. The mixture of sweat and blood in my goggles was like pink Champagne. I raised them, and the mess sluiced down my face....'

Jack, running third near the end, '.... was almost collapsing at the wheel, so I broke all the windscreen away to try and get some air. Every car I got near showered me with bricks and stones and the Coopers were absolutely destroyed at the front.... I was coasting into corners rather than braking because my feet were so badly burnt I could hardly put any pressure on the pedals.... I had to be lifted out...'

Fight to the line – young Bruce McLaren just failed to wrest second place from Moss's pale-green BRP BRM P25 after a lengthy duel in the British GP. Here they are, streaking between pits and Grand National grandstand with only ten more yards to go

5 July, 1959, French GP, Reims-Gueux – Brabham, outgunned by Ferrari V6 horsepower, drove hard in oven-like heat to finish third. Blistering sun melted sections of road surface which the cars' tyres then rolled into missiles and tossed into the air. Here Jack's works Mark IV – possibly F2/27/59 – hurtles out of Thillois Corner towards the pits with its nose badly damaged by flying stones and tarmac. He smashed out windscreen himself to win some 'cooling' air

Bruce finished fifth and climbed unaided from his car, then '... took off my helmet and started to cry my eyes out. I don't know why... but I wept uncontrollably for several minutes. This was the first race Mum and Pop had seen abroad and they were staggered to see it develop into a bloodbath....'

Trintignant had run strongly second between Brooks and Brabham, but spun on lap 20. He called at the pits with the engine off-song and was personally revived with a bucket of water. Later his engine died and he pushed a long way home to finish 11th, despite the heat. Scorning facial cuts he still cheerfully tackled the F2 race in Walker's re-engined ex-Cooper-BRM, along with the works drivers.

Two weeks passed before the British GP. At Hollyfield Road a new race mechanic had just joined the team. His name was Mike Barney, taking Bill James's place as he would be emigrating to Canada: 'I'd been a garage mechanic in Croydon, but it was boring and I got a job on the production side at Hollyfield Road. I'd only been there three or four weeks and didn't enjoy it at all. Then Ernie Looker – the works foreman – asked if I'd like to join the racing team. They'd had a young helper who was probably too keen. He was always in the driving seat of the racing cars. I was 6 ft 4 in. so they figured I couldn't fit in, so they'd have no trouble from me....' Now with Mike Grohmann and Mike Barney in the team 'Noddy' and 'Big Mike' became normal useage.

For Aintree all three works cars had gearbox oil pumps; Jack's a Holbourn-Eaton on the end-plate; Masten's and Bruce's similar pumps mounted on the side of the casing and driven by skew-gears. Ball-races inside the gearbox were replaced by roller-bearings. John was ill, and missed the meeting, watching anxiously – he was always a great worrier – on TV.

It started well. Jack qualified 27/59 on pole with Trintignant's Walker car and Gregory on row two, and Bruce behind

177

Home win – four years after his Grand Prix debut in the British race at Aintree with his own Bob-tail special, Jack Brabham won the 1959 event in terrific style here in '27/59'. The raised tailfin-spine on the engine cowl had first appeared on the works cars with 1.96 engines at the Monaco GP, 1958, some 14 months previously

them beside Moss's pale-green BRM. Masten's car ran with its windscreen side-pieces removed and suspension adjusted to increase understeer.

Jack, using the only big-valve, straight-inlet tract Mk II-headed FPF engine in the race, got away brilliantly to lead while Masten duelled with Moss for 10 laps until a fault in his car's clutch-lock mechanism caused clutch slip, curiously on alternate laps, which made the pit crew rewind and shake their stopwatches every other lap! When his engine began overheating the Kansan dropped back.

Moss closed on the leading Cooper as fuel burned down, while Trintignant and Schell were battling for third with McLaren watching every move. On lap 50 of the 75, Moss stopped for a fresh rear tyre. Bruce was up to third and closed on the BRM. The Cooper crew waved a fresh wheel and tyre at Brabham, but let him decide for himself. He had first noticed signs of wear on lap 35, and took care from then on. Moss stopped again for fuel, and Bruce took second behind his team leader: 'I set off on the irreverent task of keeping Moss the Master behind me. The Cooper was all over the place, I was really caning it and using most of the track with spinning wheels and sliding tail. . . .' Moss still hacked ahead, Bruce fought back as the maestro missed a gear; '. . . wondering if Stirling was getting annoyed I glanced across. To my surprise Stirling was thoroughly enjoying himself and gave me an encouraging thumbs-up sign!'

While the crowd concentrated on this battle for second, Jack had adapted his driving to conserve his tyres – for a stop on those bolt-on wheels would have been disastrous. His gearbox was holding together and he won handsomely in the race and on the circuit where he had made his Grand Prix debut for Cooper four years previously. McLaren and Moss meanwhile set new lap records and out of the last corner Bruce almost drew alongside the BRM, with the Cooper nose abreast its cockpit as they took the flag. Trintignant was fifth

and Gregory seventh. Jack reported the new-head FPF would pull from 4000 rpm. He never exceeded 6700 and when the engine was stripped it was in fine condition.

But could the Coopers prove competitive against the powerful Ferraris and BRMs on the high-speed courses late in the season? On 2 August, the German GP was held on Berlin's notorious Avus track with its high-banked North Curve. Preparation included 'solid' dampers to resist G-loadings on the brick-paved banking and the highest possible final-drive ratios to save the engines. Both Jack's and Bruce's drop gears were wider than standard to accommodate extra load – but the team did not notice they had been wrongly machined. . . .

As practice began, Masten calculated his car was 14 mph slower than the Ferraris. Walker fielded two Coopers, the regular car for Trintignant and a brand-new machine – probably *FII/19/59* – with the usual 2½ FPF and Colotti gearbox for Moss, back in the Cooper fold while BRP ran their BRM for German driver Hans Herrmann. The organizers grudgingly gave a reserve entry to Centro-Sud for Ian Burgess.

The 1959 Formula 1 Manufacturers' World Championship fell to the Cooper Car Company on 13 September, 1959, in the Italian GP at Monza when Stirling Moss – seen here cornering inside Dan Gurney's tall Ferrari at the Parabolica *– won at over 124 mph after 257 miles racing, and Jack Brabham – leading Cliff Allison near the same spot – placed third. By this time the Walker cars had dispensed with the Francis top rear rod and adopted double rear wishbones like the works'. Stirling ran Borrani wire rear wheels with knock-off hubs in case a rear-tyre change should prove necessary. It did not, though the Walker crew signalled Stirling in. As arranged, he just drove on, but seeing the signal Ferrari called all their cars in! The left-front tyre was the one which suffered*

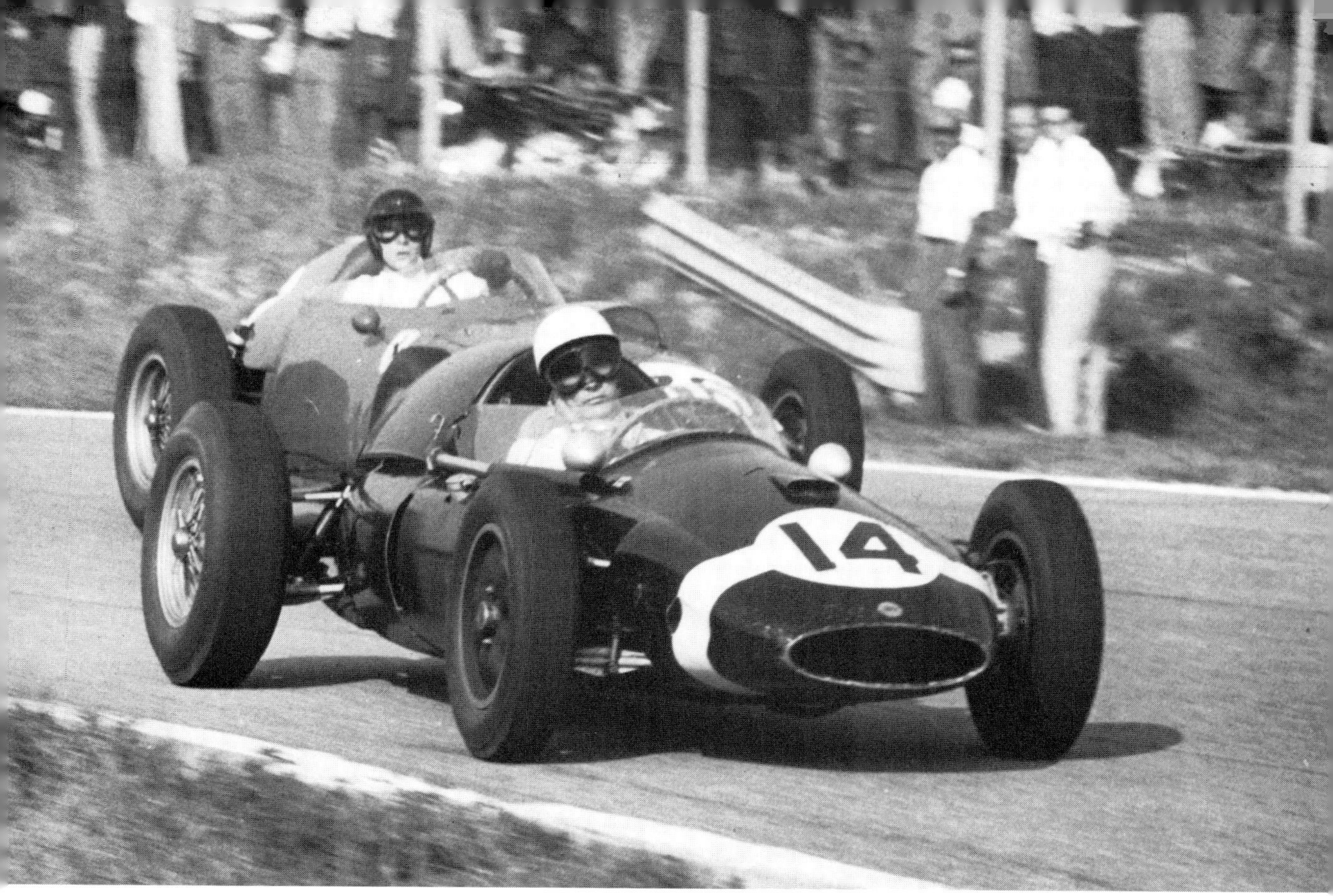
14

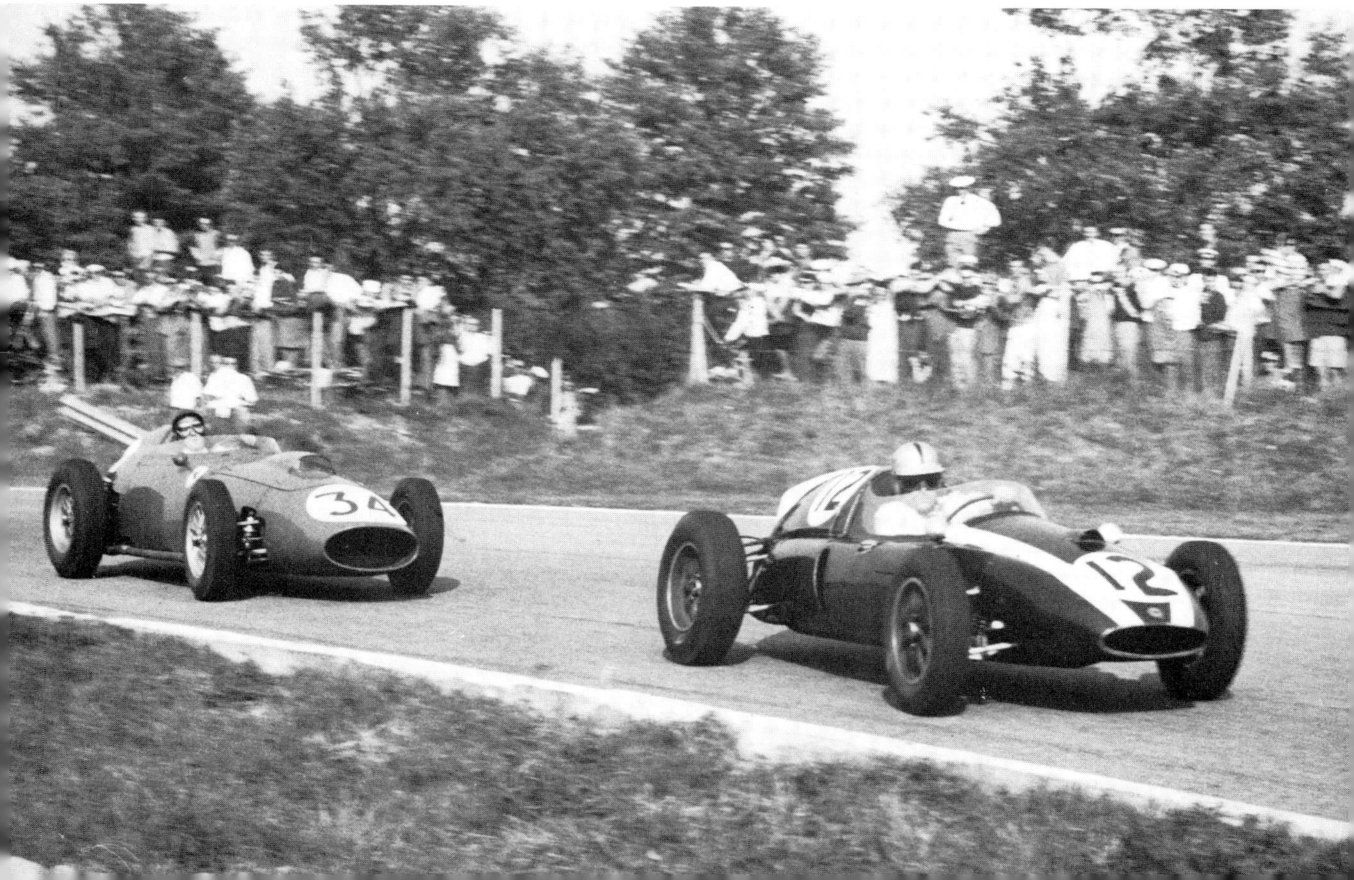
34
12

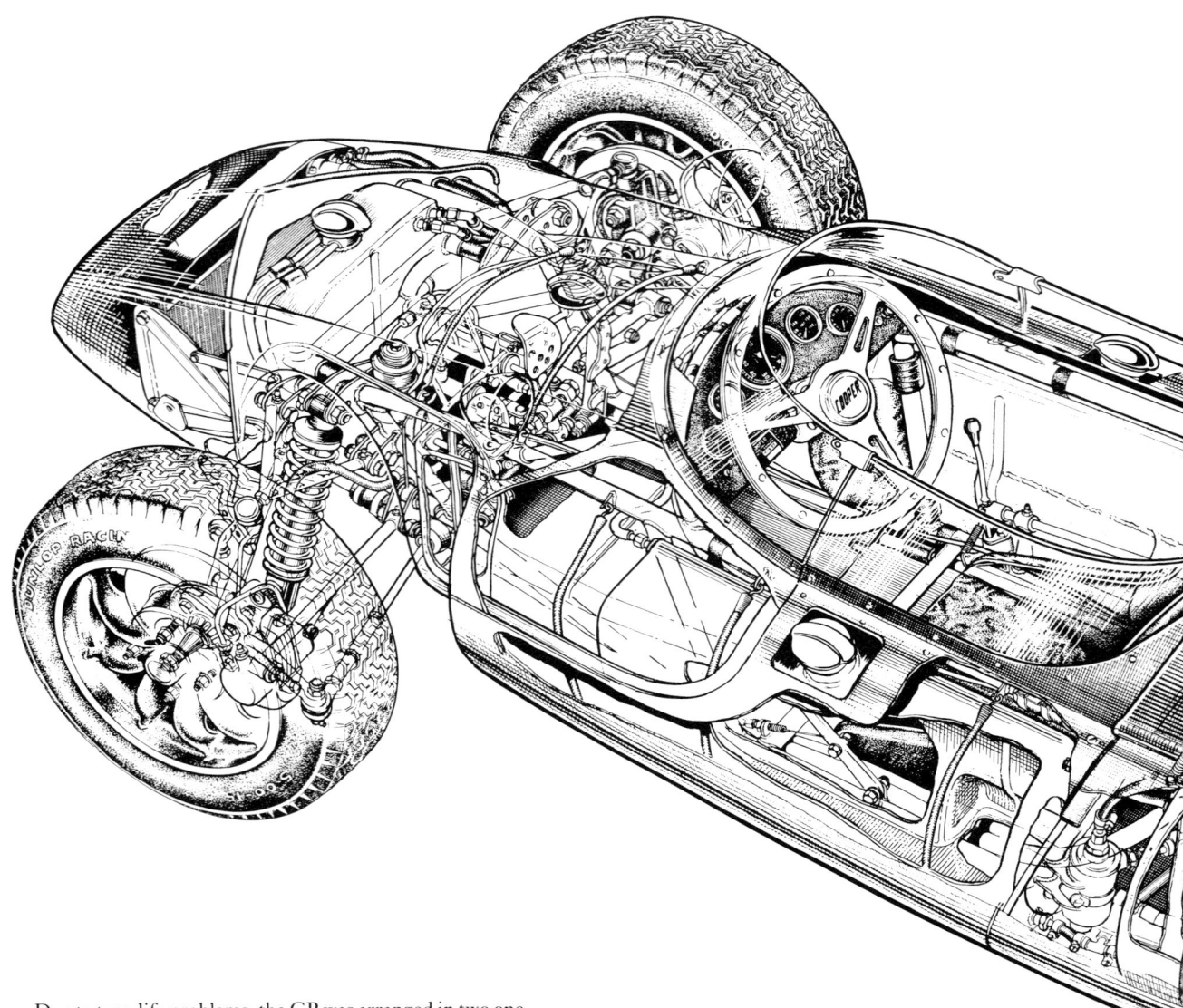

Due to tyre-life problems, the GP was arranged in two one-hour Heats with the overall result decided on aggregate time; qualifiers for Heat Two depending on the results of Heat One. In the sports car race on Saturday, Jean Behra's Porsche crashed on the rain-swept banking and he was killed. This cast deep gloom over the meeting.

Brooks took pole for Ferrari, nearly 2 sec quicker than Moss, then Gurney's Ferrari followed by Brabham, Gregory, McLaren, Trintignant and Burgess, each one row down.

On only the second race lap Moss's step-up gears stripped. Gregory sling-shot round the Ferraris on the banking, slithering round in a brave, barely controlled slide. Brabham was there too, up among the Italian cars, but while Gregory was in his element wheel-to-wheel at 180 mph, Jack wisely sat back and watched. On lap 24 the Kansan's engine plumed smoke and flying pieces as an FPF con-rod bolt broke and the block was sawn in two by the flailing rod. Jack's step-up gears stripped so Bruce was the only works team survivor,

1959 – WORLD CHAMPIONS

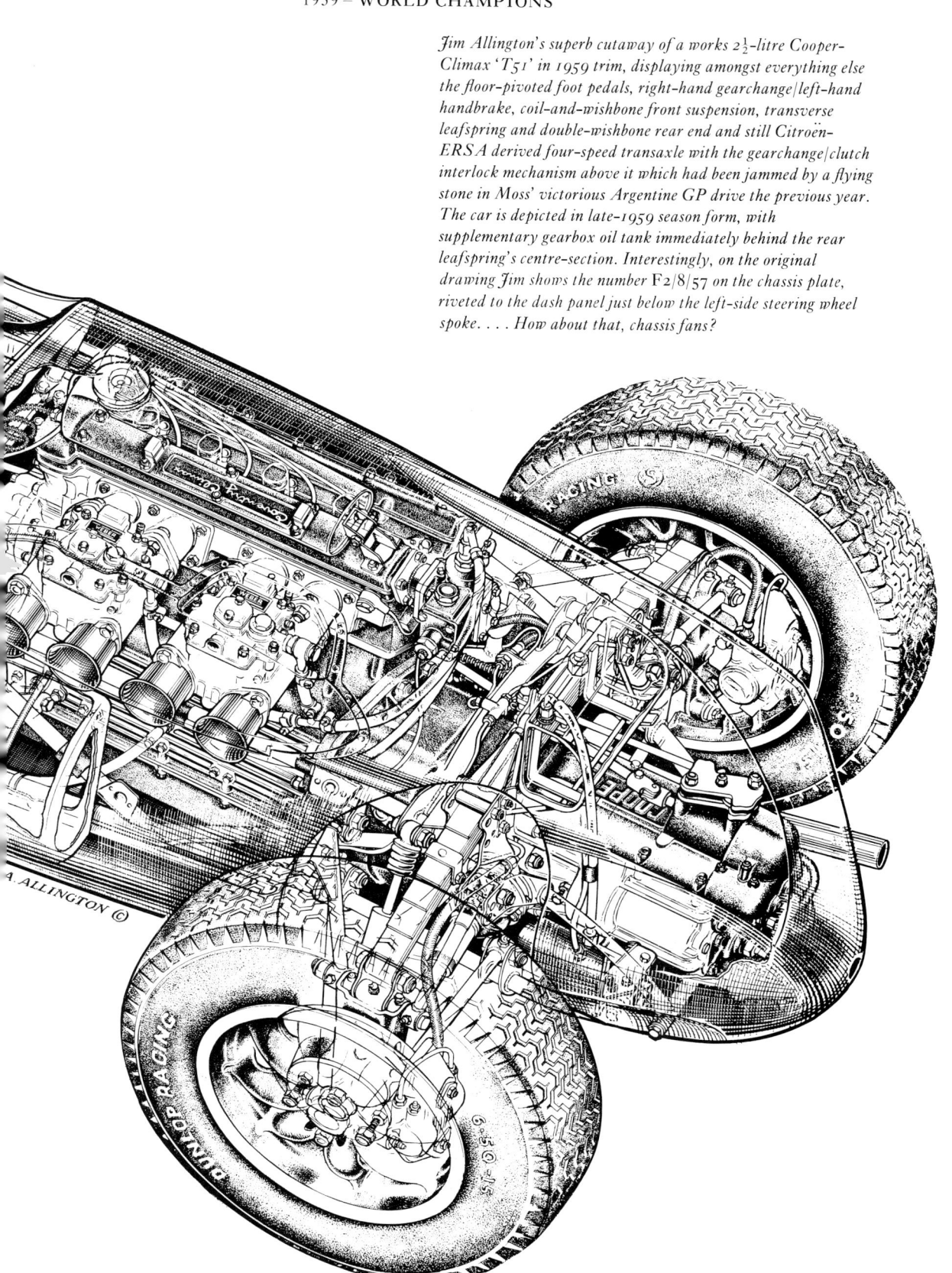

Jim Allington's superb cutaway of a works 2½-litre Cooper-Climax 'T51' in 1959 trim, displaying amongst everything else the floor-pivoted foot pedals, right-hand gearchange/left-hand handbrake, coil-and-wishbone front suspension, transverse leafspring and double-wishbone rear end and still Citroën-ERSA derived four-speed transaxle with the gearchange/clutch interlock mechanism above it which had been jammed by a flying stone in Moss' victorious Argentine GP drive the previous year. The car is depicted in late-1959 season form, with supplementary gearbox oil tank immediately behind the rear leafspring's centre-section. Interestingly, on the original drawing Jim shows the number F2/8/57 on the chassis plate, riveted to the dash panel just below the left-side steering wheel spoke. . . . How about that, chassis fans?

fourth from Trintignant sixth and Burgess ninth. In Heat Two Bruce was the meat in a Ferrari sandwich until his lower drop shaft and step-up gears broke, leaving Trintignant and Burgess to finish fourth and sixth. On aggregate their placings were the same.

On 23 August, the Portuguese GP was held at Lisbon's fast Monsanto road circuit, where only Moss, Gregory and Phil Hill had raced before. The trip began badly for Brabham – he nearly lost a toe dragging a boat up the beach, then had his pocket picked and wallet stolen. Moss's Walker car took pole from Jack and Masten, Coopers 1–2–3, Trintignant and McLaren in the next two rows. Centro-Sud ran a Cooper-Maserati for local ace Mario Araujo Cabral, and in practice he spun across the path of Schell's BRM and was lucky a collision was averted.

Moss, Brabham, McLaren and Gregory led away 1–2–3–4 for Cooper while Trintignant began a long duel with Gurney's Ferrari. On lap 24 Jack's luck ran out as he came up to lap Cabral, who moved across his line in a 130 mph right-hander. The Australian was squeezed into the straw bales, his car climbed on top of them, hit a telegraph pole just off-centre and rolled back into the road, tossing out its driver....

'I sat up in the middle of the track – and found myself looking straight into the radiator of Masten Gregory's car!' Masten glimpsed the fallen pole and cables across the road and shrank his fingers and toes 'away from the metal parts of the car in case they were live electric'. He missed Jack who was then scooped-up and taken to hospital in a terrifying ambulance ride, but was found to be only sore, cut and bruised.

Bruce's step-up gears failed again on lap 39 while Masten soldiered on, hot and bothered but second behind Moss's ever-increasing lead. Trintignant stopped to have water sluiced over himself, and out on one hairpin Bonnier was standing beside his retired BRM, splashing water from his helmet over any driver who cared to pass slow and close.... Stirling won in masterly style for Walker, Cooper-Climax and the much-berated Colotti gearbox, with Gregory firmly second and Trintignant fourth.

That night Jack's smashed car was heaved into the works transporter after two engines and all three transaxles had been loaded onto a charter flight home. A Cooper van collected them at Gatwick, rushing the FPFs to Coventry, the gearboxes to the works. There, frantic work had begun to build up the spare care for Jack in the Italian GP three weeks hence. John's Zodiac was laden down with spares, engines and gearboxes, a trailer with the spare car was hitched on behind and he drove to Monza to meet the transporter, which had trailed direct from Lisbon; with only Noddy and Big Mike to care for all three cars.

There was also a telegram awaiting John at the Milanese Hotel. Masten had broken bones in a Tojeiro crash at the Goodwood TT. Now Jack was to race Bruce's faithful '23A/58 in the GP, Bruce took Masten's regular 7/59 and experienced Maserati driver Giorgio Scarlatti would take over 4/59, with the team gaining suitable inducement from the Milan club.

Jack Fairman was to drive the Atkins' Cooper-Maserati, now using the latest works-type gearbox with endplate-mounted oil pump and oil tank, and Centro-Sud's two similar cars were down for Burgess and Colin Davis. The Walker transporter had also come straight from Lisbon with the usual cars for Moss and Trintignant. Stirling's ran in practice with the team's knock-off rear-wheel kit fitted in case tyre wear should prove marginal on this very fast course. But it was the left-front tyre which caused anxiety, so k/o rear hubs would not help much if the bolt-on fronts needed changing. At Zandvoort, Jack had accommodated excessive left-front wear by fitting a sports car Dunlop tyre with full 8 mm tread depth. Now the works borrowed a similar tyre from Centro-Sud, and Walker took one from a very fast Lotus Elite which had been racing in the accompanying Coppa Inter-Europa until Ada Pace spun in its path and caused a multiple shunt.

The Championship lay between Moss, Brooks and Brabham, and they qualified in that order, Bruce on row three with Trintignant behind him. Brooks's Ferrari clutch burned out at the start, robbing him of drive, and Phil Hill led away from Moss, Gurney and Brabham. Fairman stalled, Trint's throttle linkage fell apart and Scarlatti's gear linkage broke very early on. He gave Noddy and Mike a terrific wigging for allowing it to happen. Moss sat contentedly between the two Ferraris up front while Brabham settled back to save his tyres. Bruce's race ended in piston collapse and a thrown rod. When the Ferraris made their inevitable tyre-change stops Moss inherited the comfortable lead he held to the finish, winning from Phil Hill, with Jack third and Trintignant ninth. Denis Jenkinson wrote: 'Moss won still with ample tread left on his tyres whereas Brabham in third place had worn his tyres dangerously thin ... it is the ability to go fast and conserve his tyres, and to plan strategy while he is racing, that makes Moss the great artist that he is....' Cooper-Climax had clinched it – the Formula 1 Manufacturers' World Championship.

Now Brooks, Brabham and Moss had won two GPs each that season, and the Championships would be decided between them, in the United States GP, which had just been inserted into the calendar at Sebring on 12 December. It was a long, tense wait....

Meanwhile, on 26 September, the non-Championship Oulton Park Gold Cup was run to Formula 1 with a £2000 first prize. Brabham, McLaren and Moss drove Cooper-Climaxes against Salvadori's Cooper-Maserati and 21-year-old Chris Bristow in BRP's formerly F2 Mark IV fitted with a low-compression ex-Moss Monaco sports car 2½ FPF giving around 216 bhp. BRP – the Ken Gregory/Pa Moss partnership – had won sponsorship from the Samengo-Turner

1959 – WORLD CHAMPIONS

In 2 hr 12 min time Jack Brabham would be World Champion and Moss and Brooks would have lost their chances for another year. Here the US GP at Sebring is flagged away with Moss's Walker car (7) flanking Brabham (8) and Schell (19), followed by Trintignant's Walker car on mag wheels front and rear (6), Brooks (2), Phil Hill (5), Cliff Allison (3), von Trips (4) all Ferraris, Bruce McLaren (9) diving for the inside, Innes Ireland's Lotus (10), Salvadori's Cooper-Maserati (12), Alan Stacey's Lotus (11), de Tomaso's Cooper-Osca F2, George Constantine's Cooper-Climax, Blanchard's Porsche, d'Orey's TecMec-Maserati and extreme left/top Rodger Ward's Kurtis Kraft-Offy midget. His length-of-the-grid starting deficit against the big Coopers convinced him of their Indianapolis potential, and he said as much to the works team . . .

family's Yeoman Credit finance house and this race marked their debut under that name, with cars still beautifully prepared by Tony Robinson.

Brabham jumped the start to lead Moss, Bristow, McLaren and Salvadori until Stirling's still wire-rear-wheeled Walker car moved ahead. Bruce's car jumped out of gear and he went off at Esso Bend. Stirling won by 5.2 sec from Brabham, the similarly sideways Bristow, and Salvadori. Paul Emery drove Geoff Richardson's Cooper-Connaught, essentially an F2-chassised *Libre* car in this race.

Another minor F1/F2 race followed at Snetterton on 10 October, the 25-lap Silver City Trophy. Brabham ran his own Mark III 2.2 Cooper there against works BRMs and Lotuses and finished second behind Flockhart's Bourne machine.

One week later Moss was in upstate New York for the Watkins Glen *Libre* GP. He drove Yeoman Credit's large-engined Mark IV, starting from the back of the grid after missing first practice – due to watching TV – while the second session was wet. Tiny track-racing midget cars and some sports-racers made up the field; Moss was unstoppable and won by seven laps from Ed Johnson's Offenhauser Midget.

Meanwhile, in preparation for the vital race at Sebring, Stirling had prevailed upon Alf Francis and the Walker crew to fit his Cooper with coil-spring rear suspension, recalling how much the Vanwall had been improved by the change from transverse leaf-spring to coils. His regular car – new at Avus – had a hefty frame welded onto the top rear frame rails as top abutments for coil-spring/damper struts, which passed down through the top wishbones to pick up on the upright just above the hubs. Rob: 'It was Stirling's idea, so it had to work. . . .'

To beat Brabham for the World Championship, Stirling had to win and make fastest lap. If he won but Jack set fastest lap, Brabham won the title. Tony Brooks had to win and set fastest lap with his rivals lower than second for a clear victory. If Jack was second, the two would tie on points and Brooks would become Champion through having won three GPs to the Australian's two. The works team appreciated that fastest lap could be the key. John planned to concentrate on two cars only, for Brabham and Gregory, with the American to go all out for fastest lap regardless of finishing. He could drive extremely quickly; it was a task he would relish. But his TT accident had been serious, and he was still unfit come Sebring time. Bruce McLaren took his place and as yet he was not as quick.

Meanwhile, Jack had been offered an entry in the Bahamas Speed Week at Nassau the week before Sebring. His 2-litre Monaco sports was prepared and shipped out in company with Tim Wall. It was geared with 25:28 step-up gears for the fast Oakes Field course, but they were fitted upside down and Jack found it incredibly under-geared. Chasing Mike Taylor's Lotus for second place in the race, a stone was tossed up which smashed Jack's goggles. He finished fourth, but had splinters in one eye. After treatment, fearful for his fitness for Sebring, Jack still raced in the Nassau Trophy feature, which Moss won for Aston Martin, and he was fourth again. John, Jack and Tim Wall then flew to Miami and two days later began practice at Sebring. . . .

Noddy Grohmann met them with two impeccably prepared works cars. According to Jack they were his Lisbon crash car repaired and Masten's regular 7/59, which Sebring medical examination confirmed Bruce must drive as Gregory was still unfit. In fact Jack's car was an all-new replacement for the Lisbon write-off, originally completed with half-cutaway body panels for the London Motor Show. It probably travelled on the late Portuguese car's paperwork, so had inherited its chassis number, though of course this too might be only a transient feature.

Equipe Walker presented the coil-spring rear suspension car for Moss still with Borrani wire rear wheels, plus Trintignant's unchanged regular mount. Both works cars and Moss's carried FPFs with the latest Mark II 'big-valve' heads. Salvadori was present with the Atkins special, Harry Schell his F2 Mark III with 2.2 installed, and Mike Taylor was ill so his 2-litre F2 went to American sports car driver George Constantine.

The works cars had terrible practice problems. Jack dented the side of his car in first practice and its nose in the second session. His engine overheated with head seal problems. Bruce's stripped its step-up gears and overheated. Tim Wall was a good engine fitter – he rebuilt Jack's that night, but the drivers swopped cars. Bruce tried Jack's to see if any changes might be required, and within two miles its crown-wheel and pinion broke. If Jack had just put it away ready for the race he would not have survived the opening lap. . . .

Bruce had been dubious about his original car's handling, now Jack double-checked and found its frame twisted $\frac{3}{4}$ in. out of line, presumably by Masten clouting a kerb in Lisbon. Jack reset the suspension to level the frame, then the brakes began to judder. Bruce stripped his re-assigned car's gearbox and found broken cwp teeth had mangled the gears. Another major rebuild began. Jack's 'box was opened for a precautionary survey and its mainshaft was found cracked. The spare 'box replaced it. Briggs Cunningham kept the small works team supplied with copious supplies of hot coffee and chicken soup. Dr Frank Falkner, English-born, US-domiciled paediatrician and great racing enthusiast, was helping John 'manage', and around 1 am on race morning he briskly ushered Brabham and McLaren away to bed.

During practice, the unruly Harry Schell had a 'wheeze' . . . he took a short-cut across the airfield circuit's desolate infield, chopped off distance and time and somehow the course marshals didn't report it. Consequently, he was credited with a very good lap time and now he claimed his place on the front row, in Brooks's place! His time was impossible but the voluble Franco-American forced the inexperienced American organizers to accept it. Ferrari were beside themselves as Brooks's car was rolled back onto the second row. It quite possibly cost him the World Championship.

Moss led away with Brabham and McLaren hot on his heels, and down in the pack poor Brooks was rammed by his team mate Trips and made a stop for inspection, surrendering all real chance. It happened as quickly as that.

1959 — WORLD CHAMPIONS

Left *The master stroke — Stirling Moss might conceivably have been World Champion several times had he been content to wield his matchless skill in a standard car, if one could have been provided for him. But improvement was the name of the game, and here at Sebring, Florida, for the 1959 World Championship-deciding US GP his Walker Cooper appeared with coil-spring rear suspension, like this, and still with the Borrani wheels*

Michael Tee of Motor Sport *recorded the new World Champion's thirst-quenching Coke as he regained his breath after pushing his fuel-dry Cooper to the Sebring finish line. Fourth place was good enough, while young Bruce McLaren did the winning. The team's cup was full. In retrospect Jack suspects the crew miscounted the fuel churns when filling his car; the fourth version of the story . . .*

After just a quarter-lap Brabham's heart almost stopped when his engine fluffed onto three cylinders, but almost instantly it chimed-in again on all four. He took second place from Bruce and sat in Moss's wake. Stirling was confident, happy he could pull out another 2 seconds a lap if necessary. He was not hurrying, but after only six laps his Colotti gearbox broke. . . . Constantine's car blew its head seal, Schell's its clutch and Salvadori's Atkins Cooper-Maserati its transmission. . . .

Tony Brooks had rejoined and was driving as quickly and smoothly as ever. He was still a danger should the field be decimated. The works Coopers moved together, Brabham giving a thumbs-up wave. Trintignant was hot in pursuit and John signalled as the gap closed. Jack paced his drive carefully: 'I had never driven flat-out from the start, and if necessary I had enough in hand to pour on the coals at the end. It seemed in the bag. . . .'

His idea was that if anything happened to his car, Bruce — close behind — would go ahead and beat Brooks to the line; Tony still needing both to win and set fastest lap for the title.

'I went past the pits and nodded to John and off we went into that final lap. . . .'

Now came the drama in what had been a terribly dull race: 'I was about a mile from the finish when the car started to run on two cylinders. I was shocked. I just couldn't believe it.' He knocked the gearlever into neutral as his engine died, out of fuel. Bruce saw him slowing and almost stopped, Jack furiously waving him on. The youngster snatched second gear and tore away for the line to win his maiden GP victory by only 0.6 sec from Trintignant. Brooks was third, these points demoting Moss to third in the Championship standings.

Jack was out of his car pushing it over 400 yards slightly uphill to the line. It was hot. Heart pounding, soaked in sweat, he crossed the line fourth and flopped to the ground; gulping down a cold Coke proffered by John Cooper, who was ecstatic for his team's and his friend's success.

Jack Brabham: '. . . they helped me into an official's caravan. I flopped out for a quarter of an hour or so to get my breath back. Then it suddenly dawned on me. I'd won the World Championship — the first British driver in a British car to do so. I just couldn't believe it. Bruce was there smiling away in a daze, and hardly believing his luck. . . .'

Three stories explain the fuel shortage. Jack relates that Bruce finished with almost 4 gallons in his tanks, and since he had been towed most of the way by Jack's car he would have burned less — but only 2 gallons or so at the most. So there must have been a leak, and right at the start when his engine fluffed it had probably lost fuel through the overflow and the breather tube had spilled down past the carburettors and made it run rich. Once the fuel level fell it began running properly again.

John Cooper recalls how they would always run their fuel consumption tests in practice and base their calculated fuel load for the race upon them. 'Then to be on the safe side I'd always add a couple of gallons just for luck. At Sebring I vividly remember Jack saying "I don't want to lug all that lot around" and he had the extra couple of gallons drained off again. . . .'

Closer to the events of that historic day Bruce recorded: 'Jack, often a last-minute-change man, had gone slightly smaller on choke-tube size, which made the engine run a little bit richer, and the fact that he had been towing me in his slipstream helped save my fuel and exhaust his. Moss had gone down 2 mm on choke-tubes in practice and had found a considerable improvement in lap time. Jack had spotted this by looking at Moss's carbs and changed his accordingly. Probably Moss would have run out of fuel had he lasted the distance, as the tanks on both Coopers were presumably the same size. . . .'

Whatever the full sequence of events that day, one thing was indisputable fact. Both the 12-year-old Cooper Car Company and Jack Brabham were Champions of the World.

CHAPTER EIGHTEEN

1960 – The greatest triumph

During 1959 Cooper-Climax cars had dominated Formula 2 and their first World Championship season had seen them win eight of the year's 13 F1 races compared to Ferrari's three and two for BRM. Small wonder then that their rivals were beginning to build new GP cars the Cooper way....

During practice for the Italian GP at Monza the first rear-engined BRM had emerged, and now into 1960 Colin Chapman's highly innovative Lotus company was also committed to engine behind the driver in a multi-purpose F1/F2/Formula Junior design. At Maranello even the arch conservative Enzo Ferrari had authorized construction of such a car, if only '... for experimental purposes'. The so-called rear-engined revolution was well under way.

At Hollyfield Road, Charles Cooper was immensely proud of his company's success, if a little nonplussed by the congratulations being showered upon him by the establishment. Andrew Ferguson went with him to the BRDC dinner at the Washington Hotel. Standing sipping cocktails, The Earl Howe and Raymond Mays came to shake hands: 'Congratulations, Charles – delighted for you....' they said in their public school tones. Small talk began, Charles standing silent, uncomfortable. 'Then, I think to keep his end up, he suddenly said, "'Ere, 'ave you 'eard the one about this Irishman wiv 'is dog – really good joke this is...."'

Bruce McLaren recalled them all going to the BBC TV *Sportsman of the Year* function. Charles was introduced to Herb Elliott, the great Australian middle-distance runner. Later he turned to Bruce and asked suspiciously, 'That bloke Elliott, who does he drive for?'

Now he was intent upon capitalizing on the World Championship and preserving his company's profitability. While John knew they must progress to match the genius of Lotus and resources of BRM and Ferrari, his father was more dismissive, but even John was too. When Owen Maddock asked if he should calculate the stresses in their chassis to see if he could save weight John said: 'Colin Chapman does that with his cars and he's up all night welding 'em when they break! Why change it when we're winnin'?'

Why indeed, and why could the cars described as 'the English beetles', the 'backyard specials', the 'blacksmith's kit cars' outperform the toolroom masterpieces from Ferrari and BRM and Aston Martin?

The handling eccentricities of the prewar Auto Unions had given rear-engined designs a bad reputation. Their 1934–37 cars had been the real culprits. The pundits claimed their long V16 engines forced the driver so far forward he couldn't sense the tail swing until it was too late to correct it; and the huge engine in the rear made it swing like a pendulum. Few seemed to appreciate the optimism of a design attempting to transmit around 550 bhp through swing-axle suspension and tyre treads only 6 in. wide.... In 1938–39 the de Dion rear-suspended V12 Auto Unions had the answer, but they were not long fully developed to raceworthiness before the war broke out. If racing had continued into 1940–41 it seems probable that the rear-engined GP car could have proved itself nearly 20 years before Cooper did the trick. As it was, mud stuck, and while rear-engined designs were widely accepted in minor Formulae it seemed virtually taboo for the splendour of Formula 1, and that was largely due to Auto Union's bad press prewar.

A few adventurers saw the way. Alfa Romeo toyed with a car in 1940. Connaught developed a rear-engined design with a monocoque fuselage but couldn't raise the money to

Two of the ex-works Mark IVs went down-under to New Zealand while the other two were despatched to Sebring. Here in the New Zealand GP at Ardmore, January 1960 the new World Champion leads from Moss's Yeoman Credit team car, McLaren, David Piper's Lotus 16 (18), Bib Stilwell (6) with Ian Burgess behind him, then the local front-engined brigade with Roycroft's big Ferrari V12 on the outside, the Maserati 250Fs of Mansell, Glass and Jensen bunched inside, Teddy Gray's Tornado-Corvette and in the little Cooper nipping-out the Tornado is young George Lawton

Two in a row for Bruce McLaren as having inherited victory in the 1959 season-closing US GP he did the trick again in the 1960 season-opening Argentine race at Buenos Aires. Here an elated John and Charles Cooper bring in their winner to enthusiastic local support. Bruce's tinted goggles have lost the right-side lens but the Mark IV works car ran impeccably. Still the team had been alarmed by the pace of their opposition – major change was on the way

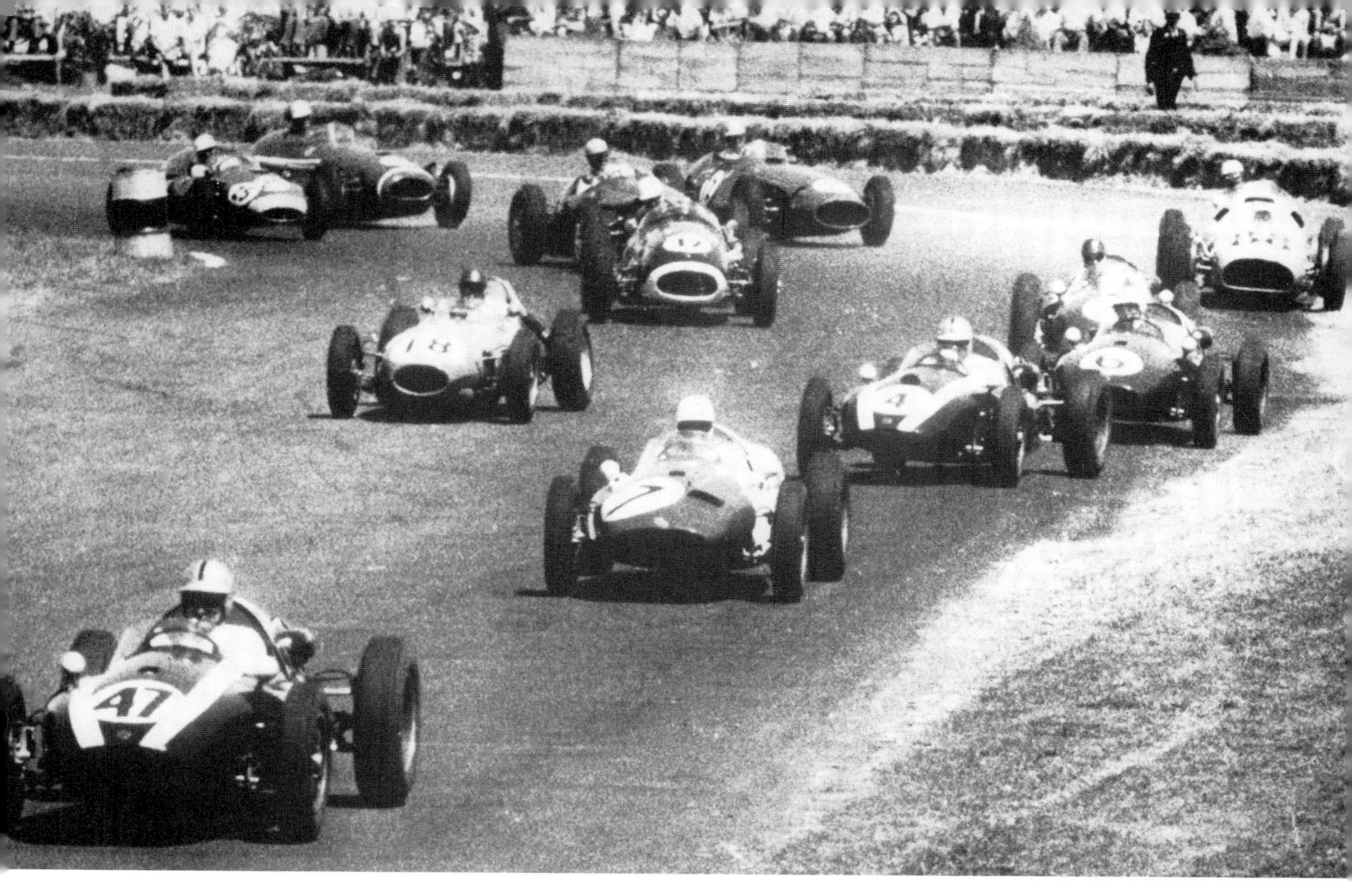
41
18
4

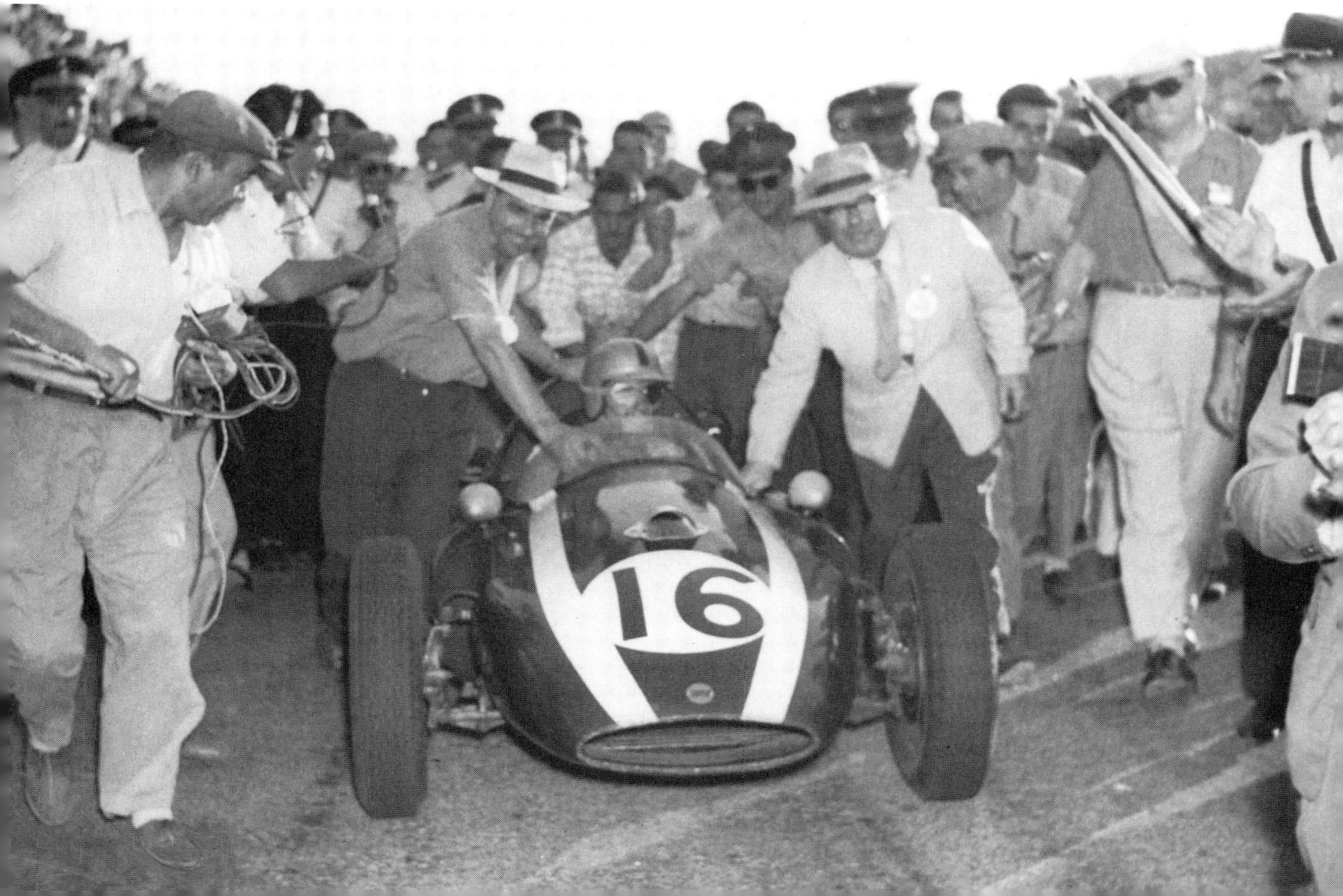
16

Having won again at Longford Tasmania in his 1960 down-under programme, here Jack Brabham lines up in the faithful Mark IV with Bib Stilwell and Jon Leighton outside him on the front row at Phillip Island, Victoria, Australia. In this two-day March, 1960, meeting he won four races, using oversize thinwall rear tyres specially flown out from the UK by Dunlop. Cooper cars of all shapes and sizes dominated Antipodean racing during this period

His type of circuit – Maurice Trintignant was brought up on some fairly rough-and-ready public road circuits in Europe around the war. He found Cordoba's course much to his liking and won the so-called Buenos Aires City GP handsomely there after the works cars' defection. He is taking the flag. The masses had a good, close view of the racing . . .

build it. Cisitalia-Porsche and Sacha-Gordine went the same way. Bugatti financed a transverse 2½-litre rear-engined GP car in 1956, but then couldn't support a race programme for it. So Cooper had to prove the idea, and make it acceptable; obviously the way to go. . . .

Without a prop-shaft beneath his seat, the driver could drop low to minimize frontal area. There need be no power-wasting driveline angularities to pass alongside his seat. Save one square foot frontal area, you've saved 25 wasted bhp. No prop-shaft, you save its weight. With engine and final-drive mounted in unit, torque reactions self-cancel and support structures can be built lighter. Lighter weight aids acceleration, brakes can be smaller, which means lighter, and so on, in a descending spiral.

Back in the 1930s Mercedes designer Dr Hans Nibel propounded the advantage of a high polar moment of inertia in a racing car. He split the major masses of engine, front suspension transmission and rear suspension far apart in a chassis set up for understeer. This gave his drivers an inherently stable platform which they could put into a balanced drift at will by exploiting the vast power and minimal tyre adhesion available to them.

As long as high power was available, designers followed where Nibel led, but in the postwar unblown Formulae there was no longer power to spare and understeer absorbs it while an oversteering high polar moment car demands brilliant artistry to control it.

During the mid-Fifties designers came to appreciate the rapid-response advantages available from reducing polar moment. The Coopers became good, if not outstanding in this respect, by evolution, having started out too nervous, too low in polar moment. Engine, driver and fuel were housed as

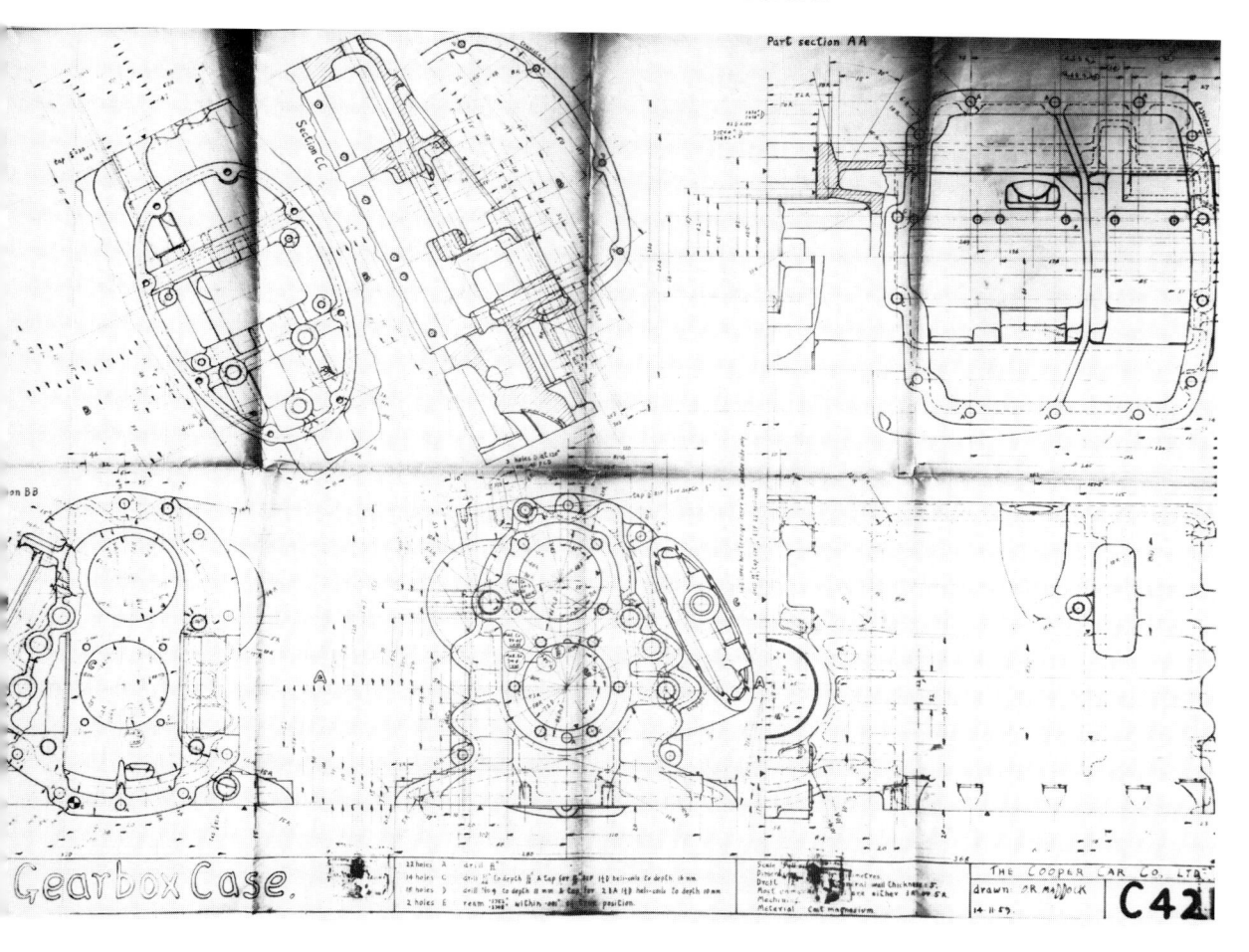

Owen Maddock's drawing of the 'C5S' gearbox casing, dated 14 November, 1959. Owen's drawings were complex and fine-detailed and he was regarded very much as the artist of Hollyfield Road. But Charles Cooper always objected to his large lettering as here in 'Gearbox Case' – 'Why can't you do it proper boy?'

conveniently within the wheelbase as in only the very best front-engined designs, although gearbox and radiator were still overhung at either end. The 44/56 front/rear weight distribution of most Coopers was surprisingly similar to that of most front-engined cars with their tail fuel tanks.

As similar double-wishbone geometry had been adopted front and rear on the cars into 1959, so Cooper fitted 5.00–15 Dunlop Racing front tyres and 6.50–15 rears so that the greater loads applied to the rear tyres would be offset by the greater cornering force they could generate. Jack Brabham had a feel for suspension adjustment and improvement which – in parallel with Colin Chapman's Lotus developments (and those of Eric Broadley in his sports Lolas) – virtually founded the modern art of setting up a racing car.

Using alternative rear wishbone pivot holes to raise or lower roll-centres, plus threaded-joint adjustment of top wishbone effective lengths to change wheel cambers, Jack had the knowledge and sensitivity to set up his car to suit differing circuits more closely than could most opponents. Much of his skill rubbed off on Bruce McLaren, and so the Cooper works team could make the most of their other advantages; not least a close and friendly relationship with Coventry Climax – with whom they didn't whinge and whine, and paid their bills on the nail – and the use of wide for their time 6.50 section tyres.

Weight was a major factor. The Cooper-Climax T51 Mark IV in Formula 1 trim weighed-in around 1008 lb *sans* driver, compared to some 1481 lb for a front-engined BRM, which was considered light for its type. For the Cooper to load its tyres in a corner to the same degree as the heavier car it would be generating higher G, so would be travelling faster. Some theoreticians dubiously claim as much as 10 per cent faster. . . .

In real life the wishbone rear end with those chubby tyres could promote terrific traction when well set up. Front roll-stiffness was high with the anti-roll bar through the front cross-member, and weight transfer front-to-rear under power would wave the inside front wheel high in the air. Thus absolute adhesion at that end was slashed and the car gained an important degree of stable understeer to kill its incipient tail-wag. Certainly the Coopers might have been more a product of practical enthusiasm and cumulative experience than of academic genius, but with fine drivers in the cockpit they were highly effective, and very much products of their time, built and run with common-sense efficiency . . . and no frills . . .

Now also the seeds were being sewn for the production road-going 'Cooper GT' car, which the public would most identify with the company. This was the Mini-Cooper project, John and Ginger Devlin having toyed with a very early production car from around the time of the Italian GP the previous year. For some time prior to that they had experimented with hotting-up the Renault Dauphine by dropping 1100 Climax engines into its rear engine bay. The layout was right for Cooper's, the buyer would be able to identify with the rear-engined racing cars, but the Cooper-Dauphine's handling was never adequately tamed and the impact of the transverse-engined front-wheel-drive Mini in comparison, with its taut wheel-at-each-corner handling, can well be imagined. . . .

What seems to have been the only serious Cooper-Dauphine prototype has survived, owned today by Tony Mantle whose Climax Engine Services company perpetuates the otherwise defunct line of classical British racing engines. The extent of modification to 104 NPK as the car is registered surprises Tony, who isn't easily impressed. It has transverse-leaf rear suspension, with specially-made spring abutments, a 1220 cc Climax engine and four-speed 4DS9 transaxle by ZF of Germany with Cooper cast side-plates. This gearbox could handle up to 120 bhp, and the car rides on wire wheels, enclosing disc brakes. Andrew Ferguson recalls driving Charles Cooper up to Oulton Park in the car, when they were overtaken by a Ford Zephyr. 'Oo's that?', demanded Charlie Cooper. It was Colin Chapman and Graham Hill with their wives, and all grinning as they swept by. The Old Man had little time for Chapman, 'Flash 'Arry' he called him, and worse . . . . When Andrew told him who it was, he roared 'Don't let 'im beat us boy, git after 'im!' and reached over with a big horny hand, grabbed the steering wheel and steered the Dauphine out round the lorry which had been baulking them, into the oncoming traffic stream to chase the Zephyr. . . .

The works Formula 1 team also had a new home, moving about a quarter-mile uphill towards Kingston from Hollyfield Road, into new premises which John Cooper had just bought from Roy Salvadori, in Langley Road. Roy had run a motor business there under the name Langley Motors. It was quiet, next door to a church in an otherwise largely residential street, and the team would settle in there quite comfortably with the Beddings joining them to do their panel-bashing.

After winning the 1959 World titles at Sebring, the works team had split. Bruce McLaren flew home to New Zealand, Tim Wall to Australia, while Jack Brabham and the English members returned to London for various functions before the new World Champion went home to Australia for Christmas, and a hero's welcome. It was obvious that effort should be concentrated on only two cars for 1960. At Sebring John had broken the news to Masten Gregory. He would not be retained: 'He was very upset. . . .'

The annual NZ GP was due on 9 January, 1960. The works

1960 – THE GREATEST TRIUMPH

*Major teams bought their Coopers from Hollyfield Road normally in chassis form, then completed them in the way they wanted with the modifications they thought might show advantage. This Ken Gregory print shows the Yeoman Credit team's new cars under preparation in their Hounslow workshops, emphasizing the simple if apparently random design of the Mark IV chassis frame, and the superb workmanship of the rolled, welded and riveted all-aluminium body panels. The car closest the camera here is rather special, with coil-spring rear suspension. It shows off its typically BRP/Yeoman Credit induction scoop, trunked along the body side to the engine bay, and the exaggerated tailfin which they adopted. Their three 1960 season cars appear in the surviving Chassis Register as FII/24/59, 25/59 and 26/59 dated that October. These are probably those three cars being completed. Ill-fated Chris Bristow drove the Yeoman cars with terrific verve and Moss tipped him for greatness (**left**), tail out as usual and very quick, Easter Monday Goodwood, 1960*

had long since shipped its other two F1 cars to Auckland, while the Sebring machines returned home. They were serviced in six days and rushed on to the *Scottish Star* bound for Buenos Aires and the Argentine GP, opening the new Championship season, on 7 February. If Jack's memory of the two Sebring cars is correct the New Zealand pair would have been 4/59 and 23A/58, probably in that order, for himself and for Bruce.

In fact the new season opened on New Year's Day at East London, South Africa, with the nation's first postwar GP. The promoters restricted overseas entries to 1500 cc, leaving their local cars unlimited, which was reasonable. BRP-Yeoman Credit ran two of their Cooper-Borgwards for Moss and Bristow, while the Belgian Equipe National Belge fielded two Cooper-Climax F2s for Paul Frère and Lucien Bianchi. Dick Gibson and Bruce Halford ran private cars. It was a long, very hot race which Moss allowed Bristow to lead before a moment sent Stirling ahead again until he had an injection pipe break. Bristow's gearbox had broken and Frère took the lead six laps from the end and won. Bianchi menaced Moss's second place until a plug lead came off, and Stirling finished second from Syd van der Vyver's Cooper-Alfa Romeo special and Bianchi. Van der Vyver was a good practical engineer, and he was briefly to join Equipe Walker in 1961 at Pippbrook Garage, but found life with Alf Francis quite difficult. . . .

Serious work at Hollyfield Road as the prototype 'Lowline' all coil-spring car for 1960 is completed there before the works team's move up the hill to their new Langley Road 'shop. These Mike Barney shots show progress: **left to right – top**, *the new straight-tube frame showing off its new double wishbone rear suspension as it is squared-up on the shop floor: test engine and*

1960 — THE GREATEST TRIUMPH

seat installation – note Charles' electric lighting being used; new body panels from the Beddings in background; seat-back bulkhead profile in place, Bradnack lugs in evidence: **bottom** – Owen Maddock's prototype Jack Knight-manufactured 'C5S' transaxle case is offered up, exhaust runs clear: back down on our knees again with the prototype on trolley jack and wheel-and-tyre, Morrison shelter chassis jigs still there in right background: John and Fred Bedding offer-up the prototype body panels. Fred died in 1982, aged 87, while still working at Motor Racing Developments' F1 Brabham factory in Chessington . . .

Tuesday, 10 May, 1960, second test session for the new 'Lowline' Cooper-Climax, Silverstone, Geoff Goddard photographed the new straight-tube engine bay **left** *with Cooper-Knight 'C5S' transaxle, coil-spring rear suspension, gearbox oil temperature test gauge, and carburettor air-box sealing panel around twin-Webers. Chassis finish was pale grey enamel. Note rear anti-roll bar linkage above top wishbone, betraying the bar's presence within top-rear frame cross-member. Gathered around the car in the circuit lay-by* **right** *out near Abbey Curve (background) where testing was habitually based in those days are left to right: lofty journalist David Phipps; Bill Aston of Mintex who acted as team timekeeper at most races; a Dunlop fitter; Vic Barlow, Dunlop racing tyre engineer; Ginger Devlin; John Cooper (leaning on tyre) and bearded Owen Maddock. Beyond Owen are Jo Bonnier and Graham Hill – BRM must have been testing as well, or were they just having a good look as Jack lowered the lap record . . .*

One week later at Ardmore, Moss arrived ahead of his Yeoman Credit Cooper's engine, still on its way from Sebring. It was found in an airline shed at San Francisco and rushed out. Jack took pole on methanol in his works car, from Stirling on petrol.

The Englishman won one prelim from McLaren, Jack led the second until his fuel pump broke and Ian Burgess won in his 2.2. In the feature race a fierce duel between Moss and Brabham ended when Stirling's transmission collapsed; his goggles had already been smashed and his face cut by flying stones. Jack led Bruce to the line by just 0.6 sec. Bib Stilwell and Stan Jones placed 3–4 in Mark IV 2.2s; Burgess's clutch failed and Hulme and Lawton both ran well in their 1.96s. Australian Len Lukey retired his ex-Brabham Mark III after running fifth. This interesting car was *F2/10/58*; originally the Tom Bridger BRP car wrecked at Casablanca in 1958. Jack took it home with him that winter, had won the South Pacific Road Race Championship with it at Orange on 27 January and then sold it to Lukey, who won the CAMS Gold Star in it. The car is still in Australia today; one of the few Antipodean Coopers to have a recorded serial matching that in the original works Register. . . .

Jack won again in the Wigram Trophy, with Burgess third and Bruce fourth in a local special after his Cooper's engine had tossed a rod and sawn itself in half in practice. The works drivers then flew off to Argentina, leaving a low-key New Zealand series to end with Burgess losing the lead at Dunedin, when his single-wishbone 2.2 split its gearbox casing, and Syd Jensen's F2 winning. The Englishman then won at Teretonga. Entries from Burgess and fellow-traveller David

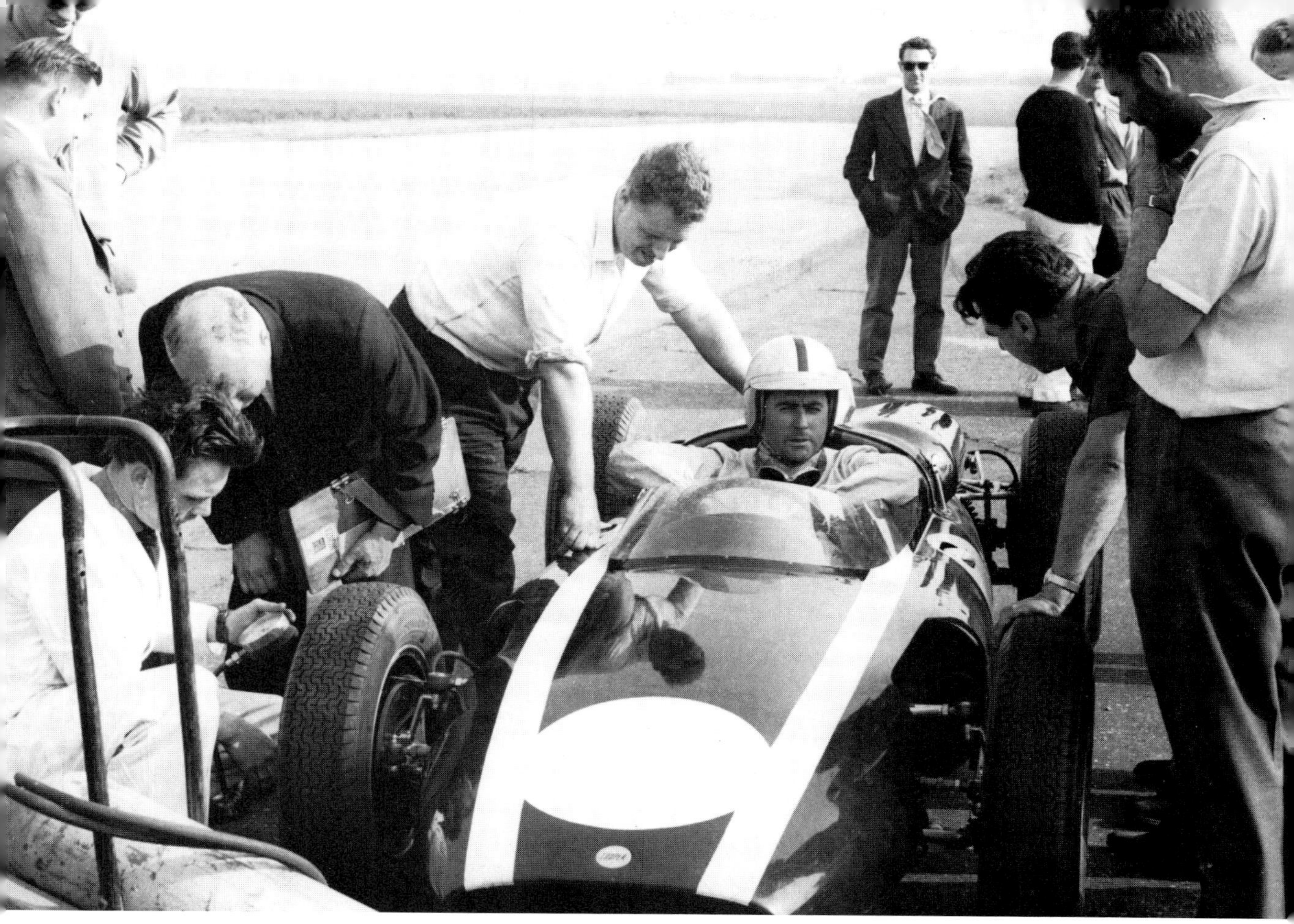

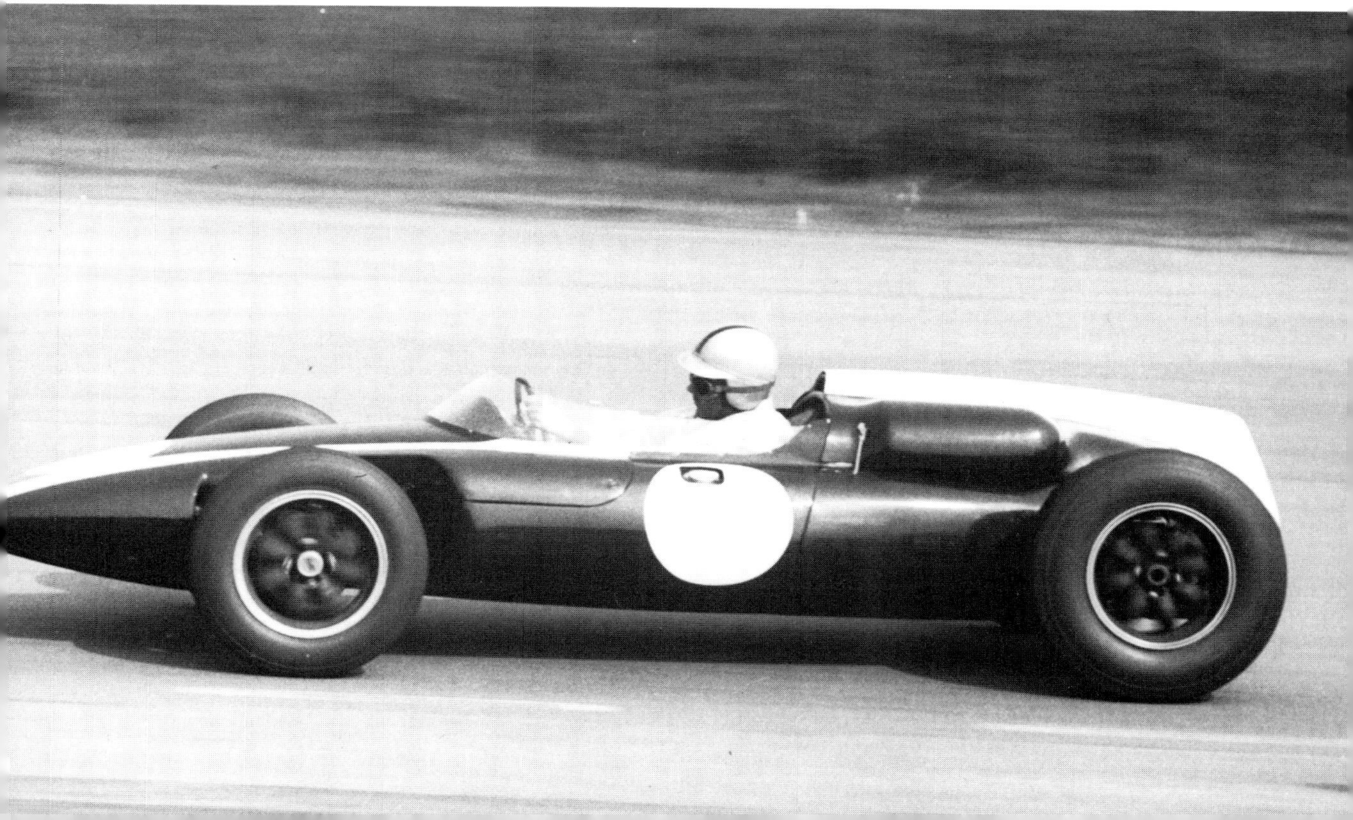

Piper's 2½ Lotus 16 were then refused at Waimate, where Jensen placed third.

For their performances in 1.96 Coopers, Denis Hulme and George Lawton were elected jointly as NZIGPA 'Drivers to Europe' for 1960. In the long term it brought one the World Championship; sadly it brought the other disaster. . . .

At Hollyfield Road, customer Formula 1, Formula 2, the new Formula Junior and Monaco sports cars were all in production, while preparation for Argentina had seen Andrew Ferguson fall out with the Old Man: 'R. & J. Parks had made us three excellent crates for our cars and Tommy Atkins's Cooper-Maserati for the Sebring trip. When they returned, I'd hired a mobile crane to swing them off the truck on to our forecourt, and Tommy was sharing the cost. Charlie was with me watching the unloading when the crane swung round and the counterweight on the back went smash, smash, smash, and knocked all the glass tops off his petrol pumps.

He just couldn't believe his eyes. "You bloody useless twerp! Look what your crane's done to my pumps!" He went on and on without repeating himself, and then spluttered out the worst thing he could think of. "You're a bloody useless *poof*! Get out; you're sacked!"'

Andrew had had enough and stayed home for days. Then a message came via Charles's secretary. Would Andrew see him? 'I had to sit in one office while he sat in his and the secretary ran messages between us. Eventually she came out with a kind of apology; Charlie explained his dog had died that morning, and he'd just taken it out on me. I went back to work and when he saw me he said, "I shouldn't have bawled at you, boy – but you're still a *poof*!"'

'He was a lovely old bugger really. . . .'

At his Box Hill home, *Shoushan*, Charles kept poultry, his horse Buster and his special pride and joy – pigs. One year at the London Motor Show he bumped into Stirling Moss and his girlfriend Sally Weston. He paid her the greatest compliment he could. 'Ere Sally,' he called excitedly, 'I've named my best sow after you.' She didn't appreciate this great honour. . . .

George Saunders was running a country club in Box Hill village: 'I'd often see Charles out in the mornings on his horse. I don't think he ever really got the hang of riding it. He used to say, "'Ere George, what d'you think's the matter with Buster this morning, I couldn't get 'im started and now 'e won't go." It sounded as though Buster was a car. Charles had a gardener who used to get upset sometimes when he rollicked him, and then he'd get his own back by feeding Buster oats. Makes 'em frisky you know, then Charles couldn't ride him at all. . . .' The Old Man also kept horses at his Restronguet cottage, near Falmouth in Cornwall. He had bought one from Stirling Moss's sister, Pat.

The ship returning the Sebring cars had arrived in the middle of a London Docks strike. Its American master berthed regardless, without assistance, but he'd chosen a meat quay and the unions refused to unload her. Andrew and John beseeched various officials to allow stevedores to unearth the crated cars amongst 4000 tons of boxed lard, crane them into lighters and then on to the dockside. There were only six days left to strip and and prepare them before reshipping to Buenos Aires and then the *Scottish Star* developed engine trouble. It was only after three days' continuous work by Blue Star Line engineers – loudly encouraged by Cooper Cars – that she could bear her precious cargo away to the South Atlantic.

More engine trouble followed, plus an Argentine dock strike, a five-week postal strike which fouled communication between Cooper and the club, and poor Bruce spent two days flying from Auckland to New York only to find his Argentine connection cancelled. He just missed a PanAm Boeing and found himself on a decrepit DC3, which creaked down to Buenos Aires in a further 36 hours! He was limp as a dishrag and slept 20 hours before emerging for practice; but there were no works cars . . . one of the *Scottish Star*'s giant pistons had collapsed.

The Cooper crew, Charles, John, Noddy, Big Mike and the drivers, cooled their heels at the Autodrome watching Innes Ireland's brand-new rear-engined Lotus 18 going shatteringly fast. The Walker Coopers were there for Moss and Trintignant, Schell had his F2 special and Centro-Sud fielded their Maserati hybrids for local drivers Carlos Menditeguy and Roberto Bonomi. Moss and Walker let Jack do some laps in Stirling's car, but there was no news of the works machines.

John tried to get some news on a wind-up telephone in the pits. But the club had no English, he had no Spanish. In angry frustration he finally tore the whole telephone set clean off the wall and hurled it to the floor, showering bells, springs and Bakelite splinters everywhere. Still no cars. . . .

Late Saturday afternoon they stood on the dockside peering hopefully into the River Plate haze. At last the ship appeared, and nosed alongside at 5.15 pm. John had commandeered a lorry and by 7 pm the still-crated cars were offloaded at the circuit, 20 miles away. The crates were broken open, the cars numbered, fuelled and oiled, discs scoured free from grease and with the dusk Jack and Bruce tore away for a few brief reconnaissance laps.

There was a final race morning session; tyres scrubbed, brakes bedded and Thermos flasks of iced orange juice fitted in the cockpits. Just before the start thermometers stood at 110°F on circuit.

Ireland's sensational Lotus led the GP before spinning, letting the BRMs then Moss through to lead. Stirling pulled away until his car broke a wishbone after 41 laps. Hot and tired, he rested briefly before Rob Walker called in Trintignant for the maestro to take over his car. Bonnier's BRM led, while Jack lost fifth place when his step-up gears broke through faulty heat treatment. With 20 laps to go Bonnier led from Ireland and McLaren. Abruptly the BRM broke,

1960 — THE GREATEST TRIUMPH

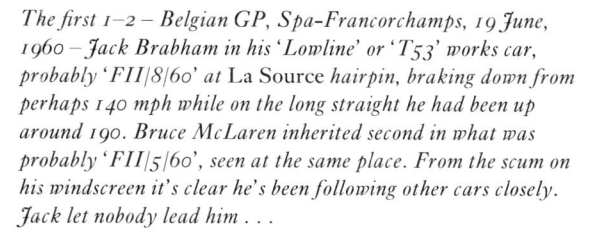

The first 1–2 – Belgian GP, Spa-Francorchamps, 19 June, 1960 – Jack Brabham in his 'Lowline' or 'T53' works car, probably 'FII/8/60' at La Source hairpin, braking down from perhaps 140 mph while on the long straight he had been up around 190. Bruce McLaren inherited second in what was probably 'FII/5/60', seen at the same place. From the scum on his windscreen it's clear he's been following other cars closely. Jack let nobody lead him . . .

Ireland led until his steering tightened and Bruce suddenly awoke to the signal 'first' waved frantically at him. He pulled away from Cliff Allison's pursuing Ferrari and disbelievingly found himself winning his second consecutive *Grande Epreuve*, by some 26 sec.

'As I rolled into the pits I thought I had found a riot. There were spectators fighting, police struggling with them, officials pushing, cameras shoved in my face, people screaming. I was dragged into the grandstand . . . my feet weren't touching the ground. . . .'

Once the pandemonium had settled down and the team could analyse the race, they realized they were in trouble, despite sweet victory. The BRMs had out-cornered them, Lotus had the edge on acceleration and showed prodigious potential and Ferrari were not too far behind, with so much power.

Meanwhile they were contracted for a second race, the Buenos Aires City GP, which to John's horror they found was to be run in Cordoba, 500 miles up-country. Mike Barney: 'When we saw the circuit we just couldn't believe it, round the city boulevards with trees at the kerbside and a huge statue slap in the middle of the road at one point. We asked the guide which side the cars were meant to go round it, and he just grinned and said, "Either side, ees up to da driver." John said, "Right boys, one race lap, collect the start money and home." He didn't like it at all. . . .'

Still Jack started from pole beside Trintignant, who was really at home on such a good old-fashioned road circuit, and in the race the works Coopers ran 1–2 until Bruce pressed too hard and clouted a hay bale, splitting the oil cooler. He stopped after 29 laps with temperatures sky-high, and on lap 40 Jack was out with vapour locks in the 100-degree ambient heat. Gurney's BRM led until its gearbox faltered and Trintignant won comfortably for Rob Walker, despite an ailing clutch. In the pits – wooden benches set up between the kerbside trees – all eyes had been riveted on a local Maserati 250F, which careered past lap after lap with its dampers obviously totally shot. 'It kept going by bouncing like a rubber ball at well over 100 mph,' Mike Barney remembers, 'with the crowd packed five deep on either kerb with their toes in the gutter. We were all wound up tight waiting for the accident to happen . . . but it never did. . . .'

On the flight home John tells how: 'Jack said, "We've really got to do something or we'll be left for dead this year," and we began planning a new Formula 1 car right there on the plane. . . .'

They landed at Heathrow on 17 March and what would become known as the 1960 'Lowline' Cooper or 'T53' was designed and built ready for the International Trophy Silverstone meeting on 14 May.

Owen Maddock's new five-speed purpose-built transaxle was just entering small-quantity production at Jack Knight's Battersea works. Owen himself was almost recovered from his 'road accident' in the glider. Now the full team combined to discuss the new car. Owen was on his own still in the drawing office, so Bruce's college drawing experience was enlisted to lay out suspension and accessory blueprints. Jack spent hours studying sketches and thinking, while John vigorously

197

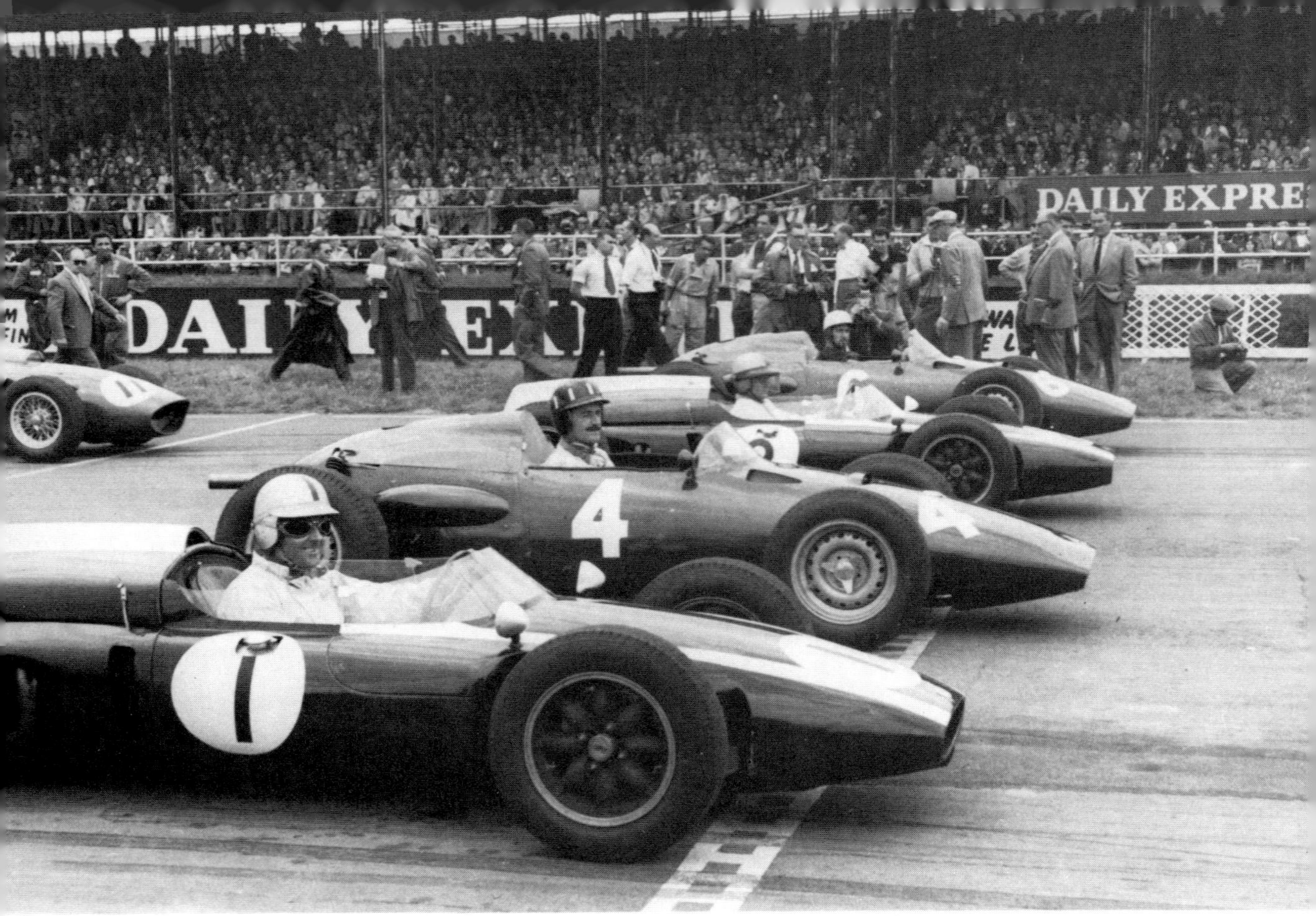
DAILY EXPRE

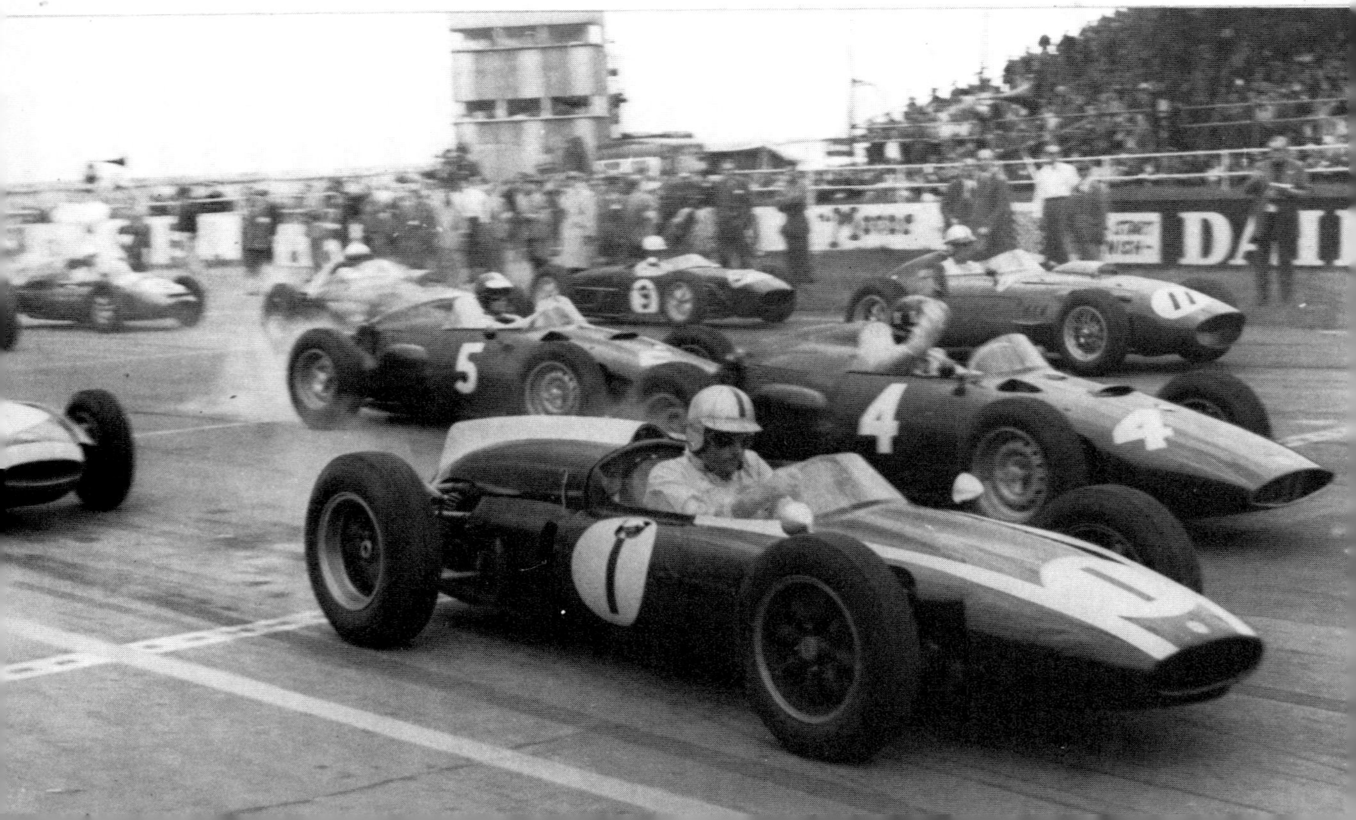
DAI

chased progress. Charles stolidly kept the production business going and when he heard they planned to fit a coil-spring rear end he positively insisted they maintain the leaf-spring option, in case coils didn't work out. He was also adamant that only one car would be built and a second would follow only when the first was proven.

It was obvious that if the prototype would only just make Silverstone it would be suicide not to lay down a second car until so late in the season. In fact work on it began secretly.

Everyone but Charles had great faith in the new design. Every part of the old leaf-spring Mark IV was re-examined, with the accent on simplification, lightness, strength and efficiency. The old car's deficiencies had been seen on the faster venues like Reims, Spa and Avus, where ultimate road-holding, good torque and traction were not enough. Now the 'Lowline' was to offer reduced frontal area with a lowered engine and slimmer body and a longer nose to improve 'penetration', while the pedals, steering gear and radiator moved further forward to allow the driver to lay back lower.

All Cooper chassis have been described simply as 'a series of brackets held together with tubes' and this was certainly true of the 1960 'Lowline' model. The frame was still a basic four-tube affair, with $1\frac{1}{2}$ in. diameter 18-gauge top rails and similar diameter but 16-gauge wall-thickness bottom rails. Diagonals braced the frame bays ahead of the cockpit opening, but the centre bay itself was unbraced save for small tube ties welded across the joint apices. Even here there were the usual Cooper anomalies, for only three of the top frame corners were braced in this way, the fourth being left open to allow a water pipe to pass through. The long rear bays were untriangulated top and bottom, other than by the engine and gearbox assembly once it was inserted, but there were two diagonals in each side with a common apex half-way along the bottom rail. These diagonal tubes also carried engine and suspension mounts, so they were sited more by geographical than structural considerations. The engine mounts themselves were welded on to curved tubes to reduce the length of the mounts, and both ends of these curved tubes were then welded to main frame members – as usual half-way along

Mike Barney shot this brief sequence of the British GP start at Silverstone, 16 July, 1960. Jack on pole position is grinning wolfishly at starter Dean Delamont of the RAC while Graham Hill's goggles are down and his BRM P48 has just arrived on the front row, flanking Bruce McLaren and team-mate Jo Bonnier outside him. Trips' Ferrari (11) is on row two. But when the flag falls the grin has gone, Brabham's clutch is home, rear wheels spinning as the works 'Lowline' bites. Hill has stalled his BRM, his arm flinging high in warning as team-mate Dan Gurney dodges round (5). Ireland's Lotus 18 is no. 7, Trips (11), Surtees (9)

their free length. This was heresy to a structural engineer like Chapman, but the main tubes were strong enough to accommodate such loading. What's more, the engine mount-carrying tube on the right was slightly longer than that on the left, simply because the diagonal on that side had to meet the top rail some distance behind the engine bulkhead to allow the magneto to protrude. . . .

To reduce frontal area, the engine was dropped 1 inch by increasing the centre-offset between the step-up gears and allowing the half-shafts to rake upwards to the wheels when static. The steering was lengthened and moved ahead of the front axle line, from behind it. This allowed the foot pedals to move forward and gave a more nearly horizontal steering column. The driver was laid back more in his longer cockpit, with his shoulders tucked beneath rolled-in cockpit sides. The oil tank capacity was unchanged, but the triangular-planform tank was now wider and shallower, still sited behind the radiator to deflect hot air out through the suspension arches in the bodywork. The radiator moved forward on separate mountings to reduce nose height.

The FPF engine and new Cooper-Knight 'C5S' transaxle were mounted at five points to stiffen the frame. Torsional stiffness was around 25 per cent better than on the 1959 cars. Suspension wishbones had been improved, with slightly wider bases on the frame, and the rears were further reinforced, with cross-braces.

Dunlop had meanwhile produced lower-silhouette tyres requiring wider rims. Front wheel sizes were up from 3.5 in. wide to 4.5 in. and the rears from 4.5 in. to 6. The extra rim width was added outboard so marginally increasing tracks front and rear.

By far the greatest investment in time and money was made in the new transaxle, which really became Owen Maddock's *magnum opus*. If anything Owen usually tended towards over-design. His drawings were incredibly finely detailed and those for the gearbox betray the manhours invested in them. His mechanisms could be quite complex and tricky to make and assemble, but in this case they worked brilliantly well and totally justified the trouble and care taken.

The new unit was larger than its predecessor, but liberal use of magnesium in the strengthened casings reduced weight increase to just 5 lb. Owen retained the step-up gear ratio-change feature, with a range of 22 to 29 teeth available. This gave 11 combinations of gear ratio. The five all-indirect gearbox ratios were fixed at 1.0:1, 1.17:1, 1.38:1, 1.78:1 and 2.38:1, and the spiral-bevel cwp ratio was 3.44:1. By swopping step-up gears this final-drive could be varied between 4.36 – as used at Monaco – and 2.94, which was never called for, even Reims demanding only 3.04:1.

The lower of the two step-up gears was co-axial with the clutch and had one inboard bearing, with the other end spigoted into a needle roller bearing in the crankshaft. The upper gear was supported by bearings on either side and incorporated a flexible quill-shaft to cushion the drive. Bending loads from this gear were absorbed by a large-diameter conical aluminium sleeve surrounding the quill-shaft, and this assembly passed above the ZF differential into the overhung gearbox. This was arranged as a four-speed with a further two-speed section added behind. In the forward section were gear clusters for 2nd to 5th, front to rear. Shaft centres had been increased compared to the earlier gearbox, from 75 mm to 89 mm, and the tooth size was also enlarged. Each gear-wheel was 16 mm thick. In the rear of the 'box resided first and reverse gears. This was a three-bearing 'box, replacing the old two-bearing layout.

One disadvantage of a two-shaft 'box is that reduction is made in one step, which inevitably leaves a very small number of teeth on the first-gear pinion. In Owen's 'box this meant cutting the first-gear teeth integral with the shaft, smaller than the other four ratios, but 20 mm wide to compensate, this being the same width as the step-up gears.

All gears were in constant mesh, with selection made by internal teeth on each gear-wheel engaging with external teeth on the selector dogs. To smooth engagement, every other internal tooth on the gear-wheels was cut back slightly. To prevent jumping out – the great bugbear of the Citroën-derived units – these teeth were cut at a 5-degree angle, matching that on the selector dogs, to create a wind-in effect. This was the precise opposite of what had happened in the '58–'59 gearboxes once the dogs had been twisted under power.

First gear was to be used only for starting, so the orthodox gate positions were 2-3-4-5, with a spring-loaded interlock mechanism preventing accidental engagement of first or reverse out to one side.

The lubrication nightmares of 1959 led to the 'C5S' being remote-sumped in the gearbox section with a splash-feed for the final-drive gears. A Holbourn-Eaton oil pump was driven off the end of the first motion shaft, drawing from the large finned sump casting to feed a gallery in the gearbox top from which drillings aimed oil jets on to the gear clusters and step-ups. An external pipe was subsequently rigged to provide a jet feeding into the nip of the crownwheel and pinion.

A fully dry-sumped gearbox would require scavenge as well as pressure pumps. This remote sump-unit placed its gears above oil level so only a pressure pump was needed.

This transmission was basically trouble-free during Cooper's amazing 1960 season, and everyone concerned with its design and manufacture are rightly proud of it. Jack Knight recalls the 'vast amount of machining involved. It cost a fortune for those days,' and Owen remembers its price to Cooper being around £1000 per gearbox, which was almost prohibitively expensive. John managed to hush it up, telling his father they cost around £400 each – and the Old Man was far from delighted with that. . . .

The new Lowline *Works Car 1* appears in the Register as chassis *FII/5/60* amongst 17 other serials listed for '1960 Formula II Racing Car Mark VI' machines. There is no Mark V in the Register; presumably applying in the Cooper mind to the contemporary FJ production model, which in its own sphere started a new series as the 'FJ Mark I'. Of course the Lowline was utterly different from the production F2 Mark VIs, but both the prototype and its two subsequent sisters, *8/60* and *12/60*, were included for paperwork purposes. Purchase tax of £980 5s. 10d. was paid on the prototype on 27 April, 1960, when it was completed officially with *FPF/430/3/1171* installed.

Meanwhile both works drivers assisted BRM in initial trials of their P48 rear-engined car at Goodwood, with Cooper's blessing. BRM had made offers for both to drive for them in 1960, to Charles and John's horror as the younger explains: 'I had to appeal to Sir Alfred Owen's Christian nature and explain that if his team stole our drivers we'd be wiped out, and we were only a tiny outfit making an honest crust compared to his gigantic empire. It worked a treat. He called off his people at Bourne and away we went. . . .'

In the middle of Lowline design, Jack returned to Longford, Tasmania, with his ex-NZ GP works car – presumably *4/59* – and he won all three races, two from Stilwell's 2.2 and Mildren's 2½ Cooper-Maserati and one from Mildren second and Stilwell third. Mildren's hybrid was an Australian concoction making its debut at Longford, with a new 250S engine, No. 2440, giving 258 bhp at 6700 rpm, mated to the latest '59-style pressure-fed Cooper-Knight transaxle. A 2.9 Tipo 61 Maserati engine, No. 2475, would be installed in 1961, plus Colotti Type 21 gearbox. Mildren eventually cannibalized the car to build his Mildren-Maserati sports-racer. The original frame – *22/59* – was reputedly tossed on to a rubbish tip . . . shades of Walker Racing. . . .

While down-under, Jack drove his works car in a two-day meeting at Phillip Island, Victoria and won four races with merciless ease. As he flew out for the Havana GP in Cuba (fourth with his Monaco) and the European F2 opener at Syracuse, his old works car stayed behind awaiting his return.

While the Lowline was being finalized, Easter Goodwood's Glover Trophy F1 race saw Chris Bristow's Yeoman Credit 2½ Mark IV sensationally take pole from Moss's Walker car and his own senior team mate, Harry Schell. Roy Salvadori's Atkins Mark IV Climax – one of the ex-works '59 cars, possibly *23A/58* – qualified ahead of Bruce's works car, which appears in some rare surviving works team records as *F2/5/57*; according to the Register one of the original School cars! It may have been the works' old F2 used occasionally during '59 and now uprated to 2½-litre trim as a 1960 team back-up. Syd Greene's Gilby Engineering concern entered the proprietor's son Keith in the ex-Atkins '59 Cooper-Maserati which they had just bought. A second works '59 car was sold to Fred Tuck of Weston-super-Mare.

1960 – THE GREATEST TRIUMPH

Bristow made a meteoric race start, but it became a duel between Moss and Innes Ireland, whose Lotus eventually won; Bristow and McLaren placed 3–4 while Greene, Schell and Salvadori all retired. Stirling's new F2 Walker Porsche was also beaten by Ireland in one of the new Lotuses and the maestro thought long and hard. He and Rob knew there was an updated F1 Cooper on the way, but they could not have one. The works relied heavily on Esso sponsorship, Walker and Moss were with BP, and Esso had made noises about arming the opposition. . . . Clearly the old-style Cooper chassis had been rendered obsolete by the new Lotus, and Stirling wanted one.

Jack Brabham was not at Goodwood. He was at Pau that day, winning the F2 GP, as related elsewhere in these pages. The year's Aintree '200' also was run to Formula 2, and then came Silverstone on 14 May.

The prototype Lowline was actually completed as a runner at Hollyfield around 9 am, Friday, 6 May after an all-nighter by Noddy, Big Mike and their helpers. It was taken immediately to Silverstone, arriving around 1.40 pm. The weather was warm and dry. Jack drove some shakedown laps, then went faster, and faster. Within ten laps he was 2 sec inside the official lap record and then both he and Bruce went faster still. The Lowline flew. . . .

The test report has survived. It reads in part *'Prototype gearbox; Selector mechanism needed slight adjustment – otherwise perfectly okay. Lap times; Down to 1 :34.6. Notes: Both JB and BM had cut at least 6 sec off old times . . . Total laps: 55 (thereabouts) . . . .'*

The team were euphoric. Bruce later claimed: 'The grin on John's face was only excelled by that on Charles's, who promptly claimed the coil-spring rear suspension as his own idea!'

In fact, on the test report 'CNC' wrote soberly: '$\frac{3}{4}$ *of circuit resurfaced & new D9 speed tyres (2 sec each?).*' He was nobody's fool and he was crediting four seconds of the improvement to circuit and tyre changes; junking his beloved rear leaf-spring and the other changes only made two seconds difference – but he was delighted with that; his boys had done it again.

On Tuesday, 10 May, another test session saw the Press invited. Again warm and sunny, Jack drove 20 laps, best 1 :34.4. The new gearbox was freeing-off and much easier, but he thought the selector plungers seemed inclined to stick in the magnesium due to being too short. Jack Knight was asked to make longer plungers with tube relieved in the middle.

Official practice for the Trophy race followed. Bruce tells us he took the new car, readied too late for the first session; Jack had the prototype. The surviving team records state otherwise, unless the prototype was indeed numbered *8/60* and the second car *5/60*. This is quite possible; since the rush had been so great I suspect they were numbered retrospec-

Leaning 'Lowline' – Brabham hammering on in the 1960 British GP could not hold off Hill's BRM recovering after its stalled start. When Graham took the lead Jack fought back and was closing as 'Noddy' Grohmann signalled 'Position 2nd, 2 sec behind, 7 laps to go' with the Hill BRM whipping under the Motor *bridge towards Copse Corner. There he misjudged his failing brakes, and spun off, Jack inherited the lead and won. On the pit counter here, right to left are Martin Fothergill, John Cooper, Noddy, Mike Barney and Ginger Devlin. The 'Position 5th, 30 sec behind' board is ready for McLaren . . .*

201

tively when carnets became necessary for travel abroad. In any case *8/60* is listed there as Jack's regular car; *5/60* as Bruce's.

That first practice day saw an embarrassed Moss shoot out of the paddock on to the wet track, drop the Walker Cooper and spin into a new Aston Martin standing innocently in the pit lane! Next day, Friday the 13th, the track was again rain-soaked. Bruce's car arrived, but John was terribly tweaked by the inauspicious date and kept running to the barest minimum. Moss took pole, but out at Abbey Curve popular Harry Schell's luck ran out. His Yeoman Credit Cooper crashed into the breeze-block retaining wall and he was thrown out. His neck was broken and he died almost instantly. The car was hardly damaged.

Race-day was drier; Moss led briefly, but Ireland's Lotus overwhelmed all opposition once a front wishbone broke again on Stirling's car and the wheel started to lean inwards. Jack finished second in his new Lowline, but complained it wasn't handling as well as he felt it should. Bruce was 14th after a stop to free his sticking throttle, and his successor as NZ 'Driver to Europe', Denny Hulme, was 12th in his F2 Cooper.

The whole team was alarmed to find the flimsy biscuit-box Lotus still faster than their latest cars, and Walker had bought one for Moss to debut at Monaco two weeks hence... Charles never had much time for Colin Chapman and his products and now was hurt by what he saw as Rob's desertion to the opposition. Equipe Walker would still have a Cooper at Monaco; Stirling would choose between them.

The works ran their two new Lowlines with old *5/57* as spare, and both drivers had tested at Brands Hatch to test tight-corner handling and set up the carburetion. Front ground clearance was thought to be about an inch too high, as the springs were rated for 35 gallons of fuel. Roll seemed excessive, with the rear roll-centre too low at '*5/16 in. below ground*'. They dialled-in oversteer and set the Weber carburettors for low-down torque. But in practice at Monaco Bruce's car misfired and handled badly. Next day he spun and smashed a wheel at the *Gazométre*. Then the timekeepers missed his quicker laps. He was in danger of not qualifying. With new springs, new brake pads and reset carburetion he took off in the penultimate session only for complaints about oil gushing from his car. In the pits no leak could be found. John was just telling Raymond Mays of BRM and Colin Chapman that 'It must have been water' when a Ferrari spun on a great puddle of oil at the hairpin and practice was stopped. In fact the Cooper's gearbox bung had fallen out. It was below undertray level, so the oil dropped clear without leaving tell-tale streaks. Now the problem was to find a suitable plug. Despite Graham Hill's helpful suggestions Wally Hassan found a rev-counter drive which fitted. Now Bruce had to qualify on his own oil. He did it on the team's timing, but again the officials missed it. By this time his tanks had been topped-up for full-load testing, and it was only after the club rechecked their tapes, that night, that they gave him 11th place on the 16-strong grid.

Meanwhile, Moss concentrated totally on his new Walker Lotus to take pole by a clear second from Jack's trouble-free Lowline and Brooks's Yeoman Credit Cooper, whose 0.4 second slower time was matched by his team mate, Chris Bristow. Ken Gregory rated Bristow amongst the best: 'He actually set his Monaco time before Tony, so he should have been on the front row, but we knew Tony's experience would make best use of the advantage in the race so we persuaded the timekeepers it was the other way round....'

Salvadori qualified in the Atkins Cooper-Climax – Aston Martin staying away – and Trintignant just got on to the tail of the grid in one of the three Centro-Sud Cooper-Maseratis entered for himself, Masten Gregory and Carlos Menditeguy, but at the last moment the Argentinian could not make the trip and Ian Burgess took his place; only the French-driven Centro-Sud car made the grid. Signor Dei's entries were being handled by Andrew Ferguson in his spare time. He had bought a low-loader racing car transporter for the team, and when they didn't need it, it became his private, personal transport. He was also making travel arrangements for Masten Gregory and other drivers, using a different name while he worked for each of them. At times he became terribly confused and had hoteliers regretting they had no vacancies since a Mr X had just booked their last room; Andrew himself under another alias. He'd then assure them that he had Mr X's blessing to cancel the original booking and make a new one! It was all extra money for him to supplement Cooper's pittance. Charles wouldn't contemplate a raise, Andrew told John he was leaving, and typically it was John who said 'I'll pay you extra, boy: but it'll be in cash out of the start money – and don't let my father know....' So some of the staff would get part of their wages in francs one week, deutschmarks the next, and perhaps lire the week after....

Another Monaco non-qualifier was Bruce Halford in Fred Tuck's ex-works car, and an interesting newcomer named the 'Cooper-Castellotti' also failed. This car used a Ferrari *Squalo*-type four-cylinder engine, with the late Italian ace's name 'Eugenio' cast into the cam covers, and Colotti transaxle. It was entered by the 'Scuderia Eugenio Castellotti' and was driven by both Giorgio Scarlatti and Gino Munaron. Its engine was too bulky to allow conventional side-draught Webers to be squeezed between it and the frame rails, so a pair of twin-choke downdraughts were substituted on a quaint 90-degree cast aluminium inlet manifold. All rather strange, and slow....

In the race Moss took the lead from Bonnier's BRM, but as rain greased the road surface Jack caught and passed the Walker Lotus for first place. On lap 38 the sun came out and three laps later Jack was skating round 3 sec clear when his Lowline snapped into a slide and hit the wall at Ste Devote.

1960 — THE GREATEST TRIUMPH

Those tramlines were almost Brabham's undoing in the Portuguese GP, Oporto, 14 August, 1960. Here he is, winning his fifth successive World Championship GP in the faithful '8/60', if team records are to be believed. What number was on the chassis plate that day could be another matter

Meanwhile Bruce's troubles persisted. Heat had affected his car's rubber brake seals. Overnight the calipers were changed and bled to prevent the brakes sticking on. Ten minutes before the start Mike Barney found the rear circuit master cylinder piston was stuck, and one of the new gearbox plungers had jammed out. The car was on the grid with its nose and tail off, gearbox apart and the brakes jammed on! Mike and Noddy worked feverishly and as the flag fell Bruce found the car perversely 'going like a rocket'.

He lay third after Jack's incident before himself spinning off beside the World Champion's car. Jack himself had realized there would be few finishers and had just returned to see if he could restart. Now he directed Bruce back into the race, then disentangled his own car's dislodged rear anti-roll bar from beneath the frame and rejoined.

Bruce's left goggle lens had steamed up and he spun at *Gazométre*; then petrified Phil Hill by passing the Ferrari almost broadside on the pavement leaving the tunnel....

Moss won in the Walker Lotus, but Bonnier went off and Bruce was second; thrilled with his car after all that drama. Phil Hill's Ferrari was fourth ahead of Brooks, but Jack was too far behind to be classified as a finisher, though he took the flag. The gearbox plungers in his car were the wrong size, and his gearbox had jumped out of gear repeatedly before his spin. Thumping the wall had also bent *8/60*'s frame out of line.

Both cars had been set up for street racing, with seat backs up and forward 3 in. and steering wheel moved forward. Now the Dutch GP was only a week away and the transporter was to head straight to Zandvoort, but Jack's bent car had to be rebuilt. Noddy and Mike hammered the old truck to Dunkirk, despite losing the trailer and Jack's car en route and having to back-track, finding them safely at rest in the roadside long grass! They arrived midnight Tuesday. The works trailer with Jack's car was unhitched and shipped to Dover. One of Ken Tyrrell's vans took it to Langley Road, arriving lunchtime Wednesday. Noddy accompanied the car, while Mike and Hollyfield production mechanic Martin Fothergill – who had gone to Monaco to spectate but who would stay with the team for the rest of the year – went on to Zandvoort.

At Langley Road, Noddy stripped, straightened and rebuilt Jack's car working his usual way; non-stop, immersed and irritable. At 10.30 am Friday he drove the Zodiac plus trailer and *8/60* off to Southend Airport and the air-bridge to Ostend. But it was Whitsun, flights were packed. Andrew telephoned desperately, but had to split the trip, Noddy taking the Zodiac on one plane, the trailer and Lowline going on another. Noddy boarded for Ostend and his plane landed at Calais!

Fortunately, rather than drive up to Ostend he chose to return to Southend, and there discovered the trailer and car forlorn and forgotten still in the car park. Noddy exploded and contrite airline officials hastily bundled him, his Zodiac, trailer and racing car all on to a direct flight. He drove into

203

Zandvoort circuit 9.30 am Saturday morning, just in time for practice. The Cooper chief mechanic still hadn't slept – nor would he.

At Zandvoort, Bruce McLaren, still the youngest driver in Formula 1, was leading the World Championship after his win in Argentina and second at Monaco. Jack Brabham, defending Champion, still hadn't scored a point. 'It was getting awkward,' Bruce admitted, 'but it was typical of Brabham's character that this made him more determined than ever....'

Both Lowlines ran 3.58:1 back-axles, noted: *'too high – wanted to have 3.43 really – if high wind had been present engines might have been overrevved.'* They hit 7000 rpm on the long straight and the street-racing driving position proved impossible. The seats were laid back and buffeting decreased. Jack ran engine *1176* as at Monaco, while Bruce had new FPF *1181* in place of his Monaco engine *1171*, serving as spare, together with *1162* in the old spare car and *1182* in the truck.

Jack was beaten for pole by Moss and 0.2 sec, but he found he could lap within half a second of his best time even on full tanks. Bristow qualified ahead of McLaren, for this was the Kiwi's first visit to the Dutch course. A pre-race spot check on gearboxes revealed a half-tooth chipped from Bruce's cwp, probably after the oil loss in practice at Monaco. It was changed. Jack's 'box was perfect. Brooks and Henry Taylor drove the other two Yeoman Credit 2½s. Trintignant's Centro-Sud hybrid started on the back of the grid on the understanding that Dei would only get start money if the car made the top ten in the first ten laps. Predictably the shoe-string Italian gambler put his car on the line with only a gallon in its tanks, compared to 28 in Jack's Lowline....

Carel Godin de Beaufort was also running a brand-new F2 Cooper – chassis *FII/10/60* – specially built for his huge figure with a 4 in. longer than standard cockpit. Masten Gregory's Cooper-Maserati was the only Surbiton-built non-qualifier.

The race saw a terrific battle between Brabham and Moss, Cooper and Lotus, until lap 17, when the Lowline tossed up a chunk of concrete kerbstone which smashed a Lotus front wheel. 'He seemed to think I'd done it on purpose,' the Australian recalled, but he was free to win untroubled; his first *Grande Epreuve* of the season and the first victory for the Lowline Cooper.

Bruce broke a UJ cross and was out of third place after 10 laps, his rev-counter tell-tale left at 8000 as the load came off the engine. Brooks's gearbox broke, while Bristow had waited calmly on the grid as Yeoman's mechanics feverishly fixed his car's throttle-linkage, broken on the warm-up lap. His engine failed in the GP, while Taylor had been instructed to 'finish in one piece even if you are last', and he was seventh of the eight finishers – ahead of de Beaufort – even though maladjustment of the clutch lock-out on his car prevented him ever getting into top gear.... Trintignant jumped the start from the back of the grid, won his team start money by taking tenth place then refuelled before his step-up gears stripped. Moss rejoined with fresh wheel and tyre and finished fourth. Bruce led the Championship with 14 points to Moss's 11 and Jack's eight for this Dutch victory.

The Belgian GP at Spa saw the Lowlines arrive with engines lifted a quarter-inch at the rear and moved forward $\frac{7}{16}$th to ease half-shaft angularity after Bruce's Dutch UJ failure. With Charles's blessing, a third Lowline was now under construction at Langley Road....

Both works drivers found their cars superb on the high-speed Ardennes road circuit, and Jack lapped over 2½ sec faster than anyone else, 7 sec inside Hawthorn's standing 1958 lap record. That evening both cwps were changed due to heavy wear.

On the second practice day, Bruce cracked 4 minutes alone and decided to follow one of the aces to find the right way round. He chose Moss's Lotus and was just in time to see Stirling crash mightily and after a too-long wait for the ambulance go off to hospital.

Tony Brooks always loved Spa and excelled there. Now he put his Yeoman car alongside Jack's on the grid with Hill's Ferrari outside them, and the Belgian ace Olivier Gendebien's second Yeoman Cooper just behind, ahead of Bristow; Bruce mutedly back on row five. Strangely the club had rejected Centro-Sud's entries and took the Fred Tuck Cooper instead for ENB man Lucien Bianchi to drive.

Jack led from Hill's powerful Ferrari until lap 29 of the 36, when the V6 car broke. Mindful of Brabham and John Cooper stories of the 1958 Belgian GP, when only one of the first four cars to finish was still fit for another lap, Bruce played a waiting game, but lapped 7 sec faster than during practice in contact with Gendebien and Graham Hill's rear-engined BRM. Poor Brooks's gearbox broke on lap 3 and Bianchi's snapped an inboard half-shaft UJ, which he set about replacing in the pits.

Meanwhile Bristow was deep in battle with Willy Mairesse – who was handling a Ferrari on his home circuit. On lap 19 the young Londoner passed the Ferrari by the pits and led away over the hill and flat-out in top gear towards Burnenville and the scene of the Moss crash. Bristow seemed to enter the curve on the wrong line, tried to correct his error and died instantly in a horrible crash through a wire fence.

Bruce saw the blanketed body lying by the track-side and the mildly damaged Yeoman car. He was racing with Gendebien; '... it could only be Brooks or Bristow.' Six laps later, tyre marks and a huge fire in the bushes marked Alan Stacey's fatal accident in a works Lotus.

The heelrest came loose in Bruce's car and jammed under his pedals. He hooked it out and tossed it overboard, but this let Gendebien and Hill pull away. Then as Jack entered his last lap Hill's BRM blew up, Gendebien coasted-in with his gearbox shot and Bruce inherited second place for another

Above *18 April, 1949*—John Cooper in his 'works' 500 Mark III attended by tall 'Boots' Hume and George Pace on the Brands Hatch grid in the days when 500s raced round the Kentish former grass track anti-clockwise. Colour photography of motor racing even at Grand Prix level was rare in those days, but Guy Griffiths who shot this frame was exceptionally far-sighted . . .

Below *13 May, 1950*—big day for the new International Formula 3, as the Final begins at 'Royal' Silverstone's British GP meeting. King George VI and family see four Cooper Mark IVs dominate the rolling-start front row: John Cooper (42 on pole) leading away from the Parker Special '48' driven by Reg Parker, and Coopers driven by 'Red Devil' Eric Brandon (15), Bill Aston (21) and Stirling Moss (30). Photo by Tom March, another of the earliest British motor racing photographers regularly to shoot colour

Right *10 May, 1952—International Trophy, Silverstone, with Mike Hawthorn showing his class in the nitro-fuelled Cooper-Bristol Mark I, starting from pole position to win Heat One and sharing fastest lap in the Final with Peter Whitehead's Ferrari. Within months Hawthorn would be offered a works Ferrari drive, en route to Grand Prix greatness. Another Tom March photo*

Below *9 May, 1953—International Trophy, Silverstone— Ken Wharton's unmistakable Cooper-Bristol Mark II beat Hawthorn's works Ferrari 500 by one second to pole position for Heat Two, but this position was reversed in the race. Ken eventually finished fifth in the Final. Where Hawthorn's Mark I pole-time in 1952 had been 2 min 00.0 sec, Wharton's in the 1953 Mark II, magnificently depicted here by Guy Griffiths' camera, was just 1 min 52.0 sec*

Right *20 July, 1957—British GP, Aintree—that wonderful day when Moss and Brooks in the Vanwall beat 'Those bloody red cars' for the first time, scoring the first all-British* **Grande Epreuve** *victory since 1923! Roy Salvadori—captured here by Tom March setting up his 1960 cc F2-based T43 for Tatts Corner—finished fifth, Cooper's best World Championship race finish of their maiden F1 season with these rear-engined cars. So who needs flame-proof overalls?*

Below *7 April, 1958—Glover Trophy, Easter Monday Goodwood—Edward Eves' view of the start: Moss's stalled 'Argentine' T43 being push-started by the Walker team's mechanics while Archie Scott-Brown's Bernie Ecclestone-entered Connaught (12), Tony Marsh's Cooper T45 (white nose), Keith Campbell's red Maserati 250F, Harry Schell's BRM (part hidden behind Don Christmas, pushing Moss), Stuart Lewis-Evans' Ecclestone Connaught (14), Jean Behra's BRM (3), Hawthorn's Ferrari Dino 246 (1) which will win, and the Coopers of Salvadori (18) and Brabham (19) charge away. Jack's red-nosed 1960 cc T45 finished second*

Left *2 July, 1960*—during practice for the French GP at Reims-Gueux, Cooper's great driving force through their finest years—Jack Brabham—poses for the camera in his faithful 'Lowline'. He was about to achieve his hat trick of consecutive World Championship-qualifying GP wins the following afternoon . . . and there would still be two more consecutive victories to follow!

Below left *15 July, 1960*—colourful practice scene in the Silverstone pits as Tony Brooks tells Yeoman Credit chief mechanic Tony Robinson his latest thoughts on Cooper T51 'F2-26-59'. Brooks had proved himself one of the greats with Connaught, BRM, Vanwall and Ferrari, but could never show his best in the privately-entered rear-engined cars available to him. Tony Robinson's Cooper career spanned the Alta-engined Moss specials of 1953 to the works team's swan-song in 1968

Above right *26 March, 1961*—InterContinental Formula Lombank Trophy, Snetterton—Cooper cars were fast, manoeuvrable, rugged, often tail-happy but forgiving . . . at least that's presumably what Roy Salvadori was hoping here as he sorted out Yeoman Credit's new T53P 'Lowline' production car—'F1-2-61'—en route to fifth place. Geoff Goddard's shot highlights the anti-roll bar linkages working overtime front and rear . . .

Right *3 June, 1962*—Monaco GP, Monte Carlo—New Zealander Bruce McLaren was the last of Cooper's great long-term faithful F1 drivers and this was his third and final *Grande Epreuve* victory for them as he drove a typically reliable race in the T60 'F1-17-61'. The plastic pipes taped to the alleged 'roll-over protection' bar behind his head are fuel-tank breathers; the Climax V8 engine's cooling system filler is visible beneath

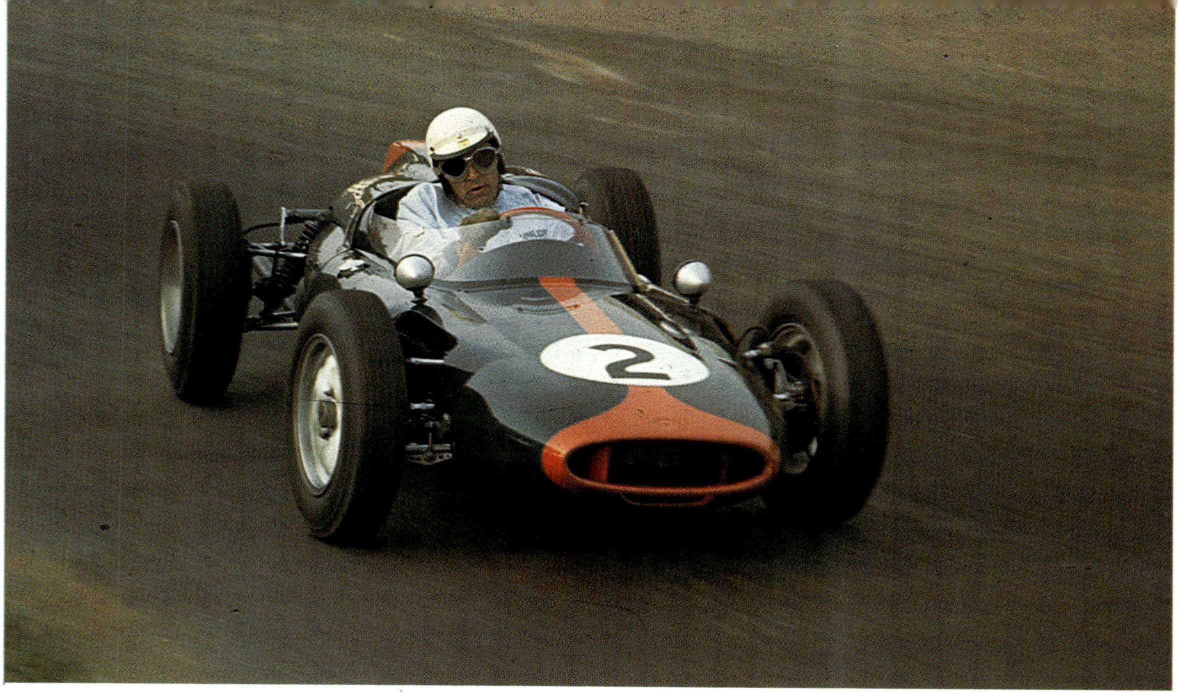
2

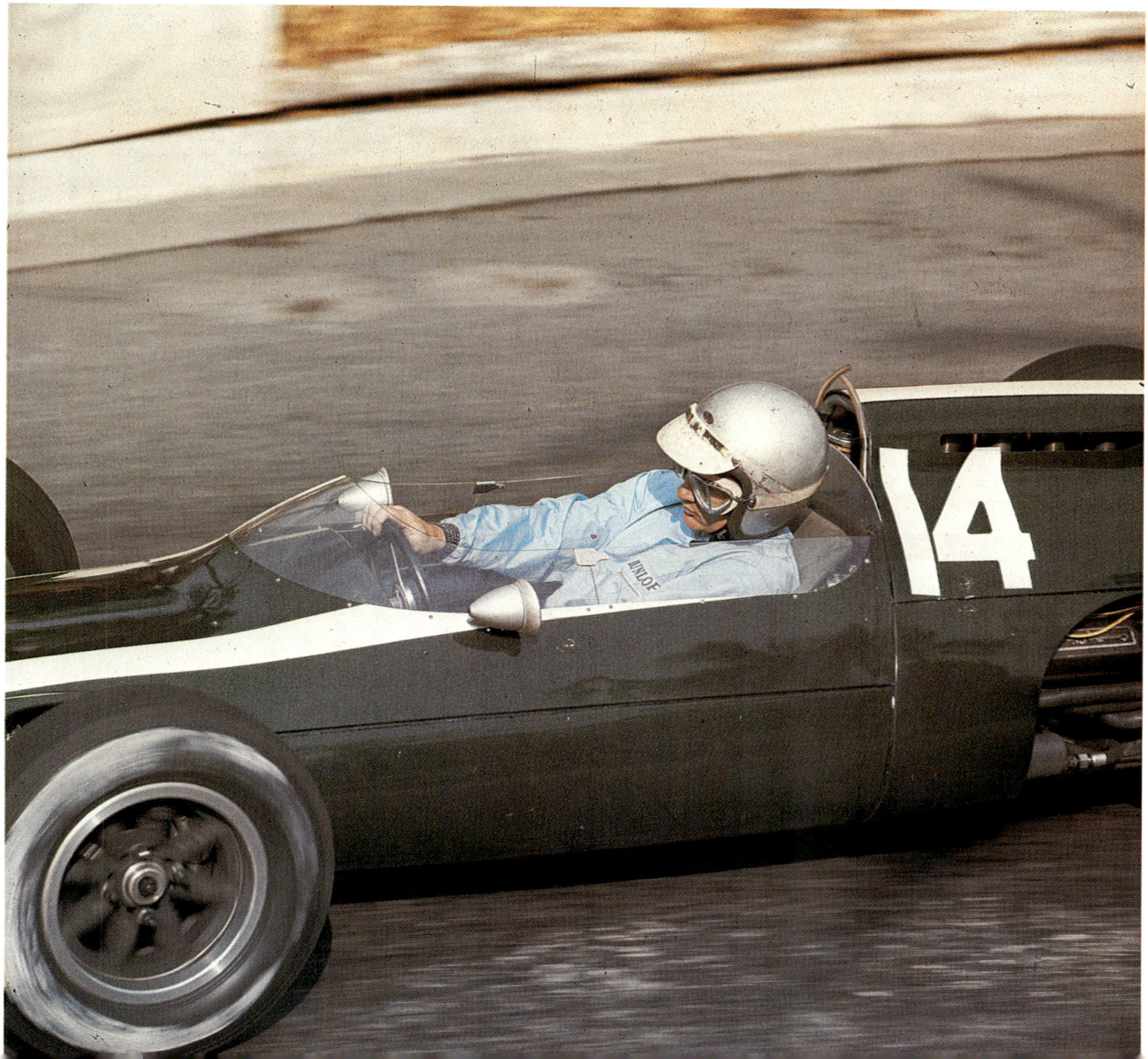
14

Above *19 July, 1958—British GP, Silverstone*—Maurice Trintignant on his way to eighth place in Rob Walker's now 2-litre 'Argentine' T43 special, displaying the tricolour motif in honour of its French driver and its Alf Francis modifications—the single top-rear radius rod suspension, nose ducts etc. Another Tom March shot

Left *10 May, 1959—Monaco GP, Monte Carlo*—the Cooper Car Company's great day as Jack Brabham accelerates his rippled and travel-stained 2½-litre T51 works car out of the Station Hairpin and down towards the sea front, Monte Carlo beach and the works team's first-ever World Championship-qualifying Grand Prix victory! This shot was taken by Max Boyd, reproduced by permission of the National Motor Museum, Beaulieu

11 May, 1959—morning after the night before; Cooper's works team celebrates its maiden Grande Epreuve *victory at the Diodato outside Monaco; the cars are Masten Gregory's (26) which had been Brabham's originally-assigned mount, troublesome in practice, and which broke after six race laps; Jack's winner (24) and Bruce McLaren's (22) which finished fifth and last. Masten had already left, but Jack's journalist friend 'Dev' Dvoretsky's shot here shows (left to right) 'Noddy' Grohmann, John Cooper, 'Blackie' himself, Bill James, Bruce McLaren and his New Zealand pal Phil Kerr with the team cars and transporter. No multi-million sponsorship budgets in Cooper's heyday . . .*

19 June, 1960—Jack Brabham won five consecutive World Championship-qualifying GPs in the 'Lowline' Cooper. Here on the entry to La Source hairpin at Spa-Francorchamps, Jack brakes hard from high speed on the way to the team's second win of that historic series. The car's nose has been stripped by flying grit and pebbles

23 October, 1966 — Mexican GP, Magdalena-Mixhuca, Mexico City — John Surtees on his way to Cooper's penultimate Grande Epreuve *and F1 win in the big Maserati V12-engined T81 'F1-6-66'. These cars had proved ever more competitive since Surtees' mid-season arrival from Ferrari. In the next GP, opening round of the 1967 Championship, Pedro Rodriguez would score Cooper's final victory but it was lucky — Surtees' Mexican win, recalled here in this Michael Tee* Motor Sport *shot, was Cooper's last on merit*

26 May, 1968 — Monaco GP, Monte Carlo — Geoff Goddard recorded the Cooper works team's swan-song outing where their F1 ambitions had first flowered in 1957. Lucien Bianchi placed third and Ludovico Scarfiotti fourth, but both were four laps down amongst only five finishers. Here Scarfiotti follows in Brabham's one-time World Champion Cooper wheel-tracks, accelerating his neatly Monaco-nosed BRM V12-powered T86B 'F1-2-68' out of The Old Station Hairpin, the station itself now demolished

The Cooper-Knight 'C5S' five-speed remote-sump transaxle was quite a hefty, complicated lump and its cost – had Charles Cooper been told the proper figure – would have caused uproar at the works, but it proved phenomenally reliable and was instrumental in securing their second consecutive World Championship title, and in such a convincing manner. Here in the Oporto paddock Noddy examines the works, the 'box lying on its side, top towards the camera, input end at right

works Lowline 1-2 finish. Jack averaged over 134 mph in this race to score Cooper's first works back-to-back GP victories, but with two fatalities and Moss and Michael Taylor of the Taylor & Crawley private Lotus team badly hurt there was little joy that night.

The winning engine, *1182*, was in its first race and finished in fine order, having been taken to 6800 and returning 11½ mpg. Bruce's engine, *1171*, had hit 7000 rpm – 180 mph along the Masta Straight – and was less happy. Climax were asked to investigate its oil loss and periodically flagging oil pressure. It was also due for a routine overhaul, having also done the Monaco GP. There was no gearbox trouble, the 'C5S' units were unchanged.

For the French GP at Reims in July, larger-capacity gearbox oil pumps were adopted to improve cwp life. By this time the team had on call 10 2½-litre FPFs, five from 1959 plus five new ones. Normally they would return the two raced engines to Widdrington Road after each event, taking four with them on the next trip. At Reims Jack began practice with *1182* ex-Spa, changing to the new *1184* for the race. Bruce used the 1959 engine *1153*.

Brooks's Reims record was 2:19.4 and Jack soon got down to 2:20, then 2:17, then pole at an imperious 2:16.8. The Australian's Lowline was uncatchable, but Bruce's was only ninth fastest. Yeoman Credit's three cars were driven by Gendebien, Taylor and Bruce Halford, the Belgian's with an ex-Walker Colotti transaxle. Brooks was out in a lightweight Vanwall. Trintignant, Gregory and Burgess drove Centro-Sud Cooper-Maseratis, Gino Munaron one of two Cooper-Castellottis entered and Bianchi Tuck's car. Trint's Centro-Sud hybrid had lowered suspension and Burgess's late-arriving model carried a brand-new improved Maserati engine.

The GP was a bitter battle between Brabham and the Phil Hill and von Trips Ferraris; the American crumpling his car's nose against a Cooper rear wheel at one point. This scrap raged for 29 laps, in which Brabham set a new 2:17.5, 135.8 mph lap record, and won his third consecutive *Grande Epreuve* of this fantastic season.

Bruce had another long dice with Gendebien, but the radiator ducting inside his Lowline's nose broke loose and partially blanked the radiator. Temperature soared to 115°C, oil pressure flopped and oil temperature hovered around 140°C, but still the engine pulled. Gendebien's 'vintage' Mark IV showed more power out of the slower corners, but the Lowline had an edge flat-out at the end of the straights. Bruce decided to dive ahead into a braking area, let the Belgian repass and hope he would make a mistake. Booting their way out of Muizon on one lap Gendebien went sideways, bouncing straight off the kerb. As they rocketed away side by side Olivier glanced across at his young adversary and gave the continental, in this case self-deprecatory, gesture with thumb and forefinger. Bruce signalled back – he wanted to be second. . . .

But with 10 laps to go his engine flagged. Two laps to go and the engine semi-seized, and as Bruce abruptly slowed a gaggle of just-lapped backmarkers almost ran into him; Masten Gregory was one who staged a phenomenal avoidance. Yet Bruce's engine freed and in one last death-or-glory attempt to repass Gendebien he instead flogged up the Thillois escape road. Last lap, the engine tightened again and Bruce toured in third behind the elated Belgian and ahead of Henry Taylor's other Yeoman Credit car, which was fourth, for a Cooper-Climax 1-2-3-4 finish – humbling three Lotus 18s to the family's intense glee. Yeoman Credit were delighted; Ken Gregory: 'Reims was the team's best result that year. . . .'

The works team report on Reims comments: '*Slight marking on pinion in JB's gearbox due to overheating (due to not running in properly? – JNC)*.'

For the British GP at Silverstone a new external pipe and oil jet to the pinion was rigged on Jack's gearbox, while Bruce's simply ran a fresh cwp. Lance Reventlow's ill-conceived American Scarab F1 programme had run onto the rocks at Reims and now John offered him *F2/5/57* for the British race. He accepted, but then developed 'flu, so his team driver Chuck Daigh took over.

Brooks was back in a Yeoman Credit Cooper after his one-off return to Vanwall at Reims. Halford was dropped, and

Tony's car used a Colotti gearbox like Gendebien's, while the Belgian's car used knock-off wire wheels at the rear. Henry Taylor's third car was standard. Gregory and Burgess drove for Centro-Sud, Bianchi for Tuck, Fairman for Tommy Atkins and Keith Greene his father's Cooper-Maserati. The Castellotti team did not arrive until practice was over, with a car for Munaron.

Jack Brabham was on the crest of a wave. He took pole from Graham Hill's rapidly improving rear-engined BRM, and Bruce was third ahead of the Bonnier BRM. In the race Bruce led initially before moving over for his team leader, then being passed by Bonnier and Ireland's Lotus. The race developed with Jack being chased by three Lotus 18s – John Surtees, Clark and Ireland – and Bruce falling behind, fifth.

Graham Hill had stalled on the startline, as had Brooks and Taylor. But the BRM driver was to tiger his way through the entire field until on lap 55 of the 77 he barged past Jack for the lead.

Towards the finish Jack saw '... John Cooper waving at me madly so I started pressing on and was gradually picking Graham back'. The BRM's caned brakes were playing tricks and Jack had just begun to think he might get within striking distance when, with six laps to go, the BRM dived into Copse Corner too deep, passing one back marker too many, and ran out of brakes, spinning on to the verge. Jack was handed victory on a plate, and took it gratefully; Cooper's second consecutive victory in their home GP, and their fourth successive GP win that season. Brabham had been troubled by fluctuating fuel pressure and a seizing clutch thrust race. Bruce was fourth behind two Lotuses, disappointed with his own performance after that promising practice time, while the works spare car in Daigh's hands had battled with Henry Taylor for much of the race until a head seal popped and he retired on lap 57.

The new cwp oil system worked a treat on Jack's car as the terse team report records: '*Jack: ... New jet on pinion – result 1st class. Bruce: No new jet on pinion – shagged.*'

There was no World Championship German GP, the AvD opting to give Porsche some glory by running their race to Formula 2, but the following day was August Bank Holiday Monday and it saw a non-Championship F1 race at Brands Hatch. The works ran Jack Brabham in his usual car while Bruce took over old *5/57* ex-Daigh, fitted with engine *1147*, freshly rebuilt from the New Zealander's 'cut-in-half' Wigram unit. Newcomer Jimmy Clark took pole for Lotus from Brabham's Lowline with Brooks and Salvadori (in the Atkins car) on row two, followed by numerous Coopers: Bruce beside Henry Taylor and Dan Gurney in Yeoman Credit cars, George Wicken in his maroon vehicle, Halford in a fourth Yeoman car, Bianchi, Greene, Burgess, Munaron and Scarlatti in Cooper-Castellottis, Geoff Richardson's Connaught-powered Cooper-RRA and Masten Gregory's Centro-Sud Cooper-Maserati on the back alongside Brian Naylor's Cooper-like JBW-Maserati special.

Jack Brabham won the race by 4.4 sec after Jimmy Clark's Lotus gearbox failed; the young Scot making his first vivid impression in Formula 1 in this race. Bruce was third, fascinated by the difference in handling between the '59-style car and the latest Lowline. He found the inside front wheel of the rear-leaf-spring car would lift and could be rested comfortably on the raised inner kerb in corners, but if he tried that same trick in the coil-sprung Lowline it would clump the kerb with a terrific jolt. Jack's winning Lowline – his regular *8/60* – had started with $3\frac{1}{2}$ gallons of oil on board but finished with only $1\frac{1}{2}$ left after the 50 laps. Pressure was fluctuating severely near the end.

Then it was off to Oporto for the Portuguese GP on 14 August, with the works new Lowline *F2/12/60* at last on hand as spare. Moss was recovered and racing a replacement Walker Lotus 18, and as Jack went out to warm up his Cooper, Moss whizzed by on a flying lap. Instantly some luminaries of the British Press cabled home stories about Moss passing Brabham the instant he got back into a racing car. . . .

Yeoman's three entries placed Brooks in a Colotti gearbox car, Gendebien with Cooper four-speed 'box and wire rear wheels, and Taylor standard. Walker had a Cooper as spare

206

1960 — THE GREATEST TRIUMPH

to the Lotus for Moss, while Centro-Sud ran their lowered hybrid for Gregory and rented a second to Jack's old friend from 1959 – Mario Araujo Cabral.

Jack shunted the bales lightly while running-in and Taylor crashed much more heavily, bending his car's frame and hurting himself. On the eve of the race the front suspension and smooth-changing new gearbox from the new Lowline were fitted on to Jack's faithful 8/60 frame, then the three mechanics went to bed early. Next morning, much to the drivers' horror, the cars were stripped again in readiness for Jack to start from pole and Bruce from row three.

Gurney's BRM led the first eight cars tightly bunched, but on lap 2, Jack got caught on the cambered cobbles between tramlines which matched the Lowline's track perfectly. He hurtled down an escape road but luckily the pack all missed him. He rejoined eighth, on Bruce's tail. Jack led his team mate in the fight back. Retirements elevated them to run 3-4 behind Surtees's Lotus and Phil Hill's Ferrari. After a brief but intense battle Jack took second, and ahead of him Surtees found trouble as his car's fuel tanks had split and leaking petrol was making the pedals slippery. On lap 36 he flew off the road and Brabham and McLaren flashed by for another Cooper 1-2 victory; Jack's and the team's fifth consecutive

October 1960, Bathurst 100-Miles, Mt Panorama, NSW – Brabham leads away in the 'Old Nail' from Mildren's Mark IV-Maserati (2) and Stan Jones' 2.2 Climax model (4). Jon Leighton and Bib Stilwell are on row two, Leighton's car having survived a trailer roll-over en route from Melbourne. Austin Miller's 2.2 (60) flanks Noel Hall's old 1.96 and Glass's Maserati 250F on row three; John Youl's new 2.2 (striped helmet) is on row four ahead of Alwyn Rose's DalRo-Jaguar (28), quickest of the local specials

Grand Prix victory in an unprecendented show of strength; allied to some good fortune. Now the Australian was virtually assured of back-to-back World Championship titles as only Bruce could challenge his points total, and even then only by winning both the Italian and United States GPs; the only two left on the calendar.

Bruce did have a small fright at Oporto when his car's fuel pressure zeroed with eight laps to go, but he switched to the auxiliary tank and finished comfortably.

Then the Italian GP organizers insisted on including the banked Monza speedbowl in their circuit and the British teams ganged together and boycotted the race; after their Avus experiences banked tracks were considered too dangerous for lightweight modern F1 cars. Jack Brabham and Cooper-Climax were confirmed as World Champions for the second successive year.

At Monza, Ferrari predictably finished 1-2-3, but Giulio Cabianca was fourth in a Cooper-Castellotti.

Then two non-Championship British F1 races were held before the US events at Watkins Glen, NY, and the second United States GP at Riverside, California. In the Lombank Trophy at Snetterton, works Lotuses and BRMs humbled private Coopers, though Salvadori was fourth in the Atkins car despite gearbox problems. Henry Taylor – still uncomfortable from his Oporto practice injuries – was joined in the Yeoman Credit team by Denny Hulme, making his Formula 1 debut. Denny's fellow-traveller George Lawton had been tragically killed in an F2 Cooper crash at Roskilde, Denmark, shortly before. At Snetterton the Kiwi placed fifth, while Taylor ran well early on before being delayed by further gearbox trouble. Rather curiously the Ecurie Ecosse Cooper Monaco sports car was accepted for this race, ready-adorned with a hefty rollover bar in preparation for US racing that autumn. There was also a large F2 section.

One week later the Oulton Park Gold Cup saw the works Lowlines racing again, with older-style cars for Taylor, Salvadori, Flockhart and Halford, the Centro-Sud hybrids for Gregory and Trintignant and the Cooper-RRA for Richardson. Ian Burgess drove Centro-Sud's latest Maserati-powered F1 device – a Lotus 18. Charles grunted something about 'That bugger Burgess . . . ' but he still worked at Ewell Road, running the School with Andrew Ferguson; not that it would last much longer. . . .

Moss's Walker Lotus took pole from Clark's works car and Brabham's Lowline. The double World Champion led briefly before Ireland, then Clark moved ahead. Moss was locked in combat with the Lowline and when Clark crashed and Ireland took to an escape road their battle was for the lead. Innes had rejoined and caught *and passed* both superstars which drew well-earned praise. Jack's clutch began slipping and he dropped back, while poor Ireland's clutch broke and put him out. So Moss won from Jack second, Bruce was fourth and Taylor and Halford 7-8 for Yeoman Credit.

By the end of September the Lowlines and spare car were crated and off to America in the *Loch Gowan*. Ferguson wrote ruefully: 'True to form a dock strike was in progress as our cars departed. . . .'

In early October Jack went home, racing his old works Mark IV left in Australia at Bathurst, where he won from Bill Patterson's white 2.2, recently uprated from 1.96, and Stilwell's 2.2. Jon Leighton placed fourth in his ex-Brabham/Lukey Mark III 1.96 ahead of Noel Hall's Mark IV with similar engine. First non-Cooper finisher was Arnold Glass's Maserati 250F. . . . He was about to buy the ex-Atkins/Greene Cooper-Maserati. . . .

One week later, the Formula 1 circus reported for duty at Watkins Glen for a 100-lap 230-mile International Grand Prix, non-Championship race. Moss's Lotus took pole from Jack, followed by Bonnier and Gendebien's Yeoman Credit cars and Salvadori in the Ecosse Monaco. US entries included John Plaisted's F2 Cooper, which withdrew after practice bearing failure, Stutz Plaisted's sister car and Bill Bradley's F1 Cooper-Climax. Brabham led until baulked by a backmarker, when Bonnier dived ahead. Jack fought back and ran first again until Moss began his charge and took and held the lead to the finish, with the works Lowline second from Salvadori. Both Yeoman cars again suffered gearbox failures, though Bonnier was classified fourth. The Plaisted F2 was sixth.

Riverside hosted a financially catastrophic second United States GP in November. In the heart of sports car country there was minimal public interest in a badly publicized Formula 1 race. The works ran their regular Lowlines for Brabham and McLaren plus the older spare for Ron Flockhart – Jack's flying instructor and regular airborne co-pilot. Yeoman Credit fielded four cars for Brooks, Gendebien, Taylor and Phil Hill – Ferrari staying away. Centro-Sud ran Cooper-Maseratis for Trintignant, Burgess and von Trips; Salvadori was in Tuck's car and Pete Lovely in a Cooper-Ferrari bought by Fred Armbruster. Brian Naylor's JBW-Maserati appeared after its promising run at Monza.

Moss again took pole from Jack and Gurney's BRM – the Californian racing within whistling distance of his home. Gendebien was quicker than Brooks and McLaren. This was to be the last 2½-litre Grand Prix and a lot of tired machinery took the start. Jack led initially, but his car's tanks were topped to the brim to avoid a repetition of Sebring, and under a hot sun the fuel warmed and expanded and dribbled from a breather. It blew back over the engine and the exhaust pipe was soon hot enough to ignite it. The explosion scorched Jack's back and he stopped after four laps to investigate. All seemed well. He rejoined ninth, but four laps later another fireball erupted in his car on the straight. By the time he braked to a halt the fire had gone from the cockpit, but the engine bay was still sizzling. He drove into the pits, singed wires were taped and the breather pipe shifted. The engine wouldn't run cleanly thereafter and he finished a distant fourth. Moss won from Ireland in Lotus 18s, while Bruce was third, Phil Hill sixth, Salvadori and Trips 8-9, Lovely and Gendebien 11-12, and Taylor and Trintignant 14-15. Flockhart retired early on and neither Brooks nor Burgess finished. . . . Jack set fastest lap – it was another *Grande Epreuve* he could have won.

And animal-loving Charles Cooper and keen Chinchilla breeder Alfred Moss spent much of their Californian stay touring the rabbit farms around the State. . . .

It was the end of 2½-litre World Championship racing, and the end of an era in which Cooper cars had changed the layout of Grand Prix car design; and had reached the pinnacle. . . .

CHAPTER NINETEEN

Interlude for Two – 1958-1960

While the works Formula 1 team was putting together its back-to-back World Championship titles, Cooper cars continued to dominate Formula 2, at least during 1959, while success became more sparse that second season.

The significant development for 1959 was the British Racing Partnership's approach, in conjunction with Rob Walker, to septuagenarian Carl Borgward in Bremen, asking to use his company's powerful fuel-injected dohc 16-valve 1500RS sports car engine in F2 Cooper frames for Formula 2. The German sports-racing cars had shown terrific pace during 1958 and the Carl Ludwig Brandt-designed power unit obviously had great potential. Ken Gregory approached Borgward through their London concessionaires, Metcalfe & Mundy. Carl Borgward himself was interested, but only if Moss would drive, so a deal was done on that basis; the Borgward engine would power two F2 Coopers for BRP drivers Ivor Bueb and George Wicken, and a Walker car for Moss.

Walker mechanic John Chisman went over to Bremen for a few days to build the first fuel-injected F2 engine into what had been Trintignant's '58 Monaco-winning Mark III Cooper. Works engineer Fritz Jüttner test-drove this prototype locally and would accompany BRP as technical rep in their race programme ... at the team's expense. Their F2 cars were brand-new Mark IVs, chassis *F2/1/59* and *2/59*, completed respectively with Borgward engines *30009* and *30005*, with £1176 7s. PT on each of them, paid on 3 March.

The cars used twin-coil ignition with batteries mounted in the nose for twin plugs per cylinder. The throttle butterfly for the fuel injection was housed in a large intake trunk by the driver's left ear, and these extended intakes would become characteristic of the cars.

Jack Brabham ran an independent F2 programme with his own ex-works Mark III – probably *F2/22/58* which he had bought in September. It was progressively modified by his ex-Walker friend and mechanic Tim Wall. He and Atkins mechanic Harry Pearce ran their cars from lock-ups behind the 'North Star' pub, opposite Jack Brabham Motors in Chessington. Tim was another very quiet Australian – if anything even less talkative than Jack himself, which took some doing. The other two works drivers, McLaren and Gregory, were invited by Alan Brown and Ken Tyrrell to handle their team cars in F2, while Roy Salvadori would feature in Tommy Atkins' Mark III *15/58*, still in harness from the previous season.

When 1959 F2 commenced at Goodwood on Easter Monday, Brabham just beat Salvadori to the line, with Jim Russell's smart green-and-silver Downham Market-built private car third. Both BRP Cooper-Borgwards had a disappointing debut, but two weeks later at Oulton Park Russell won in awful weather from Tony Marsh's drum-braked car and Bueb once fuel blockage had forced Brabham out of the lead. Brian Whitehouse – son of the late, much-missed 'Big Bill'

GPs de France F2 Champion 1959 – Stirling Moss in Rob Walker's Mark III-Borgward on his way to victory in the Coupe de Vitesse, Reims-Gueux, *as his main opposition, Hans Herrmann in the Behra-Porsche, has been lured into misjudging his braking at the end of the long downhill Soissons Straight, and goes flurrying straight on up the escape road at Thillois Corner! It was typical Moss. Here he looks relaxed as ever. Note Borgward's four-into-one megaphone exhaust, and Walker team's immaculate preparation. At Reims one Walker car had its engine cowl blow open during practice, scraping its tail. The mechanics under Alf Francis cut a different-shaped hole to remove the damaged section. They were delighted to find several other teams copying their 'latest tweak', unaware why the new-shaped hole was there ...*

– was eighth in this race driving the ex-Wicken Mark III. The first eight cars were all Coopers.

Ivor Bueb led the F2 category at Aintree until his clutch broke. Mike Taylor eventually won the division in an Alan Brown car from Keith Greene and Jack Lewis; another Cooper-Climax 1–2–3. Maurice Trintignant gave the Walker Cooper-Borgward its debut, but it also disappointed.

A frantic charter-flight scramble whisked five Coopers and a Lotus ex-Aintree to the Syracuse GP, where Moss's Walker Cooper-Borgward won easily from Behra's front-engined Ferrari Dino 156. This was not only Cooper's first victory over Ferrari in a pure F2 race, but also the first ever for the Borgward engine and the new Colotti gearbox. Brabham and Gregory were lapped 3–4, Bueb fifth and Wicken seventh. Stuart Dodd's 1957 ex-Sopwith all-leaf-spring Mark II car and John Campbell-Jones's drum-braked sister both broke their gearboxes.

Another scramble took the stars back to the May Silverstone race, where Jim Russell won the category from Bueb's Cooper-Borgward, with Marsh third. Formula 2 cars then attempted to qualify at Monaco; the contingent including four Coopers. Two were new Mark IVs – 9 and 10/59 – for Bianchi and de Changy of Equipe Nationale Belge. Jean 'Lucien-bonnet' ran his own Mark III – reportedly the ex-Salvadori '58 German GP/Jack Brabham F2 Casablanca winner – and the United Racing Stable entered another new Mark IV – 8/59 – for Ivor Bueb. This team was a partnership between Bob Gibson-Jarvie of the UDT finance house and Col. Ronnie Hoare, a businessman-motor trader whose wide interests would soon include the UK Ferrari concession. Bueb was quick enough to qualify until the dying embers of practice, when Cliff Allison's Ferrari 156 bumped him off the grid. The Ferrari, Lotus and Porsche F2s which did make the race were all eliminated in a second-lap collision.

At Whitsun there were F2 races in the UK and at Pau. Salvadori beat Bueb and Chris Bristow at Crystal Palace after Russell's clutch faltered soon after taking the lead from Roy. Bristow was driving Tom Payne's Bradstock Motors-entered Hume-Cooper, a much-modified rebodied car developed by John 'Boots' Hume. Bristow, from South London, had driven well in earlier events that year, and was watched with great interest by Pa Moss and Ken Gregory.

At Mallory Park that day Tim Parnell – son of Reg – won in his Mark III 7/58 from Dodd and School pupil Keith Jack's Cooper, while the *Libre* race there fell to Naylor's Cooper-copy JBW-Maserati from Parnell and Jack. Chris Summers rolled George Nixon's new Mark IV – 3/59 – violently at Devil's Elbow, but emerged almost unscathed.

Meanwhile at Pau it was a Cooper benefit. Trintignant won in his wire-wheeled Walker car fresh from F1 at Monaco and now re-engined as a 1500. He had a battle with Behra's Colotti-built open-wheeled Porsche special and Masten Gregory's luridly driven Brown-Tyrrell car; Behra spun and the Kansan's final-drive broke. Norman Barclay crashed his Cooper heavily in late rain – detuning McLaren, who witnessed the incident. Bianchi and Marsh placed 3–4.

In the long break before Reims the Borgward engines were fully race-developed. The F2 race followed that blindingly hot French GP by 30 minutes and 17 Coopers ran in the 24-strong field. Moss won easily in his Walker Cooper-Borgward; his ex-Monaco and Dutch GP Mark III with its usual 2½ Climax FPF engine replaced by the 1500 Borgward unit. Hans Herrmann was second in the Behra Porsche ahead of Bonnier's German works car; then Trintignant in Walker's former Cooper-BRM, now in Climax F2 trim. Henry Taylor drove Nixon's repaired Mark IV home sixth, and Chris Bristow made his debut in Wicken's place in a BRP Cooper-Borgward, but retired; as did George in his own Climax car. Brabham became semi-conscious with heat exhaustion following his GP efforts and rammed Bueb in one of the hairpins, putting them both out, while Bruce found himself semi-conscious and driving far too hard and took Ken Tyrrell's pre-race advice and retired.

Now the Cooper-Borgwards were coming on full song. Moss was uncatchable again at Rouen once Brabham's car split an oil line and spun on its own oil. Harry Schell – driving his own Mark IV – 17/59 which had been new at Reims – was second from Gregory, who just skated by McLaren near the end, the Kiwi suffering hands blistered at Reims and a deflating tyre. Chris Bristow's BRP car was fifth, by a nose from Trintignant's Walker Cooper-Climax.

An F2 category was included in the British GP at Aintree, with the BRP Borgwards of Bristow and Bueb facing Henry Taylor, Peter Ashdown – the Lola sports car driver – and Mike Taylor in Parnell and Brown-Tyrrell Cooper-Climaxes. Bristow won convincingly from Taylor, Ashdown and Bueb's gearbox-crippled team car.

F2 Coopers in a Libre *rae at Mallory Park, but still an interesting bunch here at Shaw's Hairpin, 13 September, 1959 – Ian Raby in the bulbous Hume Cooper with Porsche-like bodyshell enclosing an all leafspring Mark II frame, leads the way, Chris Summers' Nixon car runs wide while Henry Taylor tries hard to find some way past them both. It was 'best dice of the day' – a typical scene in Cooper's heyday . . .*

29 August 1959, Kentish '100', Brands Hatch – Chris Bristow's BRP Mark IV-Borgward with distinctive induction ram-duct leads Graham Hill's works Lotus 16 (32), Moss's Walker Mark IV-Borgward (2), Salvadori's Atkins Climax version (10), Mike McKee's Russell Car (9), Ireland's Lotus 16 (33) and on the inside Bonnier's early works Porsche 718 round Paddock Bend on the opening lap. Look closely and you'll see Bristow's car has no upper rear wishbones, but they are fitted on Moss's and will handicap it. Brabham's works car has already gone by . . .

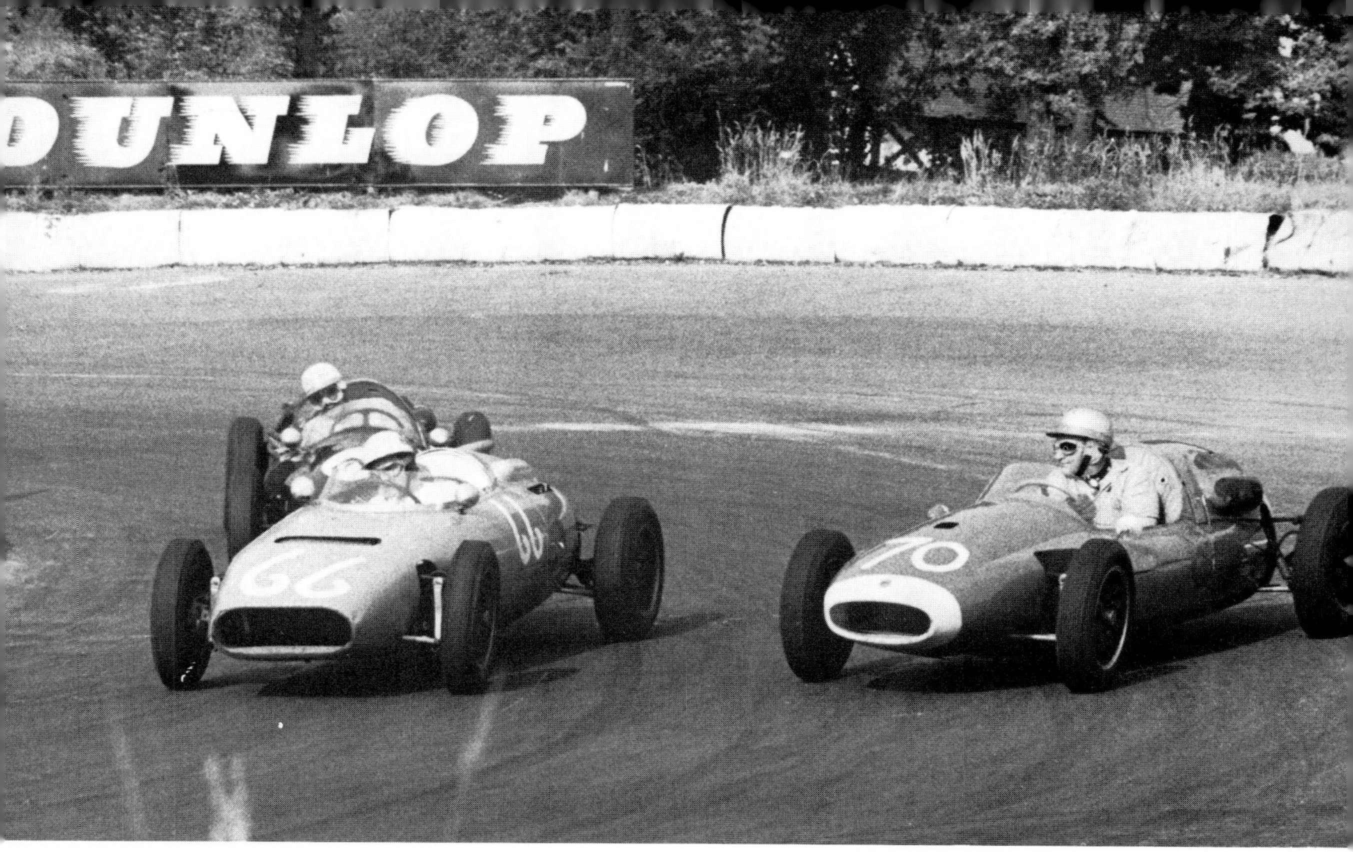
DUNLOP

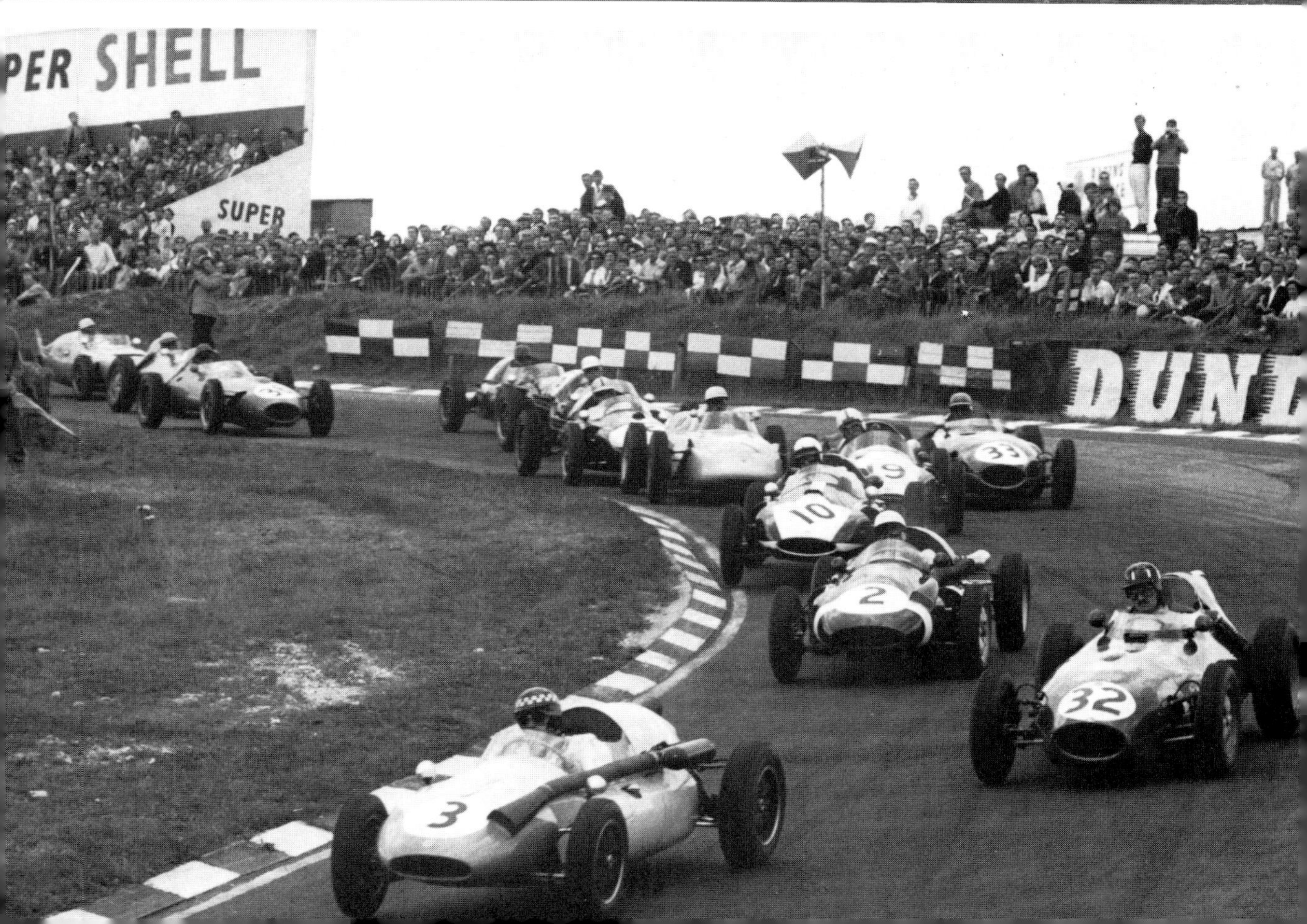
PER SHELL
SUPER
DUNL

On 26 July the F2 circus appeared at Clermont-Ferrand. Moss's Walker Borgward was blocked by starter Toto Roche on the line and he chased Bristow's BRP sister for four laps before taking the lead he held to the end. Ken Gregory asked his opinion of young Bristow's driving: 'He never put a foot wrong,' Stirling answered. But tragically Ivor Bueb had, losing his BRP Borgward over a hump in a fast curve. He was thrown out as the car rolled and sustained severe internal injuries from which he died six days later. Today Ken feels if they could only have got Ivor into a British hospital he could have survived. His loss was a terrible blow to all who knew him; it hit Hollyfield Road hard.

Meanwhile Bristow's head seal failed and Henry Taylor placed second from McLaren, Gregory and Olivier Gendebien's ENB car in a Cooper 1–2–3–4–5 clean sweep. John Campbell-Jones was seventh behind a Lotus in the Hume-Cooper.

Clermont saw Moss's third French F2 victory and assured him of the year's *GPs de France* title, but after Bueb's accident few left Clermont happy, least of all Chris Bristow, who was initially prepared to retire from racing.

Brands Hatch on August Monday persuaded him otherwise as he beat Brabham, Salvadori and McLaren for his and BRP's first major F2 victory. He had the advantage of single wishbone rear suspension against the double-wishbones of his rivals, which gave less controllable oversteer. At Brands you needed to be able to hang the tail out predictably, and the single-wishbone Cooper-Borgward simply did it better....

Keith Greene won a minor F2 race at Snetterton, then on 29 August the circus returned to Brands for the major Kentish '100'. Most serious Cooper runners had learned their lesson on August Monday and arrived with single-wishbone rear ends; but Moss had missed the earlier race and his Walker Borgward had doubles and suffered in consequence. Jack won both heats from a Lotus, Moss third. Jack did a lap of honour with John Cooper perched on his engine cover, clutching the trophy, and Surbiton had again won the F2 Championship.

The 1959 F2 season ended at Snetterton in the *Autosport* 3-Hours meeting, where the Silver City Trophy F1/F2 supporting event saw Bristow win again for BRP and Borgward from Mike McKee in the Le Mans-injured Jim Russell's car, and Campbell-Jones third.

With 14 major victories this was another superb Cooper season to add to the F1 World title and Monaco sports car successes, and success was split equally–seven-each to Climax and Borgward power. Carl Borgward was delighted, but then decided to rest on his laurels and withdrew the engines for 1960, after a BRP-Yeoman Credit foray to South Africa.

Now Formula 2 had extra significance as Porsche and Ferrari were preparing carefully for 1500 cc Formula 1 racing in 1961. Both concerns – plus Lotus – were building rear-engined cars and Cooper would find success harder than ever. Of 11 significant F2 races in 1960, Cooper would win only

two, against Porsche's four, Lotus's three and Ferrari's two; one with a front-engined car, one their new rear-engined challenger.

While the works concentrated totally upon their Lowline programme to defend the World title, Jack Brabham continued to run his own much-modified F2 car as a privateer, now using a special five-speed gearbox in a Cooper-Knight casing, as did young Jack Lewis from Stroud in his H & L Motors machine. BRP, now with new sponsorship, the Yeoman Credit Racing Team, had bought three new Mark IV cars – chassis *FII/24*, */25* and *26/59* – mainly for 2½ F1 but also occasional F2 use, on which £980 5s. 10d. each PT had been paid on 28 October, 1959.

When the 1960 F2 season opened at Syracuse there were 10 Coopers in the 18-strong field, including one of Yeoman's new Mark IVs for Harry Schell and an older single-wishbone car for Bristow. Both used Cooper four-speed gearboxes with end-plate oil pumps, and had long ram ducts in the old Borgward style feeding the twin SU carburettors from an intake on the nose. Ron Flockhart drove what had been Gregory's Brown-Tyrrell car in 1959, while Gendebien and Frère handled ENB's entries, fresh from South African success. Maurice Trintignant was now racing independently with his ex-Walker Cooper, now Climax instead of Borgward-powered but retaining the Colotti five-speed gearbox. This double-wishbone car was maintained for him by Centro-Sud in Modena, for whom he was driving F1 that season. Brabham, Chris Threlfall and the Frenchmen Jo Schlesser and Bernard Collomb completed the Sicilian entry.

Rob Walker had been loaned a Porsche for Moss's use and by Monaco time would have a Lotus for Formula 1, temporarily ending a long and fantastically successful exclusive allegiance to the Cooper marque.

The Syracuse race was of absorbing technical interest with the flat-4 air-cooled Porsche leading Ireland's new ultra-light Lotus 18, Brabham's hefty but practical Cooper and Trips's front-engined Ferrari V6. The Ferrari's luck was in and Trips won as the others faltered. Brabham's magneto sparked-out, and Trintignant was second from Gendebien, Frère, Schlesser, Schell and Ian Raby in the Hume-Climax. Flockhart bent his car.

Two weeks later, at Oulton Park, Innes Ireland's new Lotus 18 won at record-shattering pace, while Ken Tyrrell gave World Champion motorcyclist John Surtees his F2 debut in one of his Coopers, having previously introduced him to four-wheeled racing with a new Formula Junior Cooper at the opening Goodwood clubbie. Surtees was sensational, finishing second ahead of Salvadori, Bristow, Schell and Bruce Halford. Mike McKee had led initially in the Russell Cooper before Ireland rocketed by, and then he rolled his car on the last lap. Undeterred he climbed straight into a Team Lotus FJ Type 18 and was third in a team 1–2–3 finish! Lotus were attacking Cooper successfully in F1, F2

INTERLUDE FOR TWO – 1958–1960

Champions again – clinching the Formula 2 title at Brands Hatch provided this happy moment for the team; Jack Brabham, John Cooper, and the works 'T51' Mark IV-Climax. Jack had just won both heats of the Kentish '100'. Note driver ventilation holes drilled through windscreen base, and rear suspension set-up without top wishbones to impart more oversteer

Pau GP, 18 April, 1960 – Jack Brabham spoiling Maurice Trintignant's chances of a memorable hat-trick by leading throughout though the Frenchman's ex-Walker car sprayed pale-blue with the tricolour stripes across its nose was never more than 5 sec adrift. It was prepared by Scuderia Centro-Sud, whose badge appears on the nose. Jack's private car was Tim Wall-maintained, used a special five-speed Citroën-Cooper-Knight gearbox. Trintignant's had a Colotti five speed

and FJ; it was strange for Surbiton to have that backs-to-the-wall feeling....

The inaugural Brussels GP on the Heysel street and *Auto-route* circuit followed and Brabham's special won on aggregate; second to Moss's Porsche in the first Heat and winning with Stirling only third in Heat Two. Trintignant was third overall – making a fine start to his private-entrant season. ENB ran an extra new Cooper – *3/60* – and the German amateur Wolfgang Seidel fielded his ex-Atkins car. Marsh's Cooper had disc brakes at last, Campbell-Jones drove a Mark IV and Keith Ballisat the Dick Gibson machine. Trint's blue ex-Walker car had the tricolour stripes across its nose....

Easter Monday Goodwood was later in the programme than usual, and there Innes Ireland's Lotus 18s won both F1 and F2 races from Moss, convincing Stirling that he too must have a Lotus. Salvadori was third F2 in the latest Atkins car, from Bristow, Halford and McKee.

Meanwhile at Pau, Brabham won, using single rear wishbones on the tight street circuit and foiling Trintignant's hopes of a Pau GP hat-trick; the Frenchman finishing just 1.5 sec behind. Jack Lewis made his mark in practice, starting fourth on the grid, but his gearchange came apart in the race. Centro-Sud ran a new F2 Cooper-Maserati with 1500 cc four-cylinder engine on twin 45DC03 Webers in a 1959 frame with a Cooper gearbox casing, Maserati-made four-speed internals and lubrication.

The Aintree '200' was cut from miles to kilometres and run for F2 cars on 30 April. No less than 21 Coopers ran, including Surtees in his own new F2 Cooper – *FII/4/60* – just completed with engine *FPF/430/3/1159*. Brabham and Salvadori led away, just like old times, were passed briefly by Ireland until he spun off, and then on lap 26, with the Porsches closing and Surtees just behind them, both Coopers broke, Jack's losing its fuel pump drive and Roy's with valve-gear trouble. Porsches won 1-2-3, from Surtees, Trintignant and Bristow and the great motorcycling ace set fastest lap. He was blindingly fast but inclined to be unruly in close company, which his rivals did not appreciate....

Denny Hulme and George Lawton, fresh from New Zealand, respectively finished tenth and retired in this race, while at Silverstone Denny actually won the F2 class of the Interna-

213

tional Trophy, from Marsh and Campbell-Jones.

A long F2 hiatus followed, as even the Reims organizers preferred Formula Junior; it was cheaper for a larger field. Then the week following the British GP in July the Solitude GP was held outside Stuttgart and von Trips won in the new rear-engined Ferrari Dino 156. Jack raced there in a new machine described as 'a 1959 car built up from bits and pieces', while Seidel had bought the Australian's early-season car though with four-speed gearbox in place of Jack's personal five-speeder. The German had sold his own ex-Atkins car to Trips for his private Scuderia Colonia, which was aimed at developing new German driver talent. It was lent to Edgar Barth for this race, surprisingly left without a drive through Porsche muddling their entries. Centro-Sud had conjured up 'a new standard car' for Cabral; this may have been *FII/13/60* sold to Claudio Corini in June 1960. . . . Jack Lewis qualified well and led the Coopers in the race, but the Ferrari won from four Porsches, and the best Cooper was Gregory's Maserati-powered Centro-Sud car, ninth. Times were changing.

The German GP was run to F2 for Porsche's benefit; Jack's lightened Cooper qualified third amongst them and Bruce made his F2 debut that season in one of the NZIGP team Mark IIIs as team mate to George Lawton, while Denny was away winning with his FJ Cooper in Italy. Gregory crashed heavily – even by his standards – and wrecked his Centro-Sud Cooper-Maserati during practice, and inevitably Porsche finished 1–2, with Brabham nursing his overheating Cooper home third followed by three more Porsches and two Lotus 18s. McLaren was next Cooper home, ninth. Times really were changing – an awful warning for the following season's Formula 1 . . . Jack took note. . . .

Mike McKee won an Aintree *Libre* race in Russell's F2 car next day and took the Vanwall Trophy at Snetterton that weekend from Lewis and a young South African named Tony Maggs, who set fastest lap in Essex farmer and Tojeiro Cars' sponsor John Ogier's Mark III. George Lawton jumped the start and was penalized a minute, while Jack Sears drove a Yeoman Credit car, but its timing slipped.

Going into the Kentish '100' on 27 August Cooper and Porsche were virtually neck-and-neck for the F2 Championship, but there Lotus won and the Championship was split jointly between the marques. Lawton beat Marsh, Lewis and 19 year-old club driver Stan Hart – son of speedway star Oliver Hart – for fifth place, all in Coopers, while Hulme clouted McKee, whose car again overturned. Again he emerged unflustered, and promptly came close to winning the FJ race in his Lotus! Neither works driver took part, Salvadori went out in a collision and the Centro-Sud Cooper-Maserati for Gregory had its rear suspension auto-destruct. Poor George Lawton then hit a bank during a Copenhagen GP which Brabham won on September 11 at Roskilde, Denmark, and was killed as his Cooper somersaulted. . . . He was only 21.

Formula 2 ended its four-year life with a make-weight category in the Italian GP, then Lewis beating Halford and Sir John Whitmore – in Ogier's car – in the category at Snetterton's Lombank Trophy F1/F2 race, before three European internationals.

At Zeltweg, Austria, on 18 September, Moss and Porsche won while Jack Brabham retired with fuel pump trouble. At Modena, Porsche beat Ferrari, Trintignant was sixth for Cooper. Without factory opposition Jack Lewis won at Montlhéry from Bianchi, Vic Wilson, Collomb and Dickie Stoop, all in Coopers.

The Formula 2 story ended on 16 October, 1960, at Brands Hatch, where Tony Marsh won, but in a Lotus 18, beating Lewis and Stan Hart. It was the end of an era. For Cooper, the writing was on the wall. . . .

John Surtees made tremendous impact upon the motor racing scene in his first few outings, 1960. Here he is in his own brand-new production F2-Climax, Aintree '200', 30 April, 1960. He and his father Jack maintained the car, and here had changed an oil-pipe immediately before the start. Geoff Goddard captured the motorcycle World Champion streaking through Melling Crossing as he set fastest race lap, the new F2 record, at exactly 90 mph

CHAPTER TWENTY

Monaco – mighty sports car

Sports car racing had been growing in popularity worldwide since the Second World War, but in the UK it seemed to pulse, interest grew and waned. It was on a high through 1958, with memorable Aston Martin versus Lister-Jaguar battles, and then for 1959 Hollyfield Road at last announced a new rear-engined sports car, a replacement for the highly successful old central-seat Bob-tail. It was named the 'Monaco' in honour of Trintignant's 1958 victory there and mindful of that race's worldwide lustre.

The prototype was shown to the Press at Hollyfield in November 1958. The factory extension and rebuilding had provided the necessary space to build both sports and single-seater cars more comfortably, and naturally both sports and production Mark VI Formula cars shared a number of common components. The same weight distribution was maintained to minimize development problems. Owen sketched out a new spaceframe in which the four main $1\frac{1}{2}$ in. diameter 18-gauge tube longerons swept outwards amidships to two-seat width, with additional diagonals in the scuttle and side bays and cross-linked by a series of hoops and straight cross-members. The Hollyfield Road chassis jigs were actually old Morrison air-raid shelter frames, one for the Monaco, two for single-seaters....

Since the rear engine mounting required no central transmission tunnel, the two seats could be crowded together either side of the centreline. The FPF engine was to be used in $1\frac{1}{2}$- or 2-litre form, mounted at four points on rubber bushes and tilted 18 degrees to the right. The Citroën-ERSA four-speed transaxle with step-up gears was now virtually all-British apart from its Cooper-developed Parisian-cast casing, for the internals were all tailor-made by Jack Knight's specialist company. In the Monaco the 'box had a right-hand change pivoted on the bottom chassis rail and operating via a long universally jointed linkage weaving alongside the engine. The 1958 single-seater locking mechanism was retained to prevent gears jumping out.

A single 12-gallon welded aluminium fuel tank was strapped outboard onto the left-side chassis rails to separate it as far as possible from driver and outboard battery on the right-hand side. The fuel load offset driver weight.

A bottom-ducted radiator resided in the nose, split 3/1 water/oil, with the dry-sump oil tank sited just behind on the top front cross-member. The spare wheel lay horizontally above the foot pedal area, with the hydraulic master cylinders for the brake and clutch. Steering wheel and column were inclined outwards from the centrally-placed rack-and-pinion, angling the whole driver position, for the foot pedals were pushed inboard by the front wheel housing.

Front suspension was by double wishbones and coil-spring/damper units as on the Marks III, IV and 1960 Mark VI single-seaters, while the faithful transverse leaf-spring was retained at the rear, with a single lower wishbone. The front anti-roll bar passed through the bottom-front frame cross-member. The rear leaf-spring was located laterally by the short link of the Mark III/IV rather than the now superceded 'curly leaf'.

Girling disc brakes appeared front and rear, $10\frac{1}{4}$ in. diameter. The front calipers were behind the axle line with the steering arms ahead, while the behind-axle rear calipers bolted direct to the cast magnesium hub carriers. The wheels were four-stud-fixing Cooper cast-magnesium eight-spoke; 4.50–15 fronts and 5.50–15 rears.

Bodywork was neat and stubbily attractive, reminiscent of the old 1100 Bob-tail with the razor-edges around the tail transom now rounded off, and a more handsome side intake treatment of the engine cover. Owen recalls how John preferred the curvy look to sharp edges.... There was a full-length undertray in two parts, and both these and the main body panels – clamshell-opening nose and tail and bottom-hinged doors above the wrap-round undertray sills – were in 18-gauge Noral sheet. The rear deck was styled with a central recess to clear mirror vision. An intake in each side of the tail cowl admitted induction air on the left and engine bay cooling air on the right, where the exhaust was gathered into two tail-pipes, with a small absorption-type silencer if needed.

Wheelbase was 7 ft 7 in., track 3 ft $10\frac{1}{2}$ in., overall length 11 ft 9 in., width 4 ft $9\frac{1}{2}$ in., height 2 ft $9\frac{1}{2}$ in. and ground clearance $5\frac{1}{2}$ in. at specified ride height. The turning circle, at two turns lock-to-lock, was 40 ft and approximate dry weight was 1120 lb. Cooper claimed 20.5 mph per 1000 rpm in top using a 4.01:1 final-drive, and a weight distribution split 44/56 front/rear, including driver and a half-tank of fuel.

There were no plans to run a works car. There was no

'*My dad made it . . .*' *Young Mike Cooper with the prototype Cooper Monaco sports-racing car posed on the Hollyfield forecourt, November, 1958, ready for the 1959 sales and racing season. The new car's lines were reminiscent of the Bob-tail but layout as can be seen with nose and tail cowls removed was very much contemporary F1/F2 big-tube frame widened to accommodate two legal seats. Nose radiator is ducted down through undertray, dry-sump oil tank wraps high over the ducting, sparewheel above footbox, fuel tank far from driver as possible, partly to counter-balance his weight. The right-hand gearchange is visible, note also centre dash glovebox!*

published Monaco price in the UK; it was open to discussion and several cars were sold as tax-free kits or collections of parts for the customer to assemble or have assembled himself. Significantly the US export price was published; $7700 for a 1500 and $8250 for a 2-litre.

Only eight Monacos appear in the Register for 1959; No. 1 going to Curt Lincoln in Finland, the second direct to Sebring for Hernano da Silva Ramos and Jean Lucas to drive in the Floridan 12-Hours race, third to an American named W. S. Bowman, who would race it at Silverstone in May before taking it home. Chassis *CM/4/59* was completed for Jack Brabham – to be prepared and run by John Coombs's Guildford garage – in April, when Jack was described as '*Australia – Temporary overseas resident*'. The fifth car went to Centro-Sud courtesy BP Trading in May; sixth to Henry Blanchard, USA, in June; seventh less engine to Hap Sharp, Texas, and eighth to N. J. Hartman, USA, both in September.

The Monacos were immediately successful. They had a slight edge over the Lotus 15s in sports car races accompanying most major British race meetings. Coombs had a 2½-litre Maserati-engined version built-up for Roy Salvadori to drive, while Jack's, liveried as a sister Coombs car, used a 2-litre Climax FPF. Roy did particularly well while Jack shone in some fearsome duels, usually with Graham Hill's works Lotus in 2- or 2½-litre trim.

The Coombs Monacos were built-up by mechanic Ken Stratton within the motor business, and the 2½-litre Maserati unit was the biggest they could lay their hands on at that time to fit the car. It was painted off-white with blue flashes and, typically Coombs, was always immaculate.

Jim Russell had a 2-litre built for him at Downham Market by Pip Preece: '. . . who came to work for me when Ivor Bueb went to BRP for Formula 2 and Lister for sports cars that year. I loved that Monaco. It was the *best* Cooper I'd ever driven,' Jim recalled in 1982, 'and *I* liked them all. . . . We were running an F2 car at the same time, and we tried consciously to make the sports car handle the same, and we succeeded, although the gearbox was never properly sorted out. It was a very forgiving car, you could do anything with it. . . .'

On 11 April at Oulton Park he won both the F2 and sports car races in these two Coopers and went on to lead the *Autocar* F2 Championship and achieve more Monaco success before sharing the sports-racer at Le Mans with Bruce McLaren.

During practice the car was very fast, really frightening

Ferrari's 2-litre Dino crew. Running into the night the Monaco lay ninth, leading the Dino by 6 min when Jim: '... went into White House corner to find oil all over the road and the Whiteheads' Aston Martin lying right in my line, and I hit it. The impact broke my leg and some ribs and I was struggling to get out when Faure's Stanguellini hit me, right in the fuel tank, which ignited. I got out of the fire in a pretty bad mess, and spent three to four months in hospital. My season was ended, I'd lost my chance in the F2 Championship and the Monaco was history....'

Meanwhile, Stirling Moss had taken to the Monaco and was to drive one in pale green and white prepared and entered for him by Mike Keele, a friend with an engineering business in Stirling's home town of Tring. They collaborated in building and promoting Trobikes; £30 a time with 50 cc lawnmower engines. Keele Engineering later went into the racing kart market very successfully, and Mike's son Roger achieved fame as a kart and later Formula 3 racing driver.

They fitted their car with one of the still rare $2\frac{1}{2}$-litre Climax FPFs with the original low-compression Mark I head, and Colotti transaxle, and Stirling qualified it on the front row for the British GP sports car race at Aintree, only to stall at the start and be rammed from behind. The impact restarted his engine and after checking for damage he was rushing through the field when the car caught fire....

Stirling's diary records that the Monaco was geared to 160 mph at 7000 rpm and comments: '*Clutch bad, brakes bad, oil leaks & suspension seizing otherwise OK. Oil pipe burst & oil fire....*'

He later took it on a Scandinavian tour, racing at Karlskoga in Sweden, and Roskilde near Copenhagen in Denmark. '*Karlskoga – bad brakes, broken roll bar, jumping gears etc.... Led start to finish, beat Brabham & Bonnier; 137 at 7000 gearing, got 6700....*'

At Roskilde's tiny track he was lapping in 46 sec and never got above 105 mph; he and Brabham sharing victory between them in a multiplicity of race heats. He didn't really care for the car very much.

The Coombs Monacos of Salvadori and Brabham were the most successful of the UK season. Roy always excelled on the wide open expanses of Silverstone and had expected to drive for Aston Martin there in the May International sports car race: '... but Stirling became available so Aston took him and I took the Coombs car instead. It went very well indeed and I managed to lead Stirling, then the car started to handle very badly and I just scraped home narrowly ahead to win, which pleased me enormously – feeling I'd got my own back. Coombs asked me how the car had been going and I said "well it did handle rather badly towards the end", and he looked it over, slammed the rear bonnet down and told me the chassis had broken! Ever after he'd say I must be as thick as two short planks; the only driver who could win a race with a broken chassis and not know it! The chassis was beefed-up, but it broke again, on occasion; I always had reservations about it. We were always worried about that Maserati engine and gearbox; had to be careful with it, and eventually the engine broke. We later found the pistons should have been lifed-out and replaced – we'd just run them over-life. The car was sold to Brian Naylor for 1960 and he was quite successful with it in lesser races....'

Colin Davis drove the Centro-Sud Monaco-Maserati very well at Messina in August to beat Giulio Cabianca's 2-litre Ferrari Dino, despite having to stop for refuelling while the Dino ran non-stop. In the RAC TT at Goodwood, Jack Brabham qualified eighth fastest with the Coombs $2\frac{1}{2}$ Monaco-Climax FPF fitted for the occasion with k/o hubs borrowed from Rob Walker, but early in the race a steering arm bolt sheared and after hub trouble he was out.

Chris Bristow drove his own Monaco that season but had a string of spins and mechanical misfortunes; Formula 2 would make his name. Prize for the unluckiest Monaco of the year went to The Chequered Flag dealership's car – the first to appear in fact – which was totalled within minutes of first practice beginning at Snetterton's season-opening meeting in March. Driver Percy Crabbe dropped it on a rain-soaked surface and was quite badly hurt. The car's remains were sold to hillclimber Josh Randles, who rebuilt it with supreme success.

On 28 February, 1960, the Havana sports car GP in Cuba saw strong Monaco representation; Jack Brabham losing third place with magneto trouble, Davis finishing fifth in the Centro-Sud Monaco-Maserati and Trintignant sixth for Maserati proper only after a race-long duel with George Constantine's private Monaco. Sir Jack also recalls another Coombs Monaco '... a 2-litre that we raced at Riverside, then sold to an ex-fighter pilot chap from Sacremento. He ran it in the next race at Laguna Seca, crashed and killed himself...'.

Slightly modified Monaco Mark IIs appeared for 1960, with subtly improved longer-nose body styling, but still transverse leaf-spring rear suspension. The first Registered car – *CM/1/60* – went to Swiss hillclimber Harry Zweifel in March. It had 2-litre FPF power and an ungainly tall regulation windscreen. He attacked the European Mountain Championship with it, facing works Porsches and finishing the season fourth behind two of them and a 'Birdcage' Maserati. Among his opposition was the Centro Sud Monaco-Maserati Mark I *CM/5/59* driven by gentlemanly Gianni Balzarini and another Italian sports Cooper driven by Peroglio.

In the UK, Coombs fielded a new car with $2\frac{1}{2}$ FPF power for Salvadori which promptly cleaned-up, winning virtually everywhere it went. Ron Flockhart replaced Salvadori at the wheel for the British GP meeting, and won, naturally. Jimmy Blumer's 2-litre Monaco featured strongly, and Tony Marsh was competitive in his $2\frac{1}{2}$-litre. Naylor's ex-Coombs Monaco-Maserati won at club level, while Ecurie Ecosse bought a $2\frac{1}{2}$

FPF car in kit form from Mrs Green's well-stocked shelves at Hollyfield Road, and had it assembled in a Surbiton lock-up by 'Wilkie' Wilkinson and completed by Stan Sproat. It was driven regularly by diminutive Tommy Dickson, with great success.

Jimmy Blumer on his Monaco: 'My first car came in 1960 in component form, for a 2-litre FPF, and we screwed it together in my garage in Middlesbrough. It cost about £1200 with the engine and gearbox extra. It was never road-registered; we just painted our trade-plates on it. It took quite a bit of sorting, we rejigged and reassembled the whole thing. There have been, ah, more accurate jigs made than Cooper's....'

He ran the car in the 1600 cc Spa GP in June, with a 1500 FPF fitted, and was sensationally fast in practice, pushing local star Paul Frère hard in a works Porsche. Then it rained on race day and the starter kept the field waiting because Frère was not ready: 'My Monaco started to overheat and I got a bit edgy, then the flag dropped and Frère rushed off with me right behind him, in his spray. It was cockpit thrombosis, you know, a dangerous clot between steering wheel and seat. I should have sat back and waited, but instead I sat in his spray where I couldn't see and I spun off at Burnenville into

Owen Maddock's architect father designed the famous curved-frontage Cooper Car Company factory which replaced the old Cooper's Garage front-workshops, 1957–58. Here, November '58, the prototype Monaco poses on far forecourt, facing works F1/F2 Mark IIIs and a production F3 Mark XII. The production workshop is through the large doors and ground-floor windows, original drawing office in building at this time is first-floor right, Charles and John's office – which became – and remains today – oak-panelled, is first-floor centre. At grand opening a pair of oil-soaked overalls were run-up one flagpole. 'Oo's are they?' roared the Old Man, 'Sack that Man!' 'But dad, they're Jack Brabham's . . .'. The petrol pump orbs are those smashed by the counterweight on Andrew Ferguson's hire crane. In the 1980s the building complete with its penthouse former drawing office added in 1961 is a police patrol car depot

the biggest rock in Belgium, and Bob Hicks's Lola rammed me up front while I'd demolished the tail, and banged myself about quite a bit . . . not very bright of me. . . .'

Jimmy's mechanic, Jack Dowson, really understood the car and he rebuilt it and it was sold to Aston Martin and Lister-Jaguar entrant-driver Jim Diggory from Wrexham. The 1960

MONACO – MIGHTY SPORTS CAR

Roy Salvadori did more winning than anyone else at serious level in John Coombs' various Monacos. Here at Aintree in the original 1959 Monaco-Maserati he shows off its neat if not exactly pretty lines, clipping the apex at Melling Crossing. Coombs' colours were ivory-grey with red flashes. This car sold to Brian Naylor who eventually fitted a 3-litre Ferrari 4-cylinder engine, ex-Peter Whitehead Tasman car. The two Italian units were interchangeable. Naylor sold the car as a Cooper-Ferrari via George Pitt to Phil Barak, the 2.7 Maserati engine to Fred Tuck

Coombs Monaco-Climax driven by Salvadori was apparently sold to the Hon. Eddie Portman for 1961, and he road-registered it 99 MBH and ran it with a 2-litre FPF. Portman found it all rather quick and willingly sold it to Blumer, who raced it with considerable success for two more seasons before selling it in 1963 to Greg Wood in Bradford, who raced on at club level, Jimmy taking a Cooper FJ in part-exchange. He found this second Monaco much better than the first: 'It was terrific fun to drive; you had to hang it out at what felt like 30 degrees to the direction of travel and just keep your foot hard on the power to corner rapidly . . . it really was a joy. . . .' Wood later sold the car to George Pitt who restored it before selling it on to Ken Yates of the BARC.

Jim Diggory was impressed with his Blumer Monaco: 'I'd been driving a Lister-Jaguar, and moving over from that to the Monaco was like climbing down off a dinosaur to ride a race-horse. My car was yellow with a black stripe and it was prepared at my garage by Ken Wild. I sold it in the end to John Fitch in the USA. . . .'

Some owners were not so impressed by the Monaco; Tony Marsh was one: 'It was the only one of my Coopers that I didn't like. Going into a fast corner like Woodcote at Silverstone you'd flick the steering to set it up and you could feel the chassis twist around you. Then when you straightened up on the exit and put the power on you could feel it flex straight again! I didn't really enjoy my drives in it at all, and it soon moved on. . . . I can't even remember where to. . . .'

Mancunians Alfie Osbiston and Colin Escott bought it from Brian Naylor and George Pitt, who had bought it from Marsh in the Silverstone paddock. Osbiston crashed it heavily.

Late in 1960 David Murray, Ecosse's patron, entered their Monaco for the Watkins Glen *Libre* and US West Coast professional sports car races. It was rigged with an SCCA-regulation roll-over hoop to suit, and driven by Salvadori. The Edinburgh team's mechanics had to hack away part of the dash and raise the steering column to fit him in; the car had been tailored to little Tommy Dickson. Roy was third at the Glen, first sports car home, and at Riverside – 2700 miles away on the other coast of America – came drama as he spun and stalled on lap 2. He rejoined 31st and last, but fought his way back through the field and to finish sixth.

Murray invited Jack Brabham to drive at Laguna Seca, but stone-damaged tyres and brakes put him out of contention. Moss was there in a brand-new rear-engined Lotus 19 sports car. Colin Chapman named it the 'Monte Carlo! . . . Stirling's Lotus had won there in that year's GP. He was taking the juice out of Cooper.

Through 1961, with the swing towards GT racing, interest in sports cars declined apart from the BRP-managed UDT-Laystall Racing Team Lotus 19s, which, when driven by Moss, Henry Taylor and Cliff Allison, could slaughter the Monacos. They placed 1–2 ahead of Dickson's Ecosse car at Easter Goodwood, and 1-2-3 at Oulton Park ahead of the Dickson and George Pitt Monacos. Same again at Aintree from Dickson and Naylor's now 2½-litre Ferrari-engined four-cylinder ex-Coombs car.

Pitt's Monaco was ex-Bristow. He had crashed badly into a tree first time out at Oulton Park due to the frame still being distorted after a Bristow incident. George hit a tree backwards and wrote off the chassis, later rebuilding the car totally around a new frame.

What seems to have been the first 1961 Monaco Mark III emerged at May Silverstone; Roy Salvadori in an unpainted floridly styled new car clearly aimed at the US market.

The new Mark III was based upon the 1960 Lowline F1 design, with the double-wishbone and coil-spring rear end at last supplanting the faithful old transverse leaf-spring. This move had clearly been in mind during 1960 – the first drawings for the change being prepared that season, when there was also some experimentation. The Mark III chassis frame was markedly different from the Marks I and II, with Lowline-type straight tube runs where possible replacing the original types' bends and curves.

The Bedding's new body panels featured a low sweeping nose with an attractive wide radiator intake, while the rear wings rose to flashy pointed tail fins 'to appeal to the Yanks'. . . . At Silverstone Roy split the 19s, second to Moss. Tom Dickson headed Henry Taylor's UDT 19 in fourth place, but it was running only a 1500 engine. . . .

At Crystal Palace on Whit-Monday the Lotuses appeared with new k/o wheel fixings in preparation for the Nürburgring 1000 Km, but they threw wheels and Salvadori and Blumer scored a now rare Monaco 1-2.

Ecurie Ecosse, meanwhile, had prepared their car – registered DS 288 – for Le Mans, where Dickson would co-drive with Bruce Halford. The notorious French scrutineers saw the Monaco as a two-seat racing car, a cheater rather than a 'proper' sports car. It took David Murray's special relationship with secretary Acat of the organizing club to get the car accepted; Ecosse Jaguars had won the 24-Hours twice, after all. In the race the car was running well until the evening and its 34th lap, when Halford went missing. Unsighted by rain and parallax through the tall regulation windscreen he had crashed under the Dunlop Bridge and was hurled along the road as the Monaco pounded itself into virtual scrap. A few laps later the team's second entry, a Sprite, also rolled and young Bill Mackay was more seriously hurt. Both survived.

Only three Monaco Mark IIIs appear in the Register, excluding the prototype machine, and they went to Texan Hap Sharp in June, Philadelphian Roger Penske in August and to British private entrant Peter Berry in September. This third car was originally a cancelled order, which Bruce McLaren heard about one day. The previous autumn, while Brabham and Salvadori had handled the Ecosse Monaco, he had driven a Jaguar for Briggs Cunningham in the West Coast professional races. The money was fantastic and it was all terrific fun.

Now in late 1961 Bruce was preparing to take Tommy Atkins's InterContinental Formula ex-works Lowline single-seater down-under for Tasman racing, and Climax had agreed to sell him a 2.7 FPF engine of the type developed that year for the Indianapolis project described in Chapter 21. Bruce had developed the Atkins car into the best-handling of all Coopers that season, and now he figured that a Monaco, set up the same way, with a 2.7 engine, should earn real money in America.

He couldn't finance the idea himself – being fully extended by the Tasman trip – but he sold the idea to Peter Berry, for whom he had been racing 3.8 Jaguar saloons that year. Peter gained backing from Castrol and bought the car next day. Frank Falkner fixed entries for Riverside and Laguna, and Bruce arranged to ship the precious 2.7 engine on from San Francisco to Auckland to meet his single-seater in time for the new year's New Zealand GP.

Bruce and Mike Barney completed the car at Hollyfield Road and in testing at Silverstone it lapped a second inside Moss's Lotus 19 times. Larger Aston Martin-type calipers and thicker discs were used for the first time on a Monaco,

MONACO — MIGHTY SPORTS CAR

and the engine was Jack's Indy race unit rebuilt.

But the Monaco was rigged to full Appendix 'C' spec with lights, screens, two proper seats, etc., and at Riverside Bruce and Mike discovered the Americans just didn't bother with such niceties and Tim Wall had been there a week preparing Hap Sharp's lightweight stripped Monaco for Jack Brabham to drive; using the practice 2.7 ex-Indy engine!

Bruce chose to run in full 'C'-spec just in case he should win and somebody protest. Jack stole pole on sticky wet-weather Dunlop D12 tyres; it was worth $200. Moss (Lotus 19) and Bruce both considered running D12s in the race but opted out due to 103°F ambient temperatures. Jack took the gamble in his lightweight car and won after Bruce's engine blew water on to his rear tyres in the closing laps and cost him the lead. Jack won $7000, plus bonuses, plus a Pontiac Grand Prix sedan, while Bruce was compensated in lap money for leading most of the way. At Laguna one of his 2.7's big pistons collapsed – they would prove suspect after four or five hours' running. Peter Berry then sold the car to Cunningham and the precious Indy engine sailed away to New Zealand.

Now Cunningham sent the car to Reventlow Automobiles Inc. in Venice, California, where a lightweight aluminium-block Buick V8 engine was fitted. Rodger Ward's older-model leaf-spring rear Monaco had run Buick power that season, as at Laguna, where it ran well before overheating. Reventlow's own Scarab sports car programme had investigated the Detroit V8s in everything from 3- to 4.2-litre form; the standard displacement being 215 cu. in., or 3.5 litres. A 3.8 gave 280 bhp at 6200 rpm with 250 ft/lb torque from 5000 rpm.

As delivered to RAI the ex-Berry Monaco weighed 1480 lb, with a 20-gallon left-side pannier tank and a 7-gallon tank by the driver's right knee. Bruce had retained his own special Cooper-Knight 'C5S' transaxle with Citroën-derived large-diameter sliding-spline half-shafts, and it was replaced by a standard Cooper-Knight, which RAI mated to the Buick block with a special bell-housing. The engine breathed through two Weber 45DCOE carburettors, and exhausted through 8-into-2 pipes, swept low, whereas Ward's had run high over the rear suspension.

The frame cross-member abaft the seat had to be dropped 4 in. to clear the front of the V8, while tower mounts supported it on each side. In basics the Buick was said to be 20 lb lighter than the 2.7 FPF it replaced, so it was hoped there would be no handling problems.

Cunningham's chief engineer, Alfred Momo, soon decided the Monaco was far more practicable than the Maseratis they had been running. But the Buick engine was less convincing. Soon after returning to London after the 1962 Tasman races,

Having made his initial mark in US racing with Maserati sports-racing cars, Roger Penske rubbed it in with this red-hued Monaco Mark III sponsored by Du Pont. Here he is on the infield road circuit loop at Daytona, Florida, in the Daytona 3-Hours race, 1962

Left *Aimed at the American market, the 1961 Monaco Mark III was the first production model to replace the transverse rear leaf-spring with coil-and-wishbone suspension as standard. Rear frame tubes were straighter than Mark I/II practice, drawing on 1960 Formula 1 Lowline experience. Here is Roy Salvadori, his Coombs-entered new car still unpainted, passenger seat unupholstered, at the Silverstone May Meeting, 1961. He had his hands full with BRP's similarly 2½-litre Climax FPF-powered Lotus 19s which had more sophisticated suspension and spaceframe design, and were usefully lighter*

Bruce was telephoned by Frank Falkner, saying Cunningham was flying to Monza in three days to test the latest Maserati, and a new Monaco Mark IV with a 2.8 Maserati four-cylinder engine. This was *CM/1/62* – signed-off from Hollyfield Road in January and engined at Maserati's Modena works. Bruce was due to return to Australia for a Tasman race, but Frank asked if he could test at Monza beforehand, then race one of the cars at Sebring the weekend after. . . .

By this time Jack Brabham had left Cooper to go independent and Bruce was number one, but English snow made F1 testing impossible, so with a clear conscience he accepted the Cunningham offer. At Monza he lapped the Monaco-Maserati far quicker than the company's own new *Tipo* 64, and then shared it with Roger Penske at Sebring. After brake, electrical and lighting troubles the car still finished the 12-Hours in fifth place behind three Ferraris and a Porsche – and in John Cooper's presence.

To finish so well in such company after 12 hours' racing was a fantastic result, a glowing tribute to the strength of the Owen Maddock and Jack Knight transaxle in particular. Bruce and John returned to Hollyfield Road elated, with John insisting such a car had immense potential for Le Mans and the Nürburgring 1000 Km. But old Charles was unimpressed. He was still sore at Brabham's defection, and didn't want young Bruce leading John up the garden path. As much as possible he would distance Bruce from Cooper design and policy-making, and no way would he sanction time and money for a long-distance Monaco programme. . . . 'I'm not 'avin' it!' became his new theme song, and he meant it.

Three more Monaco Mark IVs were exported to the States that year; to Van Housen Motors in April, Alan Connell in May and Roger Penske in October. The Register also lists a Mark IV bound for Jack Hinkle in November, but this was actually the second of the 1963 'T61M' models; the old Roman numeral system being dropped at this time.

During 1962, Penske defended the SCCA Championship, which he had won with his *Tipo* 61 'Birdcage' Maserati and Monaco the previous year. He was second in professional races at Bossier City to Dan Gurney, and in the Player '200' at Mosport Park, Canada, where Masten Gregory won in a UDT Lotus 19. Penske also won amateur SCCA races in his $2\frac{1}{2}$ Monaco-Climax at Marlboro, Danville, Cumberland and Lime Rock. Alan Connell's similar pointed-tail-fin car ran at Mosport, where USAC track star Rodger Ward drove the Monaco-Buick. In September the Canadian GP was run for sports cars back at Mosport and Gregory won again for UDT Lotus. Gurney put the Arciero Bros 19 on pole and Penske was second quickest in his Monaco, now with one of the ex-Indy 2.7s installed. After running well it succumbed to its characteristic piston ring land breakage. Jack Brabham drove a little Lotus 23 with a 1500 Holbay-Ford engine in this race, and won the 2-litre class. McLaren's new Monaco-Climax was not finished in time to take part.

That same day, at Watkins Glen, Cunningham's pointed-tail-fin Monacos placed 1-5 in the annual sports car classic; Walt Hansgen's with a '4-litre' Buick V8, and Augie Pabst's, the ex-Sebring car, with a 2.8 Maserati engine. Hap Sharp's Monaco-Climax 2.5 was second, but was lapped by Hansgen as he and Pabst both spun repeatedly on the slick surface.

In Britain only the Guards Trophy race at Brands Hatch on a wet August Monday catered for international sports racing cars. Penske was invited over with his bright-red Monaco and he finished fifth behind Mike Parkes's dominant works-loaned Ferrari Dino SP. Jimmy Blumer's Monaco ran hard on Penske's tail before retirement. He had considerable club race success with this car.

Meanwhile Bruce's prototype T61M Monaco for the 1962 US series was approaching completion at Hollyfield Road. The new model used the 1962 F1 car's suspension in a modestly revised tubular sports chassis, with a new 2.7-litre engine installed at a 30-degree inclination to the right and driving through a $7\frac{1}{4}$ in. twin-plate clutch to a 1960-type 'C5S' five-speed Cooper-Knight transaxle. Pannier fuel tanks amidships contained a total 28 gallons and Owen had restyled the bodywork considerably, the voluptuously curvaceous new panels giving the car a broader, lower and more handsome appearance than hitherto. The panels were all-aluminium, formed by the Beddings, and all-detachable by Dzus fasteners. The prototype car for Bruce to drive in the Fall West Coast professional races had abrupt elbows on the rear of the front fenders, leaving a channel between fender and screen which was intended to allow direct airflow over the broad, flat nose to pass through to the intakes abaft the cockpit. I thought this looked terrific, especially in profile, a handsomely aggressive car with praying mantis wings, ready to pounce. After initial shake-down tests at Goodwood John thought otherwise, as Eddie Stait recalled: 'I think somebody like Ken Tyrrell saw the car and said "Huh, you'll never sell it with wings like that!". John was always very sensitive to that type of criticism and so the chopped-off styling remained unique to that car, and the others we made subsequently had smoothly blended-in wings in the traditional style. . . .

The T61M Monaco ran on GP-sized Cooper cast magnesium wheels with 5.00-15 front and 6.50-15 rear tyres, and the 7 ft 7 in. wheelbase was also identical to the current V8 F1 car. Tracks front and rear were 4 ft 7 in., overall length to the rounded-edge Kamm-type tail 12 ft 1 in. and overall height only 2 ft $7\frac{1}{2}$ in., there being a hefty roll-over frame running full width beneath the body lip behind the cockpit. The 2.7 Climax engine – which Lee and Hassan had now rather reluctantly put into modest production for sports and Tasman racing – was said to deliver 250 bhp at 6200 rpm, while the T61M's capacious engine bay was tailored to allow easy installation of alternative American V8 power units.

Bruce was worried that the roomy body would prove too big and heavy in US competition, and he was right. Roger

Bruce McLaren's prototype T61M for the 1962 US West Coast professional series races, photographed stripped on the Hollyfield forecourt one dreary autumn day, 1962, mated that year's F1-type suspension with revised frame, accommodating canted 2.7 Indy FPF and 'C5S' transaxle. Again radiator is ducted with a flat oil tank wrapped above ducting, but there are now large long-range fuel tanks bungee'd either side. On initial testing at Goodwood the car showed-off its notch-wing body styling, idea being to allow clean airflow over nose, through valleys between wing and windscreen, and past either side of cockpit into the engine bay intakes on rear wing leading edge. Colour was Cooper's standard dark BRG with white stripes and roundels, natural cast-mag wheels

Penske was set to scoop the money on the West Coast with a startling new Cooper special.

He had studied the regulations closely and set out to stretch them tight. At the US GP at Watkins Glen in 1961, Walt Hansgen had crashed Cunningham's production T53 F1 car very heavily. It was chassis F1/16/61, and Penske bought it on the spot and added the ex-Indy 2.7 engine from Jack. That winter at Newtown Square, Pennsylvania, Roger's mechanic, Roy Gaine, straightened the bent F1 frame, added body outriggers and laid it out as a central-seat sports racing car. Wheel-enveloping bodywork was added by Bob Webb and Harry Tidmarsh's Molin Body Shop up the road in Wayne, Pa. Molin is still there as I write and still has an outstanding reputation. A light passenger seat was slung in the outrigger frame beside the driver's and with the 2.7 FPF astern the result was light, potent and aerodynamically highly penetrative.

Penske had been sponsored by DuPont chemicals for some

Penske's historic Zerex Duralite Spl *sports-racing car began life as a Cunningham Team production Formula 1 'Lowline'. Here at Riverside before the* LA Times GP *which it won, 14 October, 1962, the car's single-seat Cooper origins lay revealed. Note welded-on additional body mounts, regulation 'audible warning of approach' (bulb-horn), fuel tank on left in this view and regulation passenger seat outrigged to right. Penske himself (in overalls and driving shoes) stands at right*

Bruce McLaren bought the Zerex for 1964 and after winning twice with 2.7 Climax power had the chassis centre-section completely rebuilt to restore rigidity. With a 3.5 Oldsmobile F85 V8 fitted Bruce took the car to the Players '200' at Mosport Canada in June, and won. Here he is enjoying his victory lap

time, under their *Telar* anti-freeze brand name. Now the quasi-Cooper rule-bender for Riverside emerged resplendent in Penske red livery, as the *Zerex Special*, another DuPont brand name.

News of the car leaked to the American press, and before arrival for Riverside practice it was already dubbed the 'FUBAR' – 'Fouled-Up Beyond All Recognition'. Its exquisite finish proved that was a lie and after edging Bruce's new works T61M off pole position in practice Penske romped away to a superb win. Bruce could only finish fourth, Connell's Monaco-Climax 2.5 was 17th and one George Grinzewitsch 18th in a 2-litre version; the ninth 2-litre home.

The 1100 lb *Zerex Special* won its creator $8350 plus a $4000 Pontiac Grand Prix, and its sponsor reaped huge publicity dividends. The McLaren Cooper was hastily stripped of non-essentials by Mike Barney for Laguna Seca the following weekend where Hansgen, Connell and Graham Hill also drove Monacos. Penske took pole again for the two-heat race. Gurney's Lotus won Heat One from Roger after Bruce spun early on, finishing third with a broken clutch. In Heat Two he started clutchless from the back of the grid and finished fourth while Gurney retired, Lloyd Ruby's Lotus won the heat and Penske was second again to take the money on aggregate. Walt Hansgen's Monaco-Buick was third in Heat Two after overheating blew out a core plug in the earlier race. On aggregate Bruce was placed third overall.

Penske's 'Updraught Enterprises' team pocketed another $8000 to add to the $700 he'd won gambling at Las Vegas between races. He couldn't lose that October....

On 11 November the *Zerex* completed its hat-trick of wins at Puerto Rico's Antilles circuit, Penske beating young Timmy Mayer, who had just bought Roger's old Monaco-Climax, with Sharp's Monaco fourth. Timmy then won the day's FJ race in his Cooper-BMC; he was a Corporal in the US Army at the time, based in Puerto Rico teaching English.

Then a storm broke. The US Professional race series had employed its own version of FIA Appendix 'C' regs, loosely applied, but even they stated that at least two seats of equal dimensions should be fitted, located on either side of the longitudinal axis. The *Zerex* didn't comply, but nobody had

224

protested, and during construction Penske had carefully consulted the authorities. But now several visiting entrants had made it clear they wouldn't bother to return if such cars were again allowed to start. In Paris the CSI now enquired how 'a car not conforming to Appendix "C" has been allowed to compete in an International race for sports cars?'. In early December the 'FUBAR' was banned.

Penske was prepared, as always, and had bought the McLaren T61M. He raced it in John Mecom Racing Team light metallic-blue livery at Nassau, but hit trouble while Sharp won the Governor's Trophy for the marque. The T61M ran a new nose section with smooth fenders in the main event, but died again with ignition and gearbox problems after lying 2nd behind Ireland's Lotus 19. Sharp was 3rd.

Meanwhile, in Australia, Bib Stilwell had been winning with his 1959-series Monaco. He had discovered it laid-up at Hollyfield Road during a visit in mid-1961. It was reputedly ex-Moss – therefore, if this was true, the Keele car – and he bought it on the spot. It ran a 2.5 FPF and Cooper-Knight gearbox and won most times, although Frank Matich's Lotus 15 and later Type 19 would have Stilwell's measure. For the 1963 Australian TT the Monaco used a 2.7 FPF and was timed at 160 mph at Longford.

In the UK, indefatigable club driver Chris Summers fitted the 4½-litre Chevrolet V8 from his *Libre*-racing ex-F2 Cooper into a Monaco – according to George Pitt, his 'ex-Bristow' car. Jackie Epstein/Bill Wilks also ran an ancient Monaco in 1963, and tackled the mighty Targa Florio with it. . . .

Across the Atlantic, on 3 February, the new USRRC season commenced with Jim Hall – Texan constructor of Chaparral cars – winning at Daytona in his white-painted T61M from three Porsches, a Dino and Corporal Timmy Mayer's ex-Penske Monaco-Climax.

At Chessington, Tommy Atkins had a new T61M built-up by Harry Pearce with 2.7 FPF power for Roy Salvadori to drive. This pale metallic-green-and-white car became virtually unbeatable, and humbled even the Lotus 19s as at May Silverstone, where Innes Ireland drove his heart out for UDT but had to be content with second place as Roy won at record speed. Summers's V8 rumbler was seventh.

Later in the year, Dan Gurney drove Mayer's 2.7 Monaco into third at the Player's '200' in Canada, while Roger Penske had sold his cars to Texan oil millionaire John Mecom Jr. The now pale-blue-and-white *Zerex Special* had been rebuilt with proper side-by-side seating, its main-frame longerons cut and curved wide apart, and its torsional rigidity 'low', and Roger was fourth in both heats and on aggregate at Mosport – reputedly on 2.5 FPF power as the 2.7 had blown up in a USRRC round at Pensacola, after Hap Sharp had relieved Penske at the wheel. Mayer was fourth there, and he led the Championship. . . . Later in June, Penske was running away with the Elkhart Lake race only for another 2.7 failure.

At Reims a sports car race over 25 laps supported the French GP. Salvadori fought wheel-to-wheel with a Ferrari *Testa Rossa* in Atkins's Monaco until his stretch FPF, perhaps predictably, lunched a piston. Victory was Roy's at the British GP meeting, with Summers fourth, and on August Monday at Brands Hatch US support included Penske's remodelled *Zerex*, which led from start to finish. Roy's T61M and Tim Mayer's visiting tail-finned Mark III were second and third for a surprise 'Cooper' 1-2-3 – just like old times! Roy set fastest lap, at 91.73 mph for the twisty 2.65-mile circuit – a good impression of the Monaco's potential at that time.

Meanwhile, Ecurie Ecosse had continued to run their venerable Mark II car with Bruce Halford, Tommy Dickson, Jimmy Blumer and a youngster named John Young Stewart at the wheel. They notched some success, particularly with Stewart, in minor events. At the time of its Le Mans mangling, Stan Sproat had left the team for a year: 'Then David Murray telephoned me and asked me to come back, for a major increase in money! I found the Monaco still being straightened out in Merchiston Motors, but it never was done properly and it always had one wheel higher than the others.' He was building rear-engined Tojeiro-Climax coupés for the team's 1962 Le Mans effort, and took time to hack the back off the Monaco frame and replace its leaf-spring with a coil-and-wishbone system. 'Then Jackie Stewart came along and drove it very well indeed, considering . . . all the wishbones were far too short and the wheel arcs of movement had to be seen to be believed. Then at Oulton Park – Spring meeting 1964 – 'he hit a tree, and we scrapped the car and used the salvage to build the Ecosse-Climax single-seat *Libre* car around the engine and gearbox. I tested the old Monaco occasionally, and it was terribly cramped; the suspension bent back and folding-up the chassis at Oulton Park was a good enough excuse to get rid of it. . . .'

Jimmy Blumer had been invited to drive the Ecurie Ecosse car after regularly beating Tommy Dickson in his own Monaco before selling it: 'That Ecosse car was the worst Monaco I ever drove, I'm not surprised you have heard its frame was twisted – mind you, I believe they *all* were as standard when they left the works – but the Ecosse car really was awful, a terrible thing to drive. You could tell just how good Jackie Stewart would be when he was so successful with it. . . .'

Late in September 1963 the Canadian GP saw no Monacos entered, but at that time, at Carroll Shelby's works, the former RAI establishment in Venice, California, the 'King Cobra' Cooper Monaco-Fords had recently been completed.

Shelby's Cobra road and race cars were running well and he wanted a tilt at the West Coast races, using a V8 Ford race engine in a genuine sports-racing chassis. His people believed there was no margin left in the spidery Lotus 19 frame, and no time to build their own, so it would have to be a Cooper Monaco. 'Ole Shel' called John Cooper and two rolling chassis were rapidly supplied, tailored for Ford V8 block and Colotti gearbox. They seem to have been frames *CM/1* and *CM/3/63*, obviously all coil-and-wishbone suspended, and were stripped to bare frame and totally rewelded on arrival. Special over-sized radiators were rigged, and 289 cu. in. – 4.7-litre – Ford V8 engines were race-prepared for them by Phil Remington's crew. Shelby and his collaborators, Al Dowd and Pete Brock, were more anxious about making the races than the niceties of finish, and with vertical stack-pipes poking through rough-cut slots on the rear deck the unpainted first car was tested briefly at Riverside by team driver Dave MacDonald. He got round in 1:34, the fastest-ever Riverside lap at that time.

The two new Monaco-Fords were ready and running at Kent, Washington, on 29 September, driven by MacDonald and his senior, Bob Holbert, but both overheated in the race after Holbert shattered the lap record in practice. The cars were too new to be reliable, but Shelby's men were dismayed by the winner – Lloyd Ruby in J. Frank Harrison's Lotus 19 . . . with a Ford V8 engine. Chapman's charger *was* strong enough after all. . . .

The *Los Angeles Times GP* at Riverside was the richest race of the series and the MacDonald and Holbert cars appeared painted kingfisher blue and titled 'King Cobras' for the first time. Jim Hall's Chaparral caught fire early on, and MacDonald just powered away from the rest to win by a lap from Penske. Holbert's car overheated again, blowing a head gasket.

At Laguna it was Holbert's turn to shine in practice while MacDonald broke his engine and later went off the road before qualifying. Holbert led away, leaving Jimmy Clark's Lotus 19 floundering in his wake, only to squash his car's nose on a back-marker. He re-inherited the lead after a stop to open the nose aperture, but overheating claimed him again, and MacDonald stormed through to win. The project really was paying off rather well. . . .

A total Shelby-Cobra débâcle followed at Nassau, where the Monaco-based cars retired and the roadsters were well blown-off. Penske's reportedly brand-new *Zerex Special* was a Monaco with a Chevrolet V8 installed, and it led the Nassau Trophy before terminal overheating when a radiator hose pulled off. He also raced the old, born-again, FUBAR 2.7 FPF in its legalized form. Skip Hudson ran a Monaco-Chevvy, MacDonald a King Cobra and Bob Holbert took over Ray Heppenstall's Monaco-Ford V8.

Into 1964 Shelby American built its Daytona Coupés aimed at the World GT Championship, and the sports-racing Cooper-Fords took a back seat while Ford product identification concentrated the bucks and brains elsewhere. Still Shelby had ambitions on the USRRC title for 1964 and in that competition a full Group 7 car like the King Cobra was necessary as the opposition could clamber all over an ordinary Cobra roadster.

Cobra historians Dave Friedman and John Christy describe the cars as 'probably one of the least expensive World class racing cars ever built – you probably could have had a duplicate, less engine, for around $8000 . . . about 12 big ones would have put you in the racing business, with a chance, if you had the will and the skill, to make it back in less than a season. Little wonder that when the 1964 season opened there were so many Cooper copies some SCCA National events had to hold consolation races. . . .

Right *Ready to strike – Dave MacDonald testing the prototype 4.7-litre Ford V8-engined Monaco 'King Cobra' (number 98) at Riverside, 1963, when he set fastest lap-time yet. Extra nose ducts help dissipate heat from the 4.7-sized radiator, makeshift stub exhausts project through rear deck slots and the carburettor ram pipes inspire through deck-centre cut-out. Rear-brake cooling ducts are trunked onto the tail top. In second shot No 97 is Ed Leslie's special Pete Brock-styled Lang Cooper leading Bob Bondurant's Shelby King Cobra and Jerry Grant's Lotus-Chevrolet 19 at Laguna Seca, 18 October, 1964. Penske won the Monterey GP for Chaparral from Gurney's Ford V8-engined Lotus 19, but Bondurant salvaged third for Shelby, Leslie fifth behind a Lotus 30. King Cobra's reign was brief, but memorable*

Left *King-maker – Jackie Stewart's performance in the Ecurie Ecosse Monaco, 1963, led to Goodwood track manager Robin McKay recommending the young Clydesider to Ken Tyrrell for '64 Formula 3. Considering how the Le Mans-damaged Monaco Mark II was always reckoned to be a pig to handle thereafter Stewart's performances were little short of staggering. Here he is breaking the Charterhall lap record in a Scottish borders club meeting, 29 September, 1963 . . . despite the car's strong smell of pork. Jackie eventually totalled it against a tree at Oulton Park, early 1964, and surviving parts were robbed to form the Ecosse-Climax single-seat* Formule Libre *special*

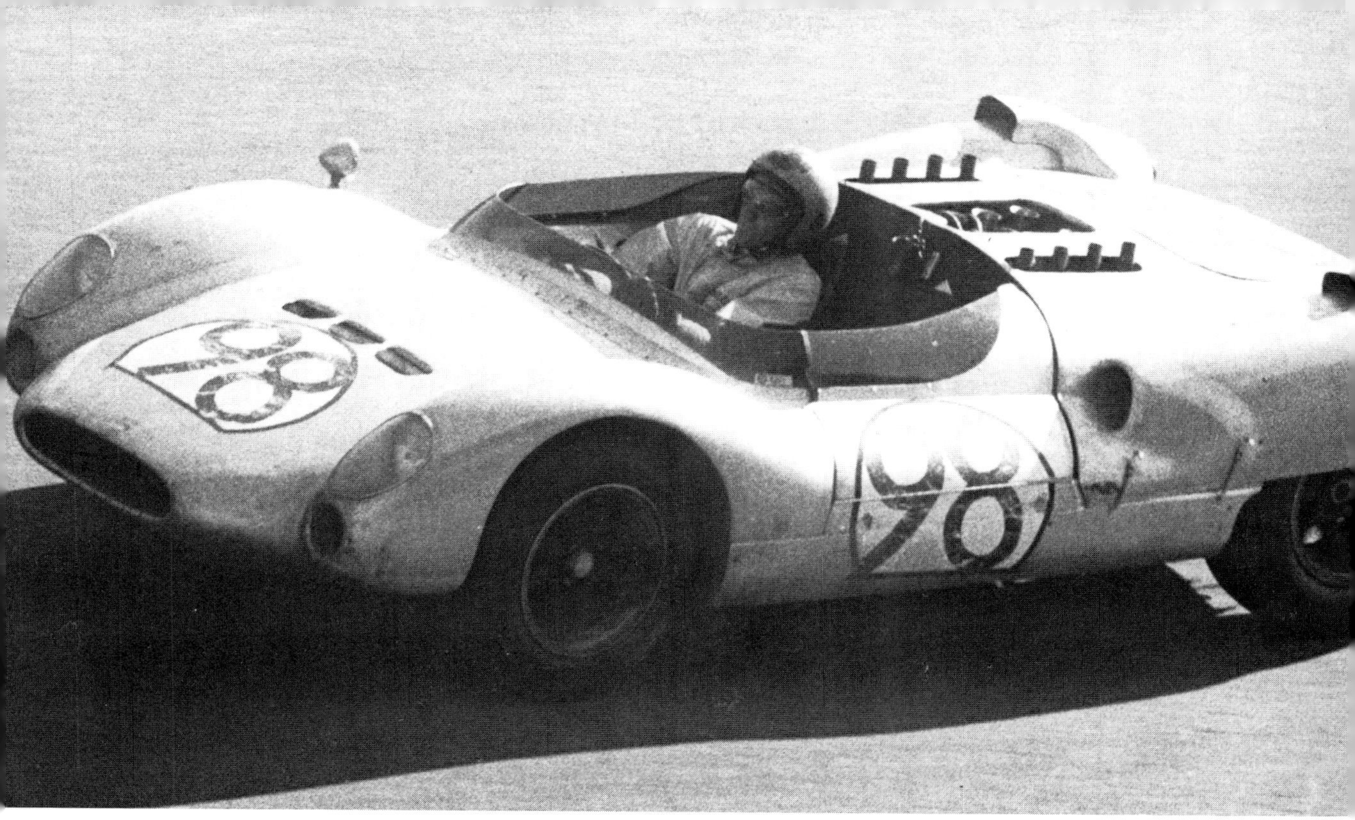

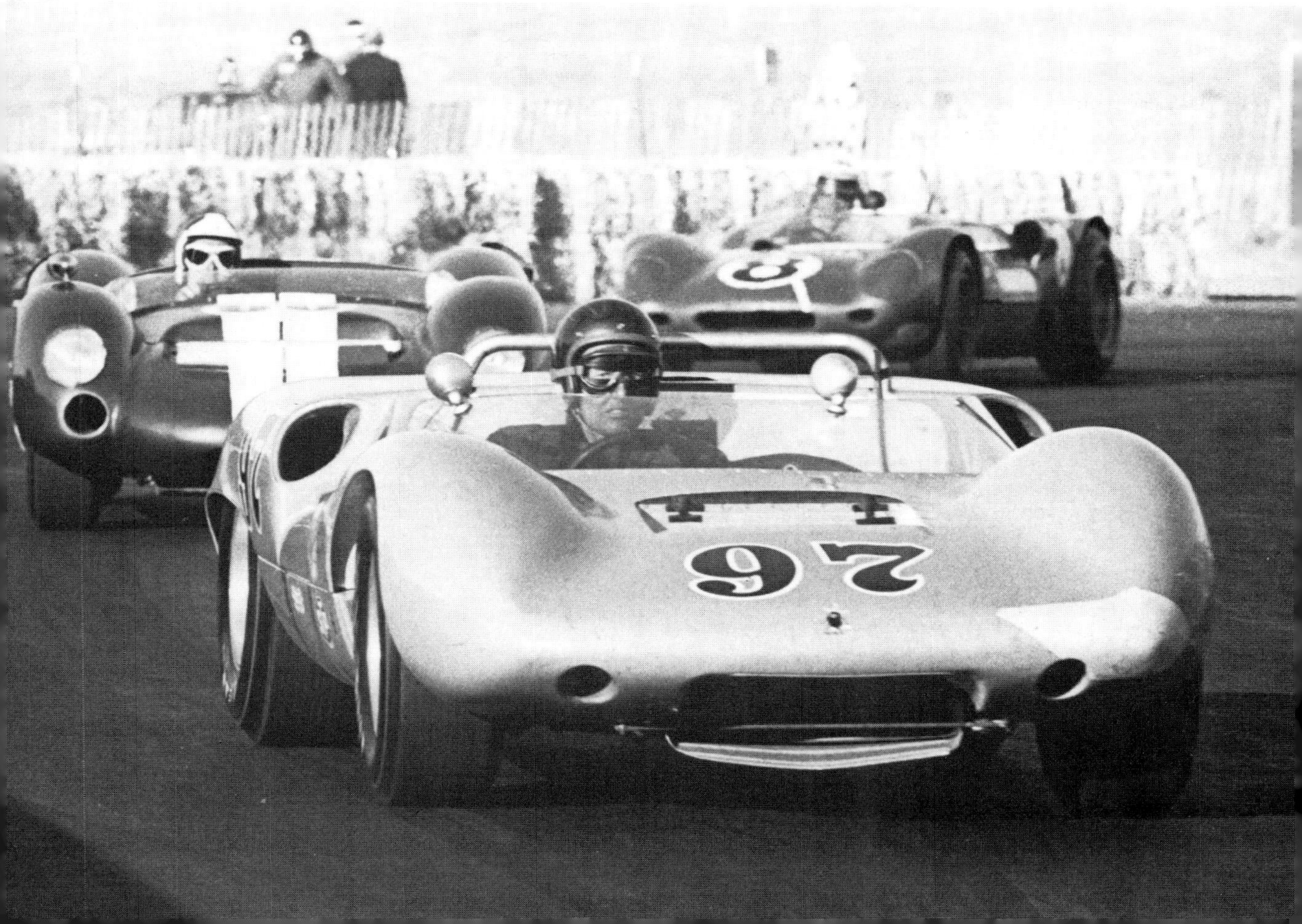

The 1964 works King Cobra season began at Kent, a few days prior to the Indy '500', where Dave MacDonald had been invited to drive for Mickey Thompson's team. Meanwhile a customer car had been completed at Venice for Craig Lang of the Olympia Brewery family from Seattle, a friend of Shelby and Dowd. MacDonald raced it at Phoenix, Riverside and Laguna early in the year, and then Holbert took it out in practice at Kent, but he lost control and totalled the car against others parked in the unguarded pit lane, and burned himself painfully. MacDonald took over Holbert's originally assigned works car and won on race day, then left for Indy, where he was killed. Holbert retired from racing forthwith.

At the Mosport Player '200' Bruce McLaren's re-engined ex-*Zerex Special* Jolly Green Giant (see shortly) won with Oldsmobile V8 power. Third behind him in one heat, second in the other, was Augie Pabst – the Milwaukee brewery heir – who had taken over Ken Miles's non-qualifying Shelby King Cobra after his own listed Mecom Lola-Chev had blown its engine in practice. Canadian Ludwig Heimrath's Comstock Racing Team Monaco-Ford from Toronto was fourth.

At Lexington, Ohio, the Chaparrals of Hap Sharp and Jim Hall were 1-2 from George Wintersteen's Monaco-Chevy and Miles's Shelby King-Cobra. Back at Mosport in September for the Canadian GP Heimrath was sixth in his Comstock Ford V8-engined car, while Wintersteen and Hudson represented the Cooper-Chevy flotilla.

Shorn of their name drivers, the King Cobras had raced relatively quietly until that Fall and the West Coast series, for which three Monacos were ordered and prepared with test-driving assistance from Richie Ginther. Indy star Rufus 'Parnelli' Jones led the team with Bob Bondurant, Ronnie Bucknum and Ginther, while a new Lang Cooper, which wore a sleek aerodynamic Pete Brock-designed bodyshell – emerged for Ed Leslie. At Riverside the fleet finished 1-4-5-7 in the order Jones, Leslie, Bondurant, Ginther, while Bucknum's engine failed.

The team reappeared at Laguna Seca, less Ginther after a difference of opinion. Penske was driving a monocoque Chaparral and he won from Gurney's Lotus-Ford 19B, with Bondurant third in the King Cobra. Bucknum was fourth on aggregate and Leslie seventh, but Parnelli Jones had an early spin on spilled oil, and later crashed heavily and had to watch his car burn luridly, for hours.

Thereafter Shelby's interest and effort was elsewhere in Ford's GT programme, and the now Guardsman-blue King Cobras lay fallow through 1965, although Charlie Hayes raced the Lang Cooper in USRRC before Craig Lang sold it to Skip Scott's Essex Wire Racing Team. It was no longer near-competitive with the monocoque, alloy-engined Lolas, Chaparrals and Bruce McLaren's new CanAm cars, Chevrolet were on the charge, and the old Ford-powered car was soon set aside.

Late that year Shelby's famous garage sale saw two of the three surviving Kings offered for $3000 apiece as assembled rolling chassis sans engine and gearbox, and the third disassembled for $2500. Their used four-speed Colotti 'boxes were priced at $800 each and a newer unused five-speeder at $1800 – and away they went into bush-league obscurity. . . .

German immigrant mechanic Lothar Motschenbacher bought the Jones Riverside-winning car and was fifth in it at Mt. Tremblant, Canada, on 19 September. Former Monaco-Chevy man George Wintersteen had upgraded to one of the first production McLaren-Chevs. In the Canadian GP, Motschenbacher was sixth, a Monaco-Chevy running there for a driver named Evenden. Way down amidst the field that day was a Hungarian immigrant named George Fejer, driving a Merlyn-Chevrolet. He would later build competition cars under the name Chinook, and in four years' time would buy all that remained of the defunct Cooper Car Company racing team's hardware, jigs and drawings. . . .

Meanwhile the legalized *Zerex Special* had been set aside after Nassau 1963 and sat under dust sheets in a corner of the Mecom workshops. They had a 3.5-litre aluminium Oldsmobile F85 V8 engine sitting beside it in a crate waiting to be fitted. By this time Bruce McLaren Motor Racing Ltd had been formed, with Bruce in partnership with Timmy Mayer's brother Teddy, to run a pair of special Tasman Formula Coopers in January–March 1964. With Bruce's mechanic, Wally Willmott, and Timmy's mechanic, Tyler Alexander, plans had been laid to build a *Zerex*-type sports car for 1964 to use up the stock of otherwise redundant 2.5–2.7 FPF engines, which would remain from the Tasman tour. A prototype tube frame had been built, and Bruce was convinced a reliable lightweight car with Climax power could still be a winner. Teddy and Tyler had seen the American big-gun V8s at Nassau and were not so sure.

Bruce was eventually persuaded to buy the redundant *Zerex Special* plus spare Oldsmobile engine from Mecom. It arrived in the UK in April 1964, just three days before the Oulton Park spring meeting. Wally and Tyler hurriedly fitted the regulation luggage boot and spare wheel, and the car made the race, using the 2.7 FPF engine, but lost its oil pressure. At the Aintree '200' it was right, and Bruce beat Jimmy Clark's brand-new Lotus-Ford V8 Type 30. At May Silverstone he beat another V8 car, this time Roy Salvadori's latest Tommy Atkins Monaco, packing nothing less than a 5-litre four-cam Maserati unit. . . .

This Atkins car was the ultimate Cooper Monaco. It had a tube frame reinforced with stressed 20-gauge steel sheet undertray riveted and welded in place. Its independent coil-and-wishbone suspension followed contemporary F1 practice save for outboard rather than inboard front coil/damper mounts. The Maserati V8 engine had bore and stroke of 94 × 89 mm, displacing 4941 cc, and produced around 430 bhp at 7000 rpm. It was a mighty lump and drove through a hefty Colotti Type 37 gearbox with Mercedes SL-derived half-shafts. A giant radiator resided in the nose, ahead of the regulation useable-size spare wheel, which necessitated a 3 in. higher-than-normal profile humped into the nose body panelling. The car made its race debut unpainted at Silverstone, and soon after won its first race at Whitsun Goodwood.

It was a disappointing car to Roy: 'Maserati claimed so many horsepower, and Climax were keen to see it on their test-bed and they found considerably less horsepower and valve-bounce at 6000 rpm. There was little power below four-three/four-four so we were operating on a rev band of about 1600 rpm. This made if a difficult car to drive, especially in the UK, where we wanted to compete. It would have been better on fast circuits, but we had to be so careful off the line; it would just eat gearboxes. I guess we'd have regretted it if we hadn't tried it, but the combination really was no good. And with that narrow power band it was lethal in the wet – when the power came in it just took over. In fact I had two mag switches, and I'd turn one off in the wet to slash the power output, and that helped enormously to keep it under control!' Tommy Atkins' health was failing. This was his last racing car. Convinced he had cancer, he chose his own way out, in December, 1965.

Meanwhile, the day after the Silverstone win, the McLaren car was stripped and its centre-section scrapped in Bruce's tiny workshop in New Malden. Penske's conversion to side-by-side seats had necessitated cutting clean through the original F1 car's main tubes and inserting curved piping 'which would have delighted a master plumber'. The frame thereafter had 'the torsional rigidity of a wet bus ticket'. Now a new McLaren-designed centre frame was welded-in, using main longerons as oil and water pipes like the recent Cooper single-seaters and the Atkins Monaco. The Oldsmobile V8 was dropped into the frame, mated to an old Colotti Type 21 five-speed gearbox from Bruce's Tasman car. There was no time to make up proper exhaust manifolding, so eight stub exhausts projected through the tail deck.

The frame was completed on a Sunday morning and Bruce's secretary Eoin Young was despatched to buy some paint. All he could find was 'garden gate green' – an 'appalling' shade – and in his excellent memorial book to Bruce he related how the car had three names; 'The Jolly Green Giant', the 'Zerex Special' or – to smooth matters with Charles Cooper – the 'Cooper-Oldsmobile'.

It was flown to Canada, where Bruce immediately won the June Player '200' at Mosport Park, then back at Brands Hatch on August Monday it won again, Salvadori running second until a rear upright broke. Roy then retired from race driving. By that time Bruce's tiny new team was housed in Belvedere Works, behind the new Feltham shopping centre, and the first spaceframe McLaren-Oldsmobile sports-racing car was being laid down, based along 'Jolly Green Giant' lines, and the old *Zerex* was at last retired.

Salvo's last season – Roy on the grid, Silverstone May meeting, 1964, in Tommy Atkins' giant 5-litre Monaco-Maserati V8 special, brand-new, still unpainted. The vented bulge on nose-top housed the regulation usable size spare wheel, while the Italian 5-litre 4-cam V8 engine's intake trumpets reside under mesh bubble on rear deck. The owner stands beyond in rally jacket, sharing a joke with Keith Greene of Armstrong dampers, in the holey cardigan. A. F. Rivers-Fletcher, Sir Alfred Owen's PA at BRM, strolls by in the wellies. This ultimate Monaco is preserved today in Germany in the collection of Peter Kaus

Into 1965 the new generation of Group 7 sports-racing cars really took hold in the UK as much as in their American birthplace, and the new monocoque-chassis Lola T70s and production tube-frame McLarens, all with 'big-banger' American V8 engines, reigned supreme. Back in 1961–62 Cooper had a real foothold in the American market but had failed to capitalize upon it. Eddie Stait recalls one visit by Masten Gregory to Hollyfield Road, when they sat with Charles Cooper in the Royal Oak pub just round the corner and discussed racing as a business: 'Masten I remember spelled out the importance of the American market and really emphasized to the Old Man just what potential lay there, but Charlie dismissed it. In retrospect perhaps that's the moment when we really missed the boat....'

Eddie was also impressed on that visit by Masten's apparently part Red Indian girlfriend: 'She disappeared while we were chatting and when Charles went back to his office he opened the door and there she was upside down in the corner humming to herself in some sort of Yoga or meditation posture. Old Charlie didn't really know how he should react in such a situation so he just closed the door and didn't go back into his office until she eventually emerged. Ever after he connected Masten Gregory with rather strange young ladies....'

Irrespective, Masten had been right, and by the end of 1964 the days of the Cooper Monaco family were over, Cooper dropped out of the sports car market, and the progenitor of the successful rear-engined production sports racing car was no more.

CHAPTER TWENTY ONE

1961 – The Indy project

It had begun at Sebring in 1959 when Jack Brabham clinched Cooper's first World title. USAC track driver Rodger Ward was all set to blow off the visiting cars with his Offenhauser-powered dirt track midget racer. Before practice began he had told the Cooper boys how they were wasting their time. He was sure the midget's cornering power would more than compensate for the F1 machinery's extra power on the straight. Next day he, Jack and Bruce all arrived together at the first corner, and he was sorely disabused of the idea as they streaked away from him through it and the midget slewed spectacularly, but relatively slowly, in their dust. . . .

To his credit, he took it well, and said the experience really opened his eyes to the way Formula 1 cars could corner. What's more, he thought such a car could set Indianapolis alight.

The annual Indianapolis 500-Miles track classic was the world's richest motor race. Rodger Ward worked on John Cooper throughout the Sebring meeting and his enthusiasm was sparked, while Jack Brabham's eyes gleamed at the prospect of Indy-size prize money. Dr. Frank Falkner was there, and he set about organizing an Indy trip for the team. Late the following year, in October 1960, the Cooper boys returned to the USA to race at Watkins Glen and Riverside. One Lowline was despatched first to Indianapolis for Jack to try his hand on those hallowed brick setts.

He flew in direct from his Bathurst victory in Australia, and Rodger Ward met him and took him straight to the Speedway, where John Cooper and Noddy Grohmann were ready with the car in Formula 1 form. Ward drove Jack round, showing him the accepted racing line through the four near-identical banked turns; the line all Indy racers aspired to in their heavy 4.2-litre Offy-engined Roadsters. USAC Competitions Director Henry Banks insisted Jack complete the usual driver's test for Indy newcomers. Jim O'Connor and John Gullery from Dunlop's Buffalo base had the car ready on standard R9 and R10 racing tyres, and Noddy had fitted a 3.3:1 final-drive. Jack took out the car to warm it up and on his second lap averaged 128 mph.

The officials were shocked. Indy Chief Steward Harlan Fengler flagged him in and in Jack's words: 'Gave me a hell of a rocket – after that I had to judge my speed by my revs – but going around at 125 mph was unbelievably slow. . . .'

The trouble was that the normal Rookie test began with a '115 mph acclimatization phase'. Jack dutifully covered eight laps around that mark; Fengler allowed him to skip the 120 mph phase, then followed 10 more around 125 mph. With carefree precision the green Cooper – itself an anachronism at superstitious Indy, where anything green had been taboo for years – covered another 10 laps at up to 135 mph while officialdom allowed Jack to skip the 130 mph section. As rain began to fall Jack stopped, and everyone crossed the street for lunch at the Holiday Motel.

That afternoon, word had got round and several Indy regulars emerged to watch this strange green 'bug' drone round their Speedway; going so fast, with so little drama. Jack covered 16 more laps, stopping only for tyre changes. Clay Smith – Indy Qualifications Timer – was stunned when the Australian slammed in three straight laps spot-on 142.857 mph, according to his apparatus. He then added two more at 143 mph before stopping for the day. Pole for that year's '500' had fallen at only 146 mph. . . . This was sensational.

Jack couldn't understand all the fuss, the course had only four left-hand corners, and he'd seen only 6400 rpm before the shut-off point at the end of each straightaway. Next day, with a lower 3.45:1 back axle, he'd go faster . . . and he did.

His engine was peaking at 6800 rpm on the back straightaway. He averaged 125 mph from a standing start and ran 11 laps with a best of 143.6 mph. He wanted more speed through the turns. John and Noddy fiddled the car's roll-centre through midday with little effect, while Jack chatted to Rodger Ward and was introduced to a stream of Indy personalities attracted to the Speedway like moths to a flame. Drivers present included A. J. Foyt, Tony Bettenhausen, Duane Carter, Paul Russo, Gene Hartley and Eddie Johnson. Jack obliged by lapping easily around 143 mph, then banging-in three final laps at 144.3, 144.6 and 144.834 mph. That would have put his 2½-litre car on to eighth place in the 33-strong grid for that season's '500'. Of the drivers watching, only Ward and Bettenhausen had ever lapped faster – and it was 'their' track.

Through the quarter-mile-long first turn Jack had equalled Johnny Thompson's official Roadster record of 6.5 sec, set during the 1958 '500', although it had since been lowered

230

1961 – THE INDY PROJECT

Outside the Langley Road works, next door to the church, John and Charles Cooper look on while Jack Brabham tries the newly-completed Indianapolis Cooper-Climax for the benefit of the press. Inside the works keen amateur photographer Noddy Grohmann, in typical British works mechanic overalls, winds on his Leica. These two shots show USAC regulation seat harness, roll-over and nerf bars – all strange items at that time to British eyes – twin fuel fillers, suspension offset to set the chassis to the inside of the left-turn only corners, and specially-made Dunlop 16-in. wheels, on three-eared knock-off cap hubs, though special-tread tyres are not ready yet. The car used a 2-speed version of the 'C5S' gearbox, for which Jack Knight had cut special new step-up gears.

during Firestone tyre testing. Times were also taken on a short marked stretch from the exit of Turn Four to the finish line. Here the Cooper took 11.7 sec, almost 2 sec slower than a self-respecting Offy Roadster. The little European car was clearly cornering as fast as only the very best, but ran out of steam away from the Turns. With more power from an enlarged engine, a 950 lb car like the Cooper could close the power-to-weight ratio with a 4.2-litre 1700 lb Roadster.

Two Indy regulars watched; one complacent: 'If they go another five miles an hour faster,' he said, 'they're gonna be in trouble.' His friend grunted: 'Listen buddy, if they go another five miles an hour faster, there are gonna be *a lot* of people in trouble....'

The ripples of Brabham's October runs washed icily through the conservative Indy establishment, but the team was elated by its friendly reception. Their F1 engine burned AvGas at the rate of 12 mpg against the Offy's usual 2-3 mpg on alcohol. There was a tyre problem. Dunlop's road-racing tyres were inadequate at the Speedway due to their relatively soft compound and flexible casing, which allowed the right-front to wear out in as few as 12–20 laps. This would mean a minimum 10 tyre stops in a 200-lap 500-miler.... To com-

231

At the Speedway the right-side filler has been removed and body orifice covered assymmetric-tread Dunlops have been fitted and a tall deflector pane fitted to the raised cockpit coaming within the wrap-round windscreen. With Jack by car are John Cooper (left) and Rodger Ward. Behind stand (left to right), Noddy Grohmann, Harry Stephen, Bob Smiley, Kimberly's pilot, Marshall Lewis and Jim Kimberly the Kleenex millionaire and project sponsor himself...

ply with USAC regulations an Indianapolis Cooper-Climax would need a 5 in. longer wheelbase, nerf bars, a roll-over bar and other special fittings.

Jack was happy, sure that even with only 230 bhp he could have lapped still quicker with more practice and adjustment. Rodger Ward drove briefly and returned fascinated by its smooth ride and stability compared to the normal tooth-rattler Roadster. He added '... damn shame it doesn't have more steam....'

Frank Falkner then introduced the visitors to Jim Kimberly, head of the Kleenex empire and a great racing enthusiast. On the spot he offered to sponsor a special Cooper-Climax for the coming year's '500', and they flew to Chicago to finalize the deal. John emerged with the widest grin ever and a cheque with sufficient noughts to build the car and return next May.

Qualification, a month-long process at Indy, would be a major problem as the period coincided with the Monaco GP, but Kimberly waved it aside and offered to arrange private air travel to connect with the necessary trans-Atlantic flights. The Englishmen and Aussie hitched-up their car and trailer and drove away happily to Watkins Glen....

The change in Formula 1 regulations for 1961 would affect the British teams badly, for in their opposition to the proposed 1½-litre limit and high minimum weight restriction they had spent too long promoting a continuation of 2½-litre racing in the so-called InterContinental Formula. This had allowed Porsche and Ferrari to go ahead quietly with developing suitable 1½-litre F1 racing engines, and both Coventry Climax and BRM began their serious development of multi-cylinder 1500s too late to be competitive during the new regulation's first season. Cooper's income from Formula 1 racing in 1961 could be slashed, as it had been already by the end of Formula 2, despite the number of private F1 cars then being ordered instead. Kimberly backing and the Indy project had come along at just the right time.

Back at Hollyfield Road, Owen Maddock was tearing his hair out with overwork. On 10 October a new draughtsman joined him. This was Eddie Stait, brother of Tyrrell mechanic Alan Stait, and he came to Cooper from five years' experience with the Royal Aircraft Establishment at Farnborough. Eddie's first job was to set down the fuel tank design for the 1961 F1 cars: 'Owen would draft what he wanted and I had to set them down properly on paper. He did the thinking, the designing, and I just detailed it. Then in mid-November we started seriously on the Indy car. Owen laid out most of it – obviously in conjunction with John and Jack – while I did much of the transmission and running gear detailing....'

Work proceeded feverishly and the car was eventually completed on Thursday, 4 May, 1961, wheeled-out for press photography on the forecourt and then flown out direct to Indy, never turning a wheel on native soil.

Meanwhile Charles and John had approached Leonard Lee and Wally Hassan at Climax to stretch the FPF further, to make it as large as possible. Climax were anxious not to start a rush. They didn't want other constructors to use Cooper's lead and start demanding over-sized FPFs for what was now 3-litre InterContinental Formula. Widdrington Road was already fully extended supplying new 1½-litre F1 FPFs and in development of the new FWMV V8. Therefore, while agreeing to do the stretch for Cooper's Indy project a statement was issued reading in part: 'The small dimensional increase which is physically possible leaves the capacity still well below three litres. It imposes considerably greater inertia loadings and because of this the permissible crankshaft speed is reduced, and also, therefore, the potential power ... we have agreed somewhat reluctantly to produce one special engine for this race in which the bore and stroke have been increased to give a capacity of 2750 cc. While this may prove an interesting experiment we are not at all happy as to the reliability of the engine....'

In fact two engines were built, necessarily, with bore and stroke increased by 0.08 in. and 0.02 in. respectively. Using a 50/50 methanol/AvGas fuel mix the 2.7-litre unit delivered around 251 bhp at 6250 rpm, while in the mid-range, at

5000 rpm, the stretch yielded an extra 25 bhp compared to the standard 2½-litre. The engine was mounted inclined in the Cooper frame at 18 degrees to the left – instead of the right as in the F1 cars – to aid left-side weight bias for the left-turn-only course. Re-aligning the engine/gearbox adaptor plate had caused some build problems when a plate was made up with the bolt holes drilled in the wrong place. It touched John on a raw nerve and Eddie Stait witnessed his first 'scream' from John: 'He went right through the roof. There was a terrible scene for about half the day. . . .'

The USAC technical committee were very understanding where the Kimberly-Cooper project was concerned, seeing it as an additional attraction for their great annual showpiece race to have the double World Champion Formula 1 constructor and driver taking part. They waived their 8 ft minimum wheelbase rule, and the new car emerged with a wheelbase of 7 ft 8¼ in., stretched by only 1¼ in. from F1 standard merely to avoid the rear Weber carburettor fouling the tyre.

The normal-type tubular frame was welded-up by Terry Kitson at Langley Road and had the depth between the top and bottom longerons increased from 12 in. at the front to 16 in. behind the cockpit to accommodate the Webers below the left-side top longeron. All frame tubes were 1½ in. diameter, but those supporting the rear suspension components were heavier gauge than in Formula 1. The wishbones themselves were also fabricated from heavier-gauge stock, and the fronts were 1 in. longer than Formula 1 spec. Inboard pivots of both front and rear wishbones on the right side were cantilevered 1 in. further outboard than those on the left to offset the body/chassis assembly to the inside of the banked turns. Front track was therefore 3 in. wider and rear track 1 in. wider than Formula 1.

Enlarged steering ball joints were fitted, those for the right wheel larger than the left, and the rack-and-pinion steering was lower-geared than normal with an eight-tooth instead of normal nine-tooth pinion. Fuel load was also offset to the left, with an 18¾-gallon left-side tank and only 11½ gallons on the right. The larger tank was divided into two and changeover cocks on the floor enabled Brabham to empty the right tank first, then the rear portion of the left tank, followed by its forepart until the refuelling stop would be made. The bottom halves of both tanks were sheathed in fibreglass as puncture protection. The left-side inclination of the engine enabled the right-side tank to be extended rearwards, where in Formula 1 the magneto prevented such a move.

Girling disc brakes were retained, 10¼ in. diameter at the front and 9¾ in. at the rear, Jack intending to steady the car on them during the race as well as use them hard in the scheduled pit stops. A regulation USAC roll-bar behind the driver's head was fitted, together with driver harness and rear bumper. A two-speed Cooper-Knight transaxle was employed.

Since tyre wear was a major factor at Indianapolis, Dunlop's aid had been enlisted, and they happily took on Firestone's monopoly, developing 5.50–16 front and 7.00–16 rear covers – ½ in. wider in section than Cooper's normal F1 wear, and 1 in. greater in diameter. The Birmingham company also supplied perforated disc centre-lock light-alloy wheels with beautiful eared k/o hub nuts to speed wheel-changes.

The lone T54 Indy car was joined at the Speedway by one of the works 1960 Lowlines – possibly *12/60* modified with USAC attachments and 16 in. centre-lock wheels to act as a practice and back-up car. After placing second at May Silverstone, Jack flew out to commence Indy practice. His hectic travel programme took him to Monaco practice on 12 May, back to Indy qualification next day and back again into Nice Airport at 11.30 am on 14 May for the Monaco GP that afternoon. If he failed to qualify at Indy that weekend he would have to return for the second session on 20 May, jet back to Zandvoort for the Dutch GP practice and race on 21–22, then return to Indy for the 500-Miles on 30 May. . . .

Bill Kimberly provided spotless garages in Gasoline Alley plus his own mechanics, all rigged in KIMBERLY-COOPER overalls. The works crew included Charles and John Cooper, Noddy Grohmann, Alf Francis, Bill James and Tim Wall, while Leonard Lee was also present. Noddy's cussedness surfaced as he dumped his battered tool kit on the polished workshop floor and, scattering tools and rags everywhere set to work on the car. When a Kimberly crewman asked if he intended to strip the engine after practice Noddy snapped: 'What for? It's only another race – you people only race here once a year. We're out racing every weekend and our engines are built to stand that kind of thing. . . .'

John recalls the pained silence which followed. The ice soon thawed; any friction was not of their American hosts' making.

Jack's first rush from Silverstone proved unnecessary as Indy was rained out. That afternoon it dried and he completed the official driver tests; '. . . going round the bends almost as fast as if we were really trying for a best-ever lap, but dawdling up the straights with only 5000 rpm on the clock. . . .'

Roll-bars were changed front and rear, but the next two days were rained out. On the Wednesday morning he managed two hours' running, with 146.4 mph the best lap. It looked as if 144 mph would qualify safely. The Monaco flit took place, and he covered his four qualifying laps back at Indy at 145.144 mph to find himself on the fifth row of the grid; the pace having risen higher than predicted.

On the Friday after the Dutch GP, Jack, his wife Betty and small son Gary flogged back across the Atlantic for the 500-Mile race. The second 2.7 engine had shown an extra 7 bhp on Climax's dyno and was chosen for the race, though the original was still running perfectly.

Problems included the filler necks filling too slowly, and the screen design causing buffeting around the World Champion's head. Modifications were made. On race eve a final planning session included Jack, John, the pit crew, Kimberly and Vic Barlow from Dunlop. Sadly they didn't pay enough attention to Barlow's prediction that they'd need three stops. They felt instead that the circuit would 'rubber-down' as the race progressed and allow them to get by with only two stops. That would give them an immense advantage, but John and his driver agreed privately that a finish in the top 10 'would be good enough'.

Even the unflappable Australian felt tense at the start. Indy's reputation was lurid and the notoriously unswervable

Pit stop drama, Jack holds forth with the car stationary on its pneumatic lift platform. Note race-trim changes; right-side scuttle filler has been restored, there's a scoop shroud in place of left-hand filler and it's been re-sited on the left-side pannier top in an ugly bodywork hole hacked clean through one sponsor's decal! The screen has a top-lip deflector tacked-on and is liberally plastered with bugs and oil smears. The little green car will finish ninth, but the message had been put across and two years later a rear-engined Lotus would finish second and very nearly win. Once again Cooper had shown the way...

1961 – THE INDY PROJECT

Roadsters loomed high above the little green Cooper. But in the first 30 laps he found it wasn't half as terrifying as he'd expected and he ran comfortably sixth. But his offset-tread Dunlop tyres wore out 4–5 laps earlier than anticipated and at 42 laps he made his first stop. The right-rear hub-nut was damaged at this time, and later had to be hammered all the way off and all the way back on, rather than just finger-spun most of the way. Kimberly-Cooper stops cost up to 64 sec each – against 20 sec or so for the USAC regulars....

Jack drove on determined to conserve his tyres and make only one more stop, but he miscalculated and slowed too much. Stop two was not made until lap 110, but he still needed another change before the end. Had they planned three stops he would have run harder in between and could undoubtedly have finished higher. As it was he placed ninth, warmly applauded by the 280,000 crowd, having averaged 134.116 mph.

He had only one bad fright, soon after the first stop when he tried to pass Don Davis's *Dart Kart Special* in the Finishing Straight and its engine abruptly blew and it began spinning wildly. Jack dodged between the careering car and the outside wall and next time round was fascinated to see that four more Roadsters had been unable to dodge and had become involved with the first.

During each stop Noddy had supplied a glass of water, fresh goggles and a new stick of chewing gum, while the tanks were filled and both rear wheels and the right-front changed. The left-front tyre survived the full 500 miles – typical Cooper, it probably wasn't touching the road very often. It lost just 4 mm tread. The right-rears wore a total 23 mm, the others 14–15 mm each. The car covered a total 460 practice and race laps – 1180 miles – and weighed 1050 lb dry against 1700 lb for the lightest US entry. Jack never exceeded 6000 rpm and the engine needed no more oil. His best time through the Turn 1 trap was 6.2 sec, 143 mph, the best in the race, against only 135 mph for Dick Rathmann's best Roadster. The Cooper's quickest laps were its 36th and 37th at 146.104 mph. It averaged 142 mph for the first 40 flying laps. Foyt won in his *Bowes Seal Fast* Watson-Offy at a race average of 145.903 mph.

John Cooper: 'We picked-up around $9000 prize money, plus the lump sum advance from Jim Kimberly and the great time we had at Indy for the best part of a month was an experience that I wouldn't have missed for the world....'

His team would not return, but in 1962 Cooper-like Indy cars were entered by Mickey Thompson with Buick engines, and Gurney made the grid in one and ran well. Dan had Colin Chapman in tow, examining the Indy scene, and in 1963 a Lotus-Ford would stand the establishment on its ear by finishing second. In 1965 another Lotus-Ford, also driven by Jimmy Clark, would win, and the F1-style rear-engined cars had toppled American track racing's holy of holies.

The Kimberly-Cooper which began it all in 1961 spawned a Buick rear-engined Kimberly for 1962, but one Porky Rachwitz didn't make it to the 500. In 1963 Pedro Rodriguez attempted to qualify California BMC distributor Kjell H. Qvale's Aston-Martin-engined ex-Kimberly Cooper, modified with the stretched wheelbase USAC now demanded, but at 146.687 mph was too slow to make the grid. Two Kimberly-Buicks were entered that year for our friend Porky and Jim Davies, neither made it. Today the team's back-up Cooper-Climax 12/60 ex-Jim Hall stands dignified in the Indianapolis Speedway Museum. It was sold to Hall's partner Hap Sharp at Indy '61. It survives today with 2.5 FPF engine '430/17/1176'.

Now we must turn the clock back, to look at Cooper's early forays into a much less-elevated form of motor racing; for in 1958–59 the racing world had produced Formula Junior....

While Jimmy Clark's Lotus-Ford stood Indy 1963 on its ear the old Brabham Cooper returned, in Kjell Qvale's ownership, stretched to meet USAC's re-imposed minimum wheelbase limit and powered by Aston Martin 6-cylinder dohc engine. Running regular Firestone track tyres and driven by Pedro Rodriguez the white-and-blue liveried BMC Aston Martin Spl *failed to qualify, too slow for the grid at 146.687 mph. In 1961 only five drivers had qualified in the 146 mph bracket, Brabham's average was 145.144. Such is progress...*

CHAPTER TWENTY TWO

The Junior Coopers

It came from Italy. In the mid-Fifties the AC d'Italia was anxious to bring on new driver talent to replace the greats like Ascari, Villoresi and Farina. On 30 November, 1956, they held a meeting at San Remo to discuss proposals for new single-seater schoolroom classes. Count Giovanni 'Johnny' Lurani Cernuschi was the eloquent advocate of 'Formula Junior', which would use a 1-litre engine based upon a 1000-off production unit then available. The gearbox should also come from production, though the internal ratios could be altered but without structural alteration to the casing. Front suspension should come from the same source as the engine; overhead-camshaft units were banned to minimize cost, and only pump petrol would be allowed. Induction should be the same type as production and the brakes had to be the same system as on the production car from which the engine was taken.

Into 1957, Lurani's proposals were accepted and Fiat-based specials began construction in Italy. Then in January 1958 the CSI appointed a sub-committee to study this national formula, and they granted it international status for 1959 – when in effect it replaced that other national formula which became great; 500 cc Formula 3. The sub-committee held one meeting at that year's Italian GP meeting and asked two Englishmen for their views.

Colin Chapman said Lotus would never be seen dead building a Junior, while equally typically John Cooper just bubbled with enthusiasm and thought it was a great idea.

In October it was confirmed that FJ would go international for 1959 and run to the end of 1963. Capacity limits were 1000 cc with a minimum weight limit of 360 kg (about 792 lb) or 1100 cc with a limit of 400 kg (about 880 lb). Minimum wheelbase was 200 cm, track 110 cm and maximum body width 95 cm. The open single-seat body had to carry a roll-over bar to protect the driver and onboard starters were required. It was forbidden to use dohc, self-locking diffs and to change the number of crankshaft bearings, or camshaft. Other Italian national requirements survived intact.

Of course the first FJ season in 1959 was dominated by the well-developed Italian cars from Stanguellini, Volpini, Raineri, Taraschi and Foglietti. British interest was initially sparse. Cooper for one was deeply committed to F1, F2 and Monaco sports car production. On a broader front Britain's own Monoposto Formula was just beginning, but it would never aspire to international status.

By the middle of 1959, however, it was obvious there would be demand for Junior, and the prototype Cooper T52 or 'Formula Junior Mark I' made its bow in November 1959, ready for the 1960 season.

The car was very much a cobbled-together device drawing heavily on redundant F2 parts and practice. It resembled the slim-bodied 1956 F2 Mark I and carried the old, early-design '500' style Cooper cast wheels with integral brake drums.

Yet again Owen Maddock had laid out a frame in $1\frac{1}{2}$ in. diameter steel tube, 18-gauge wall thickness for the top longerons and 16-gauge for the bottom. The wheelbase of 7 ft 2 in. was an inch shorter than that of the contemporary 500 cc Cooper but well above the CSI's 6 ft $6\frac{3}{4}$ in. minimum. Like Frank Nichols of the Elva concern, John had chosen to use the British Motor Corporation 'A' series Austin-Morris four-cylinder in-line engine; the old familiar 64.4×76 mm, 948 cc unit with pushrod ohv. Externally the FJ version resembled that used in the Austin-Healey Sprite, with the exception of

The British Mark I Juniors seem all to have been delivered to their owners in kit form, tax-free for self-assembly. Here on the rain-slick starting grid for the inaugural British FJ race, Boxing Day, Brands Hatch, 26 December, 1959, is Mike McKee in Mike Taylor's new car, with Ian Burgess behind in the Cooper School prototype. McKee led but could only finish fourth, while lurking beyond dark duffle-coat is Alan Stacey's unpainted aluminium-bodied Lotus 18 FJ prototype. Like the Cooper's its engine was behind the driver, and it marked the start of Lotus' take-over of Surbiton's markets . . .

BMC's humble A-series in-line 4-cylinder production engine was always quite amenable to performance tuning, and 1959-64 provided Cooper's minor-Formula mainstay, as here in one of the earliest 1959 Formula Junior Mark Is. Note twin SU carburettors, complete with airbox inner-panel ready to seal against the closed engine cowl intake blister, hefty curved-tube chassis frame, typically Cooper cooling system header tank and clutch cylinder and operating rod at left. There was nothing very complicated about the cars . . . just big Meccano really . . .

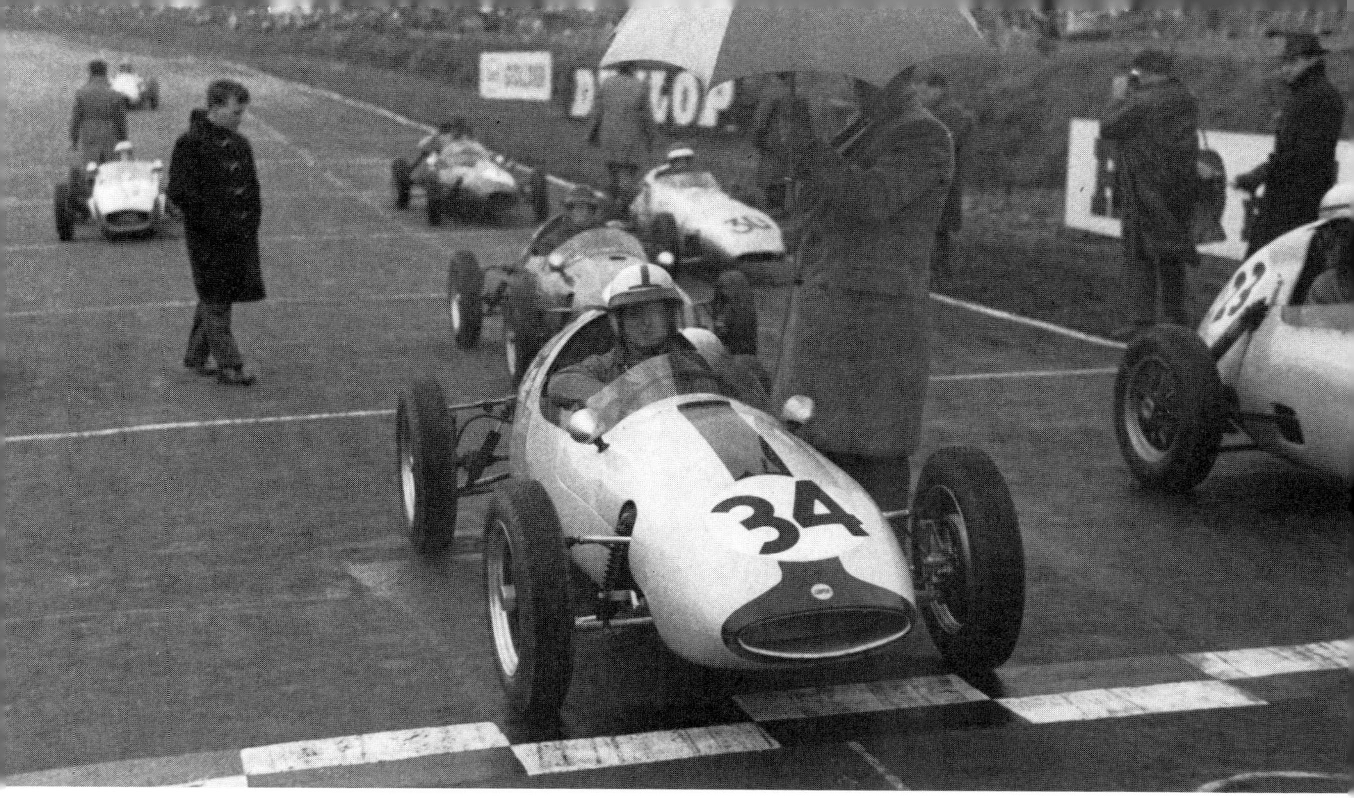
34

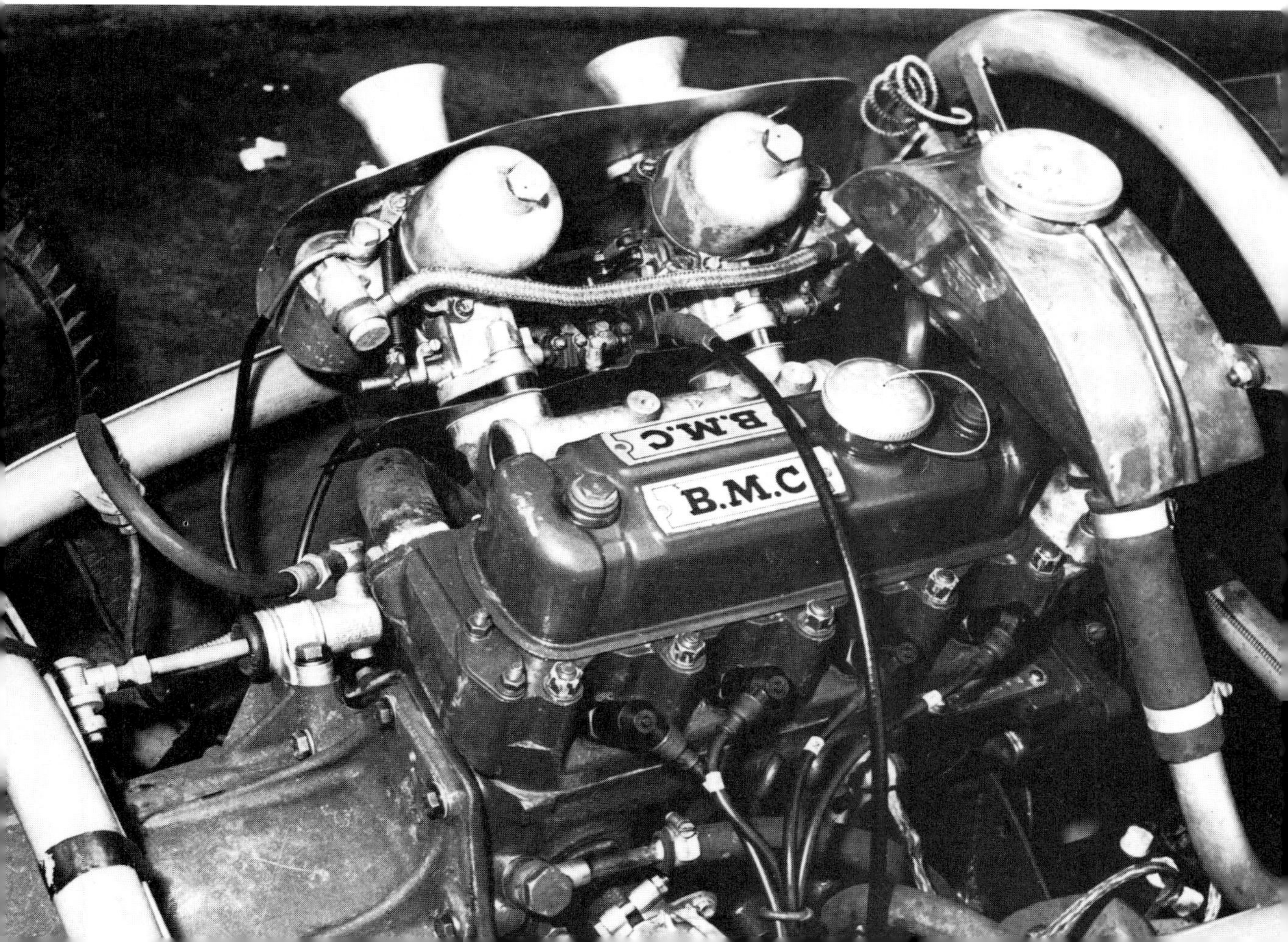
B.M.C
B.M.C

the electric fuel pump and the fitting of a gilled tube oil cooler ahead of the water radiator. Tuned as regs allowed, this modest little unit with two SU carburettors delivered around 70 bhp at 6500 rpm. It was mounted upright and bolted to a tailor-made bell-housing mating it with a Citroën-ERSA transaxle with Jack Knight internals and the familiar lock-out mechanism demanding that the clutch should be depressed to allow gear engagement. The single fuel tank mounted in the scuttle over the driver's legs. He had a right-hand gear-change and a left-side handbrake operating the foot pedal. On the dash ahead of him were a Weston 8000 rpm tach-ometer, oil and water temperature gauges, oil pressure gauge and starter and ignition switch. Behind his bucket seat ahead of the engine lay the battery, fuel pump and the high-mounted brass header tank.

Suspension retained the coil-and-wishbone F2 front end but returned to the economic transverse leaf-spring and lower wishbone at the rear, with transverse link locating the spring laterally. An anti-roll bar appeared on the front, and brakes were 8 in. diameter Lockheed drums common with the F3 car, operated by twin master cylinders. Kerb weight was quoted as 798 lb with oil and water but no fuel, distributed 44/56 per cent front/rear. Price complete was quoted as 'around £1300', and the prototype car was tested by Ian Burgess in the rain at Brands Hatch during School sessions.

A major factor in persuading Cooper to enter the fray was the great and growing interest in FJ shown by the American market. The new Cooper's US price was $3700....

In testing, the prototype oversteered wildly until a heavier front anti-roll bar was fitted. Then Ian Burgess ran it as pace car at the School. It was bug-free, and four Cooper FJs raced at Boxing Day Brands Hatch, 1959; two works cars for Burgess and star pupil Bill Lacy, one from Mike Taylor for Mike McKee to drive and the other Edward Hine's private car. McKee led initially but finished fourth behind two Elvas and a Lola – all front-engined. The track was greasy and they handled better than the under-developed Cooper, and the prototype rear-engined Lotus 18, which had engine trouble.

While 17 FJs appear in the surviving Register, many more were built in kit-form for British customers, Douggie Johnson and his men bolting together suspension corners ready for the new owner to hang them on the frame, install the engine and attach the body panels. At Hollyfield Road the amazing Mrs Green running the stores would make good any shortfall in the kits. She had an encyclopaedic knowledge of Cooper components and generally knew her way around the cars better than many men in motor racing.

Walt Hansgen christened the baby Cooper in its interna-tional debut at Sebring on 25 March, leading before retire-ment in a Cunningham entry. Meanwhile, in the UK, Ken Tyrrell's little team was gearing-up for Junior, and gave John Surtees his four-wheeled racing debut in one. John had test-driven Vanwall and Aston Martin cars and now he and his dealer father had ordered a new F2 Cooper. While at the

First time stunner – John Surtees, already with multiple motor-cycle racing World Championship titles to his name, making his four-wheeled racing debut, Goodwood, 19 March, 1960. Here in Ken Tyrrell's shiny new Cooper-BMC Mark I he hurtled round, locked in combat with Jimmy Clark's similarly bright and shiny – though already painted – works Lotus-Ford 18. Surtees and Cooper finished second. Winning was difficult for the Mark I FJ. Note the Colin Darby-designed early-type cast Cooper road wheels and single wishbone rear suspension, with leafspring providing lateral location. Hence the oversteer . . .

works one day John met Ken Tyrrell. His big worry was obtaining his competition licence from the RAC in time for the F2 opening meeting at Oulton Park. The RAC would accept one club race for him, and AFN Ltd offered a Porsche for the opening March meeting at Goodwood. Then Ken made the better offer of a new Cooper FJ. In private practice John was sensationally quick; 2 sec faster than Bruce McLaren. Much could be made of that, but many F1 drivers found the step-down into an under-powered formula quite difficult. Ian Burgess had already lapped Brands faster than Brabham in the prototype Mark I.

Still Surtees qualified on pole at Goodwood faster than Jimmy Clark and Trevor Taylor in their Team Lotus 18s with Cosworth-Ford 105E engines against the Cooper's milder BMC. He finished second between them, won his licence and two weeks later at Oulton Park was second F2 and bent the gear-lever in his Tyrrell FJ car. Henry Taylor drove the team's other Mark I into fourth place, but the Lotus 18s were in a class of their own. . . .

This was the pattern for the year, and Cooper cars were eclipsed in a minor formula, really for the first time since

Money spinners—the 1961 FJ Mark II prototype and Mini saloon share the limelight on the now familiar, often-photographed, Hollyfield forecourt. The miniature 'Lowline' styling of this hugely-improved FJ is evident. Note also all coil-spring/double-wishbone suspension and improved later-series Maddock-designed eight-spoke cast wheels. The Mini-Coopers were to become an integral part of the company's business throughout succeeding years, including a saloon racing works team run by Ginger Devlin from the Hollyfield works, and later Canada Road, Byfleet . . .

their introduction. The Lotuses won all the races and titles which mattered in the UK, while in Europe the Italian-organized 'World FJ Championship' fell to Colin Davis's works OSCA.

Surtees drove for Tyrrell whenever motorcycle and later Lotus F1 commitments allowed, for he catapulted straight into the GP class that same season. But he was always unlucky, even when Tyrrell bought him a Lotus 18 late in the year. While Surtees was elsewhere, Henry Taylor was joined by Keith Ballisat or Ian Raby in the Tyrrell Cooper team, and when Henry's F1 rides with Yeoman Credit became more regular, Keith and Ian were joined by Jo Schlesser – at Reims – and later by Denny Hulme, who had been trailing his own Cooper Mark I round Europe as a penniless privateer – though he harried Davis on occasion and beat him at Pescara.

Alan Stait and Neil Davis – still working for Tyrrell in 1982–83 – cared for the Juniors and had a busy year. At Aix-les-Bains, Chris Threlfall died when an overloaded spectator bridge collapsed in the path of his Elva. The local police chief commended Ballisat's presence of mind for spinning his Cooper deliberately to avoid hitting the wreckage. The Tyrrell car was still badly bent, and John Cooper loaned the School car to replace it, after Ken ran just one – for Taylor – at Monaco, and he promptly won the most prestigious FJ race of the year. The winning car was then mangled at Crystal Palace when Ballisat spun while leading into the first corner, and within four days the mechanics prepared the sister car and the loaned schoolie and whizzed them down to Albi for Taylor and Raby to drive. They each won their heat and then took the Final 1–2, 0.4 sec apart. John Love's Fitzwilliam Team Lola was third, and this Rhodesian garagist from Bulawayo was later co-opted into the Tyrrell Organisation at Pescara, finishing third outclassing Ballisat. . . .

Don Rickman – a well-known motorcycle scrambler – had some races in the Cooper school car, but generally the season confirmed Cooper's eclipse. The Mark I had not been a great success, and as early as Easter Goodwood its third straight defeat by the Lotuses had convinced Ken something drastic had to be done to control its tail-happiness. He bought smaller 13 in. diameter wheels cast by Ted Whiteaway's Grosvenor Garage at nearby Worplesdon for the Condor FJ. With the Condor wheels, a lowered chassis and the BMC engines themselves lowered in the frames, the Tyrrell cars were much improved thereafter.

In the USA competition was less intense. Walt Hansgen was at his aggressive best in Cunningham's Alfred Momo-prepared car and at one stage won five FJ races on the trot without touching the engine. At the United States GP meeting at Riverside in November, Walt gave the new Mark II prototype car its race debut, unpainted, and won easily after a battle with Billy Krause's Lotus.

The new Mark II was a very important car for Cooper. F2 had died and FJ was the only alternative market, save for the expansion in F1. Cooper relied upon production and parts sales for income and whereas the 1960 FJ Mark I had been a spare-time cobble-up, the new 1961 Mark II showed far greater investment in time, thought and money.

The car emerged virtually as a scale model of the highly successful Formula 1 'Lowline'. The chassis itself, virtually all straight tubes apart from a simple sweep-down of the top longerons at the nose, was lowered, retaining $1\frac{1}{2}$ in. diameter main longerons – 16-gauge at the bottom, 18-gauge at the top – cross-braced by $1\frac{1}{4}$ in. diameter members. The leaf-spring rear end was junked in favour of unequal-length double wishbones with interposed coil-spring/dampers, as at the front, but all wishbones were now wider-based on the frame to give better control and rigidity. The usual through-the-frame anti-roll bar was retained at the front and there was provision for one at the rear, although prototype tests suggested this was not necessary.

Where the Mark I car had been rather short and tall, the new Mark II frame was lengthened 3 in. to move the driver and power unit further forward, and the battery was located behind the radiator instead of behind the driver's back; the rack-and-pinion steering also moved forward, with the steering arms facing forward instead of back, so allowing the foot pedals to move forward too. The driver reclined more than before, stretching out in his slightly longer cockpit, and these changes took some six per cent weight off the rear wheels.

Taking a leaf out of Tyrrell's book, the car now ran as standard on 13 in. rather than 15 in. wheels, using Cooper's contemporary eight-spoke cast magnesium design, and this reduced ground clearance from $4\frac{1}{2}$ to 4 in. The single scuttle fuel tank of the Mark I was replaced by twin panniers well forward alongside the driver's legs and built as low as possible. For the first time fairly extensive use was made of fibre-glass in the bodywork and the driver's seat – the panels being made in moulds formed over an aluminium original beaten and rolled by the Beddings.

While the BMC 'A' series unit suitably developed and tuned under the watchful eye of Eddie Maher of BMC's Engine Division was retained, tests had been run with a Ford 105E alternative. Similarly, while the Citroën-based Jack Knight gearbox was standard, there was a Renault-derived option now available which was lighter. While the BMC engine still ran upright in the frame, the alternative 105E Ford was inclined to the right at 15 degrees from vertical. Part of the engine development had been to adopt a single Weber 45DCOE4 carburettor as an alternative to the well-proven twin-SU H4 $1\frac{1}{2}$ in. set-up, showing improvements in both power and torque. With special pistons, crankshaft and camshaft, plus a considerably reworked cylinder head, the 64.4×76.0 mm engine was now out to 994 cc as standard, with 11.5:1 compression ratio.

Amongst detail changes on the Mark II were the ducted radiator, exhausting air to each side through the suspension cut-outs in the body and from the lower half of the radiator matrix downwards beneath the car. The alternative Renault transaxle was married inverted, with four all-indirect ratios and half-shafts running almost straight out to the outboard UJs and hub carriers outboard. With the Citroën 'box the half-shafts raked back to the hubs at a considerable angle, the joints operating satisfactorily – it was claimed – at angles of up to 35 degrees.

The new Mark II had a wheelbase of 7 ft 5 in., front track of 4 ft and rear track of 3 ft 11 in., overall length was 11 ft 6 in., width 4 ft $6\frac{1}{2}$ in. and height 2 ft 7 in. Kerb weight was 795 lb and in kit form complete the asking price was £1350. Lotus, meanwhile, had ingeniously reduced the size of their production Junior and clothed it in exceptionally sleek fibreglass bodywork. They called it the Type 20; it would carry on winning where the 18 had been so dominant, and its kit price was £100 more than the new Cooper – Colin Chapman knew that his customers would stand it. . . .

Ken Tyrrell invited John Love and South African newcomer Tony Maggs to join his Mark II team for 1961. Love's early racing had been with an allegedly ex-Moss Cooper-JAP back home, replaced by a much more successful Cooper-Norton, then a D type Jaguar, the famous OKV 3. He had come to Europe to drive the Fitzwilliam Lola FJs in 1960, and was now committed full-time to the Tyrrell Racing Organization.

Anthony Francis O'Connell Maggs, meanwhile, had started racing in 1958 in an Austin-Healey. During 1959 he gained experience with a Lotus 11 and Ogier's Tojeiro-Jaguar in the UK, and in 1960 drove Ogier's F2 Cooper to a second, third, fourth and the Snetterton lap record in five outings. He also drove Gemini FJs and with Tyrrell in the new Mark II the lanky, fair-haired South African would win eight major

THE JUNIOR COOPERS

Works foreman Roy Golding attending a new Mark II in the Hollyfield production 'shop, 1961, note curved panel-joint aluminium body section unlike subsequent slimline Mark III panels. The straight-tube frame is apparent here, continued use of typically Cooper 'Bradnack lugs' for wishbone pick-ups and also the marque's pragmatic disregard for engineering niceties in the way top-rear wishbone forward pivot is half-way up an unsupported tube which itself joints into the unsupported centre-section of the rearmost side-bay diagonal. The extended top rear cross-member can accommodate an anti-roll bar, the forward bar running inside the foremost cross-member, its operating linkage just visible ahead of left-front wheel

1961 FJ races at Goodwood, Magny-Cours, Monza, Karlskoga, Zandvoort, Oulton Park and Montlhéry, where he dead-heated with his team mate! Tony shared the European FJ Championship title with a Swiss Lotus driver, an ex-motorcyclist named Jo Siffert. John Cooper invited Maggs to become Bruce McLaren's works F1 team mate for 1962-63....

Love, meanwhile, lost the lead at Cesenatico when a plug lead fell off and at Oulton the same problem cost Maggs. At Monaco the season's major FJ prize fell to Peter Arundell's works Lotus – he would become virtual 'King of Formula Junior', but the so-called 'Tyrrell Twins' placed 2-3 behind him in the Final, and Tony won his Heat, and John was second in his.

The Twins were also 1-2 at Chimay, $\frac{1}{10}$ sec apart, and they did it again at Magny-Cours, where Raby's Cooper set fastest lap. Love beat Siffert at Caserta and won again at La Châtre. Maggs won the Monza Lottery GP at 106 mph average, where Paddy Gaston was fourth in a sister Cooper entered by Bob Gerard. At Reims the FJ race was run in three heats. Each saw a Maggs-versus-Trev Taylor duel, Taylor winning on aggregate by 0.8 sec. Love was fifth and Denny Hulme sixth in the new Cooper he had built-up at Hollyfield Road, under McLaren's close scrutiny. The FJs reached 142 mph on the long straights. So it went on – Maggs and Love 1-2 at Karlskoga, 1-2 again in reverse order at Roskilde, then the Montlhéry dead-heat. Ken sold one of his cars to Robert Bouharde, who was to make good use of it.

The amateur Midland Racing Partnership team from Wolverhampton also did well in their co-operative Cooper FJ efforts that season; drivers including John Rhodes, Dick Attwood, Bill Bradley, David Baker and Jeremy Cottrell. Ian Raby and Chris Andrews formed the Empire Racing Team with Mark II-BMCs, the latter winning his heat at Teramo, Italy.

The Austrian-based Ecurie Vienne team of Kurt Bardi-Barry and Rolf Markl had some success, Bardi-Barry very fast but often over-exuberant. Markl led Andre Liekens's sister Cooper home 1-2 at Portoroza, Yugoslavia; Formula Junior races were being held everywhere. In Scandinavia Curt Lincoln was a force to reckon with, and fellow Finns Jouko Nordell and Leo Matilla did well, including a 1-2 for Cooper in the Halle-Saale races in East Germany. Lincoln won at Budapest Airport, while at Messina the 1961 NZ Driver to Europe, Angus Hyslop, beat Denny Hulme.

In the US, Walt Hansgen had another good year for Cunningham, and the boss himself drove FJ occasionally, notably with a Mark II OSCA-Fiat. At Sebring Hansgen had been beaten by Charlie Kolb's new rear-engined Gemini, but Pedro Rodriguez was fourth in a Pepsi-Cola-sponsored Cooper, which his schoolboy brother Ricardo had used earlier to win a $10,000 Junior race in Mexico City that January!

There was even an FJ race around Las Vegas streets and a parking lot, where Fred Work's Cooper was third. At Nassau, Roger Penske placed third in his FJ Cooper . . . at the time he was a sales executive for Alcan.

The Mark II had performed well, but still the Lotus 20 in good hands posed formidable opposition and there was also the new Jack Brabham and Ron Tauranac-produced 'MRD' – later Brabham – FJ car in the wings showing advanced suspension thinking and daunting promise. . . . Jack was leaving Cooper to go his own way, and his production FJ cars would be followed by his own F1 in 1962.

For Cooper during 1961, the performances particularly of the Tyrrell cars had been most satisfactory, and for 1962 the T59 or Formula Junior Mark III model was altered, mainly in profile, from the Mark II, the body being narrowed no less than 5 in. and overall height reduced by 2 in. to minimize frontal area. Track widths were increased to 4 ft $2\frac{1}{2}$ in. front and 4 ft $1\frac{3}{4}$ in. rear to provide more bite on turning into corners, while roll centres were allegedly raised to 4 in. and 5 in. respectively.

Suspension was still by unequal-length wishbones and outboard coil-springs. The springs wrapped round Armstrong GT7 adjustable tele-dampers which were softer and shorter than the Mark II's, non-adjustable dampers being used as standard at the rear, though owners quickly experimented. . . . The front suspension was set up standard, with 9 degrees castor and zero camber – the wheels upright – but at the rear there was a half-degree negative camber. A front anti-roll bar was fitted in the usual way, and again there was provision for one through the top rear chassis cross-member, although it was not supplied as standard and the light weight of the normal BMC engine hardly demanded it.

There had been rule changes. From the 1961 Prix Monaco Junior, the CSI allowed free brake systems and the Mark III as designed used Lockheed discs front and rear, with Mini-Cooper saloon calipers clasping enlarged $9\frac{1}{4}$ in. front and 9 in. rear discs, mounted outboard in the cast mag wheels, carrying their 5.50–13 and 4.50–13 Dunlop tyres.

BMC had developed a full 1100 cc version of their 'A' series FJ engine fitted with a Weber 40DCOE9 twin-choke carburettor, and the unit was fully dry-sumped with the oil tank located behind the driver. Twin moulded pannier tanks appeared either side – 6 gallons to the left and 4.5 gallons to the right – and the nose-mounted radiator incorporated an integral oil cooler, the pipe runs for water and oil being exposed to the airstream to minimize cockpit heat and improve cooling.

The engine cylinder bores had been enlarged to 67.6 mm, compression raised to 12:1, and with the 76.2 mm stroke the new engine displaced 1095 cc. Power output was claimed to be 95 bhp at 7500 rpm. There were larger valves, an entirely new camshaft giving longer valve-opening periods and increased overlap, and the crankshaft was stiffened, though bearing sizes were unchanged. Spur gears drove to the Citroën-based five-speed gearbox, and first gear was now robust enough to be used in racing and no longer merely for starting.

During prototype testing at Silverstone, with front and rear roll centres raised from the Mark II's 3 in., at 4.66 in. front and 4.72 in. rear, it was found that the new car gave much improved 'feel' as the cornering limit approached and a consistent $1\frac{1}{2}$ sec per lap improvement in time was recorded.

In February 1962, orders for 30 Mark IIIs were announced, the more modern style 'Mark 3' gaining currency, and their price was released as £1600 unassembled. Only 28 are recorded in the Register, excluding Tyrrell's of course, which were built at Ockham from works-supplied parts. Again these cars gave Cooper's FJ season a firm backbone, Maggs still driving when F1 allowed and John Love frontlining beside Denny Hulme. Ken's team also ran the works Mini-Cooper racing saloons this season, and John Love won the BRSCC British Saloon Car Championship in one. It was a frantically busy year. . . .

But Peter Arundell had taken a firm stranglehold with his Team Lotus 22s and success was harder to find for Cooper. Maggs and Love were often 2–3 behind a Lotus, and it was usually Arundell's, or the Brabhams, which also used Cosworth-Ford engines. At Roskilde, Love and Hulme notched Tyrrell's first 1–2 of the year. Love won at Magny-Cours, José Rosinski at La Châtre, Rhodesian Dave Riley at Schleiz and Sachsenring in East Germany with his Cooper, and Bardi-Barry's car with SuperSpeed Ford engine at Vallelunga and Nürburgring. Yet another South African, Trevor Blokdyk, won for Cooper at Nogaro (in a Mark II) and Kurt Ahrens Jr took honours at Budapest and Brno. Russell Cowles's Mark 3 was victorious at Mettet, and Rosinski again at Chimay, where Bill McCowen's Fitzwilliam Team Mark 3-Ford spun out of the lead. Jay Chamberlain, the American driver, toured Europe in F1 and FJ, and had several good placings in his ex-Cunningham Mark II. McCowen was badly burned in a practice crash at Monza, while at Monaco former Cooper F2 exponent Dennis Taylor had crashed fatally in his new Lola.

At last Tony Maggs won a race, at Clermont-Ferrand, and again at Brands Hatch. At Karlskoga and Roskilde the Tyrrell Twins took their 1961-style 1–2 victories and in September at Albi, Love and Hulme were 2–3 in Heat One, but in the Final Maggs spun, and while Denny placed third poor John Love crashed heavily and broke his arm.

This was an unfortunate end to a season in which the Cooper boys had fought hard, but come off second best to Lotus and had their problems dealing with the dozen production Brabhams then finding their feet.

In the USA, Hansgen had finished third in Cunningham's new Mark 3 at the important Sebring race accompanying the 12-Hours, with Penske's Mark II-Fiat fifth and, more signifi-

THE JUNIOR COOPERS

Another wet morning in Surbiton with the 1962 FJ prototype lined-up alongside its 1961 Tyrrell team predecessor – note worn tyres – to emphasize smaller frontal area, shallower frame, revised suspension geometry etc. The overhead shot demonstrates new Mark III's slender lines, and the exaggerated blister necessary to enclose the carburettor. The bodywork is arranged with small cockpit side-panels and screens, Dzus-fastened behind the large nose/scuttle/screen section. Front anti-roll bar resides in forward chassis cross-member, operating-linkages visible either side. There is no rear anti-roll bar fitted

cantly, being beaten by Timmy Mayer's old Mark II, which was second. Cunningham bought a Brabham before season's end, but at Riverside Hansgen's Cooper was second to Pete Lovely's old Lotus 20, and at Puerto Rico the 'Rev-Em' Team of Tim Mayer, Bill Smith Jr and Peter Revson placed 1–2–3 for Cooper. Timmy became SCCA National FJ Champion for the year. In 1963, aided by his lawyer brother Teddy, he would come to Europe.

This 1962 Junior season was rather distastefully marred for Cooper when the German club suspended Kurt Ahrens Jr's licence on suspicion of his using over-sized engines in his Cooper Mark 3.

The class ran to its close through 1963, to be replaced by 1-litre production-based F3 and racing engine F2 in 1964. The UK's annual Racing Car Show in London had become the great showcase for the racing industry, and the 1963 Cooper T65 car made its bow there in January. It is listed as 'Formula Junior Mark IV' in the Register, but became known popularly as the Mark 3A. And the Show car used BMC Hydrolastic suspension. . . .

John had been charging around in a pre-production BMC 1100 the previous summer, going off on holiday down to Charles's much-loved holiday house at Restronguet on the River Fal. Eddie Stait remembers how he returned '. . . raving about Hydrolastic, so preliminary suspension drawings for the new Junior were tossed into the drawer and we began grafting Hydrolastic onto the new frame. . . .'

The idea was to transfer the 1100 saloon's essentially pitch-free ride into racing. This was taken further by building-in anti-dive and anti-squat angularity into the front and rear wishbone pick-ups. By raking the pick-up axis downward 3 degrees towards the nose at the front, and rearward 9 degrees at the rear, dive or squat in the chassis would seek to induce an upward movement of the wheels, which braking or acceleration would resist. The option was retained to fit conventional coil-spring/damper units. In the Show prototype, Alex Moulton's Hydrolastic units were fitted with the rubber displacers coupled front-to-rear by small-diameter water pipes. Extra duralumin activating levers linked the lower wishbones to the Hydrolastic displacers, but the system was tricky to set up and control in practice, and the marked degree of anti-dive made the steering deaden unpleasantly under braking. The

Hydrolastic system is recalled as 'one of John's flights of fancy', and it was not to be raced.

The latest frame was lighter, of $1\frac{3}{8}$ in. and 1 in. diameter 16-gauge tube, two main longerons doubling as water pipes from radiator to engine, and the other two carrying oil. Wishbones were Rose-jointed at their outboard ends and on Vandervell bushes inboard. An extra lateral link locked-off rear wheel toe-in in addition to the normal bottom wishbones.

Jack Knight had been responsible for gearbox modifications within the familiar Citroën-type casing, now enclosing six straight-cut indirect speeds, while the magnesium-cased sump was shallower and wider than before, with full-pressure lubrication. It was unnecessary to change ratios for any British circuit and at Monaco one simply used the bottom four ratios. It was intended to adapt the gearing for Reims and Monza either by changing the crownwheel and pinion or by fitting larger rear wheels. Metalastic Rotoflex rubber couplings replaced splines in the half-shafts, and the engine was mounted upright as before on Silentbloc bushes. BMC were now extracting 98 bhp at 7800 rpm with a single Weber twin-choke carburettor. As standard the car rode on the usual Cooper cast-magnesium wheels, with $5\frac{1}{2}$ in. rims carrying 4.50–13 and 5.50–13 Dunlop tyres. Once again Lockheed disc brakes were fitted, outboard all round.

Thirteen Mark IVs appear in the Register for 1963, plus two more early in 1964. Out of 37 major European FJ races that season, Coopers won eight. Kurt Ahrens Jr's Ford-engined 'Mark 3A' won four times, at Aspern, Collemaggio, Nürburgring and Innsbruck. Bardi-Barry won at Vallelunga, while a wild young newcomer named Jochen Rindt ran his ex-Bardi-Barry Mark 3-Ford into first place at Cesenatico.

José Rosinski's Tyrrell 'Mark 3A' was victorious at Magny-Cours, and on 18 August the marque had a joy-day at Roskilde, where Peter Revson's Cooper won from Georg Duneborn's Mark III-BMC, Peter Procter and Mayer in Tyrrell Mark IVs and Sven Andersson's Mark III-BMC.

Mini-Cooper star John Rhodes returned to FJ with Tyrrell early in the year, but the BMC engine was by this time outclassed on faster circuits like Silverstone, where John was eighth and Procter crashed in his efforts to keep up. Timmy Mayer was injured in his Tyrrell car when a brake caliper failed approaching the infamous Goodwood chicane in the TT meeting, and he smashed into the brickwork, disrupting the race and its organization.

A major FJ international at Brands Hatch in September saw Peter Revson being loaned a Tyrrell car after his own had failed in practice. He crashed, and wasn't asked again. Mayer won his Heat but was back in sixth place in the Final.

Formula Junior died on 31 December, 1963, with Cooper in decline. Meanwhile, what had been happening in Formula 1...?

The Tyrrell Twins, 1962 – John Love from Rhodesia leading Tony Maggs from South Africa in their Tyrrell Racing Organization Cooper-BMC Mark IIIs at Karlskoga, Sweden, where they finished – as so often – first and second. The FJ Cooper Mark IIIs were increasingly referred to as 'Mark 3s' though this more modern form did not gain widespread use until 1963 and the latest 'Mark 3A', which of course the surviving Cooper chassis register still lists as 'Formula Junior Mark IV'. Pity the poor historian, please...

CHAPTER TWENTY THREE

The 1½-litre years – 1961-65

International motor racing exploded with new-found vigour in 1961. Many former F2 entrants and drivers were attracted to 1½-litre Formula 1 racing, as it was potentially inexpensive and 1960 F2 cars could easily be used in the new class. The Cooper Car Company's order book bulged for F1 cars which were effectively replicas of the World Championship-winning T53 Lowline, while Owen was drawing new T55 slimline cars for the works team which were improved in detail, lower, slimmer and more streamlined.

The Register lists 20 '*1961 Formula 1 Cooper-Climax Mark I 5-speed gearbox*' cars, actually including the three works T55s – chassis *10, 11, 12/61* – and at the end of the list there are two new T60 V8 cars for 1962. One interesting entry in December 1961 records *F1/19/61* bound for Okura Trading Co in Japan – this being acquired for investigation and test by Honda with Climax FPF *430/27/1237* installed.

Production T53s sold to Yeoman Credit (three cars), Lucky Casner's new Andrew Ferguson-managed Camoradi International F1 team, to Jack Lewis, Rob Walker, Terry Bartram for his driver Shane Summers, to Bernard Collomb, BP Trading (Centro-Sud), Bib Stilwell, Roger Penske, Hap Sharp and Briggs Cunningham.

In January it was announced that the Driver Training Division was closing down. With Formula 1, Formula Junior, Monaco sports car and Indy commitments resources were stretched too far. Something had to go, and with vigorous competition from Jim Russell's establishment, and the Vanderbyl and Motor Racing Stables schools on the way, return from the Suez stop-gap idea was on the wane.

Andrew Ferguson went off to join Lucky Casner's motor racing division at Masten Gregory's invitation, Ginger Devlin and Terry Kitson merged into the regular set-up at Hollyfield and Langley Road, and 'The School' was gone but not forgotten.

Andrew: 'Some extraordinary things happened on our School days at Brands. Like the time we had 22 airline pilots arrive for a course, and 21 of them flew off the road and crashed in their first few laps.... Then there was the remarkable case of – well – this chap arrived and said "Me Busgith very good South American racing driver", so we put him in a car and told him all about it and it soon became obvious that "Me Busgith very good South American racing driver" was the only English he could speak. Sure enough he up-ended the lot in the biggest possible way and we went rumbling down in the ambulance to pick him up. But he wasn't going to be carted off to some English hospital and he jumped up, fought off the ambulance men and literally ran away across the fields, out of Brands Hatch, out of the School and out of our lives. For all I know he went straight back to Heathrow, bleating "Me Busgith very good South American racing driver" and flew off home, all battered and bruised and still with Brands Hatch mud on his overalls.... The School was like that. It was a wonderful period at Cooper's and I never regret a day of the time I spent there....'

Racing began on 2 January at East London, South Africa, where Bruce Johnstone's Cooper-Alfa Romeo won from the Maserati- and Climax-engined models of John Love and the German Wolfgang Seidel. Few Europeans made the trip. Meanwhile, after Riverside the works Lowlines and their 'old nail' spare car had been shipped to Auckland, New Zealand, for the NZ GP, accompanied by three Yeoman Credit cars, two Coopers and a Lotus 18. John went out to run the works team for Brabham and McLaren, while Flockhart ran the spare car under the Scottish Border Reivers team banner. Reg Parnell's Yeoman crew prepared one of their Coopers for Bonnier and the Lotus for Salvadori, while local entrant Feo Stanton rented their second Cooper for Denny Hulme. There was the strongest-ever opposition, from Team Lotus and BRM.

The Lowlines ran methanol fuel and both fuel pressure and float levels were set very low to improve response out of the slow Ardmore hairpin. But engine demand was so high they were starving at the end of the straight. Bruce tried hard to beat his team leader in this his home GP, but his car starved worse and Jack beat him again, with Flockhart fourth. Jack was on a winning streak; next day in the Bay of Plenty he hooked a 206 lb Mako shark – another ambition fulfilled.

The Wigram race was ruined by torrential rain; Jack winning again from Moss's damaged Walker Lotus, Angus Hyslop's 1.96 Cooper and McLaren, with Hulme fifth as at Ardmore. Then the tourists split, some heading for Sebring, Bruce included, some for Australia. Yeoman Credit stayed in New Zealand, where Bonnier won the Levin race in their Cooper-Climax from Salvadori's Lotus. At Dunedin, Denny

245

Hulme won a national race in his rented Cooper from a private Ferrari and farmer Angus Hyslop's ex-Jensen 1.96. Sister cars were 3–4 driven by David Evans and Tony Shelly – his car ex-Hulme.

At Teretonga, Bonnier again beat Salvadori for Yeoman Credit and a six-lap 'Flying Farewell' race ended the day. Bonnier promptly went flying off into the scrub and demolished the Yeoman Cooper, leaving Roy to win in their Lotus. Reg Parnell chose to abandon the mangled frame in Invercargill....

Meanwhile the works Lowline for Jack, the T51 spare for Flockhart, Team Lotus, Walker and BRM had gone to the Warwick Farm '100' in Sydney, Australia. Moss won in Rob's 18 after temperatures of 110°F cooked Jack's chances and Flockhart pushed his car home fifth. The Coopers of Bib Stilwell and Austin Miller were 3–4.

The New Zealand season ended with Hulme, Gold Star Champion, selling his ex-Yeoman car to Johnny Mansell. He fitted a Maserati engine. Hyslop was voted the year's 'Driver to Europe'.

This Tasman tour ended in Tasmania with the first big Longford road race. Jack smashed all records in the Lowline, lapping the 4½-mile country road course at 108.57 mph and hitting 168 mph on the straight. But UJ failure put him out and Roy won in the ex-Flockhart 'old nail', beating Bill Patterson's 2.5 Cooper-Climax, local man John Youl's 2.2, then Austin Miller before Davison's Aston Martin and Mildren's Cooper-Maserati.

Len Deighton's alleged Cooper FJ ran in this race, this interesting car having been acquired from one Bill Smith of Sunbury, England, who had fitted a Ford 105E Junior engine into an ex-F2 frame, which he claimed to have bought from Rob Walker. The car looked like a Walker Mark I F2 from 1956–57, with the Alf Francis nose cone with additional air intakes either side. It probably was not the 1958 Argentine GP winner as claimed, because Rob had long-since sold that car to John Pringle, from Bangor, Northern Ireland, the Ulster garage owner running the car there in 1959–60 although there was a law suit over its background too.

Back in Europe, the international season saw former F2 race promoters now running a plethora of non-Championship F1 events – 21 of them – plus the new English crop of Inter-

THE 1½-LITRE YEARS – 1961-65

Left *'Lowlines' down-under* – after their resounding World Championship success in 1960, the works 'T53s' were shipped from California's Riverside circuit to Auckland, New Zealand, for the NZ GP, January 1961. But it was Jack Brabham's flying instructor, Ron Flockhart, who initially took the lead in the team's faithful 'Old Nail' spare 'T51' seen here, leading McLaren (47), with Brabham on his tail, Moss's Walker Lotus 18 (7), Ireland's works 18 (1) with team-mate Jimmy Clark on the outside, Denny Hulme in rented Bowmaker-Yeoman car (20) with Graham Hill's BRM P48 on its tail, Lotus 18, Aston Martin DBR5/250 and Cooper-Maserati in rear. The works Coopers finished 1-2-4

The 'Old Nail' again – standard British team nickname for an ancient, much-raced war-horse – Salvadori in command at Longford, Tasmania, March 1961, where Roy won after Jack Brabham retired his 'Lowline'. From the mess under the carburettors it looks as though the ancient 'T51' was running very rich, and running methanol . . .

Continental Formula races, which served briefly to perpetuate 2½-litre racing. Cooper cars provided the bulk of the entry in all these races and enjoyed considerable success, although Lotus were far more successful overall and Ferrari's V6 cars utterly dominated the World Championship, save for two miraculous drives by Moss in Walker's year-old Lotus 18.

Cooper failed to win a single World Championship GP for the first time in four years; Ferrari taking five of the seven they entered, Lotus beating them twice courtesy Moss, and Team Lotus driver Innes Ireland winning the US GP at Watkins Glen, where Ferrari abstained. Of course Ferrari won the 1961 Constructors' Cup from Lotus, but Porsche then headed Cooper-Climax into third place. It was a sorry fall from the heights of 1959-60. In the 21 non-Championship races held, Lotus won no less than 11, while Cooper won five, Ferrari two and Ferguson-Climax, BRM and Porsche one each.

Cooper's wins came in the Lombank Trophy at Snetterton and Glover Trophy at Goodwood, where John Surtees's Yeoman Credit cars did the honours; at Crystal Palace, where team mate Salvadori confirmed his local standing as 'King of the Palace'; at Brussels, where Jack Brabham won in his privately entered re-engined ex-works Lowline – possibly F2/5/60 – and at Aintree, where his brand-new slim-bodied works T55 won the '200' on its debut.

The Cooper picture was far more rosy in the inconsequential InterContinental Formula meetings. Five were held, two at Silverstone, one combined with F1 at Snetterton, one at Goodwood and one at Brands. The 2½-litre FPF-engined T53s won them all; Jack taking the Lombank Trophy at Snetterton in Tommy Atkins's pale-green ex-works Lowline – possibly FII/8/60 – and the Guards Trophy at Brands in his own car fitted with the 2½-litre FPF. Moss won the Lavant Cup at Goodwood and the International and British Empire trophies at Silverstone in his new Equipe Walker T53 Lowline – chassis F1/7/61. Bruce was always competitive in his well-developed Atkins Lowline.

John and Charles initially chose to campaign the works cars only in World Championship races after early forays at Aintree and Syracuse. But in mid-season they appeared in the minor Silver City Trophy F1 race at Brands; normally the lesser events were covered by Brabham's own car or Bruce McLaren's Atkins entry in F1 or ICF trim.

The new T55 works cars were virtually identical to the production 1960-design-based T53s, retaining the same coil-and-wishbone suspension front and rear. The engine, however, had been slung slightly lower in the frame to enable a lower bodyshell to be devised which was also slimmer and included a bulbous multi-curvature Perspex windscreen. To enable the tight-fitting rear bodywork to sweep down around the gearbox the fuel pump was now mounted beneath the Weber carburettors instead of bolted onto the rear end of the inlet cambox and driven by vee-belt and pulley from the crankshaft. What the team tried to keep secret from onlookers was the fact that they were now using a six-speed version of the faithful 'C5S' gearbox, outwardly little different from its 2½-litre predecessor. At Hollyfield Road, Owen Maddock and Eddie Stait were working as and when they could on a completely new six-speed for the forthcoming Climax V8 engine. In the meantime the reduced power and torque accompanying the change from 2½- to 1½-litre engines allowed them to slim down the gearwheels and so pack in six where formerly five had lived. It worked well, and helped the drivers in balancing the car on the Climax engine's relatively narrow torque band, particularly when the roads were wet.

Meanwhile, at the beginning of the year, Harry Mundy observed in *The Autocar*: 'With Brabham and McLaren as drivers [Cooper] have a well-balanced and disciplined team. This, together with Cooper's meticulous preparation of the cars – for none have proved more reliable in the past two years' racing – must give Charles and John Cooper every confidence. . . .'

Such confidence – if indeed they really were that optimistic – was not fulfilled. Porsche's 180 bhp and Ferrari's 185 was too much for the Brits, struggling (if they were lucky) with stop-gap FPF Mark II four-cylinder engines built around the big 2½-litre bottom-end, delivering around 151 bhp at 7500 rpm and 116 ft/lb peak torque at 6250. New 1½-litre V8s were on the way, but would not be generally available until 1962. A pilot batch of eight Mark II engines ran at Monaco in the opening Championship round; Cooper and Lotus having two each, Yeoman Credit, UDT-Laystall, Rob Walker and BRM one each.

On the works slimline T55s' debut at Aintree Bruce McLaren recalled how they still did their best to keep the gearbox secret, and in rain it contributed to a works 1–2 success, Brabham first, Bruce second. They used Dunlop's new D12 high-hysteresis wet-weather compound tyres, which proved admirable on the streaming surface.

The Brits were dragged back to earth with a bump three days later at Syracuse. Unknown Italian Giancarlo Baghetti's new Ferrari V6 slaughtered all opposition, winning from two German Porsches; Jack fourth in his private car ahead of Salvadori's Yeoman Credit entry, and both Coopers had been lapped....

In Surbiton a new face had joined the company in March. Major Terry Owens was married to John's cousin, and freshly retired from the Army he became general manager at Hollyfield Road, relieving Charles and John of day-to-day administration. As one of the staff put it: 'He was an ideal front man to protect John from the likes of Junior customers whingeing about late delivery....' He drove a magnificent vintage straight-eight supercharged Alfa Romeo; Bruce's secretary Eoin Young describing it as 'the longest two-seater I've *ever* seen....'

With the Major's arrival a new penthouse drawing office was built on top of the Hollyfield Road works, Owen and Eddie Stait moving up there while the Major took over their old office down below. Extensive work on the Indy project knocked back development of their all-new six-speed V8 transmission. Eddie: 'We had a Lotus gearbox to look at, very nice, compact, light and ingenious, but unfortunately the gearchange went right through the middle of the shaft; it was a nice idea but it didn't work well in practice, dog life was excessively short. Owen set about the new layout and casing, and I just did the detailing work.... On all our work at Cooper's John had a lot of the original ideas and then Owen would add some very original thinking in developing those ideas; they were a team, like all racing design outfits ... and Jack of course contributed a lot.'

Up at Langley Road, as the Indy deadline approached, some frantic all-nighters were going in on the Kimberley-Cooper. After two in a row the mechanics were out on their feet. The car was up on trestles, at a comfortable leaning height, and they had just taken a much-needed break, leaning on the car with Noddy Grohmann reading the latest *Autosport*, when Charlie Cooper walked in. 'What's all this?' he demanded, slapping at Noddy's magazine: 'I don't pay you to read the *Autosport* on my time!' It was unfair, but understandable, and for Noddy it was the wrong time.... He exploded in fury, swatted Charles with the magazine and threw the Old Man out of his own Formula 1 'shop. Down at Hollyfield Road Roy Golding recalls Charles coming in, looking bemused: ''Ere Roy', he grumbled, 'That Noddy Grohmann's just told me to f—— orf....' The Major was sent to sort it out. 'The tail's been wagging the dog long enough,' he said. It was the beginning of the end for Noddy and Cooper's....

Yet when the pressure was off and Noddy was in the mood Langley Road saw some remarkable goings-on. Terry Kitson first told me about Noddy's fearsome interest in gunnery: 'He decided to make himself a spud gun, using our usual 1½ in. tube with one end welded-up, charge it with acetylene, force a spud down it, flash-off the gas and *boom* away it went, terrorizing the church next door. Then he got ambitious. He had a length of probably 3- or 4½ in. tube – old Connaught de Dion material I think it was – and he built himself a mortar....'

Mike Barney: 'Noddy's mortar was something else. He'd welded a plate into one end, and a spark plug and he had a big pair of calipers, which he took down to the greengrocer's to measure up his stock of turnips. If you got some just the right size to seal adequately you could charge the tube with acetylene, load it, put a battery across the spark plug and off she'd go ... turnips tended to break up – a good, big, hard spud was best....'

Eddie Stait: 'One day they set up Noddy's mortar on the flat roof at Langley Road trying to bombard us and I was on the 'phone in the penthouse at Hollyfield Road spotting the fall of shot for them. They never quite managed to hit us, but they were getting closer all the time....'

Mike Barney: 'We were on town gas up at Langley Road, and Noddy sat up one day and said "we're going to make a balloon bomb". He filled a big balloon with gas so it would fly and filled a smaller balloon with acetylene and tied it under the first. Then he attached a length of Jetex toy rocket fuse to the balloon-full of acetylene and went up on the flat roof and lit the fuse and launched them. They'd float away 'til the burning fuse touched off the acetylene and there'd be an almighty bang. He'd do this occasionally at night when the flash was really spectacular. One time – a dark, foggy night – he filled a huge balloon with acetylene and it took several more full of gas to lift it. Unfortunately the wind backed and took it over the hospital and it went off like a V2, shaking the windows for miles around and blowing people out of bed. The police stopped it all after that – they hadn't liked the mortar at all in the first place.... Chris Skeaping was working with us as the boy then. He was standing on the roof about to launch a pair of balloons with the fuse already lit when the wind flipped the burning fuse up; it touched the balloon

THE 1½-LITRE YEARS — 1961-65

Busy days at Hollyfield Road, with Owen 'The Beard' hard at work on the V8 Climax car's new gearbox. Notice on the wall above his head advises all to 'DO IT TOMORROW – you've made enough mistakes today'. After leaving Cooper in 1963 Owen went to live and work in the Isle of Wight hovercraft industry, but his health failed him. In 1983 his still considerable energies concentrated upon his old love, music. Down in the workshop, production 'T53' or '1961 Formula 1 Cooper-Climax Mark I' production jostled for space with Monaco Mark III tail-finned sports cars. Note integrated water/oil radiator design, the small matrix (left) handling oil, larger matrix water. There's an interesting curved-tube drum-braked coil-spring car just intruding bottom-right, but we don't know what it is . . .

What were apparently the two ex-works World Championship-winning 1960 'Lowlines' in formation at the non-Championship Brussels GP, 9 April, 1961, running 1½-litre FPF 4-cylinder engines; Brabham leading McLaren (in Tommy Atkins' metallic-green and white car) with Surtees' production 'T53' in Bowmaker-Yeoman's dark BRG and maroon right on their heels. Car No 3 is Jack's brand-new 'T55' or so-called 'Slimline' car specially-tailored for the new 1½-litre Formula 1, making its debut and winning in the rain-soaked Aintree '200', 22 April, 1961. Two of these very pretty little cars were built, recognizable by their multi-curvature windscreen mouldings and regulation roll-over bars. Dunlop's new high-hysteresis D12 rain tyres contributed greatly to Cooper's last works team Formula 1 1–2 finish . . .

and it blew-up in his face. You know how oxy-acetylene leaves flakes of ash floating down when it's flashed-off, well young Chris was standing there with his ears ringing, no eyebrows and covered in grey ash. . . .' He would recover, and in later years raced sports and formula cars with considerable success at modest level. . . .

At Monaco, Moss's Lotus denied Ferrari a 1–2–3–4 finish and Brabham – briefly returned from Indy – ran in midfield before ignition trouble put him out. Bruce had carburetion problems throughout, stopped to add fuel and took a single Championship point, sixth but five laps behind Moss's Lotus.

At Zandvoort for the Dutch GP, Stirling tried Walker's spare T53 with 1½ FPF but preferred the Lotus for the race. The works T55s qualified 7–13, and they were outclassed in the race, Jack finishing sixth and Bruce 13th. Tuning the Mark II engine's Weber DCOE9 carburettors was a tricky business; this was thought to be the cause and Bruce's again suffered very badly, stuttering along on three cylinders.

Both works cars ran at Brands' non-Championship race on 3 June, but Jack's oiled its plugs in practice, which was then thought to be the root cause of the earlier trouble. With a rebuilt engine he took fourth place in the race, then the plugs fouled again. Bruce's luck was even worse. Trying to pass a back-marker at Dingle Dell he crashed heavily into the marshal's post, severely damaging his precious T55. Tragedy befell Shane Summers in Terry Bartram's Scots-blue T53 during practice. This promising young driver struck the tunnel parapet at Paddock Bend and was killed instantly. Moss won the race in a UDT Lotus.

At Spa both works cars retired from the Belgian GP. Jack's *10/61* when a piston collapsed and Bruce's repaired *11/61* with misfiring. The latest Weber carburettors were not the beautifully hand-crafted instruments of yore, and their mass-produced float chambers had tiny imperfections which fouled the float. The effect was obvious, but the cause desperately difficult to trace.

At Reims in the French GP Jack pulled into the pits when he saw the oil pressure zero. On stripping, the engine proved undamaged, only the gauge was faulty. Bruce did better, finishing fifth.

THE 1½-LITRE YEARS — 1961–65

Entering this season, Jack Brabham's private business interests were growing rapidly. His Chessington Garage was thriving, and he had invited an old engineering acquaintance from Australia – Ron Tauranac – to join him in England to lay down a line of production FJ cars; hopefully to be followed in 1962 by his own Brabham F1 car. It was a ticklish situation politically, for 68-year-old Charles in particular thought Brabham an ingrate 'after all we've done for 'im', but John could understand Jack's need to progress further. Both Coopers suspected 'something was up', but the double-World Champion did not finally tell them he was leaving until late in the year. It was understandable.

The British GP at Aintree saw Brabham finish fourth in another rain-swept Liverpudlian outing on D12 tyres, while Bruce – outgunned – was eighth.

Now at long last the prototype Coventry Climax V8 engine was ready to make its debut in a Cooper frame at the German GP. This jewel of an engine, with chain-driven dohc per bank, 63 × 60 mm bore and stroke and 1495 cc, had two valves per cylinder and produced around 181 bhp at 8500 rpm, allied to 118 ft/lb torque at 7500 rpm.

The first V8 build had taken place in May but power was disappointing. A last-minute change in port shape was suspected to be responsible, and Walter Hassan decided to butcher a precious head and sleeve its ports. This expedient worked and the original port shape was settled upon. By July, the test engine was yowling away on the Climax dyno, giving 174 bhp. While a second unit was being assembled, the first was rushed to Langley Road, arriving on Friday, 28 July. Just four days later it was installed in the tailored T55-based 'T58' frame – F1/12/61 – and the first British 1½-litre V8 F1 car was ready to run.

Its raucous scream rattled Surbiton windows before it was taken to Silverstone for shake-down testing. On the wrong anti-roll bars the new car wallowed through fast curves, but Jack still lapped at 1:38, enthralled by the engine's smooth response and wide torque band. Its over-run braking effect was considerably less than the FPF's and he had to use the 2½-litre-sized disc brakes harder than ever. Bruce had a brief steer, lapping in 1:38.2. The 2½-litre lap record was 1:34.2.

After 27 test laps the car was trailed home and then taken to Nürburgring. There were immediate practice problems. The distributor had been turned to give the plug leads a better run clear of the hot exhausts. This had blocked an oil hole and seized the distributor drive spindle. Jack practised in his T55 before the V8 was ready again, in late afternoon. The T58 car bottomed, its suspension was wound higher. It still bottomed, but he lapped in 9:15 from a standing start and was much encouraged....

Through Friday night the engine was raised 1 in. at the front and they retuned the downdraught Weber carburettors, which had run rich in slow corners. Jack got down to 8:58.2, but the gearbox was jumping out of second. That afternoon the sun beat down, and in 20 miles running the V8 overheated, but it still proved some 8 mph quicker on the straight than the FPF.

John Surtees made a terrific start to his 1961 season with the Bowmaker-Yeoman team, as here at Goodwood, Easter Monday, captured in this superb Geoff Goddard shot fisting-on left lock in the ess-bend at St Mary's, on his way to winning the Glover Trophy feature race. This is one of the definitive 'T53' 'Lowline' production cars for the new season, probably F1/1/61 chassis

Ending practice, Dunlop broke the bad news. Their 6.00-15 rear tyres would not survive the race at practice wear rates. Without any experience of running 6.50s on the T58 the team had to adjust gear ratios and suspension settings by guesswork to carry these larger tyres in the GP.

Then rain fell. John was haring around trying to find 6.50 rain tyres. There were none. Jack went to the grid with D12s on the front and ordinary 6.50s on the rear, all unscrubbed. It was a dangerous but enforced gamble, and hardly surprisingly he flew off the road after leading into the first corner, and his GP was over before it had really begun. But 'it was a wonderful feeling as I let in the clutch and the Cooper shot away like a shell'. And he had qualified second quickest to Phil Hill's Ferrari . . . the V8s were coming.

Bruce had qualified down the grid and finished sixth, behind Surtees' Yeoman Credit car – of which more shortly.

The V8 looked promising for Monza, where Climax's second prototype unit would be available to Moss in a Walker Lotus. BRM's exquisite new V8 car would also appear there, but in practice only. Cooper managed just one day's testing between Nürburgring and Monza. Silverstone was rainswept, temperatures low and the straight was much shorter than in Italy.

At Monza Jack ran happily for only six laps before the V8's coolant blew out. Noddy and Co rigged a stand-pipe hoping the boiling water wouldn't reach the relief valve at its head. Jack qualified 10th, Bruce utterly outpaced 14th. In the opening race laps the V8 held the Ferraris for speed and led briefly round the banking.

Jack: 'When nothing went wrong after the first six laps I began to hope the plumbers had found a solution . . . but it wasn't long before the trouble recurred. . . .' He boiled his way into retirement, but Bruce drove superbly to take third place in his T55-FPF. Jack Lewis – the Ecurie Galloise privateer with a T53-Climax Mark II – drove another polished race to give Cooper fourth place, 12 sec behind Bruce. The Welshman – who had been through the Brands Hatch School – looked set for a bright motor racing future, but in 1962 he would invest in a private BRM V8, become discouraged and bow out of racing.

Climax engineers eventually traced the V8's overheating to an elusive head-seal failure under load, which could not be reproduced on the test-bed.

On 23 September, Jack ran his works T55 as a private entry in the Oulton Park Gold Cup and finished second to Moss's Walker-entered four-wheel-drive Ferguson – the season's other great novelty. He had a long battle with Bruce in Tommy Atkins's Lowline, which Jack freely acknowledged as 'probably the best-handling Cooper in the business today, owing a great deal to development Bruce has put in himself. . . .'

Atkins had originally asked Bruce to drive a Monaco for him, but the Kiwi suggested better prospects in minor F1 and ICF events; so Tommy had bought ex-works Lowline 8/60 for him. After Jack had driven it successfully at Snetterton, Bruce set to work, wanting to set up the car from scratch. He'd done considerable FJ testing with Ken Tyrrell and 'found lifting the rear roll centre had a pronounced effect. . . . Previously Jack had been chief test driver and I didn't always completely agree with him. . . .' Harry Pearce prepared the Atkins car, as always, and it used a Colotti gearbox – the first to be mated to a $1\frac{1}{2}$-litre engine for Formula 1 – and was transported in an ex-BRM truck.

The works entered the T58 V8 for Jack and the usual T55 for Bruce in the US GP at Watkins Glen, where practice saw the V8 suffer its usual misfiring and handling problems, but overheating seemed under control. Jack qualified on pole 1.1 sec clear of all opposition.

The race saw a magnificent battle between him and Moss, with the four-cylinder Walker Lotus. Jack had a go to prove the V8's superiority and drew 7 sec clear in three laps. Suddenly the water temperature soared clean off the clock and 'he roared into the pits. John, big panic as he sometimes did, grabbed the water cap and of course it blew straight off in a column of steam and boiling water, John understandably dropped it and it clattered down into the cockpit under Jack's seat. Jack was out of the car and he grabbed John by the legs and jammed him up and down on his head in the seat bawling "*Cooper!* Where's the *Caaap!*"' recalls one who was there. But the water pump spindle had sheared and the great Australian driver retired on lap 57 – from his last race in a works Cooper; the team he had served so wonderfully well for six long years.

One moment during that race would stay with him: 'When the car boiled, it gushed its water out of the overflow onto the back wheels as I was going down into a right-hander. The car slid wildly towards the edge of the track, and continued like that for a distance before two of the wheels slipped off onto the dirt. Just at that point there was a corrugated metal safety barrier which I just grazed at about 70 mph before lurching back onto the track. . . .'

The season had seen the works team make 22 race starts, 19 with T55s and three with the V8 T58. The slimline cars returned 13 finishes and six retirements, and the V8 never finished a race. But we must now add the intense activity of the Cooper privateers, with Brabham and McLaren at their head.

Jack's private season with his Lowline – 5/60 – had begun at Pau on Easter Monday when the Tim Wall-prepared car retired with water pump breakage. Six days later it won at Brussels, then followed the ICF programme with $2\frac{1}{2}$FPF replacing the 1500 before its F1 return at Karlskoga and Roskilde in August, then the Modena and Zeltweg races in September. In Sweden, duelling for third place with Surtees, the faithful 'C5S' gearbox stripped third gear: 'It was the first time this had happened to that gearbox, which had proved incredibly reliable....' One week later at Roskilde, Moss's UDT Lotus just beat Jack in one heat by 0.2 sec. Next day the Australian collided with Ireland's works Lotus, but chased Moss in second place until a pinion race seized.

The Modenese invited 30 entries but would only accept 14 starters, at least three of whom would be Italians, so practice was a hectic affair in itself with no money available for non-qualifiers. Jack covered 72 laps to qualify after a broken valve spring robbed his engine of 400 rpm. Off for a bite that evening before stripping the engine, he and Tim Wall returned to find their borrowed garage locked tight. So the sick engine had to do the race, and Jack nursed it home fifth.

At Zeltweg in Austria on the way home from Monza, he finished second behind Ireland's winning works Lotus. A week later at Oulton Park he ran his T55 slimline under his own name.

Meanwhile the Yeoman Credit team, based in Hounslow, managed by Reg Parnell and staffed by ex-Aston Martin personnel, enjoyed considerable success. After six early wins in New Zealand and the UK they had taken the Brussels lap record, placed 2–3 in the first Silverstone ICF, first and the lap record for Roy at Crystal Palace, 2–6 in the second Silverstone ICF, sixth in the British GP, 5–10 in Germany and sixth for Roy at Monza. Talking of John Surtees, 'Uncle Reg' believed 'his best drive was in the Belgian GP at Spa when he finished fifth behind the four Ferraris; he drove wonderfully well that day. The other outstanding drive was Roy in the US GP, when he blew-up near the end when lying second to Ireland's Lotus and challenging for the lead.'

The dark-green Coopers with their maroon noses and stripes were immaculately prepared by Jimmy Potton, Peter Bryant and Gerry Hones and were transported in Albion and Thames Trader transporters. One of the cars – chassis *4/61* – was completed in their workshops as the 'VR' – 'Very Rapid' – Cooper-Climax with slimmer, streamlined bodywork wrapping the cockpit and engine bay more tightly. It was a private slimline, in effect, originally suggested by Surtees, who raced it at Syracuse in April, leading two laps before retirement, but it was not raced again until the British GP. At Karlskoga it was used to save mileage on John's normal race car *1/61* and placed third. At Roskilde a cam follower failed.

1 August, 1961; Cooper-Climax 'T58' V8 first tests at Silverstone. Goddard was there again to capture Jack settling back into the multi-cyclinder prototype, John on the left ('Good God I'm wearing braces!'), engine designer Wally Hassan with hands in pockets on right, Charles in the regal stance far right. In the background stand the legs of the famous Silverstone water tower, still a landmark down by that onetime hard-used layby just beyond Abbey Curve. Today even testing centres on the pit area and the layby is half-forgotten

V8 debut – Jack Brabham giving the latest Coventry Climax racing engine its competitive debut during practice for the 1961 German GP, here diving down into the 'ditch' in the Karussel turn. The car is basically similar to the 'T55 Slimlines' with revised engine bay structure and rear bodywork to accept the new multi-cylinder engine. Jack's race ended on the opening lap, when on unsuitable tyres he slithered off the wet road and into the springy bushes, as captured here by Mike Barney's camera; Ginger Devlin, John and Jack examining the damage. Note proprietary Alford & Alder forged uprights, still in use

Appreciating that a lighter, more compact car could offer some advantage, the team then built-up an FJ-sized special T56 with the 2 in. shorter wheelbase, carrying F1 suspension and brakes, plus a Mark II engine in unit with a new Colotti Type 29 five-speed gearbox, with different engagement systems to the preceding Types 10, 21 and 32. Wearing modified FJ bodywork this interesting little special was tested briefly at Modena with 13 in. front wheels prior to the Italian GP, but only practised there. John then raced it at Zeltweg; placing tenth, in trouble. The Gold Cup saw magneto failure and it didn't go to Watkins Glen.

Lovable old 'Mimo' Dei's Scuderia Centro-Sud persevered through the year with Cooper-Maseratis using Colotti transmission, and one old frame was modified with double wishbones and coil-springs at the rear. At Syracuse newcomer Massimo Natili impressed using an old C-S frame with the latest 1½ Maserati engine, but the cars were also-rans. Dei began the year with two old T51s – one Cooper-, the other Colotti-'boxed – for Mario Cabral and young Lorenzo Bandini at Pau. They finished 3–4 in the team's best result of the year. The Italian was third again at Naples, then C-S dropped from sight until the British GP, where BP and Andrew Ferguson won adequate terms for Bandini and Natili to reappear; the former in a new T53 – *13/61*. He finished 12th, while Natili's gearbox broke on lap 1. Bandini's Maserati engine broke at Nürburgring and Modena, but he was eighth at Monza. The team T53 reappeared at Zeltweg, driven by Renato Pirocchi and Bandini to place a troubled 11th and last.

Meanwhile, Maurice Trintignant had driven for Count Volpi's Scuderia Serenissima, using Cooper-Maseratis with Colotti transmission. Trint's old F2 frame was used initially, then replaced by a T51, in which he was seventh at Monaco. At Spa the F2 car reappeared with additional torsion bars and helper springs, plus a second T51 with modified bodywork. The team ran this car alongside a Cooper-derived De Tomaso-Alfa Romeo for much of the year.

At Pau, Gino Munaron ran a leaf-spring Cooper fitted with

a Conrero-tuned Alfa Romeo engine and redesigned bodywork as the 'F1 Conrero', and now Serenissima took up this theme, without success worth recalling. Trintignant's special-bodied T51 was ninth at Monza, and in Nino Vaccarella's hands was third in the obscure *Coppa Italia* at Rome's Vallelunga circuit in October.

Other Cooper owners' activities that year may be traced in the appendices, but the US GP was interesting in that seven Coopers ran in the field of 19; the works T58 and T55, Yeoman's two T53s, and three sister Lowlines for valued US customers Hap Sharp, Roger Penske (entered by John M. Wyatt III) and Walt Hansgen (Cunningham's car). Pensk was eighth, Sharp tenth and poor Hansgen crashed heavily. His car would become the *Zerex Special* sports racing phenomenon.

In November John suddenly appeared in the penthouse drawing office with a scheme for a rear-engined Mini-Cooper special, a sports two-seater for road use. Eddie Stait: 'It never got off the ground, but it took up a lot of time. John was quite keen on projects like this, but when he went off on some wild adventure Charlie would get terribly upset because he was very conscious of keeping production going all the time.... We were really getting down to fine details of the six-speed V8 gearbox at that time, and a new chap called Neil Johanssen had joined us in the drawing office. The winter was hectic with FJ testing, John Whitmore took me round in a Mini-Cooper, tyre-testing, which is an experience I'll never forget ... and never a day with enough hours in it....'

After the long European season two tours occupied the winter of 1961–62; the Springbok series in South Africa and the Tasman series. Yeoman Credit ran Surtees's regular Lowline plus their FJ special for Tony Maggs and Bruce Johnstone in the Rand GP at Kyalami, these two facing works Lotus and Porsche opposition plus a flock of local machinery including several Coopers; Johnstone was fifth. In the Natal GP neither Yeoman car finished and Johnstone crashed the FJ special. On Boxing Day, the non-Championship South African GP saw Maggs fourth, and with this experience plus a wonderful Tyrrell Cooper FJ season behind him, John invited him to join the works F1 team as number two to Bruce McLaren for 1962–63. Meanwhile Yeoman Credit sold the well-raced but still glistening ex-Surtees T53 to Mike Harris, who raced it widely in Africa with an Alfa-Romeo engine.

One last Springbok race was run at Killarney, near Cape Town, on 2 January, 1962; Maggs placing fifth in the car. The hectic 1961 season, with so much racing to recount, had seen Cooper cars make a grand total of 130 starts in 29 races, compared to Lotus's 125. By coincidence, in World Championship GPs both Cooper and Lotus made 55 starts. Lotus equalled Hollyfield Road in customer F1 car production and in years to come would move ahead as Cooper's competitive edge became blunted. The change in balance was immediate. The old magic was waning fast....

Coopers still featured strongly in the 1962 season-opening Tasman series. The NZ GP at Ardmore was again marred by blinding rain. Newly married Bruce McLaren led in Atkins's Lowline using the 2.7 engine fresh from the Peter Berry Monaco in California. After Bruce lost his way in the rain and found himself on the wrong side of the course markers, Moss won in Walker's new Lotus 21 from Surtees's now Bowmaker-Yeoman-sponsored 2.7 T53. The Atkins car finished third, Salvadori's B-Y $2\frac{1}{2}$ fourth and Bandini's 2.8 C-S Cooper-Maserati was fifth.

Jack Brabham broke a gear selector in his ex-works T55 when running third with $2\frac{1}{2}$ FPF fitted instead of the 2.7, which he also had available. The third Bowmaker-Yeoman Cooper had been sold to Lex Davison, while Centro-Sud entered Johnny Mansell in one of their Cooper-Maserati 2.8s after he had become disillusioned with his own car in recent races.

Moss drove the Walker T53 at Levin, saving his Lotus for more important events. In more rain Brabham won from Moss, Surtees and Bruce. Fierce sun beat down on the Lady Wigram Trophy race; Moss won in his Lotus, from Brabham, Surtees, McLaren, Salvadori and Hyslop – a Cooper 2–3–4–5–6, and with Mansell eighth. Bruce had qualified on pole but made an awful start.

Bowmaker-Yeoman then took off for Australia and missed Teretonga. Harry Pearce set up Bruce's Atkins car with only the left-side fuel tank for the short, mainly left-turn race, and after beating Moss's Lotus in the prelim he 'had one of my most pleasing drives, picking up more than a second a lap on Jack and Stirling', and he had almost lapped Brabham when the chequered flag was shown. He also won the Flying Farewell race that day.

In Australia, at Warwick Farm, Hyslop and Bandini arrived ahead of their cars travelling surface from New Zealand, and they learned the circuit in Bib Stilwell's ex-Moss Cooper Monaco. Practice was stopped after Salvadori had an enormous accident when his brakes grabbed, after a scrambled wheel change to fit soft wet-mix qualifying tyres. There were initial fears for his life, but he escaped with severe concussion. Jack led before his home crowd until his private T55's gearbox split, leaving Moss victorious in Walker's 2.7 Cooper from Bruce, Stilwell's $2\frac{1}{2}$ and Bandini, with Hyslop sixth.

Meanwhile, at Dunedin, poor Johnny Mansell missed the start in his Cooper-Maserati, and joined in long after the rest of the field, in pouring rain. He lost control, rammed a power post and the car broke in two, and he died.

The Australian tour continued at Lakeside, near Brisbane. Tim Wall had cannibalized the gearbox from Salvadori's wreck to put Brabham on the grid and he won from Stilwell's ex-Bowmaker car. Bruce had arranged to sell his Atkins car to Australian motoring writer and team patron David McKay, but used it at Lakeside and stripped fourth gear. He then made his trip to Europe to test Tyrrell's latest FJ Cooper and on to Italy with the Cunningham Monaco and Maserati.

John Surtees had also been home, to get married, and returned on his honeymoon for the Longford meeting, where his 2.7 Bowmaker-Yeoman car beat Brabham's; the pair reaching 171 mph through the speed-traps. Davison wrecked his ex-Bowmaker car in practice, bouncing from a tree into the wall of a pub. Leaving the steaming wreck where it lay, he stumped into the bar and crisply ordered a double brandy. . . .

There were 12 starters, of which 10 were Coopers, and one – right on the back of the grid – was Ernie Clay's ancient front-engined Cooper-Bristol. Stilwell finished third, Hyslop fourth, McKay fifth, followed by Patterson, Youl's 2.2 and Ron Marshall's $1\frac{1}{2}$. . . .

The tour ended at Melbourne's new Sandown Park course, where McLaren and Surtees fought wheel-to-wheel in the prelim, the motorcyclist edging the verdict. Brabham was unbeatable in the Final, though Surtees tried his lurid best and failed by only 0.8 sec. Bruce was third in what was now the ex-Atkins McKay car. Jack used his ex-Indy 2.7 engine, having sold the $2\frac{1}{2}$ to Stilwell and his older ex-works T53 to Davison as a replacement for his Longford wreck. 'Davo' asked Salvadori to drive the new car at Sandown, using the FPF engine salvaged from Roy's Warwick Farm crash. The Cooper star was yet to wane in Australia. . . .

During 1962, Coventry Climax prepared new Mark II V8 engines for Cooper, Lotus, Bowmaker-Lola – the Reg Parnell-managed team having now forsaken Cooper chassis – and Brabham's new marque. They faced Ferrari's ageing V6 and Porsche's new flat-eight, plus the V8 BRMs.

The World Championship would commence at Zandvoort on 20 May. Before that seven non-Championship F1 races were run. Bowmaker, awaiting delivery of their new Lolas, ran the FJ-based Cooper T56 special at Brussels and Snetterton for Salvadori, but it finished neither event. Ian Burgess also reappeared on the scene in his Mrs Louise Bryden-Brown-owned Anglo-American Equipe's T53 – chassis *3/61*. Bernard Collomb practised his T53 – *9/61* – at Brussels, but had the misfortune to see it burn to the waterline when a fuel fire got out of hand.

The works made their bow at Easter Goodwood with new team leader Bruce McLaren driving his Mike Barney/Ginger Devlin-built T55 – *11/61* – in the Lavant Cup race specially organized for four-cylinder F1 cars only. He started from pole, won easily and set fastest lap on the way. In the Glover Trophy, against V8 cars, he was second again behind Graham Hill's new multi-cylinder BRM. It was this race which saw the end of Stirling Moss's career, against the earth bank at St Mary's. . . .

At Pau, Burgess drove the Aiden-Cooper special, built by Anglo-American's mechanic Aiden Jones and based on an FJ frame with Climax FPF $1\frac{1}{2}$ engine and Cooper five-speed gearbox, hip-mounted radiators and a pointed nose. It finished eighth.

Bruce's 'old nail' T55 ran again in the Aintree '200' and was excellent, finishing second, just like the previous year. He was elated at having beaten the Ferraris of Phil Hill and Baghetti – but they were a spent force this season. At Silverstone, Bruce finished fifth in the old four-cylinder car, and two weeks later came the Dutch GP and the debut of the new Cooper-Climax T60 V8. . . .

In effect the car was a creation of Owen Maddock, Bruce McLaren and John Cooper plus accumulated knowledge and experience elsewhere in the team. As always it was design by evolution rather than revolution, and the construction was carried out at Langley Road in the Formula 1 team shop. One description of the new car commented that whereas 'the Cooper chassis used to be a series of mounting brackets connected by tubes . . . now it's a series of mounting brackets connected by water and oil pipes.' The top-left and bottom-right longerons were used to carry water from radiator to engine, the other two carried oil. Top longerons were 18-gauge $1\frac{1}{2}$ in. material, bottom 16-gauge $1\frac{3}{8}$ in. and the frame was as strong as ever and, thanks to Bruce's influence, considerably more rigid. Cross- and triangulation members were all 18-gauge.

Bruce's thinking was also revealed in the relatively high roll centres, at around 5 in. front and 6 in. rear. Jack habitually preferred lower centres but acknowledged how well the Atkins Lowline had cornered. Alternative bolt holes were provided to raise or lower wishbone pick-ups on the chassis.

Top *End of the road – Jack Brabham's last race as a works Cooper driver was here in the United States GP, Watkins Glen, 8 October, 1961. His 'T58' V8 leads Moss's Walker Lotus, Hill's BRM, Ireland's ultimately victorious works Lotus 21 and Bruce's team 'T55', with on the inside Gurney's silver Porsche and Clark's Lotus 21 spoiling for a fight. The Cooper in the background, distinctive with its twin white stripes, is Hap Sharp's 'T53'*

The Cooper empire after 25 years' effort, depicted in this montage promotional photo; Charles and John supposedly blocking Hollyfield Road with their Mini-Coopers, No 243 Ewell Road on the corner with the family flat above where first Mr & Mrs Cooper Snr then Mr & Mrs Jr lived before buying properties elsewhere; the corner showroom where Stirling Moss spotted his first Cooper 500, where Owen Maddock studied the ThinWall Special and from where Ian Burgess and Andrew Ferguson used to run the Drivers' School. In the background is the rebuilt production factory, now with the drawing office housed in the penthouse extension, while Major Owens had taken over the old drawing office behind the 'Esso' sign. Inset, the Cooper Spl 'T1', John up, in the Brooklands paddock

36

AUSTIN COOPER

62

Building a winner – Mike Barney's photography preserves Langley Road construction of the prototype 1962 'T60' Formula 1 car, tailor-made for Climax's new production V8 engine. On trestles it shows how the main-frame longerons doubled as water and oil pipes, and how detachable frame rails in engine bay ran over twin cam-boxes each side. Down below is the prototype six-speed 'C6S' transaxle case intended to carry inboard rear brakes in the new V8. Owing to a freely-confessed 'cock-up' they wouldn't fit in the car. The Maddock-designed Cooper-Knight 'C6S' was never as reliable nor popular as the World Championship-winning five-speeder. It was on the roof here at Langley Road that Noddy Grohmann's mortar and acetylene balloon bombs rocked Surbiton's normal suburban calm . . .

Monaco was the only circuit on which the highest holes, providing the lowest roll-centre, would be used, and even at Nürburgring the centre height was maintained, although in the rain which fell there it might have been a good idea to drop them.

An Alford & Alder proprietary forged front upright was used, as on the Triumph Herald saloon car, ball-jointed top and bottom and so giving the designer two fixed starting points. Front suspension was by quite narrow-based double wishbones, with partially inboard coil-spring damper units picking-up on a brace half-way along the bottom wishbone and reacting against a top chassis abutment. All joints were fitted with grease nipples. Screw-threaded outer ends gave camber adjustment.

At the rear magnesium uprights were used, located by double wishbones, the lower component being longer and in three pieces to control toe-in. Again co-axial coil/damper units were mounted outboard, this time ahead of the axle line. The springs were very soft Aeon bump rubbers mounted around the Armstrong damper piston rods sharing the load. The thickness and therefore rate of these rubbers could be altered as required, giving further adjustment and adaptability to differing circuits and conditions. Relatively thin anti-roll bars were fitted fore and aft, passing above the frame, not through it.

Girling disc brakes were mounted outboard in the wheels at front and rear, $10\frac{1}{4}$ in. and $9\frac{3}{4}$ in. diameter respectively. It was intended originally to mount the rear brakes inboard on the transaxle cheeks, but due to a self-confessed 'cock-up' in the drawing office insufficient space was left between the casing and the frame. This sparked another of John's famous eruptions. The brakes were hastily remounted outboard, and there they stayed.

Steering was by modified Morris Minor rack-and-pinion, with alternative pinions available to vary ratios. A 13 in. steering wheel was fitted.

The latest version of the Cooper-Knight gearbox provided six speeds in constant mesh, selected by internal dogs, and ratios could be changed rapidly by removing the end cover and sliding out the gears. Now it carried 'C6S' cast onto the casing. There were 17 alternative ratios, while final-drive gearing was fixed at 9:41. There were to be early problems with the V8 installation, but as always the 'box proved pleasant to use, and quick with its spring-steel selector forks and minimal power-loss and relatively lightweight by the standards of its time.

Variations in drive-shaft length due to suspension movement were accommodated by adapting a Citroën DS19 drive-shaft coupling with the UJ itself housed within a large-diameter splined casing at the inboard end of the shaft; the spline size and siting reducing binding to a minimum.

This new T60, or 'V8 Mark II' car, ran on 13 in. front wheels to improve penetration and unsprung weight, wearing

THE 1½-LITRE YEARS — 1961–65

5.50-section Dunlop Racing tyres on 6 in. rims of familiar spoked design. The rears were 15 in. diameter, carrying 6.50 tyres on 7 in. wide rims. Wheelbase was 7 ft 7 in., front track 4 ft 3½ in. and rear track 4 ft 2½ in. The bodywork by the Beddings made this the most handsome single-seat Cooper yet, and the pannier fuel tanks formed the outer body sides.

The first two T60s appear in the 1961 'Mark I' section of the surviving Register as '*Works No. IV*' and '*Works No V*', numbered F1/17/61 and F1/18/61 respectively. The purchase tax on each of them at that time was no less than £1813 12s. 6d, with a surcharge of £181 7s. 3d. . . .

In Holland, Colin Chapman sprang his monocoque Lotus 25 on the racing world and Porsche also unleashed their *Typ* 804. Of the three débutantes the Lotus was the most impressive. Tony Maggs made his bow in the works T55 while Bruce drove the new V8, but in practice its transmission quill-shaft broke. The only replacement was an identical spare, so Bruce went into the race with little confidence and the shaft broke again; but he was running second, pleased with the car's feel. Maggs finished fifth, and Jack Lewis eighth in his old T53.

For Monaco the 'C6S' gearbox was converted to only four speeds, and a redesigned quill-shaft installed. Bruce led the field from third place on the grid, before sitting back to let Graham Hill's BRM set the pace. Clark's Lotus 25 took second place before retiring, and Bruce was then following Hill's leading BRM comfortably when he became aware of excitement in the crowds. The BRM was in trouble and died, and all Bruce had to do was maintain the lead for the last five laps. . . .

'Phil Hill was 17 sec back so I could slow a little and make absolutely sure. . . . With three laps left, Mike Barney and John began feverishly hanging signals on the board. They had been timing the gap on one side of the pits and hurriedly putting it on the board for me to read as I went past the other. . . . I had time to chuckle. Phil was still 5 sec away, even if he were on my tail there was nowhere to pass on that last half-lap. . . .'

Bruce won by 200 yards and his first words to John were 'This is a terrific car!' He later wrote of the T60: 'It was

What a way to go racing. The works team travelled to Monaco 1962 with two cars, two drivers and just two mechanics – Mike Barney and Wally Willmott. Mike's sequence here shows (top), Bruce's V8 'T60' in the Renault garage by the quayside just prepared and, once body has been attached, ready to start the race. (Centre) Graham Hill's wheel-spinning BRM V8 beats Bruce's Cooper – far side – and Clark's Lotus 25 V8 – bottom right – off the line as Louis Chiron against the Armco flourishes the starting flag. (Bottom) – job done, Bruce's victorious car with its laurels, back in the Renault dealers'

259

JAMES.A.ALLINGTON.

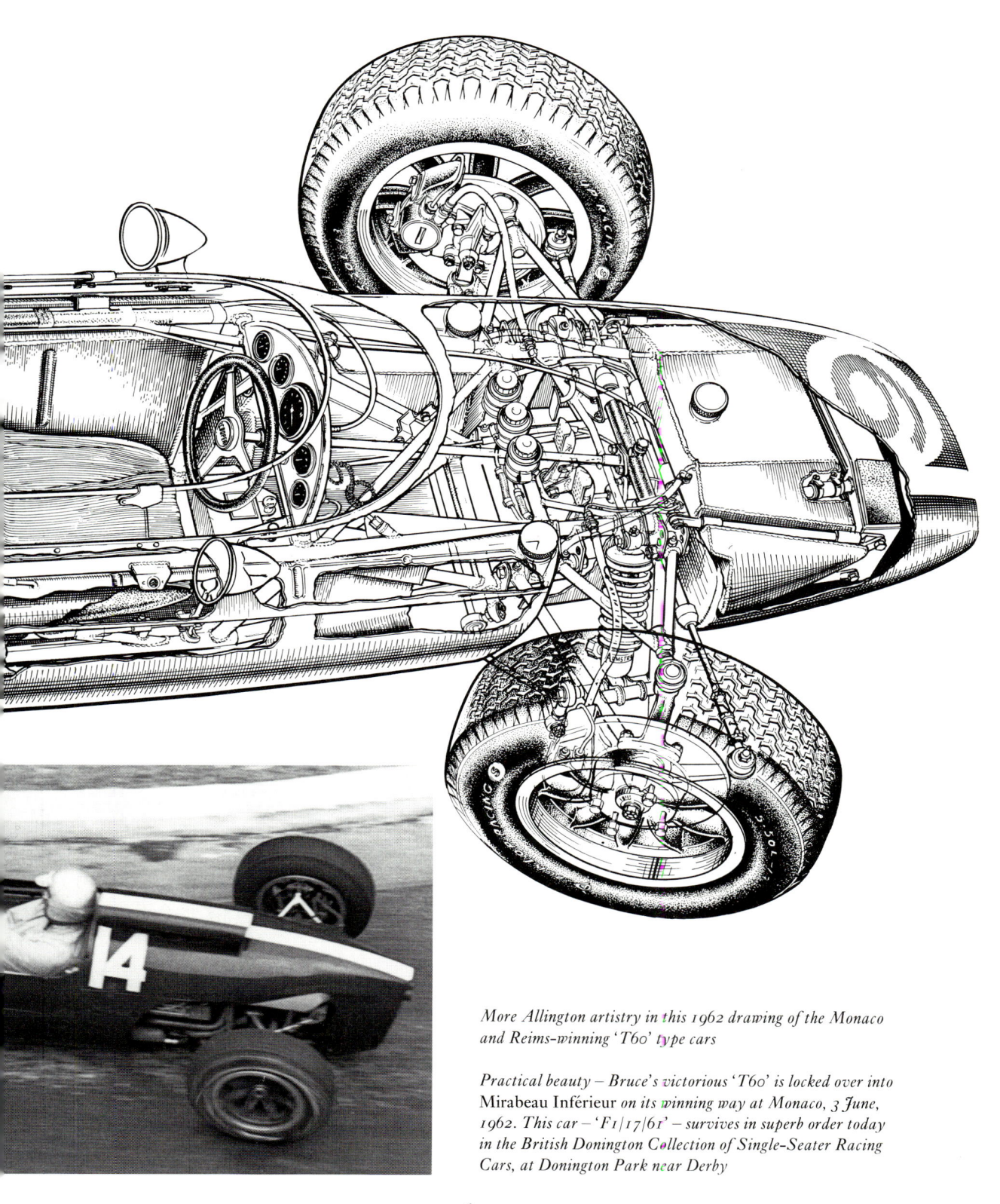

More Allington artistry in this 1962 drawing of the Monaco and Reims-winning 'T60' type cars

Practical beauty – Bruce's victorious 'T60' is locked over into Mirabeau Inférieur on its winning way at Monaco, 3 June, 1962. This car – 'F1/17/61' – survives in superb order today in the British Donington Collection of Single-Seater Racing Cars, at Donington Park near Derby

a well-thought-out car, with nothing liable to fall off . . . not particularly light, nor particularly original, but I had proved it was a winner. . . .'

Mike Barney and Wally Willmott crewed the team at that race. Noddy 'threw a wobbly for some reason before we left, and just didn't come. That's all there was to it. . . .' The mechanic who had contributed so much effort, skill and capability to the team through such crucial and historic years followed Jack Brabham to his new Formula 1 team, and the old partnership struck up anew. . . .

Meanwhile, at Monaco the pit crew had been worried sick by their car, which hooted past with a peculiar sibilance lap after lap. They never did locate the cause, and it never happened again. Mike Barney: 'It was possibly something to do with the twin exhaust pipes tucked inside the tail-cowl – it sounded as though it was acting like a big whistle!'

The second T60 was running in time for Spa. Bruce qualified on the front row of the grid and ran third until a big-end bearing failed. Maggs was impressive in his V8 until the shrunk-in centre of a gearwheel pulled out in the six-speed gearbox.

On 1 July, a non-Championship F1 race was held at Reims, since that year's French GP was at Rouen. Bruce had a feeling about this race and slipstreamed Clark's Lotus until it broke, then took the lead. His six-speed gearbox gave him an advantage on the uphill sections of the course. Jack Brabham was racing a private Lotus 24 V8 that season, pending completion of his own new F1 car, and he and Graham Hill duelled with the new Cooper number one until Bruce overdid his braking

End of an era – Bruce McLaren had been an integral part of the Cooper team throughout their front-line Formula 1 career and here at Reims-Gueux, 1 July, 1962, his victory with 'T60' chassis 'F1/18/61' was the Cooper Car Company's last until Mexico 1966 under new management and in a new Formula. Here Bruce rounds Thillois, the photographers behind emphasizing the low build of modern F1 cars as Jack Brabham's private Lotus-Climax 24 V8 and Graham Hill's BRM P57 lock over behind

It was nothing unusual to find competitive Coopers being built-up in lock-ups and backyards all round the UK, but particularly in the Surbiton and Chessington area. Here is Bruce's 'T60'-framed 4-cylinder 2.7 Climax FPF-engined 'T62' Tasman special waiting to go to New Zealand for the start of the 1963 down-under series. Another exceptionally handsome member of the marque, and it was a winner. But Bruce sold it to Lex Davison for 1964. Rocky Tresise crashed fatally in it at Longford in 1965

and shot up an escape road. He rejoined 100 yards astern and 'next time past the pits I could see the despondency amongst the Cooper crew. They looked at me as though to say, "Oh no, what have you done?"'.

Bruce took his engine to 8800 rpm and within one lap was back with the leaders, then slingshot back into the lead and pulled away a second a lap to win through strength, not mere reliability, Bruce driving *18/61* – the Maggs car from Spa.

THE 1½-LITRE YEARS — 1961–65

Tony drove the old T55 and retired with failing oil pressure. Bruce was always excellent on the fastest circuits: Reims, Spa, Monza.... But this was to be Cooper's last Formula 1 win for more than four years.

One week later Bruce was again on the front row, for the French GP at Rouen, but soon found gears jumping out. This caused a spin, but after two stops he finished fourth. Only later was it found that the chassis had cracked and a wishbone been bent in the spin. The other favourites had trouble, Gurney won in his flat-eight Porsche and Tony Maggs was second in his works T60. John was delighted for him, but less happy when Bruce's gearbox was stripped to reveal that the centre of fourth gear, now brazed-in, had pulled out. The selector dogs had been jumping out.

Clark's Lotus 25 won at Aintree, and Bruce was outpaced by Surtees's Lola and finished third; Maggs was sixth. At Nürburgring, Tony crashed his T60 in practice on oil spilled after Graham Hill's BRM had run over a movie camera which had fallen from another car. Bruce was fifth, Tony ninth in the T55.

Meanwhile, at Hollyfield Road, Bruce's Monaco was under construction for the US Fall series and at Tommy Atkins's Chessington works, Harry Pearce and Wally Willmott were assembling a special Tasman Cooper for Bruce's winter campaign. Back at the start of the year, Atkins had arranged to buy a T60 frame and running gear to accept a customer BRM V8 engine. Bruce would drive in minor F1 races which the works chose not to enter, as with the Lowline the previous season. But come June the V8 engine was still not available, so when Bruce was contacted by the Australian GP organizers about entering their race – to be run with the Commonweath Games at Perth that November – he bought the frame to fit a 2½ FPF.

The European F1 season continued, with the Oulton Gold Cup on 1 September where Bruce qualified yet again on the front row. An earnest fire-extinguisher salesman had plagued the team the previous day, and ironically Bruce lost a good race placing when the T60 caught fire!

The works team was back to full T60 strength in the Italian GP, in which Bruce headed Mairesse's Ferrari to the line by 0.4 sec for third place, with Maggs placed seventh.

Around this time the Tasman special first turned a wheel at Goodwood. Initially the frame flexed through the engine bay, so it was braced, the front wishbone pick-ups reinforced and larger steering arms fitted. Stiffer springs were borrowed to control roll, with two coils amputated for the required ride height. A second test session at Goodwood saw Bruce smashing the lap record, at 1:10.8.

At Watkins Glen on 7 October the works T60s placed third and seventh in team order in the US GP. Cooper F3 and Monaco sports car driver Timmy Mayer drove a T53 under the works banner, but retired with ignition problems. Sharp's old T53 was 11th. On 4 November, the inaugural Mexican GP took place as a non-Championship event. Bruce ran *17/61* as the lone works entry, while Alan Connell fielded his T53 – *16/61*. Bruce led from lap 13 to lap 34, and felt he could win, until his engine broke; Connell's had long since failed....

263

Two weeks later at Caversham, outside Perth, Bruce crashed his new 2.7 Tasman special mildly in practice, but recovered to win the Australian GP comfortably. Jack Brabham's new Brabham-Climax, using McLaren's spare 2½ FPF, had led until a back-marker sent him off the road.

One round remained in the 1962 World Championship, the South African GP, and it was to decide the titles between Graham Hill and Jim Clark, BRM and Lotus. It would be held on 29 December, after three preliminary Springbok races. Tony Maggs drove what had become his ex-works T55 at Kyalami without success and then sold it to John Love, who was sixth in it at Natal. At East London, Graham Hill became World Champion for BRM while McLaren and Maggs finished strongly 2–3 for Cooper-Climax and Love was eighth.

In practice there Bruce's T60 had run a vee-shaped radiator within a cut-back nose. It was hastily replaced by a conventional set-up for the race, amidst some Cooper family embarrassment. It had been Charles's idea, tailor-made at colossal expense by Serck Services; it was a rare and expensive flight of fancy on the Old Man's part.

While the 1963 season commenced with eight races in the Tasman tour, the year would see 24 Formula 1 events in which Cooper cars made only 34 starts compared to Lotus's staggering total of 161; no doubting which marque now had the greater customer support, but Cooper still had some good races to come.

The traditional Tasman opener, the NZ GP, was transferred this year to the new Pukekohe road circuit in Auckland. Tony Maggs had signed with Reg Parnell's Bowmaker team for this tour and the coming Formula 1 season, alongside Surtees, and they were running Lolas in New Zealand with 2.7 Climax FPF engines, plus a 2.7 T53 as spare. Bruce McLaren fielded his latest Cooper special fresh from its Caversham victory. He led before his home crowd and set fastest lap before a cooked magneto and split fuel tank put him out. Surtees won from Hyslop's 2½ T53. Young Jim Palmer celebrated his 21st birthday with third place in the loaned Bowmaker T53.

At Levin, Jack Brabham scored in his own new 2.7 Brabham-Climax. Bruce tried too hard to overcome a lowly grid placing after missing the prelim with magneto and clutch trouble, and he bent his car's steering in a spin. At last his home-country luck changed at Christchurch, where he won the Lady Wigram Trophy. Incredibly it was his first long-distance race win in New Zealand, but it was a close thing, with oil pressure dangerously low near the end, and only 0.5 mm tread left on the outside rear tyre. Jack Brabham, sweetly beaten into second place, was on completely bald tyres at the flag. . . .

Bruce won again at Teretonga, holding off Brabham before the former World Champion's car punctured. Angus Hyslop placed well, his exploits winning the Gold Star Championship. Bruce also enthralled the crowds with a Mini-Cooper that he had shipped out for the supporting saloon car races, suitably modified by Pearce and Willmott.

Again it was blisteringly hot for the Australian GP at Warwick Farm, run confusingly only two months after the previous year's event. Brabham won in a new car having sold his New Zealand mount to David McKay to replace the Aus-

Bruce said it felt as though it was jacking itself up into the air and getting up on tip-toe, and he was right. The unpainted 1963 F1 prototype 'T66' (or 'T63' according to the works Register) made its debut in the Glover Trophy race, Easter Monday Goodwood, and is captured here wheel-waving its way through Madgwick Corner after the pits. The driver isn't happy . . . are we surprised?

tralian's ex-Atkins Lowline, which went to young Chris Amon in New Zealand. Bruce was third, close to exhaustion, but ahead of the McKay and Stilwell Brabhams. Now Coopers were becoming *passé* even down-under, in their last great stronghold. Bruce wryly recalled the arguments with John over using chassis rails for water and oil: 'I'd heard the Lotus boys needed morphia for burns in one particularly hot race in South Africa, and John replied, "Well, boy, we'll just have to carry morphia!"'

At Lakeside, in tropical rain, Bruce and Tasmanian grazier John Youl lined-up abreast on the front row in their Coopers, the Tasmanian's car being the ex-Brabham T55. Bruce spun off after hitting a puddle and almost dropped it into the lake. Best-placed Cooper at the finish was 19-year-old Chris Amon's ex-Bowmaker car, fourth in McKay's Scuderia Veloce colours.

Bruce won again at Longford, where only Brabham and Maggs of the international circus opposed him. Jack broke an oil pipe, Youl and Palmer finished 3–4. Lex Davison won the supporting race from Amon and Youl, Bruce having broken a UJ yoke after stalling on the line and recovering to take the lead. During practice 'Davo' had broken his ex-Bowmaker car's gearchange near the pub he'd hit the previous year. 'Why hallo Mr Davison, back again?' remarked the landlord's wife as he entered. . . .

At Sandown Park there were eight Coopers in a 19-strong field; McLaren, Davison, Youl, Patterson, Palmer, Amon, Thompson and Frank Gardner in the ex-Moss/Walker T53. It was the last race of the series and McLaren and Brabham duelled wildly, ignoring rev limits. With 1½ laps to run, Jack was ahead when a big-end bolt let go in his 2.7 and Bruce dodged by to notch his fifth win of the tour; most of which were at Jack's expense. Youl was fifth, the other Coopers out of luck. Gardner's actually shattered its right-front brake disc going into a corner and crashed heavily. He was unhurt.

In Europe, the F1 season commenced at Snetterton on 30 March where Bruce was fourth in the faithful T60. The new year's T66 – *F1/4/63* – would make its debut unpainted at the Goodwood Glover Trophy. Meanwhile, down-under Lex Davison continued Bruce's winning ways in the Cooper Tasman special to take the Bathurst '100' from the Brabhams after McKay's engine had blown.

Wally Willmott had joined Mike Barney, Ray Rowe and Hughie Frankland as the race mechanic strength at Langley Road, 'Noddy' Grohman having at long last followed Jack to Brabham's, while Terry Kitson welded frames and worked on the team as required. The new T66 largely followed the successful straight-tube formula of the 1962 T60, but it was narrower and size and weight were saved. The floor section between the front and rear bulkheads was reinforced with mild steel sheet instead of aluminium. The main longerons still carried water while the bottom-left rail acted as the oil catch tank for the engine and transaxle breathers. Main changes involved the suspension. The T60 had been prone to marked pitch, particularly under braking, when the front wheels would take on marked negative camber and up-edge their tyres. The move towards squarer tyre crown profiles could not tolerate such camber change. So the axis of the top front wishbone pick-ups on the chassis was inclined 5 degrees down towards the nose to give anti-dive, and the rear

Almost! – Bruce was second in the Belgian GP at Spa, 9 June, 1963, running the high-penetration nose-cone seen here. In torrential rain at the finish he caught and passed Gurney's Brabham, but was still over 4 minutes behind Clark's uncatchable works Lotus. He and the Coopers would always shine on the fastest circuits, however low fortunes sank elsewhere. The anti-dive angle of the front wishbones, forward pivots lower than aft, and anti-squat angle of the rear wishbones, forward pivots higher than aft, can be clearly seen. Note also low anti-roll bar mounting at front, high at rear, and still Alford & Alder uprights

11 degrees down towards the tail for anti-squat. On the rear suspension the top wishbones were shorter and more steeply inclined than before to lower the roll-centre – Bruce's thinking having developed further in this area.

The slimmer aluminium body was achieved in part by reducing the pannier fuel tanks' capacity and using an 8-gallon integral seat tank beaten in aluminium. These tanks each had separate fillers, and breathed through the roll-over bar behind the driver's head. The 'C6S' transaxle was retained unchanged. The front anti-roll bar was coupled to the bottom wishbones, while at the rear an over-chassis bar used long links to couple to the bottom wishbone.

The car was to use the first of Climax's new short-stroke Mark III FWMV V8 engines; 67.94×51.56 mm, displacing 1495 cc and with compression raised to 11.0:1. With Lucas fuel injection replacing the Weber carburettors this unit revved to 9500 rpm and gave 195 bhp with 118 ft/lb torque at 8000 rpm. The new car's wheelbase was 7 ft 7 in., front track 4 ft 3½ in., rear track 4 ft 2½ in., and again it ran on 13 in. diameter front wheels, 15 in. rears.

In most published Cooper type number series, the 1963 F1 cars are listed as the T66 model. The surviving factory Register in fact enters them under the heading '*1963 FORMULA I TYPE 63*'. Six cars are included, numbers 3–6 being works cars – chassis *FI/2/63* being reserved for Rob Walker, whose driver would be Jo Bonnier; while the first frame listed – *1/63* – was actually a *Libre* version of the T60 supplied to Ulsterman John Pringle to accept the engine and gearbox from his existing car. In fact the prototype 1963 car debuted by McLaren at Easter Monday Goodwood appears to have been *FI/4/63*, the subsequent sister car for Tony Maggs was *FI/5/63* and *3/63* was the number applied to Walker's new machine when it finally appeared at Spa to supplement the ex-Maggs T60 – *18/61* – which Rob had hired early in the year and subsequently bought for JoBo's use. All rather confusing....

Bruce was second in the unpainted new car at Goodwood, using the latest short-stroke, fuel-injected Climax V8, and at Aintree Tony Maggs rejoined him in the older works T60, for Bowmaker had abruptly retired from racing. Bruce was desperately unhappy with the new car there, lapping a second slower than his T60 time the previous year. A Silverstone test session was planned to sort out the new car's handling prior to the May International, but the weekend before this could happen, on 4 May, John Cooper had a severe road accident....

He had been at Biggin Hill airfield where somebody had taxied into his light plane and creased it. He was due at a dinner party at Roy Salvadori's new Esher house that evening, and he drove home – not best pleased – in the twin-engined Mini prototype with which they had been experimenting at Hollyfield Road.... He awoke in hospital badly knocked about, with cracked ribs, amnesia and very severe concussion, the car having rolled several times on the Kingston Bypass, reducing itself to scrap. Its twin transmissions had possibly selected conflicting gears, but the damage was so extensive a precise cause for the accident was never established. John would be back in harness quite soon, but it would be many months before he was fully fit. Many of his men believe he was never the same man ... not while Cooper Cars were in racing.

Ken Tyrrell stepped-in to help Charles – himself an ailing man with heart trouble – to run the team, and after a successful Silverstone test session Bruce confidently qualified on the front row for the Trophy race and finished second. Tony was sixth in his new, unpainted, second-string T66.

Ken took the team to Monaco, where the cars ran with bumper bars protecting the gearbox oil pumps and pipework; Bruce and Tony finishing very well, third and fifth. At Spa for the superfast Belgian GP, Bruce's car was rigged with more aerodynamic front body panelling, with a tiny nose aperture and more enclosing screen. Despite a late-race rainstorm sweeping the Ardennes course, Bruce finished strongly second and Maggs was classified seventh, after they had qualified 4–5 on the second row of the grid. Bruce was leading the World Championship by a point from Graham Hill, Clark and Richie Ginther, but it would not last.

Both T66s ran the sleeker bodies at Zandvoort, Bruce qualifying again on the front row, but both would retire, with gearbox failure and overheating. Nose apertures were enlarged slightly for the French GP at Reims, and there Tony Maggs survived to finish strongly, second, while Bruce's ignition 'black box' overheated and cut-out his engine. At the British GP meeting the Coopers were remarked upon as being the only F1 cars still without radius-rod rear suspension location. Bruce's engine snapped a con-rod, Tony was ninth

The Cooper 'T70' Tasman cars built for Bruce McLaren and Teddy Mayer's new Bruce McLaren Motor Racing Ltd team's down-under programme in January–March 1964 aimed towards a form of semi-monocoque construction to approach Lotus 25 rigidity. Here panel men Fred Bedding and his son Pete are seen with Bruce at Langley Road, working on the prototype. Pete is offering up the freshly-welded roll-over bar frame. The stressed side panel can just be seen, closing off the cockpit bay at foot of photo. The completed car at Langley Road shows off its small Tasman fuel tankage compared to Formula 1, including the shaped aluminium seat structure, stressed side panels and single top radius rod rear suspension originally designed by Owen Maddock for his Formula 1 monocoque. Euan Sarginson's superb race photo shows Bruce (nearest camera) and team-mate Timmy Mayer in formation at Teretonga, New Zealand, 25 January, 1964, where Bruce led a team 1–2 success, 0.1 sec between them at the finish. Colours were Cooper BRG but with silver stripes

THE 1½-LITRE YEARS — 1961–65

after being left at the start. Ken Tyrrell was still running the team come August and the German GP, where Bruce uncharacteristically crashed during the race and like John before him awoke in hospital unable to remember what had happened. Examination of the wreck suggested the right-rear wishbone had broken, allowing the wheel to turn out, sending the car diving away to its left into the bushes and trees at over 100 mph. This was a most unusual failure for a Cooper, and it knocked Bruce's confidence, already dented by his string of retirements.... Therefore, he was far from delighted when during practice at Monza an experimental new rear hub carrier seized its bearings at 140 mph on the banking and hurled the Cooper sideways. During unofficial practice they had tried long rear radius rods, but reverted to normal wishbones for the timed sessions and the race itself. The results were better, Bruce third and Tony sixth.

At Oulton Park the works pair struggled 5–6, and at Watkins Glen and Mexico City engine breakages sidelined them both. Bruce described it as 'a disastrous year for me. Since that brief spell at the top of the Championship ladder after Spa, I finished in only two motor races....'

The monocoque Lotus 25 was unquestionably the car of the year, and Jimmy Clark walked the World Championship with that incredible tally of seven GP wins. When John had returned after his Twinny-Mini accident he had urged on Owen Maddock's latest project, which was for a very stiff monocoque-chassised Formula 1 Cooper. All the Cooper boys vividly recall his scheme – Eddie Stait: 'It was a bloody good idea. It was the traditional oval-section cigar shape, with a hole for the driver and two booms out the back for the engine. It had an aluminium outer skin, but inside that was aviation aluminium honeycomb, on the inside of which was bonded fibreglass to stabilize the whole structure without ribs or formers. The Beddings made the aluminium panels and Owen got Peter Jackson of Specialized Mouldings – the fibreglass racing car bodywork specialists – to put the honeycomb and fibreglass in it. I think it was one of the most complicated things he'd had to do. Thickness of the structure varied according to load and the tanks were rubber bags bonded-in. It was eventually intended for the Climax flat-16 engine for 1965 because we couldn't get its exhausts out of a spaceframe car. It wasn't very heavy, and it was fantastically rigid, but it was expensive to make, and development took a long time....'

So long in fact that it outlived its creator at Cooper's. Owen was feeling trapped on a drawing office treadmill: 'It was nothing but drawing and more drawing by that time. I missed not going to the races any more, the fun had gone out of it. Add to that the fact that I'd fallen in love with the hovercraft – I wanted to design and build a racing hovercraft – and in August 1963 I told the Major I was leaving. Old Charlie came to see me and just said "I think you're doin' the right thing cock...." John tried to talk me out of it, but off I went.'

He freelanced on designs for Bruce McLaren's 1964 Tasman specials and items for the first McLaren sports cars which would follow that year, including the four-spoke cast McLaren wheel, which was immensely stiff and very successful for its type. Then he moved to Cowes on the Isle of Wight and began building hovercraft ... and founded the Hover Club of Great Britain.

Meanwhile Rob Walker had returned to the Cooper fold for 1963, ordering the new T66 for his new driver, Jo Bonnier. While awaiting delivery he hired the works old T60 – *18/61* – which JoBo raced in early-season events before the new car emerged at Spa, complete with flat-plane crank Climax V8 engine and Type 34 Colotti six-speed gearbox. The older T60 was retained as team spare. He finished fifth there, sixth at Nürburgring and fifth again in Mexico City.

Meanwhile Scuderia Centro-Sud had been revived by Signor Dei, and had emerged early in the season at Imola, where old T53 and T51 Cooper-Maseratis were driven by Bandini and Carlo Mario Abate, who finished fifth there and followed-up that result with third at Syracuse. In the mid-season Solitude GP, Mario Cabral appeared in the team's old T53 and the following weekend at Nürburgring was armed with the team's ex-works T60 – *17/61* – retiring with gearbox failure. Bonnier was fourth and Cabral seventh in Walker and Centro-Sud T60s respectively in the Mediterranean GP at Enna, Sicily, and then in the Italian GP meeting the Portuguese failed to qualify. Something of a mystery Cooper entry was made for the Mexican GP by one Frank Dochnal in a 1959 T51 car with 1500 FPF engine. He failed to qualify, after crashing in practice.

The season ended with the Rand and South African GPs; John Love's faithful T55 – *11/61* – finished fourth in the former event at Kyalami, while one of six other Cooper entries was Alex Blignaut – the man who would make Johannesburg's

THE 1½-LITRE YEARS — 1961–65

Kyalami circuit the South African GP's regular home – in the ex-Mike Harris/ex-Yeoman Credit T53. In the World Championship round at East London on 28 December the works and Walker T66s all finished; McLaren fourth, Bon-

Below left *The fantastic concept – all the Cooper men who were there at the time recall Owen's Formula 1 monocoque this way. Here it is, pictured long after development had been dropped, in the tyre rack at Langley Road. It was years ahead of its time in using glass-fibre internal sheathing and honeycomb composite to stiffen a simple aluminium outer stress skin. Metalwork by the Beddings, glass-fibre by Peter Jackson's men at Specialized Mouldings Ltd. The project was dropped when development took too long for comfort and the management probably quite rightly feared for problems repairing crash damage. When the order was given to scrap it, at the Byfleet works, it proved almost impossible to break-up!*

Two of a kind – with an Austin Cooper 'S' in the pit lane at Goodwood, Bruce wheels out for initial testing of the 1964 Formula 1 'T73' slimline, with Tasman-proven stressed-skin panelling around the cockpit section, and in many ways the sleekest and best-looking F1 Cooper bodywork yet. Those are 13-inch diameter wheels front and rear, wearing the new generation broad profile Dunlop Racing tyres. Note single radius rod rear suspension. Ginger Devlin stands by with clipboard and stop-watches. It was probably this car F1/1/64 which sold to hillclimber John Macklin on 17 August '65 – invoice No. 2495, price £1300 – after duty as team spare that season. Macklin fitted a 3.5-litre Buick V8 engine, but completely destroyed the car in a crash at Harewood hillclimb in April, 1966

nier and Maggs 6–7; John Love was ninth and Trevor Blokdyk's Scuderia Lupini T51-Maserati – *16/60* – placed 11th.

Bruce McLaren finished only sixth in the World Drivers' Championship and Cooper-Climax were fifth in the Constructors' Cup. Bruce might have drawn some consolation from heading Jack Brabham by three points in the Drivers' competition, but there was little comfort for Cooper as the Brabham-Climax marque lay third in their Championship, three points ahead of Cooper at season's end.

This was a difficult period for all concerned. Charles at 70 was in failing health with his heart trouble. John was still not fully recovered from his road accident. Bruce McLaren was frustrated by Cooper's slowing development and his own lack of success. His close friend Eoin Young wrote: 'People were beginning to comment on the dimming of the McLaren star, and there were those who blamed Bruce for the Cooper lack of success.... He felt he knew what had to be done, but it was becoming increasingly difficult for him to have his suggestions acted upon. . . .'

He wanted to build a pair of special Coopers for the new 2½-litre limit Tasman Championship series to be held that winter, and run them as works cars. Charles blocked the idea. 'I'm not 'avin' it', he would say. He believed the regular F1 cars would do; Bruce was utterly convinced they would not. He wanted to build special slimline lightweights to make the most of the regulations. Tony Maggs was leaving the F1 team and would be replaced by the Young American FJ driver Timmy Mayer, and it was planned for him to accompany Bruce down-under. But he was unknown there, and Charles said bluntly that if there were any problems with entries and adequate appearance money then he'd cancel the whole project.

At this point Bruce opted to go it alone and with Timmy's elder brother Teddy Mayer set up Bruce McLaren Motor

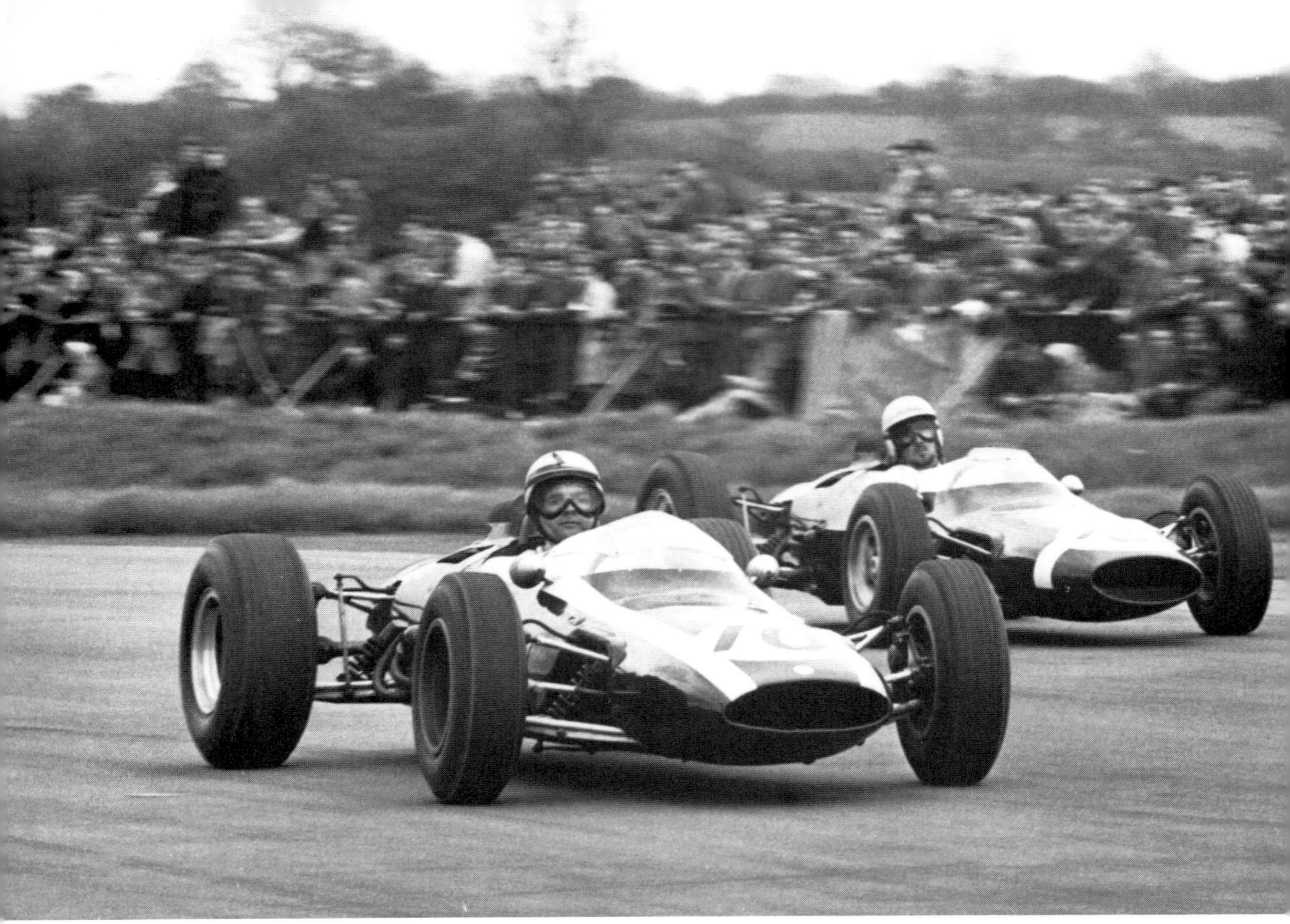

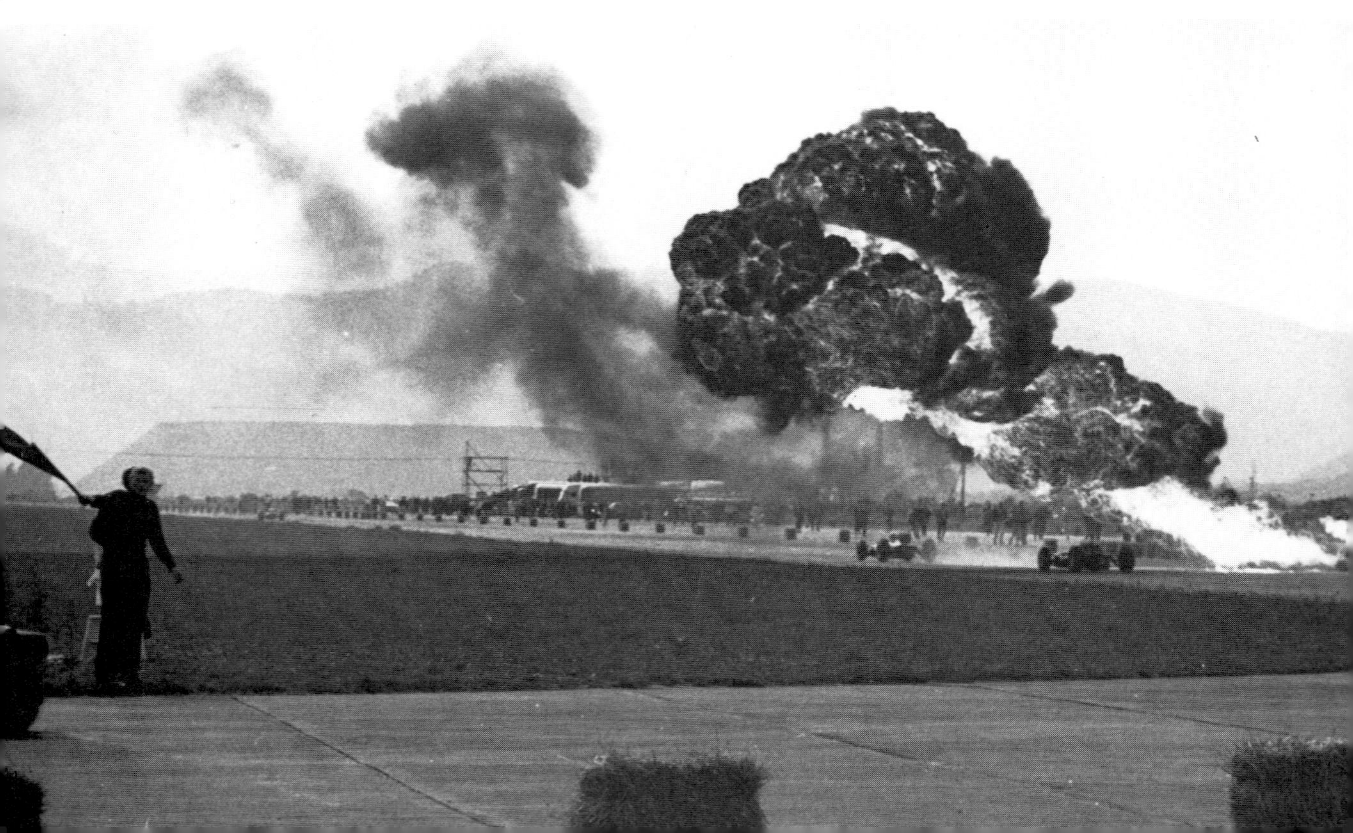

Racing Ltd to run the cars as he wanted. They were produced at Surbiton, drawing on T66 experience, but the basic tube frame made by Terry Kitson and the Beddings was stiffened by stressed-skin steel panelling amidships, where the cockpit was only 25 in. wide. Rear suspension incorporated the top rear radius rod tried at Monza, which was actually the layout intended for the monocoque car, and $2\frac{1}{2}$ FPF four-cylinder engines were to be mated to Cooper-Knight five-speed transaxles. The first car was completed and on test in September 1963, and the team's debut was made at Levin on 4 January, 1964, where they were trounced by Hulme's new Brabham, Mayer and McLaren finishing 2–3.

In eight attempts Bruce had never won the NZ GP. Now mechanics Wally Willmott and Tyler Alexander – Timmy's American minder – painstakingly prepared the new Coopers. Bruce had realized that by shortening the stroke of a 2.7 FPF to pull it within $2\frac{1}{2}$ litres you would have a better engine than a standard $2\frac{1}{2}$. Typically, Jack Brabham had had the same idea, and he set Repco in Australia to making special parts while Bruce's were produced in the UK. Just before the Pukekohe race Bruce discovered his engine's pistons gave too low a compression ratio and a replacement set was hurriedly fitted. The only place available to run them in was Auckland's Western Springs banked cycle track, and he grumbled round it for an hour and a half to do the job, dizzied by covering three laps a minute! In the GP it was Mayer who led initially, then Brabham, before Bruce forged ahead. Jack crashed and Bruce was able to win his home GP at long, long last, with Hulme second and Timmy third. Torrid battles with Brabhams at Wigram and Teretonga were also resolved in favour of the McLaren Cooper, but the team's luck slumped in Australia; Bruce and Timmy 2–3 at Warwick Farm, Timmy losing the Lakeside lead when his engine blew, and Bruce placing third behind Youl's Cooper and Hulme's Brabham. Then, in practice for the final race of the Championship at Longford, Tasmania, Timmy's Cooper was thrown into the air over a bump just before a braking area and smashed into

Old fellers – works and Walker 1963 Coopers in the 1964 International Trophy race at Silverstone, still on the narrow tread tyres of year-old technology; Phil Hill in the works car (10) and Jo Bonnier in Rob Walker's, beyond . . . . It was not a happy year for the American former World Champion, culminating in his fiery accident at Zeltweg aerodrome in the inaugural Championship-qualifying Austrian GP, as seen here, 23 August. Having smashed his 'T73' in practice, Phil had the team's old spare 'T66' 'F1/6/63' ex-Silverstone, break loose and charge the straw bale barriers, rupturing its fuel tanks and erupting – after he had scrambled clear – into this spectacular blaze. The old car was subsequently rebuilt as a Tasman special . . .

a tree; Timmy died instantly. Next day Bruce drove a muted race, finished second to Graham Hill's Brabham and he won the Tasman Championship title.

In the middle of the down-under tour, Jack Brabham returned for the Racing Car Show, to be told the shocking news that Noddy Grohmann was dead.

It was on 24 January 1964: Noddy had been driving home to Godalming from Brabham's New Haw works near Byfleet when he evidently felt unwell and pulled into a lay-by beside the road. He was found there in his car, killed by a cerebral haemorrhage. . . . He was just 32. His friends put it down to years of overwork.

Lean, mean, hilarious Mike Grohmann had contributed hugely to the Brabham-Cooper World Championship story. Before the days of bayonet-fitting racing engines he was master of every part of the cars in his care. Just how much he meant to the double Cooper World Champion comes through in what Jack wrote in his *Motor Racing* magazine column for March that year: '"Noddy" Grohmann was a racing mechanic in a million. Indeed, he was far more than a racing mechanic, because he had the ability to build and develop racing prototypes. . . . Our association went back to my Cooper days, and his preparation of the cars was a very important factor in the two years when I managed to pull off the World Championship. Nothing was ever too much trouble, and though he was sometimes feeling off-colour he would always insist on plugging on with a job right through to the end.

'Noddy was a great character, liked and respected by everyone intimately connected with motor racing, and his death at such an early age will be an enormous loss to the sport as a whole. I would rate him as one of the finest racing mechanics in the world. I remember that when Dan Gurney teamed up with us at the beginning of the 1963 season he told me, "It sure is an honour to have my car prepared by him." Everyone in motor racing will miss him deeply. . . .'

Back in England for the full 1964 season, Bruce was third in his works T66 at the Snetterton F1 opener, behind Bonnier's Walker car. At Goodwood on Easter Monday the Kiwi was swept off the road in a collision with Ireland's BRP monocoque car, and Bonnier also crashed. At Syracuse the young Swiss Jean-Claude Rudaz emerged in a Fabre Urbain-entered T60 – old *18/6* – the ex-Walker spare car from the previous year. In time for the Aintree '200' on 18 April, Bruce had a new team mate – the veteran American Phil Hill. While the Californian ex-world Champion retired his T66 with the gearbox casing split – legacy of Bruce's Goodwood shunt in the car – Bruce's brand-new T73 challenged for second place before boiling and the driver calling it a day before something expensive could break. 'I was thrilled with its potential,' he said. 'I haven't been that far up in a Formula 1 race for at least 12 months!'

The new car was a quickie replacement for the flagging

monocoque idea based on the Tasman slimlines, with fluid through the frame tubes and stressed steel skin, and had been assembled at Langley Road by Mike Barney and Hughie Frankland. The 1964 F1, F2 and F3 cars were all basically similar in layout, four straight tubes forming the basic frame. The top tubes angled down from the scuttle to the nose and the horizontal cockpit side members terminating in the seat-back bulkhead. The top members in the engine bay ran lower down, below the V8 heads. The stress panels spot-welded onto this tube frame were in 24-gauge steel sheet, wrapped under the car and up to the top frame longerons. Drilled steel sheet also stiffened the front and rear bulkheads. By eliminating large pannier tanks and using four separate cells instead, overall body width was cut to 26 in. As on the 1963 car an aluminium seat tank was used, augmented by a saddle over the driver's knees and two smaller cells either side of his legs.

The new T73's bodywork was neat, close-fitting and sleek with a high tail spine around the injection trumpets wrapped down to the gearbox with twin tail-pipes protruding through a neat orifice in the extreme tail.

Cooper had followed other manufacturers in adopting rocker-arm front suspension with inboard coil/damper units, the wide-based bottom wishbones being braced forward on the frame's nose. Anti-dive was again built in. At the rear a lower wishbone was used with a third arm to control toe-in, and the 1963 double-wishbone layout was at last abandoned in favour of a single top link and long radius rod anchored on the roll-over hoop, as in the Tasman specials. Since Cooper had run 13 in. wheels on the T66s they did not have the geometry change problems of other teams in adapting to the new season's wide-tyre innovations. Neither did they have to reduce brake diameter, relying on 1963-style Girling equipment. The Climax V8 engine was mounted rigidly to enhance frame stiffness, and there were extra tie-rods from block to chassis. The 'C6S' gearbox was probably the most reliable in contemporary Formula 1, though large and heavy, and it was retained almost unchanged, though the old Citroën-type drive-shaft joints were replaced by normal UJs and sliding splines. But the mechanics never liked the 'C6S', as one describes: 'It worked after a fashion; there was loads of room for six speeds in the old five-speeder from the 2½-litre days and that would have been a better bet, it worked all right in the slimline '61 cars. Owen's second gearbox finally worked, but the selector mechanism was fiendishly complex and a pig to assemble with its locking mechanisms. And we used to get new 'boxes delivered bone dry and so tight you had no chance of turning them by hand. One time we assembled a car and had to tow it up and down Hollyfield Road to make the wheels and gears go round ... it was back to the old days of '59 when we had to spend hours honing-down the drop gears before they would fit on the splines, because Jack Knight only had an old broach; Coopers wouldn't buy him a new one....'

There was another splendid Langley Road flap at this time, as new wide rims were anxiously awaited to carry the new generation doughnut tyres. Eddie Stait: 'We had a bloke who came in to work evenings, after his normal day job, turning wheels. He worked on an ancient lathe with no proper turning copying attachments; he'd just work away like a wood turner. He'd come in after most people had gone home, and find a fresh wheel casting and a drawing left there for him to work from. This particular night the long-awaited wide-wheel castings had arrived at last and they were put out ready for him, but there'd been a muddle and somebody had left a drawing for an old narrow rim, only about 4–4½ in. wide. The turner must have thought, "cor they're getting their money's worth out of me tonight," and when we came in next day there were these beautifully turned narrow little wheels and a gigantic pile of swarf! John went *spare*....'

At Silverstone, Bruce's new car threw a front-wheel balance weight while Phil finished fourth in his old T66, and Rudaz and Bonnier both ran Coopers – the Walker driver after his new Brabham-BRM had burned-out during practice. Monaco saw both works drivers in new T73s, Phil's so new it hadn't turned a wheel before going there. Bruce's broke a steering arm in practice so he raced the T66, but it leaked oil and ran its bearings while Phil's race ended with a broken suspension link. He had qualified quicker than McLaren. Bonnier's Walker T66 placed fifth.

The steering arm breakage was attributed to the front suspension allowing flap under braking. Before the Dutch GP at Zandvoort radius rods were added to the top rocker arms, picking-up on the chassis by the dash panel and Mike Barney bolted stiffening brackets to the suspect steering arms while new castings were due at Spa. Seventh and eighth, out of the points, was a poor result. Jo Bonnier's replacement Walker Brabham proved far quicker than the Cooper spare, but it placed ninth in the race.

At Spa the T73s used new beefier front upright castings with stronger steering arm lugs. Bonnier crashed the Walker Cooper at La Source in practice, but in the race Bruce finished strongly second on merit, while the others retired. He was second to Graham Hill's BRM on the last lap when it ran dry and stopped, and so the Cooper led to the last corner only to splutter with electrical trouble, being caught and passed by Clarke's Lotus before coasting across the line. Bruce's car had experimental rear suspension geometry changes, with altered radius rod location to reduce bump-steer and more vertical coil dampers. It worked, and both cars were set up that way at Rouen for the French GP, where Bruce and Phil finished 6–7 after McLaren had an early spin.

The British GP was at Brands Hatch for the first time; the cars ran with gauze injection covers, and while Bruce's gearbox failed it was Phil's turn to take sixth place and another Championship point.

By this point in the season morale was low. Owen was

THE 1½-LITRE YEARS — 1961-65

The Bruce McLaren team 1965 'T79' Tasman slimline was based on the 1964 Formula 1 works team's 'T73' but a last-minute contract with Firestone – who at the time had only 15-in. tyres available – meant a change from 13-in. wheels as originally intended. This upset the suspension geometry and gave drivers McLaren and Phil Hill (in the surviving 1964 'T70' updated) some real headaches for most of the New Zealand/Australia series. Here at Christchurch for the Lady Wigram Trophy race, Bruce demonstrates the notorious 'bump' there; only the left front tyre touching ground, Euan Sarginson's camera capturing the other three Firestones all airborne, and some strange suspension angles .... Note the front coil/damper units have been tucked away inboard as on the 'T73'.

working as a freelance for Bruce and others while planning his beloved new hovercraft, and in June Neil Johanssen left and Eddie Stait followed – joining Bruce McLaren's private company to build sports cars – in July. One draughtsman, a newcomer named Mike Chambers took over to keep things going, but soon a new designer would join the company, recommended by John Coombs and Roy Salvadori, who had worked closely with him before. He was South African Derrick White, formerly with Connaught in the Fifties and more recently running the chassis engineering side of Jaguar's lightweight E type programme; Coombs was at that time entering the works development car for Salvadori and others.

The Solitude GP was run without a single Cooper starting, but at Enna, Gerard Racing fielded their ex-Centro Sud/ works T60 V8 – *17/61* – for John Taylor, who had formerly driven their 1500 Ford-engined T71/73 hybrid in UK F1 and Libre events. He finished seventh.

At Nürburgring the German GP saw both works T73s described frankly as 'tatty', both retired early with valve gear derangements and Edgar Barth drove Walker's T66 on home ground but had its clutch break.

The Austrian GP at Zeltweg airfield is best forgotten by Cooper people. Poor Phil Hill crashed his T73 in practice, drove the spare T66 in the race and crashed again, possibly when a wishbone broke, escaping unhurt as the car – *6/63* – burst into flames and was destroyed. He and John, both good men, had never 'clicked', communication was never easy and now in a fearful bust-up Phil was effectively fired. Bruce's engine failed, again . . . no longer were Cooper a prime Climax customer, and it showed.

In the Walker camp Jo Bonnier had never taken to the very high-revving BRM V8 engine in his Brabham, and now the Climax engine and Colotti gearbox from the spare Cooper had been dropped into a Brabham frame for him.

Bruce always performed well at Monza in the Italian GP and it was to provide the highlight of his 1964 Formula 1 season. He qualified on the second row in first practice, it rained next day and he made the most of this advantageous position and the best Climax engine he had used all year to finish second. John Love was summoned from Rhodesia to take Phil's place, but with little realistic chance he failed to qualify. His car was dumped in the truck and the whole team

273

concentrated on Bruce's. How it showed! Differences were patched for the US GP in October, when Phil returned, but both drivers were out of luck again. Bruce had the consolation of a highly promising debut with his new McLaren-Oldsmobile sports racing car at Mosport Park's Canadian GP meeting. He had these other irons in the fire, and had been winning all season in his former Zerex Special sports car. Charlie Cooper had long regarded Bruce's extramural activities with suspicion since Jack Brabham's defection. But he was no longer around, for while the team was at Watkins Glen, on 2 October, 1964, Charles Cooper suffered a fatal heart attack, and died in his bedroom at *Shoushan* on Box Hill. . . .

His obituary in the US GP edition of *Motoring News* said it all: 'Charles Cooper took an active part in all his company's ventures . . . blunt and forthright in his views, he was often reluctant to change the design of a car. However, he must take credit for changing the face of World motor racing and for creating the modern breed of lightweight rear-engined racing cars as well as helping to bring many British racing drivers . . . to the forefront of the motor racing world. . . .'

Andrew Ferguson: 'For me the real measure of the Old Man was the size of the crowd which turned out for his memorial service. Everybody but everybody in British motor racing turned out for him. . . . You'll find everybody has Charlie Cooper stories, but don't think for one moment we didn't respect him . . . he could be a lovely old boy. . . .'

Ken Gregory: 'Give Charles credit – you'll hear all kinds of stories about him, because he was a character, a rough diamond; but he kept his feet firmly on the ground, he was as honest as the day is long and his word was his bond. He was rightly proud of what his company had achieved, and British motor racing owes him a great debt. . . .'

Bruce McLaren tugging his 'T77' down through the gears in the braking area for La Source Hairpin, Spa, Belgian GP, 13 June, 1965. He finished third but lapped. One year earlier he had led from this last corner on the last lap, only for the engine to cut dead allowing Clark to steal another win in his Belgian GP four-in-a-row for Lotus. Here the 'T77' displays its strap-on long-range fuel tank for this fast, thirsty race, high-level exhausts in the inferior Climax V8 engine and the old Cooper 'C6S' transaxle. In fact the cars' fuel capacity proved too small, and the extra tank became almost standard everywhere as on Jochen Rindt's yumping 'T77' (right) during practice for the 1965 German GP. The car is wearing its strap-on right-side fuel tank now permanent and painted. Note front suspension at full droop, showing off cast Cooper front uprights

He was 71.

In Mexico City the works T73s finished 7–9, and the 1964 World Championships were decided with Bruce McLaren down to seventh, Phil Hill 20th with his solitary point and the marque fifth behind Brabham in the Constructors' competition.

Through the winter John – missing his father desperately and still not really fit after his road accident – talked to friends like Roy Salvadori about the company's future. Roy was able to make introductions – see Chapter 25 – and in May the following year the Cooper Car Company would become part of the Chipstead Motor Group, headed by Jonathan Sieff – former racing driver and member of the Marks & Spencer family. Formula 1 regulations would change to 3 litres unsupercharged on New Year's Day, 1966, and there was the unspoken prospect of 'St Michael' Marks & Spencer brand sponsorship for Cooper come the expensive changeover. Maserati featured large in the Chipstead Group's interests, and here was a potential source of 3-litre F1 power, for Coventry Climax had made it clear they were not interested in investing in the new Formula; their last hurrah would be a flat-16 cylinder 1500 engine for 1965, and the last races of the 1½-litre era. . . .

That winter saw Bruce McLaren Motor Racing building a new Tasman Cooper for the 1965 series, to be painted white with a green centre stripe. It was based on the T73 stress-panelled spaceframe, slightly wider than the '64 Tasman super-slimliners, but now including inboard front suspension with forward bottom radius rod and rearward upper rod, and using the new lightweight Hewland five-speed trans-axles. It was designed around 13 in. wheels and since race distances were not to exceed 100 miles fuel tankage was restricted to only 8 gallons in the seat tank, and 3 gallons in two tanks either side of the driver's knees. Bruce had high regard for Phil Hill and invited him to drive the '64 T70.

The little team then concluded a new contract with Firestone tyres, who were making their entry into European-style road racing, and initially they only had 15 in. tyres available, so a last-minute conversion to 15 in. wheels had to be made. Phil's car remained in England to test tyres and was flown out to Auckland at a cost of £1880 just in time for the NZ GP. The sudden change in wheel size and tyre-ware rendered both cars almost unmanageable and it was not until the final race of the tour – the Australian GP at Longford – that Bruce managed to win, on new 13 in. covers. It was Firestone's first Grand Prix win.

Other Cooper aspects of the series included New Zealand Speedway rider Bruce Abernethy rebuilding the cremated remains of Phil's Zeltweg-wrecked T66, winning sponsorship from Rothmans tobacco and fitting a 2½ FPF. After two gearbox failures the colourful and controversial Abernethy was dropped by Rothmans and replaced by fellow-Kiwi Roly Levis, who spun at Teretonga and wiped off a wheel on a parked truck. In Australia most of the local aces were Brabham-mounted by this time. Lex Davison was one, his ex-McLaren Cooper now being driven by his young protégé Rocky Tresise. Tragedy struck at Sandown Park, Melbourne, where 'Davo' – one of Australian motor racing's most respected personalities – crashed fatally in his Brabham during practice for the Tasman round. His Ecurie Australie team still went to Longford; in mourning but determined to run the Cooper effectively for Tresise. He groped for gears off the line and had to work his way back through the field. Pulling out to pass a back-marker at 120 mph past the start–finish line the road narrowed and he found himself on the verge. The Cooper hit a drain, lost a wheel and somersaulted, killing Tresise and luckless photographer Robin d'Abrera. . . .

During 1965 there was little point in making expensive Formula 1 developments since all 1½-litre cars would be redundant by the end of the year. The flat-16 Climax engine was still-born and would never race, though Cooper, in common with Lotus and Brabham, built a suitable chassis to accommodate it. The new season's T77 F1 cars emerged at the Race of Champions in March, little changed from the preceding model. At the 1964 Austrian GP, John had signed-on Jochen Rindt – fresh from making a meteoric name for himself in Formula 2 – binding him to three seasons with Cooper Cars. This was to be Bruce McLaren's last of eight years with Cooper, but in World Championship GP races he would score only four times; fifth at East London, Monaco, and Monza, and third at Spa – where he always excelled. Rindt finished fourth at Nürburgring and sixth in the US GP. They were ninth and 13th respectively in the Drivers' Championship, while Cooper remained fifth in the Constructors' table.

The successor to Owen Maddock joined the team during 1965. Derrick Atherstone White was a South African, born in East London on 20 March, 1929. His father, Bob, a lawyer, had helped organize the first South African GP in 1934, as vice-chairman of the East London Committee. Derrick was educated at Witwatersrand University, held a pilot's licence and built two specials in the 1940s before moving to the UK, where in 1952 he became an experimental chassis draughtsman/engineer. In his spare time he worked with Kieft and Mezzolitre 500 cc F3s. He spent 1954–55 with Connaught – an astonishingly advanced F1 team hamstrung by financial worries – as a chassis and suspension man. That second season there he built his own 750 Formula special.

Four years followed back home in South Africa, where he designed a prototype sports racing car, then from 1959 to 1964 he was with Jaguar, where he was responsible for the E type i.r.s. system and the lightweight racing version's chassis engineering. With his Impala 750 special he finished third in the Goodacre Trophy club racing Championship, and during 1964 raced Fraser Imp saloons. With this considerable experience and obvious enthusiasm, he was invited to join Cooper by former Coombs/works development E type driver Roy Salvadori.

At Zandvoort the team's spare car appeared with the lighter Hewland gearbox in place of the six-speed Cooper-Knight, but there was minimal further development and the team showed all the signs of just going through the motions, although Rindt charged furiously whenever he could.

Roy Salvadori had been instrumental in setting up the Chipstead merger, as we shall see. He had just retired as a racing driver after the 1964 season, and he became effective team manager from Monaco, where there was an early problem with Rindt, whose car would not perform at all and failed to qualify. Jochen could be a very abrasive character and while Roy rapidly developed immense respect for his talent their relationship was less than close. Now he made a point of explaining to the Press that the Austrian's failure was in no way the driver's fault, it was a car problem; '. . . and we paid him the start money he would have got if he'd qualified. I felt that got me onto a better basis with Jochen.'

What had happened was that Mike Barney discovered Jochen's mechanic had quietly modified his car to ease tank fitting, by hacking-off a lug which supported one end of the Bowden throttle cable outer sleeve. He would then fix the sleeve after each rebuild by taping it to the chassis tube. Since the tube carried water it heated up when the car was running and the cable fixing slackened. Since such controls operate by relative movement between sleeve and inner core it was vital that the sleeve should be rigidly anchored. Consequently as the tape softened Jochen wasn't achieving full throttle opening. His 'down on power' engines were only on part-throttle. Rindt's minder overheard Mike explaining his discovery to Salvadori – inevitably the unfortunate mechanic responsible was fired on the spot.

Mike Barney: 'This made me think back to the previous year with Phil Hill. He'd regularly do ten laps in practice and come in complaining that the engine had 'gone flat'. Climax could never find anything wrong in the engines and I don't think it did much for the atmosphere between Phil and John. I think his throttle cable had been taped the same way; when the frame tubes got hot the tape would melt and the throttle cable slid forward. I had a lot of respect for Phil Hill, I was sorry he had the troubles with us that he did. . . .'

Better things were round the corner, but first we must look at the minor formulae and the final years of Cooper's production racing car story.

CHAPTER TWENTY FOUR

The minor formulae – 1964-69

On 1 January, 1964, while Bruce McLaren's first team of Tasman Coopers was preparing to do battle down-under, and the Shelby King Cobras had just been laid to rest in the States, two new 1-litre racing classes replaced Formula Junior. Formula 2 allowed virtually pure-bred racing engines, while Formula 3 restricted stock-block engine modifications, banned overhead camshafts and specified use of production-based transmissions with five- or six-speed conversions banned to minimize cost.

Into the winter of 1963–64, Owen Maddock had left after his years of faithful service to Cooper, and Eddie Stait and Neil Johanssen were working in the penthouse design office on Bruce's Tasman car and then on the family of F1, F2 and

John Taylor in Bob Gerard's Mark 3 A-based Formule Libre/ F1 *special with twin-cam Lotus-Ford 1500 engine is seen here winning the* Formula Libre *feature race, Mallory Park, Boxing Day, 1963. Gerard Racing ran this car in several 1964 Formula 1 events and John Taylor always impressed with his quick and neat driving. 'Mr Bob' added the ex-works Monaco-winning 'T60' V8 to his equipe that season . . . but John was a regular winner at club level in the 4-cylinder*

F3 machines based upon it. The two 1-litre cars were respectively the Cooper T71 and T72. Like the Tasman specials and the new F1 T73, the new chassis used semi stressed-skin construction with a 20-gauge sheet steel floorpan wrapped up either side of the basic tubular frame and spot-welded to it. The main frame longerons were 16-gauge round tube with diagonal members in each engine side bay and on the flat above the driver's legs. Under his feet an 18-gauge sheet bulkhead stiffened the front end and accepted suspension loads.

Contemporary Formula 1 practice persuaded them to adopt top rocker arm inboard front suspension; the T71/72 being the first Cooper to appear with its front coil/damper units tucked away out of the airstream. Lower front location was by wide-based tubular wishbones extending forward to an anchorage just behind the radiator out in the nose. At the rear the lower wishbone was augmented by a lateral link behind the axle line to offer screwed adjustment of rear wheel toe-in. At the top a single lateral link and long radius rod appeared, the rod anchored at the junction of the top chassis longeron and cockpit bulkhead-cum-roll-over hoop. The top link had screwed rod-ends and alternative inboard pivot mountings to adjust camber, while the radius rod was also length-adjustable to alter bump-steer effect. As at the front,

Presenting John Young Stewart, star of Formula 3, Formula 2 and Formula 1 progressively through the 1964 season. Here the wee Scot is pushed off in the Tyrrell Racing Organization 'T72'-BMC in which he took a stranglehold on the new 1-litre Formula 3 class that season. Even the minor-class Coopers that year used new cast-magnesium front uprights in place of the faithful old Alford & Alders. The inboard front coil/damper mounting uses fabricated top rocker arms, and there's single top radius rod rear suspension

Timken roller bearings were used in cast magnesium hub carriers. An anti-dive angle of 5 degrees was built into the front suspension with 11 degrees anti-squat at the rear.

The Formula 3 engine was developed by Eddie Maher's men at BMC from their Mini-Cooper 'S' base with a special short-throw – reduced by 0.25 in. – crankshaft to reduce it from 1071 cc to within the 1000 cc limit. Bore was 71.6 mm, stroke 61.9. The crankshaft was in EN40 steel nitride-hardened with a 2 in. diameter centre main bearing. Lubrication was dry sump. The main oil tank was mounted between the car's foot pedals and radiator, carrying 2½ gallons in its 4-gallon volume. The oil cooler was built into the water radiator, made by Serck on a Mini core with four elements. The lower-right frame longeron carried oil to the engine, through a filter at the end of the engine bay, then returning through the top-left longeron. Cooling water similarly used the other main frame members, while the cross-tube behind the driver's shoulders formed the 'header tank'. With a single SU HS6 carburettor, restricted as the regulations demanded by a 36 mm, 1.42 in. throttling flange orifice, the new engine delivered 88 bhp at 7750 rpm.

Transmission was via a Lockheed single-dry-plate diaphragm-spring clutch to a Knight-developed Hillman Imp-cased transaxle, the casing being used inverted and fitted with the standard cwp. The normal Imp 'box was all-indirect and Jack now inserted constant-mesh dog-engagement internals, with 16 interchangeable sets, which he had designed himself. Any ratio could be changed in around 20 minutes, as the two-shaft assembly slid out of the casing easily once it had been unbolted from the final-drive housing.

The engine was installed on three Silentbloc rubbers, steadied by a stay on the right-rear, while the cross-member carrying the single rear engine bearer was detachable to help in removal.

The all-disc braking system was little changed from the preceding FJs', though front disc diameter was now 9.5 in. As F1 was leading the move towards wider tyres, so F3 followed, and Cooper now specified 6 in. wide cast-magnesium rims for the T72, with the usual 4.50–13 and 5.50–13 Dunlop tyres wider-based than usual. The F2 T71s rode on 7 in. rims, with 6.00–13 rear tyres.

Wheelbase was 7 ft 7 in. and the wide track reached 4 ft 4 in. front and 4 ft 3 in. rear; overall length 11 ft 4½ in.; height 2 ft 4½ in.; ground clearance 3¾ in. and weight 870 lb with oil and water only, in F3 form. Complete with BMC F3 engine the price was published as £1740 complete, or £1325 less engine and gearbox. In F2 form the cars included an extra long-range fuel tank fitted under the seat in addition to the standard 8-gallon panniers, plus a reshaped engine cowl; price was £1415 basic and they would accept a variety of new F2 engines.

While the first prototype F3 car had an upswept nose with rounded aperture and Gibraltarian carburettor bulge on the engine cowl, the final body shape was very attractive, with a toppled-D air intake and lowered bulge on the tightly tapered tail cowl. The more bulbous F2 cars were less pretty.

Tony Hegbourne shows-off his Normand Racing 'T71'-Cosworth SCA F2 car at Pau, running wheel-to-wheel with Jacques Maglia's private Brabham. The 'T71s' were a real headache for their mechanic Colin Knight, and major suspension modifications could only improve them marginally. The Normand livery of white with bright blue and red stripes and flashing really made these troublesome little cars look superb. The team were nice people too . . .

During initial tests in January 1964 the weather was dreadful, but the F3 looked highly promising and Bruce McLaren was pleased with its general behaviour. Timmy Mayer was killed soon after, and Ken Tyrrell was left looking for a new driver for his quasi-works F3 team. Robin McKay, who was the Goodwood track manager, suggested he try young Jackie Stewart, whose handling of the difficult Ecosse Monaco had impressed him. Ken knew Jackie's elder brother Jimmy vaguely from the 1950s and called him; 'Is your brother serious about going racing?' he asked. Jimmy assured him the sky was the limit in Jackie's view and the young Scot was invited to a test session at Goodwood. Bruce was present to set a target time, and Stewart promptly demolished it. Bruce tried harder. Jackie was faster still. Bruce worked-up a sweat. Jackie still challenged his times without looking bothered. Ken signed him on the spot, to join former Turner sports car club-driver Warwick Banks in his F3 team.

It is familiar history today, how Jackie Stewart's career rocketed away from that point. He won 11 major F3 races in his Tyrrell Cooper-BMCs, and was second in another when afflicted by clutch slip. Warwick Banks – who had won more club races than anyone else in 1963 – won a 12th F3 race for the team and this latest pair of 'Tyrrell Twins' took 1–2 finishes at Oulton Park, Silverstone, Mallory Park and Rouen and utterly dominated the new Formula's first season. Banks was also driving Tyrrell's Mini-Cooper saloons, and while he was away in Budapest winning the European Touring Car Championship in one, John Love returned to take fourth at the Oulton Gold Cup meeting, where Jackie rolled his brand-new 1965-spec Cooper T76 in practice, but happily won the race in the repaired car. Stewart had no equal in Formula 3 and poor Banks – himself a very good racing driver – caused Ken heartache when he understandably could hardly believe that the two team cars were essentially identical.

By mid-season Stewart was into Formula 2 with Ron Harris's quasi-works Lotus team. He sampled Jimmy Clark's F1 Lotus at Brands Hatch during British GP practice and after refusing offers from Cooper and Lotus for Formula 1, he signed for 1965 with BRM. His F1 debut was actually made in a Lotus at the non-Championship Rand GP that winter.

Certainly Stewart and the Tyrrell Coopers had some advantages during that 1964 F3 season. Not least was the BMC Engine Division's concentration of effort upon maintaining their half-dozen F3 engines, while Holbay Engineering, for instance, had around 50 of their Ford-based units to overhaul and prepare for the opposition. Cosworth Engineering – formerly the scourge of Formula Junior – concentrated upon their SCA Formula 2 racing engines that season and could only offer linered-down ex-FJ Ford 105E units to F3 customers. The Tyrrell Racing Organization was undoubtedly the best-prepared, best-organized and best-equipped team of that maiden F3 season, and it was to Cooper's immense benefit.

In France the Volant-Shell driver-training scholarship for 1963 had been won by Jean-Pierre Jaussaud. His prize was a brand-new T72 in which he won at Pau before demolishing the car – and very nearly himself – at Monaco, where Stewart won, of course. Jaussaud returned before year's end with some more good results, for example, second behind Pierre Ryser's Cooper at Nogaro and fourth to the good Belgian Jacques Bernusset's sister car at Albi.

Jean-Claude Franck won with BMC power at Nürburgring, and in September it was Bernusset's turn there, where Ryser and the Hon Charlie Crichton-Stuart placed 5–6 for the marque. Young French former motorcyclist Eric Offenstadt did well in a converted FJ Lola early in the season before taking a fancy to Franck's Cooper, so they swopped cars and Eric won at Montlhéry and one of the Heats at the big Monza meeting. Crichton-Stuart, Leo Cella, Ryser, Franck and

Formula 2, 1965 – Jackie Stewart in Ken Tyrrell's Cooper-BRM 'T75' heads ex-F2 Cooper driver Graham Hill in 'Noddy' Coombs' replacement Brabham, Richard Attwood in the Midland Racing Partnership's monocoque Lola T60 and Denny Hulme's works Brabham out of Thillois corner, Reims-Gueux, Coupe de Vitesse. While the Cooper-BRM was another good-looking car its BRM 1-litre 4-cylinder fuel-injected engine proved a real disappointment, and its unreliability allowed the prime opposition's Cosworth SCA engines to dominate

Right *Gran Premio do Portugal, Cascais, 26 July, 1965 – a far-cry from the World Championship GP of the 1959–60 period but still a good win for Cooper's beleaguered F3 'T76s' by this time in the marque's production customer car fortunes. Here John Fenning leads team-mate Rodney Banting in their Stockbridge Racing entries. They finished t'other way round, Banting victorious, after the 45-lap 94-mile race*

Michel Dagorne all did well for the marque, while at Zandvoort on one occasion Rob Slotemaker and John Rhodes were 3–4 in guest Tyrrell drives.

Meanwhile the first season of 1-litre Formula 2 saw 18

races, of which Brabham won nine, Lotus seven, one fell to Lola and one to Cooper – and every winner used a Cosworth SCA engine.

The surviving Register tells that only three 1964 F2 T71s were delivered; the first pair to Normand Ltd, the London car distributor, for their immensely likeable team drivers Mike Beckwith and Tony Hegbourne. They had campaigned Lotus 23 sports cars formerly. Stocky, cheerful Beckwith ran the team.

Initial Cooper F2 plans had been laid for a quasi-works effort with Tyrrell, using a new BMC F2 engine. The F2 Cooper-BMC would be something appetizingly different to set before race organizers in a Cosworth-dominated field, but the project turned round and bit its instigators. The BMC F2 engine was an unmitigated disaster. Preliminary tests showed it would be quite inadequate and it was never raced in Formula 2. Tyrrell confined his activities to F3 and operation of the Mini-Cooper saloon team, while the opportunity to race something different amongst a horde of Brabhams and Lotuses persuaded Normand that an SCA-engined Cooper programme would be a good idea. Unfortunately they were plagued by woefully poor handling.

Chief mechanic Colin Knight slaved all season to make the cars work properly. Tony Hegbourne proved they were quick in a straight line by winning both heat and overall at Avus, where both cars' underbellies were badly scored by bottoming. Knight then raised the front suspension and removed the anti-dive. The rear anti-squat was reduced by chopping the forward wishbone anchorage, and more fundamentally the standard bottom wishbone and extra link were removed and replaced by a reversed wishbone with inboard apex, controlled by an additional bottom radius rod. The cars were more comprehensively instrumented than their F3 sisters, and used five-speed Hewland transaxles in place of the Hillman-Knights. This moderate season saw the Normand pair 2–3 on aggregate at Vallelunga in the Rome GP, and Hegbourne fifth at Mallory Park and sixth at Pau and Crystal Palace, while Beckwith was third at Karlskoga in one Heat and fifth at Albi.

The third F2 Cooper-SCA of the year was delivered to John Coombs for Graham Hill to drive. He needed all his stoic grit to win the Heat with it at Crystal Palace on Whit Monday before he and the other stars present were crushed convincingly by Jochen Rindt's Brabham – this being the race at which the young Austrian erupted into the international limelight.

During practice, Graham had discovered that the grey Cooper suffered from overworked rear dampers, their leverage ratio was excessive. They were filled with thick castor oil to delay inevitable failure and the ploy worked for 3–4 laps until they died on him. Graham recalled 'the wheels were flapping up and down as if not attached to the car at all. . . . But during the race the rear anti-roll bar came adrift when a bracket broke. This gave the rear wheels tremendous grip and completely upset the balance of the car; all of a sudden it developed colossal understeer. . . . I had to literally throw it into corners to get the tail out or I wouldn't have got round at all. . . .' Rindt barged by, and Graham's broadsiding then kept all other opposition behind. The Cooper was set aside and replaced by a Brabham. Coombs sold it the following year to an earnest young racing car trader named Frank Williams. He found it quite untameable. Friends like Piers Courage, Roy Pike and Jonathan Williams tried it for him to see what they could suggest. 'You're on your own mate,' was one suggestion; another 'Sell the bloody thing before it kills you....'

Clearly what worked very nicely indeed with F3 power could not cut it with 115-horsepower in Formula 2.

For 1965 the Tyrrell team cars – numbers *FIII/4/64* and *FIII/5/64* – were sold to Tony and Jean Denton and to W. Dulles for UK minor-league racing, with BMC engines *XSP 222436/437* respectively. I understand the Stewart car was sold eventually to a young Irish enthusiast, with his father's blessing. Dad expected a 'Cooper' to be a small box-like saloon car and was horrified when an open-wheeler arrived. The car sat around unused and was then sold to a rally enthusiast who cannibalized its suspension and other parts for a special saloon. The frame was a waste of space, so he literally sawed it into bits small enough to fit into a dustbin, and out it went, to be rebuilt in the 1980s by a Midlands enthusiast.

The 1965-spec T76 car differed mainly from the T72 in its suspension. Front rocker-arm leverage was now on a ratio

F2 Coupe de Vitesse, Reims-Gueux, 2 July 1966 – Bob Anderson in Gerard's 'T82'-Cosworth SCA (No 36, right) during its slipstreaming battle on the pits straight from Thillois to Gueux, wheel-to-wheel with Bill Bradley's Brabham-Cosworth, (42), Henri Grandsire's works Alpine-Renault (22), Graham Hill's Coombs Matra-BRM (28) and Pete Arundell's Lotus 44-Cosworth (4)

of 2:1 instead of 3:1, promoting better damper life and more control. Anti-squat was removed from the rear suspension and adjustable Armstrong dampers replaced the inverted non-adjustable type of the T72s. The damper-foot also picked-up further inboard on the lower wishbone to make the barrel more vertical. Long radius rods trailed from the outboard ends of the front rocker arms to anchorages abreast the dash panel on the top frame longerons, reacting to braking forces better. Adjustable anti-roll bars became standard front and rear. BMC and new Cosworth-Ford MAE engines could be specified, and after Stewart's fantastic performances the Hollyfield Road order book was bulging with 19 T76s.

Rather more surprising, in view of their struggles in 1964, were orders for eight similarly uprated T75 cars for Formula 2. According to the Register two of these were retained by the works and two sold to Ken Tyrrell, who would campaign all four with new BRM four-cylinder F2 engines for Jackie Stewart and John Surtees to drive. A fifth spare car was added in August. The prototype *FII/1/65* was entered in the Register in January, using the still-born BMC F2 engine *XSP 222442*. Chassis *7/65* went to Eric Offenstadt with BRM engine *8003* that spring, and two cars – *2* and *3/65* – were supplied to Alf Francis, now working closely with Valerio Colotti in a company named Gear Speed Developments, GSD, in Modena, Italy.

In March it was reported that Colotti-Francis were developing a Cooper T72 for Formula 2 racing with an Alfa Romeo engine developed by *Ing.* Giancarlo Rebecchi, formerly with the ill-fated ATS concern. He had based his work on the production Giulietta engine, reduced to 996 cc and fitted with twin Weber 45DCOE carburettors – while BRM used fuel injection as standard and Cosworth were testing it. Transmission was via a Colotti-modified VW transaxle. Power output was claimed to be 115 bhp, just like the purpose-built SCA. The cars were to be entered by Ecurie Alf Francis, and would be driven by Jo Siffert and Bernard Plaisance.... They would fail to qualify at Crystal Palace, and generally had a most unhappy time.

The BRM engine in the Tyrrell and Offenstadt Coopers was essentially one bank from the Formula 1 V8. It was visually one of the most elegant racing engines ever built, but it had fundamental problems. Up to 127 bhp was claimed for it, but early in the year bearing problems saw V8-sized shells being adopted. This did not prevent three failures on Surtees's Tyrrell car, which had three big-end bearing collapses, usually resulting in a rod smashing its way out of the block. The season started promisingly, with Stewart second to Hulme's works Brabham-Cosworth at Oulton Park, but they would never finish so strongly again. At Enna, Chris Amon came into the team and took fourth place in his heat, while Offenstadt's private car was fourth in his. The Cooper-BRM's only other top-six placing was Stewart's fifth at Pau. Jackie could only manage eighth place in the *Autocar* F2 Championship that season, and Tyrrell's team was sixth in the French Championship. Another way of looking at that result is to say they were second to last....

In Formula 3, 1965 saw 61 major races held of which Cooper won three. Warwick Banks succeeded for Tyrrell early in the year at Silverstone in the rain, Devonian Clive Baker finishing third there in his Stockbridge Racing Team car; Stockbridge's Rodney Banting and John Fenning placing 1–2 at Cascais in Portugal, and later in the year Fenning won at Knutstorp in Sweden, where Banting and Yngve Rosqvist were 4–5, also in T76s.

Banks retired from racing, while private Cooper-BMCs to place in Internationals that season were driven by Paul Poty, Lars Bjuhr, Sven-Olof Gunnarsson, Jean Blanc and Sven Furstenhof. None, then or now, were exactly names to conjure with.

Cooper-Fords placed well in the hands of Mike (son of Jerseyman Bill) Knight, Ryser, Bernusset in Paul Swaelens'

Long faces at Goodwood during the unsuccessful tests of the 1966 Formula 3 Cooper 'T83'. The car generated such aerodynamic lift – although it was not recognized at the time – that it suffered immense and apparently intractable understeer. Here John Fenning (bearded), John Cooper in the hat and journalist/driver management consultant Paul Watson (with camera) show mutual disappointment. The inboard front suspension, outboard rear and curious low-level front anti-roll bar mounting are visible here. Only seven of these cars were built

Belgian team car, Sven Andersson, Leo Matilla, Hardy Sandstrom, Georg Duneborn, Ake Lindberg and Hasse Nilsson. Scandinavia was still a Cooper stronghold, but Formula 3 was now thoroughly dominated by Brabham cars, his company's New Haw, Byfleet, works now taking over the mantle once held by Cooper at Hollyfield Road.

Matters were worse for Cooper in 1966 as only Swedish newcomer Reine Wisell notched Cooper wins in F3 internationals, and then only in minor meetings at Roskilde and Bengtsfors in Sweden. Sister Coopers driven by Lars-Ake Teijby and Hasse Nilsson were respectively third and fourth in those events.

Paul Watson wrote of Cooper's attitude to production racing cars after their merger: 'John Cooper had all his previous enthusiasm, but the rest of the hierarchy seemed, rightly or wrongly, more interested in their F1 projects than in the little 1000 cc class. The result was that John Fenning and Clive Baker of Stockbridge Racing were so disappointed with the cars when they tested them at Goodwood that before long they were out of the new Type 83 Coopers and into Brabhams. Cooper sold few of these cars over the winter of 1965-66....'

The remains of the Owen Maddock design staff, Neil Johanssen and Eddie Stait, had long gone, replaced by Derrick White ex-Jaguar and Bob Marston ex-Marcos, and they concentrated on Formula 1. The factory at Hollyfield Road had been turned into a car showroom and a new production

Gerard Racing's two F2 Coopers harrying Jackie Oliver's works Lotus Components spaceframe Type 41B at Crystal Palace, Whit-Monday, 1967 – Mike Beckwith in the latest 'T84' with inboard-of-upright front brakes locking over for South Tower Corner ahead of team-mate Peter Gethin in the team's older 'T82' with discs buried in the wheels. This Cosworth FVA-engined trio finished 3-4-5 here in Heat One, then 6-9 and crashed in the Final

and F1 team facility established in former Thomson & Taylor premises in Canada Road, Byfleet, Surrey, on a small industrial estate just across Oyster Lane from the looming remains of the old Brooklands Outer Circuit banking.

The 1966 Type 83 Cooper F3 was even more sleek and streamlined than the preceding Type 76 and looked promising on the Racing Car Show stand, but Bob Marston recalls how it was dogged by apparently incurable understeer: 'In retrospect, in producing a body which we thought would be superfast on the straights, we'd made a perfect lifting aerofoil, which made the thing try to become airborne at any kind of reasonable speed. We tested continuously to find some front-end grip and got nowhere. If we'd known then what we know today about aerodynamics, it just wouldn't have happened....'

Seven of the cars were built at Canada Road, all Cosworth-Ford MAE-powered as BMC interest in the Formula had expired. They went to Clive Baker, Andre Choukron in Paris, Paul Swaelens, Len Selby in Essex, John Kendall from London, Pierre Ryser in Geneva and John McKechnie of Cheltenham.

In an effort to kill the dreaded understeer the car's front suspension was altered to an outboard coil/damper affair like the successful Lotus 41's. There was little improvement and it was as well that most T83 outings were confined to British events.

Older cars in Europe carried Jean Sodreau, 'Josse', Hasse Nilsson and James Eatherley to top-six placings with BMC power, matched by Jean-Pierre Cassegrain, Hans Sjosted, Hughes de Fierlandt, Heinrich Brendt, Mike Herbertson, Leo Matilla, Tico Martini, Barry Collerson and Kurt Keller with Cosworth-Ford power.

While Cooper F3 production was down to just seven cars, Brabham that season built over 50 and did most of the winning from Lotus and French Matra products. Among Matra's customers was Ken Tyrrell, having abandoned Cooper after so many years' faithful and highly successful service.

In Formula 2, the Brabham-Hondas were untouchable, and down on the back of the grid were two Cooper T82s. The first was sold to ever-faithful Bob Gerard for Cosworth SCA power, the second to Ecurie Suisse for a BRM engine. Bob Anderson retired Gerard's car from virtually every event started. Max Johansson was 10th at Keimola, in Finland, and Beckwith took over for Brands Hatch in November where 'Mr Bob' also ran an old T73 for promising former kart champion Chris Lambert. He finished 12th.... The Ecurie Suisse car was driven by Jo Bonnier, Jo Siffert and Sten Axelsson; his ninth place at Karlskoga being their best of the season.

Into 1967 Cooper was very much a Formula 1 team rather than a broad-based racing car manufacturing company in the old sense. A new 1600 cc Formula 2 began that year, but the projected Cooper T84 attracted no interest at all, and only two T85 F3 cars appear to have been produced – 'Works Car I' in December 1966 and a replica going to E. A. Coates Ltd of Frimley, Surrey, in April 1967.

Neither made its mark and it was left to the Belgian Baron Hughes de Fierlandt to win twice in his T83 – both times from nobody of much note – at the East German Bernauer-Schleife in May, and at Zandvoort in July, where Rene Scalais's T76 was fifth....

Meanwhile Gerard Racing's old T82 was eventually augmented by the one-off still-slimmer T84 car, both being prepared by chief mechanic Ralph Gilbert for John Cardwell, Mike Beckwith, Trevor Taylor, Harry Stiller and Alan Rollinson – none of whom could fathom their quirky handling. Beckwith retired from four of his six races in the cars, Trev Taylor twice from two, but Cardwell finished three of his five outings in the T84 and placed 13th at Mallory Park after a stop to change his muddy shoes, because he'd had to lift the car bodily out of a ditch along the way.... Stiller, the Bournemouth businessman who would later give Alan Jones one of his first big breaks *en route* to the World Championship, had two races in the T82; ninth both times, but then Rollinson achieved fifth at Mallory, sixth at Hockenheim and 10th at Langenlebarn in the older car.

This was more encouraging, and Peter Gethin was enlisted for third in the minor Hockenheim race with the T84, and was fifth in Heat at Crystal Palace with the T82 before colliding with Gardner's Brabham in the Final.

Graham Owen ran a Cooper T83-Cosworth SCB hybrid at Mallory Park driven by Brian Myers, and David Darby then non-started with it at Crystal Palace. Another oddball was Luigi Bertocco's Cooper-Alfa Romeo special, which retired from the Rome GP at Vallelunga. Right at the end of the UK season Julian Gerard drove his father's old T73 twin-cam at Brands Hatch and finished a distant 11th.

In November the Graham Owen T83 qualified on pole for the Macau *Libre* GP in the tiny Portuguese colony clinging to the Chinese coastline. It was driven by Peter Gaydon, but unfortunately, after setting his time, he crashed in practice and was able to start the race only after aid from a Portuguese sergeant, a Chinese welder and the local Naval dockyard staff. A wheel nut was left loose as the car took the start and Peter lost control while leading and the car rammed the bank. It summed-up Cooper's eclipse.... There would be no production minor-Formula Coopers in 1968, for the first time in over 20 years, and by the start of the 1969 season, the lights had finally gone out at Cooper Cars....

Alan Rollinson's Gerard 'T82' with in-wheel front discs and that untidy front anti-roll bar layout on the aerodrome circuit at Tulln-Langenlebarn in the Austrian F2 round, 16 July, 1967, day after the British GP. He finished tenth. While Jochen Rindt was disappointed in his F1 Cooper 'T86' at Silverstone, here he won on home soil in his Roy Winkelmann Racing Brabham. Winkelmann had learned some of his early racing in the old Cooper-Bristol 2-litre sports ...

CHAPTER TWENTY FIVE

The Maserati project – 1966-67

Mario Tozzi-Condivi was a salesman – a very good one. Tall, angular, a heavy smoker, he could charm customers out of the trees. He had known Ray Salvadori for years, and had worked for his Elmbridge Motors dealership in the late-Fifties, first as a salesman but soon a director. He was an Italian who had come to England soon after the war. On Roy's introduction he had acted as Cooper's go-between when they began taking the Bob-tail sports cars to venues like Imola and Rome in 1956. He was uniquely well-connected to obtain the best possible starting money and bonuses. 'I was in the Italian Air Force and at the end of the war Dr de Minicis of the Italian Auto Club and I were stranded for a week together in a village up in the mountains. . . . Now I could call him and he'd tell me who I should speak to in the organizing clubs, and how much they could *really* afford. . . .'

Roy had great respect for his salesman's abilities: 'I asked him once what his ambition was and he said he wanted to have *me* working for *him*. . . . I couldn't help but think one day it might just happen.'

Tozzi-Condivi had known Adolfo Orsi, owner of Maserati, since 1947, when the industrialist had wanted a contract man in Britain to promote imports of Maserati batteries, spark plugs, horns, machine tools and, yes, maybe also their early attempt at a production GT car. Eventually the British concession went to a trader in Lancashire while, through Fangio, Maserati concluded a massive contract with the Perón regime in Argentina to supply machine tools. When Maserati collapsed in 1958 it was largely due to Perón's fall and the new Argentine authorities reneging on the deal. Maserati did eventually get its money, but it was a slow and painful process and meantime engineers Alfieri and Selmi had designed and built the prototype 3500GT production car in an effort to remain viable. At this point the British concessionaire set off for pastures new, and Adolfo Orsi contacted Tozzi-Condivi again to take over the franchise. He did so in conjunction with Clifford Taylor of Taylor & Crawley, a major London motor trading company. Clifford's son Mike Taylor raced Cooper and Lotus cars. Tozzi-Condivi later bought-out Taylor's half-share on behalf of his new company – the Chipstead Motor Group. This was an organization which Salvadori's former salesman had formed 50:50 with another businessman named Peter Hodge, who ran Chipstead Motors. They were joined by Jonathan Sieff, grandson of Lord Sieff of the Marks & Spencer retail chain-store empire. He had done some racing in a variety of cars, but had been grievously injured in a Lotus Elite crash during practice for the 1961 Le Mans 24-Hours race, and retired from competition thereafter.

They were keen to expand and looked around for companies to buy. Tozzi-Condivi knew that Salvadori might be receptive and made an offer for his motor trading businesses, which Roy accepted. 'It was a most satisfactory arrangement,' he told me in 1983, 'I was relieved of most business worries, I was retained on a service contract and enjoyed working with Mario, Peter Hodge and Jonathan Sieff; they were very nice people and it worked out very well. . . .'

Then Charles Cooper died in October 1964, and John – still feeling the lingering after-effects of his road accident – was obviously uncomfortable and unsure how to approach the future. Roy talked to him about selling – 'I have and I've got a super deal' – and the Chipstead people were very interested in buying. Cooper had a fine reputation, and was making good money from racing in addition to the Mini-Cooper royalties. The production racing car business was also quite successful. Some surviving figures show that in 1962 car exports from Hollyfield Road totalled £65,262 15s. 3d, spares exports adding another £28,483 15s. 8d. In 1963 the rise of Lotus and Brabham competition saw car exports slashed to £33,424 15s. and spares down to £14,040 17s. 5d, while home car sales were up to £13,016 3s. 3d. With the advent of Formula 3 and Jackie Stewart's success in 1964, car exports had soared again, to £45,953 1s. 9d, while home car sales added £16,867 9s. 3d – spares exports totalling £9,620 13s. 6d. The graph was volatile, but the company had all the prerequisites to be an imposing feather in Chipstead's cap.

John: 'When I decided to sell to Jonathan Sieff I knew that potentially he had Marks & Spencer behind him, 3-litre Formula 1 was going to be very expensive by our standards, and through Tozzi-Condivi they had the Maserati tie-up and there could be a captive source of engines to replace Climax. There was also the unspoken possibility of commercial 'St Michael' sponsorship from M&S, if only their directors would wear it . . . which we subsequently discovered they wouldn't, but at the time it all felt right – good vibrations; know what I mean?'

THE MASERATI PROJECT — 1966–67

Big, beefy, but not brutal – the Cooper-Maserati T81 was the first monocoque Cooper to see public limelight, and during that first season of 3-litre racing in 1966 they rapidly reached fully competitive development. This is Jo Bonnier's private car – 'F1/5/66' – on display in Sweden. Here the inboard-of-upright front brake disc mounting is evident, along with top-ducted nose to allow hot radiator air to escape, rear horn extensions of monocoque pontoons to support the big 60-degree V12 engine, modern double-radius rod rear suspension and electronic ignition and injection gubbins packing the engine valley. This car was sprayed orange with white stripes. It survives today in the displays at Donington Park, near Derby, England

The Cooper Car Company was sold to Chipstead for something over £200,000. John retained title to the property and took a service contract to continue working for the company. It was all made public at the end of April 1965, only six months after Charles's death.

On 27 April, 1965, Peter Cattle of Bullock & Turner Ltd, public relations consultants, issued a press release headed 'COOPERS AND CHIPSTEAD MERGER'. It read as follows:

'We have merged with the Cooper Car Company and Coopers Garage because we feel that we are complementary organizations.' That was how 31-year-old Mr Jonathan Sieff, Chairman of the £500,000 Chipstead Motor Group, explained the deal signed at the weekend with his company by Mr John Cooper, head of Coopers.

'Chipstead have the administrative and marketing set-ups to take a great many of the worries off John Cooper's shoulders,' Mr Sieff went on. 'We believe there is an even greater market potential for the Mini-Cooper which has so far been untapped.

'With Roy Salvadori to help him with the racing administration, John can also forget many of these worries, too, and can concentrate on the development of Formula One, Two, Three and sports cars and – perhaps most important of all – on the development of the Mini-Cooper.

'So far as Chipstead are concerned, we get a ready-made, first-class racing set-up which we have never had.

'Since the BMC Mini was given a high-performance Cooper engine in 1961, Mini-Coopers have become among the leading sports saloons in the world. They won the last two Monte Carlo Rallies and scores of other awards.

'One of our main objectives at Chipstead, in the closest possible association with John Cooper, will be to bring the links with BMC even closer,' said Mr Sieff.

'Let there be no doubt that Cooper will continue in World Championship motor racing this year and next, when the new 3-litre Grand Prix Formula begins. It is our intention to expand our motor racing interests in all forms.'

Mr John Cooper, who will remain in sole control of the technical side of the Cooper Car Company – which stays as an entirely separate entity within the Chipstead Group – stated, 'This joint venture with my long-standing friends at Chipstead will relieve me of administrative headaches and let me devote my energies to the construction of racing cars and to my very special interest in furthering the competition development of the BMC Mini-Cooper.

'I am sure that future developments will bring our links with BMC even closer.

'The appointment of 42-year-old Chipstead executive and veteran racing driver Roy Salvadori as a racing administrator with Coopers takes him back to the scene of some of his former triumphs. At one time he was number one works driver with Coopers.'

An *Autosport* editorial read:

'The acquisition of the Cooper Car Co, Ltd, by the Chipstead Motors Group [*sic*] should lead to an even more competitive representation of Coopers in both formulae and sports-car racing. While John Cooper will remain in charge of motor racing activities, he will have the assistance of that very experienced driver Roy Salvadori in planning for the future. Chipstead's chairman, Jonathan Sieff, has stated that the group's

COOPER CARS

On loan from Honda, works development driver Richie Ginther tries the prototype T81 for size in the new Canada Road works at Byfleet, 1966, discussing progress with new chief designer Derrick White (left) while youthful mechanic Ron Dennis looks on (right). The engine is a Maserati slave unit, half-dismantled here, on Weber carburettors and coil-ignition whereas the finalized team and customer cars ran fuel injection and electronic ignition. Ron Dennis would later work for Brabham, then run his own Formula 2 teams before taking control of the Formula 1 team which had been founded by Bruce McLaren, into the 1980s

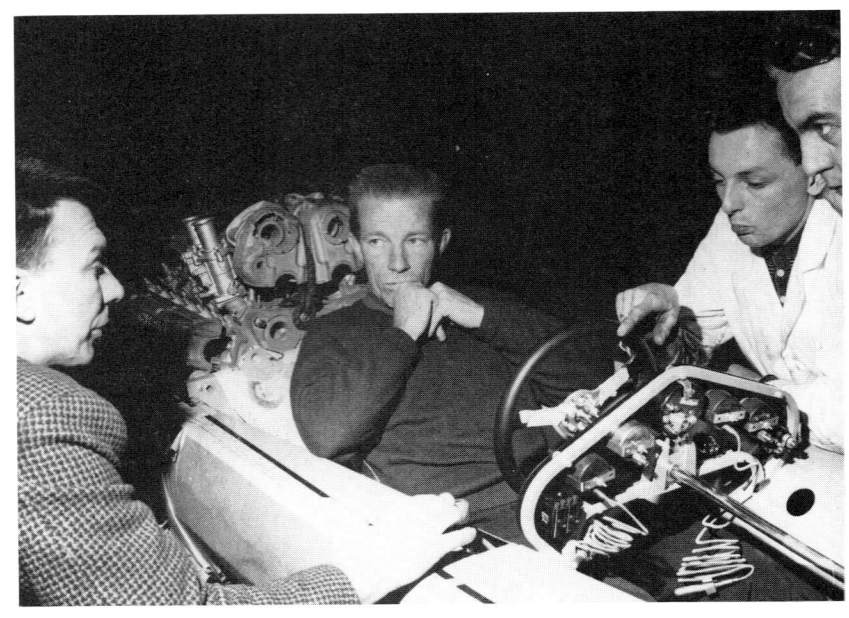

Left *3-litre Formula 1 racing was billed as the return of power. It certainly produced some impressive-looking mechanical assemblies, like the T81-Maserati seen here, Monaco 1966, Richie Ginther locking-over into Mirabeau Inférieur on the descent from the Station hairpin. Geoff Goddard's shot shows the twin-plug ignition (two distributors) of the V12 engine, protective gauzes over injection trumpets, three-into-one exhaust systems, ZF transaxle and lashed-on oil catch tanks. The front brake discs and calipers are visible out in the breeze while rears are buried within wheels. Note hefty half-shafts, right-hand gear linkage and rear anti-roll bar working hard!*

Right *12 June, 1966, Belgian GP, Spa-Francorchamps: Jochen Rindt in his works T81 – F1/3/66 – drove a marvellous, instinctive race in awful conditions to lead the race before finishing second behind Surtees' Ferrari. The hefty Cooper-Maserati with its relatively modest power output (though good at that time) felt more stable on the slick surface than most. Catch-tank layout has changed on the transmission since Monaco. Note aluminium windscreen extension for the super-fast Ardennes public road circuit. But it wasn't all roses for the Cooper drivers. As the field tore into that first-lap downpour here at Burnenville Jo Bonnier spun into this embarrassing position with his private 'T81's front end hanging over an uncomfortably long drop. He edged his way gingerly back to safety over the hot, steaming engine. Jack Brabham and Lorenzo Bandini splash by on the right line. The pub on the inside gave a terrific close-up view of racing through the bar window. Racing as it was . . .*

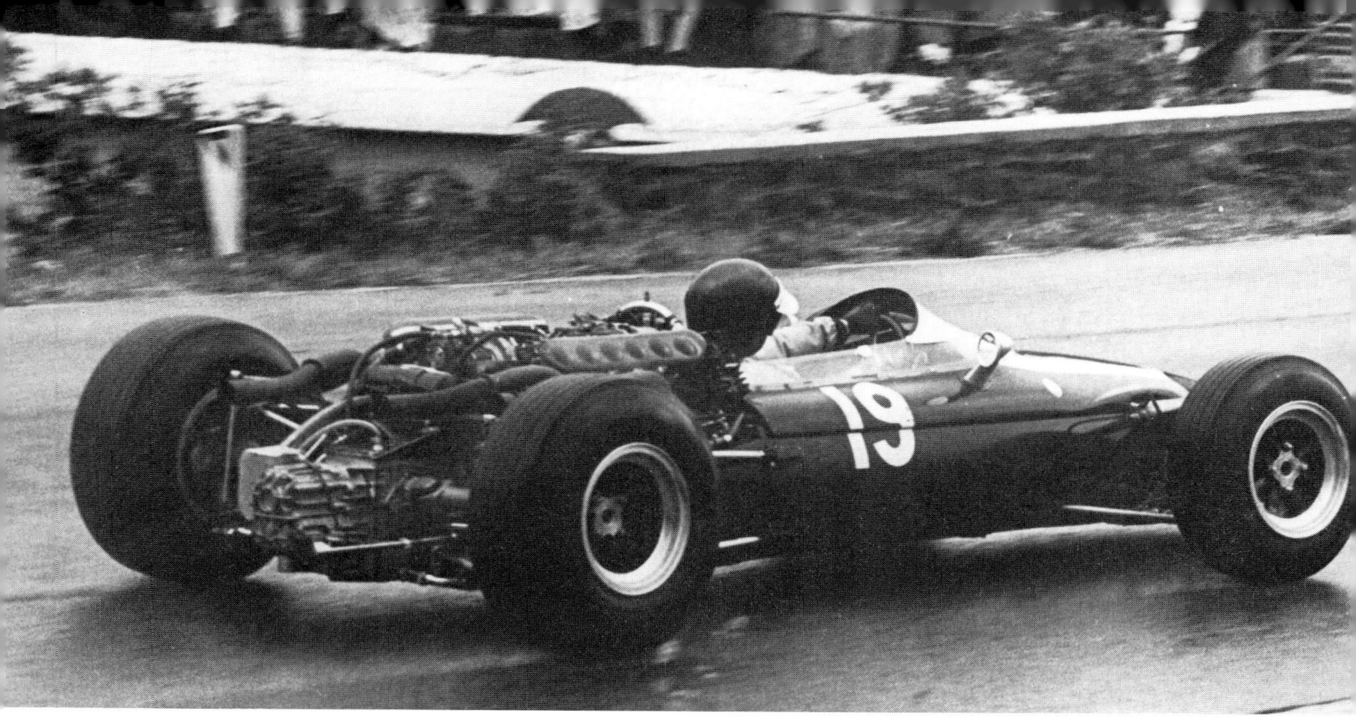
19

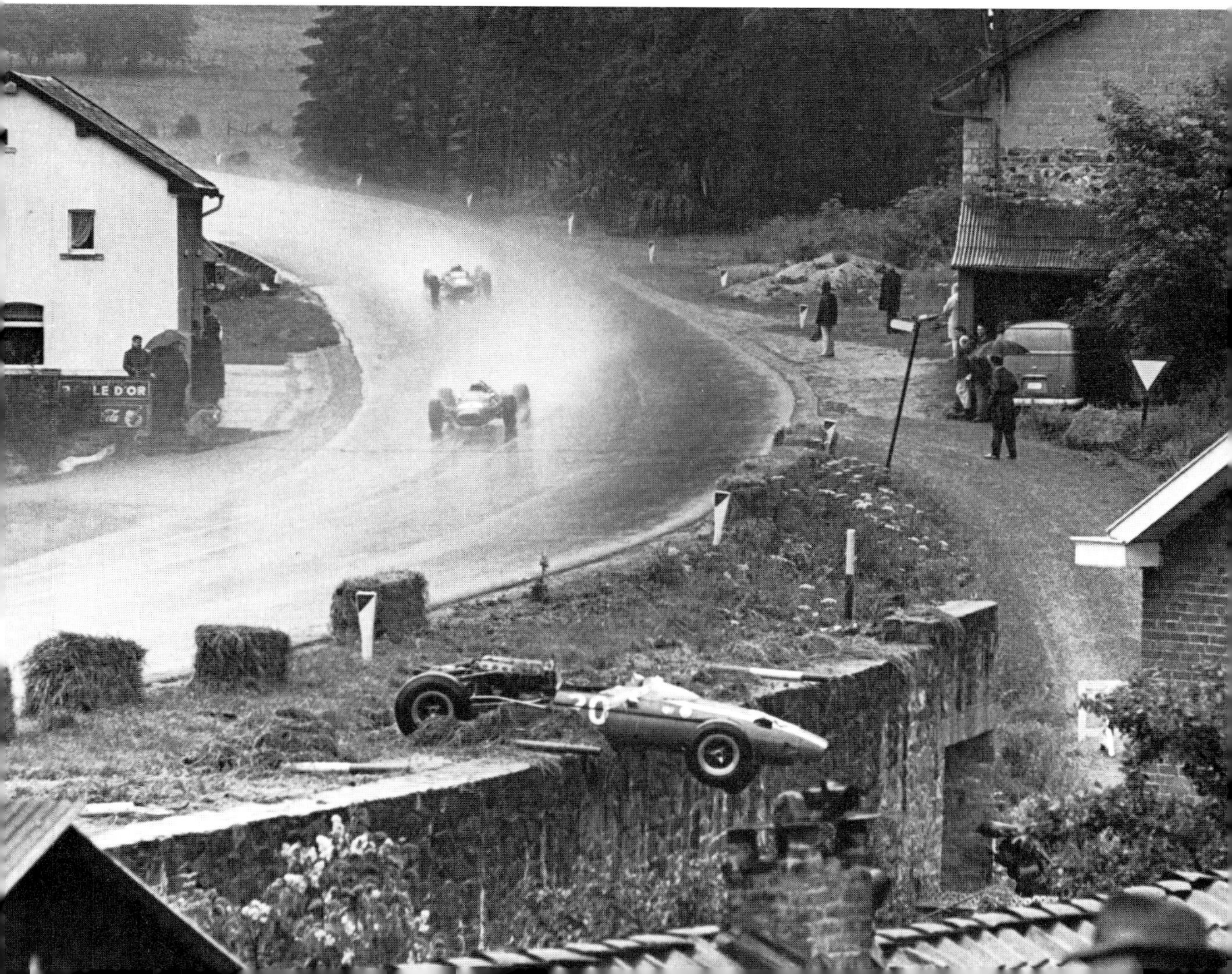
LE D'OR

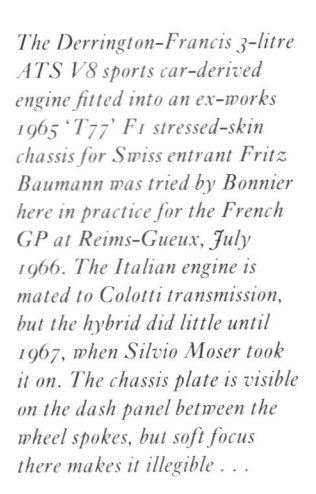

The Derrington-Francis 3-litre ATS V8 sports car-derived engine fitted into an ex-works 1965 'T77' F1 stressed-skin chassis for Swiss entrant Fritz Baumann was tried by Bonnier here in practice for the French GP at Reims-Gueux, July 1966. The Italian engine is mated to Colotti transmission, but the hybrid did little until 1967, when Silvio Moser took it on. The chassis plate is visible on the dash panel between the wheel spokes, but soft focus there makes it illegible . . .

policy will be to continue racing Coopers, as well as to establish an up-to-date sales and service organization for Mini-Coopers within its ever-expanding structure. Chipstead's main interest is in high-performance machines, and the board believes that a motor racing programme is the ideal method of furthering its policy. Coopers . . . could well return to their former glory in Grand Prix racing, backed by the finance and undoubted enthusiasm of the Chipstead concern.'

Rumours began immediately that Chipstead's Maserati ties would produce works Maserati-engined F1 cars for 1966. *Motoring News* – the British racing weekly newspaper – was at its wild and woolly best: '. . . it is rumoured that the 3-litre Formula 1 Cooper will use two of the 1½-litre V12 Maserati engines.' One detects John's sense of humour in that 'leak'.

One immediate effect of the merger was predictable, a certain degree of ill-feeling among the Cooper old hands. One recalls: 'Suddenly we had all these new people walking about as though they owned the place . . . it was hard to realize they actually did. . . .' Chipstead split Cooper into two, the Car Company and Cooper Car Sales, which would market new and used performance cars of all kinds. John was made responsible for day-to-day management of the racing car works, plus preparation of the Formula 1 team cars, while Roy Salvadori ran the team as such, negotiating with the drivers, oil companies, tyre suppliers, etc. Major Owens ran team movements, bookings and so on.

Mario Tozzi-Condivi found the company was showing a good profit from its activities, but recalls alarm at the size of Climax's supply and service bills for their V8 engines: 'We were buying our engines, and there had to be a better way for the new formula. . . .'

So in preparation for 1966 he approached Adolfo Orsi and his son Omer during 1965 to suggest co-operation in a 3-litre Formula 1 project. Tozzi-Condivi was the lynch-pin, without him the Cooper-Maserati would never have come about.

'Adolfo was in favour, but naturally they were all terrified of the financial involvement because I was not going to commission them to develop an engine and then underwrite its cost. The Cooper Car Company Ltd would instead become sole concessionaires for a 3-litre Cooper-Maserati V12 engine and customers buying our cars would also buy their engines through us. The works engines would be Maserati's property. They would commit themselves to providing sufficient engines for three works cars, to development to keep them competitive and to all necessary servicing. We would pay them a fixed fee per rebuild, irrespective of the amount of work necessary. It was around £700 per rebuild, I think. . . . And they agreed. . . .'

Cooper paid Maserati an advance sum to launch the project and through the summer of 1965 *Ing.* Giulio Alfieri and his team in Modena's Viale Ciro Menotti dusted-down their old 1957 2½-litre V12 racing engine and set about a major updating programme.

Late in the year a prototype engine was taken out on test in the rear of a lashed-up spaceframe car actually based on the one-off T80 frame, which had been standing around waiting for the still-born flat-16 Climax engine. Mike Barney's last job for Cooper was to help complete this car. Then he left for McLaren's. While this hack tested suspension, tyres and other ideas, *Ing.* Alfieri developed fuel injection to supplant the test V12's carburettors, and transistorized electronic ignition to replace the remarkable array of coils and contact-breakers arranged on the test car's tail. Derrick White, with his vast Jaguar E type experience behind him, was detailed to produce a robust and practical monocoque car to carry this powerful but thirsty new engine. Amongst his papers he noted '14 weeks to design and build. 15 weeks develop design & build 5 (cars)'. To stiffen the team with experience of monocoque racing car construction, Tony Robinson – late of Equipe Moss Cooper-Alta, etc. – was enlisted from the now-defunct British Racing Partnership BRP team; with whom he had helped design and build both Formula 1 and Indy monocoque cars.

The prototype 3-litre Cooper-Maserati T81 made its bow at the Racing Car Show in January 1966. It was the first fully-fledged British 3-litre to make its bow and attracted intense interest, though by $1\frac{1}{2}$ litre standards it looked enormous.

The monocoque tub followed Lotus practice in forming an open-topped 'bath-tub' with two stressed-skin booms either side united by a stressed floor and three widely spaced bulkheads. The booms extended the full length of the wheelbase and were skinned in duralumin, save for the inner skins in the engine bay, which were in steel to protect the fuel bags within; there being a single 25-gallon cell each side. These cells were actually so long that the booms had to be free of internal obstruction, only a midship bulkhead fabricated from top-hat section steel like the ribs of a boat providing stiffening.

The front suspension hung from a hefty front bulkhead comprising two steel diaphragms sandwiching inboard coil/dampers. A midships beam braced the booms apart and provided front engine mounts, while a sloping seat-back panel was riveted to the top of the beam and to the side skins and floor to stiffen the tub. Behind this bulkhead assembly the side booms tapered rearwards to a box-section steel ring, which anchored the rear springs and suspension links. The Maserati V12 and ZF five-speed transaxle sat on two dural bearers front and rear, while two lugs cast on the final-drive cover bolted through the rearmost ring bulkhead. These rigid fixings allowed the engine/transmission assembly to stiffen the chassis structure.

Suspension followed $1\frac{1}{2}$-litre practice, but was all new in detail. Redesigned cast-magnesium hub carriers were required to accommodate the extra braking torque in such a fast and heavy car, and to accept a new brake layout in which the discs were stepped inboard of the upright and wheel at the front to expose them and their calipers to direct, uninterrupted airflow. At the rear the carriers were designed to place the wheel bearings as near the rim centreline as possible to minimize overhang loadings and reduce angular movements at the drive-shaft UJs by permitting the longest-possible shafts.

The inboard front suspension retained Cooper's normal anti-dive angularity, while the split lower wishbones used a trailing torque stay aft of the lateral link instead of ahead of it as in the $1\frac{1}{2}$s. As compression members they now fed loads direct into the meat of the tub, anchored in small channel sections riveted into the side booms. The deep rocker arms themselves were steel sheet fabrications.

At the rear, a reversed lower wishbone was used with single lateral top link, twin radius rods and outboard coil/dampers. Adjustable length on the top links determined wheel camber and roll-centre height, while the trailing radius rod lengths determined toe-in.

White's adoption of 'inboard-outboard' front brakes driven by live stub axles gave extra freedom of front-wheel diameter, since the discs no longer had to be housed within the rims, as well as offering better cooling. The ploy was bulky, but no heavier than normal because the conventional hub was eliminated and the upright itself was lighter. White cited reduced unsprung weight with 13 in. front wheels and improved brake cooling as advantages of the system.

The wheels themselves were new castings on the old spoked magnesium theme, 8 in. wide fronts and 10 in. rears. Front brake discs were fully 10.75 in. diameter, rears 10.3 in., cooling airflow through the spoked wheels being especially vital there.

Ing. Alfieri had modernized his late-Fifties V12 engine by broadening its notoriously top-endy original torque curve with different ports and revised cam profiles. Whereas the original 68.5×56 mm $2\frac{1}{2}$ litre F1 engine of 1957 had been stressed to 10,000 rpm, the 68 mm stroke 3-litre sports-car version revved lower, to around 8500. Now Alfieri cut that stroke to 64 mm and enlarged the bores to 70.4 mm to reproduce the original 10,000 rpm limit with the increased capacity.

It was a classical 60-degree V12 with twin gear-driven ohc per bank and two valves per cylinder. Initially ignition was by two Marelli double-deck distributors coupled to Lucas transistorized systems. The test hack used 24 coils, one for each plug, with matching contact breakers in banks. Lucas initially provided two six-cylinder fuel-injection metering units, later replaced by a proper 12-cylinder system. Unusually, Alfieri adopted separate Dell'Orto motorcycle-type piston slides to control air intake. They were made by Maserati anyway, so were there on the shelf, but problems were anticipated with eddying in the tracts at part throttle. Their friction area was also considerably greater than a conventional throttle slide as used with injection systems on BRM and Ferrari engines. The linkage for 12 individual slides was also enormously complex and potentially troublesome.

Initially there were no power figures released, but into the 1966 season they began talking of an honest 360 bhp at 9200 rpm. This was transmitted via a Lockheed $7\frac{1}{4}$ in. dry-plate clutch to the Ford GT40-type ZF 5DS25 transaxle. Wheelbase was 8 ft 2 in.; front track, 5 ft; rear track, 4 ft $9\frac{1}{2}$ in.

The spaceframe test car based on the T80 flat-16 frame

is Registered as tax exempt on 30 November, 1965, given the chassis number *FI/1/66* and was fitted with Maserati V12 engine No *9001*. In fact the car had been out on test at Goodwood earlier that month, driven by Roy Salvadori and Denny Hulme, who quickly scotched rumours that he was signing for Cooper, and confirmed he would stay with Brabham. Jochen Rindt tested later in the year. In addition to the works monocoque cars three would be supplied to customers; Rob Walker again – *2/66* with engine *9006* – a second car to the Swiss Scuderia Felipe Pemeti emerging in French blue for wealthy public works contractor Guy Ligier to drive as a private entry – chassis *4/66*, engine *9005*; and finally to Jo Bonnier, genuinely Swiss-based, chassis *6/66* engine *9007*.

There were to be nine World Championship rounds that year and four minor F1 races. The cars were the first proper 3-litres to appear in quantity, but were too late for the first minor F1 South African GP at East London on New Year's Day. The team moved from Surbiton into its cavernous new HQ at Canada Road, Byfleet, while the private cars made their debut at Syracuse on 1 May, with both the Walker and Ligier cars appearing, the dark-blue British-entered machine being driven by Jo Siffert. Ligier spun his into a wall during practice, its right-front suspension being repaired with Walker spares. It was suspected that the rear torque arm of the lower wishbones was whipping under braking, so the Walker machines were stripped of their chrome and had bracing ribs brazed along both sides. While Surtees's new 3-litre V12 Ferrari took pole position, Siffert was third fastest and Ligier fifth in the small field.

In the race Siffert suffered misfiring until a half-shaft broke, and after a pit stop to correct ignition faults Ligier finished sixth, but outside the time limit and 17 laps behind Surtees's winning car.

André Wicky, the Swiss privateer, ran an ancient Cooper with 2-litre BRM V8 engine in this race, but qualified *37.4 sec slower* than Surtees and retired at the start as his battery refused to start the engine. . . . Roberto Bussinello, the Alfa Romeo test driver, was entered by Alf Francis in one of the 1965 works Coopers now fitted with a 3-litre ATS engine, but it failed to appear.

Two weeks later, May Silverstone saw Jochen Rindt and his new team mate Richie Ginther – on loan until the 3-litre Honda would be ready – give the new works T81s their debut. Jack Brabham's low-powered, uncomplicated, beautifully-handling Repco V8 car ran there and won handsomely. The car espoused all the old Cooper virtues, and some. . . . Bonnier, Ligier and Siffert were also running and all the T81s had reinforced front wishbones after the Syracuse failure. Rindt's car handled peculiarly in the race and dropped from third to fifth at the finish. Bonnier's orange car inherited third place, while Ginther's went out with overheating and Siffert and Ligier both broke their precious engines in practice. Rob Walker's man was loaned the spaceframe T80 hack for the race, but its clutch failed, while poor Ligier could not start at all.

Monaco followed and the start of 3-litre World Championship racing. Four T81s appeared; the works cars for Rindt and Ginther, plus Ligier and Bonnier. Walker's team, now co-sponsored by stockbroker Jack Durlacher, ran Siffert in their old Brabham, now fitted with a 2-litre BRM V8 engine. It should be a good proposition around Monte Carlo streets, in the 1957–58 Cooper-Climax mould. The T81s ran with the extension piece removed from their nose cowls for greater cooling area and less vulnerability in traffic, and with cut-down screens. They still proved too cumbersome for the tight course, and qualified poorly, but both privateers survived to the finish, though too far behind to be classified after lengthy stops with ignition and injection maladies. Rindt ran as high as third until his engine broke, while Ginther survived until lap 80 in fifth place when a drive-shaft broke.

Spa-Francorchamps was a more suitable circuit, and all five T81s then extant appeared; two works and three private. After the half-shaft pounding at Monaco, redesigned components appeared on all the cars, and while Surtees's Ferrari took pole, Rindt was next up, followed by Bonnier, Ginther, Ligier and Siffert in the Cooper-Maserati pecking order.

But on the opening lap of the Grand Prix the pack ran into torrential showers and nine cars went missing. Bonnier's T81 fetched-up dangling its front end over a consider-

Back on form – the revamped Cooper team with its Maserati-engined cars proved truly competitive again from the German GP, here at Nürburgring, 7 August, 1966. This is John Surtees who played such a large part in the team's transformation, splashing past the Startplatz *and* Sporthotel *grandstand into the* Südkehre *roundabout corner. The detachable nose cone is visible here, quickly providing enlarged cooling intake, the screen is cut low and the mirrors have tripod tube mountings unlike the Rindt-Spa faired type. 'John the Great' started second fastest qualifier, and finished second ahead of Jochen, third. Jack Brabham won in his own team car*

Winning again! – Surtees in the open-nosed 'T81' – F1/6/66 – on Mexico City's Magdalena Mixhuca circuit en route to winning the Mexican GP, closing round of the year's World Championship series, 23 October, 1966. The car is running faired mirror mounts and shaped aluminium draught-includers over the injection stacks. Broadsiding luridly in John's wake, just like the old days, is Jack Brabham – having already clinched his third World Championship Drivers' title – with Jochen Rindt next up, the nose fuel pump mounting visible in his car's radiator intake. Strange experience for Brabham to be sandwiched by two works Coopers – even stranger to be beaten by one of them . . .

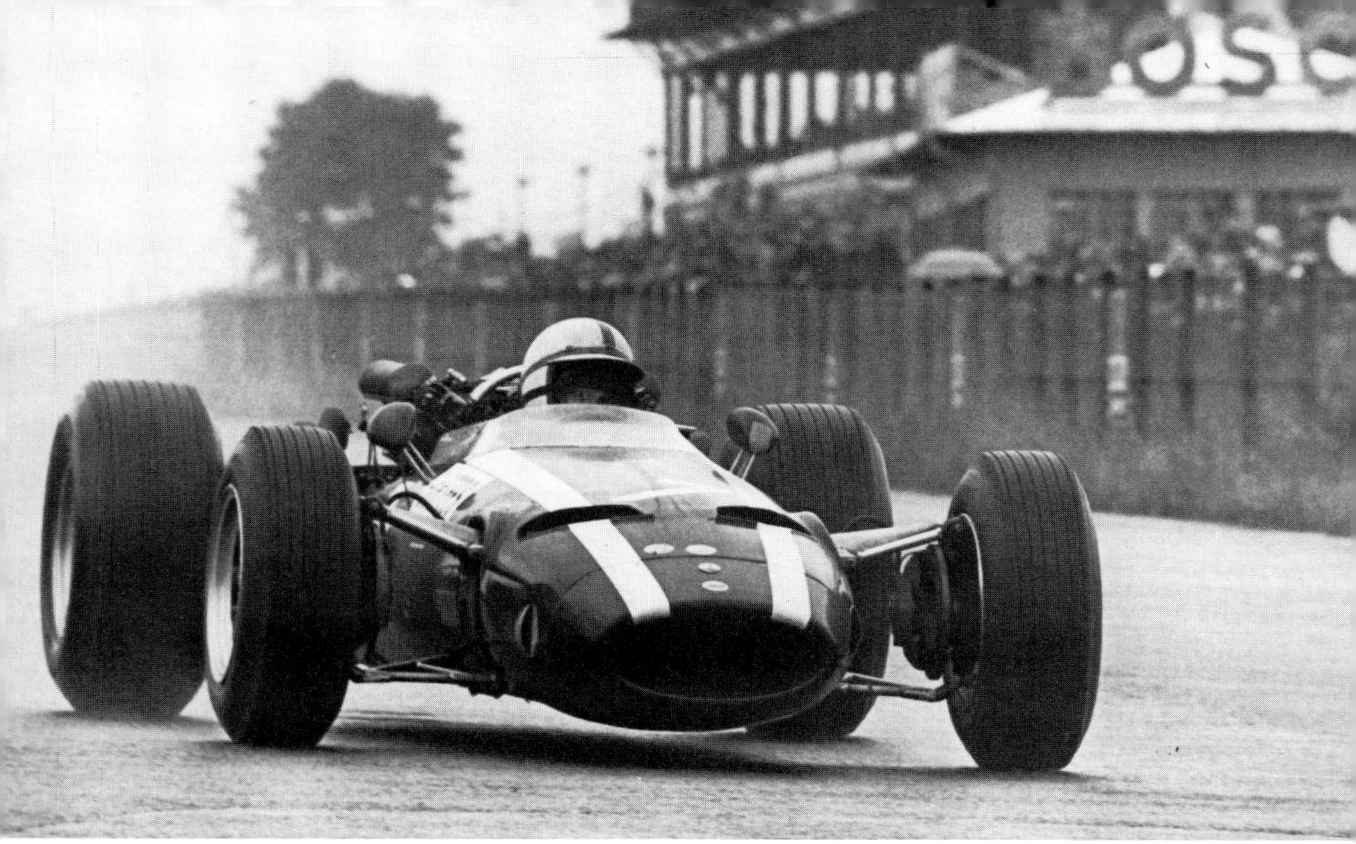

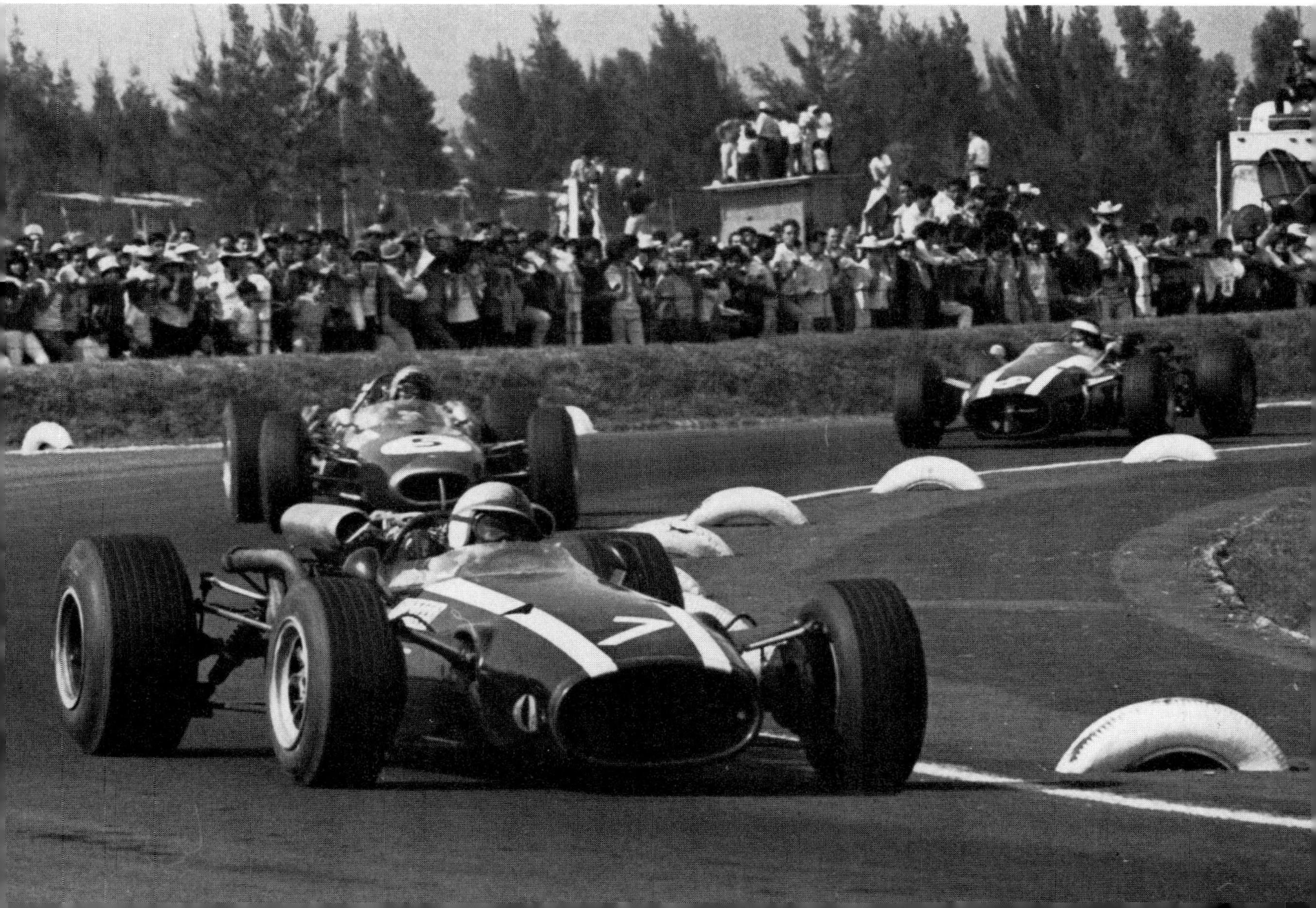

able vertical drop on the outside of Burnenville Curve, the Swede having to inch his way gingerly to safety over the steaming engine. Siffert crashed Walker's car and Rindt spun mightily in Surtees's spray through the Masta Kink – the latter stages of his high-speed gyration featuring in MGM's awful feature film *Grand Prix*. The Austrian nervelessly gathered it all up and rejoined sixth behind Ginther and Ligier. By lap three he was third and then forced past the works Ferraris to lead the Grand Prix. . . .

Surtees sat back, content to let the Cooper driver set the pace. By lap 8 they had lapped Ginther, but by lap 20 the rain had eased, there was less spray and Jochen was in trouble with his ZF diff faltering, causing queasy handling on the damp surface. Surtees could now see where he was going and regained the lead to win easily, with Rindt second for Cooper and Ferrari's rival firm in Modena. Richie was fifth and Ligier was still running at the finish, but too far behind to be classified after a stop to adjust the clutch and lower tyre pressures.

Jochen had shown the Cooper-Maserati's potential in practice and drove splendidly in daunting weather conditions. It was no disgrace to be beaten by John Surtees and the V12 Ferrari. Spa had always been kind to works Coopers. . . .

In the three weeks preceding the French GP at Reims on 3 July, Ginther was recalled by Honda, whose new V12 car was ready for testing in Japan. Roy called on Chris Amon – McLaren's spare driver, still without a car – to take over the second Cooper-Maserati.

Then Surtees unexpectedly became available after long-simmering troubles had erupted at Ferrari. John left the team he had served so brilliantly during the preceding three and a half years and Mario Tozzi-Condivi received the intelligence from Modena in a 3 a.m. telephone call '. . . from a very reliable source. He told me Surtees was leaving Ferrari and would be available for Formula 1. I called my co-directors and got them out of bed to meet me at Canada Road at 5 a.m. that morning, and I beat down all resistance and had a new team car built that week. Roy was part of this plot, and we just built the extra car and made it known generally we had a spare chassis available and then waited for the phone to ring. . . .'

Contacts were made and once problems of clashing fuel company contracts had been resolved Cooper and Maserati delightedly welcomed *Il Grande John* into their fold. Jochen would retain his regular car at Reims, Surtees took over Ginther's and Amon was given the brand-new spare – 7/66 with engine *9010* signed-off on 27 June, just six days before the race. Bonnier's T81 was still under repair and he reappeared in Alf Francis's rather dubious Cooper-ATS V8 special instead. Siffert and Ligier were out in their usual cars.

Ferrari missed the first practice session and amidst the golden cornfields it was a glorious day again for Cooper as Surtees and Rindt set the pace, their raucous V12s singing exultantly across the Champagne country. Alfieri had bolted together a '370 bhp' engine for Surtees, but Bandini's Ferrari stole pole from him by 0.6 sec with Parkes's Ferrari third and Brabham and Rindt on row two. Amon suffered brake and sticking throttle problems, while Bonnier judged the Cooper-ATS unraceworthy and took the spare Brabham with 2.7 FPF instead for the race.

In the race Cooper came down with a bump. Poor Surtees was in trouble from flagfall with fuel vaporization and was struggling 13th before stopping. Amon, Siffert and Ligier also stopped to have water splashed over their overheating fuel pumps, tucked away out of the airstream by the gearbox.

Last victory – Pedro Rodriguez driving his reliable race at Johannesburg's Kyalami circuit, South African GP, 2 January, 1967, which brought him victory – Cooper's last in Formula 1. The fuel pump has retreated once again to the tail, fed with cooling air through that huge flexible trunk sprouting between the injection gauze and roll-over bar. The car is chassis F1/6/66 again

Rindt stopped too, but managed to salvage fourth place, while Amon was eighth, Ligier again unclassified, and Surtees and Siffert both retired.

This was a shattering end to such high hopes, and John Cooper's observation that the fuel pumps should be mounted in the nose aperture to keep cool caused some bitterness among the Chipstead directors; it was too late to say so now, but he felt they hadn't been listening earlier; '. . . by this time the design was by committee and I'd always wanted the fuel pump moved from on top of the gearbox into the nose.'

At Brands Hatch for the British GP the T81s again proved too big and cumbersome, until the surface became slick and damp, when the works pair Surtees and Rindt ran briefly 2–3 as the cars' weight made them feel stable and relatively secure. As the surface dried so they dropped back, Jochen finishing fourth and Surtees dropping out when diff failure made his car uncontrollable. Ligier and Siffert tailed in at the finish, while Chris Lawrence was last in the J. A. Pearce Cooper-Ferrari special, confected by levering an sohc Ferrari 250GT V12 engine into the rear of the old works F1-2-64 frames.

The Dutch GP followed a week later at Zandvoort, where the fast swerves through the sand-dunes didn't suit the cars at all. Bonnier's was repaired and running again, but Jochen bent his works car early in the race when he found the wrong gear, and it was later savaged again as Parkes's spinning Ferrari landed beside it in the catch-fencing. Surtees suffered electrical trouble, Siffert's engine broke and Bonnier and Ligier finished 7–9. The works cars broke two engines in practice, an expensive weekend for Maserati. . . .

Only four T81s ran at Nürburgring in the German GP as the Walker-Durlacher team failed to agree terms with the organizers. Lawrence reappeared in the metallic pale-green Cooper-Ferrari special. In practice Guy Ligier uncharacteristically crashed and was thrown out of his severely damaged car with a broken knee and abrasions.

Surtees was on top form on this difficult circuit and qualified second to Clark's nimble 2-litre Lotus-Climax on pole. Rindt was in row three. Rain fell at the start and John was the early leader, coming to grips with his now well set-up car, before Brabham slithered by. With only two of the 14.2-mile laps to run John was still second, just 2 sec behind the former Cooper team leader, but then his clutch pedal refused to return and as the fuel load diminished so the lightened T81's handling deteriorated, and Surtees had to settle unhappily for second place at the finish. Meanwhile Jochen held third virtually all the way. Bonnier was in trouble with the Firestone tyres on his car, against the works on Dunlop, and he gave up. Lawrence was running last until lap 11, when a front suspension ball-joint failed under braking. He fought the car to a safe halt. Cooper-Maserati relished their 2–3 finish, for Ferrari had languished way behind them.

The unfortunate Guy Ligier was out of racing for the rest of the year, and his car was damaged beyond repair. Meanwhile Alfieri's men in Modena set about preparations to out-do Ferrari in the Italian GP. Revised works engines emerged with inlet ports inclined inwards to make the whole unit more compact. Surtees tried an original spec V12 with Marelli ignition at Monza on the Saturday and split the Ferraris, while Siffert's engine threw a rod and a replacement V12 was borrowed from the works. Bonnier was in fuel injection-pump trouble. John finally qualified fourth fastest and Rindt eighth.

In the GP, Surtees led the third lap across the timing line but could not match the Ferraris for sheer pace. His car then began handling peculiarly because leaking fuel was spraying onto a rear tyre, and as it grew worse he retired. Rindt finished fourth, despite having the left-front tyre deflate completely and leave the rim as he approached the finish line – the car scuttering off onto the grass verge with the wheel locked. Bonnier's throttle linkage put him out on lap 4, while Siffert's second engine of the meeting went bang on lap 47. It was not a good day for Cooper-Maserati. John Cooper was responsible for the preparation of the cars at that time and 'it is true I did have a clash with Condivi at the Italian GP, because of the leak in Surtees's fuel tank. . . .' Sir George Harriman wanted him to concentrate upon Mini-Cooper race preparation in any case, and he would miss several GP races into 1967.

Alfieri's latest-spec engine had the distributors arranged in tandem within the vee, driven back-to-back instead of sitting side-by-side above the engine. The unusual barrel throttle system survived, but one engine appeared with Lucas injection upstream of the throttles and another downstream. Alfieri would try anything; he bubbled with quiet enthusiasm and there was no doubting that Maserati's heart was in the project, as Salvadori emphasizes: '. . . but they had their problems with strikes at the works, and lost time could never be adequately made up. Heini Mader, Siffert's former mechanic, worked for us at the Maserati factory, would go with Bertocchi to watch the engines on the dyno and oversaw much of the rebuilding and preparation there. Alfieri was a wonderful type and gave as much time to the project as he could, but he was involved in other work – like the Citroën-Maserati – and eventually the F1 engine was overtime, most of the work going on outside conventional business hours. . . . All things considered, it did well. . . .'

Chris Lawrence ran the Cooper-Ferrari in the sparsely supported Oulton Park Gold Cup on 17 September, finishing fifth and last, and then at Watkins Glen Surtees ran an original-head V12 and Rindt the latest type. John was truly competitive, hounding Brabham and Bandini, only to be put off the road by a back-marker as he tried to lap him. The Cooper driver lost three laps limping back to the pits for a check-over, but there were many retirements and he soared back through the field to finish third behind Jochen – another Cooper 2–3, and fourth too as Siffert finished there.

In Mexico City the works fielded their third car for local ace Moises Solana using a late-style engine, and after carefully adapting mixture and injection settings to suit the high-altitude Mexico City circuit, Surtees qualified strongly on pole with Rindt fifth. In the opening laps John's engine fluffed off-song 'until it got really hot, when it cleared and ran like a bird'. In two laps he caught and passed his team mate, then closed on Brabham and in another lap was leading. He held that lead to the chequered flag, Brabham – the year's new World Champion – settling for second place. It was Cooper's first Formula 1 race victory since Reims in 1962; back home John Cooper heard the news with mixed feelings. He was delighted, but it would have been nice to be there....

Both Rindt and Siffert were put out by left-front suspension ball-joint failures, and Solana retired with no oil pressure after an early stop to complain of overheating. Jo Bonnier was sixth for his World Championship point of the season.

In this race Richie Ginther's Honda V12 set fastest lap, and mindful of the Japanese concern's slowish start in motorcycle racing before total domination, John Surtees signed for them for 1967–68 Formula 1. Salvadori had to find a new team mate for Jochen Rindt in the 1967 season, when 11 GPs would make up the World Championship and there were six minor F1 events on the calendar.

The season's frustrations were more than offset by the World Championship placings at its end, which saw Jack Brabham World Champion driver and constructor, but John Surtees was runner-up with his Ferrari and Cooper-Maserati points, and Jochen Rindt was third overall purely for Cooper-Maserati. The marque was third in the Constructors' competition, just one point behind Ferrari, though 12 behind Repco Brabham. In these terms it was Cooper's best season since 1962....

Cooper's second – and final – season with Maserati power was summed-up by David Phipps in the annual *Autocourse*: 'The Cooper-Maserati was handicapped by low power, high weight and slow development.... For most of the season the cars were much the same as in 1966 – except that they were not so reliable. Rindt finished two races, compared with six in 1966....'

In his search for available drivers Roy had offered the Mexican Pedro Rodriguez a one-off outing in the South African GP at Kyalami on 2 January. After the Mexican success there was optimism among new chief mechanic Trevor Orchard's crew at Canada Road. Kyalami was another high-altitude circuit. Both cars for Rindt and Rodriguez used old-style headed engines and Marelli coil ignition. Rodriguez took over the Surtees Mexico car – 6/66 – and Rindt retained his usual mount. Siffert and Bonnier were running their usual T81s while John Love appeared in his ex-McLaren Tasman Cooper-Climax 2.7, and was second quickest in the Friday practice session. The works car noses were cut back to improve cooling and their mechanical fuel pumps were reversed and spaced outboard behind the engine, with flexible ducting to feed cooling air around them. It worked well; Pedro qualified fourth fastest, but Love was ahead of Rindt – only 1.1 sec covering the three Coopers – two V12s and the ancient but impeccably well-prepared four-cylinder.

In the GP, both Siffert and Bonnier broke their engines; by lap 24 Jochen was third behind two Brabhams, but on lap 39 his engine dropped a valve. Pedro had fallen back, behind Love's incredible 2.7, Gurney's Eagle and Surtees's Honda. Then Brabham's leading car stopped with fuel vaporization. His team mate Denny Hulme led with Love second from Gurney, but then the Californian's suspension broke. So Surtees and Rodriguez were running 3–4. With 21 laps to go Hulme abruptly cut off into the pit lane with brake failure and the impossible was happening; John Love was leading what was virtually his home Grand Prix in one of the local cars! The Honda went out and Pedro was second and Love – handicapped by the Tasman Cooper's tight fuel capacity – had to stop to refuel. While he was stationary, the Mexican works driver sailed by to win by 26.4 sec from the disappointed, but wildly fêted, Rhodesian. It had been a confused race of attrition, but Cooper-Maserati had now won two consecutive GPs, the first round of the new World Championship, their new driver led the Drivers' standings and they had seen another Cooper 1–2 at World Championship level, quite like old times....

From this point forward it was all downhill.

At Monaco the works team re-emerged with the spare chassis carrying Alfieri's latest engine, using the 1966 *Tipo* 9 bottom end with new *Tipo* 10 three-valve-per-cylinder Heron

THE MASERATI PROJECT – 1966–67

British GP, Silverstone, 15 July, 1967 – Cooper trio at Maggott's Curve with Rodriguez's T81B –F1/6/66 showing the way to Moser's Baumann-owned ATS V8-engined special, carrying inboard-of-the-upright front disc brakes like the T81s, and in rear Alan Rees enjoying his guest drive in the spare works T81 – F1/3/66. Silverstone can't have been hotter than Kyalami, but those pumps are back in the nose. In the pit-lane, vastly different to that which witnessed the Cooper victory in 1960, Jochen sits ready to start practice in the dramatically ugly magnesium-skinned T86 prototype. Roy Salvadori has an expression of apparent distaste at left, next to him are Bob Marston and crew-cut Derrick White, behind him Jabby Crombac with, in cape and deer-stalker, John Bolster. Ron Dennis is at the right-rear wheel from this angle, with Siffert trundling Walker's Torrey Canyon *into view beyond*

heads. Included angle between the valves was now so narrow that both camshafts could be enclosed by a single cover. The inlets were re-sited within the vee in true cross-flow form with the exhausts outboard. Twin spark plugs per cylinder lay beneath the exhaust ports in the side of the combustion chamber instead of more conventionally in the centre. Internal-toothed flexible belts drove from the front of each inlet camshaft to 12-pole distributors fed by Lucas transistors. All three works cars ran ZF transaxles with new one-piece half-shafts with rubber doughnut couplings to provide plunge. Designers White and Marston had also developed an experimental smaller, lighter radiator, and new fabricated magnesium dish wheels, but they remained unused at this meeting.

Siffert was faster than both works cars, Rodriguez's car ran badly and Rindt hit a kerb 'harder than usual' and broke a rear wheel and wrenched the chassis. He stayed with the leading group until his gearbox failed, while Pedro nursed his car home on 10 cylinders to finish fifth. His crew were reluctant to call him in for attention, knowing how cantankerous the V12 could be in restarting when hot.

A new lightweight T81B was assembled with aluminium instead of duralumin skins and a Hewland transaxle, plus the magnesium disc wheels for Rindt in the Dutch GP. While Jim Clark and Graham Hill set new performance standards with their Lotus-Cosworth Ford DFVs on their debut, the Cooper-Maserati pair were undismayed and lined-up on the second row of the grid. Rindt's car became too unmanageable to drive and Pedro's broke its gearbox. Jochen was then fourth at Spa and Pedro blew-up after dicing with him. Salvadori was far from pleased. . . .

On the laughably tight Bugatti circuit at Le Mans for the French GP the T81 and T81B were outpaced; Jochen broke a piston after a wild early spin and Pedro coasted into the pits with fuel spouting from the pressure gauge piping. At Silverstone for the British GP a new Cooper-Maserati T86 made its debut, its magnesium-elektron-skinned monocoque a lower, lighter, narrower version of the T81. Suspension was similar and the flat-scuttled car had quite the ugliest nose treatment ever seen in the 3-litre Formula. The car was powered by the 36-valve *Tipo* 10 engine mated to a Hewland transaxle. Overall the T86 saved some 112 lb against the T81. Rindt was half a second quicker in it than Rodriguez in the

T81B but could see oil smoke in his mirrors during the race. He stopped to investigate, but it was only catch-tank overflow spraying onto the hot exhausts. After rejoining his engine 'made nasty noises', so he parked. Rodriguez finished fifth, lapped, while Alan Rees made a one-off appearance in the third works car and placed ninth. He told me the car was 'big and bulky, but really very nice to drive. . . .'

For Nürburgring, the team prepared the T86 and T81B for Jochen plus two T81Bs for Rodriguez, all with Hewland gearboxes. In practice the flywheel on Jochen's spare car disintegrated, smashing the crankcase and starter and gashing the tub. The T86's steering failed in the race, while Pedro was a distant eighth.

On 27 August, before the Italian GP, a new Canadian race was added to the World Championship programme, at Mosport Park. Rodriguez had hurt himself in an F2 accident at Enna and Richard Attwood took his place alongside Rindt. A plague of disintegrating starter rings afflicted the Cooper-Maseratis and in torrential rain they proved almost unmanageable on race day; Jochen's electrics drowned and Attwood splashed home tenth.

In testing, the T86 had shown a disturbing tendency to lift at speed and after the initial palliative of adding 30 lb of lead, a front-end spoiler was fitted for Monza. Jacky Ickx made his F1 debut in the second car, both machines using 36-valve engines with revised combustion chamber form. Both cars used Hewland transaxles and had the rear brakes inboard of the uprights. Jochen drove his heart out to finish fourth, Ickx was sixth and both Cooper-Maseratis finished ahead of Amon's lone and disconsolate Ferrari!

Roy took Ickx with Rindt to the US GP, where the T81B used a 36-valve twin-plug engine and the T86 a new 36-valve three-plug! While the more conventional engine carried its plugs in pairs on the outside of the vee, the 36-plug unit carried its extra dozen down the inside of the vee. Keith Duckworth, designer of the epochal new Cosworth-Ford V8, snorted, 'If one plug per cylinder isn't enough to make it go *Bang* then something's radically wrong!' His eight-cylinder would always use only eight plugs. . . . The Maserati engine was betraying its 1950s' roots.

In the race, Ickx and Rindt both retired with chronic overheating and burned pistons. Jochen's close friend Heinz Prüller told the tale: 'When his mechanic asked what was the matter with the engine Jochen said, "This time it blew up really spectacular! When I realized it was about to go, I gave the accelerator pedal an extra kick and shot the revs up to 12,000, just to make quite sure. . . ."' It was the Austrian charger's last appearance for Cooper; Salvadori was standing behind him at the time, with his sound right ear cocked, not – as was usual – the deaf left one. . . . Jochen would drive for Brabham in 1968.

Pedro Rodriguez ran the lone works car in the Mexican GP, the older T81B, and Alfieri recommended using the 36-valve, 36-plug V12, so all the extra coils had to be accommodated on the older car. The Bonnier and Siffert T81s were also present for this race, having been quietly picking up occasional finishes during the year, while Guy Ligier had re-emerged before selling his repaired T81 and replacing it with a Brabham. After losing his original car *4/66* at Nürburgring in 1966 he had bought *7/66* ex-works to carry his engine in the new year. But he crashed it at Brands Hatch during practice and appeared only in the International Trophy, Belgian and French GPs before buying the Brabham. Pedro finished sixth, Bonnier 10th, and Siffert retired when a small plastic oil pipe collapsed and blocked feed to one camshaft.

The Cooper-Maserati requiem came at Kyalami in the South African GP of 1 January, 1968. Fortunes had sagged dramatically; the heavy, fuel-thirsty Maserati V12 was to be replaced by a new BRM 12-cylinder, but none were yet available. John Cooper had signed-on the ex-Ferrari driver Ludovico Scarfiotti and Brian Redman for this new year, and they drove the T86 and aluminium-hulled T81B respectively, while Siffert and Bonnier ran their usual cars and the Love Tasman 2.7 was entrusted to local man Basil van Rooyen. On only the second race lap Scarfiotti's legs were scalded when a water pipe burst, and two laps later Redman stopped with overheating, later to retire when an out-of-line camshaft caused a massive oil leak. Bonnier lost a rear wheel, replaced it and continued before being beset with the traditional overheating. Siffert's Walker-Durlacher car – affectionately labelled *Torrey Canyon*, after the stranded supertanker whose oil had polluted miles of British coastline the preceding year – finished seventh behind Beltoise's tiny Matra F2, running under ballast in Formula 1. Van Rooyen retired when his FPF engine blew a head seal and the penultimate chapter in Cooper's racing history had ended.

Grand Prix debut – Jacky Ickx had been making a terrific reputation for himself in Formula 2 and won this maiden F1 drive in the works T81B – F1/1/67 – Italian GP, Monza, 10 September, 1967. He finished sixth and took his first World Championship point. The cast-magnesium disc wheels carry Firestone tyres, tyre company and BP fuel sponsorship revealed by the cockpit side stickers

CHAPTER TWENTY SIX

Those final years . . .

The move to what had been Thomson & Taylor's cavernous premises in Canada Road was made between December 1965, and February 1966. Hollyfield Road, with its world-famous curved frontage, and the tacked-on penthouse drawing office on the roof, became a Cooper Car Sales dealership. The old team workshop in Langley Road was sold. John would later buy it back and rent it to a printer. Many of the old team moved with their company; the Beddings, Roy Golding, Douggie Johnson and 'Ginger' Devlin with his works Mini-Cooper crew. Ernie Looker was one who opted out, Byfleet was too far to commute; another was Terry Kitson. . . .

Chipstead had great plans for their new interest. Mario Tozzi-Condivi: 'We were making a substantial profit out of racing, the image promoted our sales of other cars and we were intent on exploiting the Mini-Cooper, but we wanted to renegotiate the terms of the original agreement with BMC, our royalty from each car built was laughable. One idea through my personal friendship with Nuccio Bertone – we were Bertone agents – was a Bertone-bodied Mini-Cooper, for which we would hold sole distribution rights. A prototype was built, but then we ran up against warranty problems – we wanted world marketing rights, but not the problems of warranty administration, and BMC, or BL as it later became, wouldn't take them on, perhaps understandably. . . .'

John Cooper: 'There were plans really to capitalize on the Cooper name, as in the Mini-Cooper. They were talking about Cooper road wheels, Cooper steering wheels, Cooper exhausts, and we were going to produce hotted-up production versions of other BMC or BL cars like the 1300 and 1800 – but it never really came off. . . .'

While the Formula 1, production and Mini-Cooper teams found their feet in their new home, the yard at the back was jam-packed with Moskvitch saloons in store after import from Russia. Another Chipstead company was Russian Car Concessionaires, but from the number of Moskvitches standing silent and apparently unwanted beside their new workshops the Cooper fraternity felt sure they couldn't be doing very well. One young man charged with keeping Moskvitch-mould at bay was named Ron Dennis. He would later aspire to the Cooper F1 team, then join Brabham, and in the Eighties take over McLaren International – the F1 team descendant of Bruce McLaren Motor Racing Ltd.

Tozzi-Condivi was the boss so far as the Cooper boys were concerned. John was technical director and Roy Salvadori team manager, but Mario was the man with the real power of 'yes' and 'no'. Designer Bob Marston remembers '. . . everybody was frightened of him, but he always seemed very pleasant to me.' Roy got on with his former employee particularly well: 'Mario was always decisive. If he wanted to go some particular way he'd make the decision and go. We'd get an immediate "yes" or "no" from him. We were never bogged down by a long chain of command, which is just what you need in Formula 1. He put up the right political umbrella over us. But then he became deeply involved in setting-up BMW's British concession for the Group and sometimes it was difficult to get hold of him. Sometimes I felt that if only we could get him he would make the right decisions and bale us out and put things right. As time went by he became less obtainable and we began to drift. . . .'

Differences then surfaced between Tozzi-Condivi and the rest of the Chipstead board and suddenly he was gone. Jonathan Sieff, chairman at 37, was still enthusiastic but now had many interests. David Blackburn, ex-Cavalry officer, flyer and Parliamentary candidate – described in one Chipstead release as 'the most experienced foreign car import man in Great Britain' – was brought in as managing director. Anthony Towner was financial director and Cliff Holden – ex-racing motorcyclist turned highly successful Mercedes-Benz distributor – would become perhaps the most familiar board member to the Cooper team, supporting their activities enthusiastically at numerous race meetings. From February 1967, their company would be known as Cooper Car Holdings Ltd, and way into the Eighties the Cooper name remains a major force in the UK motor market, wielding many of the acquisitions made in those formative years.

John Cooper would attend the 1967 Monaco GP with the new executives, but thereafter spent 'most of my time involved with BMC. By that time the Mini-Cooper was selling very well and we were receiving a lot of money from BMC. Sir George Harriman wanted me personally to give more time to Mini-Cooper competitions and future developments of the car, so I didn't return to the works Formula 1 team until 1968. . . .' One gets the impression he didn't really miss it except when they won. . . .

It was inevitable that the change from family business to Group subsidiary should produce some shock-waves. There had always been friction in the team, old Charles, for instance, had thrived on it; but flare-ups were brief and it always gave someone another good story to tell, another laugh in the pub, and kept everyone on their toes. It was constructive, dynamic, an itch to be scratched.

Among the hierarchy at Canada Road there was little of this.... Neither did John relate very well to chief engineer Derrick White – which frankly was a pity, because if they had 'clicked' the story could have been different.

Perhaps Bob Marston put his finger on the problem: 'John was a doer – "We're racing in four days' time, make it *now*!" – while Derrick was a thinker from a background of Jaguar and major manufacturing – "Let's work this out and do it *right*...." Both were very nice blokes but they just thought differently. Derrick was directly answerable to Roy, who insisted he should be given his head, and John – who'd had great faith in Tony Robinson, who was another doer, brought up in the same practical mould – was effectively cut out of it....'

Bob had immense respect for White's abilities: 'He was a damn nice guy and a great theoretical thinker, and perhaps that didn't suit him too well to a racing environment. At Jaguar he couldn't express himself enough – if he'd taken Bill Heynes's job there I'm sure he'd have excelled himself – but at Cooper's he was totally wrapped-up in his work yet never really happy under racing pressure. He'd give himself time to think out problems by trying to work 25 hours a day. I lived in Byfleet, he lived in Great Bookham, some miles away, and we'd go down to the pub or he'd come back to my house and we'd discuss suspension theory or whatever for hours on end. One time he'd come home and we were eating dinner when he suddenly leaped up and said "Ooh! – I'm meant to have gone home tonight!" We'd just lost ourselves in discussing something about the cars. "Make sure Derrick leaves on time tonight," became a standing joke between Laura White and I....'

Also in the drawing office at that time was draughtsman Ian Bailey, later to work for Brabham designer Ron Tauranac in his hugely successful Ralt production racing-car company into the Eighties. He recalls White as: '... a highly strung, intense man, who simply lived and breathed the job. You could merely be walking out to your car on the way home and he'd see a car parked across the road with its wheels at a funny angle and he would say, "What do you think of that?" and go off into a great searching discussion on suspension and steering theory. You could stand there with him for hours....'

The pressures did him no good at all. His health seemed fragile. He apparently suffered ulcers, and migraine. Eventually he left Cooper as their 1968 F1 car was being planned. He moved to John Surtees's Honda team towards the end of the 1967 season, where he helped produce their Italian GP-winning 'Hondola' RA301; again in only 14 weeks' design and build. He left Surtees in 1969 to join Spen King's engineering team at Standard-Triumph. In the autumn of 1970 he was taken ill while on a sailing holiday in Brittany. Back home he was admitted to Stratford Hospital, where viral meningo-encephalitis was diagnosed; a very rare, almost invariably fatal infection of the brain tissues. Ten days later he died there, on 22 September. He was only 41.

Byfleet's BRM prototype – the first T86B-BRM V12 being shown to the press outside the Canada Road works, early-1968. John Bolster of Autosport *has a point explained by Tony Robinson (in cardigan) and a distracted John Cooper. This is a full-monocoque car in the racing technology sense, with the stress-panelling rolled 360-degrees over the driver's legs, as can be seen in the scuttle structure ahead of the low screen lip. The nose again has a separate detachable tip cowl. Note very lightweight cast magnesium disc wheels. Overhead view emphasizes slim lines possible with BRM's neat sports car-intended V12, scuttle fuel filler, driver's restraint harness, dark piping of onboard fire extinguisher system – mandatory that year – on either cockpit sill, and the off-the-shelf Hewland transaxle. Front brake discs and calipers are still in the airstream, but so are the rears, as on the 'ugly duckling' T86-Maserati prototype the preceding summer*

At the end of the Maserati era, John Cooper was back in charge of the racing team. Roy Salvadori was offered the plum dealership of Thomson & Taylor at Cobham, and in partnership he bought it and retired from active involvement with competition. John had always been close to Sir George Harriman, head of BMC at the time the Mini-Cooper was born, and of British Motor Holdings since BMC had merged with Jaguar's group in 1966. Harriman and Cooper 'got on like a house on fire', and when discussions began on the future of the Mini-Cooper and the wider BMH association evidently Harriman made it clear that if John wasn't deeply involved he wasn't interested....

In one respect this relationship backfired on Cooper's future in Formula 1. The Cosworth-Ford DFV engine was available to interested teams other than Lotus for 1968, but clearly with their BMH interests Cooper daren't take up Ford's offer. The DFV clearly rendered the hefty Maserati V12 obsolete. Servicing and liaison had always been a problem simply because of the distance between Byfleet and Modena; team base in one country, engine shop in another. BRM's sports-car-intended customer V12 engine was being uprated for Formula 1 use and so the Cooper-BRM T86B came about.

Roy Salvadori had been vigorously opposed to the BRM idea: 'In fact I wrote to Chipstead, making my position clear and saying that really the *only* way to go was for the Ford engine and condemning the BRM arrangement. The Mini royalty business was very small indeed and was going to be phased out anyway so I didn't think that should prejudice Formula 1, but my views were not in favour. Some of the new directors were very keen to become closely involved with racing, and it was obvious to me they would rather I left. They offered to sell me Thomson & Taylor, a super motor business at Cobham on the A3. This was one hell of a carrot, which I took with a friend of mine, Robert Perry, and that was the end of my association with the Cooper team....'

The former Cooper works number-one driver reflects on a rather peculiar finale to his long association with the team, as he felt nobody seemed concerned with the sponsorship links he had established, and for 1968 the team had little support and looked doomed: 'In my three years the F1 division made a profit – I hated to see them go down. Bear in mind I was always a very close friend of both John and Charles – Charles was a superb man – I always thought so much of Coopers....'

There had as yet never been serious money problems for the team. When Chipstead took over Cooper they inherited a five-year deal which John had made with BP for around £25,000 a year – 'which was quite good considering we'd won the World Championships on no more than 10....' For 1967, Roy had done another lucrative deal with Firestone to test and race their tyres. Bob Marston can never recall being pressured to keep costs down, in fact only once '...did Roy jump up and down, when I dropped a clanger on a casting, but otherwise there was little problem with the money we spent....'

Now, during 1967, BP abruptly announced their withdrawal from motor racing sponsorship, and it was a nasty blow to Coopers. Worse followed that September when Firestone followed suit. For 1968 Cooper would have to buy their F1 tyres.

Work progressed on the new Cooper-BRM T86B, using the magnesium-panelled Maserati T86 as starting point. The new cars were laid out by Derrick White and Bob Marston and built largely under the direction of Tony Robinson, who had returned to the team at John's invitation after his early involvement with the original T81 monocoques in 1965–66.

The new T86B tub was skinned principally in 18-gauge NS4 malleable aluminium sheet formed over three mild steel bulkheads made partly from 22-gauge tube. The BRM engine was considerably smaller and lighter than the Maserati and would demand less fuel, so there was no need for the magnesium lightweight skinning of the 1967 car. The T86B used a full-length monocoque again, extending either side of the engine to pick-up a rear cage bulkhead carrying the engine and Hewland transaxle mounts and suspension. Fuel was housed in FPT Industries rubberized bags extending the full length of the side booms. With a 6-gallon scuttle tank, capacity was still over 40 gallons.

Suspension drew largely on existing T81B and T86 stock, and the very light disc wheels, which weighed as little as 9 lb each, were cast in magnesium halves, which were then machined and welded together. They used four-stud fixing and Firestone tyres. Front rims were 11 in. wide and rears 14 in. There was still pronounced anti-dive built into the front suspension, with the chassis pick-ups raked downwards to the front some 5 degrees.

The BRM V12 needed less cooling area than the Maseratis, and so the T86B escaped with a slimmer nose, housing a four-row Serck radiator with a large 6-gallon vee-shaped oil tank behind it, hung ahead of the front cage bulkhead. The BRM's initial outings in Bruce McLaren's car the previous season indicated high oil consumption. Water and oil pipes were routed through vee channels formed beneath the tub.

The Group also had an Alfa Romeo interest, and in the Tasman Championship Frank Gardner had campaigned an Australian-owned Brabham-Alfa Romeo V8 with some success. It was a 2½-litre sports car unit in basics, with four cams and all the proper noises. Cooper attempted to set-up a deal with Autodelta – the Alfa Romeo competitions arm – to run a 3-litre V8 in Formula 1, copying the Maserati arrangement. One T86C tub – number *F1/3/68* – was prepared for this engine. Its rear booms were shortened 4 in. to accept the shorter V8 and, with a 2½-litre T33 sports car engine installed, it was tested at Silverstone by Alfa works driver Lucien Bianchi. But the 3-litre F1 engine did not emerge that season, and the T86C lay fallow in a corner of the works....

Meanwhile the 24-valve BRM V12 was claimed to deliver 'just under 400 bhp' at 6500–7000 rpm. It gave more mid-range torque than the antiquated Maserati, pulling from around 6500–7000 rpm, and it weighed only 375 lb against the *Tipo* 10's 390. The T86B-BRM still weighed-in around 1220 lb, or some 118 lb above the minimum limit. Wheelbase was 8 ft 2 in., compared to 7 ft 10 in. on the T86C-Alfa Romeo; tracks front and rear were 5 ft 0 in., at the tread centres.

After the Cooper-Maserati swan-song at Kyalami, the prototype T86B-BRM made its debut at the Brands Hatch Race of Champions, driven by Lancastrian sports-car star Brian Redman. Like his Porsche team mate Ludovico Scarfiotti he would be available to the team whenever endurance racing commitments did not clash. He finished fifth at Brands, where Jo Siffert shunted Rob Walker's brand-new Lotus 49 during practice. That evening in Dorking, while Tony Cleverley and John Chisman were stripping the car, drained-off fuel ignited. Rob's racing workshop, together with the Lotus, the prepared-for-sale Cooper-Maserati, his priceless ex-Seaman Delage straight-eight, all his racing records and souvenirs, including Moss's threadbare Cooper tyres from Argentina 1958, were lost or virtually destroyed.

This was a shocking blow for the most popular private entrant in motor racing – the man whose enthusiasm and generosity had first launched Cooper into Formula 1.

The Silverstone non-Championship race followed, but it clashed with the Monza 1000 Km sports car race, so Frank Gardner was given the choice of the two T86Bs. His later car with the '400 bhp' BRM engine went bang in the race when he was running eighth.

Before the Spanish GP at Jarama, Tony Robinson shifted the bottom rear radius rod pick-up on Redman's prototype tub, raising it together with the top rocker arm pick-up at the front to reduce camber change between bump and droop. The steering had to be revamped to suit. Scarfiotti's second car had its rear suspension similarly altered, but the front unchanged. The move didn't help; as there was so much anti-dive both drivers complained they couldn't sense when the front brakes were about to lock. Their practice was punctuated by spins and Scarfiotti crashed quite heavily. The grid was only 13 strong, and they started on the back of it, but a reliable race saw them finish 4–5 – well in the points.

Redman was driving for Porsche at Spa on Monaco GP weekend, so Lucien Bianchi joined Scarfiotti – all the nicest guys drove for Cooper. Both cars retained the revised rear suspension, but the prototype returned to original front geometry. Scarfiotti had a nasty moment, reminding him of his Kyalami scalding, when during practice his car's oil tank burst and soaked his legs in hot oil. But again the cars proved remarkably reliable during the race, Bianchi finishing third and Scarfiotti fourth amongst only five finishers....

Scratch one Cooper — Brian Redman was most unfortunate to suffer right-front wishbone failure under braking for Les Combes corner at Spa, Belgian GP, 9 June, 1968, but considering the state of 'F1–2–68's wreckage he was very fortunate to emerge with 'only' a badly broken arm. The T86B hurdled the barrier and collided with a parked marshal's car. The crumpled and burned monocoque is beyond repair. Even the dash panel is distorted and the right-side mirror smashed. The whitish powder coating everything is extinguishant

At this point the Cooper-BRMs had a better reliability record than any other team in F1 that season. It was all working better than the team could have hoped, but the cars were profiting from reliability, inheriting good finishes rather than looking like serious contenders to win top honours. Brian Redman was available for the Belgian GP at Spa – driving *2/68* – alongside Bianchi, while Scarfiotti was away at Rossfeld in Germany driving a works Porsche *Bergspyder* in a European Mountain Championship round.

Bianchi was lucky to escape injury in practice at Spa when a bird hit him in the face at speed, and he returned to the pits shaken and with blood and feathers on his helment. This was apparently what had killed Alan Stacey on this circuit in 1960.... Lucien finished sixth in the race, but the unfortunate Redman had a wishbone break on his car while braking for Les Combes corner on lap 7. The car charged the roadside barrier, vaulted over it and smashed into a parked marshal's car beyond, bursting into flames. Brian was hauled clear with a badly broken arm and his F1 career never recovered from this set-back. The car was destroyed, its tub charred and battered and only one wheel remaining attached. The cause of the accident was only established when *Autosport* photographer Peter Burn saw his colour films, and found he had captured the wishbone in the act of breaking, just before the first impact.

As if this blow was not enough, the news then came through from Rossfeld – 'Lulu' Scarfiotti had crashed his Porsche, and was dead....

On that fateful day Canada Road's team had lost one car, but both its drivers. Only the prototype T86B was taken to the Dutch GP, its front wishbones remade in $\frac{7}{8}$ in. diameter, $\frac{1}{8}$ in. wall thickness tube in place of the original $\frac{3}{4}$ in. 14-gauge. The 5-degree anti-dive was removed from the front suspension. Camber change was reported to be reduced from the original 1.08 degrees-per-inch deflection to 0.70 in., more in line with modern Formula 1 thinking. Bianchi crashed out of the Dutch race on lap 10, spinning off the fast *Bos Uit* right-hander entering the long main straight.

Vic Elford – former rally star-cum-works Porsche sports-car driver – turned out for the team at Rouen, accompanied in this French GP meeting by the young French F2 star 'Johnny' Servoz-Gavin. Both were making their Formula 1 debut, and in Vic's case this was only his second-ever single-seater race! His car was brand-new – *4/68* – matching the specification of the blonde Frenchman's prototype. They qualified on the back of the grid, but the race was ruined by rain, marred by Jo Schlesser's fatal accident in the air-cooled Honda; however, Vic's rally-bred car control won him and the Cooper-BRM a good fourth place. Servoz, earning the team good appearance money on his home soil, lost control comprehensively and rammed a tree when 10th.

The new T86B was further updated for the British GP at Brands Hatch. A top-ducted nose exhausted radiator air upwards instead of sideways out through the suspension cut-outs, to kill lift. John gave another promising F2 driver – Robin Widdows – his F1 debut in *1/68*, and teamed him with Elford. They qualified 17–18 on the grid and both retired with engine and ignition failures. This was the first time the BRM V12 had let them down since Gardner's breakage at Silverstone early in the year. One Tom Jones was entered at Brands in a mysterious Cooper-Maserati, but did not report for duty.

Bianchi brought some experience back into the team for Nürburgring, where both T86Bs sprouted fashionable strutted airfoils above the engine bay. Vic knew the circuit like his own back room and qualified fifth among the established front-runners. This was a tremendous boost for the team, but raceday was wet and misty. Vic was blinded by spray on the opening lap and he crashed heavily, ripping two wheels off his car. Bianchi qualified poorly and retired with leaking bag tanks.

Alfa Romeo's 3-litre V8 was not ready even for the Italian GP at Monza, where only one T86B ran for Vic Elford. It was his German car, repaired and now fitted with a spring-loaded rear wing, which was intended to feather under air pressure at speed along the straights and then flick into a download position as he hit the brakes for a corner. In practice he crashed after catching the welt of his walking shoes under the brake pedal. On lap 3 of the race he found the pedal but there were no brakes behind it, and he ploughed straight off into the *Parabolica* sand-traps at around 130 mph. . . .

Only the North American races at Ste Jovite, Canada, at Watkins Glen and Mexico City now remained to Cooper. Elford and Bianchi were teamed together; and in Canada Vic was fifth – though four laps behind – with Lucien seventh. Vics two points were the last that Cooper would score in World Championship Racing. The Englishman's car used the spring-loaded wing, the Belgian's was decently wingless. At the Glen both were way off the pace; perhaps more seriously uncompetitive than ever as money was at last perilously tight and BRM engine rebuilds were restricted by cost. Elford broke a camshaft and Bianchi his clutch.

In Mexico City both qualified way down on the back of the grid; Vic finishing eighth while Lucien – that gentlemanly, extremely likeable Belgian ex-racing mechanic – retired with engine failure.

Derrick White had long since left the team, and Bob Marston followed – joining Surtees's Honda operation before the season's end. Eighth place and retirement at the Magdalena Mixhuca circuit on 3 November, 1968, was an undramatic, low-key swan-song. But under the Mexican sun, this was the Formula 1 Cooper works team's last hurrah. . . .

In November 1968, British Motor Holdings merged with Standard-Triumph to form the British Leyland monolith. Sir George Harriman was out, and the Mini-Cooper arrangements came under scrutiny. For years Cooper had been a spent force in Formula 1, and the briefly promising surge with the Cooper-Maserati in 1966 had proved impossible to sustain. The marque had lost its production racing-car market and now, far worse, it had lost its prestige. To hard-headed business it was no longer a promotable asset; and to retrieve that one-time charisma would take money, and time, and incalculable good fortune.

Plans were laid to continue with Cosworth-Ford power for 1969, regardless of Mini-Cooper manufacturing sensibilities, and negotiations were well advanced for sponsorship from Wilkinson Sword. A production Formula 5000 car to use 5-litre American V8 engines in the new European single-seater class was also produced, and two were displayed at the 1969 Racing Car Show, but no customers stepped forward to buy. . . .

When the new year's World Championship season commenced at Kyalami on 1 March, there were no Coopers on the grid. *Motoring News*'s front page for 6 February had carried this news paragraph under the headline 'NO COOPERS TO SOUTH AFRICA':

'No works F1 Coopers will take part in the South African Grand Prix, though a new car which has been designed can be ready in two months if sponsorship can be found. Financial support has been the drawback since Firestone withdrew their help in November and a number of large firms have been approached. John Cooper hopes to have the new car in action when the European season gets under way with the Spanish GP on 4 May, and suggests that he might enter one driver only this year. Robin Widdows is under contract and Vic Elford's has an optional renewal clause. If and when it's built the 1969 F1 car will probably have a Cosworth-Ford V8 engine, since the full 3-litre Alfa Romeo V8 still shows no sign of materializing.'

In the 20 March issue of *Autocar*, former F1 driver-turned-sports editor Innes Ireland wrote: 'It looks as if we shall not be seeing the familiar name of Cooper in the starting grids of Formula 1 events this year. In the past few years the cost of running the team has been borne by the Chipstead Group . . . but since they have been unable to find a sponsor this season, the Group feel they will have to withdraw from Grand Prix racing. . . . We can but hope that John Cooper will find a sponsor who would be interested in Grand Prix racing as an advertising and sales promotion medium, for John Cooper and his cars will be sadly missed round the circuits this year. . . .'

One car did keep racing; Vic Elford having agreed to drive for Colin Crabbe's Antique Automobiles Ltd team, perhaps appropriately enough, in the old Cooper-Maserati T86 *F1/2/67*. The car was pristine in their maroon livery for the International Trophy at Silverstone, where Vic finished 12th and last in the rain. Historic racer Neil Corner then drove the Crabbe car in the combined F1/5000 Madrid GP at Jarama and finished fourth, the car using a 36-valve, 24-plug engine.

The tiny team then gained a private entry at Monaco, only 16 being accepted and no need to qualify. Vic started from last place on the grid, 2.3 sec slower than next man, Swiss privateer Silvio Moser's Brabham, and fully 8.2 sec slower than Jackie Stewart's Matra on pole. He kept the Cooper-Maserati going and finished seventh, six times lapped.

This was Cooper's last outing in a World Championship Grand Prix. Antique Automobiles patron Crabbe then acquired an ex-works McLaren M7-Cosworth for Elford's reappearance in Formula 1.

On 22 May, the news was broken in the weekly comics that the Cooper Car Company's owners had finally, regretfully, concluded they should close down the racing operation. Innes Ireland: 'The final Cooper Formula 1 coffin nails are to be driven home at 11 a.m. on 11 June when the two remaining works car will be sold by public auction at British Car Auctions, Frimley Bridges, Farnborough. The cars are the 1968 Type 86B-BRMs (3-litre vee-12), valued at over £5,000 each.

'D. C. Blackburn, the managing director of the Cooper Group, said: "Until we can arrange major sponsorship for

THOSE FINAL YEARS...

By mid-season, having lost both Redman and Scarfiotti, the works team was giving F1 debut drives to newcomers, like F2 Champion Johnny Servoz-Gavin seen here in F1/1/68 during practice for the French GP at Rouen-les-Essarts. Dive planes tacked onto the nose mark the birth of real aerodynamic awareness for the marque. He hit a tree in the rain-soaked race, and was not asked again

a Cooper works Formula 1 team we will not be re-entering Grand Prix racing. It never had been our policy to do it in a half-hearted manner, we do it properly or not at all. Without sponsorship there is no point in hanging on to these cars."'

His reasoning cannot be faulted. At BCA's auction centre the third T86C car was offered engineless while the two T86B-BRMs and the two F5000 T90s extant – one only a rolling chassis – went under the hammer. It would appear that only *Autosport* – the magazine founded by Gregor Grant, who had been so close to the 500 movement which had given Cooper life – was sufficiently interested to report the outcome:

'John Scott-Davies picked-up Vic Elford's T86B F1 car complete for £1500, which is what a reasonable Formula Ford would cost. The complete T90 F5000 was bought for just £2,225 by former Lotus-Bristol driver Chris Warwick Drake.

Two T86B rolling chassis went for £530 and £500 respectively, while the T90 rolling chassis went for £500. Another rock-bottom price was £650 for the BRM V12 engine, less than the cost of a twin-cam Ford! Alain de Cadanet bought one of the transporters beforehand, and so all that remains of Cooper's equipe are some F1 and F5000 jigs, and several spares, wheels and so on, which they wish to sell as one lot. . . . Meanwhile, despite rumours of a Cosworth DFV Ford-powered Cooper being tested by a top-line F1 driver and imminent sponsorship, it seems that the famous name has no future in F1 at the present time. . . .'

Chris Drake was offered the entire Cooper stores for a song, but couldn't think what he would do with it; only when he found himself in the classic car and historic racing business 10 years later would he regret it.

On 28 August, 1969, *Motoring News*'s front page carried a paragraph reading: 'In Toronto this week George Fejer, a Hungarian-born Canadian who builds Chinook sports and formula cars, announced that he had "acquired control of the assets of the Cooper Car Company Ltd and will now build various types of car using the name Chinook-Cooper". Asked to comment Mr Jonathan Sieff, chairman of the Cooper Group of Companies, said on Tuesday: "I've never heard of him. The story is completely untrue. . . ."'

In its rather grandiose wording Fejer's statement made rather more of his purchase of all remaining Cooper parts, jigs, stores and drawings than it really merited, but the bare bones of the one-time double World Championship racing concern were indeed on their way across the Atlantic; Chinook-Cooper making virtually zero impact thereafter.... By the late-Seventies another Canadian dealer was advertising the original drawings and surviving record books for sale at a hugely inflated value – with no apparent takers....

It was the end of the Cooper story, they did not survive as a racing car company to celebrate the 10th anniversary of their first World Championship....

John Cooper and Major Terry Owens ran the Canada Road Mini-Cooper team with Ginger Devlin through 1969 and then the man whose enthusiasm had really started it all with Eric Brandon back in 1946 took a garage at Ferring on the Sussex coast and settled for a more peaceful life in the motor trade. The Major helped him set it up and it ticks over happily as I write, John worrying as always but genial as ever, puffing *bon mots* round his pipe and always delighted to see old

Last Grand Prix, where it had all begun – initially with Harry Schell's Cooper-JAP twin in 1950, but more seriously with the Rob Walker/works Cooper-Climax 1.96 driven by Jack Brabham in 1957. Here, 12 years later, 18 May, 1969, Vic Elford drives Colin Crabbe's ex-works T86-Maserati with in-vee injection home into seventh place at Monaco; Cooper's last hurrah on the stage they had once dominated. Colours here were dark maroon, with white stripes

friends, while his son Mike and son-in-law John Angelo seem to do most of the work. Close-by Goodwood, memories must abound; but the only tangible clues to past endeavour are Charles's old veteran de Dion Bouton standing beside a 500 in one corner of the garage, paintings of Cooper-Maserati and the European Championship Mini-Cooper on John's office wall, and a framed photo of him with Jack Brabham at Indy. 'They were good times, boy; good times....'

APPENDIX ONE

The Mini-Coopers

Within these covers I have tried to tell a comprehensive story of Cooper racing cars. But to the general public the Mini-Cooper production saloons are the marque's major product. We must include them, but their story has been told in immense detail many times and the Mini-Coopers' fantastic world-wide rally successes are fully chronicled elsewhere. In essence it was only the circuit racing Mini-Coopers which had a direct connection with the Cooper Car Company and its bases at Hollyfield Road, Surbiton, and later Canada Road, in Byfleet. We don't have space here to cover their activities in the kind of detail devoted to the open-wheelers and sports-racing cars, but this must not be construed as a reflection of the programme's unimportance to the company as a whole for it was very important, and its roots went back to the late 1950s.

Colin Chapman unveiled his gorgeous Lotus Elite prototype road car at the London Motor Show in October, 1957. John thought it was fantastic '. . . a beautiful thing', while Charles felt his company was being upstaged but couldn't suppress a chuckle; 'Wot's he got 'imself into now? . . .' Both would like to produce some kind of performance road car of their own, but a project of Elite proportions was totally out of the question. They tried to jazz up the Renault Dauphine by fitting a Climax engine and ZF gearbox in its tail. The rear-engined link was good, but the car's handling was never properly sorted although much work was done, including casting new uprights, adapting a ZF Hanomag transaxle and so on.

Then while researching a source of suitable proprietary engines and other components for their 1960 production Formula Junior car, John came into closer contact with BMC technical director Alec Issigonis. John had known the Smyrna-born engineer from early postwar hillclimbing days, when Issigonis campaigned his striking monocoque Lightweight Special. Now they frequently discussed FJ requirements and racing in general, and Issigonis's forthcoming Mini saloon was mentioned. John was fascinated by the thought of such a tiny car with east-west engine, front-wheel drive and rubber suspension. Compared with the stodgy conventional production saloons of the period it should be quite something. . . .

He was loaned a pre-production car for the Italian GP trip to Monza in September 1959. John had to rush a works F1 car down there by trailer behind his Zodiac, but Roy Salvadori obliged by hustling the Mini along and they used it during the meeting. Roy was thrilled. He was driving for Aston Martin at the time but had covered the ground to Monza faster than team manager Reg Parnell; and he was driving an Aston Martin DB4GT. . . . It was typical Salvadori road driving, but this little Mini really was something special.

Ferrari's former chief engineer Aurelio Lampredi, then with Fiat, saw the car in the Monza paddock and asked if he could borrow it. He was gone for hours and John was convinced he'd rolled it into a ball by the time he came hurtling back, breathless and excited: 'If it was not so ugly I would shoot myself!' he raved.

Back home John was keen to hot-up a Mini. He was sure this could be the basis of the road car he'd always promised himself. He put the idea to Issigonis, 'It would make a great little grand tourer', but the car's creator was unconvinced – he still saw it as a modern people's car.

At Hollyfield Road Ginger Devlin set about tuning a production Mini engine simply for more power, as John says: '. . . just to make it go, and then we knew we'd have to fit disc front brakes to make it stop.' He went straight to the top, to see Sir George Harriman, and after a brief drive in the Cooper-modified prototype to see what could be done with more power the BMC Chairman returned immensely impressed, enthusiastic about the charisma of a tie with the double World Championship team. There was a minimum of further negotiation and paperwork. Harriman suggested a royalty per car should the deal go through and John received a simple letter of intent through the post; a hand-shake and the Mini-Cooper had been born. . . .

Harriman sanctioned a trial run of 1000 Mini-Coopers to test reaction. BMC engineers and the Cooper Car Company kicked the idea around and it was calculated that 55 bhp was required for a top speed around 85 mph. To increase torque while keeping the capacity under 1 litre, the standard 'A'-series Mini engine's stroke was stretched from 68.3 mm to 81.3 mm, and the bore reduced from 62.9 to 62.4. Twin SU carburettors were fitted and the compression raised slightly. Bigger valves, altered ports, modified exhaust and a stiffer

Spirit of Mini-Cooper racing: Sir John Whitmore waving a redundant un-driven rear wheel at Brands Hatch's Paddock Bend in the early-'sixties when his performances in private and works team cars became legend

Right *Later years – wheel extensions, fat tyres, broadside cornering and John Rhodes' Mini-Cooper brilliance at the wheel added up to enthralling saloon car racing in the decade*

engine bottom-end followed, and a remote gear-change was fitted for racy changes. Second and third gear ratios were raised to improve their spacing. The standard car's inadequate drum brakes were replaced at the front by 7 in. diameter discs. This 'ADO50' 997 cc Mini-Cooper was introduced in July 1961 with the name still basking in the glory of back-to-back World Championship titles and the recent attack on Indy – the heartland of American motor racing.

The cars received a terrific reception 'and soon one simply had to have one'. Thereafter Eddie Maher of Engine Division and consultant specialists like Daniel Richmond of Downton Engineering and their engineers did most production Mini-Cooper engineering on the various succeeding models. The 1071 cc Mini-Cooper 'S' was followed by a 998, replacing the original 997; then 1275 and 970 'S's, the Hydrolastic-suspended range from September 1964; Mark II 'ADO20' bodies on all models from October '67 and so on, until July 1971, when after 10 years the Mini-Cooper story ended as the Mark III Cooper 'S' was discontinued.

The Cooper Car Company earned a small royalty on every car sold bearing their name, and when the original Harriman agreement lapsed in August 1971 the Mini-Cooper was dead. Super-salesman Donald (later Lord) Stokes had risen to the top of the pile when British Leyland had been created and Cooper's 'consultancy agreement' was one of several which he sought to buy-out as soon as he took control. He told John that the Cooper name was depressing sales because it instantly meant high insurance ratings. The Mini-Cooper's successor would be called the Mini GT; and the insurance rating stayed where it was. . . .

At that time Cooper had been earning about £2 for every car sold. In Italy the Cooper name ran on because Geoffrey Robinson, MD of Leyland's Innocenti subsidiary, refused to give it up. When Robinson was transferred to Jaguar in Coventry, the Innocenti-Cooper also bit the dust.

In the old days of BMC they had formed a Competitions Department at MG's Abingdon works, initially to go both racing and rallying. Tragic involvement of MG and Austin-Healey sports cars in accidents at Le Mans and Dundrod persuaded the conservative BMC board to opt out of racing to concentrate upon rallying. Racing was farmed out to private teams. If they did well with BMC products, the group would bask in reflected glory. If something went terribly wrong, well, we weren't involved were we?

From 1962 the Cooper Car Company received a measure of financial and material support to represent BMC in saloon car racing with the new Mini-Coopers. The previous year had seen exuberant young Sir John Whitmore win the BRSCC British Saloon Car Championship in his hotted-up ordinary Mini, and now for 1962 Tyrrell's Rhodesian Formula Junior driver John Love scooped the pool in a works 997 Mini-Cooper, with Whitmore in support; Ginger Devlin running the team and caring for the cars. Music teacher Christabel Carlisle drove brilliantly in her Don Moore-prepared private car and often humbled many male drivers.

In 1963 the works Cooper-Mini team was represented by Sir John Whitmore, Timmy Mayer and in several races by Paddy Hopkirk, the Irish rallyman. Jack Sears won the Championship in his giant 7-litre Ford Galaxie, but the tyre-smoking cornering antics of the Mini-Coopers were a spectacular and enormously crowd-pleasing feature of every major saloon car race. Dutchman Rob Slotemaker drove a Downton-entered car in the European Championship that season, and won the 1300 cc class.

For 1964 it was Cooper's turn to farm out part of their

works racing responsibilities, to Ken Tyrrell's team based down in the timber yard at Ockham, a few miles outside Guildford. He would campaign two cars in the European Touring Car Championship, which was then gaining great importance. While Ken's F3 Coopers dominated their class that season driven by Jackie Stewart and Warwick Banks, the latter won the European title outright in his 1-litre Mini-Cooper. His team mate, Belgian Mini specialist Julien Vernaeve, chose a 1275 for the larger-capacity class. While Tyrrell campaigned his cars in Europe, the Ginger Devlin-run works team contested the British Championship with drivers John Fitzpatrick and Paddy Hopkirk. 'Fitz' won the 1300 cc class outright and was runner-up overall.

For 1965, John Rhodes and Warwick Banks joined the Hollyfield Road team, respectively tackling the 1300 and 1-litre classes of the British Championship. Rhodes was to became the Mini-Cooper king of British motor racing. He had driven FJ Coopers with the Midland Racing Partnership in his days as more mechanic than driver, but in the Minis he was almost arrogantly spectacular and incredibly quick. Abingdon Competitions Manager Peter Browning wrote that he 'drove Minis in a style that gave pleasure to everyone. . . .'

He won the 1300 class of the British Championship in 1965, while Banks took the 1000 class and was runner-up overall. The cars used engines prepared by Eddie Maher's BMC Engines outfit, but for 1966 the switch was made to Daniel Richmond's Downton company, and only the Cooper team received BMC financial support. Again Rhodes dominated the 1300 class.

Fuel-injection engines emerged for '67, when Rhodes was joined in the works team by John Handley. With tyre development having progressed so dramatically the Mini-Coopers were hard-pressed to keep in touch with the Ford Anglias, but they remained competitive on reliability.

Rhodes could have taken the Championship overall in the last round, but was pipped narrowly at the post.

Racing tyre developments for Mini-Coopers fill a large section of Peter Browning's excellent history *The Works Minis*. The first 10 in. Mini racing tyre – the CR48 – emerged from Dunlop in 1964, paralleling F1 developments in its wider, squatter profile and use of lower pressures than hitherto. By mid-'65 when the Minis were churning out 10 more bhp a new CR65 was introduced. There were problems with tread pattern stability in the luridly driven front-wheel-drive cars. John Rhodes's works entry would destroy a fresh set of fronts in only 7–8 laps flat out! A change of pattern to Dunlop's CR70 fixed that, but Mini handling now demanded different tyres front and rear, differing patterns imparting much-needed extra stability at the tail.

Into 1966 yet more power created more headaches. The tyres were so small and rotated at such a pace, and had to carry such high load, that they overheated easily. A Formula 1-based design was produced in the CR81, introduced in May 1967 for the Cooper works cars alone. But outputs up around 105 bhp saw the tyres' inner shoulders almost molten. An asymmetric profile was adopted to compensate for the cars' marked camber, but then they understeered too much and new rear tyres had to be adopted to impart some oversteer to balance it out. Rear treads were only $4\frac{1}{2}$ in. wide against $5\frac{3}{4}$ in. at the front.

It was in 1966 that Ginger Devlin suggested fitting 12 in. wheels. This was not to fit larger-diameter tyres. Under the regulations the homologated body shape could not be altered to enlarge the wheel-arches to accommodate bigger or wider tyres, but the use of a 12 in. wheel would enable the tyre designers to cut sidewall height by an inch, and produce a stiff low-profile tyre with reduced internal stress, so less heat build-up, allowing softer and stickier compounds to be

With the Formula 1 and production racing car programmes at an end, John Cooper, Major Terry Owens and Ginger Devlin kept the works Mini-Cooper saloon car team running from Canada Road. Here their British Saloon Car Championship challenge is presented to the press, 7 January, 1969; left to right, O. A. Proctor, Chairman of Britax (London) Ltd, seat-belt manufacturing sponsors; Ginger Devlin, team manager and so-long faithful Cooper employee; Mike Heathwise, Britax's Competitions Manager; John Cooper, and driver Steve Neal. In the car sits Gordon Spice, whose performances would shine that final season of Cooper works racing . . .

deployed. It was not until the Ford Escort had been introduced to racing that the 12 in. wheel ploy was actually pulled out of the hat, in 1969, by which time the Cooper Car Company was dead in racing. BL had taken the works team in-house, but John Cooper and Major Owens ran independently from Canada Road using yellow-liveried cars co-sponsored by Britax seat belts and Downton Engineering.

John Rhodes and Steve Neal had driven their works 1275s in the 1968 British Championship, when the combined brain power of Eddie Maher, the British Vita team's Harry Ratcliffe and Harry Weslake had failed to find more power. Rhodes again won the 1300 cc division in a hard year.

Into 1969, under the new Stokes British Leyland regime, the Abingdon Competitions Department was forced to cut back on rally activity and concentrate upon events it could win in countries where there would be tangible marketing and promotional benefits. So Abingdon had signed-on Rhodes and Handley to drive its in-house works cars, while the Britax-Cooper-Downton team run by Ginger Devlin fielded cars without Leyland support for Steve Neal and Gordon Spice.

Peter Browning: 'I'd tried to persuade John Cooper to run in the 1-litre class of the British Championship. It was clear that a competitive 1-litre Mini stood a very good chance of success. John, I know, would have liked to have done this – even with one car – but I suspect he was influenced by his two forceful drivers, who were reluctant to drive in the small car class and were desperately keen to prove a point against the works men, Rhodes and Handley! Jim Whitehouse of Equipe Arden prepared and entered a 1-litre car for Alec Poole and he successfully pulled-off the Championship. . . .'

In the larger class the Mini-Coopers had no chance against the Ford Escorts, but Gordon Spice's brilliance gave Ginger's cars the edge over BL's best from Abingdon. Browning: 'Both the Mini teams provided some of the closest racing of the season and I am sure that both lost out to Ford on many occasions because they were racing against each other and not racing together against the Escorts. In front of the pits, where John Cooper and I could see what they were up to, the boys behaved themselves, but I have seen some very alarming pictures of what was going on around the rest of the circuit. . . .'

At the end of that season the Canada Road operation finally closed down, and so far as its original instigator was concerned the Mini-Cooper racing story was at an end. . . .

APPENDIX TWO

The minor leagues . . .

Cooper cars naturally provided the backbone for British minor-league motor sport during the Fifties. In particular they utterly dominated the hillclimb scene and cornered the British Hill-Climb Championship from 1951 to 1962. For 11 of those 12 seasons the title fell to the 'big twin' Cooper-JAPs.

These cars were ideally matched to the demands of short-distance British hillclimbs, few of which exceeded 1000 yards, a far cry from the mighty mountain climbs of Europe, or those in the USA. The requirement for torque, good traction, lightweight and nimble handling – plus an overall size suitable for the farm-drive narrow-track character of the hills – matched the Cooper-JAP 1000s and 1100s perfectly.

Hillclimbing had a most significant place in the structure of British motor sport. We had never been allowed to close public roads for circuit racing on the mainland, so the highly artificial Brooklands Motor Course stood alone until 1933, when Donington Park opened for cars, and at last we had a proper mainland road-racing course. Against this background, sprints and hillclimbs gained extra importance, giving the public at large their only chance to see competitive motoring short of making the pilgrimage to Weybridge.

This type of competition against the clock was so popular that clandestine sprints and hillclimbs were run widely on suitable stretches of public road until 1925, when a Bugatti charged the crowd at Kop Hill, near Princes Risborough, and authority stamped hard on such activities. Thereafter these events were confined to venues on private land, like the old-established Shelsley Walsh climb near Worcester, and from 1939 Prescott near Cheltenham. Postwar circuit racing caught hold initially around airfield perimeter tracks, but the hills still retained an importance of their own for many years.

The RAC British Hill-Climb Championship had been instituted in 1948, when the doyen of the sport, Raymond Mays – father of ERA and BRM – took the title in his legendary ERA 'R4D'. In 1949 Sydney Allard's fearsome Steyr V8-engined Allard special took the crown, and in 1950 it fell to industrialist Dennis Poore in his raucous prewar GP Alfa Romeo 8C-35.

That season saw Allard share the Championship runner-up position with Smethwick garage proprietor Ken Wharton, who had replaced his self-built 750 Special with a new Cooper-JAP twin 1000. John Cooper and Stirling Moss had shown how well the cars were suited for short-distance hillclimbing, and now Wharton would ram the message home.

From 1951 to 1962 the RAC British Hill-Climb Championship was resolved like this:

1951 Ken Wharton (Cooper-JAP)
1952 Ken Wharton (Cooper-JAP)
1953 Ken Wharton (Cooper-JAP & ERA)
1954 Ken Wharton (Cooper-JAP & ERA)
1955 Tony Marsh (Cooper-JAP)
1956 Tony Marsh (Cooper-JAP)
1957 Tony Marsh (Cooper-JAP)
1958 David Boshier-Jones (Cooper-JAP)
1959 David Boshier-Jones (Cooper-JAP)
1960 David Boshier-Jones (Cooper-JAP)
1961 David Good (Cooper-JAP)
1962 Arthur Owen (Cooper-Climax)

Ken Wharton dominated the Championship on driver ability, aggressively competitive preparation of all his considerable armoury of cars and engines, and on the eminent suitability of the 'big twin' Coopers for this role. For 1951 he had replaced his original Mark IV-based car with the lightweight F2/F3 Cooper frame ordered by the late Raymond Sommer. Wharton fitted a 996 cc JAP twin engine and supercharged it. Blown engines of this type had a ghastly reputation, although Brooklands tuner Robin Jackson had achieved success with one in the Fry family's legendary special, the *Freikaiserwagen*. With cars of this type, Wharton was to achieve his fantastic run of four Championships on the trot, and his activities included a whitewash by winning every qualifying round and no less than six consecutive ftds at the annual Bouley Bay 'climb on Jersey in the Channel Islands.

Wharton's prowess during 1951 persuaded wealthy Peter Bell, married to Mary McAlpine of the McAlpine construction family, to invite Wharton to campaign his ERA 'R11B' in Europe. Wharton was quite successful with the car, while his 500-engined Cooper also placed second to Moss in the Freiburg F3 class.

Into 1953 Wharton was shooting at a hat-trick of British Championships and he drove his own Cooper-JAP and the Bell ERA and at several climbs would set ftd in the Cooper

The Cooper big-twin Champions: Ken Wharton in his basically Mark IV ex-Sommer car – Tony Marsh's basically Mark VIII extremely highly-developed super-lightweight – David Boshier-Jones in his later pale-green and red model – David Good, the brilliant one-handed hillclimb star, in his similar black-and-white lightweight. More than a decade of RAC British Hill-Climb Championship domination here...

and second ftd in the larger car! He was also racing his quasi-works Cooper-Bristol Mark II that year and his hectic schedule was typified by the Ulster Trophy at Dundrod, where he was second to Hawthorn's works Ferrari, then flew overnight to Cheltenham to win at Prescott in the Cooper-JAP and ERA next day.

Come 1954 and the hillclimb fraternity wondered briefly if Wharton would bother to defend his title for another season. He would, and he bought Mays's 'R4D' to do so, supplementing the blown basically Mark IV/V Cooper-JAP 1100. With Wharton running his own ERA the man who had become his main rival, Michael Christie, drove Bell's ERA and blown Cooper-JAP 1100, in addition to his own unblown Cooper-JAP.

Wharton was unstoppable, and seemed hungry for five in a row come 1955, but after missing the early-season climbs with his Silverstone Vanwall burns he could only tie on points with young Tony Marsh, the RAC Competitions Committee then breaking the tie in the newcomer's favour.

Tony Marsh had burst upon the scene in 1953, after buying the ex-Peter Collins long-chassis Cooper with 1260 cc JAP twin engine. At Shelsley Walsh, Michael Christie beat him only narrowly and next day at Westwood Park sprint Marsh set ftd and was on his way.... At the end of 1954 he bought a new Mark VIII 1000, ran both cars and won the title in the later model. In 1956–57 he had a special thin-tube car built in the Mark VIII G which weighed only 560 lb or so, and wore a special body which he had made. He looked little more than a boy, but was both a highly controlled and capable driver and a good practical engineer. He was a quiet, reserved young man, almost shy. His father was a director of a large pie and sausage-making company, and Tony ran his farm for him at Kinver, Warwickshire. Marsh added a Bob-tail sports 1100 to his stable during the first Championship season and would later graduate to an F2 car, which he also hillclimbed. But just as Ken Wharton had lost his crown when circuit racing took more of his time, so Tony Marsh would lose out to new Champion David Boshier-Jones come 1958.

The 'Welsh Wizard' from Newport had first come to notice in 1952, driving a new 500 Kieft at his local Lydstep hillclimb. He lost control in the deceptive top corner and uprooted the finishing-banner posts! Next time at Lydstep he set ftd. In 1954 with a Cooper he smashed the Shelsley 500 record, before turning again to the JAP twin 1100 recipe, and achieving his personal championship hat-trick in 1958–59–60. His cars were immaculate in pale green with red striping and the Welsh dragon rampant on their scuttles. He was an elegant driver, 'the automaton' as one contemporary report put it. In 1959 he emulated Ken Wharton's feat of achieving a Championship round whitewash, winning every event, and after his hat-trick title he announced his retirement.

Throughout this period Michael Christie, founder of Alexander Engineering, the tuning and accessory concern from Haddenham, Bucks, had featured prominently in the Championship. He was Wharton's closest rival, then Marsh's but would never win the title. He had bought his first Cooper, Chassis number 17, in 1949, a long-wheelbase model for either 500 single or 1000–1100 twin-cylinder engines. He was credited with running an 1107 cc engine in most appearances, and car, man and performance were always immaculate. He favoured polychromatic mid-green livery with red seat and wheel trims and red helmet, and when Wharton bought 'R4D' for 1954, Christie took over the Peter Bell ERA and blown Cooper to support his own unblown car, which was 'the best of them all'. He put up the three top times of the day on one memorable occasion at the Scottish Rest-and-be-Thankful climb; fastest in the unblown Cooper, then Bell's supercharged car, then the ERA. That was about the right 'pecking order' in hillclimbing at the time. He also drove works Kiefts and would later handle Rob Walker's Connaught and both F2 and F1 Cooper-Climax cars on the hills; 'The little 1500 first time I drove it, without any practice, at Prescott – my favourite hill – was utterly fantastic. . . .' but in 1958 he adopted a specially tailored F2 Lotus-Climax, selling the last of his 'about a half-dozen' Cooper 'big twins' to Phil Scragg. Before season's end the Lotus was on its way to Tony Marsh and he was buying back the Cooper, which was a very special lightweight version. Then he decided to retire and the Cooper went to Mike Hatton, who began to build a considerable reputation with it on the hills.

Several cars had long competitive careers as they passed through various owners' hands. Bulky Walsall industrialist Bertie Bradnack had campaigned a supercharged 1000 through 1951, and subsequently sold it to John Broad. He competed energetically before selling it on to genial hotelier Dick Henderson, who had already proved himself a terrific wet-weather driver in a 1000 twin. In Henderson's hands the twin-rear-wheeled ex-Bradnack 1100 *mit kompressor* and humped engine cowl always looked somehow larger, more a 'proper racing car' than its sisters and was very successful. The Jerseymen Arthur Owen and Bill Knight campaigned a 1000 twin, and this ex-works car with 1100 engine went subsequently to former ERA driver David Good. He was director of a West Country dairy concern and like the great Archie Scott-Brown was a one-handed driver; lacking a right-forearm and hand from birth. It made little difference to his driving; he looked like Boshier-Jones's natural successor and proved it in 1961 by taking over his Championship title. Robin Jackson had built up a fearsome 1132 cc part-Norton, part-JAP twin engine for Ray Merrick's early long-chassis Cooper and it gained notoriety as the 'Cooper-NorJAP'. It passed to Australian-born Midlands resident J. D. 'Bill' Sleeman, who handled it with great verve and was always in the running. The supercharged car was driven occasionally by rally star Mrs Nancy Mitchell, until Bouley Bay 1955, when the unfortunate owner rolled it and was killed . . . a very rare occurrence in British hillclimbing.

On a lighter note Nancy Mitchell also drove the works 'big twin' on occasion, cornering the Ladies' award with it at Prescott in 1953–54. Owen Maddock and mechanic Derek Felix trailed the car there behind a Cooper Car Company van one year, but on the way home Owen – who had been working nights – fell asleep at the wheel and the rig rolled 360 degrees, the works car toppling off its trailer into the road. People stopped to help, and the Cooper had just been bounced back onto its wheels when a police car cruised by, unconcerned. Owen: '. . . was terrified of what the Old Man would say, but to my surprise it was John who blew up. When he'd finished old Charlie just took me to one side and said, "Listen cock, you don't want to go drivin' when your're tired cock. No cock . . . You always ought to 'ave a kip cock first. . . ."'

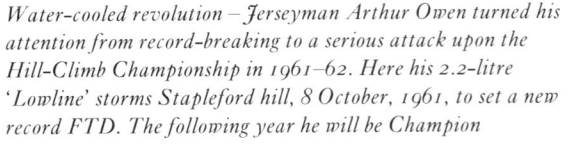

Water-cooled revolution – Jerseyman Arthur Owen turned his attention from record-breaking to a serious attack upon the Hill-Climb Championship in 1961–62. Here his 2.2-litre 'Lowline' storms Stapleford hill, 8 October, 1961, to set a new record FTD. The following year he will be Champion

Michael Christie's immaculate driving and superbly-prepared cars always seemed fated to be eternally second in the Championship. Here at Shelsley Walsh, 16 June, 1956, he enters the Esses en route to 2nd FTD...

Meanwhile hillclimbing had suffered particularly badly when Ken Wharton was killed in the New Zealand Ferrari accident early in 1957. Current Grand Prix drivers would no longer feature strongly on the hills; it became a more confined sport, a backwater, but the Cooper influence remained vivid. After Wharton's death his car stable was acquired by Tom Norton – the inveterate special builder whose early forays had been under the pseudonym 'T. Dryver'. One of the Wharton engines went later into the shared Mike Hatton/Peter Gaskell early-model Cooper twin to set Castel Farm ftd in Wales come 1958. Dick Henderson had a huge shunt at Prescott that season, rolling the aged ex-Bradnack car. Ray Fielding, from Forres, Inverness-shire, had bought the ex-Ivor Bueb 1100 Bob-tail through Walker's Pippbrook Garage and emerged on the hillclimb scene. The following year he modified it with centreline chassis brace, side-by-side seats, full-width screen and twin headrests, and continued an extremely successful programme in both the sports car and Championship classes.

When Mike Hatton bought the ex-Christie lightweight 1100, his former partner Peter Gaskell acquired the ex-Tony Marsh very special, also very lightweight, 'big twin'. These cars just managed to stave off the increasing number of F2 Cooper-Climaxes then taking to the hills. Fearless George Keylock from Hay-on-Wye – another former Cooper twin exponent – supercharged his F2 car. In 1957 Reg Phillips had produced his fearsome Fairley Special version, based on a Cooper twin frame with 1460 cc Climax FWB engine mounted transverse in the rear, driving through the original motorcycle gearbox and chains to the rear wheels! Phillips used no radiator, merely relying on the water in the block to keep matters cool enough to reach the summit... one was fitted later. That same year at Bouley Bay local driver Mac Daghorn erupted from obscurity in a very ancient 1000 twin, to beat Christie, Henderson and Boshier-Jones for second ftd behind the inevitable Tony Marsh. The Jerseyman's old Mark IV-based car remained a force to be reckoned with at Bouley Bay until 1961, when local businessman Peter Wakeham bought the Boshier-Jones Championship car for him, and he became truly competitive on any hill.

Back in 1955, Ivor Bueb hillclimbed his works F3 car very successfully, facing notably Mervyn Kearon's Ecurie Arklow model. Newcomers to the class that season included Douglas Haigh and Pauline Brock, who shared husband-to-be Jack Welton's Cooper. He was a Cheltenham motor trader and is not to be confused with Cooper-owning northern quarry owner Jack Walton. The Weltons notched many Cooper hillclimbing successes until 1960, when their ex-Bueb Mark X was sold to Ian McLaughlin, a Birmingham coach operator, who would maintain the big twin's challenge in its declining years. Wally Cuff was another Cooper exponent who had shone on the hills for many years with his famous 500s 'Hell's Hammers' and a big twin....

In 1960, change was fast approaching. Arthur Owen in

THE MINOR LEAGUES . . .

Genial hotelier Dick Henderson at Shelsley, June 1959, always instantly recognizable in the ex-Bradnack supercharged Cooper with its twin rear wheels and that enormous blower blister on the engine cowl

Forres garage owner Ray Fielding travelled thousands of miles from home ground in the north of Scotland to pursue his enthusiasm for hill-climbing. Here he is in his ex-Bueb works Bob-tail sports car. He bought it 29 August, 1958, from Walker's Pippbrook Garage, Dorking, with the 500 cc F3 chassis number 'Mk 8/15/54' and sohc Climax FWB engine '400/8/6632'. Jock Watson re-worked the car with a centre chassis brace and conventional side-by-side seating as shown, plus twin-headrest tail. Colour was Aston Martin 'peacock blue'. After initial competition 'the frame proved agricultural enough for us to remove the centre brace, leaving the cockpit completely open, and it still didn't fold in the middle'. Ray bought an Emeryson sports-racer in 1960, selling the Bob-tail to Spean Bridge, Connaught owner Alan Bateman

effect reintroduced Formula 1 machinery to the hills with his 2.2 Cooper-Climax T51, and split Boshier-Jones and David Good's Cooper twins in second place in the Championship. While the compact, nimble and torquey Cooper-JAPs had run circles around the traditional, heavy front-engined F1 car, now their descendants – the modern rear-engined F1s – were in turn putting them out to grass. In 1961, Tony Marsh would occasionally unleash his F1 Lotus 18 (with Cooper gearbox) on the hills to great effect, and in 1962 Owen's 2½-litre Cooper-Climax would take the Championship and prove near-unbeatable. The key here would be Dunlop's new range of high-hysteresis wet-weather racing tyres. The narrow edge between high power and uncontrolled wheelspin had always limited water-cooled multi-cylinder racing engines in face of JAP twin opposition on the hills. Now sticky tyre compounds allowed Owen and his followers to make use of their power advantage, and only

then did the long day of the Cooper big twin's domination draw to a close.

In turn the day of the F1 car would quickly pass as even more torque was available – and much less expensively – simply by adopting British or American production V8 engines. Chris Summers dropped a 5.3-litre Chevrolet into his ex-F2 Cooper-Climax to dominate club *Formule Libre* racing in 1962–63, and his hillclimbing appearances set both crowds and track surface alight. Simultaneously, Peter Westbury had fitted a 2.6 Daimler V8 into his ex-F2 Cooper and found competitive times on the hills, and he capitalized on this recipe in 1963 with his Championship-winning Felday-Daimler V8 special.

The Cooper flag flew particularly high in the sports car classes with Josh Randles's 2-litre Cooper Monaco FPF. This was actually the ill-fated Chequered Flag car crashed in its first few laps of life by Percy Crabbe at Snetterton in

Chris Summers' fearsome Cooper-Chevrolet V8 special smokes off the Weston-super-Mare startline, 29 September, 1962, on its way to an 18.34 sec FTD over the 800 yard sprint course, repeating the combination's Brighton success that season. Summers fitted a V8 in the ex-Bristow ex-Pitt Monaco sports car at this time. With a 3½-litre Buick V8, Bob Waters later campaigned his Anglo-American Monaco hybrid, and V8s also caught-on widely in the sprint and hillclimb scene

Josh Randles' Monaco sports-racing car, believe it or not, Loton Park 'climb, 20 October, 1963 – here at Museum Bend the veteran enthusiast shows off his Monaco's cut-down sprint body, cycle wings, original full-body registration number and tax disc for road use. Old 536 TEH had begun life as the Chequered Flag's short-lived Monaco-Climax, written-off on its debut, Snetterton, March 1959. The entity survives today, restored to full enveloping body form

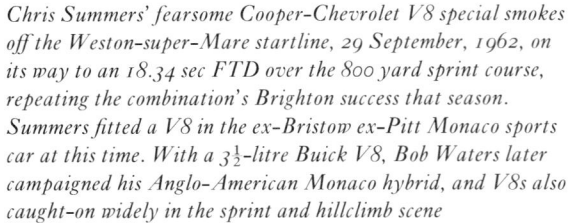

March 1960. Randles bought the wreck and rebuilt it in his garage at Stoke. He enjoyed two extremely successful seasons with the car – registered 536 TEH – in 1961–62 and won the latter season's Sports Car Hill-Climb Championship. He held every hillclimb sports record except Prescott and Great Auclum. At 48, with a mane of silver-grey hair, Randles had big plans for 1963, but was run over in a road accident and almost died. He staged a remarkable recovery, and fitted the Monaco with a peculiar open-wheeler body, then replaced the Climax engine with the ex-Brian Naylor 3-litre Maserati four-cylinder. The Cooper-Maserati promptly set ftd first time out in the sports class at Great Auclum, and its front-line success continued.

During 1963 David Good chased Westbury's Felday-Daimler hard with his supercharged F2 Cooper-Climax, but at May Prescott the potential of the American V8 was underlined when Brian Eccles scored a surprise ftd in his ex-Yeoman Credit Cooper with 4.7 Chevy V8 and Cooper gearbox. Unfortunately the US V8 hybrids proved unreliable on some occasions and overpowered on others! Good compromised and fitted a 2.6 Daimler V8 like Westbury's before season's end. George Keylock campaigned a 3.5-litre Cooper-Buick and Scots husband and wife team Gray and Agnes Mickel the ex-Arthur Owen Championship 2½-litre Cooper Climax 'Lowline', Gray mangling the car badly at Rest-and-be-Thankful.

Any visitor to Ulster had to contend with Bangor garage owner John Pringle and his Coopers. He had reputedly bought the ex-Moss Argentine GP-winning Walker car in 1959 with a 2-litre FPF engine and had since replaced it with 2½-litre cars and shone at Craigantlet and on the Irish circuits, to which several other ex-F1 and F2 Coopers had retired.

In 1964 Pringle had a 2.7 engine, while John Macklin's ex-Keylock Cooper-Buick led the Cooper rearguard action in the Hill-Climb Championship against Westbury's four-wheel-drive Ferguson and the ever-developing Tony Marsh specials. The Mickels' ex-Owen car had survived to fight again, while perennial F2 Cooper campaigner Patsy Burt put up some immaculate performances in her pristine pale-blue-and-white car. Wally Cuff ran the ex-Good Cooper-Daimler, and in 1964 replaced its SP250 V8 with a 4.6-litre big-banger taken from a Daimler Majestic limousine, while David Good himself had taken to a Lola-Chevrolet sports car! Bearded John Macklin was a regular with the ageing Cooper-Buick, while David Hepworth had little luck in his 4.7 Cooper-Chevrolet. Ian Swift did better with his Cooper-Cobra, using a 4.7 Ford V8, but late in the year he lost

THE MINOR LEAGUES...

Martin Brain who did so much to enliven the latter years of Cooper's minor-league activities, in his 'T81B' 'F1/1/67' with 7.2 Chrysler V8 engine, setting 2nd FTD, Willow Bend, Harewood, 28 April, 1968. The big car's monocoque was kinked in a trailer mishap in the Shelsley paddock, May 1970, and considered written-off. Brian died soon after in his 'T86B-BRM V12 at Silverstone, and the big hillclimb car was bought from Sun Alliance insurance by John Northcroft and repaired. In 1971 Johnty Williamson bought it, and through the hands of Terry Smith, Bob Ascot, and Clive Osbourne it passed to John Hewitt – one of the country's most capable historic car engine rebuilders, working with Crosthwaite & Gardiner in Buxted, Sussex where 16-cylinder Maseratis and V12 Auto Unions hold no fear

control on mud at Dyrham Park and smashed the car against a tree. He rebuilt it as the Swift-Ford special and his hillclimbing career continued for some years. Colin Watts scored Championship points in his Mark VIII Cooper-JAP 1100, and that had become quite a feat by this time.

John Macklin ran the 'ex-McLaren' 1965 F1 Cooper-Buick T77 in 1966, but at Harewood, Yorkshire, it was written off in an extensive accident, and its owner subsequently reappeared in a Ford GT40.... David Harrison ran a Cooper-Buick, then fitted the engine in an Irish Crosslé frame. David Blankstone emerged in an F3 Cooper T65, and a rather dilettante newcomer named Martin Brain made his debut in the ex-Westbury Cooper-Daimler, and began talking of having a new 7.2-litre Chrysler-powered F2 Cooper built for 1967.

Brain was a director of Brames Ltd, a tube-manufacturing company based in Birmingham, and his early slightly 'playboy' image was rapidly submerged as he became one of the most committed and determined competitors in the Hill-Climb Championship.

He retained his Cooper-Daimler for the early part of the 1967 season, until the tailor-made T84 was ready, whereupon the 2.5 V8 engine was transferred, but the results did not come and at the end of the year he bought the ex-Rindt lightweight F1 Cooper T81B to accept the threatened 7.2 Chrysler V8. The Hill-Climb Championship standings for 1967 underline Cooper's eclipse: Ian Swift 15th in his special; Roy Lane 17th, having replaced his early-season 1.6 Cooper-Ford Mark 3 supercharged twin-cam with a Brabham; David Blankstone's ex-Mike Hawley F1 Cooper-BMC T67 19th; Brain 22nd; Ray Langdon's 4.7 Cooper-Ford T62 23rd and David McDougall's F3 Cooper-BMC T72 26th....

Martin Brain led the way into 1968 with his T87 Cooper-Daimler special – chassis *FL/1/67* – and the ex-Rindt/Redman South Africa T81B – *F1/1/67* – into which the 7.2 Chrysler V8 had been fitted at Cooper's Canada Road works. It was in near-standard tune, but even so gave around 430 bhp at 3500 rpm and 490 ft/lb torque! A change to new carburetion and manifolding in mid-season yielded about 40 bhp more. Brain planned to use the 225 bhp T87 on the tighter hills and the T81B on the power venues, like Shelsley Walsh, but in practice the larger car was always faster. The T81B was in dock at Great Auclum time, so the small Cooper-Daimler was used to notch its only Championship points of the year. The cars were sponsored by Golden Knight Oils, but Brain's season was spoiled by 'moments' and he could do little about Peter Lawson's Champion 4WD

317

Left *End of the line – Tony Robinson studies progress at Canada Road as the Beddings' beautifully-made 'T90' Formula 5000 prototype monocoque nears completion on its jig. The F1 Cosworth-engined 'T91' was never completed, and the final team sell-off from Canada Road to George Fejer in Canada eventually included over 2000 works drawings housed in their original oak drawing cabinets, including the earliest known – dated 7 November 1946 No. C100 for the 500 cc cars, and the last, dated 12 February 1969 No. 2420 for the 'T91'*

Brain's special – the stark, highly-specialized little Cooper-Daimler 'T87' chassis 'FL-1-67' completed that July for Martin Brain, then sold to Clive Oakley in August 1968 and fitted subsequently with a 3.5 Rover engine. Here is Oakley with the Daimler still installed, 28 March, 1969

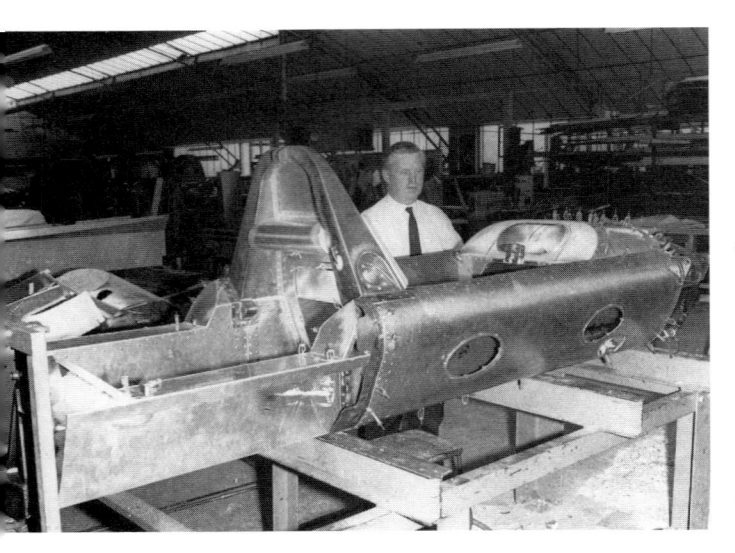

BRM, and finished the season in second place. The next-up Cooper was Ray Langdon's 4.7 Ford V8 T62 way back, equal 25th!

The Cooper-Daimler T87 was then sold to Clive Oakley, while Martin Brain said he would retire. But the lure of the hills was too great, and after Cooper's closing down auction he returned in 1969, sharing his new ex-works T86B-BRM V12 F1 car with Tony Griffiths. The T81B-Chrysler lay fallow, requiring vital parts, until August, by which time Brain had already won the Craigantlet climb. Then on 17 August at Shelsley Walsh he and his Cooper-Chrysler smashed the two-year-old climb record with a scintillating 30.72 sec; it was probably the highlight of his career. He finished the season fourth in the Hill-Climb Championship.

Meanwhile, in British club racing, the exploits of Chris Summers's Cooper-Chevrolet in 1962–63 *Libre* racing were but fond memory. Alan Eccles had raced-on in the Cooper-Chevy, while 750 MC Chairman Mike Eyre's 3½ Cooper-Buick V8 was successful, but mainly in level sprints. John Taylor had been the star of Mallory Park racing in 1963 with Bob Gerard's 1½-litre 112 bhp Cooper-Ford twin-cam and he actually smashed John Surtees's F1 Lola outright lap record with the car, Gerard replacing it with the new F1/2/3/*Libre* hybrid for 1964. Taylor was to shine in *Libre* racing at club level, and did as well as could be expected with his four-cylinder car in the non-Championship F1 races contested. When Gerard later adopted the Monaco GP-winning V8 T60, John, Taylor and Rhodes both did the obsolete car justice. Then, driving a Brabham for the Bridges brothers in the 1966 German GP this very pleasant Midlander crashed and was badly burned, dying some weeks later from his injuries.

Another ex-F1 Cooper to perform well at club level was John Axon's 1963 ex-Walker T66, fitted with a 4.7 Cobra-Ford V8 engine for the 1966 season, in which the combination won eight races, and Axon's ex-MRP mechanic David Depper also drove on occasion. Kartist Chris Lambert raced an F3 Cooper T83 briefly for entrant Alan McKechnie – another club character, Barrie 'Whizzo' Williams, winning his first race in this machine. In 1967 Tiny Littler's 1.6 Cooper-Ford twin-cam won seven *Libre* races and Julian Gerard appeared in the 1964 T73. Axon's T66-Ford had sold to Jim Charnock, who enjoyed considerable *Libre* success with it in 1968, winning five times before passing it on to John Scott-Davies.

In 1969, Formula 5000 was introduced to the UK, with F1-like single-seater cars powered by US-style 5-litre V8 engines. Chevrolets were the thing to have; Cooper's projected production T90 flopped as the company lay down and died, and only two chassis regularly represented the marque that year. One was the ex-Rob Walker/Axon/Charnock/John Scott-Davies T66 with Shelby-Ford V8, which had been acquired by Mike Coombe and John Dean. After two early races they rebuilt it with a new rear frame and modernized rear suspension and wheels. It was sprayed bright yellow and won them some money on reliability; Coombe later bought a second-hand Lola T142 for 1970. The other F5000 Cooper was the purpose-built T90 prototype bought by Chris Drake at the Frimley auction. It used a Mathwall-prepared wet-sump Chevy V8 engine which was a disaster and the new owner couldn't really afford it all – 'Just the gearbox cost the same as a new Mini'. He inadvertently turned the British F5000 Championship decider into an anticlimax by putting both contenders, Trevor Taylor and Peter Gethin, off the road during their final duel at Brands Hatch, and was only then black-flagged from the race for being uncompetitive.

The T90 prototype had been completed at Canada Road

in the autumn of 1968 and a deal had been arranged with Vegantune Engineering – a Lincolnshire concern founded by two ex-BRM technicians – to provide suitably modified Chevrolet V8 engines for the planned (if wildly optimistic) production run of 'not more than 24 of these cars'.

The full-length monocoque tub was based on the T86B's, with three 18/24-gauge steel bulkheads in the forward nacelle, skinned with 18-gauge Alclad aluminium and malleable NS4 sheet. The rear chassis horns were in 16/18-gauge aluminium. The centre bulkhead was skinned up into an integral roll-over structure, while the front and rear sections were very similar to T86B practice. F5000 races were comparatively short, so the FPT rubberized fuel bags held only 26 gallons, residing in the pontoon structure beside the cockpit, and there was no scuttle tank over the driver's legs. Suspension followed the T86B layout, and 'inboard/outboard' brakes sat in the airstream front and rear, 10.75 in. diameter front and 10.5 in. rear. The wheels were Cooper magnesium disc, 9 or 11 in. wide front and 12 or 14 × 15 in. at the rear. Vegantune's projected Chevy engine was to use Lucas F1 fuel injection and ignition and claims were made for 500 bhp at 6500 rpm and 415 ft/lb torque at 5500. Drive passed through a $7\frac{1}{4}$ in. Borg & Beck triple-plate clutch fitted to a lightweight steel flywheel, and through a five-speed Hewland LG600 gearbox.

Using a slave engine on Webers, the prototype T90 – chassis *F1C–1–68* – was tested at Goodwood by Robin Widdows, but hefty (around 1350 lb) and underpowered cars often feel very good to handle. So it proved in Drake's ownership, but the car like the Beddings' other monocoque Coopers, was beautifully built; it was just the pedigree and the times which failed it.

At club level the ex-Antique Automobiles Cooper-Maserati T86 had gone to Falken Racing Developments, and Tony Lanfranchi scored its first-ever race win in a Silverstone meeting where John Scott-Davies crashed the other T86B-BRM mildly, then Lanfranchi won again at Brands Hatch.

At club level *Formule Libre* lost its American-engined would-be competitors to Formula 5000. Two Coopers were adapted; Aston Martin development engineer Peter Hawtin fitting a 5-litre Chevy V8 in a T86B monocoque, while one Fred Place adapted the T86C tub (originally intended for the Alfa Romeo V8 engine) to accept a Ford Boss 302.

In the hillclimb world the competitive Coopers had all but disappeared by this time, although twins and 500s were being preserved lovingly by a growing band of enthusiasts. The opening Hill-Climb Championship meeting at Prescott on 3 May was tragic on two counts. Newcomer Stuart MacQuarrie rolled his Cooper-Ford T72 and was killed as the roll-over bar collapsed. Fatalities were very rare in hillclimbing and they were keenly felt. At the same meeting, Martin Brain's mighty Cooper-Chrysler was damaged in a transport-unloading accident, and thorough investigation of the kinked monocoque revealed fundamental structural damage. Since the ex-Canada Road chassis jigs had been sold to Canada, Brain regretfully concluded that his car was beyond economic repair, and it was judged a write-off though in fact it survives to this day.

He had ordered a new McLaren M10B F5000 car for hillclimbing, and on 21 May his F1 Cooper-BRM T86B was advertised for sale, just completely rebuilt, for £4500. On 25 May he raced it at the Notts SCC Silverstone club meeting, qualified on pole beside Graham Eden's 1600 Chevron and led off the line. Eden darted ahead and Brain drove desperately hard to repass. On lap 7 they came barrelling down the runway straight, rushing up onto two back markers. Eden flashed through between them, while Brain

Last hurrah – One of the two prototype 'T90' F5000 Cooper-Chevrolets seen on its stand, London Racing Car Show, 8–18 January, 1969 in the National Hall, Olympia, parked tail-to-tail with its sister. This bright-yellow, black-striped car had no rear wing, and an oil cooler above the gearbox. Its red-hued sister car with white stripes looked more complete, with oil coolers either side of the fabricated integral roll-over protection, and a strutted rear wing anchored on the rear uprights. Note all inboard-of-upright brakes, just visible front and rear. This car has the planned Vegantune V8, the other carried a Mathwall

dodged to the outside. Somehow the Cooper-BRM put a wheel on the verge, then it slewed, dug in and flipped, cartwheeling crazily, far into the long grass, killing its intrepid owner-driver.

This tragic season also saw Cooper-Chevrolet originator Chris Summers suffer fatal injuries when his F5000 Lola had a tyre deflate. He crashed on the straight at Snetterton and was thrown out. Summers, with his short-sleeved sports shirt and disdain of restraint harnesses, had epitomised a passing era of 'come as you are' club racing. Peter Hawtin was a driver in the same mould, but at the closing round of the 1971 Formula 5000 Championship at Oulton Park, something appeared to seize on his ill-handling Cooper-Chevrolet T86B and it smashed into a marshal's post at Hill Top, on the fastest part of the course. It broke into two and caught fire and Hawtin – another club driver who scorned flame-proofs and seat belts – could not survive.

Apart from historic events, and what had become virtually the curiosity classes of sprints and hillclimbing, the Cooper saga had reached its close; I must emphasize a highly untypical end, for Cooper's own team had never lost a driver in 23 years' racing and they would always be regarded as strong, robust, and safer than most other racing cars. . . .

Yet one cannot avoid the thought that the marque's demise coincided with that of two very-British drivers, who perhaps typified the old spirit of Cooper's proper time; the Cooper era – a happy-go-lucky age of uncomplicated motor racing where enthusiasm was the spur, monetary profit a pleasant bonus. Cooper Cars as originated had no place in the hardening, commercialised, sanitized and self-consciously sophisticated modern era of the Seventies and Eighties.

Their time for being had passed, but the cars had been active in four decades at major level. For all concerned it had been quite a party. . . .

APPENDIX THREE

The record cars

During the Fifties, Cooper cars attacked and established 56 class World records with a series of specially modified versions of their production road racers.

It began late in 1951 and the prime mover of the project was the veteran racer-cum-fruit farmer Bill Aston. He had long cherished ambitions to go record breaking with a modified version of his long-chassis Cooper big twin, and John Cooper typically took little persuading. What emerged was the first entirely new car to be built in Britain for record-breaking since John Cobb's Railton Special. The new record car was based on a Mark V stretch chassis and the Beddings – Fred and Pete – worked weekends to fit it with outrigger supports and shape the 18-gauge aluminium streamlined body panels, with Mrs Cooper Sr '. . . coming down from their flat above the corner shop with cups of tea and biscuits', as Pete recalls. Body design was the usual committee effort, Owen Maddock recalling that '. . . I just drew a record car the way I thought a record car should look', while fellow 500 cc engineer Gordon Bedson – whose full-time employer was Vickers Aviation, for whom he worked on the Valiant V-bomber project, subsequently constructed a scale model of the proposed design and gained permission to test it in a Brooklands wind tunnel: 'He would be able to warn us if it was about to flip over onto its back at 60 mph; I think we did alter the nose a little bit in line with his findings. . . .'

To lower the body as much as possible, the driver reclined in a hammock seat, cockpit access being through a large hinged panel flat on the body deck, with only the tiniest opening for the driver's head and a Perspex screen wrapped tightly round his face. Frontal area was only 6 sq ft. One victim of the lowering programme was the conventional steering wheel. Now instead of it being splined normally onto the steering column, a bevel-box was fitted at the scuttle and driven by a virtually horizontal wheel set above the driver's lap. Suspension, brakes, rack-and-pinion gear and wheels were standard Mark V, and the co-owners intended to attack International Class I (500 cc) and Class J (350 cc) records that October at Montlhéry. Transmission was via the standard Norton racing gearbox, and to sustain the attack on records up to 200 km fuel tankage within the broad body sponsons totalled 21 gallons.

The car was tested briefly on an airfield with Aston's 1098 cc JAP twin installed, and he took it up to around 140 mph with no sign of the dreaded nose lift. The green-cellulosed record-breaker with its red upholstery attacked the records at Montlhéry on 8–9 October, 1951, with these results:
Attempt I – John Cooper – 350 cc JAP Class J
50 km – 90.62 mph; 50 miles – 92.02 mph; 100 km – 92.13 mph; 1 hour – 90.27 mph; 100 miles – 91.80 mph; 200 km – 91.98 mph.
Attempt II – Bill Aston – 500 cc Norton Class I
50 km – 99.30 mph; 50 miles – 99.56 mph; 100 km – 99.59 mph; 1 hour – 99.41 mph; 100 miles – 99.41 mph; 200 km – 99.13 mph.

This Mark V stretch chassis record-breaker was later used by John Cooper to win the Grenzlandring and Avus high-speed circuit races as described earlier. It then sold to John Fox Jr of San Francisco, California, USA, finished in American national racing colours for record runs at Bonneville, Utah.

During 1953 John and Eric Brandon decided to take a new streamliner to Montlhéry to attack existing Class H (750 cc), I and J records. The car to be used was the prototype Mark VIII, fitted with a modestly redesigned version of the '51 streamliner body, lightened and designated the Mark VIII(R). By saving as much weight as possible they hoped to compensate for the 350 cc Class J Norton engine's lack of ponies. One weight-saving ploy was the adoption of smaller dampers, which was a mistake. The bankings hammered the suspension mercilessly in the Class H 600 cc Norton runs on 4 October, 1953, the dampers gave out and their brackets began to break up. Brandon hammered on until a drive-chain broke and the attempt had failed. Ginger Devlin, Eric's Ecurie Richmond mechanic, and John Cooper then fitted a 500, remade the damper mounts and fitted new dampers before John raised seven Class I marks. On 6 October, with a Ray Petty-tuned Norton 350, John succeeded in taking another seven Class I records. Further runs with the sidecar-derived 600 saw the team leaving Montlhéry with 15 World records in the bag:
Attempt III – Eric Brandon – 600 cc Norton Class H
Failed.

Attempt IV – John Cooper – 350 cc Norton Class J
50 km – 105.71 mph; 50 miles – 104.93 mph; 100 km – 105.10 mph; 100 miles – 104.39 mph; 200 km – 103.87 mph; 200 miles – 103.46 mph; 1 hour – 104.32 mph.

Attempt V – John Cooper – 500 cc Norton Class I
50 km – 111.14 mph; 50 miles – 111.22 mph; 100 km – 111.40 mph; 100 miles – 112.35 mph; 200 km – 112.89 mph; 1 hour – 112.61 mph; 200 miles – 103.62 mph (taken on first run).

Attempt VI – John Cooper – 600 cc Norton Class H
200 km – 114.08 mph.

On 1 October, 1955, Jerseymen Arthur Owen and Bill Knight brought Cooper back into the records business, mounting an attack upon Class G (1100 cc) world records using a specially modified Bob-tail sports car. They had attacked 250 cc records at Montlhéry that April, and although the FIA subsequently refused to ratify them as Owen described in his book *The Racing Coopers*: 'I had developed the record-breaking itch. . . .'

He and Bill Knight commissioned the Cooper Car Company to build them a Bob-tail around a heavier-than-normal gauge tubular frame, fitted with uprated dampers, long-range fuel tanks, auxiliary fuel pump and specially designed comfy seat intended for runs up to six hours in duration at Montlhéry. For the higher-speed records Jim Russell was included in the team. He lapped at 126 mph in practice, before attacking and taking records up to 1 hour on 17 October, 1955. Owen and Knight then took over to take records up to 1000 km and six hours. The car ran on Esso Golden pump petrol, and returned 35 mpg!

Attempt VII – Jim Russell – 1100 cc Class G
50 km – 128.27 mph; 50 miles – 127.43 mph; 100 km – 127.36 mph; 100 miles – 125.86 mph; 200 km – 125.37 mph; 1 hour – 125.34 mph.

Attempt VIII – Arthur Owen and Bill Knight – 1100 cc Class G
200 miles – 118.35 mph; 500 km – 115.30 mph; 3 hours – 115.26 mph; 500 miles – 112.88 mph; 1000 km – 111.55 mph; 6 hours – 111.63 mph.

Eleven months later, on 22 September, 1956, Wing Commander Freddy Sowrey sprang a surprise by attacking Class G (1100 cc) records on British soil, at Bedford aerodrome, using his Mark VI Cooper fitted with a blown 1097 cc JAP twin and a fibreglass body taken off the 1953 Mark VIII(R) panels. Sowrey's targets were the standing-start kilometre and mile marks. He had planned the project with fellow Cooper big-twin campaigner Peter Hughes the previous year, when they had met during the Brighton Speed Trials. Unfortunately, returning from Le Mans, Hughes was killed in a road accident, but Sowrey persevered and took the records at 87.64 and 93.88 mph. This was the first such record attempt to be staged on British soil since the war.

Within the month, Arthur Owen and Bill Knight had returned to the fray, this time attacking Class G (1100 cc) and Class E (2-litre) marks at Monza in Italy, with high-speed support from Roy Salvadori. A Mark II Bob-tail was prepared around a heavier-gauge chassis frame, and fat 5.00–15 front and 5.50–15 rear tyres were adopted to withstand high speeds around the *Pista de Alta Velocita* speedbowl. The Jerseymen felt the Class F (1500 cc) marks were untouchable, having been set up on the vast expanse of Bonneville Salt Flats in the USA, but by boring an FWB engine beyond 1500 cc they would be into the 2-litre class, where the mark was attainable.

Climax co-operated by casting a more capacious block which they could overbore to 1530 cc, whereas the basic FWA 1100 unit had already been taken to its sensible limit in the FWB 1460. A bubble-canopy Team Lotus Type 11

THE RECORD CARS

Looking right – the 1951 flat steering wheel record-breaker emerged with this gorgeous Beddings bodyshell, here in Hollyfield Road showing off its wheel spats, tiny cockpit opening, thin-padded headrest and large forward hinging cockpit entry hatch. The slots in the headrest fairing would accommodate single or twin-cylinder exhaust pipes, as required. In the paddock at Montlhéry the streamliner is opened-up, mechanic Chris Brew tending the twin-cylinder engine while owner Bill Aston (left) and John Cooper – with inevitable pipe and less inevitable BRDC badge – looking on. The car's nose carried a BRDC decal and 'COOPER-JAP' lettering

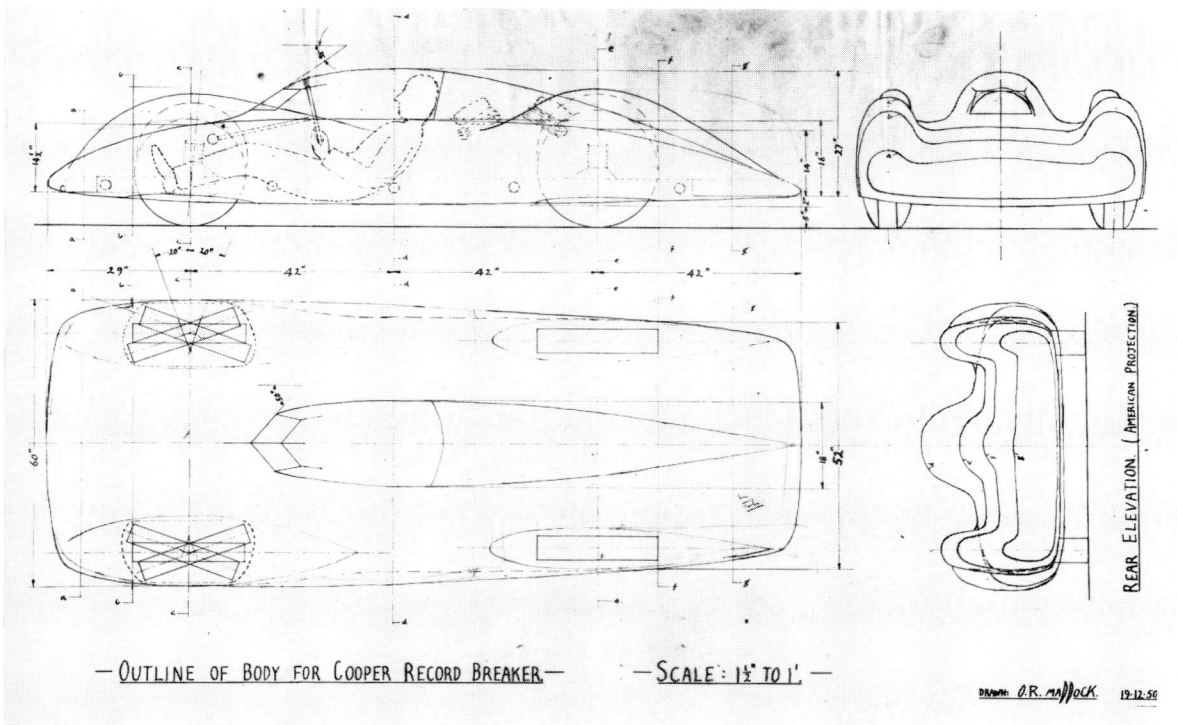

Owen Maddock's original bodyline drawing for the record-breaker – dated 19 December, 1950 – show vee-section windscreen set into bubble fairing, and a standard upright steering wheel disposition. To lower the car overall a flat-wheel and bevel-box system was substituted before the design was finalized. There's nothing new about placing driver's feet ahead of the front axle line!

Right *Wing Commander Fred Sowrey of the RAF in his Mark VI 500 fitted with glass-fibre bodywork moulded on the Mark VIII(R) aluminium panels from 1953, powered by a supercharged 1097 cc JAP twin while attacking Class G records successfully at Bedford airfield, 22 September, 1956. The works streamliner sold to America, and ostensibly became Pete Lovely's Porsche-engined 'Pooper' sports racing car. Ken Miles also Porsche-engined a Bob-tail, fitting air-cooling vents on its tail, and racing it with great success 1956–57 . . .*

Bill Knight in the specially beefed-up Bob-tail which he shared with Arthur Owen (far left) in so many record attempts, seen here at Montlhéry, 17 October, 1955, when 13 marks fell to them. Jim Russell (hand bandaged) is by front wing, Charles and John Cooper in duffle-coats at tail. The car is a specially-prepared Mark I, on Darby wheels. During practice for the runs Jim found the car jumping out of gear. John cured it by fitting a bungee cord which 'whanged the gear-lever back into top and held it there over the biggest bumps'. Cooperism at its practical best . . .

THE RECORD CARS

Monza Autodrome, October, 1957 – **Below** *Ron Searles (left) and young Frank Butler wheel-out the strengthened heavy-gauge tube Owen-Knight Bob-tail ready for the record runs in which poor, popular Ron would lose his life. The car's radiator has been removed with the body, but the large battery to sustain lighting for night running and bulky long-range fuel tanks are visible. In the background is the small team's borrowed Jack Brabham transporter, while tail of the Underhill's of Jersey glass-fibre bodied streamlined Mark IV-framed 250 protrudes from lock-up 2. The unpainted streamliner wheeled out by transporter* **left** *shows off its detachable cockpit roof and centre section, and fixings for wheel spats*

November, 1959 – back at Monza again, Arthur Owen pounding round the high-banked Pista de Alta Velocita *in his 2-litre Mark IV single-seater – probably 'FII/6/59' – on his way to the one hour class record – he took it, closing a Cooper record-breaking era in the chilly Milanese mist on the deserted, echoing Autodrome...*

sports racing car had just taken all the old Cooper 1100 cc records at Monza when the new contender set out for its attempts on 15 October, 1956. George Saunders had brought out the new record car together with Salvadori's works 1500 Bob-tail, *en route* to the Rome GP at Castelfusano. New Zealander Ray Thackwell accompanied George as mechanic.

Owen lapped comfortably at around 137 mph, Knight took it up to 141.5 mph, then a damper broke. After 338 laps the dynamo broke adrift, the water drained out and the engine seized, 90 miles short of the intended target, though with seven records already in the bag.

A spare 1100 cc FWA engine was installed, John Cooper re-welded a minor chassis crack, and four new dampers and tyres were fitted. On 16 October Salvadori tried the car to see if it could approach the contemporary bubble-canopy Lotus 11's class figures. Its aerodynamic form proved woefully inferior and the crew fell back upon their own 1955 200-mile and six-hour records, rather than attack Lotus for the hour. Salvadori held the throttle flat to the boards and took the Jerseymen's 200-mile Montlhéry mark from 118.35 mph right up to 131.89! They would never dream of driving so hard; John encouraged them to do so and it proved fatal, a fibre timing-wheel breaking up just before the 500 km mark with Knight driving.

Attempt IX – Arthur Owen and Bill Knight – 2-litre Class E
1 hour – 135.072 mph; 200 miles – 131.685 mph; 500 km – 127.885 mph; 3 hours – 128.642 mph; 500 miles – 126.969 mph; 1000 km – 125.787 mph; 6 hours – 125.716 mph.

Attempt X – Roy Salvadori – 1100 cc Class G
200 miles – 131.890 mph.

Owen and Knight returned to Monza in October 1957 with the heavy-gauge chassis Bob-tail Mark II and a new fibreglass bodied streamliner to attack 1100 cc and Class J (350 cc) and K (250 cc) records, using Climax and Ray Petty Norton engines.

The streamliner was based on their old 1955 Mark IV hillclimb frame. They had borrowed the Mark VIII(R) streamliner body drawings from Hollyfield Road and had a new shell made from them in Jersey by Eric Bisson and the Underhill coachwork company. An original plan to attack shorter-distance records with a Marshal-Nordec blower were shelved when the made-to-order supercharger flopped. They aimed at the 1000 mile, 2000 km and 12-Hour marks instead with this car.

Such distances demanded a third driver and Hollyfield Road works manager Ron Searles pleaded to be included. John could not take part as his wife Pauline was expecting a baby around the time of the attempts. Bespectacled Ron was running the Brands Hatch school, competed in occasional races with the air-cooled single-seaters and had an ambition to qualify for the BRDC. He was a most capable and humorous chap to have around.

Cyril Posthumus of *Autosport* magazine at that time knew Ron Searles very well. 'He was a lovely, engaging bloke with a really zany, goonish sense of humour. "Ooh," he'd say, "... you coming for lunch? We're having cats' bums and custard, my missis often gives me that, I love 'em..." We'd frown at each other and wonder what on earth he was talking about. "What d'you mean, Ron? Cats' bums and custard?" – and he'd beam and say "Have you ever *looked* at a sliced banana?..." That sort of thing was typical....

Bill Knight set five new Class K records in the streamliner before the nearside front hub race seized, shearing the stub axle and losing the wheel. After six hours' running the first Bob-tail attempt failed with a thrown con-rod. Plans were made to run again the following Monday, 14 October, 1957. Ron should have been back at work that day but a phone call to John set matters straight, provided he would bring home a report 'on what Lotus have been up to'. A new stub axle for the streamliner was ordered from Switzerland and on arrival machined at Gilera's factory – free of charge although they were attacking a Gilera record. . . .

Bill Knight ran the streamliner with its 350 cc engine and lapped at 112 mph, but after only 49 km a valve dropped in.

The team's last hope was the Bob-tail 1100 and the endurance records so, on the Monday, Owen set out on the run at 7.00 a.m. To approach MG's records they had to lap at over 120 mph. The car was running well, and into the dusk Ron Searles took over for the final 1 hr 35 min. Heavy winking lights had been placed on the track by the Monza officials where the banked *Pista de Alta Velocita* curved away from the flat road course. Ron slowed as it grew dark and the crew feared their record would slip away. A driver change at that late stage with only 20 minutes to go would lose it for sure. The only alternative was to signal 'FASTER'. Standing in the glare of the pit lights they waved him on. One of the winking lights at the circuit intersection may have gone out. In any event poor Ron Searles struck it with the right-front tyre, the car cartwheeled into the air and slid upside down along the concrete, where its fuel load exploded, and its driver was killed.

Arthur Owen and Bill Knight returned to Monza in November 1959 to tackle the 2-litre hour record in Arthur's interim-F1 Mark IV. That misty run ended the Cooper record-breaking story. Monza owed it to them. . . .

Attempt XI – Bill Knight – 250 cc Norton Class K
50 km – 96.326 mph; 50 miles – 97.602 mph; 100 km – 97.786 mph; 1 hour – 97.260 mph; 100 miles – 97.184 mph.
Attempt XII – Bill Knight, Ron Searles and Arthur Owen – 1100 cc Class G
1000 miles – 120.55 mph; 2000 km – 120.74 mph.

APPENDIX FOUR

Cooper type numbers

This listing is that normally issued by the Cooper Car Company in response to interested inquiries. It does however contain some anomalies as mentioned in the text and in the chassis register. The team itself never worried overmuch about Type numbers, and one written record inevitably often differed from another. Typical Cooper – getting the cars ready on time and winning races is what mattered . . .

T1	Austin 7 Special	1936	Built by Charles Cooper
T2	Prototype Cooper-JAP 500 Mark I	1946	Built by Charles and John Cooper with Eric Brandon
T3	Mark I 500	1947	For Eric Brandon
T4	Triumph-engined sports car	1947	
T5	Production 500s Mark II	1948	
T6	Cooper-Vauxhall sports car	1948	For John Cooper
T7	Production 500s Mark III	1949	
T8	The Cooper trailer	1949	
T9	Stretch-chassis for 1000 twins	1949	
T10	Cooper 'sports-racing car'	1949	
T11	Production 500s Mark IV	1950	
T12	Stretch-chassis for twins Mk IV	1950	
T13	1100 cc JAP twin sports car	1950	
T14	Cooper-MG production sports	1950	
T15	Production 500s Mark V	1951	
T16	Stretch-chassis Mark V	1951	
T17	Mark V streamlined record car	1951	
T18	Production 500s Mark VI	1952	
T19	Production stretch Mark VI	1952	
T20	Cooper-Bristol Mark I	1952	Front-engined Formula 2
T21	Latest Cooper-MG sports	1952	
T22	Cooper-Bristol sports car	1953	No allocated to Alan Brown
T23	Cooper Mark II Formula 2 — Bristol	1953	
T24	Cooper-Alta Formula 2	1953	
T25	Cooper-Bristol sports car	1953	Planned for 25-off production
T26	Production 500s Mark VII	1953	
T27	Stretch Mark VII	1953	
T28	Mark VIII (R) record car	1953	Built for Eric Brandon
T29	'Sports car'	1953	
T30	Vandervell F1 chassis	1953–54	
T31	Production 500s Mark VIII	1954	
T32	Stretch Mark VIII	1954	
T33	Cooper-Jaguar Mark I sports	1954	Built for Peter Whitehead etc.
T34	'Cooper-Norton sports car'	1954	
T35	Cooper-Lea Francis sports car	1954	Built for John Goldschmidt
T36	Production 500s Mark IX	1955	
T37	Stretch Mark IX	1955	
T38	Cooper-Jaguar Mark II	1955	
T39	Bob-tail 1100 sports	1955	Presumably Mark I *and* II?
T40	Brabham Cooper-Bristol F1	1955	Modified Bob-tail
T41	Mark I F2-Climax	1956	
T42	Marks X-XIII production 500s	1956–59	
T43	Mark II production F2-Climax	1957	

COOPER TYPE NUMBERS

T44	Cooper-BG-Bristol F1 special	1957	Built by Bob Gerard
T45	Mark III production F2-Climax	1958	
T46	Experimental F1 streamliner	1959	Unsuccessful one-off
T47	Cooper-Anzani 3-wheel road car	1958	Project shelved
T48	Bob-tail sports (2-off)	1958	For US customers
T49	Mark I Monaco sports car	1959	
T50	Cooper Dauphine	1959	Renault Dauphine saloon with Climax FWE engine conversion
T51	Mark IV production F1/F2	1959	Mark VI in 1960
T52	Mark I production Junior	1959	
T53	1960 Lowline works F1 cars	1960	
T53P	Production or Mark I 1500 F1	1961	
T54	Indianapolis one-off	1961	Built for Bill Kimberley
T55	Works slimline F1s	1961	
T56	Formula Junior Mark IIs	1961	
T57	Mark II Monaco sports car	1961	Coil-spring irs
T58	T55 with Climax V8 prototype	1961	
T59	Mark III Formula Juniors	1962	
T60	Works Climax V8 F1 'Mark II'	1962	
T61	Monaco Mark III	1962	
T61M	Monaco '63	1963	
T61P	Monaco-Maserati	1964	Built for Tommy Atkins
T62	Tasman Formula	1962–63	Ex-Atkins/McLaren Spl
T63	Mark IV Formula Junior prototype	1963	Or F1 cars that year!*
T64	Formula 1 prototype project	1963	with Hydrolastic suspension
T65	Formula Junior 'Mark IV'	1963	With Hydrolastic suspension, known as the 'Mark 3A'
T66	Formula 1	1963	
T67	Claimed as Mark 3A Junior	1963	According to some lists
T68	Monaco GT project	1963	Contrary to 'Register' entry shelved
T69	F1 monocoque prototype	1964	Register credits works and Gerard F1s as Type 69s
T70	Tasman Formula	1963–64	McLaren Racing team cars
T71	Formula 2 1-litre cars	1964	For Normand and Coombs
T72	Formula 3	1964	
T73	Formula 1	1964	In Register under 'Type 69'
T74	Interim 1964–65 F3 car	1964	Supposedly Tyrrell car
T75	Formula 2	1965	For BRM engine
T76	Formula 3	1965	
T77	Formula 1	1965	
T78	Monaco sports car	1965	Allegedly one built
T79	Tasman Formula	1964–65	One for McLaren
T80	Cooper-Maserati prototype hack	1965–66	
T81	Cooper-Maserati F1 monocoques	1966	
T81B	Cooper-Maserati lightweights	1967	
T82	Formula 2	1966	
T83	Formula 3	1966	
T84	Formula 2	1967	
T85	Formula 3	1967	
T86	Cooper-Maserati lowline F1	1967	
T86B	Cooper-BRM V12	1968	
T86C	Cooper-Alfa Romeo V8 F1 tub	1968	
T87	Hillclimb/Libre project	1968	Daimler V8 for M. Brain
T88	Formula C — 1-litre BRM 4-cyl.	1968	To Peter Rehl, USA
T89	Formula 3 project	1968	Not built
T90	Formula A/5000 prototypes	1969	
T91	Cooper-Cosworth V8 F1	1969	Never completed

*There are discrepancies between this well-known list and the surviving Chassis Register. The first 'T-number there is 'T63'-1963 Formula 1. 'T69' is listed as 1964 Formula 1 instead of 'T73' as here, though 'T71-72' both agree as do later nominations

APPENDIX FIVE

Cooper chassis records

Surviving factory records of cars built 1946-1969 are fragmentary and incomplete, but here we reproduce basic data from them, starting with the 1951 mark Vs.

MKV/1/51 – Cooper Car Co (Experimental) 500 cc.
MKV/2/51 – Cooper Car Co (Experimental) 500 cc – to Ken Carter.
MKV/3/51 – Cooper Car Co (Experimental) 500 cc – to Bill Whitehouse.
MKV/4/51 – Cooper Car Co (Festival of Britain) 500 cc – 'White cellulose, red wheels' deleted, green with green wheels substituted, 'red' upholstery altered to black.
MKV/5/51 – N. Prosser & Sons Ltd Order No. B208 30-10-50 – 500 cc JAP less engine – Belco 284 Nile Blue, red upholstery, wheels unpainted – Card issued 12-1-51.
MKV/6/51 – Mr Hobart (deleted) South Africa substituted* – 500 cc – Colour/upholstery originally 'As Alan Brown', changed to Sky Blue to pattern, to match. With spare engine.
This may have been first Cooper imported into South Africa for Tony & Doreen Fergusson, 1951.
MKV/7/51 – Alan Brown – 500 cc unpainted, blue upholstery, plated suspension – Card issued 12-1-51.
MKV/8/51 – Gerrard (sic) Cars Order No. 1767 13-11-51 (sic) – 500 cc Norton fittings – racing green, cream wheels, green upholstery, Norton gearbox, 2 spare front, 2 spare rear wheels – Card issued 12-1-51.
MKV/9/51 – C. D. Headland – 500 cc Norton – cream with red upholstery – Card issued 22-2-51.
MKV/10/51 – N. J. Gray – 500 cc JAP 4-stud alloy barrel – gun-metal grey with red upholstery – plus trailer – Card issued 9-4-51.
MKV/11/51 – A. Rippon – 500 cc JAP – unpainted, blue upholstery – Norton gearbox to be fitted, 'Paint name on side Alan Rippon as on Carter's car'.
MKV/12/51 – D. V. Annable – 500 cc JAP – ivory with red upholstery – Norton g'box, spare set Norton mountings.
MKV/13/51 – J. Blake & Co Ltd – 500 cc – unpainted with red, trailer – Card issued 12-1-51.
MKV/14/51 – J. Richmond (deleted) America substituted – 500 cc Norton – 'As A. Brown' deleted, red paintwork and upholstery substituted.
MKV/15/51 – E. Brandon – 500 cc Norton fittings – Card issued 12-1-51.
MKV/16/51 – D. N. Brake – 500 cc Norton & JAP fittings – black & white with white wheels, red upholstery & steering wheel, 'long-range tanks, racing tyres, more leg-room'.
MKV/17/51 – A. D. Gill (deleted) America substituted – 500 cc JAP – light green with beige upholstery, set Norton mountings, Norton g'box – Card issued 6-11-51.
MKV/18/51 – D. Wilcocks ordered 27-12-50 500 cc deleted, 1100 cc substituted, less engine JAP fittings for 1100 cc – racing green, beige upholstery & steering wheel.
MKV/19/51 – Ken Wharton 500 cc less engine, Norton & JAP mountings, supplied frame only 'to be supplied less tyres and tubes and shock absorbers. Sides of scuttle to be flared a little more than standard, seat to lean further back. Quoted £465.0.0 less cost of painting, tyres & tubes & shock absorbers' – card issued 12-1-51.
MKV/20/51 – Bill Aston deleted, Noverraz substituted – 500 cc JAP Mk 1 replacing original 1100 cc chassis order – red & white with red upholstery.
MKV/21/51 – Peter Braid 500 cc Norton fittings less engine & g'box – light green, green upholstery 'Two sets mountings Norton & JAP – chassis to be + 1 inch in width'.
MKV/22/51 – 'Gerrard Cars (Clarke)' (sic) – read Gerard Cars (David Clarke) less engine Norton gearbox, unpainted, upholstery dark blue on green. Norton & JAP engine mountings. Card issued 9-4-51.
MKV/23/51 – Italy, Leonardi tests – 500 cc JAP – red with red upholstery – Card issued 22-1-51.
MKV/24/51 – Italy, Turin Show – 500 cc JAP – red with red upholstery – Card issued 22-1-51.
MKV/25/51 – Italy deleted, Turin Show, America substituted – 500 cc JAP red with red upholstery – Card issued 6-11-51.
MKV/26/51 – Mr Ecclestone – 500 cc Norton fittings – polychromatic blue with red wheels, red upholstery.
MKV/L/2/51 – Mr Norton (Tom Norton?) – 1100 JAP – black with green upholstery, 'Extras – Long range tanks, Norton gear box, ZF diff, 2″ extra off foot pedals'.
MKV/L/1/51 – Montgomerie-Charrington (cars in this order in chassis book) – 1100 cc JAP – green 'to be sprayed

with Laqualex to be supplied', green upholstery.
MKV/27/51 – Sir Francis Samuelson – 500 JAP, racing green, green upholstery – Card issued 9-4-51.
MKV/28/51 – Johnny Brise – 500 JAP (deleted) Norton double k. substituted 'less engine' – lavender grey, red upholstery.
MKV/29/51 – J. Blake T. Leigh – 500 cc fittings for Norton & JAP – Olympia blue – to Oldham, Lancashire.
MKV/30/51 – 'Gerrard Gouldbourn Feb 1st 1951 Delivery 7 weeks 22-3-51 500 cc chassis only unpainted, red upholstery' many more spec details but whole order 'Cancelled'.
MKV/31/51 – Gerrard (Issard-Davies) (sic) – 500 cc JAP – racing green with silver wheels, green upholstery plus trailer, Norton g'boxes.
MKV/32/51 – Pearson – 500 JAP less engine – blue with red upholstery – Cancelled.
MKV/33/51 – Brandon – 1100 plus Norton 500 cc – unpainted, red upholstery.
MKV/L/3/51 – Harry Schell – 1100 cc JAP less engine – blue & white, red upholstery 'Extras – long-range tanks. ZF diff taken from old car'.
MKV/38/51 – Johnny Claes cancelled, substituted 'America' 500 JAP – original 'yellow with brown upholstery' deleted, grey with red upholstery substituted.
MKV/34/51 – America – 500 cc – red with red.
MKV/35/51 – America – 500 cc – Bugatti blue with blue.
MKV/36/51 – J. Blake – 500 cc 4-stud alloy barrel JAP – light blue with black, plus set Norton mountings.
MKV/37/51 – America – 500 JAP – dark blue with beige – Card issued 6-11-51.
MKV/39/51 – J. Blake – 500 cc less engine – white with red.
MKV/40/51 – N. J. Gray – 500 cc JAP 4-stud – Gun-metal grey with red plus Norton gearbox, trailer.
MKV/30/51 – Trident Motors – 500 cc 'with engine' – green with natural upholstery – extras 'long range tanks, trailer with 500 × 15 wheels, car to be fitted with 400 × 15 wheels all round . . .'.

MKV/41/51 – John Crouch (Australian agent) – 500 cc 'with engine' – racing green on green.
MKV/4/51 – (sic) – John Crouch – 1100 cc – unpainted with black, set Norton 500 cc mountings and exhausts.
MKV/L/5/51 – John Crouch – 1100 cc – irridescent bronze with red.
MKV/42/51 – Commander Eyre – 500 cc – BRG with red, Norton g'box.
MKV/43/51 – Commander Eyre – 1100 cc JAP with 500 mountings also – BRG with red – 'Deliver to Mr K. Bains, J. Burns & Co., Chadwell Heath, Essex'.
MKV/44/51 – D. J. Wheeler, Cheam Surrey deleted, 'Finland' substituted – 500 cc JAP – BRG deleted, black with red wheels, red upholstery substituted.
MKV/45/51 – John Crouch – 500 cc – powder blue with blue.
MKV/L/6/51 – John Crouch – 1100 cc maroon with red.
MKV/L/7/51 – John Crouch – 1100 cc – colour 'Reckitts blue, upholstery to match' deleted, ivory with blue upholstery substituted.
MKV/46/51 – Symmonds (sic) – 500 cc less engine – BRG with green.
MKV/47/51 – John Crouch – 500 cc less engine, g'box & Body.
MKV/48/51 – Don Truman deleted, 'Finland' substituted – 500 cc less engine, dark blue with beige deleted, blue with blue wheels and red upholstery substituted.
MKV/49/51 – Kenani – 500 JAP – pale blue with pale blue, Norton g'box & engine mountings.
MKV/L/8/51 – Shelly New Zealand – 1100 cc – light metallic blue with beige upholstery, engine mountings also for 500 JAP.
MKV/50/51 – America – 500 JAP – light metallic blue with beige.
MKV/51/51 – America – 500 JAP – red with red.
MKV/52/51 – America – 500 JAP – black with beige.

From 1957 the surviving chassis register includes in essence the following entries . . .

500 cc Racing Cars 1957

28-12-56	Stephen Foreman	UK	MK XI-1-57
5-2-57	Joe Lubin, Los Angeles	USA	MK XI-2-57
14-2-57	H. S. Howlett	UK	MK XI-3-57
—	I. E. Raby	UK	MK XI-4-57
—	Kurt Lincoln	Finland	MK XI-5-57
—	Bremner	Finland	MK XI-6-57
18-3-57	E. Populidx	USA	MK XI-7-57
19-3-57	Ellis	UK	MK XI-8-57
29-3-57	D. Wagner	UK	MK XI-9-57
8-4-57	LER (?)	UK	MK XI-10-57
—	Biron H. Rogers	USA	MK XI-11-57

12-4-57	Don Parker	UK	MK XI-12-57
20-5-57	D. R. H. Keith	USA	MK XI-13-57
—	J. P. Cavill (?)	UK	MK XI-14-57
14-8-57	A. Zains	UK	MK XI-15-57
	Peter Glass (Brackenbury)	—	MK XI-16-57
—	A. J. Barrett	—	MK XI-17-57
October	J. Lubin	USA	MK XI-18-57* *Less engine
December	J. Lubin	USA	MK XI-19-57

1500 cc Racing Cars 1957

	Raymond Thackwell	NZ	F2-1-57 – FWA/400/6/6812*
	Ronald Moore	NZ	F2-2-57 – FWA/400/6/6833
	Works (experimental)	—	F2-3-57 – 'Roy' – FPF/430/3/1001
	Works (Aust.)	—	F2-P-56 – FWB/8/6624
	Works	—	F2-4-57 – 'School' – FWA/6/6876*
	Works	—	F2-5-57 – 'School' – FWA/6/6827*
July	George Wickens	—	F2-6-57 – less engine
	Works Roy	—	F2-8-57 – FPF/430/3/1004
	Works Jack	—	F2-9-57 – FPF/430/3/1003
	Works car 1100 engine	—	F2-10-57 – 'School' – FWA/400/6/6832
May	Tony Marsh	—	F2-11-57 – FPF/430/3/1008
	Rob Walker	—	F2-12-57 – FPF 2 litre 1011
May	Nixon	—	F2-13-57 – less engine
May	W. Whitehouse	—	F2-14-57 – FPF/430/3/1013
June	Revenlow (?)	—	F2-15-57 – FWB/400/6/7051
June	Leston	—	F2-16-57 – FPF/430/3/1014
May (sic)	Ronnie Moore	NZ	F2-17-57 – FWB/400/8/7050
May	Ray Thackwell	NZ	F2-18-57 – FWB/400/8/6630
June	R. Stoop	GB	F2-19-57 – FWE/400/6/6919
	Mr R. Gibson	—	F2-20-57 – FPF/430/3/1022
June	Bob Gerard	GB	F2-21-57 –
June	Alan Brown	GB	F2-22-57 – FPF/430/3/1021
July	R. R. Walker	GB	F2-7-57 – FPF/430/3/1023
July	Brian Naylor	GB	F2-23-57 – FPF/430/3/1025
	T. Sopwith	UK	F2-24-57 – FPF/430/3/1026
August	J. D. Lewis	UK	F2-25-57 – FPF/430/3/1018
August	C. T. Atkins	UK	F2-26-57 – FPF/430/3/1034
September	Joe Lubin	USA	F2-27-57 – FPF/430/3/1029
	A. G. Mildren	Australia	F2-28-57 – FPF/430/3/1036
October	R. Gibson (Prideaux)	UK	F2-29-57 – FPF 1038 (sic)
December	WORKS CAR No. 1	UK	F2-30-57 ⎱ Transferred to
December	WORKS CAR No. 2	UK	F2-31-57 ⎰ 1958 list

*Climax engine numbers show basic type, then third section serial reveals spec. of engine fittings, eg. F2 single-seater or sports with dynamo, etc. Final four-digit number is individual unit serial

Sports Cars 1957

12-2-57	Woodward	USA	CS11-1-57 – FWA/678?1
28-11-57	Lance Reventlow	USA	CS15-1-57 – FPF430/3/1037

1958 500 cc Formula III Racing Cars

31-3-58	R. Taylor	UK	MK XII-1-58 – "Mr Beart supplying engine"
	R. Nelleman	Denmark	MK XII-2-58 – 64027

K. Lincoln	Finland	MK XII-3-58 – "Mr Beart supplying engine No. 358"
Barnet	UK	MK XII-4-58 – less engine
Basse (*sic*) Hveem	Norway	MK XII-5-58 – less engine
Jack Fernandez	Venezuela	MK XII-6-58 – "Norton 100 stroke featherbed No. 43558"

1958 1100 cc Sports Car
Pages blank

1958 1500 cc Formula II

N. Barclay	UK	F2-1-58 – FPF/430/30/1070/(*sic*)
A. Brown	UK	F2-2-58 – FPF/430/3/1044
T. Marsh	UK	F2-3-58 – FPF/430/3/1043
G. Nixon	UK	F2-4-58 – FPF'1059
WORKS CAR No. 1	UK	F2-5-58 – FPF'1050 (1046)
A. Mackay	UK	F2-6-58 – FPF'1056
R. Parnell	UK	F2-7-58 – FPF'1049
J. Russell	UK	F2-8-58 – FPF'1048
R. Walker	UK	F2-9-58 – FPF'1060
K. Gregory	UK	F2-10-58 – FPF'1041
J. B. Naylor	UK	F2-14-58 – FPF'1075
L. Monteiro	Portugal	F2-15-58 – "Order cancelled"
C. T. Atkins	UK	F2-15-58 – FPF'1065
J. R. Stoop	UK	F2-11-58 – FPF'1061
L. F. Lulu	UK	F2-16-58 – FPF'1066
Alan Brown	UK	F2-17-58 – less engine
A. Guelfi	France	F2-18-58 – FPF'1073
H. Zweifel	Switzerland	F2-19-58 – FPF'1074
M. Neil	New Zealand	F2-20-58 – FPF'1028
A. Mildren	Australia	F2-21-58 – Less engine
B. McLaren	—	F2-12-58 – FPF'1057
S. Jensen	—	F2-13-58 – FPF'1058
J. Brabham	—	F2-22-58 –
WORKS CAR No. 1	—	F2-23A-58 – FPF'1082 2.2*
J. R. Lewis	—	F2-23-58 – FPF'1087

*This entry includes additional notes "Sold Fred Tuck 11-5-61" apparently with engine No. "FPF/430/17/1152"

1959 Model 500 cc Mark XIII Formula III

11-2-59	Jack Fernandez	Venezuela	MK XIII/1/59 – FLB 592 Norton
—	Jack Fernandez	Venezuela	MK XIII/2/59 – FLB 593 Norton
6-7-59	M. R. Sharp III (A. Dupont Jr)	USA	MK XIII/4/59 – FLB 59.82 Norton
24-7-59	Don Parker	UK	MK XIII/3/59 – less engine

1959 Model 1500 cc and 2-litre Sports "Cooper-Monaco"

January 15	Kurt Lincoln	Finland	CM/1/59 – FPF/430/15/1104
February 26	Hermanda (*sic*) da Silva Ramos	France	CM/2/59 – FPF/430/6/1095 (prototype)
April 7	W. S. Bowman	USA	CM/3/59 – FPF/430/15/1136
—	Jack Brabham	Australia	CM/4/59 – less engine
May	Signor Dei (BP Trading)	Italy	CM/5/59 – less engine
June	H. Blanchard	USA	CM/6/59 – FPF/430/15/1137
September	J. R. Sharp	USA	CM/7/59 – less engine
September	N. J. Hartman	USA	CM/8/59 – FPF/430/5/1126

1959 Model 1500 cc Mark IV Formula II

Date	Customer	Country	Chassis
7-1-59	G. Nixon	UK	F2/3/59 – FPF'1085
	WORKS CAR No. 2	UK	F2/4/59 – FPF'1061 (?)
	BRP	UK	F2/1/59 – Borgward 30009
	BRP	UK	F2/2/59 – Borgward 30005
	A. Owen	UK	F2/6/59 – FPF/430/14/1133
	WORKS CAR No. 3	UK	F2/7/59 – FPF/430/17/1139 2.5
	J. R. T. Gibson-Jarvie	UK	F2/8/59 – FPF'1098
	R. Taylor	UK	F2/5/59 – FPF'1096
April 22	Pierre Stasse	Belgium	F2/9/59 – FPF'1100
	Pierre Stasse	Belgium	F2/10/59 – FPF'1111
April 23	K. Twisk	UK	F2/11/59 – FPF'1099
May	Signor Dei (BP Trading)	Italy	FII/12/59 – less engine
	Signor Dei (BP Trading)	Italy	FII/13/59 – less engine
June	B. Patterson	Australia	FII/15/59 – less engine
	R. Hall	Australia	FII/16/59 – less engine
July	Harry Schell	France	FII/17/59 – FPF'1101
	Norman Hamilton	Australia	FII/18/59 – FPF'1083
August	Victa Consolidated Industries Ltd	Australia	FII/14/59 – FPF/430/14/114
	R. R. C. Walker	UK	FII/19/59 – less engine
August	Stan Jones	Australia*	FII/20/59 – FPF'1061
August	Mario Cabral	Portugal**	FII/21/59 – FPF'1112
October	A. Mildren	Australia	F2/22/59 – less engine
October	F. Tuck (H. Gould)	UK	FII/23/59 – less engine
October	Yeoman Credit Ltd	UK	FII/24/59 – less engine
October	Yeoman Credit Ltd	UK	FII/25/59 – less engine
October	Yeoman Credit Ltd	UK	FII/26/59 – less engine
October	WORKS CAR No. 4	UK	FII/27/59 – less engine
October	SA Power Tool & Equipment Co	S. Africa	FII/28/59 – FPF'1118

*Additional note "Transferred R. Stilwell Australia"
**Additional note "Consigned to Switzerland 23-4-60"

Formula Junior 1960 Mark I

Date	Customer	Country	Chassis
February 16	A. H. Beels	Holland	FJ/1/60 – less engine/g'box
February 26	K. Ahrens	Germany	FJ/2/60 – less engine
March 12	Briggs Cunningham	USA	FJ/3/60 – BMC XSP-581/6
April 20	G. (?) Lincoln	Sweden	FJ/4/60 – BMC XSP-1462/2
April 8	Carrol. Smith	USA	FJ/5/60 – BMC XSP 1462/3
May	Hubert Patthey	Switzerland	FJ/6/60 – BMC XSP1462/8
—	Andre Liekens	Belgium	FJ/7/60 – BMC XSP1462/10
June	L. G. Arnold	USA	FJ/8/60 – BMC XSP1462/15
July	J. R. Sharp	USA	FJ/9/60 – less engine
August	J. Nordell	Sweden	FJ/10/60 – BMC XSP.1462/18
August	T. P. Waring	USA	FJ/11/60 – BMC XSP1462/20
August	Briggs Cunningham	USA	FJ/12/60 – BMC XSP1462/22
September	J. R. Sharp	USA	FJ/13/60 – BMC XSP1462/24
SI (sic)	A. O. Stearns	USA	FJ/14/60 – BMC XSP1462/21
October	J. R. Sharp	USA	FJ/15/60 – BMC XSP1462/26
—	E. Agostini	Italy*	FJ/16/60 – less engine
November	Briggs Cunningham	USA	FJ/17/60 – BMC XSP1462/28

*Additional note "(Tempy held up. Prob dismantled)"

COOPER CHASSIS RECORDS

1960 Formula II Racing Car Mark VI

January	J. R. Pringle	UK	FII/1/60 – FPF/430/1011 2.0
March 2	G. Scarlatti	Italy	FII/2/60 – less engine/g'box
April 1	ENB	Belgium	FII/3/60 – FPF'1131
	John Surtees	UK	FII/4/60 – FPF'1159
	WORKS CAR No. 1	UK	FII/5/60 – FPF'1171
May	Ian Burgess	UK	FII/6/60 – less engine/g'box
	Stan Jones	Australia	FII/7/60 – FPF'1082
	J. Adda	Switzerland	FII/11/60 – FPF'1116
June	C. de Beaufort	Holland	FII/10/60 – FPF/430/17/1117
	Claudio Corini	Italy	FII/13/60 – less engine/g'box
	WORKS CAR No. 2	UK	FII/8/60 – FPF/430/17/1176
	J. Youl	Tasmania	FII/9/60 – FPF/430/1063
July	F. Armbruster	USA	FII/14/60 – less engine/g'box
	D. McAlister	N. Ireland	FII/15/60 – FPF'1120
October	All-Purposes Appliances Corp.	S. Africa	FII/16/60 – less engine/g'box
	WORKS CAR No. 3	UK	FII/12/60 – FPF/430/17/1184*
	Jack Brabham	UK	FII/17/60 – less engine

*Additional note "Sold J. R. Sharp USA May 1961 at Indianapolis" Chassis '5, '8 and '12 were works Lowline models for Formula 1.

1960 Sports Cooper-Monaco Mark II

March 7	Dr H. Zweifel	Switzerland	CM/1/60 – FPF/430/15/1170
September	R. P. Hogue	USA	CM/2/60 – less engine*

*Additional note "ZF fitted in gearbox No. 83"

1961 Formula I Cooper-Climax Mark I 5-speed gearbox

February	Yeoman Credit	UK	FI/1/61 – FPF/430/28/1202
	Yeoman Credit	UK	FI/2/61 – FPF/430/27/1213
	Camoradi International	UK	FI/3/61 – FPF/430/3/1122
	Yeoman Credit	UK	FI/4/61 – No entry
	J. R. C. Lewis	UK	FI/6/61 – No entry
	R. R. C. Walker	UK	FI/7/61 – FPF/430/28/1193
	R. Bartram	UK	FI/8/61 – No entry
April	B. Collomb	France	FI/9/61 – FPF/430/26/1189
	WORKS CAR No. 1	UK	FI/10/61 – FPF/430/27/1212
	WORKS CAR No. 2	UK	FI/11/61 – FPF/430/27/1210
	WORKS CAR No. 3	UK	FI/12/61 – ET/892/1205
May	BP Trading (Centro-Sud)	Italy	FI/13/61 – less engine/'box
July	B. S. Stilwell	Australia	FI/5/61 – FPF/430/17/1153
August	R. Penske	USA	FI/14/61 – FPF/430/17/1171
September	Momo Corporation	USA	FI/16/61 – less engine
	J. R. Sharp	USA	FI/15/61 – less engine
	WORKS CAR No. 4	UK	FI/17/61 – no entry*
	WORKS CAR No. 5	UK	F1/18/61 – no entry*
December	Okura Trading Co.	Japan	FI/19/61 – FPF/430/27/1237

*1962 works team V8 cars completed in the new year

1961 Formula Junior Mark II

January 6	J. R. Sharp	USA	FJ/1/61 – BMC XSP1462/27
January 17	Adolf Kern	Austria	FJ/2/61 – less engine/g'box
January 30	Kurt Ahrens	Germany	FJ/3/61 – less engine/g'box
February 15	C. D. Thomson	Detroit, USA	FJ/4/61 – BMC XSP 1462/23
March 13	J. F. Harrison	USA	FJ/8/61 – BMC XSP1434/4

March 16	Fred Work	USA	FJ/9/61 – Ford 105E 6015
March 18	Momo Corporation	USA	FJ/5/61 – BMC XSP 1717-1
March 18	Momo Corporation	USA	FJ/10/61 – BMC XSP 1717-2
April 4	Kurt Bardi-Barry, Ecurie Vienne	Austria	FJ/6/61 – Ford 105E-3611
April 8	Rolf Markl, Ecurie Vienne	Austria	FJ/7/61 – Ford 105E-3612
April 27	Curt Lincoln	Finland	FJ/11/61 – BMC XSP 1717-7
May	E. E. Mayer	USA	FJ/12/61 – BMC XSP 1717-11
June	J. Peterson	USA	FJ/13/61 – less engine
July	Kurt Ahrens	Germany	FJ/14/61 – less engine
	Momo Corporation	USA	FJ/15/61 – BMC XSP 1717-17
	Momo Corporation	USA	FJ/16/61 – BMC XSP 1717-18
	A. Liekens	Belgium	FJ/17/61 – less engine
August	J. R. Sharp	USA	FJ/18/61 – BMC XSP 1717-21
	Momo Corporation	USA	FJ/19/61 – BMC XSP 1717-19
September	R. Bouharde	France	FJ/21/61 – BMC XSP 1722-6
	J. R. Sharp	USA	FJ/20/61 – BMC XSP 1717-15
September	Momo Corporation	USA	FJ/22/61 – BMC XSP 1801-2 1100 cc

1961 Cooper-Monaco Sports Mark III

June 20	J. R. Sharp	USA	CM/1/61 – less engine, fitted 5sp g'box No. 20
August 8	R. Penske	USA	CM/2/61 – less engine/g'box
September	Peter Berry	UK	CM/3/61 – less engine

1962 Cooper-Monaco Sports Mark IV

January	Briggs Cunningham	USA	CM/1/62 – less engine
April	Van Housen Motors	USA	CM/2/62 – FPF/430/17/1235
May	Alan Connell	USA	CM/3/62 – FPF/430/17/1236
October	Roger Penske	USA	CM/4/62 – FPF/430/17/1254
November	J. Hinkle	USA*	CM/5/62 – FPF/430/17/1260

*This was prototype 1963 Monaco T61M

1962 Formula Junior Mark III

February	Kurt Ahrens	Germany	FJ/1/62 – less engine
	Steve McQueen	USA	FJ/2/62 – BMC XSP 1722-4
	Bob McLean	Canada	FJ/3/62 – BMC XSP 1809/3
March	J. R. Sharp	USA	FJ/4/62 – less engine
	Briggs Cunningham	USA	FJ/5/62 – BMC XSP 1854-2
February	Kurt Bardi-Barry	Austria	FJ/6/62 – less engine
March	Edward Mayer	USA	FJ/7/62 – BMC XSP 1854-3
April	Edward Mayer	USA	FJ/8/62 – BMC XSP 1854-4
	Curt Lincoln	Finland	FJ/9/62 – less engine
	Kurt Ahrens	Germany	FJ/10/62 – less engine
	Kuderli & Co	Switzerland	FJ/11/62 – BMC XSP 1854-5
	Kuderli & Co	Switzerland	FJ/12/62 – BMC XSP 1854-9
	Kuderli & Co	Switzerland	FJ/13/62 – BMC XSP 1854-10
	Roland Boddie	Switzerland	FJ/14/62 – BMC XSP 1854-8
	Yngve Rosquist	Sweden	FJ/15/62 – BMC XSP 1854-6
	Fibs (sic) Meub	Germany	FJ/16/62 – Cosworth 462490
May	E. McKinney	N. Ireland	FJ/17/62 – BMC XSP 1854-11
	H. Norrmann	Sweden	FJ/18/62 – less engine
	H. Patthey	Switzerland	FJ/19/62 – BMC XSP 1854-15
	D. Riley	S. Rhodesia	FJ/20/62 – BMC XSP 1854-18
May	D. Harrison	UK	FJ/21/62 – BMC XSP 1854-24

COOPER CHASSIS RECORDS

June	H. Patthey	Switzerland	FJ/22/62 – BMC XSP 1854-17
	BMC	Sweden	FJ/23/62 – BMC XSP 1854-27
August	S. Dietrich	USA	FJ/24/62 – BMC XSP 1854-20
	Scuderia Venezia	Italy	FJ/25/62 – Ford Holbay 11-62-69
	E. Mayer	USA	FJ/27/62 – BMC XSP 1854-31
	Crichton-Stuart	UK	FJ/26/62 – Ford Cosworth 462615
December	David Cole	UK	FJ/28/62 – BMC XSP 1854-25

1963 Formula I Type 63 (sic)

January	J. R. Pringle	N. Ireland	FI/1/63 – FPF/430/17/1173*
May	R. R. C. Walker	UK	FI/2/63 – FWMV/499-15
July**	WORKS CAR No. 1	UK	FI/3/63 – FWMV/499-6
May	WORKS CAR No. 2	UK	FI/4/63 – FWMV/499/6 (sic)
May	WORKS CAR No. 3	UK	FI/5/63 – FWMV/499/4
July	WORKS CAR No. 4	UK	FI/6/63 – FWMV/499/21

*Additional note "Engine and gearbox supplied by customer"
**Note late origination date for works cars, in fact they emerged much earlier in the season.

1963 Sports "Monaco" Type 61M

February	Carroll Shelby	USA	CM/1/63 – less engine/g'box
	W. Mitchell	USA	CM/2/63 – less engine/g'box
April	Carroll Shelby	USA	CM/3/63 – less engine/g'box
	Jack Ensley	USA	CM/4/63 – less engine/g'box
December	Carroll Shelby	USA	CM/5/63 – less engine/g'box & radiator
	Carroll Shelby	USA	CM/6/63 – less engine/g'box & radiator

1963 Formula Junior Mark IV Type 65

May	R. Wheelan	USA	FJ/1/63 – XSP 20361
May	Kurt Ahrens	Germany	FJ/2/63 – less engine
May	A. Liekens	Belgium	FJ/4/63 – less engine
April	J. Francks	Belgium	FJ/5/63 – less engine
April	Curt Bardi-Barry	Austria	FJ/6/63 – less engine
	D. Revson	USA	FJ/7/63 – XSP 1854-21
	P. Revson	USA	FJ/8/63 – Holbay 5B-116292
	I. Rosqvist (sic)	Sweden	FJ/9/63 – Holbay 5B-116278
May	Mr. Dernier	Belgium	FJ/10/63 – Holbay 5B-116399
	Ed Hugus	USA	FJ/11/63 – BMC XSP 20362
June	H. Patthey	Switzerland	FJ/3/63 – Holbay 5B-1163102
July	C. Crichton-Stuart	UK	FJ/12/63 – Cosworth 109E 6015
November	M. J. Hawley	UK	FJ/13/63 – BMC XSP 20363
January '64	J. Ewer	UK	FJ/14/63 – BMC XSP 1722-20
	T. Shatwell	UK	FJ/15/63 – less engine

1963 Formula Libre (sic)

October	Bruce McLaren	UK	FL/1/64 – less engine/g'box
October	E. Mayer	UK	FL/2/64 – less engine/g'box

1964 Formula I Type 69 (sic)

March	Gerard Racing	UK	FI/3/64 – less engine
April	WORKS CAR No. 1	UK	FI/1/64 – FWMV/499 - 4
	WORKS CAR No. 2	UK	FI/2/64 – FWMV/499-5

1964 Formula II Type 71

March	Normand Ltd	UK	FII/1/64 – less engine
March	Normand Ltd	UK	FII/2/64 – less engine
May	John Coombs	UK	FII/3/64 – less engine

1964 Formula III Type 72

March	D. Richomond	UK	FIII/1/64 – less engine
	K. Ballisat	UK	FIII/2/64 – XSP 22243
	J. Bernusset	Belgium	FIII/3/64 – XSP 22244
April	Pierre Ryser	Switzerland	FIII/6/64 – XSP 22245*
	J-C Frank	Belgium	FIII/7/64 – XSP 22247
	Leo Matilla	Finland	FIII/8/64 – XSP 22249
	P. Revson	UK	FIII/9/64 – XSP 222410
May	P. Swaelens	Belgium	FIII/10/64 – XSP 222412
	Bernard Baur	Switzerland	FIII/12/64 – XSP 222411
	Leo Cella	Italy	FIII/11/64 – XSP 222415
	A. Fletcher	UK	FIII/13/64 – less engine
June	E. Offenstadt	France	FIII/14/64 – XSP 222417
	H. Jackson	UK	FIII/15/64 – XSP 222418
	W. Trevor	UK	FIII/16/64 – XSP 222420
July	Andre Periat (?)	Switzerland	FIII/17/64 – XSP 222419
	J. Jaussaud	France	FIII/18/64 – XSP 222421
	M. Buis	France	FIII/19/64 – XSP 222423
October	Shingo Shiozawa	Japan	FIII/20/64 – XSP 222426

*See below separate entry for chassis 'IV and 'V

1964 Sports "Monaco" Type 61(M)

February	Carroll Shelby	USA	CM/1/64 – less engine/g'box
March	John Mecom	USA	CM/2/64 – less engine/g'box
	Jack Brewer	USA	CM/3/64 – less engine/g'box
June	Shelby American	USA	CM/4/64 – less engine/g'box
July	Shelby American	USA	CM/5/64 – less engine/g'box
August	Shelby American	USA	CM/6/64 – less engine/g'box

1964 Formula Libre Type 79? (sic)

October	Bruce McLaren	UK	FL/1/64 – less engine, gearbox, halfshafts, exhaust pipes

1964 Formula III Type 72

December	W. Denton	UK	FIII/4/64 – XSP 222436*
	W. Dulles	UK	FIII/5/64 – XSP 222437*

*Special note "Ex Tyrrell's cars"

1965 Formula I Type 77

March	WORKS CAR No. 1	UK	FI/1/65 – FWMV/499/21
	WORKS CAR No. 2	UK	FI/2/65 – FWMV/499/6

1965 Formula II Type 75

January	WORKS CAR No. 1	UK	FII/1/65 – XSP 222442
February 2	Alf Francis	UK	FII/2/65 – less engine/g'box
February 2	Alf Francis	UK	FII/3/65 – less engine/g'box
February 16	K. Tyrrell	UK	FII/4/65 – BRM
February 16	K. Tyrrell	UK	FII/5/65 – BRM
April	WORKS CAR No. 2	UK	FII/6/65 – XSP 222442
April 13	E. Offenstadt	France	FII/7/65 – BRM 8003
August 27	WORKS CAR No. 3	UK	FII/8/65 – less engine

COOPER CHASSIS RECORDS

1965 Formula III Type 76

15-12-64	D. Headley	UK	FIII/3/65 – XSP 222431
31-12-64	Pierre Ryser	Switzerland	FIII/4/65 – XSP 222432
Jan/Feb	Works car (deleted) B. J. Hough	UK	FIII/2/65 – XSP 222435
February 13	Steve Matchett	UK	FIII/6/65 – XSP 222441
February 16	K. Tyrrell	UK	FIII/1/65 – less engine
April 5	Y. Rosqvist	Sweden	FIII/5/67 – XSP 222434
April 22	J. Brindley	UK	FIII/7/65 – XSP 222439
March 12	W. Knight	UK	FIII/8/65 – Cosworth Ford 105E
March 15	L. Matilla	Finland	FIII/9/65 – Cosworth MAE 650319
March 25	H. Norrman	Sweden	FIII/10/65 – less engine/g'box
March 25	H. Norrman	Sweden	FIII/11/65 – less engine/g'box
March 27	P. Swaelens	Belgium	FIII/12/65 – less engine/g'box
April 29	Viscount Fielding	UK	FIII/14/65 – less engine
May 5	J. Vernaeve	Belgium	FIII/15/65 – less engine
June 4	R. Banting	UK	FIII/16/65 – less engine
May 21	Y. Rosqvist	Sweden	FIII/17/65 – Cosworth 650420
June 10	J. Fenning	UK	FIII/18/65 – less engine
June 23	S. Keinanen	Finland	FIII/19/65 – less engine
September 10	G. R. Crossman	UK	FIII/20/65 – Cosworth/Ford No. 650803

1966 Formula I Type 81

January	WORKS CAR No. 1	UK	FI/1/66 – Maserati 9001
January 12	WORKS CAR No. 1	UK	FI/3/66 – less engine
April 21	Scuderia Felipe Pemeti (*sic**)	Switzerland	FI/4/66 – Maserati 9005
April 15	Rob Walker	UK	FI/2/66 – Maserati 9006
May 2	J. Bonnier	Switzerland	FI/5/66 – Maserati 9007
May 12	WORKS CAR	UK	FI/6/66 – Maserati 9008
June 27	WORKS CAR	UK	FI/7/66 – Maserati 9010

*The Swiss Scuderia Filipinetti!

1966 Formula II Type 82

March 28	Bob Gerard	UK	FII/1/66 – Cosworth MAE 40407
	WORKS CAR	UK	FII/2/66 – less engine

1966 Formula III Type 83

March 7	Clive Baker	UK	FIII/1/66 – MAE 650170
	WORKS CAR No. 1	UK	FIII/2/66 – less engine/g'box
April 27	Paul Swaelens	Belgium	FIII/3/66 – MAE 66050
April 23	Len Selby	UK	FIII/4/66 – MAE 66065
May 11 (?)	J. Kendall	UK	FIII/5/66 – MAE 66090
May 17	Pierre Ryser	Switzerland	FIII/6/66 – MAE 66103
June 17	J. M. McKechnie	UK	FIII/7/66 – MAE 66123

1967 Formula I Type 81B

January	WORKS CAR No. 1	UK	FI-1-67 – no entry

1967 Formula II Type 84
No entries

1967 Formula III Type 85

January	WORKS CAR No. 1	UK	F3-1-67 – MAE 66175
April	E. A. Coates Ltd	UK	F3-2-67 – MAE 67206

No further entries . . .

APPENDIX SIX

Racing records

FRONT-ENGINED COOPER F1/F2 1952–57
Of all Cooper products those with the greatest historic racing interest today are the Cooper-Bristol/Cooper-Alta series cars built during 1952–53, and subsequently campaigned at significant level to the end of 1957. Here those significant events are listed, with date, event, race number, driver, chassis and result details. PP = Pole position; FR = Front row qualification; FL = Fastest lap; DNS = Did not start; DNQ = Did not qualify; UNC = Unclassified, too far behind winning car to be placed officially. Data in this whole record has been compiled with immense assistance from the Formula 1 Register run by Dr Paul Sheldon and Duncan Rabagliati

Date	Event	Race No.	Driver	Chassis	Result
1952					
14-4-52	Lavant Cup, Goodwood	4	Eric Brandon	CB/3/52	3rd
		10	Alan Brown	CB/2/52	2nd
		41	Mike Hawthorn	CB/4/52	FIRST FL
		46	John Cooper	CB/1/52	DNS
19-4-52	Ibsley F2	122	Mike Hawthorn	4/52	FIRST FL
10-5-52	International Trophy, Silverstone, *Heat 1*	11	Mike Hawthorn	4/52	FIRST = FL
	Heat 2	12	Alan Brown	2/52	6th
		14	Reg Parnell	1/52	Rtd
	Final		Hawthorn		UNC, = FL
			Brown		UNC
18-5-52	SWISS GP, Berne	24	Eric Brandon	3/52	8th
		26	Alan Brown	2/52	5th
8-6-52	Monza Autodrome GP	—	Eric Brandon	3/52	10th
		—	Alan Brown	2/52	13th
21-6-52	Boreham F2	18	Reg Parnell	1/52	FIRST, FL
22-6-52	BELGIAN GP, Spa	8	Mike Hawthorn	4/52	*4th*
		10	Alan Brown	2/52	6th
		12	Eric Brandon	3/52	9th
29-6-52	Marne GP, Reims	32	Alan Brown	2/52	Rtd*
		34	Eric Brandon	3/52	UNC '11th'*
	*Brown took over Brandon's car	42	Mike Hawthorn	1/52	7th
6-7-52	FRENCH GP, Rouen	42	Mike Hawthorn	1/52	Rtd
19-7-52	BRITISH GP, Silverstone	7	David Murray	CB/6/52	Rtd
		8	Reg Parnell	CB/1/52	7th
		9	Mike Hawthorn	4/52	3rd
		10	Eric Brandon	3/52	20th
		11	Alan Brown	2/52	UNC '23rd'
10-8-52	Cummings GP	38	Archie Bryde	1/52	Rtd
17-8-52	DUTCH GP, Zandvoort	32	Mike Hawthorn	4/52	*4th*

RACING RECORDS

Date	Event	Race No.	Driver	Chassis	Result
23-8-52	National Trophy, Turnberry	29	Andre Loens	CB/5/52	Rtd
		40	Ninian Sanderson	6/52	3rd
		41	John Barber	CB/7/52	2nd
24-8-52	La Baule GP	34	Eric Brandon	3/52	UNC '9th'
		36	Alan Brown	2/52	UNC '10th'
31-8-52	Grenzlandring F2	—	Eric Brandon	3/52	Rtd
		—	Alan Brown	2/52	Rtd
7-9-52	ITALIAN GP, Monza	36	Eric Brandon	3/52	13th
		38	Alan Brown	2/52	UNC '15th'
		40	Ken Wharton	6/52	9th
		42	Mike Hawthorn	4/52	UNC '19th'
14-9-52	Modena GP	28	Roy Salvadori	4/52	DNS*
	*After Hawthorn's testing crash in this car				
27-9-52	Madgwick Cup, Goodwood	14	Mike Hawthorn	4/52	DNS
		15	Eric Brandon	3/52	Rtd
		16	Alan Brown	2/52	3rd
		23	John Barber	7/52	8th
		31	Ninian Sanderson	6/52	6th
4-10-52	Joe Fry Trophy, Castle Combe	49	Eric Brandon	3/52	Rtd
		50	Alan Brown	2/52	4th
		58	Archie Bryde	1/52	Crash
		63	Ninian Sanderson	6/52	3rd
11-10-52	Newcastle Journal Trophy, Charterhall	20	Mike Hawthorn	4/52	DNS
		32	Andre Loens	5/52	5th
		34	John Barber	7/52	?
		35	Archie Bryde	1/52	?
		38	Ninian Sanderson	6/52	6th
		85	Eric Brandon	3/52	Rtd
		87	Ken Wharton	4/52	Rtd
		91	Alan Brown	2/52	Rtd

1953

Date	Event	Race No.	Driver	Chassis	Result
18-1-53	ARGENTINE GP, Buenos Aires	20	Alan Brown	2/52	9th
		22	John Barber	CBMk2/1/53	8th
		24	Adolfo Schwelm	5/52	Rtd
22-3-53	Syracuse GP, Sicily	6	Peter Whitehead	T24-Alta	5th
		10	Tom Cole	T23-Bristol	Crash
		14	Eric Brandon	'3/52	4th
		16	Rodney Nuckey	T23-Bristol	3rd
6-4-53	Lavant Cup, Goodwood	6	Stirling Moss	Alta Spl	7th
		9	Paul Emery	T23-Alfa Romeo	15th
		15	Peter Whitehead	T24-Alta	5th
		16	Bob Gerard	T23-Bristol	8th
		28	Eric Brandon	'3/52	Rtd
		30	Ken Wharton	T23-Bristol	6th
		35	Jimmy Stewart	'6/52	12th
		37	Archie Bryde	'1/52	Rtd
		41	Jeff Sparrowe	'5/52	13th
18-4-53	Snetterton F2	2	Bob Gerard	T23-Bristol	2nd
		5	Peter Whitehead	T24-Alta	3rd
		9	Joe Kelly	'Cooper-Bristol'	DNA

COOPER CARS

Date	Event		Race No.	Driver	Chassis	Result
			19	Berwyn Baxter	'Cooper-Bristol'	DNA
			21	Tony Crook	'Cooper-Bristol'	DNA
			102	Ken Wharton	T23-Bristol	Rtd
3-5-53	Bordeaux GP		—	Peter Whitehead	T24-Alta	Rtd
9-5-53	International Trophy,		7	Stirling Moss	Alta Spl	2nd FL
	Silverstone	Heat 1	35	Bob Gerard	T23-Bristol	8th=
			41	Eric Brandon	'3/52	10th
			45	Jacques Swaters	T23-Bristol	11th
		Heat 2	36	Ken Wharton	T23-Bristol	2nd
			10	Peter Whitehead	T24-Alta	4th
			14	Ninian Sanderson	'6/52	10th
			32	Archie Bryde	'1/52	11th
		Final		Wharton		5th
				Gerard		6th
				Whitehead		8th
				Moss		9th
				Sanderson		14th
				Swaters		16th
				Brandon		18th
				Bryde		Rtd
16-5-53	Ulster Trophy, Dundrod	Heat 1	7	Jock Somervail	'3/52	3rd
			18	Jock Lawrence	'6/52	4th
			8	Archie Bryde	'1/52	Rtd
		Heat 2	39	Ken Wharton	T23-Bristol	2nd
			4	Peter Whitehead	T24-Alta	4th
			5	Graham Whitehead	T23-Bristol	8th
		Final		Wharton		2nd
				P. Whitehead		4th
				G. Whitehead		7th
				Lawrence		9th
25-5-53	Coronation Trophy, Crystal Palace	Heat 1		Somervail		11th
			7	Stirling Moss	Alta Spl	4th
			21	Archie Bryde	'1/52	Rtd
			19	Ken Wharton	T23-Bristol	2nd
		Heat 2	10	Peter Whitehead	T24-Alta	FIRST
			12	Graham Whitehead	T23-Bristol	3rd
			17	Alan Brown	T23-Alfa Romeo	Rtd
			16	John Barber?		
		Final		Wharton		2nd
				P. Whitehead		3rd
				Moss		5th
				G. Whitehead		6th
30-5-53	Coronation F2 race, Snetterton		3	Jimmy Stewart	'6/52	Rtd
			66	Alan Brown	T23-Bristol	2nd
			84	Rodney Nuckey	T23-Bristol	4th
31-5-53	Eifelrennen, Nürburgring		—	Stirling Moss	Alta Spl	9th
			—	Ken Wharton	T23-Bristol	Rtd
7-6-53	DUTCH GRAND PRIX, Zandvoort		32	Ken Wharton	T23-Bristol	Rtd
27-6-53	West Essex CC F2 race, Snetterton		1	Rodney Nuckey	T23-Bristol	3rd
			6	Jock Somervail	'3/52	Rtd
			57	John Barber	'7/52	DNA
27-6-53	Midlands MEC F2 race, Silverstone		—	Tony Crook	T24-Alta	FIRST

342

RACING RECORDS

Date	Event	Race No.	Driver	Chassis	Result
5-7-53	FRENCH GRAND PRIX, Reims	36	Stirling Moss	Alta Spl	Rtd
		38	Bob Gerard	T23-Bristol	11th
		40	Ken Wharton	T23-Bristol	Rtd
11-7-53	Crystal Palace Trophy	2	Jock Somervail	'3/52	DNA
		7	Peter Whitehead	T24-Alta	5th
12-7-53	AVUSRennen, Berlin	—	Rodney Nuckey	T23-Bristol	5th
		—	Alan Brown	T23-Bristol	Rtd
18-7-53	BRITISH GRAND PRIX, Silverstone	16	Ken Wharton	T23-Bristol	UNC '8th'
		17	Bob Gerard	T23-Bristol	Rtd
		18	Jimmy Stewart	'6/52	Crash
		19	Alan Brown	T23-Bristol	Rtd
		20	Peter Whitehead	T24-Alta	UNC '10th'
		21	Stirling Moss	Alta Spl	Withdrawn
		22	Tony Crook	T24-Alta	Rtd
25-7-53	USAF Trophy, Snetterton	8	Ken Wharton	T23-Bristol	DNS
		18	Horace Gould	T23-Bristol	4th
		21	Bob Gerard	T23-Bristol	2nd
		23	Tony Crook	T24-Alta	5th
		26	Jock Somervail	'3/52	6th
	*Walton's dual-purpose '1½-seater' car	75	Jack Walton	T23-Bristol*	?
26-7-53	Aix-les-Bains F2 race	—	John Fitch	T23-Bristol*	Ht 7th
					Ht 4th
	*Brown's car			Aggregate	4th
2-8-53	GERMAN GRAND PRIX, Nürburgring	19	Stirling Moss	T23-Alta*	6th
		38	Alan Brown	T23-Bristol	Rtd
	*The '11-day Wonder', not production T24-Alta	39	Helm Glockler	T23-Bristol**	DNS
	**The ex-T23-Alfa Romeo, Bob Chase team car	40	Rodney Nuckey	T23-Bristol	11th
3-8-53	Thruxton F2 race	60	Horace Gould	T23-Bristol	2nd
		67	Jack Walton	T23-Bristol	3rd
		—	Bernie Ecclestone	'1/52	Rtd
9-8-53	Sables d'Olonne F2 GP	18	Stirling Moss	T23-Alta	Ht 1 4th
					Ht 2 5th
				Aggregate	3rd
15-8-53	Newcastle Journal Trophy, Charterhall	32	Bob Gerard	T23-Bristol	4th
		39	Ken Wharton	T23-Bristol	FIRST, =FL
		55	Jock Somervail	'3/52	?
		57	Jimmy Stewart	'6/52	?
		66	Horace Gould	T23-Bristol	Rtd
		68	Jack Walton	T23-Bristol	?
		97	Stirling Moss	T23-Alta	Rtd
23-8-53	SWISS GRAND PRIX, Berne	20	Ken Wharton	T23-Bristol	7th
30-8-53	Cadours F2 race	—	Ken Wharton	T23-Bristol	Ht 2 4th
					Final 6th
12-9-53	RedeX Trophy, Snetterton	9	Keith Hall	'3/52	Rtd
		34	Peter Whitehead	T24-Alta	2nd
		93	Bernie Ecclestone	'1/52	DNA
		100	Tony Crook	T24-Alta	Crash
13-9-53	ITALIAN GRAND PRIX, Monza	28	Stirling Moss	T23-Alta	UNC '17'
		30	Ken Wharton	T23-Bristol	UNC 22n
		46	Alan Brown	T23-Bristol	UNC '16'
19-9-53	London Trophy F2, Crystal Palace	2	Ken Wharton	T23-Bristol	DNA
		3	Bernie Ecclestone	'1/52	6th
		4	Bob Gerard	T23-Bristol	3rd

Date	Event		Race No.	Driver	Chassis	Result
			5	Rodney Nuckey	T23-Bristol	4th
			6	Horace Gould	T23-Bristol	5th
				Stirling Moss	T23-Alta	FIRST
		Heat 2		Moss		FIRST
				Gould		4th
				Nuckey		5th
				Gerard		Rtd
				Ecclestone		6th
		Aggregate		Moss		FIRST
				Gould		3rd
				Nuckey		4th
				Ecclestone		5th
26-9-53	Madgwick Cup, Goodwood		7	Stirling Moss	T23-Alta	2nd
			8	Bob Gerard	T23-Bristol	5th
			9	Jock Somervail	'3/52	9th
			21	Horace Gould	T23-Bristol	Rtd
			22	Duncan Hamilton	T23-Bristol	Rtd
			23	Ken Wharton	T23-Bristol	4th
			24	Rodney Nuckey	T23-Bristol	Rtd
			86	Mike Hawthorn	'Cooper-Bristol'	DNA
3-10-53	Joe Fry Trophy, Castle Combe		43	Stirling Moss	T23-Alta	DNS*
			44	Ken Wharton	T23-Bristol	3rd
			45	Horace Gould	T23-Bristol	2nd
			48	Rodney Nuckey	T23-Bristol	DNA
			50	Bob Gerard	T23-Bristol	FIRST
	*Drove Cooper-JAP instead, crashed		54	Jack Walton	T23-Bristol	DNA
8-10-53	Oulton Park F2		37	Peter Whitehead	T24-Alta	2nd
17-10-53	Curtis Trophy F2 race, Snetterton		–	Eric Thompson	T23-Alta*	Rtd
			–	Bob Gerard	T23-Bristol	FIRST
			–	Jock Somervail	'3/52	3rd
			–	Rodney Nuckey	T23-Bristol	T-crash
			–	Horace Gould	T23-Bristol	?

1954 – 2½-litre Formula 1 racing

Date	Event		Race No.	Driver	Chassis	Result
19-5-54	Lavant Cup, Goodwood		21	Eric Brandon	T23-Alta	6th
			23	Rodney Nuckey	T23-Bristol	DNA
			26	Jock McBain	'3/52	DNA
			39	Peter Whitehead	T24-Alta	?
			57	Dick Gibson	T23-Bristol*	Rtd
	*Ex-Tom Cole		47	Alan Brown	T23-Bristol	Rtd
9-5-54	Bordeaux GP		10	Peter Whitehead	T24-Alta	Rtd
15-5-54	International Trophy, Silverstone	Heat 1	15	Jock Somervail	'3/52	10th
		Heat 2	14	Bob Gerard	T23-Bristol	10th
			16	Horace Gould		Rtd
		Final		Gerard		8th
				Somervail		12th
5-6-54	Curtis Trophy, Snetterton		4	Jock Somervail	'3/52	3rd
			6	Tony Crook	T23-Bristol*	4th
	*Crook's new dual-purpose '1½-seater'		15	Horace Gould	T23-Bristol	?
7-6-54	Davidstow F1 race		–	Jack Walton	T23-Bristol	2nd
			–	David Watts	T23-Bristol?	4th

RACING RECORDS

Date	Event		Race No.	Driver	Chassis	Result
			–	Horace Gould	T23-Bristol	?
7-6-54	Goodwood BARC F1 race		6	Jock Lawrence	'6/52	Rtd
			7	Jock Somervail	'3/52	Rtd
19-6-54	Crystal Palace Trophy F1	Heat 1	20	Horace Gould	T23-Bristol	4th
		Heat 2	7	Rodney Nuckey	T23-Bristol	FIRST FL
			9	Jock Somervail	'3/52	Crash
		Final		Nuckey		5th
				Gould		6th
11-7-54	Rouen GP, France		32	Alan Brown	T23-Bristol	DNS
17-7-54	BRITISH GRAND PRIX, Silverstone		21	Peter Whitehead	T24-Alta	Rtd
			27	Alan Brown	T23-Bristol	DNS
			28	Horace Gould	T23-Bristol	UNC '19th'
			29	Bob Gerard	T23-Bristol	10th
			30	Eric Brandon	T23-Alta?	Rtd
2-8-54	August Trophy, Crystal Palace	Heat 1	5	Horace Gould	T23-Bristol	3rd
			7	Keith Hall	'3/52	4th
		Heat 2	6	Tony Crook	T23-Bristol	2nd FL
		Final		Gould		4th
				Hall		5th
				Crook		7th
2-8-54	Cornwall MRC F1 race Davidstow		–	Rodney Nuckey	T23-Bristol	Rtd
				Tom Kyffin	T23-Bristol	2nd
				Dick Gibson	T23-Bristol	3rd
7-8-54	Oulton Park Gold Cup		12	Bob Gerard	T23-Bristol	3rd
			14	Ninian Sanderson	'6/52	11th
			21	Alan Brown	T23-Bristol	Rtd
			29	Keith Hall	'3/52	DNS
			30	Rodney Nuckey	T23-Bristol	5th
14-8-54	RedeX Trophy, Snetterton		8	Bob Gerard	T23-Bristol	2nd
			9	Peter Whitehead	T24-Alta	Rtd
			15	Dick Gibson	T23-Bristol	6th
			19	Horace Gould	T23-Bristol	4th
			20	Charles Mauritzen	'3/52	Rtd
			28	Tony Crook	T23-Bristol	DNA
			30	Rodney Nuckey	T23-Bristol	5th
28-8-54	Joe Fry Trophy, Castle Combe		36	Horace Gould	T23-Bristol	FIRST
			49	Bob Gerard	T23-Bristol	Rtd FL
			50	Dick Gibson	T23-Bristol	?
25-9-54	Goodwood Trophy		11	Bob Gerard	T23-Bristol	4th
			12	Rodney Nuckey	T23-Bristol	DNS
			14	Horace Gould	T23-Bristol	?
			15	Bruce Halford	T23-Bristol	?
			16	Dick Gibson	T23-Bristol	?
			18	Jock Lawrence	'6/52	10th
			24	Mike Keen	T23-Alta	6th
			26	Keith Hall	'3/52	?
2-10-54	*Telegraph* Trophy, Aintree		11	Bob Gerard	T23-Bristol	8th
			14	Horace Gould	T23-Bristol	11th
			26	Keith Hall	'3/52	Rtd
			32	Jock Lawrence	'6/52	12th

COOPER CARS

Date	Event	Race No.	Driver	Chassis	Result
1955					
11-4-55	Glover Trophy, Goodwood	12	Mike Keen	T23-Alta	4th
		14	Jack Brabham	T24-Alta	Rtd
		16	Bob Gerard	T23-Bristol	j2nd
		17	Tony Crook	T23-Bristol	7th
		18	Tom Kyffin	T23-Bristol	DNA
		19	Bruce Halford	T23-Bristol	DNA
7-5-55	International Trophy, Silverstone	15	Jack Brabham	T24-Alta	7th
		17	Bob Gerard	T23-Bristol	UNC '10th'
		18	Mike Keen	T23-Alta	Rtd
29-5-55	Curtis Trophy, Snetterton	51	Tony Crook	T23-Bristol	DNA
		86	Jock Somervail	'3/52	3rd
30-5-55	Cornwall MRC F1 race, Davidstow	—	Tony Crook	T23-Bristol	?
		—	Tom Kyffin	T23-Bristol	3rd
		—	Bruce Halford	T23-Bristol	?
30-7-55	London Trophy, Crystal Palace	11	Tony Crook	T23-Bristol	Rtd Ht 1
		15	Mike Keen	T23-Alta	7th Ht 1
		16	Bob Gerard	T23-Bristol	Rtd Ht 2
		18	Tom Kyffin	T23-Bristol	5th Ht 2
		19	Alastair Birrell	'6/52	Rtd Ht 1
		20	Jack Brabham	T23-Bristol	3rd Ht 2
		21	Keith Hall	'3/52	6th Ht 1
		23	Bruce Halford	T23-Bristol	Rtd Ht 1
	Consolation Final		Gerard		FIRST FL
			Keen		2nd
			Crook		4th
	Final		Hall		7th
			Brabham		DNS
			Kyffin		8th
6-8-55	*Daily Record* Trophy, Charterhall	18	Jock Somervail	'3/52	3rd Ht 1
		19	Tom Kyffin	T23-Bristol	?
		20	Bruce Halford	T23-Bristol	
		23	Alastair Birrell	'6/52	
		26	Jack Walton	T23-Bristol	
		31	Jack Brabham	T24-Bristol	4th Ht 2
		70	Alex McMillan	T23-Bristol	2nd Ht 1
		85	Dick Gibson	?	
	Final		Brabham		4th
13-8-55	RedeX Trophy, Snetterton	123	Jock Somervail	'3/52	?
3-9-55	*Telegraph* Trophy, Aintree	10	Bob Gerard	T23-Bristol	2nd
		15	Jock Somervail	'3/52	Crash
24-9-55	Oulton Park Gold Cup	18	Bob Gerard	T23-Bristol	6th
		23	Bruce Halford	T23-Bristol	Rtd
1-10-55	Avon Trophy, Castle Combe	12	Bob Gerard	T23-Bristol	3rd

Date	Event	Race No.	Driver	Chassis	Result
1956					
21-4-56	Aintree '200'	17	Bob Gerard	T23-Bristol	Rtd
24-6-56	Aintree '100'	12	Bob Gerard	T23-Bristol	2nd
14-7-56	BRITISH GRAND PRIX, Silverstone	26	Bob Gerard	T23-Bristol	UNC '12th'
22-7-56	Vanwall Trophy, Snetterton	—	Leslie Hunt	*?-Aston Martin	UNC '5th'
		—	W. F. Morice	T23-Bristol	4th

RACING RECORDS

Date	Event	Race No.	Driver	Chassis	Result
26-8-56	Caen GP, France	—	W. F. Morice	T23-Bristol	UNC '6th'
14-10-56	BRSCC F1 race, Brands Hatch	6	Leslie Hunt	*?-Aston Martin	10th
		9	Bob Gerard	T23-Bristol	7th
	*Conceivably ex 'Mucky Pup' sports car?	10	W. F. Morice	T23-Bristol	9th

1957

14-9-57	International Trophy, Silverstone				
		Heat 2 11	Jimmy Stuart	T23-Bristol*	13th
	*The venerable ex-Gerard car	Final	Jimmy Stuart		18th

FORMULA 1 COOPER 1957–69

It has proved impossible within these pages to include adequate racing records of all Cooper products. Here their Formula 1 activities in three Formulae, 2½-litre to 1960, 1½-litre 1961-65, and 3-litre 1966-69 are recorded, with date, event, driver, race number, capacity (where significant), chassis and result details. Cooper chassis number forms with oblique slashes between serials have been instead rendered here with hyphens hopefully to ease the effect on the eye.

Driver	Race No.	Capacity/Car	Chassis	Result
7-4-57 Syracuse GP, Sicily				
Jack Brabham	12	1.5 T41	F2F2-1-56 (Walker)	'6th' UNC
George Wicken	10	1.5 T43	F2F2-6-57 (driver)	'9th' UNC
Bill Whitehouse	28	1.5 T41	F2F2-2-56 (driver)	Rtd
22-4-57 Glover Trophy, Goodwood				
Jack Brabham	10	1.5 T43	F2	4th
19-5-57 MONACO GRAND PRIX, Monte Carlo				
Jack Brabham	14	1.96 T43	F2-5-57?(Walker/works)	6th
7-7-57 FRENCH GRAND PRIX, Rouen-les-Essarts				
Jack Brabham	22	1.96 T43		Accident
Mike MacDowel	24	1.5 T43	F2	Gave car to Brabham
Jack Brabham (in MacDowel car)				'7th' UNC
14-7-57 Reims GP, Reims-Gueux				
Jack Brabham	38	1.96 T43		'12th' UNC
20-7-57 BRITISH GRAND PRIX, Silverstone				
Roy Salvadori	36	1.96 T43		5th
Bob Gerard	38	2.24 T43-BG-Bristol	F2-21-57	6th
Jack Brabham	34	1.96 T43 Walker		'8th' UNC
28-7-57 Caen GP, France				
Roy Salvadori	10	1.96 T43		2nd
Jean Lucas	—	1.5 T43	F2-22-57 (Brown)	'7th' UNC
Jack Brabham	12	1.5 T43	F2	Rtd mag.
Tony Brooks	8	1.96 T43		Rtd clutch

Driver	Race No.	Capacity/Car	Chassis	Result

4-8-57 GERMAN GRAND PRIX, Nürburgring (all F2 entries)
Brian Naylor	28	1.5 T43	F2-23-57	13th
Tony Marsh	25	1.5 T43	F2-11-57	'15th' UNC
Dick Gibson	29	1.5 T45	F2-26-57	Rtd
Paul England	26	1.5 T41	F2-1-56	Rtd
Jack Brabham	24	1.5 T41	F2-3-57	Rtd trans.
Roy Salvadori	23	1.5 T43	F2-3-57	Rtd trans.

18-8-57 PESCARA GRAND PRIX, Italy
Jack Brabham	24	1.5 T43	F2	UNC
Roy Salvadori	22	1.5 T43	F2	Rtd susp.

14-9-57 International Trophy, Silverstone
Heat 1
Tony Brooks	10	1.96 T43	Walker	PP Rtd trans.
Bob Gerard	12	2.24 T43-BG-Bristol	F2-21-57	10th

Heat 2
Jack Brabham	14	1.96 T43		2nd

Final
Brabham				Rtd oil system
Gerard				14th

27-10-57 Moroccan GRAND PRIX, Ain-Diab, Casablanca
Roy Salvadori	16	1.96 T43		Rtd trans.
Jack Brabham	18	1.96 T43 Walker		DISQ.

1958

19-1-58 ARGENTINE GRAND PRIX, Buenos Aires Autodrome
Stirling Moss	14	1.96 T43 Walker		FIRST

7-4-58 Glover Trophy, Goodwood
Stirling Moss	7	1.96 T43 Walker	(re-chassised)	PP = FL Rtd eng
Jack Brabham	19	1.96 T45		2nd
Roy Salvadori	18	1.96 T45		FR 3rd
Tony Marsh	27	1.5 T45	F2	7th
Ian Burgess	20	1.5 T45	F2	8th
Tom Bridger	9	1.5 T45	F2 F2-10-58	Crash

19-4-58 Aintree '200'
Stirling Moss	7	2.0 T45 Walker		PP FIRST
Jack Brabham	10	1.96 T45		FL 2nd
Roy Salvadori	9	1.96 T45		FR 4th

(Brooks won F2 class in Walker car, 3rd o/a)

3-5-58 International Trophy, Silverstone
Roy Salvadori	5	1.96 T45		PP 2nd
Jack Brabham	6	1.96 T45		FR 5th
Stirling Moss	7	2.0 T45 Walker		FR Rtd trans.
Maurice Trintignant	8	1.96 T43 Walker		Rtd mech.

18-5-58 MONACO GRAND PRIX, Monte Carlo
Maurice Trintignant	20	2.0 T45 Walker		FIRST
Jack Brabham	16	2.2 T45		FR 4th
Roy Salvadori	18	1.96 T45		Rtd trans.
Ron Flockhart	22	2.0 T43		DNQ

Driver	Race No.	Capacity/Car	Chassis	Result

26-5-58 DUTCH GRAND PRIX, Zandvoort
Roy Salvadori	7	2.2 T45		4th
Jack Brabham	8	1.96 T45		8th
Maurice Trintignant	9	2.0 T45		9th

15-6-58 BELGIAN GRAND PRIX, Spa-Francorchamps
| Roy Salvadori | 24 | 1.96 T45 | | 8th |
| Jack Brabham | 22 | 2.2 T45 | | Rtd eng. |

6-7-58 FRENCH GRAND PRIX, Reims-Gueux
| Jack Brabham | 22 | 2.2 T45 | | 6th |
| Roy Salvadori | 20 | 1.96 T45 | | '13th' UNC |

19-7-58 BRITISH GRAND PRIX, Silverstone
Roy Salvadori	10	2.2 T45		FR 3rd
Jack Brabham	11	1.96 T45		6th
Maurice Trintignant	4	2.0 T43 Walker		8th
Ian Burgess	12	1.96 T45		Rtd clutch

20-7-58 Caen GP, La Prairie, France
| Stirling Moss | — | 2.2 T45 Walker | | FR FIRST |
| Maurice Trintignant | — | 1.5 T45 | F2 Walker | 4th o/a |

3-8-58 GERMAN GRAND PRIX, Nürburgring
| Roy Salvadori | 10 | 2.2 T45 | | 2nd |
| Maurice Trintignant | 11 | 2.2 T45 Walker | | 3rd |

24-8-58 PORTUGUESE GRAND PRIX, Oporto
Jack Brabham	14	2.2 T45		7th
Roy Salvadori	16	1.96 T45		10th
Maurice Trintignant	12	1.96 T43		8th

7-9-58 ITALIAN GRAND PRIX, Monza
Roy Salvadori	6	2.2 45		'4th' UNC
Maurice Trintignant	2	2.2 T45 Walker		Rtd trans.
Jack Brabham	4	1.96 T45		Collision

19-10-58 MOROCCAN GRAND PRIX, Ain-Diab, Casablanca
Roy Salvadori	28	2.2 T45		7th
Jack Fairman	30	1.96 T45		8th
Maurice Trintignant	36	2.2 T45		Rtd eng.

1959

30-3-59 Glover Trophy, Goodwood
Stirling Moss	7	2.5 T51 Walker		FL FIRST
Jack Brabham	10	2.5 T51		FR 2nd
Masten Gregory	8	2.2 T51		5th
Bruce McLaren	9	2.2 T51		6th
Roy Salvadori	11	2.5 T45-Maserati	F2-15-58?	FR 8th

18-4-59 Aintree '200'
Bruce McLaren	12	2.2 T51		3rd
Stirling Moss	7	2.5 T51-BRM Walker		FL Rtd g'box.
Masten Gregory	11	2.5 T51		PP Rtd clutch
Jack Brabham	10	2.5 T51		Rtd eng.
Roy Salvadori	9	2.5 T45-Maserati		Rtd g'box.

COOPER CARS

Driver	Race No.	Capacity/Car	Chassis	Result

2-5-59 International Trophy, Silverstone
Jack Brabham	5	2.5 T51	F2-4-59	FR FL FIRST
Maurice Trintignant	32	2.5 T51 Walker		3rd
Jack Fairman	7	2.5 T45-Maserati	F2-15-58?	5th
Ian Burgess	6	2.2 T43		8th

10-5-59 MONACO GRAND PRIX, Monte Carlo
Jack Brabham	24	2.5 T51	F2-7-59	FR FL FIRST
Maurice Trintignant	32	2.5 T51 Walker		3rd
Bruce McLaren	22	2.2 T51	F2-4-59	5th
Masten Gregory	26	2.5 T51	F2-23a-58	Rtd trans.
Stirling Moss	30	2.5 T51 Walker		PP Rtd g'box.

31-5-59 DUTCH GRAND PRIX, Zandvoort
Jack Brabham	8	2.5 T51	F2-27-59	FR 2nd
Masten Gregory	9	2.5 T51	F2-7-59	3rd
Maurice Trintignant	10	2.5 T51 Walker		8th
Stirling Moss	11	2.5 T51 Walker		FR Rtd g'box.

5-7-59 FRENCH GRAND PRIX, Reims-Gueux
Jack Brabham	8	2.5 T51		FR 3rd
Bruce McLaren	12	2.5 T51	F2-23a-58	5th
Maurice Trintignant	14	2.5 T51	Walker	'12th' UNC
Masten Gregory	10	2.5 T51	F2-7-59	Rtd driver
Ian Burgess	20	2.5 T51	F2-13-59-Maserati	Rtd eng.
Roy Salvadori	16	2.5 T45-Maserati		Rtd eng.

18-7-59 BRITISH GRAND PRIX, Aintree
Jack Brabham	12	2.5 T51	F2-27-59	PP FIRST
Bruce McLaren	16	2.5 T51	F2-23a-58	=FL 3rd
Maurice Trintignant	18	2.5 T51 Walker		5th
Masten Gregory	14	2.5 T51	F2-7-59	7th

2-8-59 GERMAN GRAND PRIX Avus, Berlin
Aggregate of two heats
Heat 1
Bruce McLaren	2	T51	F2-23a-58	4th
Maurice Trintignant	8	T51 Walker		6th
Ian Burgess	18	2.5 T51-Maserati	F2-13-59	9th
Stirling Moss	7	2.5 T51 Walker		FR Rtd trans.
Jack Brabham	1	2.5 T51	F2-27-59	FR Rtd clutch
Masten Gregory	3	2.5 T51	F2-7-59	Rtd eng.

Heat 2
Trintignant				4th
Burgess				6th
McLaren				Rtd Clutch

Aggregate overall; Trintignant 4th

23-8-59 PORTUGUESE GRAND PRIX, Monsanto Park, Lisbon
Stirling Moss	4	2.5 T51 Walker		PP FL FIRST
Masten Gregory	2	2.5 T51	F2-7-59	FR 2nd
Maurice Trintignant	5	2.5 T51 Walker		4th
Mario Araujo Cabral	18	2.5 T51-Maserati	F1-13-59	10th
Jack Brabham	1	2.5 T51	F2-27-59	Crashed
Bruce McLaren	3	2.5 T51	F2-23a-58	Rtd

RACING RECORDS

Driver	Race No.	Capacity/Car	Chassis	Result
13-9-59 ITALIAN GRAND PRIX, Monza				
Stirling Moss	14	2.5 T51 Walker		PP FIRST
Jack Brabham	12	2.5 T51	F2-23a-58	FR 3rd
Maurice Trintignant	16	2.5 T51 Walker		9th
Colin Davis	40	2.5 T51-Maserati	F2-12-59	11th
Ian Burgess	42	2.5 T51-Maserati	F2-13-59	14th
Jack Fairman	22	2.5 T45-Maserati		Rtd eng.
Giorgio Scarlatti	20	2.5 T51	F2-4-59	12th

COOPER CLINCH FORMULA 1 MANUFACTURERS' WORLD CHAMPIONSHIP

26-9-59 Oulton Park Gold Cup				
Stirling Moss	7	2.5 T51 Walker		PP FL FIRST
Jack Brabham	3	2.5 T51	F2-4-59	FR 2nd
Chris Bristow	2	2.5 T51	F2-1-59	FR 3rd
Roy Salvadori	4	2.5 T45-Maserati		4th
Bruce McLaren	6	2.5 T51	F2-23a-58	Rtd g'box.
10-10-59 Silver City Trophy, Snetterton				
Jack Brabham	1	2.5 T51	F2-4-59	2nd
Roy Salvadori	10	2.5 T45-Maserati		Rtd eng.
12-12-59 UNITED STATES GRAND PRIX, Sebring				
Bruce McLaren	9	2.5 T51	'F2-27-59'/2	FIRST
Maurice Trintingrant	6	2.5 T51 Walker		FL 2nd
Jack Brabham	8	2.5 T51	F2-7-59'?	FR 4th
Stirling Moss	7	2.5 T51 Walker		PP Rtd trans.
Harry Schell	19	2.2 T51	F2-17-59	FR Rtd clutch
Allessandro de Tomaso	14	2.0 T43-OSCA Spl		Rtd brakes
Roy Salvadori	12	2.5 T45-Maserati		Rtd trans.

1960

Driver	Race No.	Capacity/Car	Chassis	Result
6-2-60 ARGENTINE GRAND PRIX, Buenos Aires Autodrome				
Bruce McLaren	16	2.5 T51	F2-7-59?	FIRST
Maurice Trintignant/ Stirling Moss	38	2.5 T51 Walker		3rd
Carlos Menditeguy	6	2.5 T51-Maserati	F2-13-59	4th
Roberto Bonomi	4	2.5 T51-Maserati	F2-12-59	11th
Stirling Moss	36	2.5 T51 Walker		PP FL Rtd susp.
Jack Brabham	18	2.5 T51	F2-27-59?	Rtd eng.
Harry Schell	34	2.2 T51	F2-17-59	Rtd —
18-4-60 Glover Trophy, Goodwood				
Stirling Moss	7	2.5 T51-Walker		FR FL 2nd
Chris Bristow	9	2.5 T51	F2-25-59	PP 3rd
Bruce McLaren	2	2.5 'T51'	F2-23-58	4th
Keith Greene	11	2.5 T45-Maserati	F2-15-58	Rtd
Harry Schell	8	2.5 T51	F2-24-59	Rtd eng.
Roy Salvadori	10	2.5 T51	Fr2-7-59	Rtd trans.

Driver	Race No.	Capacity/Car	Chassis	Result
14-5-60 International Trophy, Silverstone				
Jack Brabham	1	2.5 T53	F2-8-60?	2nd
Masten Gregory	9	2.5 T51-Maserati	F2-12-59	6th
Jack Fairman	23	2.5 T45	F2-5-58	7th
Ian Burgess	8	2.5 T51-Maserati	F2-13-59	9th
Keith Greene	7	2.5 T45-Maserati		13th
Stirling Moss	20	2.5 T51 Walker		PP Rtd susp.
Bruce Halford	16	2.5 T51		Rtd brakes
29-5-60 MONACO GRAND PRIX, Monte Carlo				
Bruce McLaren	10	2.5 T53	F2-5-60	FL 2nd
Tony Brooks	18	2.5 T51	F2-26-59	4th
Maurice Trintignant	44	2.5 T51-Maserati	F2-13-59	Rtd g'box.
Chris Bristow	16	2.5 T51	F2-25-59	FR Rtd g'box
Roy Salvadori	14	2.5 T51		Rtd o'heat
Jack Brabham	8	2.5 T53	F2-8-59	FR crashed
6-6-60 DUTCH GRAND PRIX, Zandvoort				
Jack Brabham	11	2.5 T53	F2-8-60	FR FIRST
Henry Taylor	10	2.5 T51	F2-2-59	7th
Tony Brooks	9	2.5 T51	F2-26-59	Rtd g'box
Bruce McLaren	12	2.5 T51	F2-5-60	Rtd UJ
Chris Bristow	8	2.5 T51	F2-25-59	rtd eng.
Maurice Trintignant	18	2.5 T51-Maserati	F2-13-59	Rtd trans.
19-6-60 BELGIAN GRAND PRIX, Spa-Francorchamps				
Jack Brabham	2	2.5 T53	F2-8-60	PP = FL FIRST
Bruce McLaren	4	2.5 T53	F2-5-60	2nd
Olivier Gendebien	34	2.5 T51	F2-24-59	4th
Lucien Bianchi	32	2.5 T51		'7th' UNC
Tony Brooks	38	2.5 T51	F2-26-59	FR Rtd trans
Chris Bristow	36	2.5 T51	F2-25-59	Fatal accident
3-7-60 FRENCH GRAND PRIX, Reims-Gueux				
Jack Brabham	16	2.5 T53	F2-8-60	PP FL FIRST
Olivier Gendebien	44	2.5 T51	F2-24-59	2nd
Bruce McLaren	18	2.5 T53	F2-5-60	3rd
Henry Taylor	46	2.5 T51	F2-26-59	4th
Maurice Trintignant	38	2.5 T51-Maserati	F2-13-59	Rtd Accident
Gino Munaron	30	2.5 T51-Ferrari	F2-2-60?	Rtd trans.
Lucien Bianchi	36	2.5 T51		Ret trans.
16-7-60 BRITISH GRAND PRIX, Silverstone				
Jack Brabham	1	2.5 T53	F2-8-60	PP FIRST
Bruce McLaren	2	2.5 T53	F2-5-60	FR 4th
Tony Brooks	12	2.5 T51	F2-26-59	5th
Henry Taylor	15	2.5 T51	F2-2-59	8th
Olivier Gendebien	14	2.5 T51	F2-24-59	9th
Masten Gregory	16	2.5 T51-Maserati	F2-12-59	15th
Gino Munaron	21	2.5 T51-Ferrari	F2-2-60	16th
Keith Greene	22	2.5 T45-Maserati		Rtd o'heat.
Jack Fairman	23	2.5 T51		Rtd ign.
Ian Burgess	17	2.5 T51-Maserati	F2-13-59	Rtd eng.
Chuck Daigh	3	2.5 T51		Rtd o'heat
Lucien Bianchi	24	2.5 T51		Rtd ign.

RACING RECORDS

Driver	Race No.	Capacity/Car	Chassis	Result
1-8-60 Silver City Trophy, Brands Hatch				
Jack Brabham	2	2.5 T53	F2-8-60	FR = FL FIRST
Bruce McLaren	4	2.5 T5		3rd
Henry Taylor	12	2.5 T51	F2-2-59	5th
Dan Gurney	8	2.5 T51	F2-26-59	7th
Bruce Halford	10	2.5 T51	F2-1-59	8th
Ian Burgess	30	2.5 T51-Maserati	F2-13-59	10th
Keith Greene	25	2.5 T45-Maserati		12th
Gino Munaron	22	2.5 T51-Ferrari		13th
Geoff Richardson	24	2.5 Cooper-Connaught 'RRA'		14th
Giorgio Scarlatti	20	2.5 T51-Ferrari		Rtd g'box
Lucien Bianchi	18	2.5 T51		Rtd eng.
14-8-60 PORTUGUESE GRAND PRIX, Oporto				
Jack Brabham	2	2.5 T53	F2-8-60	FR FIRST
Bruce McLaren	4	2.5 T53	F2-5-60	2nd
Tony Brooks	6	2.5 T51	F2-24-59	5th
Olivier Gendebien	8	2.5 T51	F2-26-59	'7th' UNC
Masten Gregory	30	2.5 T51-Maserati	F2-12-59	Rtd g'box
Mario Araujo Cabral	32	2.5 T51-Maserati	F2-13-59	Rtd g'box
4-9-60 ITALIAN GRAND PRIX, Monza				
Giulio Cabianca	2	2.5 T51-Ferrari	F2-2-60	4th
Piero Drogo	12	2.5 T43	F2-26-57	8th
Arthur Owen	8	T45	F2-6-59	Crashed
Vic Wilson	30		T43 F2-29-57	Rtd eng.
Giorgio Scarlatti	36	2.5 T51	F2-12-59-Maserati	Rtd eng.
Gino Munaron	4	2.5 T51-Ferrari	F2-13-60	Rtd eng.
Alfonse Thiele	34	2.5 T51-Maserati	F2-12-59	Rtd g'box
17-9-60 Lombard Trophy, Snetterton				
Roy Salvadori	9	2.5 T51		4th
Denny Hulme	4	2.5 T51	F2-1-59	5th
Jack Lewis	22	T45		6th
Bruce Halford	27		T45	7th
24-9-60 Oulton Park Gold Cup				
Jack Brabham	1	2.5 T53	F2-8-60	FR 2nd
Bruce McLaren	2	2.5 T53	F2-5-60	4th
Henry Taylor	8	2.5 T51	F2-2-59	7th
Bruce Halford	9	2.5 T51	F2-1-59	8th
20-11-60 UNITED STATES GRAND PRIX, Riverside				
Bruce McLaren	3	2.5 T53	F2-5-60	3rd
Jack Brabham	2	2.5 T53	F2-8-60	FR FL 4th
Phil Hill	9	2.5 T51	F2-1-59	6th
Roy Salvadori	14	2.5 T51		8th
Wolfgang von Trips	26	2.5 T51	F2-12-59-Maserati	9th
Pete Lovely	25	2.5 T51-Ferrari	F2-14-60	11th
Olivier Gendebien	7	2.5 T51	F2-26-59	12th
Henry Taylor	8	2.5 T51	F2-1-59	14th
Maurice Trintignant	18	2.5 T51-Maserati	F2-13-59	'15th' UNC
Tony Brooks	6	2.5 T51	F2-24-59	Rtd spun
Ron Flockhart	4	2.5 T51		Rtd brakes
Ian Burgess	19	2.5 T51-Maserati	F2-6-60	Rtd g'box

1.5 LITRE FORMULA 1 1961–65

Driver	Race No.	Chassis	Result
26-3-61 Lombank Trophy, Snetterton			
Jack Brabham	1	T53* FII-8-60	FIRST
John Surtees	3	T53 FI-1-61**	FL 3rd/FIRST
Roy Salvadori	2	T53 FI-2-61	5th
Shane Summers	16	T53 FI-8-61	8th
John Langton	15	Hume-Cooper	Rtd
Graham Eden	14	T51 –	Rtd
Bernard Collomb	10	T51 –	Rtd
George Morgan	18	T51 FII-5-59	Rtd

*2.5-litre InterContinental Formula in concurrent F1/ICF race
**Surtees first F1 home

3-4-61 Glover Trophy, Goodwood			
John Surtees	11	T53 FI-1-61	FL FIRST
Roy Salvadori	9	T53 FI-2-63	3rd
John Campbell-Jones	31	T51 –	10th
George Morgan	19	T51 FII-5-59	12th
Shane Summers	27	T53 FI-8-61	Accident

3-4-61 Pau GP, France			
Lorenzo Bandini	24	T51-Maserati FII-13-59	3rd
Mario Cabral	22	T51-Maserati FII-12-59	4th
Jack Lewis	30	T53 FI-6-61	5th
Graham Eden	34	T51 –	6th
Jo Schlesser	28	T51 –	7th
Maurice Trintignant	4	T45 FII-9-58	Rtd
Gino Munaron	26	T43 –	Rtd
Andre Wicky	38	T51 FII-11-59	Rtd
Jack Brabham	2	T53 FII-5-60	Rtd

9-4-61 Brussels GP, Belgium
Three-heat aggregate result:

Heat 1 Roy Salvadori	8	T53 FI-2-61	2nd
Jack Brabham	2	T53 FII-5-60	3rd
Bruce McLaren	4	T53 FII-8-60	4th
John Campbell-Jones	44	T51 –	9th
John Surtees	6	T53 FI-1-61	10th
Heat 2 Brabham			FIRST
McLaren			2nd
Campbell-Jones			10th
Heat 3 Brabham			FIRST
McLaren			3rd
Campbell-Jones			9th

Retirements: Surtees (Heat 2 FL); Salvadori

16-4-61 Vienna GP, Aspern, Austria			
Bernard Collomb	9	T53 FI-9-61	3rd
Ronald Wrenn	4	Hume-Cooper	7th
Shane Summers	2	T53 FI-8-61	8th

22-4-61 Aintree '200'			
Jack Brabham	3	T55 FI-10-61	FL FIRST

RACING RECORDS

Driver	Race No.	Chassis	Result
Bruce McLaren	4	T55 FI-11-61	2nd
John Surtees	5	T53 FI-1-61	4th
Masten Gregory	15	T53 FI-3-61	5th
Jack Lewis	8	T53 FI-6-61	6th
Roy Salvadori	6	T53 FI-2-61	8th
Shane Summers	9	T53 FI-8-61	12th
Graham Eden	12	T51 –	18th
George Morgan	10	T51 FII-5-59	Accident
Stirling Moss	7	T53 FI-7-61	Rtd
Bernard Collomb	14	T53 FI-9-61	Rtd

25-4-61 Syracuse GP, Sicily

Driver	Race No.	Chassis	Result
Jack Brabham	14	T55 FI-10-61	4th
Roy Salvadori	42	T53 FI-2-61	5th
Lorenzo Bandini	34	T51-Maserati FII-13-59	7th
Menato Boffa	48	T45 –	9th
Renato Pirocchi	36	T45 –	12th
John Surtees	22	T53 'VR'	Rtd
Maurice Trintignant	28	T51 –	Rtd
Massimo Natili	44	T51 FII-12-59-Maserati	Rtd

14-5-61 MONACO GRAND PRIX, Monte Carlo

Driver	Race No.	Chassis	Result
Bruce McLaren	26	T55 FI-11-61	6th
Maurice Trintignant	42	T51 –	7th
John Surtees	22	T53 FI-1-61	11th
Jack Brabham	24	T55 FI-10-61	Rtd ign.

14-5-61 Naples GP, Possilippo, Italy

Driver	Race No.	Chassis	Result
Lorenzo Bandini	34	T51-Maserati FII-13-59	3rd
Bernard Collomb	26	T53 FI-9-61	6th
Roy Salvadori	18	T53 FI-2-61	7th
John Campbell-Jones	2	T51 –	Rtd
Menato Boffa	36	T45 –	Accident

22-5-61 DUTCH GRAND PRIX, Zandvoort

Driver	Race No.	Chassis	Result
Jack Brabham	10	T55 FI-10-61	6th
John Surtees	12	T53 FI-1-61	7th
Bruce McLaren	11	T55 FI-11-61	12th

22-5-61 London Trophy, Crystal Palace

Driver	Race No.	Chassis	Result
Roy Salvadori	2	T53 FI-2-61	PP = FL FIRST
Shane Summers	8	T53 FI-8-61	4th
John Campbell-Jones	10	T51 –	6th
Jack Lewis	6	T53 FI-6-61	7th
Bernard Collomb	4	T53 FI-9-61	9th
Alan Trow	16	T45 –	10th
John Langton	18	Hume-Cooper	11th
Klaas Twisk	32	T51 FII-11-59	Rtd
Giuseppe Maugeri	34	T51 FII-19-59	Accident

3-6-61 Silver City Trophy, Brands Hatch

Driver	Race No.	Chassis	Result
Roy Salvadori	6	T53 FI-2-61	4th
Giuseppe Maugeri	50	T51 FII-19-59	10th
John Campbell-Jones	16	T51 –	12th
Bernard Collomb	14	T53 FI-9-61	Rtd
Alan Trow	54	T45 –	Rtd

Driver	Race No.	Chassis	Result
Jack Lewis	10	T53 FI-6-61	Rtd
Jack Brabham	2	T55 FI-10-61	Rtd eng.
Bruce McLaren	4	T55 FI-11-61	Accident
John Surtees	8	T53 FI-1-61	Collision

18-6-61 BELGIAN GRAND PRIX, Spa-Francorchamps

Driver	Race No.	Chassis	Result
John Surtees	24	T53 FI-1-61	5th
Jack Lewis	40	T53 FI-6-61	9th
Masten Gregory	44	T53 FI-3-61	10th
Bruce McLaren	30	T55 FI-11-61	Rtd ign.
Jack Brabham	28	T55 FI-10-61	Rtd eng.
Lorenzo Bandini	46	T53-Maserati FI-13-61	Rtd eng.
Maurice Trintignant	26	T51-Maserati –	Rtd

2-7-61 FRENCH GRAND PRIX, Reims-Gueux, France

Driver	Race No.	Chassis	Result
Bruce McLaren	4	T55 FI-11-61	5th
Roy Salvadori	42	T53 FI-2-61	8th
Masten Gregory	36	T53 FI-3-61	12th
Maurice Trintignant	32	T51-Maserati	13th
John Surtees	40	T53 FI-1-61	Accident
Jack Lewis	44	T53 FI-6-61	Rtd
Bernard Collomb	52	T53 FI-9-61	Rtd
Jack Brabham	2	T55 FI-10-61	Rtd eng.

15-7-61 BRITISH GRAND PRIX, Aintree

Driver	Race No.	Chassis	Result
Jack Brabham	12	T55 FI-10-61	4th
Roy Salvadori	36	T53 FI-2-61	6th
Bruce McLaren	14	T55 FI-11-61	8th
Masten Gregory	42	T53 FI-3-61	11th
Lorenzo Bandini	60	T53 FI-13-61-Maserati	12th
Massimo Natili	62	T51-Maserati FII-13-59	Rtd
Jack Lewis	46	T53 FI-6-61	Rtd
John Surtees	34	T53 'VR'	Rtd

23-7-61 Solitude GP, Stuttgart, West Germany

Driver	Race No.	Chassis	Result
Bruce McLaren	7	T53 FII-8-60	4th
Jack Brabham	6	T53 FII-5-60	5th
Maurice Trintignant	18	T51-Maserati -	Rtd

6-8-61 GERMAN GRAND PRIX, Nürburgring

Driver	Race No.	Chassis	Result
John Surtees	18	T53 FI-1-61	5th
Bruce McLaren	2	T55 FI-11-61	6th
Jack Lewis	28	T53 FI-6-61	9th
Roy Salvadori	19	T53 FI-2-61	10th
Ian Burgess	30	T53 FI-3-61	12th
Bernard Collomb	38	T53 FI-9-61	UNC
Jack Brabham	1	T58 FI-12-61	Accident
Lorenzo Bandini	32	T53-Maserati FI-13-61	Rtd
Maurice Trintignant	20	T51-Maserati -	Rtd

20-8-61 Karlskoga Kanonloppet, Sweden

Driver	Race No.	Chassis	Result
John Surtees	5	T53 'VR'	=FL 3rd
Roy Salvadori	3	T53 FI-2-61	4th
Geoff Duke	8	T45 FII-23-58*	Accident
Jack Brabham	2	T53 FII-5-60	Rtd g'box

*Fred Tuck entry

Driver	Race No.	Chassis	Result
26/27-8-61 Danish GP, Roskilde, Copenhagen			
Three-heat aggregate result:			
Heat 1 Jack Brabham	1	T53 FI-5-60	2nd
John Surtees	2	T53 'VR'	4th
Roy Salvadori	3	T53 FI-2-61	5th
Heat 2 Salvadori			3rd
Surtees			4th
Brabham			Rtd g'box
Heat 3 Salvadori			3rd
Surtees			Rtd
Aggregate: Salvadori 3rd			
3-9-61 Modena GP, Italy			
Jack Brabham	36	T53 FII-5-60	5th
John Surtees	44	T53 FI-1-61	Rtd
Roy Salvadori	46	T53 FI-2-61	Rtd
Lorenzo Bandini	4	T53-Maserati FI-13-61	
10-9-61 ITALIAN GRAND PRIX, Monza			
Bruce McLaren	12	T55 FI-11-61	3rd
Jack Lewis	60	T53 FI-6-61	4th
Roy Salvadori	40	T53 FI-2-61	6th
Lorenzo Bandini	62	T53-Maserati FI-13-61	8th
Maurice Trintignant	48	T51-Maserati -	9th
Renato Pirocchi	58	T51-Maserati FII-13-61	12th
John Surtees	42	T53 FI-1-61	Accident
Jack Fairman	30	T45 FII-23-58	Rtd
Jack Brabham	10	T58 FI-12-61	Rtd eng.
17-9-61 Zeltweg Flugplatzrennen, Austria			
Jack Brabham	1	T53 FII-5-60	2nd
Ian Burgess	19	T53 FI-3-61	5th
Jo Schlesser	17	T51 –	8th
John Surtees	8	T56 –	10th
Renato Pirocchi/Lorenzo Bandini		T51 FII-13-59-Maserati	11th
Roy Salvadori		T53 FI-2-61	Accident
23-9-61 Oulton Park Gold Cup			
Jack Brabham	2	T55 FI-10-61	2nd
Bruce McLaren	3	T53 FII-8-60	PP 3rd
Ian Burgess	30	T53 FI-3-61	6th
Chris Summers	20	T45 FII-4-58	12th
Graham Eden	26	T51 –	Accident
Roy Salvadori	16	T53 FI-4-61	Rtd
Chris Ashmore	27	T51 –	Rtd
John Surtees	17	T56 –	Rtd
1-10-61 Lewis-Evans Trophy, Brands Hatch			
Graham Eden	8	T51 –	5th
Chris Summers	7	T45 FII-4-58	6th
John Campbell-Jones	5	T53 FI-9-61	7th
Dickie Stoop	2	T45 FII-11-58	8th
Maurice Charles	4	T45 –	Rtd
Chris Ashmore	6	T51 –	Rtd

Driver	Race No.	Chassis	Result

8-10-61 UNITED STATES GRAND PRIX, Watkins Glen
Bruce McLaren	2	T55 FI-11-61	4th
Roger Penske	6	T53 FI-14-61	8th
Hap Sharp	3	T53 FI-15-61	10th
John Surtees	18	T53 FI-1-61	Rtd
Walt Hansgen	60	T53 FI-16-61	Accident
Jack Brabham	1	T58 FI-12-61	PP FL Rtd eng.
Roy Salvadori	19	T53 FI-2-61	Rtd

10-10-61 Coppa Italia, Vallelunga, Rome
Two heat aggregate result:

Heat 1 Nino Vaccarella	24	T51-Maserati –	3rd
Albino Buticchi	20	T45 –	6th
Luciano de Sanctis	22	T45 –	7th
Heat 2 Vaccarella			3rd
Buticchi			6th
De Sanctis			7th

Aggregate as above – Vaccarella FL

9-12-61 Rand GP, Kyalami, South Africa
Bruce Johnstone	9	T56 –	5th
Doug Serrurier	12	T51 FII-16-60-Maserati	10th
Tony Maggs	8	T53 FI-1-61	Rtd
Clive Trundell	18	T52 –	Rtd
Trevor Blokdyk	25	T52-Ford-	Accident
Bill Dunlop	28	T45-Alfa Romeo-	Rtd

17-12-61 Natal GP, Westmead, South Africa
Doug Serrurrer	11	T51-Maserati FII-16-60	6th
Adrian Pheiffer	25	T52-Alfa Romeo –	7th
Trevor Blokdyk	26	T52-Ford –	8th
John Guthrie	20	T51-Alfa Romeo FII-28-59	10th
Tony Maggs	3	T53 FI-1-61	Rtd
Dave Wright	17	T45 FII-22-58	Rtd
Bruce Johnstone	2	T56 –	Accident

26-12-61 South African GP, East London
Tony Maggs	8	T53 FI-1-61	4th
Doug Serrurier	12	T51-Maserati FII-16-60	7th
Adrian Pheiffer	23	T52-Alfa Romeo –	11th
John Guthrie	25	T51-Alfa Romeo FII-28-59	13th
Dave Wright	17	T45 FII-22-58	15th
Clive Trundell	18	T52 –	Rtd
Bill Dunlop	24	T45-Alfa Romeo –	Rtd

1962
2-1-62 Cape GP, Killarney, South Africa
Tony Maggs	8	T53 FI-1-61	5th
John Guthrie	25	T51-Alfa Romeo FII-28-59	Rtd
Clive Trundell	18	T52 –	Rtd
Adrian Pheiffer	23	T52-Alfa Romeo –	Rtd

RACING RECORDS

Driver	Race No.	Chassis	Result

1-4-62 Brussels GP, Heysel, Belgium
Three-heat aggregate result:

Heat 1 Roy Salvadori   5   T56 –   10th
         Ian Burgess   20   T53 FI-3-61   11th
Heat 2 Burgess   6th
         Salvadori   Rtd
Heat 3 Burgess   Rtd
Overall: Burgess 7th

14-4-62 Lombank Trophy, Snetterton
Roy Salvadori   11   T56 –   Rtd
Chris Ashmore   18   T51 –   8th

23-4-62 Lavant Cup, Goodwood
Bruce McLaren   22   T55 FI-11-61   PP FL FIRST*

*Race restricted to 4-cylinder F1 cars

23-4-62 Glover Trophy, Goodwood
Bruce McLaren   4   T55 FI-11-61   2nd

23-4-62 Pau GP, France
Ian Burgess   26   Cooper Spl   8th
Jo Schlesser   40   T51 –   10th

28-4-62 Aintree '200'
Bruce McLaren   16   T55 FI-11-61   2nd
Ian Burgess   17   Cooper Spl   13th

12-5-62 International Trophy, Silverstone
Bruce McLaren   6   T55 FI-11-61   5th
John Rhodes   20   T59 GR-13-62*   13th
Ian Burgess   19   Cooper Spl   18th

*Gerard Racing converted FJ-Climax

20-5-62 DUTCH GRAND PRIX, Zandvoort
Tony Maggs   7   T55 FI-11-62   5th
Jack Lewis   21   T53 FI-6-61   8th
Bruce McLaren   6   T60 FI-17-61 V8   FL Rtd g'box

20-5-62 Naples GP, Possilippo, Italy
Ian Burgess   4   Cooper Spl

3-6-62 MONACO GRAND PRIX, Monte Carlo
Bruce McLaren   14   T60 FI-17-61 V8   FIRST
Tony Maggs   16   T55 FI-11-61   Rtd g'box

11-6-62 International 2000 Guineas, Mallory Park
Mike Parkes   2   T56 –   4th
Ian Burgess   15   Cooper Spl   10th
John Rhodes   86   T59-Ford GR-13-62 Rtd

11-6-62 Crystal Palace Trophy
Bruce McLaren   2   T55 FI-11-61   3rd

17-6-62 BELGIAN GRAND PRIX, Spa-Francorchamps
Bruce McLaren   25   T60 FI-17-61 V8   Rtd eng.
Tony Maggs   26   T60 FI-18-62 V8   Rtd g'box

1-7-62 Reims GP, Reims-Gueux, France
Bruce McLaren   6   T60 FI-18-61 V8   FIRST
Jack Lewis   34   T53 FI-6-61   10th
Ian Burgess   44   Cooper Spl   11th
Tony Maggs   8   T55 FI-11-61   Rtd eng.

Driver	Race No.	Chassis	Result

8-7-62 FRENCH GRAND PRIX, Rouen-les-Essarts
Tony Maggs	24	T60 FI-18-61 V8	2nd
Bruce McLaren	22	T60 FI-17-61 V8	4th
Jack Lewis	42	T53 FI-6-61	Collision

15-7-62 Solitude GP, Stuttgart, West Germany
Bernard Collomb	19	T53 'VR'	8th
Ian Burgess	20	Cooper Spl	4th

21-7-62 BRITISH GRAND PRIX, Aintree
Bruce McLaren	16	T60 FI-17-61 V8	3rd
Tony Maggs	18	T60 FI-18-61 V8	6th
Jack Lewis	42	T53 FI-6-61	10th
Ian Burgess	36	Cooper Spl	12th

5-8-62 GERMAN GRAND PRIX, Nürburgring
Bruce McLaren	9	T60 FI-17-61 V8	5th
Tony Maggs	10	T55 FI-11-61*	9th
Ian Burgess	25	Cooper Spl	11th
Bernard Collomb	31	T53 'VR'	Rtd
Kack Lewis	31	T53 FI-6-61	Rtd

*Maggs' T60 V8 damaged in practice

12-8-62 Karlskoga Kannonloppet, Sweden
Ian Burgess	12	Cooper Spl	5th
Bernard Collomb	11	T53 'VR'	Rtd

19-8-62 Mediterrannean GP, Enna, Sicily
Bernard Collomb	12	T53 'VR'	5th
'Wal Ever'*	16	T45-OSCA FII-15-58	Rtd

*Walter Breveglieri – professional racing photographer

25/26-8-62 Danish GP, Roskilde, Copenhagen
Three-heat aggregate result:
Heat 1 Ian Burgess	18	Cooper Spl	5th
Heat 2 Burgess			7th
Heat 3 Burgess			6th

Overall: Burgess, 5th

1-9-62 Oulton Park Gold Cup
Bernard Collomb	21	T53 'VR'	9th
Jack Lewis	10	T53 FI-6-61	Rtd
Bruce McLaren	2	T60 FI-17-61 V8	Rtd fire
Ian Burgess	24	Cooper Spl	Rtd

16-9-62 ITALIAN GRAND PRIX, Monza
Bruce McLaren	28	T60 FI-18-61 V8	3rd
Tony Maggs	30	T60 FI-17-61 V8	7th

7-10-62 UNITED STATES GRAND PRIX, Watkins Glen
Bruce McLaren	21	T60 FI-17-61 V8	3rd
Tony Maggs	22	T60 FI-18-61 V8	7th
Hap Sharp	24	T53 FI-16-61	11th
Timmy Mayer	23	T53 FI-14-61	Rtd ign.

4-11-62 Mexican GP, Mexico City
Alan Connell	5	T53 FI-16-61	Rtd
Bruce McLaren	21	T60 FI-17-61 V8	Rtd eng.

RACING RECORDS

Driver	Race No.	Chassis	Result

15-12-62 Rand GP, Kyalami, South Africa
Adrian Pheiffer	24	T52-Alfa Romeo –	Rtd
Mike Harris	16	T53-Alfa Romeo FI-1-62	Rtd
Tony Maggs	15	T55 FI-11-61*	Rtd

*Entered by John Love

22-12-62 Natal GP, Westmead, South Africa
Two-heats and Final:

Heat 1	Clive Trundell	35	T51-Maserati FII-16-60	6th
	John Love	15	T55 FI-11-61	7th
	Bill Dunlop	27	T45-Alfa Romeo –	11th
Heat 2	Ray Cresp	20	T59-Alfa Romeo –	8th
	Dave Riley	37	T59-BMC FJ-20-62	9th
	Trevor Blokdyk	19	T59 Alfa Romeo –	10th
Final:	Love			6th
Final:	Trundell			13th
Final:	Cresp			16th
Final:	Dunlop			Rtd
Final:	Riley			Rtd
Final:	Blokdyk			Rtd

29-12-62 SOUTH AFRICAN GRAND PRIX, East London
Bruce McLaren	8	T60 FI-17-61 V8	2nd
Tony Maggs	9	T60 FI-18-61 V8	3rd
John Love	18	T55 FI-11-61	8th
Mike Harris	22	T53-Alfa Romeo FI-1-61	Rtd

1963

3-3-63 Lombark Trophy, Snetterton
Bruce McLaren	7	T60 FI-17-61 V8	4th

15-4-63 Glover Trophy, Goodwood
Bruce McLaren	4	T60 FI-4-63 V8	2nd

15-4-63 Pau GP, France
Andre Wicky	32	T53 'VR'	7th
Jo Bonnier	6	T60 FI-18-61 V8 (Walker)	Rtd

21-4-63 Imola GP, Castellaccis, Italy
Carlo Mario Abate	32	T51-Maserati FII-13-59	5th
Lorenzo Bandini	30	T53-Maserati FI-13-61	Rtd
Jo Bonnier	8	T60 FI-18-61 V8	Rtd

25-4-63 Syracuse GP, Sicily
Carlo Mario Abate	14	T51-Maserati FII-13-59	3rd
Lorenzo Bandini	16	T53-Maserati FI-13-61	Rtd
Andre Wicky	30	T53 'VR'	Rtd

27-4-63 Aintree '200'
Bruce McLaren	5	T66 FI-4-63 V8	5th
John Taylor	15	T59-Ford GR-13-62	9th
Tony Maggs	6	T60 FI-17-61 V8	Rtd brake

11-5-63 International Trophy, Silverstone
Bruce McLaren	6	T606 FI-4-63 V8	2nd
Jo Bonnier	15	T60 FI-18-61 V8	5th
Tony Maggs	7	T66 FI-5-63 V8	6th
John Taylor	25	T59-Ford GR-13-62	Rtd

Driver	Race No.	Chassis	Result

Rome GP, Vallelunga, Italy – 19-5-63
Two-heat aggregate result:

Heat 1 Andre Wicky	2	T53 'VR'	Rtd
Massimo Natili	46	T53 FI-13-61-Maserati	Rtd
Carlo Peroglio	48	T51-Maserati FII-13-59	Rtd

Heat 2 No Cooper starters, no Cooper finishers on aggregate

26-5-63 MONACO GRAND PRIX, MONTE CARLO

Bruce McLaren	7	T66 FI-4-63 V8	3rd
Tony Maggs	8	T66 FI-5-63 V8	5th
Jo Bonnier	11	T60 FI-18-62 V8	7th

9-6-63 BELGIAN GRAND PRIX, Spa-Francorchamps

Bruce McLaren	14	T66 FI-4-63 V8	2nd
Jo Bonnier	12	T60 FI-18-61 V8	5th
Tony Maggs	15	T66 FI-5-53 V8	7th

23-6-63 DUTCH GRAND PRIX, Zandvoort

Jo Bonnier	28	T60 FI-18-61 V8	11th
Bruce McLaren	20	T66 FI-4-63 V8	Rtd g'box
Tony Maggs	22	T66 FI-5-63 V8	Rtd o/heat.

30-6-63 FRENCH GRAND PRIX, Reims-Gueux

Tony Maggs	12	T66 FI-5-63 V8	2nd
Bruce McLaren	10	T66 FI-4-63 V8	12th
Jo Bonnier	44	T60 FI-18-61 V8	UNC

20-7-63 BRITISH GRAND PRIX, Silverstone

Tony Maggs	7	T66 FI-5-63 V8	9th
Bruce McLaren	6	T66 FI-4-V8	Rtd eng.
Jo Bonnier	14	T66 FI-2-63 V8	Rtd eng.

28-7-63 Solitude GP, Stuttgart, West Germany

Jo Bonnier	30	T60 FI-18-61 V8	9th
Mario Araujo Cabral	5	T53-Maserati FI-13-61	10th

4-8-63 GERMAN GRAND PRIX, Nürburgring

Jo Bonnier	16	T66 FI-2-63 V8	6th
Bruce McLaren	5	T66 FI-4-63 V8	Accident W/O
Tony Maggs	6	T66 FI-5-63 V8	Rtd eng.
Mario Araujo Cabral	22	T60 FI-17-61 V8	Rtd g'box

11-8-63 Karlskoga Kannonloppet, Sweden
Two-heat aggregate result:

Heat 1 Jo Bonnier	6	T66 FI-2-63 V8	5th
Heat 2 Jo Bonnier			4th

Aggregate result: Bonnier 5th

18-8-63 Mediterranean GP, Enna, Sicily

Jo Bonnier	28	T60 FI-18-61 V8	4th
Mario Araujo Cabral	6	T60 FI-17-61 V8	7th

1-9-63 Austrian GP, Zeltweg

Jochen Rindt	15	T67-Ford FJ-6-63	Rtd
Jo Bonnier	8	T60 FI-18-61 V8	Rtd

8-9-63 ITALIAN GRAND PRIX, Monza

Bruce McLaren	18	T66 FI-6-63 V8	3rd
Tony Maggs	20	T66 FI-5-63 V8	6th
Jo Bonnier	58	T66 FI-2-63 V8	7th

RACING RECORDS

Driver	Race No.	Chassis	Result
21-9-63 Oulton Park Gold Cup			
Tony Maggs	12	T66 FI-5-63 V8	5th
Bruce McLaren	11	T66 FI-6-63 V8	6th
Jo Bonnier	20	T66 FI-2-63 V8	Rtd
6-10-63 UNITED STATES GRAND PRIX, Watkins Glen			
Jo Bonnier	11	T66 FI-2-63 V8	8th
Bruce McLaren	3	T66 FI-6-63 V8	11th
Tony Maggs	4	T66 FI-5-63 V8	Rtd eng.
27-10-63 MEXICAN GRAND PRIX, Mexico City			
Jo Bonnier	11	T66 FI-2-63 V8	5th
Tony Maggs	4	T66 FI-5-63 V8	Rtd eng.
Bruce McLaren	3	T66 FI-6-63 V8	Rtd eng.
14-12-63 Rand GP, Kyalami, South Africa			
Two-heat aggregate result:			
Heat 2 John Love	8	T55 FI-11-61	5th
Trevor Blokdyk	9	T51-Maserati FII-16-60	6th
Alex Blignaut	19	T53 FI-1-61	14th
Clive Trundell	13	T52 –	18th
Heat 2 Love			3rd
Trundell			13th
Blignaut			15th
Blokdyk			Rtd
Aggregate result: Love 4th, Blignaut 12th, Trundell 15th			
28-12-63 SOUTH AFRICAN GRAND PRIX, East London			
Bruce McLaren	10	T66 FI-6-63 V8	4th
Jo Bonnier	12	T66 FI-2-63 V8	6th
Tony Maggs	11	T66 FI-5-63 V8	5th
John Love	19	T55 FI-11-61	9th
Trevor Blokdyk	23	T51-Maserati FII-16-60	11th

1964

Driver	Race No.	Chassis	Result
14-3-64 Daily Mirror Trophy, Snetterton			
Jo Bonnier	20	T66 FI-2-63 V8	2nd
Bruce McLaren	9	T66 FI-6-63 V8	3rd
30-3-64 News of the World Trophy, Goodwood			
John Taylor	12	T71/73 FI-3-64*-Ford	7th
Bruce McLaren	9	T66 FI-6-63-V8	Accident
Jo Bonnier	14	T66 FI-2-63 V8	Accident
*Gerard special with four-cyl Ford twin-cam engine			
12-4-64 Syracuse GP, Sicily			
Jo Bonnier	18	T66 FI-2-63 V8	4th
Jean-Claude Rudaz	12	T60 FI-18-61 V8	Rtd
18-4-64 Aintree '200'			
Jo Bonnier	21	T66 FI-2-63 V8	4th
John Taylor	23	T71/73-Ford FI-3-64	5th
Phil Hill	10	T66 FI-6-63 V8	Rtd g'box
Bruce McLaren	9	T73 FI-1-64	Rtd o/heat.
Tony Hegbourne*	30	T71-Cosworth FII-2-64	Rtd
*Normand Team F2 car in concurrent event			

363

2-5-64 International Trophy, Silverstone

Driver	Race No.	Chassis	Result
Phil Hill	10	T66 FI-6-63 V8	4th
John Taylor	23	T71/73-Ford FI-3-64	10th
Jean-Claude Rudaz	25	T60 FI-18-61 V8	14th
Bruce McLaren	9	T73 FI-1-64 V8	15th
Jo Bonnier	19	T66 FI-2-63 V8	16th

10-5-64 MONACO GRAND PRIX, Monte Carlo

Driver	Race No.	Chassis	Result
Jo Bonnier	19	T66 FI-2-63 V8	5th
Phil Hill	9	T73 FI-2-64 V8	9th
Bruce McLaren	10	T66 FI-6-63 V8	Rtd eng.*

*Raced spare car after latest T73 broke steering arm in practice

24-5-64 DUTCH GRAND PRIX, ZANDVOORT

Driver	Race No.	Chassis	Result
Bruce McLaren	24	T73 FI-1-64 V8	7th
Phil Hill	22	T73 FI-2-64 V8	8th

14-6-64 BELGIAN GRAND PRIX, Spa-Francorchamps

Driver	Race No.	Chassis	Result
Bruce McLaren	20	T73 FI-1-64 V8	2nd
Phil Hill	21	T73 FI-2-64 V8	Rtd eng.

28-6-64 FRENCH GRAND PRIX, Rouen-les-Essarts

Driver	Race No.	Chassis	Result
Bruce McLaren	12	T73 FI-1-64 V8	6th
Phil Hill	14	T73 FI-2-64 V8	7th

11-7-64 BRITISH GRAND PRIX, Brands Hatch

Driver	Race No.	Chassis	Result
Phil Hill	10	T73 FI-2-64 V8	6th
John Taylor	22	T51/73-Ford F1-3-64	14th
Bruce McLaren	9	T73 FI-1-64 V8	Rtd g'box

19-7-64 Solitude GP run in Germany without a single Cooper starting . . .

2-8-64 GERMAN GRAND PRIX, Nürburgring

Driver	Race No.	Chassis	Result
Phil Hill	10	T73 FI-2-64 V8	Rtd eng.
Bruce McLaren	9	T73 FI-1-64 V8	Rtd eng.
Edgar Barth	12	T66 FI-2-63 V8	Rtd

16-8-64 Mediterranean GP, Enna, Sicily

Driver	Race No.	Chassis	Result
John Taylor	36	T60 FI-17-61 V8*	7th
Bruce McLaren	9	T73 FI-1-64 V8	Rtd eng.
Phil Hill**	10	T66 FI-6-63 V8	Accident

*Ex-works, ex-Walker, ex-Cabral Climax V8 car bought by Bob Gerard
**Spare car burned out in race after accidental damage to his T73 in practice

6-9-64 ITALIAN GRAND PRIX, Monza

Driver	Race No.	Chassis	Result
Bruce McLaren	26	T73 FI-1-64 V8	2nd
John Love	24	T73 FI-2-64 V8	DNS*

*After practice engine failure – Love replacing Hill in works team

4-10-64 UNITED STATES GRAND PRIX, Watkins Glen

Driver	Race No.	Chassis	Result
Bruce McLaren	9	T73 FI-1-64 V8	Rtd eng.
Phil Hill	10	T73 FI-2-64 V8	Rtd ign.

25-10-64 MEXICAN GRAND PRIX, Mexico City

Driver	Race No.	Chassis	Result
Bruce McLaren	9	T73 FI-1-64 V8	7th
Phil Hill	10	T73 FI-2-64 V8	9th

RACING RECORDS

Driver	Race No.	Chassis	Result

12-12-64 Rand GP, Kyalami, South Africa
Two-heat aggregate result:
Heat 1 John Love   9   T55 FI-11-61   5th
        Trevor Blokdyk   11   T59-Alfa Romeo –   Rtd
        Dave Clapham   19   T51-Maserati FII-16-60   Rtd
Heat 2 Love
        Blokdyk
Aggregate result: Love 8th

1965

1-1-65 SOUTH AFRICAN GRAND PRIX, East London
Bruce McLaren   9   T73 FI-1-64 V8   5th
John Love   17   T55 FI-11-11-61   Rtd
Jochen Rindt   10   T73 FI-2-64 V8   Rtd elec.

13-3-65 Race of Champions, Brands Hatch
Two-heat aggregate result:
Heat 1 Bruce McLaren   9   T73 FI-2-65 V8   12th
        Jochen Rindt   10   T77 FI-1-65 V8   13th
        John Taylor   22   T60 FI-17-61 V8   14th
Heat 2 McLaren   5th
        Rindt   7th
        Taylor   8th
        John Rhodes*   T71/73 FI-3-64 – Ford   11th

*Gerard reserve entry allowed to start second heat

4-4-65 Syracuse GP run with no Coopers starting . . .

19-4-65 Sunday Mirror Trophy, Goodwood
Bruce McLaren   9   T77 FI-2-65 V8   4th
John Taylor   19   T60 FI-17-61-V8   7th
John Rhodes   20   T71/73 – Ford FI-3-64   8th
Jochen Rindt   10   T77 FI-1-65 V8   DISQ*

*Disqualified for missing-out chicane

15-6-65 International Trophy, Silverstone
Bruce McLaren   9   T77 FI-2-65 V8   6th
John Taylor   15   T60 FI-17-61 V8   11th
John Rhodes   16   T71/73 – Ford FI-3-64   Rtd
Jochen Rindt   10   T77 FI-1-65 V8   Rtd eng.

30-5-65 MONACO GRAND PRIX, Monte Carlo
Bruce McLaren   7   T77 FI-2-65 V8   5th
Jochen Rindt   8   T77 FI-1-65 V8   DNQ*

*Did not qualify, engine lacking throttle opening in practice – see text

13-6-65 BELGIAN GRAND PRIX, Spa-Francorchamps
Bruce McLaren   4   T77 FI-2-65 V8   3rd
Jochen Rindt   5   T77 FI-1-65 V8   11th

27-6-65 FRENCH GRAND PRIX, Clermont-Ferrand
Jochen Rindt   20   T77 FI-1-65 V8   Collision
Bruce McLaren   18   T77 FI-2-65 V8   Rtd steering

10-7-65 BRITISH GRAND PRIX, Silverstone
Bruce McLaren   9   T77 FI-2-65 V8   10th
Jochen Rindt   10   T77 FI-1-65 V8   14th
John Rhodes   20   T60 FI-17-61 V8   Rtd.

Driver	Race No.	Chassis	Result

18-7-65 DUTCH GRAND PRIX, Zandvoort
Bruce McLaren	18	T77 FI-2-65 V8	Rtd cwp.
Jochen Rindt	20	T77 FI-1-65 V8	Rtd eng.

1-8-65 GERMAN GRAND PRIX, Nürburgring
Jochen Rindt	12	T77 FI-1-65 V8	4th
Bruce McLaren	11	T77 FI-2-65 V8	Rtd trans.

15-8-65 Mediterranean GP, Enna, Sicily
John Rhodes	22	T60 FI-17-61 V8	Rtd susp.

12-9-65 ITALIAN GRAND PRIX, Monza
Bruce McLaren	16	T77 FI-2-65 V8	5th
Jochen Rindt	18	T77 FI-1-65 V8	8th

3-10-65 UNITED STATES GRAND PRIX, Watkins Glen
Jochen Rindt	10	7tt FI-1-65 V8	6th
Bruce McLaren	9	T77 FI-2-65 V8	Rtd eng.

24-10-65 MEXICAN GRAND PRIX, Mexico City
Bruce McLaren	9	T77 FI-2-65 V8	Rtd trans.
Jochen Rindt	10	T77 FI-1-65 V8	Rtd ign.

3-litre Formula 1 1966-1968
1965 dress rehearsal race to 3-litre regulations

4-12-65 Rand GP, Kyalami, South Africa
John Love	10	T79 FL-1-65	4th
Tony Jeffries	11	T55 FI-11-61*	10th

*Entered by John Love

1966

1-1-66 South African GP, East London
John Love	12	T79 FL-1-65	6th
Tony Jeffries	14	T55 FI-11-61	9th

1-5-66 Syracuse GP, Sicily
Jo Siffert	2	T81-Maserati FI-2-66	Rtd
Andre Wicky	8	T53 'VR'-BRM V8	DNS
Guy Ligier	26	T81-Maserati FI-4-66	DNS

14-5-66 International Trophy, Silverstone
Jo Bonnier	8	T81-Maserati FI-5-66	3rd
Jochen Rindt	6	T81-Maserati FI-3-66	5th
Richie Ginther	5	T81-Maserati FI-1-66	Rtd O'heat
Jo Siffert	7	T80-Maserati prototype	Rtd.
Guy Ligier	9	T81-Maserati FI-4-66	DNS

22-5-66 MONACO GRAND PRIX, Monte Carlo
Richie Ginther	9	T81-Maserati FI-6-66	5th UNC
Guy Ligier	21	T81-Maserati FI-4-66	6th UNC
Jo Bonnier	18	T81-Maserati FI-5-66	7th UNC
Jochen Rindt	10	T81-Maserati FI-3-66	Rtd eng.

13-6-66 BELGIAN GRAND PRIX, Spa-Francorchamps
Jochen Rindt	19	T81-Maserati FI-3-66	FR 2nd
Richie Ginther	18	T81-Maserati FI-6-66	5th

RACING RECORDS

Driver	Race No.	Chassis	Result
Jo Bonnier	20	T81-Maserati FI-5-66	Accident
Jo Siffert	21	T81-Maserati FI-2-66	Accident
Guy Ligier	22	T81-Maserati FI-4-66	6th UNC

3-7-66 FRENCH GRAND PRIX, Reims-Gueux

Driver	Race No.	Chassis	Result
Jochen Rindt	6	T81-Maserati FI-3-66	4th
Chris Amon	8	T81-Maserati FI-7-66	8th
John Surtees	10	T81-Maserati FI-6-66	FR Rtd o'heat
Jo Siffert	38	T81-Maserati FI-1-66	Rtd o'heat
Guy Ligier	42	T81-Maserati FI-4-66	9th UNC

16-7-66 BRITISH GRAND PRIX, Brands Hatch

Driver	Race No.	Chassis	Result
Jochen Rindt	11	T81-Maserati FI-3-66	5th
Guy Ligier	19	T81-Maserati FI-4-66	10th
Chris Lawrence	24	T73-Ferrari V12 FI-2-64	11th
Jo Siffert	20	T81-Maserati FI-2-66	12th UNC
John Surtees	12	T81-Maserati MI-6-66	Rtd trans.

24-7-66 DUTCH GRAND PRIX

Driver	Race No.	Chassis	Result
Jo Bonnier	30	T81-Maserati FI-5-66	7th
Guy Ligier	36	T81-Maserati FI-4-66	9th
Jochen Rindt	26	T81-Maserati FI-3-66	Accident
John Surtees	24	T81-Maserati FI-7-66	Rtd ign.
Jo Siffert	28	T81-Maserati FI-2-66	Rtd eng.

7-8-66 GERMAN GRAND PRIX, Nürburgring

Driver	Race No.	Chassis	Result
John Surtees	7	T81-Maserati FI-6-66	FR FL 2nd
Jochen Rindt	8	T81-Maserati FI-3-66	3rd
Jo Bonnier	17	T81-Maserati FI-5-66	Rtd trans.
Chris Lawrence	20	T73-Ferrari V12 FI-1-64	Rtd susp.
Guy Ligier	18	T81-Maserati FI-4-66	DNS*

*Practice crash

4-9-66 ITALIAN GRAND PRIX, Monza

Driver	Race No.	Chassis	Result
Jochen Rindt	16	T81-Maserati FI-3-66	4th
Jo Bonnier	38	T81-Maserati FI-5-66	Rtd.
John Surtees	14	T81-Maserati FI-6-66	Rtd fuel
Jo Siffert	36	T81-Maserati FI-2-66	Rtd

17-9-66 Oulton Park Gold Cup

Driver	Race No.	Chassis	Result
Chris Lawrence	10	T73-Ferrari V12 FI-1-64	5th

2-10-66 UNITED STATES GRAND PRIX, Watkins Glen

Driver	Race No.	Chassis	Result
Jochen Rindt	8	T81-Maserati FI-3-66	2nd
John Surtees	7	T81-Maserati FI-6-66	FL 3rd
Jo Siffert	19	T81-Maserati FI-2-66	
Jo Bonnier	22	T81-Maserati FI-5-66	11th UNC

23-10-66 MEXICAN GRAND PRIX, Mexico City

Driver	Race No.	Chassis	Result
John Surtees	7	T81-Maserati FI-6-66	PP 1st
Jo Bonnier	22	T81-Maserati FI-5-66	6th
Jochen Rindt	8	T81-Maserati FI-3-66	Rtd wheel
Jo Siffert	19	T81-Maserati FI-2-66	Rtd susp.
Moises Solana	9	T81-Maserati FI-7-66	

1967

2-1-67 SOUTH AFRICAN GRAND PRIX, Kyalami

Driver	Race No.	Chassis	Result
Pedro Rodriguez	4	T81-Maserati FI-6-66	FIRST
John Love	17	T79 FL-1-65	2nd
Jo Bonnier	15	T81-Maserati FI-5-66	Rtd
Jochen Rindt	3	T81-Maserati FI-3-66	Rtd eng.
Jo Siffert	12	T81-Maserati FI-2-66	Rtd

12-3-67 Race of Champions, Brands Hatch
Two-heat aggregate result:

	Driver	Race No.	Chassis	Result
Heat 1	Pedro Rodriguez	4	T81-Maserati FI-6-66	8th
	Jo Siffert	12	T81-Maserati FI-a2-66	11th
	Guy Ligier	14	T81-Maserati FI-3-66	16th
	Chris Lawrence	19	T73-Ferrari V12 FI-1-64	17th
	Jochen Rindt	3	T81-Maserati FI-1-67	18th UNC
Heat 2	Rodriguez			5th
	Siffert			8th
	Ligier			15th UNC
	Lawrence			Rtd clutch
	Rindt			Rtd trans.
Final	Rodriguez			4th
	Siffer			3rd
	Lawrence			8th
	Rindt			Rtd trans.
	Ligier			DNS*

*Car used for Final by Rindt

15-4-67 Spring Trophy, Oulton Park ran with no Coopers starting

29-4-67 International Trophy, Silverstone

Driver	Race No.	Chassis	Result
Jo Siffert	9	T81-Maserati FI-2-66	3rd
Jo Bonnier	14	T81-Maserati FI-5-66	Rtd fuel tank
Guy Ligier	15	T81-Maserati FI-7-66	Rtd eng.

7-5-67 MONACO GRAND PRIX, Monte Carlo

Driver	Race No.	Chassis	Result
Pedro Rodriguez	11	T81-Maserati FI-6-66	5th
Jochen Rindt	10	T81B-Maserati FI-1-67	Rtd chass.
Jo Siffert	17	T81-Maserati FI-2-66	Rtd eng.

21-5-67 Syracuse GP, Sicily

Driver	Race No.	Chassis	Result
Jo Siffert	?	T81-Maserati FI-2-66	3rd
Jo Bonnier	6	T81-Maserati FI-5-66	5th
Silvio Moser	10	T77-ATS V8 FI-1-65*	Rtd clutch

*Fritz Baumann's ex-works special

4-6-67 DUTCH GRAND PRIX, Zandvoort

Driver	Race No.	Chassis	Result
Jo Siffert	20	T81-Maserati FI-2-66	10th
Pedro Rodriguez	14	T81-Maserati FI-6-66	Rtd g'box.
Jochen Rindt	12	T81B-Maserati FI-1-67	Rtd susp.

18-6-67 BELGIAN GRAND PRIX, Spa Francorchamps

Driver	Race No.	Chassis	Result
Jochen Rindt	29	T81B-Maserati FI-1-67	4th
Jo Siffert	34	T81-Maserati FI-2-66	7th
Pedro Rodriguez	30	T81-Maserati FI-6-66	9th
Guy Ligier	32	T81-Maserati FI-7-66	Rtd eng.

1-7-67 FRENCH GRAND PRIX, Le Mans

Driver	Race No.	Chassis	Result
Jo Siffert	18	T81-Maserati FI-2-66	4th
Pedro Rodriguez	14	T81-Maserati FI-6-66	6th
Guy Ligier	16	T81-Maserati FI-7-66	7th UNC
Jochen Rindt	12	T81B-Maserati FI-1-67	Rtd eng.

15-7-67 BRITISH GRAND PRIX, Silverstone

Driver	Race No.	Chassis	Result
Pedro Rodriguez	12	T81-Maserati FI-6-66	5th
Alan Rees	14	T81-Maserati FI-3-66	9th
Jo Bonnier	23	T81-Maserati FI-5-66	Rtd eng.
Jo Siffert	17	T81-Maserati FI-2-66	Rtd eng.
Jochen Rindt	11	T86-Maserati FI-2-67	Rtd oil
Silvio Moser	22	T77-ATS V8 FI-1-65	Rtd eng.

6-8-67 GERMAN GRAND PRIX, Nürburgring

Driver	Race No.	Chassis	Result
Jo Bonnier	16	T81-Maserati FI-5-66	5th
Pedro Rodriguez	6	T81-Maserati FI-6-66	8th
Jo Siffert	14	T81-Maserati FI-2-66	9th UNC
Jochen Rindt	5	T86-Maserati FI-2-67	Rtd eng.

27-8-67 CANADIAN GRAND PRIX, Mosport Park

Driver	Race No.	Chassis	Result
Jo Bonnier	9	T81-Maserati FI-5-66	8th
Jochen Rindt	71	T81-Maserati FI-6-66	Rtd elec.
Richard Attwood	8	T81B-Maserati FI-1-67	10th
Jo Siffert	14	T81-Maserati FI-2-66	DNS*

*Starter motor, see text

10-9-67 ITALIAN GRAND PRIX, Monza

Driver	Race No.	Chassis	Result
Jochen Rindt	30	T81-Maserati-Maserati FI-2-67	4th
Jacky Ickx	32	T81B-Maserati FI-1-67	6th
Jo Bonnier	26	T81-Maserati FI-5-66	Rtd o'heat.
Jo Siffert	6	T81-Maserati FI-2-66	Rtd eng.

16-9-67 Oulton Park Gold Cup

Driver	Race No.	Chassis	Result
Harry Stiller	24	T82-Cosworth F2-1-66*	10th
John Cardwell	25	T84-Cosworth F2-1-67*	12th

*Gerard-Cooper Racing Team in F2 division of combined race

1-10-67 UNITED STATES GRAND PRIX, Watkins Glen

Driver	Race No.	Chassis	Result
Jo Siffert	15	T81-Maserati FI-2-66	4th
Jo Bonnier	16	T81-Maserati FI-5-66	6th
Jochen Rindt	4	T81B-Maserati FI-1-67	Rtd eng.
Jacky IcKx	21	T86-Maserati FI-2-67	Rtd eng.

22-10-67 MEXICAN GRAND PRIX, Mexico City

Driver	Race No.	Chassis	Result
Pedro Rodriguez	21	T81B-Maserati FI-1-67	6th
Jo Bonnier	16	T81-Maserati FI-5-66	10th
Jo Siffert	15	T81-Maserati FI-2-66	12

1968

1-1-68 SOUTH AFRICAN GRAND PRIX, Kyalami

Driver	Race No.	Chassis	Result
Jo Siffert	19	T81-Maserati FI-2-66	7th
Ludovico Scarfiotti	15	T86-Maserati FI-2-67	Rtd brake
Brian Redman	14	T81B-Maserati FI-1-67	Rtd eng.
Jo Bonnier	20	T81-Maserati FI-5-66	Rtd wheel
Basil van Rooyen	25	T74 FL-1-65	Rtd eng.

17-3-68 Race of Champions, Brands Hatch

Driver	Race No.	Chassis	Result
Brian Redman	6	T86B-BRM V12 F1-1-68	5th

25-4-68 International Trophy, Silverstone

Frank Gardner	11	T86B-BRM V12 F1-2-68	3rd
Ludovico Scarfiotti	15	T86B-BRM V12 F1-2-68	4th

26-5-68 MONACO GRAND PRIX, Monte Carlo

Lucien Bianchi	7	T86B-BRM V12 F1-1-68	3rd
Ludovico Scarfiotti	6	T86B-BRM V12 F1-2-68	4th

9-6-68 BELGIAN GRAND PRIX, Spa-Francorchamps

Lucien Bianchi	15	T86B-BRM V12 F1-1-68	6th
Brian Redman	16	T86B-BRM V12 F1-2-68	Accident W/o

23-6-68 DUTCH GRAND PRIX, Zandvoort

Lucien Bianchi	14	T86B-BRM V8 F1-1-68	Accident

7-7-68 FRENCH GRAND PRIX, Rouen-les-Essarts

Vic Elford	30	T86B-BRM V12 F1-4-68	4th
Johnny Servoz-Gavin	32	T86B-BRM V12 F1-1-68	Accident

20-7-68 BRITISH GRAND PRIX, Brands Hatch

Vic Elford	15	T86B-BRM V12 F1-4-68	Rtd eng.
Robin Widdows	16	T86B-BRM V12 F1-1-68	Rtd ign.

4-8-68 GERMAN GRAND PRIX, Nürburgring

Vic Elford	20	T86B-BRM V12 F1-4-68	Accident
Lucian Bianchi	19	T86B-BRM V12 F1-1-68	Rtd fuel leak

8-9-68 ITALIAN GRAND PRIX, Monza

Vic Elford	23	T86B-BRM V12 F1-4-68	Accident

22-9-68 CANADIAN GRAND PRIX, Mont Tremblant

Vic Elford	21	T86B-BRM V12 F1-4-68	5th
Lucien Bianchi	20	T86B-BRM V12 F1-1-68	10th

6-10-68 UNITED STATES GRAND PRIX, Watkins Glen

Lucien Bianchi	19	T86B-BRM V12 F1-1-68	9th UNC
Vic Elford	18	T86B-BRM V12 F1-4-68	12th UNC

3-11-68 MEXICAN GRAND PRIX, Mexico City

Vic Elford	18	T86B-BRM V12 F1-4-68	8th
Lucien Bianchi	19	T86B-BRM V12 F1-1-68	Rtd eng.

1969

30-3-69 International Trophy, Silverstone

Vic Elford	14	T86B-Maserati F1-2-67	12th

13-4-69 Jarama GP, Spain (F1 and F5000)

Neil Corner	14	T86B-Maserati F1-2-67	4th

18-5-69 MONACO GRAND PRIX, Monte Carlo

Vic Elford	12	T86B-Maserati F1-2-67	7th

APPENDIX SEVEN

Mini-Cooper serial number coding

Basic code pattern example: '9 F A Sa H 12345'

9 = Cubic capacity group
F = Main variation of power unit type within Mini-range power units
A = Subsidiary variation within main variation
Sa = Characteristics of transmission
H = High or low compression on Cooper, or actual cc on Cooper 'S'
12345 = Serial number of engine

Specific Cooper and Cooper 'S' codings:

Power Unit Coding	Engine Serial Numbers	Type	Capacity	Comp. Ratio	Remarks
9F/Sa/X	29001 to 29003	Cooper 'S'	970 cc	10 to 1	Production ceased June 1964
9FD/Sa/X*	29004 to 29036				
9FE/Sa/X*	29037 to 29038				
9F/Sa/X*	29039 to 30029				
9F/Sa/H	101 to 26376 (less 19201 to 20410)	Cooper	997 cc	9 to 1	Produced ceased September 1963
9F/Sa/L	101 to 28950			8·3 to 1	
9FA/Sa/H	101 to 4999	Cooper	998 cc	9 to 1	
9FA/Sa/L	101 to 3011			8·3 to 1	
9FD/Sa/H*	101 on (less 33661 to 33948)			9 to 1	
9FD/Sa/L*	101 on			8·3 to 1	
9F/Sa/H	26501 to 3360 (plus 19201 to 20410)	Cooper 'S'	1070 cc	9 to 1	Production ceased March 1964
9FD/Sa/H*	33661 to 33948				
9F/Sa/Y	31001 to 31405	Cooper 'S'	1275 cc	9·75 to 1	
9FD/Sa/Y*	31406 to 32208				
9FE/Sa/Y*	32209 to 32377				
9F/Sa/Y*	32378 on				

*Fitted with Positive Crankcase Ventilation.

Note: The following alternative compression ratios are available as Optional Extras for the Cooper 'S' without change to the prefix coding:

        970 cc   11 to 1
        1070 cc
        1275 cc   12 to 1

Vehicle types (not Cooper) index

AWE 130, 131
Alfa Romeo 11, 44, 47, 73, 92, 186, 248, 255, 292
  Disco Volante 81, 102, 103
  GP 37
  Giulietta 283
  Monza 9
  V8 302–304
Alpine Renault 282
Alta 43, 56, 58, 71, 75, 90
Aston Butterworth 63, 66, 136
Aston Martin 20, 104, 140, 166, 167, 171, 184, 186, 201, 202, 215, 217, 218, 220, 235, 238, 246
  2.6 litre 92
  DBR5/250 247
  Vantage 92
Atkins F2 Mk III 162
Austin GN 14
  MG 22
  7 10, 11, 14, 136
Austin Healey 145
  100S 131
  Sprite 236, 240

BG Bristol 148
BRM 118, 148, 150, 157, 160, 162, 164–166, 168, 172, 173, 178, 183, 186, 194, 196, 199, 201, 202, 206, 208, 229, 232, 243, 245–247, 252, 256, 262–264, 272, 273, 279, 280, 283, 285, 291, 299
BMW 328 14, 26, 40
BRM P48 247
  V12 302
BSA Gold Star 43
Beart-Rodger 136
Bedford 35, 36, 63
Behra-Porsche 162
Bentley 118
Bowmaker-Lola 256
Bowmaker-Yeoman 247
Brabham 269–273, 276, 281, 304
Bugatti 13, 14, 23, 24, 188
  type 54 10
Buick 221, 222

Chaparral 228
Chevrolet 17, 19, 22
  V8 72
Cisitalia 32, 188
Citroën Light 15 121
Connaught 58, 67, 71, 118, 122, 136, 143, 158, 273
Cosworth 282, 285
  Ford 301, 304, 305
Coventry Climax 8, 118, 119, 126–128, 143, 189, 200, 222, 229, 252, 256, 273, 275, 290
Crossley 118

DB Panhard 43
Daimler 34, 42
DalRo-Jaguar 207
De Haviland Gypsy Moth 13

De Tomaso-Alfa Romeo 254
Delahaye 136
Djinn Special 136

ERA 44, 118
Eagle 296
Effyh-JAP 43, 56
Elva 136, 238, 239
Excelsior 12

Ferguson 252
Ferguson-Climax 247
Fernihough-JAP 26
Ferrari 58, 64, 66, 71, 74, 75, 77, 87, 90, 144, 152, 160–162, 167, 172, 178, 186, 203, 207, 219, 222, 232, 247, 252, 253, 256, 288, 291, 294, 295, 298
  2 litre 47
  4½ litre ThinWall 61, 62, 64, 113, 114
  500/400 cylinder 136
  Barchetta 49, 92, 95
  Dino 146, 158, 161, 162, 172, 210, 214, 217
  GT 145
  Monza Sports 137
  Squalo 136, 202
  Testa Rossa 225
  V12 36, 38, 40, 186
Fiat 16, 23, 24, 32
  Topolino 14, 16, 18, 20, 23, 24, 46, 53
Flying Flea 10, 11, 13
Ford Anglia 16
Francis-Barnett 9, 10–11
Fraser-Imp 276
Frazer Nash 28, 47, 63, 66, 94
Freikaiserwagen 29

Gemini 240, 241

HAR Special 136
HW Alta 136
HWM 118
Harry-Hawker AC 10
Hillman Imp 278
Holbay Ford 222
Honda 285, 294, 296, 304

Impala 276
Iota-Triumph 43

JAP 16, 17, 20, 22, 27, 28, 30, 32, 35, 36, 39, 41, 43, 44, 54
  1000 sidecar 24
  1000 twin 28, 34, 37
  Speedway 16, 23, 28
  TT 14
JBS 54
  Norton 43, 44
JBW-Maserati 208
Jaguar 29, 89, 273, 276, 284, 291, 301
  D type 126, 240
  Ecurie Ecosse 49, 220
  SS100 54
  XK120 131

Kieft 111, 118, 119

Lagonda 25
Lea-Francis TT 136
Lister 136, 154
  Bristol 122
  Jaguar 215, 218, 219
Lolas 189, 238, 240, 256, 263, 281
  FJ 280
  T60 280
  Chevrolet 280
Lotus 25, 43, 126, 130, 136, 142, 143, 145, 146, 150, 162, 163, 171, 183, 184, 186, 189, 201, 202, 204, 207, 208, 210, 212, 219, 220, 233, 242, 245–248, 250, 253, 255, 256, 263, 264, 272, 274, 276, 279, 281, 282, 285, 291, 297
  11 129, 131, 134, 136
  12 148, 150
  13 225
  16 186, 190
  18 196, 208, 213, 239, 247
  19 221, 225, 226, 228, 235
  21 256
  23 222, 286
  24 262
  49 302
Climax 122
Connaught 124
Elite 182
MG 124
Maserati 145

MG 10, 11, 19, 34, 49
  MGB 24
  MG Q type 29
  TC 16, 41, 131
MPS-Ford 126
Magdalena-Mixhuca 1968 304
Marcos 284
Maserati 44, 58, 66, 71, 75, 90, 127, 142, 148, 149, 152, 162, 166, 167, 168, 208, 210, 254, 256, 275, 291, 295, 296, 302, 306
  1500 S 130, 137
  Birdcage 217, 222
Matra 282, 285, 304
McLaren Oldsmobile 274
Mercedes
  SL 229
  300 SL coupé 124, 145
  Benz 299
Merlyn Chevrolet 228
Mezzolitre 276
Mildren 200
  Maserati Mk IV 207
Miles Hawk 13
Moskvitch 299
Morgan 118
  JAP 3 Wheeler 13
Morris Minor 1000 166, 171

Norton 29, 40, 54, 112
  Manx 38, 39, 40, 112

Offenhauser 183
Oldsmobile 228
  V8 229

Packaway Caravan 13
Pontiac Grand Prix 221, 224
Porsche 74, 100, 122, 126, 130, 145, 146, 162, 163, 173, 180, 210, 212, 222, 232, 247, 248, 256, 263, 302
  550 125
  Berg Spyder 303
  Spyder 147

Renault Dauphine 8, 190
Riley 60
  9 saloon 31
Rover 41, 43, 48
Rudge 12

SS Jaguar 20
Sacha-Gordine 188
Scarab 221
Shelby American Cobra 49, 226
Shelby King Cobra 226, 228, 277
Simca-Gordini 44
Sturmey-Archer 21
Sunbeam
  S7 34
  V12 7
  Silver Bullet 10
  Talbot 39
Swift 118

Talbot 25
  Lago 44
Thomas Special (Flat Iron) 136
Tojiero-Jaguar 240
Tornado-Corvette 186
Triumph 118
  Speed Twin 16
  Tiger 20, 21
  twin 20
Tyrell 203, 209, 222, 226, 238–242

Vanwall 120, 123, 142, 144, 148, 150, 152, 158, 161, 162, 163, 205, 238
Vauxhall 16, 31, 32, 34
  Ten 31, 32
Veritas 47, 68
Villiers 125 cc 160
Vincent
  Black Lightning 28
  Comet 110
  HRD 14, 30, 31, 35–37, 40, 83
  HRD Rapide 28

Walker 202, 209, 212, 245
  Connaught 100, 104
  Lotus 247, 252, 256
Wasp 38
Wolseley Viper 10

Personality index

Abate, Carlo Mario 268
Abbott, Jim 81
Abecassis, George 24, 30, 35–37, 43, 63
Abernethy, Bruce 276
Ahrens Jr, Kurt 242–244
Aikens, Frank 21, 22, 43, 51
Aldis, John 117
Alexander, Tyler 228, 271
Alfieri, Giulio 167, 286, 290, 291, 294, 295
Allington, Jim 181, 261
Allison, Cliff 111, 130, 148, 158, 160–162, 178, 197, 210, 219
Amarotti 152
Ambrose, Bert 54
Amon, Chris 265, 283, 294. 295, 298
Anderson, Bob 110, 282, 285
Andersson, Solve 111
Andersson, Sven 244, 284
Andrews, Chris 35, 142
Angelo, John 306
Anthony, Mike 124
Armbruster, Fred 208
Armstrong, Bill 83
Arundell, Peter 214, 242, 282
Arutunoff, Anatoly 49, 93, 95
Ascari, Alberto 64, 236
Ashdown, Peter 210
Aston, Bill 36, 37, 39, 47, 55, 58, 59, 63, 67, 106, 194
Atkins, C T 'Tommy' 139, 158, 167, 168, 176, 182, 184, 196, 206, 208, 209, 220, 225, 228, 229, 247, 250, 252, 255, 263
Attwood, Richard 241, 280, 298
Axelsson, Sten 285

Bacon, Frank 22
Baghetti, Giancarlo 248, 256
Bailey, Ian 300
Baird, Bobby 74, 87, 94
Baker, Clive 283–285
Baker, David 241
Baker, Sir Herbert 31
Baldock, David 21, 49
Ballisat, Keith 157, 163, 213, 239, 240
Balmer, Donald 81, 94, 100
Balzarini, Gianni 217
Bandini, Lorenzo 254, 255, 268, 288, 293
Banks, Henry 230
Banks, Warwick 283
Banting, Rodney 280, 283
Barak, Phil 219
Barber, John 64, 68, 72, 78. 80, 102
Barclay, Norman 163, 210
Bardi-Barry, Kurt 241, 242, 244
Baring 35
Barker, Major 34
Barker, Richard 100
Barlow, Vic 194, 234
Barney, Mike 174, 177, 182, 192, 196, 197, 199, 201, 203, 220, 221, 224, 248, 254, 256, 258, 259, 262, 265, 272, 275, 290
Bartram, Terry 245, 250
Barth, Edgar 147, 214, 273
Barwell, Paul 49
Bateson, John 103
Baumann, Fritz 290, 297

Bayol, Eli 43
Beanland, Colin 154, 158–160
Beart, Francis 52, 53, 56, 57, 112, 121
Beauman, Don 103
Beckwith, Michael 281, 285
Bedding, Fred 25, 32, 55, 59, 110, 143, 173, 190, 192, 220, 222, 266, 268, 269, 271, 299
Bedding, Pete 25, 31, 32, 43, 51, 55, 59, 110, 143, 173, 190, 192, 220, 222, 266, 268, 269, 271, 299
Bedson, Gordon 34
Beels, Lex 37, 43
Behra, Jean 147, 151, 160–162, 166, 170–173, 180, 210
Bell, Peter 73, 84
Bendall, Cecil 87, 103
Bengry, Bill 18
Bentley, John 126, 129
Bernusset, Jacques 280, 283
Berry, Jim 86
Berry, Peter 220, 221, 225
Bertocco, Luigi 285
Bettenhausen, Tony 230
Bicknell, Ben 61
Bicknell, Joe 61
Bicknell, Reg 126, 136
Bilton, Percy 43
Binner, Egon 131
Birkett, Holly 14
Birks, Arthur 87
Birrell, Alistair 74, 78, 80
Biss, Roger 86
Black, Bill 118
Blackburn, David 299, 304
Blanc, Jean 283
Blanchard, Henry 216
Blanden, John 78, 90, 100
Blignant, Alex 268
Bloomer, Sylvia 35
Blumer, Jimmy 129, 131, 145, 217–220, 222, 225
Blyth, Bernard 'Bill' 84, 86, 134
Boddy, Bill 14, 35
Bolster, John 48, 117, 297, 307
Bolton, Peter 100
Bondurant, Bob 226
Bonnier, Jo 162, 172, 173, 182, 194, 196, 199, 202, 203, 206, 208, 245, 246, 266, 268, 271–273, 283, 287, 288, 290, 292, 294–296, 298
Bonomi, Roberto 196
Borgward, Carl 209, 212
Boshier-Jones, David 110–112
Bottoms, Alf 43, 44, 50, 51
Bottoms, Charles 51
Boulten 71
Bowman, W S 216
Brabham, Alf 131
Brabham Betty 123, 166, 171, 233
Brabham, Gary 233
Brabham, Geoffrey 11, 137
Brabham, Jack 11, 68, 72, 77, 79, 83–95, 89, 91, 117, 120, 122–124, 126, 130, 131, 134, 136, 137, 139, 141–150, 153–155, 158, 160–163, 165, 166, 168, 170, 171, 173, 176–178, 182–185, 188, 190, 191, 194, 197,

199, 201–206, 208–210, 212–214, 217–223, 230–233, 242, 245–248, 250–256, 262, 264, 265, 269, 271, 274, 278, 288, 292, 294–296, 306
Bradley, Bill 208, 241, 282
Bradnack, Bertie 41, 47, 86, 115, 117, 174
Brady, Pauline 20
Braid, Mjr Peter 40
Brake, David 53
Brandon Eric 12, 14–25, 27–31, 36–40, 42, 44, 47, 51–57, 61, 62, 64, 72, 78, 80, 90, 91, 106, 107, 112, 113, 122, 158, 306
Brandon, Sheila 54
Brandt, Carl Ludvig 209
Brendt, Heinrich 285
Bridger, Tom 111, 112, 126, 156, 158, 160, 163, 194
Brise, Johnny 56
Brise, Tony 56
Bristow, Chris 125, 145, 182, 183, 101, 200–202, 204, 210, 212, 213
Broadley, Eric 189
Brock, Pete 226, 228
Brooks, J H 48, 49
Brooks, P S 23
Brooks, Tony 112, 134, 136, 137, 142–144, 147, 148, 160, 163, 167, 168, 171–174, 176, 180, 182, 184, 185, 202, 204, 206, 208
Brown, Alan 39, 43, 51–54, 56, 57, 60–64, 66, 68, 71–75, 78, 87, 91–93, 95, 96, 98, 107, 113, 114, 139, 157, 209, 210
Brown, David 166
Brown, Jimmy 47
Brown, John 119, 122
Brown, John R 81, 92, 93, 100
Bryant, Peter 253
Bryde, A H 'Archie' 63, 64, 67, 75, 78
Bryden, Beryl (and her Backroom Boys) 31, 32
Bryden-Brown, Louise 256
Bucknum, Ronnie 228
Bueb, Ivor 107, 110, 112, 122, 124–127, 136, 145, 148, 160, 162, 209, 210
Burgess, Ian 44, 53, 140, 141, 148, 158–162, 167, 176, 178, 180, 182, 186, 194, 202, 205, 206, 208, 238, 256
Burgoyne 43
Burn, Peter 303
Burr, Ron 138
Burrill, Maurice 96
Burt, Patsy 125, 148
Bussinello, Robert 292
Byron 126

Cabianca, Giulo 208, 217
Cabral, Mario Aranjo 207, 214, 254, 268
Cambell-Jones, John 210, 212–214
Campbell-Blair, Niall 94, 96, 145
Camm, Sir Sidney 119
Cannell, George 72, 78
Cannon, Mike 49
Cardwell, John 283
Carter, Ken 39, 43, 47, 51, 53, 54
Carter, Duane 230
Casner, Lucky 245
Cassegrain, Jean-Pierre 283

Castellotti, Eugene 130
Castle, Eric 95
Cattle, Peter 287
Cella, Leo 280
Cengia, Frank 124
Challen, Keith 152
Chambers, David 68, 83
Chapman, Colin 113, 118, 124, 127 136, 142, 144, 145, 157, 165, 186, 189, 199, 202, 219, 235, 236, 259
Chase, Bob 56, 60, 61, 64, 66, 71–73, 78, 81, 87, 90–93, 95, 96, 98, 124
Chiron, Louis 39, 259
Chisman, John 168, 170 209, 302
Choukron, André 285
Christie, Michael 36, 143, 148
Christy, John 226
Christmas, Don 92
Claes, Johnny 44, 87
Clark, Jimmy 200, 208, 226, 228, 235, 239, 247, 256, 259, 262–264, 266, 272, 274, 279, 297
Clarke, Bill 78, 79, 88
Clarke, Rodney 58, 118, 158
Clay, Ernie 256
Clay, Freddie 91
Cleverley, Tony 302
Clifford, Hugh 81
Coad, Frank 91
Coatalen, Louis 10
Cobb, John 81
Coffey, Stan 75, 78
Coldham, Stan 24, 27–30, 35–37, 47
Cole, Tom 71, 73, 74, 87, 104
Collerson, Barry 285
Collins, Pat 27, 38, 44, 58
Collins, Peter 27, 29, 37, 38, 40, 43, 47, 51, 107, 113, 136, 144, 160–162
Collomb, Bernard 212, 214, 245, 256
Colotti, Valerio 168, 213, 283
Connell, Alan 222, 224
Constantine, George 184, 185, 217
Coombs, John 41, 48, 54, 94, 98, 124, 216, 219, 273, 280–282
Cooper, Charles Newton 7–29, 31–92, 105–274, 300
Cooper, Charles Renard 9
Cooper, Elsie (née Paul) 10, 19, 71
Cooper, John Newton 7–92, 102, 103, 105–306
Cooper, Judy 9, 61
Cooper, Lottie 9, 10
Cooper, Mike 306
Cooper, John A 44, 85, 89
Corini, Claudio 214
Corner, Neil 304
Cottrell, Jeremy 241
Courage, Piers 282
Cowles, Russell 242
Cowley, Alan 111
Cox, Bill 38
Cox, Ken 91
Crabbe, Colin 306
Crabbe, Percy 217
Crichton-Stuart, Hon Charles 280
Crook, Anthony 75, 86, 89, 96, 98–100

373

INDEX

Crouch, John 50, 83
Crosthwaite, Dick 86
Croydon, Harold 43
Cruz-Schwelm, Andolfo J 72
Cunningham, Briggs 184, 221, 222, 243, 245
Cunningham-Reid, Noel 142, 148
Currie, Mike 98
Curtis, Stephen 86, 95

d'Abrera, Robin 276
Dagorne, Michel 280
Daigh 206
Daniell, Harold 47
Darby, Colin 14, 22, 32, 71, 128, 238
Darby, David 285
da Silva Ramos, Hernano 158, 216
Davey-Milne, Earl 84
Davidson, I E 49
Davies, Jim 235
Davis, Cliff 47, 49, 88, 111
Davis, Colin 131, 176, 182, 217, 239
Davis, Don 235
Davison, Lex 136, 137, 246, 255, 256, 262, 265, 275
de Beaufort 147
de Cadanet, Alain 305
de Changy 210
de Fierlandt, Hughes 285
de Graffenreid, 'Toulo' 44, 66
'de Havilland' 71
Dei, 'Mimo' 176, 202, 254, 268
Deighton, Len 246
Delamont, Dean 84, 120, 122, 123, 199
de Minicis, Dr 286
Dennis, Ron 288, 297, 299
Dennis, Tony 126
Denton, Jean 282
Denton, Tony 282
de Villiers, Jimmy 72, 89
Devlin, Michael 'Ginger' 52, 57, 60, 63, 91, 122, 140, 158-160, 190, 194, 201, 239, 245, 254, 256, 269, 299, 306
Dickson, Tommy 218-220, 225
Diggony, Jim 219
Dixon, E A 94
Dixon, Freddy 10
Dochnel, Frank 268
Docker, Sir Bernard 34
Docker, Lance 34, 42
Dodds, Stuart 210
Don, Kaye 7, 10-12, 20, 23
Dougherty, J F 125
Douglas 12, 13
Dowd, Al 226, 228
Dowson, Jack 218
Dryden, 'Curly' 24, 26, 29, 30, 35, 37, 39, 43, 44, 51
Duckworth, Keith 298
Dulles, W 282
Dundas, Frank 49
Duneborn, George 244, 284
du Pont, Alexis 57, 126
du Puy, John 137
Durlacher, Jack 292
Dvoretsky, Dev 171

Eatherley, James 285
Eccles, Alan 125, 145
Ecclestone, Bernie 50, 75, 112, 117
Edwards, S 18
Edwards, Sir Clive 102, 103
Edwards, Derrick 154
Elford, Peter 79
Elford, Vic 303-306
Elliott, Herb 186
Ellsworth, Stan 87
Emery, Paul 73, 95, 183
Emney, Fred 9
England, Paul 147
Escott, Colin 219
Evans, David 246
Evender 228
Everard, Tony 92

Fahey, Miss 71
Fairman, Jack 78, 148, 171, 182, 206
Falkner, Dr Frank 184, 220, 222, 230, 232
Fane, AFP 28
Fangio, Juan Manual 61, 62, 72, 142, 146, 149-152
Farina, Pinin 35, 44, 62, 64, 72, 236
Faulkner, Freddie 43, 103
Fejer, George 28, 305
Fengler, Harlan 230
Fenning, John 280, 283, 284
Ferguson, Andrew 140, 141, 159, 173, 186, 196, 202, 208, 218, 245, 254, 256, 274
Field, Jack 10
Fitch, John 219
Flint, Ken 49
Flockhart, Ron 64, 80, 144, 161, 165, 166, 172, 183, 208, 212, 217, 245-247
Foglietti 236
Folland, Dudley 40
Fothergill, Martin 203, 210
Fox, Fred 71
Fox Jnr, John 56, 125, 126
Francis, Alf 74, 79, 89, 90, 126-128, 131, 136, 137, 140, 142-144, 150-153, 155, 157, 160, 162, 168, 170, 171, 173, 183, 192, 209, 233, 246, 283, 292
Franck, Jean-Claude 280
Frankland, Hughie 265, 272
Fraser, Alan 64, 78
Frazer-Jones, Ian 89
Frère, Paul 191, 212, 218
Friedman, Dave 226
Frost, Ron 47, 154
Furstenhof, Sven 283

Gaine, Roy 223
Gale, Guy 96
Galetti 143
Gammon, Peter 124, 126, 128, 131, 144
Gardner, Frank 265, 285, 302
Garnett, Miss 71
Garrad, Norman 39
Gaston, Paddy 241
Gaydon, Peter 285
Geil, Andreas 145
Gendebien, Olivier 162, 176, 204-206, 208, 212
Gerard, Bob 28, 47, 67, 73, 74, 78, 79, 81, 86, 89, 99, 123, 139, 146, 160, 241, 277, 282, 285
Gerard, Julian 285
Gethin, Peter 174, 284
Gibbons 88
Gibbs, Bluebell 125
Gibbs, Len 125
Gibbs, Ray 86
Gibson, Dick 87, 89, 100, 104, 147, 148, 154, 162, 191, 213
Gibson-Jarvie, Bob 210
Gilbert, Lenny 89, 166
Ginther, Richie 228, 266, 288, 292, 294, 296
Glasby, Bruce 89
Glasby, Eric 78, 89
Glasby, Ivan 89
Glass, Arnold 186, 207, 208
Gleed, Bruce 160
Glockler, Helm 74, 87
Goddard, Geoff 120, 194, 214, 251, 253, 288
Goddard, Jumbo 91
Goddard, Stan 24, 26
Grandsire, Henri 282
Grant, Jerry 226
Gray, Don 53
Gray, Teddy 84, 186
Greason, Reg 84
Green, Mrs 238
Greenall, Hon Edward 94, 98, 129
Greene, Keith 116, 125, 200, 206, 210, 212, 229
Greene, Syd 116, 125, 200, 201, 206
Greening, Stan 35, 41
Gregory, Ken 56, 90, 157, 168, 182, 191, 202, 205, 209, 210, 212, 214, 274

Gregory, Masten 166, 168, 170, 171, 173, 176-178, 180, 182, 184, 190, 202, 204-206, 208, 222, 229
Griffen, Miss 147
Grohmann, Mike 158, 170, 171, 174, 177, 182, 184, 196, 201, 203, 205, 230,232, 233, 235, 248, 252, 258, 262, 265, 271
Guelfi, André 100, 163
Gullery, John 230
Gunnersson, Sven-Olf 283
Gurney, Dan 182, 197, 199, 206, 208, 222, 224-226, 228, 235, 256, 265, 271, 296
Guthrie 89

Habin, John 37, 51
Hacking, Jack 49
Haig, Betty 87, 92-95
Haig, Doug 94
Halford, Bruce 87, 95, 148, 158, 191, 202, 205, 206, 208, 212, 214, 225
Hall, Jimmy 63, 225, 226, 228
Hall, John 140
Hall, Keith 111, 126, 148
Hall, Noel 207, 208
Halligan, Jake 87, 88
Hamblin, Bob 39, 40, 52
Hamilton, Duncan 9, 11, 66, 87, 95, 115
Hansgen, Walt 222-224, 238, 240-243, 255
Harper, John 117
Harris, Mike 255, 269
Harris, Ron 279
Harriman, Sir George 195, 199, 301, 304
Harrison, J Frank 226
Hart, Oliver 214
Hart, Stan 214
Hartin, Len 43
Hartin, Roy 43
Hartley, Gene 203
Hartman, N J 216
Hartwell, George 35, 41, 64, 78
Harwood, Jim 86
Hassan, Walter 117, 127, 138, 143, 157, 202, 222, 232, 251, 253
Hattle, Bobbi 78
Hawkes, Tom 84
Hawthorn, Leslie 61, 63, 67, 103
Hawthorn, Mike 56, 60, 62-64, 66, 67, 73-75, 77, 78, 81, 91, 94, 95, 103, 104, 110, 113, 122, 127-129, 131, 147, 148, 151, 158, 204
Head, Lt-Col Michael 116
Head, Patrick 117
Headland, Charles 43
Heath, Cecil 47
Heath, John 16, 24, 37, 43, 60, 118
Hegbourne, Tony 279, 281
Heimrath, Ludwig 228
Henderson, Dick 10, 148
Heppenstall, Ray 226
Herbertson, Mike 285
Hermann, Hans 130, 178, 209, 210
Hesketh, Lord 22
Heynes, Bill 115, 300
Higham, Johnnie 96, 145
Hill, Graham 56, 148, 158, 171, 194, 199, 201, 202, 204, 210, 216, 224, 247, 256, 259, 262-264, 266, 271, 272, 280-282, 297
Hill, Phil 131, 152, 172, 176, 182, 203, 205, 207, 208, 252, 256, 259, 271-276
Himble, Jack 222
Hine, Edward 238
Hoare, Col Ronnie 210
Hodge, Peter 286
Holbert, Bob 226, 228
Holden, Cliff 299
Hones, Gerry 253
Howe, Earl 30, 186
Hudson, Skip 226
Hugus, Ed 126, 129
Hulme, Dennis 166, 194, 196, 202, 208, 213, 239, 241, 242, 245-247, 271, 280, 283, 292, 296

Hume, John 25, 34, 41, 55, 145, 165, 210
Hunt, Leslie 100
Hunt, Reg 86, 91, 100
Hussein, King of Jordan 124
Huswick, Ken 24
Hutchinson, Henk 111
Hveem, Bosse 44
Hyslop, Angus 241, 245, 246, 255, 256, 264

Ickx, Jacky 298
Iglesias, Jesus Ricardo 72, 152
Ireland, Innes 145, 148, 196, 201, 202, 206, 208, 212, 213, 225, 247, 253, 256, 271, 304
Iszatt, Donald 111

Jacks, Keith 210
Jackson, Peter 49, 268, 269
Jackson, W C 136
James, Bill 158, 170, 171, 177, 233
Jaussard, Jean-Pierre 280
Jeffrey, Dick 84
Jenkinson, Dennis 58, 120, 130, 143, 146, 161
Jensen, Ross 154, 166
Jensen, Syd 136, 137, 163, 166, 186, 194, 19
Johanssen, Neil 255, 273, 277, 284
Johansson, Max 285
Johnson, Douggie 13, 25, 123, 146, 158, 16 238, 299
Johnson, Ed 183, 230
Johnstone, Bruce 245, 255
Jolly, Derck 117
Jones, Aiden 256
Jones, Alan 117, 285
Jones, Gordon 112
Jones, Max 44
Jones, Parnelli 228
Jones, Stan 84, 88, 117, 194
Jones, Tom 303
Jopp, Peter 131
Jousson, Ake 43
Jüttner, Fritz 209

Kans, Peter 229
Keele, Mike 217
Keele, Roger 217
Keen, Mike 90-92, 124
Keith, Roland 57
Keller, Kurt 285
Kelly, John 51, 55, 72, 114, 143, 160
Kendall, John 285
Kerr, Phil 154, 166, 171
Keylock, George 80
Kieft 51, 53-66, 118
Kimberly, Jim 232-235
King, Cecil 12
King, Spen 300
Kitson, Terry 72, 140, 159, 233, 245, 248, 265, 271, 299
Kliner, Henry 139
Knight, Bill 131, 283
Knight, Colin 281
Knight, Jack 24, 154, 168, 193, 200, 215, 222, 231, 238, 240, 244, 279
Knight, Mike 283
Kolb, Charlie 241
Kotze, Tony 89
Kranse, Billy 240
Kuhnke, Kurt 107, 111
Kyffin, Tom 87, 88, 94, 95

la Caze, Robert 163
Lacy, Bill 238
Lambert, Chris 285
Lambert, G H 125
Lampredi, Aurelio 64
Lancefield, Steve 43, 52, 54, 108
Landi, Chico 64
Lang, Adolf 107
Lang, Craig 18, 21, 228
Lang, Hermann 47
Langton, Steve 99

INDEX

Latchford, Dave 131
Lavender, John 31
Lawrence, Jack 49
Lawrence, Jock 49, 80
Lawton, George 166, 186, 194, 196, 208, 213, 214
Lee, Leonard 118, 157, 165, 222, 232, 233
Le Petoulet 158
Leighton, Jon 188, 207, 208
Leith 35
Leonard, Lionel 41, 47, 49, 88, 92
Leslie, Ed 226, 228
Leston, Les 51, 54, 56, 57, 107, 122, 125–128, 131, 136, 139, 140, 144, 146, 148
Lewis, Jack 139, 157, 210, 212, 214, 245, 252, 259
Lewis, Marshall 232
Lewis-Evan, Sheila 57
Lewis-Evans, Stuart 54, 56, 77, 107, 110–112, 158, 160, 162, 163
Lewis-Evans, 'Pop' 54, 108
Levis, Roly 275
Libaritz, Cecil 157
Liekens, Andre 241
Ligier, Guy 292, 294, 295, 298
Lincoln, Curt 56, 216, 241
Lindsay, Chris 124
Lindsay, Gordon 72, 78
Lipe, Tippy 126
Lister, Brian 49
Lloyd, Nevil 88
Loens, André 64, 73, 78, 111
Logan 35
Lones, Clive 14, 16, 26, 28
Looker, Ernie 55, 68, 71, 72, 177, 299
Love, John 239–242, 244, 245, 264, 269, 273, 279, 296
Lovely, Peter 125, 208
Lowe, W H 53
Lubin, Joe 139
Lucas, Jean 53, 146, 216
Lucas, John 41, 71
Lucien 303
Lukey, Len 91, 104, 194
Lurani, 'Johnny' 236

MacDonald, Dave 226, 228
Mackay, Alan 125, 130, 160
Mackay, Bill 220
Mackay, Major E M 48
Mackay-Fraser 144
MacDavel, Mike 119, 124, 126, 128, 145, 146
MacKenzie-Lorr, Robin 128, 129, 131
Macklin, John 269
Macklin, Lady 171
Macklin, Lance 58, 171
McLaren, Bruce 137, 153, 154, 158–163, 165, 166, 168, 170, 171, 173, 177, 178, 180, 182–186, 189–191, 194, 196, 197, 199–208, 210, 212, 214, 217, 220–224, 228–230, 239, 241, 245, 247, 248, 250–252, 255, 256, 259, 262–266, 268, 269, 271–277, 279, 288, 290, 294, 299, 302, 304
McLaren 'Pop' 137, 177
MacMillan, Alex 88, 96
MacPherson, Roddy 73, 77, 86
Maddock, Owen Richard 31, 59, 68, 71, 72, 102, 105–107, 109, 110, 113, 114, 120, 122, 125, 126, 128, 134, 143, 154, 155, 168, 173, 186, 189, 193, 194, 197, 199, 200, 218, 222, 232, 236, 247–249, 256, 266, 268, 269, 272, 276, 277, 284
Maddock, R H Richard 31, 143
Maggs, Tony 214, 240–242, 244, 255, 259, 262–264, 266, 269
Maglia, Jacques 279
Maher 240
Mairesse, Willy 204, 263
Majzub, Julian 87
Malcolm, Jack 88
Manney III, Henry 57
Mansell, Johnny 76, 186, 246, 255

Manzon, Robert 44, 66
Maritz 89
Markl, Rolf 241
Marr, Leslie 120
Marsh, Tony 115, 128, 139, 147, 148, 209, 210, 214, 217, 219
Marshall, Ron 256
Martin, Ray 44, 85, 89
Martin, Tico 285
Marston, Bob 284, 297, 299–302, 304
Matich, Frank 225
Matilla, Leo 241, 284, 285
May, Austen 26, 27, 38, 43, 54
Mays, Raymond 14, 186, 202
Mayer, Teddy 228, 243, 266, 269
Mayer, Timmy 225, 228, 243, 244, 263, 266, 269, 271, 279
Mayers, Jim 124
Mayman, Lionel 125, 145
Mayo, Merv 154
McAlpine 122
McBain, Jock 78
McCowan, Bill 242
McKay, David 255, 256, 264, 265
McKay, Ross 88
McKechnie, John 285
McKee, Mike 210, 212, 214, 236, 238
McKellar, Ian 146
Mecom, John Jnr 224, 225, 228
Meier, Hermann 47
Melly, George 32
Menditguy, Carlos 196, 202
Menere, Peter 91
Middlemas, Brian 88
Middleton, Ted 13
Mildren, Alec 86, 139, 168, 200, 207, 246
Miles, Ken 228
Millar, Cameron 87
Miller, Austin 207, 208
Mitchell, Tony 103
Momo, Alfred 221, 240
Montgomery-Charrington, Robin 44, 66
Monteiro 157
Moore, Ben 100
Moore, Don 100
Moore, S P 23
Morice, Flt Lt W F 79, 88, 94, 137
Morris, John 90
Morris, Peter 123
Moser, Silvio 290, 297, 304
Moss, Alfred 26, 28, 29, 35, 44, 157, 168, 182, 208
Moss, Katie 150, 151
Moss, Pat 196
Moss, Stirling 21, 24, 26–30, 35–40, 42–44, 47, 50, 54, 56, 64, 73–75, 78, 84, 85, 87, 89, 90, 100, 104, 107, 112, 123, 124, 126, 129, 148, 150–152, 157–163, 166–168, 171–174, 178, 182–186, 191, 192, 194, 196, 200–202, 204–206, 208, 209, 212, 217, 219, 221, 247, 250, 252, 253, 255, 256
Motschenbacher, Lothar 228
Mould, Peter 123
Moulton, Alex 243
Munaron, Gino 202, 205, 206, 254
Mundy, Harry 118, 122, 138, 247
Müller, Donatus 26, 27, 29
Mulligan, Mick 32
Murray, Colin 117
Murray, David 64, 79, 219, 225
Musso, Luigi 131, 151, 152
Myers, Brian 285
Myers, Jack 78

Nardwell, Jonko 241
Natali, Massimo 254
Naylor, Brian 206, 208, 210, 217, 219
Naylor, Jack 139, 145, 147, 148, 162
Neal, Kevin 91
Neale, Fred 25, 71
Negus, Syd 86
Neil, Merv 145, 154, 160, 166
Neilson, James 102, 103

Nelleman 145
Neri, Giorgio 168, 170
Newton, Jack 107
Nibel, Dr Hans 188
Nichols, Frank 236
Nilsson, Hesse 284, 285
Nixon, George 125, 126, 139, 145, 162, 210
Noble, Harvey 29
Nuckey, Rodney 54–56, 73–75, 80, 86, 107
Nurse, Austin 92

O'Conner, Dave 79
O'Conner, Jim 230
Offenstadt, Eric 280, 283
Ogier, John 214, 240
Oliver, Jackie 284
Orchard, Trevor 296
Orsi, Adolfo 286, 290
Orsi, Omer 290
Osbiston, Alfie 168, 200, 229
Owen, Arthur 13, 32, 125, 131, 132, 138, 145, 215
Owen, Graham 285
Owens, Maj. Terry 248, 256, 268, 290, 306

Pabst, Angie 222, 228
Pace, Ada 182
Page, Peter 24, 29, 30
Page, Theo 136, 155
Pahey 36
Palmer, George 79, 88–90, 137
Palmer, Jim 79, 264, 265
Parke, Mike 222
Parker, Don 36, 37, 43, 44, 51, 54, 56, 110–112
Parker, Harry 53
Parnell, Reg 14, 64, 124, 136, 145, 245, 253, 256, 264
Parnell, Tim 125, 145, 210
Patterson, Bill 117, 208, 246, 256, 265
Pattison, Harry 95
Payne, Tom 210
Pearce, Brit 60, 61, 63
Pearce, Harry 167, 225, 252, 255, 263
Pearce, J A 295
Pearman, Don 71
Penington, George 57
Penske, Roger 220–226, 229, 242, 245, 255
Perkins, Buzz 137, 158
Peroglio 217
Perry, Robert 301
Petre, Kay 140
Phillippe, Maurice 126
Phillips, Ron 117
Phipps, David 194, 296
Picard 163
Pick, Gordon 74, 80
Pike, Roy 282
Pilette, André 136
Pilkington, Richard 87, 103
Pinckney 89
Piper, David 91, 186, 196
Pirocchi, Renato 254
Pitt, George 219
Pittaway, L H 136
Plaisance, Bernard 283
Plaisted, John 208
Polensky, Helmut 56
Poore, Dennis 13, 37, 47, 67
Portman, Hon. Eddie 219
Posthumus, Cyril 8, 50, 88
Potton, Jimmy 253
Poty, Paul 283
Power, Chris 145
Preece, Pip 108, 110, 129, 216
Prescott, Bill 79
Prince, Bert 25, 26, 28, 29
Pringle, John 246, 266
Pritchard-Lovell, Brian 78
Proctor, Peter 244
Prosser, Pat 35, 36
Pycroft, Paul 20, 29

Raby, Ian 111, 131, 142, 145, 212, 239, 241
Rachwitz, Porky 235
Rainbow, Alec 43, 103
Rainey, Murray 84
Raineri 236
Rainwater, Lupton 145
Rathmann, Dick 235
Rebecchi, Ing. Giancarlo 283
Reddington, Hugh 138
Redman, Brian 298, 302, 303, 305
Reece, Jackie 36, 47, 49
Reece, Peter 49
Rees, Alan 297
Renault, Dr Philippe 117
Remington, Phil 225
Reventlow, Lance 140, 144, 147, 221
Revson, Peter 243, 244
Rhiando, Alvin 'Spike' 24, 27, 29, 30, 43
Rhodes, John 241, 244, 280
Richards, Horace 14
Richardson, Geoff 71, 183, 206, 208
Richmond, Jimmy 52, 54, 60
Ricker, Cliff 126
Rickman, Don 240
Riley, Dave 242
Rindt, Jochen 56, 99, 244, 276, 281, 285, 288, 294–298
Rindt, Nina 56
Rippon, Alan 118
Risely-Prichard, John 103, 104
Rivers-Fletcher, A F 229
Roache, Mike 168
Robinson, Charlie 14, 16, 20, 22
Robinson, Dave 117
Robinson, Phil 111, 112
Robinson, Tony 74, 85, 89, 157, 183, 291, 300, 301, 302
Roche, Toto 149, 212
Rodger, Bernie 60, 68, 73, 78, 80, 86, 91–93, 96
Rodgers, A P O 'Bert' 99, 126
Rodriguez, Pedro 235, 241, 294, 296–298
Rodriguez, Ricardo 241
Rol 44
Rollinson, Alan 285
Rolt, Tony 90, 100, 136
Rose, Alwyn 207
Rosenhammer, Arthur 131
Rosinski, Jose 242, 244
Rosqvist, Yngve 283
Ross, Gray 138
Rout, Frank 103
Rowe, Ray 265
Roycroft, Ron 136, 153, 186
Ruby, Lloyd 224, 226
Rudaz, Jean-Claude 271, 272
Rudd, A C 'Tony' 164
Russell, Bridget 149
Russell, Jim 107, 208, 110–112, 122, 124, 126, 127, 129, 131, 148, 162, 209, 210, 216, 245
Russo, Paul 230
Ryser, Pierre 280, 283, 285

Salvadori, Roy 74, 83, 87, 88, 94, 100, 116, 124, 126–132, 134, 136, 137, 139, 140, 142–149, 152, 154–156, 158, 160–162, 166–168, 170, 171, 173, 182, 183, 185, 200–202, 206, 208, 210, 216, 217, 219–221, 225, 228, 229, 245–248, 253, 255, 256, 266, 273, 275, 276, 286, 287, 290, 292, 294–301
Samengo-Turner 182
Samuelson, Dickie 140, 141
Samuelson, Sir Francis 24, 25, 29, 130, 131, 196
Sanderson, Ninian 66, 92
Sandstrom, Hardy 284
Sanville, Steve 140
Sarginson, Euan 206
Saunders, George Henry 22, 24, 27, 29, 130, 131, 196
Scalais, Rene 285

INDEX

Scarfiotti, Ludovico 298, 302, 303, 305
Scarlatti, Giorgio 182, 202, 206
Schell, Harry 41–44, 46, 47, 50, 72, 120, 123, 147, 157, 160, 162, 166, 171, 178, 184, 185, 190, 196, 200–202, 210, 212, 306
Schell, Laurie 43
Schell, Lucy O'Reilly 43
Schell, Philippe 42–44
Schlesser, Jo 212, 239, 303
Schlutter, Walter 56
Schonberg, Johnny 83
Scott, Skip 228
Scott-Brown, Archie 100, 122, 124, 136, 154
Scott-Davies, John 305
Scott-Russell, Peter 99, 102
Seaman, Dick 66, 67
Searles, Ron 8, 140
Sears, Jack 49, 214
Seelinger, Ern 84, 117
Seers, Rosemary 49
Seidel, Wolfgang 162, 213, 245
Selby, Len 285
Senior, Art 83
Servoz-Gavin, 'Johnny' 303, 305
Sewell, Hugh 60, 61, 63
Shale, David 117, 145
Shelby, Carroll 225, 228
Shelly, Tony 50, 246
Sharp, Hap 216, 220–222, 225, 228, 245, 255, 256
Siddall, John 14, 18, 30
Sieff, Lord 286
Sieff, Jonathan 275, 286, 287, 289, 305
Siffert, Jo 241, 283, 285, 292, 294–298, 302
Simpson, Barry 95
Sirkett, Freddie 52, 54
Sjosted, Hans 285
Skeaping, Chris 248, 250
Skirrow 24
Slotemaker, Rob 280
Smiley Bob 232
Smith Jr, Bill 124, 243, 246
Smith, Clay 230
Smith, C. F. 'Charlie' 24, 25, 37, 38, 40
Smith, Gilbert 113
Smith, Reg 124
Sodreau, Jean 285
Somervail, Jimmy 78, 80
Somervail, Jock 78, 80
Sommer, Raymond 43, 44, 46, 47
Sopwith, 'Tommy' 98, 116, 122, 124, 125, 139, 143
Sparrowe, Jeff 78
Spears, High 138
Sproat, Stan 80, 98, 217, 225

Stacey, Alan 125, 204, 236, 303
Stafford, Mike 139
Stait, Alan 232, 239
Stait, Eddie 141, 222, 229, 232, 233, 242, 247, 248, 255, 268, 272, 273, 277, 284
Stallwood, L B T 18
Stangnellini 236
Stanbury, Vyvyan 119
Stanton, Feo 245
Statham, Tony 103
Steed, Dick 117
Stephen, Harry 232
Sterzi, Count 36, 37
Stevens, Dave 31
Stewart, Jimmy 73, 74, 80, 86, 279
Stewart, Jackie 225, 226, 278–280, 282, 283, 286, 304
Stiller, Harry 285
Stilwell, Bob 186, 188, 194, 200, 207, 208, 225, 245, 246, 255, 256, 265
Stoop, Dickie 214
Strang, Colin 14, 16, 18, 21, 22, 30
Stringer, Alex 137
Stuart, Jimmy 145
Summers, Chris 145, 210, 225
Summers, Shane 245, 250
Surtees, John 199, 206, 207, 213, 214, 238, 247, 251–253, 255, 256, 263, 264, 283, 288, 292, 294, 295, 296, 304
Sutherland, R. Gordon 20
Swaelens, Paul 283, 285
Swaters, Jacques 71

Tadini 36, 37
Tanner, Reg 125
Taraschi 111, 236
Tauranac, Austin 83
Tauranac, Ron 83, 242, 251, 300
Taylor, Aubrey 95
Taylor, Clifford 286
Taylor, Dennis 111, 124, 126, 136, 137, 144, 160, 161, 206, 208, 242
Taylor, Geoffrey 58, 89, 118, 122
Taylor, Henry 110–112, 160, 162, 204, 206–208, 210, 219, 220, 239
Taylor, John 273, 277
Taylor, Trevor 111, 112, 239, 241, 285
Taylor, Mike 184, 205, 210, 236, 238, 286
Tee, Michael 185
Teijby, Lars-Ake 284
Tempest, Les 89
Thackwell, Ray 139, 144, 148
Thomas, George 55
Thompson, Johnny 230, 265
Thompson, Maj. 79

Thompson, Mickey 228, 235
Thornley, John 34, 41
Threlfall, Chris 212, 239
Tidmarsh, Harry 223
Tojiero 49
Tolley, Jack 43, 71, 72
Towner, Anthony 199
Towse, W A 125
Tozzi-Condivi, Mario 286, 290, 294, 299
Tredegar, Lord & Lady 149
Tresise, Rocky 262, 276
Trintignant, Maurice 44, 146, 158, 159, 161, 162, 172–174, 177, 178, 180, 182, 184, 185, 188, 196, 197, 202, 204, 205, 208, 210, 212, 213, 215, 217, 254, 255
von Trips, Wolfgang 130, 184, 199, 205, 208, 212, 214
Tuck, Fred 75, 79, 84, 108, 200, 202, 205, 206, 208, 219
Turk, Geoffrey 108
Tyrrell, Ken 79, 88, 111, 145, 157, 158, 160, 166, 203, 209, 222, 226, 238, 239, 240, 242, 252, 256, 266, 268, 279, 280, 283, 285

Ugohini, Nello 64
Urbain, Roland 117, 271

Vaccerelli, Nino 255
Vallone, Raf 46, 47
Vandervell, Guy Anthony 113, 114
van der Vyver, Syd 192
van Rooyen, Basil 298
van Rossern, Peter 95
Villoresi 36, 37, 64, 67, 236
Vine, David 81
Volpi, Count 254
Volpini 56
von Hanstein, Huschke 130, 162
Vroomen 131

Waggott, Merv 78
Walker, Peter 67, 68, 71, 77, 81, 87, 92, 136, 139, 140, 160, 161
Walker, Rob 92, 104, 131, 134, 136, 139, 143, 144, 146, 149–152, 157, 159, 161, 167, 168, 173, 184, 196, 197, 202, 209, 212, 246, 248, 250, 266, 268, 271, 273, 292, 302, 306
Wall, Tim 184, 190, 213, 221, 233, 252, 253, 255
Walton, Jack 75, 89, 96, 98, 100, 115
Walton, Tim 100, 103
Wandsworth, Edgar 119, 122
Ward, Ronnie 83
Ward, Roger 221, 222, 230, 232
Wark, Fred 242

Watkins, Ken 22, 43, 63, 64, 66, 67, 73, 74, 77, 81, 84, 86, 102, 123, 136, 137, 139, 143
Wheatcroft, Tom 91
White, Bob 276
White, Derrick Atherson 273, 276, 284, 288, 291, 297, 300, 302, 304
White, George 58
Whiteaway, Ted 240
Whiteford, Doug 117
Whitehead, Gordon 132
Whitehead, Peter 67, 73, 78, 89, 113, 114, 116, 117, 136, 137, 140, 219
Whitehouse, Bill 40, 43, 51, 53, 139, 143, 146, 148
Whitehouse, Brian 209
Whitmare, Sir John 214, 255
Wick, Cyril 115, 117
Wicken, George 43, 44, 54, 111, 126, 139, 143, 147, 148, 160, 161, 206, 209, 210
Wickham, Allan 31
Wicky, Andre 292
Widdows, Robin 303, 304
Wilcocks, D 50
Wild, Ken 219
Wiles, Geoff 137
Wilkinson, Derek 81
Wilkinson, Wilkie 217
Wilks, Bill 80, 94, 103
Williams, Frank 282
Williams, Jonathan 282
Williamson, Jack 81
Willmott, Wally 228, 259, 262, 263, 265, 271
Wilson, Vic 214
Windsor-Smith, Peter 138, 165
Winkelmann, Roy 94, 98, 285
Winterbottom, Eric 36, 37, 40
Wintersteen, George 228
Wissell, Reine 284
Wolstenhome, Dennis 94, 96
Wood, 'Dizzie' 31
Wood, Greg 219
Woodgate, Rex 56
Woods, Gordon 40
Woollett, Nigel 77
Worth, Bernard 80

Yeates, Ken 81, 92
Yorke, Cmdr. Christopher 18
Yorke, David 87
Youl, John 207, 246, 256, 265, 271
Young, Eoin 229, 248, 269
Young-Stewart, John 225

Zeltweg, Phil 276
Zweifel, Harry 217